REVOLUTIONARY DEMOCRACY

REVOLUTIONARY DEMOCRACY

EMANCIPATION IN CLASSICAL MARXISM

Soma Marik

HAYMARKET BOOKS
CHICAGO, ILLINOIS

Published in 2018 by
Haymarket Books
P.O. Box 180165
Chicago, IL 60618
773-583-7884
www.haymarketbooks.org
info@haymarketbooks.org

ISBN: 978-1-60846-729-7

Trade distribution:
In the US, Consortium Book Sales and Distribution, www.cbsd.com
In Canada, Publishers Group Canada, www.pgcbooks.ca
In the UK, Turnaround Publisher Services, www.turnaround-uk.com
All other countries, Ingram Publisher Services International,
IPS_Intlsales@ingramcontent.com

This book was published with the generous support of Lannan
Foundation and Wallace Action Fund.

Cover design by Rachel Cohen.

Printed in Canada by union labor.

Library of Congress Cataloging-in-Publication data is available.

2 4 6 8 10 9 7 5 3 1

CONTENTS

FOREWORD

It is with great pleasure that I introduce to the reader this very scholarly—but also profoundly politically relevant—book.

For too long, particularly in the West but not exclusively there, the revolutionary core of Marx's thought has been obscured by interpretations that professed to investigate superstructural elements at the expense of political engagement.

From the beginning of the twentieth century the ongoing debate centred on the relationship of the party to the proletariat and the development of a revolutionary consciousness among the working class. Even those who seemed to believe in a semi-automatic breakdown of capitalism—Kautsky or Luxemburg in their different ways—were enthusiastic about party organization (Kautsky) or such tactics as the mass strike (Luxemburg). But with the growing reformism of large sections of the working class in the West, including the Trade Union leadership, and the lack of the clear polarization of society, Lenin's idea of a "vanguard" party which would instil revolutionary ideas into the working class became attractive. With the success of 1917, the Leninist model in which the party incarnated the consciousness of the working class (as theorized by Lukács) became dominant. In the Soviet Union under Stalin, this conception was used to implement a violent revolution from above. In China the party, claiming to embody the consciousness of a largely non-existing proletariat, tended to become equally divorced from the people, in spite of such efforts as the Cultural Revolution. Those in the West, like Korsch and the Council Communists, who retained their commitment to workers' self-emancipation, were disillusioned. The Frankfurt School and the structuralists both reflected this lack of faith in the revolutionary potential of the working class. The only thinker to unite predominant interest in the superstructure with active commitment to politics was Gramsci.

It is in this context that the return to the revolutionary and democratic core of Marxism in the present work is welcome. In the careful dissection of the ways in which Marx and the Bolsheviks united theory and practice, Dr. Marik gives us an important contribution to our understanding of the relation of Marx and the Bolsheviks to democracy. There is an excellent discussion of Marx's views on the Paris Commune. The contributions of Engels, Bebel and Zetkin are well explicated. And Dr. Marik clearly shows the effect of the fateful ban on factions within the party in 1921—no control over the leadership and growing bureaucratization. It is no surprise, therefore, that the thinker for whom Dr. Marik has the most admiration is Luxemburg. It should be noted also that the analysis is much enriched by the careful attention to the question of gender displayed in the various political, and historical contexts discussed.

This is a major work of scholarship. The footnotes alone embody an excellent bibliographical guide to the vast literature involved. This book is unsurpassed as a guide to the theoretical and practical achievements of Marx and the Bolsheviks—and to their shortcomings. I recommend it to all potential readers unreservedly.

David McLellan
Visiting Professor of Political Theory,
Goldsmiths College, University of London

PREFACE TO THE 2018 EDITION

This book was in the making for many years and was produced in a different age. Originally conceived as a PhD thesis in 1986, when the Soviet Union was still in existence, its focus was on the links and discontinuities between the theories and praxis of Marx and Engels and that of Lenin and the Bolsheviks. Also, it aimed to examine the recurrent charge that Lenin's ideas gave rise to Stalinism. In India, the bulk of the Marxist left was split between parties of Stalinist and Maoist origin (and often continued to be Stalinist or Maoist). Some of them had moved or were moving round to the position that democracy had only one possible form, which was parliamentary democracy, and that the Stalinist bureaucratic dictatorship had its roots in Lenin and the Bolsheviks' practices and theories. Others, in wishing to be 'orthodox', defended the 'dictatorship of the proletariat' in the authoritarian regimes of Stalin, Mao, or the Khmer Rouge. One could discern similar trends in left parties and intellectual currents of Stalinist origin worldwide. So a preliminary hypothesis was that there had in fact been a revolutionary democratic politics that existed in the nineteenth century, within which the working class played a major role, and that classical Marxism was strongly involved in that politics. It was further my position that Lenin and the Bolsheviks' relationship with Marx, Engels, and the left wing of international Social Democracy was something requiring close study, rather than making a priori assumptions based on later communist practice. I had the great fortune of having Sipra Sarkar as one of my teachers of Western political thought as well as Soviet history. While critical of the Bolsheviks for many of their ideas and deeds, Sarkar insisted on challenging such a priori thinking and pointed to the need to look at primary texts and also to contextualize them. Her lectures on liberalism also highlighted the distinctions between liberalism and democracy as political movements and ideologies, so that 'liberal democracy' was shown to be a questionable doctrine of very recent (often post-1917) origin. Many of these ideas would find their way into the work as it was completed in the mid-1990s.

Only after the completion of the thesis did it dawn on me that my own engagement with the women's movement and my positions within it found no resonance in the work. There followed some years when I was working on Marxist women and the revolutionary movement in Germany, Russia, India, and elsewhere. My political position was also being shaped by the impact of globalization in India. From 1986 to 1995, while researching for my thesis, I found much of the anti-Stalinist left to be dogmatic in their rejection of feminism or dismissive towards it and the women's movement. Furthermore, they often held an instrumental attitude to women in or around the movement and its organizations. Within the far left organizations, including those critical of Stalinism, there were sometimes women comrades personally committed to the women's liberation movement, but the organizations collectively often displayed a 'Marxism' or a 'Leninism' that continued to absorb a fair amount of sexism. At the same time globalization and the increasing brutality of capitalist exploitation made it evident to me that the feminist movement in its growing NGO-ized form was not an answer. It appeared that there were two inadequate forces at work. There was a women's movement that, in its search for ways to provide assistance to masses of women, had from the end of the 1980s been turning to donors and their funds, created NGOs, which, despite laudable intents, ended up as hierarchical organizations more concerned with lobbying and carrying out partially donor-driven agendas than with building the militant mass movements of earlier times. And there was an anti-Stalinist Marxism which appeared to claim that uttering 'working-class self-emancipation' was enough, without looking at special oppressions that kept the class fractured and which had to be addressed in an autonomous way.

It was only after the most aggressively dogmatic groups split from the Inquilabi Communist Sangathan (at that time the Indian Section of the Fourth International) that I joined it, in 1996. By then, the reformist left in India, above all the Communist Party (Marxist) CPI(M), had started adapting to the Indian ruling class and its turn to neoliberal solutions. In provinces where CPI(M)-led governments were in power, the impact was very negative for working people, and within an overall increase of exploitation, gender inequity also grew. Building a revolutionary socialist party that would also be explicitly feminist was necessary, since otherwise, for women activists, there would be the dual problem of the women's movements and the Marxist parties' downplaying of gender oppression. I began to search for the historical roots of women's struggles within Marxism, which led to a major revision of the study, with practically every chapter being rewritten to bring socialist women's struggles in conversation with a more standard narrative of Marxism and democracy. My involvement with other research and political work sometimes slowed down this process of revision but also enriched it.

As a result, when this book went off to a publisher in 2005–06, and was eventually published in 2008, certain important new studies could not be taken into account. The first temptation, on learning that a new edition would be published, was to envisage looking into it. But it is evident that were I to do so, the present volume would increase massively in size. Instead, it was better to accept that this work needs to be supplemented by certain studies and only briefly discuss them.

In chapter 6, I had argued that "while there was no direct transmission from Marx to Lenin, the early writings of Lenin reveal, if anything, an excessive veneration for the Marxist orthodoxy. The nature of the Marxist influences on Lenin must, therefore, be understood. His understanding of Marxism was deeply influenced by Plekhanov as well as by the political practice of the German Social Democratic Party (SPD) especially up to 1914." There had been further discussions on this in subsequent pages. Lars T. Lih's study has of course gone much further and presented a major challenge to any scholarship that tries to delink Lenin from the wider classical Marxist tradition and relate him to Jacobinism or Blanquism.[1] While Harding had rejected the charge of Jacobinism earlier, and Le Blanc, Vanaik, and I had been among those talking about a different reading of What Is to Be Done? than just 'stick bending', Lih certainly did more than that.[2] He established in a massive way how overrated What Is to Be Done? is in much of modern Leninology. He also enabled readers to understand the book as a polemic, something that Lenin had explained explicitly a few years after he wrote it, but something that anti-Lenin as well as ostensibly 'Leninist' scholarship has chosen to forget. So the context and the texts that the polemic addressed have been brought to life, and in the process, the 'German' orthodoxy of Lenin strongly underscored. What Lih has done subsequently, in a series of papers, is to argue that Lenin was a good orthodox Kautskyian, and it was Kautsky who was a backslider during 1914 and after.[3] At the Historical Materialism conference in London in 2011, I, along with another Indian comrade, had the opportunity to have a short exchange with Lih. We argued, and he conceded, that in 1914 and after, Lenin did accept that, at least from 1909 or 1910, there were important divergences. A difference of thrust nonetheless remains.

The point that requires discussion here is not whether Lenin saw himself as a follower of Kautsky (and whether Kautsky was a revolutionary Marxist in 1902 or for several years afterwards), but whether the revolutionary party that Lenin and his comrades helped build was simply what Kautsky and others had been talking about. Lih's work is based primarily on textual exegesis. Paul Le Blanc and I, by contrast, tried to relate Lenin and other leaders and their writings to the historical process. Lih presents the views of his critics as though they are simply treating Lenin as a foolish man who did not realize what he was doing. It is possible to present a somewhat different and more coherent argument. It is well known that in 1917, Lenin called for a socialist revolution in Russia, even though that which he had all these years defined as a bourgeois-democratic revolution had not been achieved. Land had not passed to peasants. A democratic constitution had not been won. A de facto eight-hour day was being imposed where workers had power but it was not legalized.

In other words, in 1917, moments of crises and success and an acute observation of reality led Lenin to a permanentist perspective. Marx and Engels had first theorized about the revolution in permanence in the nineteenth century, something repeatedly discussed by scholars and activists examining classical Marxism. This involved a possibility, in countries where the bourgeoisie was weak and the working class relatively mature, of proletarian hegemony leading to the revolution being pushed beyond bourgeois limits to the establishment of working-class rule. One can mention the writings of Michael Löwy, Hal Draper and also Kunal Chattopadhyay as well as the author of this book.[4] But the absence of a revolutionary situation for many years meant that until 1904, this perspective would be forgotten by Marxists, with social and political development in West Europe seeming to have overtaken the strategy. It should be noted that even in his old age, Engels in a letter to Turati proposed similar strategic perspectives for Italy, but most leaders of the social democratic parties did not look at this strategy seriously until the turn of the century.[5] It was from around the time of the Russian revolution of 1905 that a number of writers took up Marx's term and concept. But in the Russian revolutionary movement it eventually came to be associated in particular with Lev Trotsky, who would develop it during the revolution of 1905 and express it both in his writings and his speeches after 1905. Lenin would reject the possibility that the revolution could bring the 'bourgeois-democratic' and the proletarian stages together, or that the 'bourgeois-democratic' tasks that he described could be achieved only under lasting working-class rule (the 'dictatorship of the proletariat'). On a couple of occasions he categorically rejected Trotsky's stance. So, in 1917, his change of position was a major development.[6] But he did not then sit down and write an essay declaring that there had been something wrong with his earlier position. Was this dishonesty? If Lenin had been a scholar writing a PhD thesis or a major piece of research, and if he there 'forgot' to mention that he had previously opposed that standpoint, or did not carry out a survey of literature to show that one Lev Trotsky had already arrived at substantially similar positions twelve years earlier, he might face such accusations. But Lenin was a revolutionary activist in the middle of a revolution. He showed his agreement with Trotsky by seeking unity, by supporting this newcomer in the party in major ways, and he showed his change of mind by demanding that dogmatic adherence to "Old Bolshevism" be discarded.

In the same way, it is of course true that from the 1890s, Lenin's goal was to build a Marxist workers' party like that of German Social Democracy (hereafter, SPD)—(that is, a fusion of Marxist theory with large numbers of militant workers), and he believed Kautsky to be a part of the revolutionary wing. So did Luxemburg, who knew Kautsky from a much closer association. But Kautsky, very clearly from 1909 on, began moving away from his previous revolutionary position. This is further discussed when I take up *Witnesses to Permanent Revolution*, but some comments are appropriate here. His refusal to publish Luxemburg's article on the proposal for a general strike in connection with the demand for securing universal suffrage in Prussia showed an unwillingness to create any tension with the party bureaucracy.[7] On the question of militarism too, his position shifted.[8] The other important difference is the Bolsheviks eventually built a party that had a different kind of relationship with the working class, compared to that of the SPD.[9] Lenin's fury at the betrayal by Kautsky is well recorded. Clearly, he was angry because he had in the past held Kautsky in greater esteem than many of the others.

But the Bolshevik Party was a different kind of party than the SPD. There have been plenty of studies. I do not want to repeat what such studies have shown.[10] I simply want to stress that not just Lenin but also Trotsky, to take one other obvious example, would both furiously polemicize with Kautsky, indict Kautskyism and yet recognize Kautsky as one of their teachers and a teacher of their entire generation of revolutionary Marxists. But by the early 1920s, both of them would also recognize that there was some difference between the SPD, including much of its orthodox currents, and themselves.

This of course leads us to a related and significant debate. Not just Lih but others have contributed in an important way to a recovery of the heritage of the Second International. The achievement of the Marxists Internet Archive is paramount. And at least one book requiring special mention is *Witnesses to Permanent Revolution*.[11] It shows that Kautsky, before and during 1905, stood on the left wing of international Social Democracy, not the centre, and far to the left of Plekhanov, for example. This goes beyond a personal reevaluation of Kautsky, of course. Day and Gaido present a fair survey of Kautsky as the most important representative of the Marxist wing of Social Democracy, whom both

Lenin and Trotsky were keen to portray as being on their side. While Kautsky did not explicitly call for the Russian revolution to lead to the revolutionary dictatorship of the proletariat and the overturning of capitalist relations, he clearly objected to any alliance with the liberal bourgeoisie. In an article in 1905, Kautsky talked repeatedly about 'Revolution in Permanence,' saying: "The revolution in permanence is, then, precisely what the workers of Russia need. . . . Within a few years it could turn the Russian workers into an elite troop, perhaps into *the* elite troop of the international proletariat."[12] This put him alongside Rosa Luxemburg and Parvus, if not perhaps fully with Trotsky (though only with *Results and Prospects* would Trotsky's full position be articulated). Yet Day and Gaido also trace the retreat of Kautsky and his debates, not just with Luxemburg but with Mehring, Pannekoek, and Radek, over the period from 1910 to 1913. One part of the Marxist current in Social Democracy was succumbing to the pressures of party and union bureaucracy. In earlier periods, Kautsky's writings showed him taking positions critical of the trade union bureaucracy.[13] As late as 1909, when the American Federation of Labor leader Samuel Gompers travelled to Germany, Kautsky wrote articles criticizing him, and this led to hot disputes between Kautsky and the German trade union bureaucrats.[14] But by 1910, he had clearly changed his stance. Not only did he refuse to publish Luxemburg's article, as discussed earlier, but he made clear the reasons for distancing himself from her. According to his biographer, Marek Waldenberg, he felt that the fact that his dispute with Luxemburg enabled him to take a distance from her unpopular image was a positive development.[15] And in a letter to Ryazanov he was explicit: "It seems to me that in order to develop good relations between the Marxists and the trade unionists it is important to show that on this point there is a great distance between Rosa and me. This is for me the most important question."[16]

There have been a considerable number of other studies. Another requiring a brief discussion is the work of August Nimtz.[17] Nimtz argues in his earlier work that first, Marx and Engels played a major role in the nineteenth-century struggle for democracy. Second, in that work, he also discusses the stance they took on elections, which was different from both an anarchist and an electoralist position. In his later work on Lenin, he traces at length Lenin's insistence that in a reactionary situation like Russia, where from 1907 civil liberties had all but disappeared, even seemingly routine trade union work was severely attacked by the police and the electoral system was thoroughly undemocratic, all forms of work, legal and illegal, electoral and underground, had to be combined. Marx and Engels had responded in advance to all types of reformists who wanted to simply enter the bourgeois parliamentary system to carry out 'socialist' reforms, by their sole proposed change in the *Communist Manifesto*, when they warned that the Paris Commune had proved that the working class could not simply lay hold of the existing state.

In the later volumes on Lenin, Nimtz is careful to warn that Leninism cannot be reduced to the specific tactics that worked in October 1917. As a result, he urges his readers to look at the political context in which Lenin saw elections, even in tsarist Russia. Nimtz's argument fits in with the international picture elaborated in the massive work done by John Riddell, who has completed the translation, editing, and publication of the documents and debates of the Communist International, including volumes on the Third and Fourth Congresses. At these two Congresses, Lenin and his comrades, including not just a few well-known Russians but many more from various countries, worked out an alternative series of lines of inquiry for revolution. These included questions of party building, participation in elections and trade unions, and the united front of the working class. They discussed how a revolutionary party was to be built in an era when the working-class movements were split between two or more large working-class parties, what tactics to take in connection with work in trade unions and parliamentary elections as well as the large number of discussions at the Fourth Congress on the united front of the working class. Lenin and the Bolsheviks were concerned with both highlighting what they felt were the real lessons of the Bolshevik experience and avoiding ultraleft simplifications. As we approach a hundred years since the Russian Revolution, and look back at ultraleft or sectarian attempts at "Bolshevizations" these attempts have a great significance. Without mechanical transplantation to a very different age, they have lessons for revolutionaries today.

The Riddell volumes are particularly important for us. Ever since the Seventh Congress of the Communist International, what has passed for Marxist policy on working-class united fronts is in reality a class collaborationist politics. In particular, in India, the Dutt-Bradley thesis, the proposed application of Dimitrov's line for India, has been extremely harmful. For decades, the search for the progressive ('national', 'revolutionary' and so on) bourgeoisie has dominated the politics of the Communist Party of India (CPI), which was the Indian section of the Communist International, CPI, and most of its successor parties. [The CPI split in 1964 with the apparently radical wing forming the CPI (Marxist), and there have been further splits since then, the most important being the exodus of the pro-Mao forces in 1966, leading to the formation of the CPI (Marxist-Leninist) and other parties.] The working out of the tactics of the workers' united front and its clear differences with the popular frontism (involving an alliance with so-called progressive bourgeois forces) that has led to disasters, from Spain in 1936 to the rout of the left in India in recent years, is an issue of great contemporary significance. While brief references to Bolshevik experiences of the united front exist in this book (for example, the struggle against Kornilov), the experience of the Communist International was beyond its focus.

There have been other important books published in this period. I do not intend to present a full survey of the literature. But I would like to mention at least two books. Tania Puschnerat wrote a biography of Clara Zetkin.[18] This work firmly situates Zetkin as a significant Marxist leader, who was of course a crucial builder of the proletarian women's movement, but who cannot be neatly slotted as such. Zetkin's other concerns have been taken up at length. However, Puschnerat has a perspective that is certainly different from mine. She has collapsed the differences between Stalinism and Bolshevism and argued that Zetkin's critical stance on the Stalinist turn from 1928 made her feel that her decision to side with the Communists had itself been wrong. At the same time, Puschnerat also argues that though Zetkin had never openly supported the "Bolshevization" of the mid-1920s or the subsequent "Stalinization" of the KPD and the Comintern, she may be viewed as the type of communist cadre who, due to a belief in excessively tight discipline, unwittingly contributed to this process.[19]

I have attempted to argue that this subjective narrative about how tight communist discipline led ineluctably to Stalinism is not a correct view, even if we do accept that the many errors of the Bolshevik leadership in the civil war years contributed to the problems. The work of John Riddell provides us with a much more significant view of what Zetkin was doing in the early Communist International. The Third Congress debates, published in 2015, show that Lenin and his comrades, including German comrades such as Zetkin, engaged in a sustained democratic process in building an international communist movement. In a number of documents, letters and private reminiscences attached to the Third Congress proceedings, Riddell has shown the way discussions and negotiations were carried out. There was no question of imposing the will of the Russians, or even the will of a majority, in a blunt way. In a telling passage, Zetkin wrote:

> Lenin told her: "The congress will wring the neck of the celebrated theory of the offensive [the idea that Communist revolutionary work must involve an offensive under all circumstances—S.M.] and will adopt a course of action corresponding to your ideas. In return, however, it must grant the supporters of the offensive theory some crumbs of consolation. . . . You will resist this as representing a cover-up and worse. But that will get you nowhere. We want the policy adopted by the congress to become law for the Communist parties' activity as quickly and with as little friction as possible. To that end, our dear leftists must be able to return home without

being too humbled and embittered."[20]

This suggests tough conflicts as well as attempts to keep unity while maintaining principles. It does not look at all either like the Stalinist imposition of fiats or the later parodies of Bolshevism, in which every difference is seen as an earth-shaking betrayal demanding splits. Moreover, Riddell's work suggests that to say Zetkin never *openly* supported certain tendencies paints a misleading picture, since it implies she *covertly* did provide support. On the contrary, she was one of those trying out a different way of working.[21]

Riddell's volumes are crucial for an understanding of what Lenin and his comrades were trying to do in the early Communist International. The Third and the Fourth Congresses saw serious attempts at working out a different kind of revolutionary strategy for countries where some form of bourgeois democracy existed and where bourgeois stabilization had occurred compared to the Bolshevik tactics followed in Russia.

We live in a very different world. But some of the lessons of the early Comintern have a lasting significance. The Fourth Congress developed the tactics of the united front of the working class as one of the most important tools to defend working-class rights and to transform a defensive struggle into an offensive struggle. The legacy of the later Comintern has led to twin mistakes, both absorbed by many of the political forces claiming to be heirs of the Comintern. On one hand, there is the legacy of 'Third Period' Stalinism, the claim that Social Democracy is fascist (social fascist) and that the united front can only be made with the ranks of the reformist parties because the leaders are known traitors, lackeys of the ruling class, and so on. On the other hand there is popular frontism, which arose from the Seventh Congress, where in the name of antifascism, or opposition to certain designated enemies, not only working-class but bourgeois forces are to be involved, and in order to make these alliances, working-class revolutionary struggles have to be put on the back burner. Thus, the idea of a united front of the working class, implying issue-based joint struggles of working-class parties and trade unions, both revolutionary and reformist, was distorted in two ways: First, the 'united front from below' was a de facto repudiation of the united front; second, the communist goal of using the united front for developing proletarian struggles in a firm anti-capitalist direction was given up and so-called progressive bourgeois parties were roped into alliances falsely called united fronts.

There is nothing more tempting than to rewrite one's work, continuously editing it in the light of one's subsequent political experiences as well as one's subsequent readings. I have refrained from doing that. I would however stress, perhaps more than I did in my book, that my continued study of classical Marxism has shown a much greater awareness of gender and sexuality in early Marxism, including in Bolshevik practice, something I have emphasized in essays published since this book was originally written. It has also become evident that the narrowing of the definition of class and class struggle, and the imposition of a Trotskyist orthodoxy or a 'classical Marxist' orthodoxy, often meant that even anti-Stalinists failed to understand how building revolutionary parties and developing revolutionary strategy had to encompass gender and other special oppressions within class and its own organizations. Otherwise, the goal of class unity becomes meaningless inside revolutionary organizations. In connection with this, it is perhaps worth revisiting the Lenin-Zetkin conversation, which I have already examined in the main text. I had argued that Lenin had certain positions one needed to question. Looking back again, one needs to raise a different point. Lenin tells Zetkin why organizing women separately is necessary, why it is not separatism. She relays this from Lenin:

> What is at the basis of the incorrect attitude of our national sections? In the final analysis it is nothing but an under-estimation of woman and her work. Yes, indeed! Unfortunately it is still true to say of many of our comrades, 'scratch a communist and find a philistine'. Of course, you must scratch the sensitive spot, their mentality as regards women.[22]

Note that Zetkin wrote these lines not in 1920–21, when Lenin was still around, but later. I would stress that her decision stemmed from the battle she was beginning to wage, to protect and ensure the continuity of the Communist Women's International, the continuity of the autonomy of women's work within the framework of the communist politics and the continuation of the struggle against sexism, the term still lacking and the concept therefore not fully clarified but highlighted as 'philistinism'. Experiences globally have shown us that this continues to be significant. Training women cadres, ensuring real, substantive equality within organizations calling themselves revolutionary Marxist and accepting women's work in those organizations as having the same value as men's work, continue to be major problems.[23] Since Stalinist influence has been declining globally, it becomes more and more difficult to reduce sexism within revolutionary organizations to being residual traces of Stalinism. As Penelope Duggan remarks in her 1997 paper, "The Feminist Challenge to Traditional Political Organizing," there are ways in which certain types of work are valued more, and others less. A young male comrade who has been a student leader, she argues, is made a leader in some other area as soon as he stops being a student. In contrast, a woman activist who has led mass movements and is capable of understanding historical materialism sufficiently to make a critical balance sheet of Engels on the family is still seen as just a specialist on women's work.[24]

Whatever the limitations of the SPD left, or of the Bolsheviks, or the early Comintern, their achievements in mobilizing such huge numbers of women also need to be recognized. And, while we are moving further and further away from that era, it is therefore important to stress that the 'toy Bolshevism' that ignores gender or only pays lip service to it needs to learn seriously from the real revolutionary Marxist tradition.

In conclusion I would like to add another round of thanks. To IIRE, and above all to Alex de Jong, for proposing that we bring out this edition, and to Nisha Bolsey and Dao Tran for serious assistance in editing; to Mr K. K. Saxena, of Aakar Books, for agreeing to the proposal; to a community of Marxist and feminist activists and scholars, with whom I have been engaged in the course of political work and writing, even if they cannot all be formally cited in bibliographies or notes. In particular I would like to thank Paul Le Blanc, John Riddell, Sebastian Budgen, Tithi Bhattacharya, and Kunal Chattopadhyay for political exchanges and discussions.

NOTES

1 Lars T. Lih, *Lenin Rediscovered: What Is to Be Done? in Context* (Leiden: Brill, 2006).

2 Neil Harding, *Lenin's Political Thought,* vol. 1 (London and Basingstoke: Macmillan, 1977); Paul Le Blanc, *Lenin and the Revolutionary Party* (Atlantic Highlands, NJ and London: Humanities Press, 1990); Achin Vanaik, "In Defence of Leninism," *Economic and Political Weekly* 11, no. 37 (September 13, 1986): 1635, 1638-42.

3 See for example Lars T. Lih, "The Strange Case of the Closeted Lenin," in http://links.org.au/node/4186 (4 December, 2014), Links international journal of socialist renewal; and Lars T. Lih, "Kautsky When He Was a Marxist."

4 Michael Löwy, *The Politics of Combined and Uneven Development* (London: New Left Books, 1981); Hal Draper, *Karl Marx's Theory of Revolution,* vol. 2 (New York: Monthly Review Press, 1978); Kunal Chattopadhyay, "Between Revolution and Reaction: Marx and the Origins of the Idea of Permanent Revolution," *Jadavpur University Journal of History* 10 (1989–90): 60–78.

5 Engels to Filipo Turati, 26 January, 1894, in Karl Marx and Frederick Engels, *Selected Correspondence,* 2nd revised edition (Moscow: Progress Publishers, 1965): 468–72.

6 There have been attempts to make a case that even in 1917 Lenin had not become permanentist. See for a typical example Doug Lorimer, *Trotsky's Theory of Permanent Revolution: A Leninist Critique* (Sydney: Resistance Books, 1998). For responses to such arguments see Ernest Mandel, "In

Defence of Permanent Revolution," *International Viewpoint* 33, special supplement (1983); Kunal Chattopadhyay, *Leninism and Permanent Revolution* (Baroda, India: Antar Rashtriya Prakashan, 1987); or J. P. Roberts, *Lenin, Trotsky and the Theory of the Permanent Revolution* (London: Wellred Books, 2007).

7   See Helen Scott, "Introduction," especially 20–22, in *The Essential Rosa Luxemburg*, Helen Scott, ed. (Delhi and Patna: Daanish Books, 2010).

8   See, for example, Nicholas Stargardt, *The German Idea of Militarism: Radical and Socialist Critics 1866–1914*, (Cambridge: Cambridge University Press, 1994).

9   For Bolshevik penetration see Victoria E. Bonnell, *Roots of Rebellion: Workers' Politics and Organizations in St. Petersburg and Moscow, 1900–1914* (Berkeley and Los Angeles: University of California Press, 1983). See also Leopold Haimson, "The Problem of Social Stability in Urban Russia, 1905–1917," *Slavic Review* 23, no. 4 (December 1964): 619–42.

10 Apart from Le Blanc (note 4 above), see also the works cited in the two chapters of this book dealing with the Bolsheviks prior to and during 1917. Victoria Bonnell's book, (note 12) traces how the Bolsheviks built a party of worker militants in the period of Stolypin reaction and up to the First World War. Another study, from a non-Marxist position, shows how in the war years the Bolsheviks built a party based on masses of workers, while their opponents were more involved with building alliances with the liberal intelligentsia and other such forces. Haimson, "The Problem of Social Stability in Urban Russia," 619–42, and pt. 2 in *Slavic* Review 24, no. 1 (March 1965): 1–22. The key argument I am making here is that the Bolsheviks ended up building a party of militant activists capable of taking independent initiatives in a way the SPD was increasingly not. This does not discount that in earlier years Lenin (and Trotsky) had seen Kautsky (and the SPD generally) as their ideal. But it does challenge a possible outcome of Lih's subsequent arguments, which is that Lenin remained a Kautskyian, that he was not a permanentist, and that for the present, a Kautskyian strategy is adequate. This, after all, is a vital component of any discussion on Leninism—what does it mean today?

11 Richard B. Day and Daniel Gaido, ed. and trans., *Witnesses to Permanent Revolution: The Documentary Record* (Chicago: Haymarket Books, 2011).

12 Ibid., 380.

13 Karl Kautsky, 'Partei und Gewerkschaft', *Die Neue Zeit* 24, no. 2 (1906): 716–35, 749–54.

14 See for a discussion D. Gaido, "Marxism and the Union Bureaucracy: Karl Kautsky on Samuel Gompers and the German Free Trade Unions," *Historical Materialism* 16 (2008): 115–36.

15 M. Waldenberg, *Il papa rosso: Karl Kautsky* (Roma: Editori Riuniti, 1980), 673–74, as quoted in Gaido, 132.

16 Ibid., 132.

17 August H. Nimtz, *Marx and Engels: Their Contribution to the Democratic Breakthrough* (New York: State University of New York Press, 2000). See also August H. Nimtz, *Lenin's Electoral Strategy: From Marx and Engels*

through the Revolution of 1905 (London: Palgrave Macmillan, 2014), and *Lenin's Electoral Strategy from 1907 to the October Revolution of 1917: The Ballot, the Streets—or Both* (London: Palgrave Macmillan, 2014).

18 Tânia Puschnerat, *Clara Zetkin: Burgerlichkeit und Marxismus* (Essen: Klartext Verlag, 2003). Another work is Gilbert Badia, *Clara Zetkin: Eineneue Biographie* (Berlin: Dietz Verlag, 1994).

19 Tânia Ünlüdağ-Puschnerat, "A German Communist: Clara Zetkin (1857–1933)," in Kevin Morgan, Gidon Cohen, and Andrew Flinn, eds., *Agents of the Revolution: New Biographical Approaches to the History of International Communism in the Age of Lenin and Stalin* (Oxford, Peter Lang Publishing, 2005) 93–110.

20 John Riddell, ed. and trans., *To the Masses: Proceedings of the Third Congress of the Communist International, 1921* (Leiden: Brill, 2015): 1140.

21 See John Riddell, "Clara Zetkin in the Lion's Den," *John Riddell: Marxist Essays and Commentary*, January 12, 2004, johnriddell.wordpress.com/2014/01/12/clara-zetkin-in-the-lions-den.

22 Clara Zetkin, "Lenin on the Women's Question," https://www.marxists.org/archive/zetkin/1920/lenin/zetkin1.htm.

23 On this, the practical evidence within the Communist Party of India is one that I have taken up at length in several essays, which are in the process of being edited and collected as a single volume. Meanwhile, I would refer interested readers to Soma Marik, 'Breaking Through a Double Invisibility: The Communist Women of Bengal 1939–1948', *Critical Asian Studies* 45, no. 1 (March 2013): 79–118. For the Naxalbari movement, that is, the Maoist movement in India in its first phase (though nowadays in India the term 'Maoist' has been preempted by the CPI [Maoist], a party focused on work mainly among adivasis or indigenous so-called tribals), see Mallarika Sinha Roy, *Gender and Radical Politics in India: Magic Moments of Naxalbari (1967–1975)* (London: Routledge, 2010). See also Cinzia Arruzza, *Dangerous Liaisons: The Marriages and Divorces of Marxism and Feminism*, Notebook 55 of the International Institute for Research and Education, Amsterdam, 2013). For documentation of how revolutionary Marxists have tried to grapple with these problems see Penelope Duggan, ed., *Women's Liberation and Socialist Revolution, Documents of the Fourth International* (London: Resistance Books and Notebook 48, Amsterdam: International Institute of Research and Education, 2010).

24 In making her case that there is often a tendency to see men as the universal and women as a special case, and in turning women cadres into niche operators, Duggan makes the following argument:

> "There's also the political process among women and the way in which that is devalued. It is astonishing that leaders of women's movement work who have led mass movements fighting for women's rights, mass movements that have been able to create alliances with the trade union movement, with political parties, with a whole range of people; leaders of women's work who are engaged in educational work where they explain and make a critical balance sheet of Marx and Engels and place them in their context and explain historical materialism, what it really means and how you can use it to understand

women's oppression, are consistently seen and treated as just specialists of women's work. You may understand historical materialism sufficiently to be able to make a critical balance sheet of how Engels applied it to the family, but nonetheless you're just a specialist of women's work. No one suggests that these skills could be applied to any other sector.

On the other hand, the young male comrade who has just been a leader of a student struggle and has shown his capacities to be a leader of the mass movement, is a leader; now he's stopped being a student he must immediately be put somewhere else so that he can lead some other area of work and use those leadership capacities he developed in two or three years of student politics." Penelope Duggan, ed., *Women's Liberation and Socialist Revolution*, 211.

ACKNOWLEDGEMENTS

This book started life as a PhD thesis nearly two decades back. My interest in Russian and Soviet history stemmed from the teaching of Ms. Sipra Sarkar, who taught us one of the two papers on the subject at the MA level. My first ideas about the Russian Revolution and Bolshevism and Stalinism came from her. The Gorbachev era had begun at that time, and this interested me into the meaning of socialist democracy and its differences with liberal democracy, as well as the class moorings of both.

The research work was undertaken while working in the Tarakeswar Degree College, and I would like to thank Sri Bidyut Kumar Das, then Principal of the College, for providing all help, especially in ensuring that I got sufficient study leave to complete my work. I would also like to thank the Indian Council of Historical Research, and particularly Professor Irfan Habib, for the award of a Senior Fellowship. My supervisor, Professor Anuradha Chanda, Department of History, Jadavpur University, provided me with both encouragement and constant constructive criticism. I would like to record my indebtedness to librarians and research institutions in various parts of the world. They include the staff of the Central Library, Jadavpur University; the Departmental Library, Department of History, and the Library of the School of Women's Studies, Jadavpur University, and in particular to Ms. Sarbani Goswami and Ms. Srabani Majumdar; the National Library, Kolkata; the Library of the Centre for Studies in Social Sciences, Calcutta; the Nehru Memorial Museum and Library, New Delhi; the Jawaharlal Nehru University Library, especially those in the Russian language section; Ms. Usha Chattopadhyay of the Jawaharlal Nehru Library, Bombay University; Dr. Peter Drucker, who was then the Director of the International Institute of Research and Education, Amsterdam; Dr. Tom Twiss of the Pittsburgh University Library and the staff of the Maisons de Sciences de l'Homme, including in particular Professor

Gilles Tarabout. Friends and relatives who helped in getting hold of books and articles include Satyabrata Dutta and Ratna Dutta, Neelesh Marik, Amitava Chattopadhyay, Samita Sen, Ron Lare, Cheryl Peck, Paul Le Blanc, and Bodhisatwa Roy.

Discussions with a large number of people helped at different stages. Professor Buddhadev Bhattacharyya, of the Department of Political Science, Calcutta University, and Professor A. R. Desai, were two very senior scholars who engaged in regular discussions, helped in the publication of early papers and monographs. The personal library of Professor Bhattacharyya provided an unending stream of books and articles. Other personal libraries which were tapped include the libraries of Professor Sujit Ghosh, Professor Ranajit Das Gupta, Professor Achin Vanaik and Sri Gautam Sen of the Majdoor Mukti Committee. Professor Jasodhara Bagchi, former Director, School of Women's Studies, Jadavpur University, and Professor Gilbert Achcar are two others who have read and commented on parts or whole of the text.

While the book began as a PhD thesis, it underwent major mutations later on. My first interest, especially with the collapse of Stalinism in the USSR, was on workers' democracy. But my activities as a left-wing feminist, along with my experience of teaching Western Political Thought for fourteen years in the Evening Courses in the Department of History, Jadavpur University, and the history of feminism and women's struggles in Europe for eight years in the MPhil program of the School of Women's Studies, Jadavpur University, also led me to recognize the need to integrate women's history within "general" history, instead of keeping them in separate compartments. In this context, I must record my gratitude to activists from a range of organizations, including in particular Maitreyi Chatterjee, Mira Roy, both of the Nari Nirjatan Pratirodh Mancha (Forum Against Oppression of Women), Kolkata; as well as other members of the Mancha; Ron Lare, trade unionist and activist in the US organization Solidarity; Dianne Feeley, Editor of the US journal *Against the Current* and a member of Solidarity and the Fourth International and Bani Dasgupta of the Communist Party of India and the National Federation of Indian Women. I would also like to record my gratitude to students of my MA Western Political Thought course and the MPhil, Women's Studies course, both in Jadavpur University. Many arguments made in this book were hammered out in course of discussions in class over the years.

Two persons whose support I would like to acknowledge are Professor Partha Sarathi Gupta, who always had words of encouragement, and who insisted that I should publish what to many others had seemed a large and unwieldy thesis; and Professor David McLellan, who saw the book both as a thesis and as the final product, for which he kindly agreed to write a Foreword.

I am grateful to Sri K.K. Saxena of Aakar Books, as well as the editor whose meticulous care made the book virtually error free. My daughter Nayanika has designed the cover for the book. I would like to thank Ms. Anindita Bhaduri in assisting with the index. Ms. Sravani Biswas was of immense help in producing the digital version of the text, notably in checking the footnotes.

I also sincerely acknowledge the grant of leave whenever necessary by Pravrajika Bhaswaraprana, Principal, Ramakrishna Sarada Mission Vivekananda Vidyabhavan. Without this and encouragement from my departmental colleagues I could not have finished this book on time.

I would also like to express my gratitude to the women domestic help, particularly, Pinky Haldar, Draupadi Mandal, Tapashi Majhi, and Kabita Majhi, who contributed immensely by taking care of my housework while I was busy doing my research. Their lives are daily reminders of the reality of capitalism and patriarchy in extreme forms.

I would probably not have studied all the way that I did, but for the encouragement given by my mother, Krishna Marik. She also stood by me all these years, and took over many of my responsibilities whenever I was in need, from helping me raise my daughter to checking the proof of my PhD thesis, a task also shared by my aunt Sanhita Marik.

Finally I would like to acknowledge the assistance of my husband Kunal Chattopadhyay, who prodded me whenever I seemed to be slackening, and undertook many of the duties of a research assistant. We had our own distinct views, but discussed them. His knowledge of Marxist theory and history was valuable in carrying out my research. My academic debt to him is acknowledged only in part in the footnotes. I would like to dedicate this book to my mother and to Kunal.

Kolkata
January 2008

LIST OF ABBREVIATIONS

ADAV	: Allgemein Deutsch Arbeiterverein (General German Workers Association)
Cheka	: Extraordinary Commission for Combating Counter-Revolution
CWF	: K. Marx—*The Civil War in France*
DPML	: H. Draper—*The "Dictatorship of the Proletariat" from Marx to Lenin*
GCFI	: The General Council of the First International: Minutes
IWA	: International Workingmen's Association (First International)
KMTR	: H. Draper—*Karl Marx's Theory of Revolution*, 4 volumes
KPD	: Kommunistische Partei Deutschlands (Communist Party of Germany)
LCW	: V. I. Lenin, *Collected Works*
MECW	: K. Marx and F. Engels, *Collected Works*
MESC	: K. Marx and F. Engels, *Selected Correspondence*
MESW	: K. Marx and F. Engels, *Selected Works*
MEW	: K. Marx and F. Engels, *Werke*
MRC	: Military Revolutionary Committee
NEP	: New Economic Policy
NKIu	: Peoples' Commissariat for Justice
NKVD	: Peoples' Commissariat for Internal Affairs
NRZ	: *Neue Rheinische Zeitung*
RZ	: *Rheinische Zeitung*
RCP (B)	: Russian Communist Party (Bolshevik)
RSDLP/RSDRP	: Rossiiskaia Sotsial-Demokraticheskaia Rabochaia

	Partiia (Russian Social Democratic Workers Party)
RSFSR	: Russian Soviet Federated Socialist Republic
Sovnarkom	: Council of Peoples' Commissars
SPD/SDAP	: Sozialdemokratische Partei Deutschlands (Social Democratic party of Germany)
SR	: Socialist Revolutionary Party
SUCR	: Société Universelle de Communistes Révolutionnaires (International Society of Revolutionary Communists)
Tsektran	: Central Transport Committee
Vesenkha	: Supreme Economic Council
Vikzhel	: Railway Union
VTsIK	: All-Russian Central Executive Committee of Soviets
Zhenotdel	: Zhenskii Otdel (Women's Section)

1

INTRODUCTION

What is the relevance of Marxism in the contemporary world? Revolutionary socialists are today consistently confronted with the challenge that Marxism is a failed doctrine, a despotic Utopia that has been finally superseded by the coming of an eternal market-driven democracy. Throughout most of the twentieth century, revolutionary Marxism was identified with Stalinism, and the struggle for socialism was portrayed as a conflict between two camps and two systems, where the communist system led by the Soviet Union promised food security rather than democracy. As the economy of the former Soviet Union and other bureaucratized workers' states faced their terminal crisis, it seemed evident not only to ideologues of capitalism but also to many one-time socialists, that socialism was inferior to capitalism, and that Marxism's lack of commitment to genuine democracy was a major factor in the "demise of Marxism."[1] Since the Soviet Union was often projected as a living embodiment of classical Marxism, the Marxist theory was portrayed as authoritarian, without a serious examination of what it said.[2] Moreover, it has also been concluded that the Bolshevik theory, whether or not directly inspired by Marx, had an authoritarian agenda right from the birth of Bolshevism,[3] and finally, that consciously authoritarian choices on the part of the Bolsheviks, led by Lenin, caused the establishment of a totalitarian regime after the October Revolution.[4]

We are therefore compelled to make a serious study in two parts in order to explore the original democratic commitments of revolutionary socialism, with which Marx, Engels, Lenin, Luxemburg, Clara Zetkin, Trotsky, Alexandra Kollontai and others were associated. First, we need to ask whether Marx's opposition to economic liberalism turned him into an opponent of civil liberties. How democratic was the content of Marx's own theory and practice?[5] In the second place we have to look at the claim that the Leninist theory dictated the creation of Soviet totalitarianism.[6] This necessitates a discussion on the Leninist theory of party as implemented in practice, the Bolshevik strategy of revolution and the manner in which the Bolsheviks held and exercised power from October 1917. It is only by relating these two apparently distinct themes—Marx and nineteenth-century socialism on the one hand and Lenin and the Bolsheviks on the other—that we can carry out a fresh assessment of the relationship between Marxism and Bolshevism on the question of democratic theory and begin to pose an answer to the question of how far they contributed to the rise of Stalinism.

For decades, academic industries have grown up around the study of Marxist theory and Soviet history. Yet this industry has made relatively little attempt at combining the study of theory and history. In the recent past a number of scholars have begun interrogating the thesis that Marx was a totalitarian or a "totalitarian democrat."[7] But almost without exception they have done so only to accuse Lenin and Bolshevism of totalitarianism.[8] Studies on Leninism have by contrast often failed to relate it to his commitment to Marx's views.[9] If at all Marx and Lenin are combined in a study, the historical development is ignored in favor of an abstract theoretical model.[10] At the same time, new trends in history writing with the stress on history from below have produced a remarkable series of books and specialized studies on the Russian revolutionary movements, the revolution of 1917, and the early years of the Soviet state. But while many of these throw considerable light on Bolshevik practice, there is little attempt to produce an integrated conceptualization of the relationship between Bolshevik theory and practice.[11] As a result the decline of democracy is often attributed to the Bolshevik theory without asking detailed questions about this.[12]

Three methodological points should be made here. The writings of Marx himself affirm the need for a ruthless criticism of everything existing, and call for self-criticism by the proletarian revolution. This self-critical approach must be extended to Marxist theory and practice. One major area where revolutionary Marxism has updated itself, as well as shrugged off the negative legacies of social democratic reformism and Stalinism in the course of the second half of the twentieth century is over women's liberation.[13] It was therefore also felt necessary to integrate the record of classical Marxism from Marx to the Bolsheviks on this question to a general study of Marxism and democracy, rather than relegate it, as is often done, to a separate study on Marxism and women's liberation. Second, I aim at producing a social history of political theory, which emphasizes the relationship between Bolshevik political thought and the history of contemporary class struggles. While doing this, the criticism that there was a dichotomy between a democratic Marx and an authoritarian Bolshevism was interrogated by tracing whether there were discursive shifts in Marxism between the period of Marxism during the lifetime of its founders (1848–1895) and the Marxism of the Bolshevik era (1903–1921). Though theory has a degree of autonomy, it arises out of practice and can be best understood when it is placed in the crucibles of historical narrative. Thus socially conditioned, theory, too, plays its role in shaping the contours of politics and movements. In the third place, I have found it essential to challenge the view of Marxism as a set of texts detached from contemporary class struggle, with a hierarchy among the creators (for example, the once well-known utterance of Ranadive in India—Marx wrote for Lenin, Lenin wrote for Stalin, and Stalin wrote for us). No doubt, this cuts both ways. Not only liberal critics, but dogmatic defenders of texts and their particular interpretations will be subjected to scrutiny by this method.

The first part of this book, dealing with Marx and Engels, must begin with the formation of their own political thought and the emergence of the concept of workers' democracy. Marx's ideas on democracy and freedom stood in a relation of dialectical negation rather than outright rejection of liberalism and Hegel's idealism.[14] In other words, he sought to incorporate the positive elements in these systems while going beyond them. For liberalism the rational individual is the central figure. The classical liberal theory of the state envisages that the conflict of individuals in the market requires for its resolution a strong sovereign authority.[15] But at the same time liberalism views the state only as a necessary evil, whose authority over the individual had to be kept at a minimum. The realm where the state had legitimate functions was the political domain. This was the area of unfreedom. The freedom of the individual was achieved by limiting and negating excessive claims for power on the part of the state through the development of civil liberties. Thus these rights were negative rights. Collective social rights for example, the right to education, livelihood or health—by contrast—are positive rights in the sense that a public agency has to enforce them, if necessary by overriding private economic interests. Neither classical liberalism, nor modern neo-liberal advocates of democracy are able to accept such rights.[16] Marx argued that the primacy of individual property and the opposition to public control of social wealth made liberalism a political ideology of capitalism.[17] Unlike liberalism, Hegel saw in the state the overcoming of the conflicts of civil society.[18] Marx accepted Hegel's philosophical method as far as the idea of a universal agency which would ensure human freedom, but challenged the concept of the universality of the state.

In tracing the evolution of Marx's political thought, two problems have to be confronted. The first is an examination of the writings of the young Marx. For the purposes of the present study, two aspects of the debate over the young Marx are important. On the one hand there is Marx's theory of alienation, which suggests that socialism is not simply nationalization of property but free collective association of the producers. On the other hand there is Marx's defense of democratic rights—originally produced from a radical democratic paradigm—and whether it continued to be relevant in his communist phase.[19] The second problem is one whose solution is essential for settling the question of authorship. This problem is the status of Friedrich Engels. Was he a cofounder of Marxist politics or should he be considered an influential commentator on Marx? The position taken in this study is that unless there is a specific difference, which should be explicitly mentioned, the views of Marx and Engels should be treated as a unity. In supporting this position a number of facts may be adduced. Several of the most important programmatic texts, including above all *The Communist Manifesto*, were signed by both. Though the *Critique of the Gotha Programme* came exclusively from Marx's pen, Engels solidarized with it, as his contemporary letter to Bebel shows.[20] Furthermore, the most comprehensive exposition of what Marx stood for that was to be published in Marx's lifetime was Engels' book *Anti-Dühring*.[21] The dispute over its status within Marxism arises from Engels' handling of dialectics in nature, rather than over the political line.[22] Marx's own words make it clear that in their writings he and Engels worked to a plan, with a division of labour.[23] Finally, Marx had enough trust in Engels' political views to request him to write substantial political essays in his name. It can therefore be concluded that on all fundamental issues there was political agreement between them.

Central to Marx's concept of workers' democracy was the principle of working-class self-emancipation. But can the idea of self-emancipation be combined with the idea of a revolutionary party, which is by definition smaller than the class? This is the subject of considerable debate. Some writers have opined that Marx wanted to build a vanguard party, some hold that he was interested in a broad-based and basically propagandist party, while some others question how far he was at all interested in party building.[24] What very few have attempted is the very simple task of actually going through all the political writings of Marx and Engels, and of their record as militants in various working-class, communist, socialist organizations. It has been assumed only too often that they were not serious organization builders. And when their organizational activities are addressed, preconceived notions of Marxist authoritarianism immediately begin to predominate.

The next issue is the application of the principle of workers' democracy in revolutionary strategy. Did Marx advocate majority revolution?[25] In most countries the working class was not a majority, so how could a proletarian revolution be a majority revolution? This suggests the extension of proletarian hegemony over the non-proletarian oppressed masses.[26] A further consideration is required on the role of democratic slogans in the struggles for class unity and class power.[27] Moreover, how far was the advocacy of violence justified in workers' democracy in the course of breaking the old legality?[28] How did Marx address the question of universal suffrage?[29] And what were his views on the nitty-gritty of democracy, that is, how committed was he really to issues like freedom of the press, independence of the judiciary, etc.?[30] It is here that one should search for evidence of how far workers' democracy was to be more democratic than bourgeois democracy.

In discussing problems of party building and revolutionary strategy, it has been a consistent concern of the present author to keep in mind the gender dimension of the working class. Women workers have a distinct identity, and organizing them, developing a program that takes their experience adequately into account and steers a path towards the overcoming of patriarchal domination, requires conscious action. It has often been argued that classical Marxism simply subsumed the category "gender" under "class." While it is true that the writings of Marx and Engels may not have provided all the solutions, it will be argued that nor were they totally devoid of any concern for women's equality. Moreover, it will be argued that August Bebel and Clara Zetkin, and the proletarian women's movement which the latter led, made significant contributions, often underrated.

There is of course a vigorous debate over the term "dictatorship of the proletariat."[31] It will above all be necessary to disentangle Marx's use of the term from the varied ways in which it has been used in the twentieth century. It is also necessary to ask whether the term was used only in a sociological sense, as one line of defense of Marx argues,[32] or whether certain political conclusions were implied by the use of this term.[33] Some critics have contended that even considering the dictatorship of the proletariat as simply class rule opens the door to arbitrariness, authoritarianism and the liquidation of class enemies. According to this concept, Marxist politics as a whole impoverishes the Western political tradition by eliminating the opportunity of dissent and the peaceful transfer of power.[34]

Following the discussions on the founders, an attempt will be made to relate their ideas with the history and political ideology of Bolshevism. This needs to be broken up into three components—first, the emergence of Bolshevism and its history prior to the outbreak of the February Revolution, and the question of how far Lenin was conversant with the principle of self-emancipation and how far he tried to relate that to his project of building a revolutionary organization.[35] The idea of a vanguard party appears at first sight to be an extremely elitist concept.[36] Particularly in view of the Stalinist tradition of insisting on proclaiming that the independent activity of the proletariat, not sanctioned by the vanguard party, is harmful, the concept of the vanguard party has become a dirty word even to many militants on the left, who see the revolutionary party as an imposition on the actual movement of the class. At the same time, one of its weaknesses, the delay in integrating women workers' experiences and the hesitant way in which all but a handful of Bolsheviks did so, will be taken up at every moment in party history. Along with this, there will be a discussion of the Bolshevik concept of democracy and the extent of their adherence to democracy in revolutionary strategy. What strategy did they advocate in order to make a majority revolution in a country in which the proletariat was in a minority?[37] A dimension added to this study, is the attempt by a fairly large number of Bolshevik women, and their attempts at reworking the revolutionary program to integrate women's liberation within a revolutionary perspective.[38]

Further, it will be necessary to look at Bolshevism in the year 1917. This was the first major test in practice of their concept of democracy. A critical examination of the Bolsheviks in the year 1917 means looking into much of the voluminous criticism mentioned earlier. What was the relationship between the Bolshevik party and the mass organizations of the workers—soviets, factory committees and so on? What was the composition and internal structure of the party itself in 1917? Was there a genuine parliamentary democratic option present? And finally, what was the strategic line culminating in the October insurrection—was it a line of minority revolution or a coup d'etat?[39]

Finally, we need to discuss the early years of Bolshevism in power, and test two hypotheses. The first is the view that a predetermined authoritarian theory of dictatorship of the proletariat led inexorably to the establishment of a totalitarian regime.[40] This theory has two sub-sets. One group treats *The State and Revolution* as a libertarian aberration. A number of recent authors have been unwilling to make this concession, and they claim that Lenin's theory of the revolutionary state ruled out the concept of a legitimate opposition and insisted on a strict unity of the class under the "correct line" of the vanguard party. This criticism has to be examined by carefully analyzing Lenin's writings, including *The State and Revolution*.

The alternative hypothesis is that after October 1917 the circumstances changed dramatically. It claims that before October, the prospect of a workers' conquest of power was viewed with utmost hostility by Russian liberalism, not to speak of forces further to the right. This hostility turned into an armed counter-revolution, first during the attempted putsch of Kornilov, then, even more categorically in the aftermath of the Soviet conquest of power, and was supported by the imperialist powers. This, together with an attendant economic crisis, is held to have brutalized existence and terribly weakened every form of democratization, including the experiments at workers' control of production in place of bureaucratic management, the Soviet power system, and so on. It was the counter-revolution itself which contributed to the elimination of the opposition and the regimentation of the Bolshevik party according to this hypothesis.[41] The tragedy of Russian democracy was that parties of moderate socialism, who claimed to be democrats, were to turn to the right wing. They could not distinguish between their opposition to the line of the Bolshevik party and their opposition to the workers' and peasants' regime. But it is also a case that all too often, in place of admitting that acute crises were causing departures from workers' democracy, the Bolsheviks justified those departures as developments superior to bourgeois democracy. This caused a deep retreat in the theoretical field and ultimately affected their political practice seriously.[42] Nonetheless, the process of bureaucratization and the rise of Stalinism meant a decisive break with the Bolshevik legacy, rather than an essential continuity. Perhaps the clearest indications include the total retreat, under Stalinist rule, compared not only to Alexandra Kollontai, but even compared to Lenin's relatively less radical, certainly non-feminist, commitment to women's liberation. To discuss that, one needs to first of all look at the process of bringing women into the party, as well as the process of trying to change women's lives for the better, despite the hardships of the early years of the revolution.

Even today the experience of the Russian Revolution cannot be treated as a historical past that has little bearing on current affairs. Attitudes to the social and political questions of the present are substantially shaped by the stand one takes regarding Bolshevism and the October Revolution. But as this is neither an apologia nor a post-Cold War breast-beating by had-been socialists, there is a necessity of keeping a critical attitude vis-à-vis the subject of the study. The aim of the work as a whole will not be to "absolve" the Bolsheviks of their responsibility for the systematic degeneration of democracy in the early years of Soviet power. But ideologically motivated research that denies the necessity of situating the Bolsheviks in the grim context in which their ideology and practice unfolded after 1917 cannot be accepted even if it appears as the consensus of the day. Interestingly, the archival material released since the fall of the bureaucratic regime has come to corroborate, as serious scholarship has shown, the arguments contained in this book rather than the theories of premeditated Bolshevik totalitarianism.[43]

In undertaking this study, I was not motivated by a non-existent pure scholarly outlook. I believe that a commitment to revolutionary democratic socialism from below must assimilate all the lessons of the past, both positive and negative, in order to move forward. In part,[44] the crisis of the Soviet Union was caused by a global capitalist offensive, often called globalization.[45] An important dimension of this world capitalist offensive was the slogan called TINA—There is No Alternative (to capitalism). Democracy has been shorn of its traditional meaning and the citizen turned into a consumer. Pseudo-scholarship on Marxism and the Russian Revolution are essential ingredients of this anti-working class offensive. And as the old left wears out, as Stalinist or Centrist parties move towards a full scale rapprochement with capitalism, calling for reforms within capitalism and so on, they also seek to erase all memories of the October Revolution and to spread calumny about it as the herald of an authoritarian detour. Yet capitalism even in its "democratic" forms is grossly undemocratic. When we look at the former Soviet Union, or indeed the East European states, we are struck by the fact that after all the rhetoric of restoration of democracy, what has been created is elite domination and the subjection of people to the market. Since 1991, standards of living have fallen.[46] Protests have been greeted with considerable violence. Boris Yeltsin used direct military force to overthrow one elected parliament.[47] And this is not exceptional, but in tune with global developments in the name of democracy. When George Bush, Jr. brings democracy to Iraq by destroying the country, or when in India, in the name of development, mass evictions of tribals occur, or when, in the name of fighting "Naxalite terrorism," the state militarizes civil society,[48] it becomes clear that capitalist democracy is not intended for the majority and can only push the world to new catastrophes. This is a stark example of the polarity expressed by Rosa Luxemburg—"socialism or barbarism." The creation of a democratic alternative looking for social justice is a difficult task, but if we ignore the contributions of the revolutionary socialism of the nineteenth and early twentieth centuries, we will be weakening that struggle further. Precisely for that reason, undermining the socialist alternative remains perpetually on the agenda of defenders of neoliberalism. The heritage of the revolutionary socialist perspective of democracy continues to be important because it went beyond purely political democracy and attempted to overcome the state and civil society duality. It challenged the view that democracy must leave untouched all the key economic decisions. Today, the arguments about economic consensus under the aegis of the WTO-IMF-World Bank mean that even if radical political forces use the electoral process to partially capture political power, they are told that they cannot use this power in order to move towards a break with neoliberalism. In country after country in Latin America, for example, this has been the argument used when leftist parties win elections. In India, too, this has been the logic behind the transformation of the politics of the mainstream left. The consequence is a loss of historical memory. This is of fundamental importance. As Antonio Gramsci pointed out: "The subaltern classes, by definition, are not unified and cannot unite until they are able to become a 'State'. . . . The history of subaltern social groups is necessarily fragmented and episodic. There undoubtedly does exist a tendency to (at least provisional stages of) unification in the historical activity of these groups, but this tendency is continually interrupted by the activity of the ruling groups. . . . Subaltern groups are always subject to the activity of ruling groups, even when they rebel and rise up. . . . Every trace of independent initiative on the part of subaltern groups should therefore be of incalculable value for the integral historian."[49] Forgetting the real history of Classical Marxism and democracy is not accidental, but a pressure of the ruling classes globally. The Russian Revolution is portrayed as despotism, overlooking the massive creativity of the early years. Restoring its real picture, not idealized but with all lessons duly drawn, means challenging bourgeois specialists who try to control the thinking of toiling people, and also rejecting formerly leftist intellectuals in retreat who do not merely express legitimate criticisms of the shortcomings of the socialist project, but try to integrate themselves with capitalism.

NOTES

1. See F. Fukuyama, *The End of History and the Last Man*, New York, 1992; J. Dunn, ed., *Democracy; The Unfinished Journey*, Oxford, 1992.
2. L. Kołakowski, "Marxist Roots of Stalinism," in R. C. Tucker, ed., *Stalinism. Essays in Historical Interpretation*, New York, 1977; G. Leff, *The Tyranny of Concepts; A Critique of Marxism*, London, 1961; and F. A. Hayek, *The Road to Serfdom*, Chicago, 1950 are notable examples.
3. G. Lichtheim, *Marxism; An Historical and Critical Study*, London, 1961; D. W. Lovell, *From Marx to Lenin*, Cambridge, 1984.
4. L. Schapiro, *The Origin of the Communist Autocracy*, New York, 1965, A. J. Polan, *Lenin and the End of Politics*, London, 1984; S. Farber, *Before Stalinism*, London, 1990.
5. Works emphasizing the totalitarian nature of the Marxian project include K. R. Popper, *The Open Society and its Enemies*, 2 vols, London, 1962, J. L. Talmon, *The Origins of Totalitarian Democracy*, New York, 1960, and *Political Messianism, The Romantic Phase*, New York, 1960.
6. For charges about the authoritarian elitist nature of the Leninist Party, see L. Schapiro, *The Communist Party of the Soviet Union*, London, 1970; S. S. Wolin, *Politics and Vision*, Princeton, 1960, and R. N. Carew Hunt, *The*

Theory and Practice of Communism, Harmondsworth, 1978.

7. J. Plamenatz, *German Marxism and Russian Communism*, London, 1954; R. N. Hunt, *The Political Ideas of Marx and Engels*, 2 vols, London and Basingstoke, 1975, 1983; and H. Draper, *Karl Marx's Theory of Revolution* (hereafter cited as *KMTR*), 4 vols, New York, 1977–1990.

8. R. N. Hunt, vol. 1, pp. 365–67; H. Draper, *The "Dictatorship of the Proletariat" from Marx to Lenin*, (hereafter cited as DPML) New York, 1988.

9. See e.g., E. Wilson, *To the Finland Station*, London, 1960; and A. B. Ulam, *Lenin and the Bolsheviks*, London, 1969. A particularly extreme case is the psychological study, E. V. Wolfenstein, *The Revolutionary Personality; Lenin, Trotsky, Gandhi*, Princeton, 1967.

10. See in particular D. W. Lovell, *From Marx to Lenin*, p. 188, See also T. K. Bandyopadhyay, *Concept of the Party from Marx to Gramsci*, Calcutta, 1992.

11. Literature on Russian working-class and socialist movement is vast. Major studies include V. E. Bonnell, *Roots of Rebellion*, Berkeley, 1983; G. Swain, *Russian Social Democracy and the Legal Labour Movement: 1906–14*, London and Basingstoke, 1983; for the pre-revolutionary period; A. Rabinowitch, *Prelude to Revolution*, Indianapolis, 1968, and *The Bolsheviks Come to Power*, New York, 1976; D. Mandel, *The Petrograd Workers and the Fall of the Old Regime*, New York, 1984, and *The Petrograd Workers and the Soviet Seizure of Power*, New York, 1984, for the revolution of 1917; and S. A. Smith, *Red Petrograd*, Cambridge, 1983; I. Getzler, *Kronstadt 1917–21*, Cambridge, 1983 and S. Malle, *The Economic Organization of War Communism, 1918–1921*, Cambridge, 1985, for various aspects of the early Soviet era, Bolshevik policy and the problems of democracy.

12. Even a number of socialists have come to this position from the final years of Gorbachev. See for example, J. Slovo, *Has Socialism Failed?*, London, 1990, and R. Blackburn, "Fin de Siecle: Socialism after the crash," in *New Left Review, 185*, January–February 1991. However, for one of the most currently popular academic studies, one has to go to Orlando Figes, *A People's Tragedy: The Russian Revolution 1891–1924*, London, 1996. In Figes' work, capitalism and the ruling class practically disappear from view, so the nasty Bolsheviks are left in solitary splendor as the inaugurators of totalitarianism.

13. For twentieth-century advances in Marxist theoretical and practical advances in the case of women's liberation, the critical literature is vast. We can only begin by mentioning a few texts. Lydia Sargent, ed., *The Unhappy Marriage of Marxism and Feminism: A Debate on Class and Patriarchy*, London, 1986, has an excellent collection of articles around Heidi Hartmann's "dual systems" theory. Z. Eisenstein, ed., *Capitalist Patriarchy and the Case for Socialist Feminism*, New York and London, 1979, is an important collection dealing with a range of issues faced by socialist and Marxist feminism. See further Lise Vogel, *Marxism and the Oppression of Women: Toward a Unitary Theory*, New Brunswick, 1983; L. Vogel, *Woman Questions*, New York and London, 1995; M. Mies, *Feminism in Europe: Liberal and Socialist Strategies 1789–1919*, The Hague, 1983 for a text that is quite critical of classical Marxism's legacy; T. Cliff, *Class Struggle*

and Women's Liberation, London, 1987 for a rather stultifying orthodox response to socialist feminism; and S. Rowbotham, H. Wainwright and L. Segal, *Beyond the Fragments*, London, 1979 for a critique of Leninism. For political interventions, see Nita Keig, ed., *Women's Liberation and Socialist Revolution*, New York, 1979, (resolution of the Fourth International); and "Positive Action and Party Building Among Women," resolution of the Fourth international, *International Marxist Review*, no. 14, Winter 1992, pp. 109–31.

14. However, S. Avineri, in *The Social and Political Thought of Karl Marx*, New Delhi, 1977; and R. N. Berki, "Through and Through Hegel, Marx's Road to Communism" *in Political Studies, XXXVIII*, 1990, claim that Marx's communism was a product of his Hegelianism. R. N. Hunt, vol. 1, pp. 134–39 treats Marx's earliest political stand as a liberal one.

15. This is clearly stated by Locke. See, for example, J. Locke, *Two Treatises on Government*, P. Laslett, ed., Oxford, 1980.

16. Thus J. S. Mill, *On Liberty*, New York, 1956, pp. 6–7, argued that democratic government did not constitute the freedom of the individual. Some years back two US scholars described the liberal democratic state as one which is separated from control over the allocation of social labour. See S. Bowles and H. Gintis, "The Crisis of Liberal Democratic Capitalism: The Case of the United States," in *Politics and Society*, vol. XI, no. 1, 1982, p. 52.

17. This line of criticism was also developed by C. B. MacPherson in *The Political Theory of Possessive Individualism*, Oxford, 1962; *Democratic Theory; Essays in Retrieval*, Oxford, 1973; and *The Life and Times of Liberal Democracy*, Oxford, 1977. See also E. M. Wood, *The Retreat from Class; A New "True" Socialism*, London, 1988 and R. Miliband, *The State in Capitalist Society*, London, 1973 for Marxist discussions on the functioning of liberal democracy. For a rejoinder to theories seeking to dissociate Locke's liberalism from capitalist accumulation and its defense, see N. Wood, *John Locke and Agrarian Capitalism*, Berkeley, 1984.

18. For Hegel see S. Avineri, *Hegel's Theory of the Modern State*, Cambridge, 1972; and Z. A. Pełcyński, ed., *Hegel's Political Philosophy*, Cambridge, 1971.

19. Social democrats like S. Landshut and J. P. Meyer, eds., *Karl Marx der Historische Materialismus*, Leipzig, 1932, tried to put forward the conception of a humanist Marx on the basis of these writings. The Stalinist response was to minimize the importance of these texts, because the theory of alienation showed that for Marx economic freedom did not just mean an increase in the standard of living but the control by the collective producers of the entire production process. See for example, L. Althusser, *For Marx*, London, 1977. In their view, the young Marx had not yet "become" Marx, and his writings up to 1845–46 should not be viewed as Marxist. This eliminates some of Marx's most powerful writings in defense of democracy and democratic rights.

20. F. Engels, "Letter to August Bebel," and K. Marx, "Marginal Notes on the Programme of the German Workers' Party," in K. Marx and F. Engels, *Collected Works* (*MECW* hereafter), 24, Moscow, 1989, pp. 67–73, 81–99.

21. F. Engels, *Anti-Dühring*, in ibid. 25. Moscow, 1989, pp. 5–309.

22. There is a massive debate over the question of dialectics in nature. See T. Carver, *Marx and Engels: The Intellectual Relationship*, Brighton, 1983; and J. Coulter, "Marxism and the Engels Paradox" in R. Miliband and J. Seville, eds., *Socialist Register*, 1971. For a more far-ranging attack on the role of Engels, see N. Levine, *The Tragic Deception; Marx contra Engels*, Santa Barbara, 1975. S. Avineri, in *The Social and Political Thought of Karl Marx*, likewise sharply differentiates between Marx and Engels. The present author accepts the arguments put forward by R. N. Hunt, *The Political Ideas of Marx and Engels*, and especially H. Draper, *KMTR* 1. Very recently, the Argentine-born Brazilian scholar, Osvaldo Coggiola, has produced an excellent essay arguing for conclusions similar to mine. I am grateful to Professor Coggiola for sending me an English translation of his so-far unpublished essay, "*The Quieter of the Two: Friedrich Engels and Political and Internationalist Marxism.*"

23. K. Marx, *Herr Vogt*, in *MECW* 17, Moscow, 1981, p. 114.

24. The best survey is M. Johnstone, "Marx and Engels and the Concept of the Party," *Socialist Register*, 1967. For the "Vanguard party" interpretation see E. P. Kandel, "'Iskazenii Istorii bor'" by Marksa i Engelsa za proletarskuiu partiiu v rabotakh nekotorikh pravikh solsialistov," *Voprossii Istorii*, no. 5, 1958.The theory of a "propagandistic" party will be found in H. J. Laski, "Introduction" to *Communist Manifesto: Socialist Landmark*, London, 1954; J. O. Malley and K. Algozin, eds., *Rubel on Karl Marx*, Cambridge, 1981, pp. 26–81 and B. I. Nicolaievsky , "Toward a History of the Communist League, 1847–52" *International Review of Social History*, no. 1, 1956. For an example of a work that sees Marx as unserious about party building, see B. D. Wolfe, *Marxism: One Hundred Years in the Life of a Doctrine*, Madras, 1968.

25. There have been claims that insurrectionary politics cannot be majoritarian. See E. Bernstein, *Evolutionary Socialism*, London, 1909, and S. W. Moore, *Three Tactics: The Background in Marx*, New York, 1963.

26. See M. Löwy, *The Politics of Combined and Uneven Development*, London, 1981; A. Gilbert, *Marx's Politics*, Oxford, 1981, and K. Chattopadhyay, "Marx, Engels and the Peasant Question," parts I–III, *Journal of History*, Jadavpur University, vols. V, VI and VII, 1985, 1986–87, and 1987–88. For a contrary view, see B. D. Wolfe, *Marxism*.

27. See the historical narrative in O. J. Hammen, *The Red '48ers*, New York, 1969.

28. Bernstein was the originator of the claim that the use of violence renders the revolution undemocratic.

29. S. Avineri, *The Social and Political Thought of Karl Marx*, pp. 34–37 believes that Marx saw in universal suffrage the dissolution of the state. For a refutation of theories that show Marx as a champion of direct democracy, see P. Springborg, "Karl Marx on Democracy, Voting and Equality," *Political Theory*, vol. XII, no. 4, November 1984, pp. 537–56.

30. For anarchist-inspired criticisms, Marx is an authoritarian socialist. For the origin of such criticism, see S. Dolgoff, ed. *Bakunin on Anarchy*, London, 1973. The examination of these specific issues will throw light on the above charges as well.

31. For a survey of the debate over Marx's own use of the term, see H. Draper,

KMTR 3. For a survey of the modern debate see B. Bhattacharyya, *Dictatorship of the Proletariat: The Current Debate,* Calcutta, 1985, for two contrasting modern positions see S. Carillo, *"Eurocommunism" and the State* London, 1979 and A. R. Desai, ed. *Communism and Democracy,* Bombay, 1990.

32. In *KMTR* 3, Draper's central thesis is that the term has a purely sociological significance and has nothing to do with the mechanics of power.

33. For discussion of the concept of the dictatorship of the proletariat incorporating institutional forms, see S. H. M. Chang, *The Marxian Theory of the State,* Delhi, 1990.

34. A typical case is R. N. Carew Hunt, *The Theory and Practice of Communism,* p. 107, where he writes that the dictatorship of the proletariat means the rule of a single section which must eliminate all other sections. While this may be a partially recognizable picture of the Stalin era, methodologically it is unsound to deduce from Stalinism's action that Marx did want such a development.

35. See R. Pipes, "The Origins of Bolshevism: The Intellectual Evolution of Young Lenin" and the attendant discussion by a number of scholars, in R. Pipes, ed., *Revolutionary Russia,* Cambridge, 1968, for attempts to find various Russian narodnik or Blanqui-type intellectual inspirers of Lenin. See D. W. Lovell, *From Marx to Lenin,* Chapter 5, for a claim that through Plekhanov, Russian Marxism was from inception insistent upon the leadership of the intelligentsia.

36. This is claimed by L. Kołakowski, *Main Currents of Marxism,* vol. 2, Oxford, 1982. Even a pro-Lenin author like M. Liebman, *Leninism under Lenin,* London, 1980, has a similar view. R. Schlesinger, *History of the Communist Party of the USSR,* Calcutta, 1977, p. 79 argues that there is no sharp demarcation between the Leninist and the Stalinist concept of party organization. A defense of Lenin from the charge of Jacobinism is provided by N. Harding, *Lenin's Political Thought,* vol. 1, London and Basingstoke, 1977. See also L. Trotsky, *Stalin,* London, 1946 and P. Le Blanc, *Lenin and the Revolutionary Party,* New Jersey and London, 1990.

37. S.H. Baron, *Plekhanov, Father of Russian Marxism,* London, 1963 and A. Ascher, *Pavel Axelrod and the Development of Menshevism,* Cambridge, 1972, treat the Menshevik strategy of an alliance with the liberal bourgeoisie as the orthodox Marxist stand. E. Kingston-Mann, *Lenin and the Problem of Marxist Peasant Revolution,* Oxford, 1983, treats the Bolshevik strategy of worker-peasant alliance and proletarian hegemony as a departure from orthodox Marxism.

38. A large number of books has been used in elaborating upon these discussions. See, for example B. Evans Clements, *Bolshevik Women,* Cambridge, 1997; Cathy Porter, *Women in Revolutionary Russia,* Cambridge and New York, 1987; B. Farnsworth, *Alexandra Kollontai: Socialism, Feminism and the Bolshevik Revolution,* Stanford, 1980; B. Evans Clements, *Bolshevik Feminist: The Life of Alexandra Kollontai,* Bloomington and London, 1979; and several essays by the present author, including S. Marik, "Biplabi Dal O Linga Samata" (Revolutionary Party and Gender Equality), *Loukik*

Udyan, Manabi Sankhya, August 1999; "Bolshevikbad O Nari Sramik: Prayoger Aloke Tatver Punarvichar" (Bolshevism and Women Workers: A Reappraisal of theory in the light of practice), in G. Chattopadhyay, ed., *Itihas Anusandhan* 13, Calcutta, 1999; "Proletarian Socialism and Women's Liberation," *Proceedings of the Indian History Congress,* Calcutta, 2001; "A Pioneering Male Socialist Feminist: The Recovery of August Bebel," (Review Article based on *Men's Feminism: August Bebel and the German Socialist Movement* by Anne Lopes and Gary Roth , Amherst, New York, 2000) in *Against the Current,* March/April 2004; and "Gendering the Revolutionary Party: An Appraisal of Bolshevism," in Biswajit Chatterjee and Kunal Chattopadhyay, eds., *Perspectives on Socialism,* Calcutta, 2004.

39. See R. Pipes, *The Russian Revolution,* London, 1990, and E. Hobsbawm, "Waking from History's Great Dream," *Independent on Sunday,* February 4, 1990. A critique of this trend is to be found in S. F. Cohen, *Rethinking the Soviet Experience: Politics and History Since 1917,* New York, 1985.

40. See N. Harding, *Lenin's Political Thought,* vol. 2, London and Basingstoke, 1983, for arguments about flaws in Lenin's theory, as well as the works of Polan, Lovell, and Schapiro cited earlier. For a defense of *The State and Revolution* see L. Colletti, "Lenin's *State and Revolution,*" in R. Blackburn, ed. *Revolution and Class Struggle,* Glasgow, 1977, pp. 69–77.

41. For a rigid defense of Bolshevism in power, along the lines of argument sketched out above, see J. Rees, "In Defence of October," *Society and Change,* vol. VIII, no. 2, July–September 1991.

42. See in particular R. Luxemburg, "Zur russischen Revolution," in R. Luxemburg, *Gesammelte Werke,* 5 vols, Berlin 1988 –1990, Band 4, 1990, pp. 332–65. See further S. Marik, "The Bolsheviks and Workers' Democracy: 1917–1927. The Ideological Crisis of Russian Communism and the Rise of Stalinism," *Proceedings of the Indian History Congress,* 52nd Session, New Delhi, 1992, pp. 903–12.

43. See, for example, D. Mandel, *Factory Committees and Workers' Control in Petrograd in 1917,* Montreuil, France, 1993. There have also emerged works that have attempted to show the early Bolshevik regime as an inherently authoritarian one, including General D. Volkogonov's *Triumph and Tragedy,* vol. 1, Moscow, 1989. The politically motivated distortions of such works have been discussed by a number of Soviet and American scholars. For this, see M. Vogt-Downey, ed., *The USSR 1987–1991: Marxist Perspectives,* New Jersey, 1993, pp. 288–330.

44. I use the qualifying words as I do not intend to argue that the Soviet bureaucrats did not turn consciously to capitalist restoration. But that they could do so at a particular historical moment can be related to globalization. That the Soviet working class, unlike the East European, was not even able to create mass resistance, is worth noting. On these subjects, see S. Marik, "The Withering Away of Stalinism," *Society and Change,* Calcutta, vol. VI, nos. 3 & 4, October 1989–March 1990; and Kunal Chattopadhyay, "The German Reunification and the Left," and David Mandel, "Revolution, Counterrevolution and Working Class in Russia: Reflections for the Eightieth Anniversary of the October Revolution," both

in Rila Mukherjee and Kunal Chattopadhyay, eds., *Europe in the Second Millennium: A Hegemony Achieved?*, Calcutta, 2005.

45. I do not propose to analyze globalization here, but there are many Marxist studies. Some important works can be mentioned. To understand capitalism in the second half of the twentieth century one cannot do better than to start with Ernest Mandel, *Late Capitalism*, London, 1978. For more recent trends, see Eric Toussaint, *Your Money or Your Life!: The Tyranny of Global Finance*, 3rd ed., Chicago, 2005; James Petras and Henry Veltmeyer, *Globalisation Unmasked*, Halifax, Nova Scotia, 2001; Michael Chossudovsky, *The Globalisation of Poverty*, Mapusa, Goa (Indian edition), 2001.

46. According to the Russian commentator Aleksander Buzgalin, between 1991 and 2001 wages more than halved in real terms, while unemployment rose to 12 percent in a country where it was virtually unheard of. Aleksander Buzgalin, "Russia: Signs of Change," *International Viewpoint*, no. 340, May 2002, p. 29.

47. On the use of force to create a very limited and controlled "democracy" in post-Soviet Union Russia, see Kunal Chattopadhyay, "Hunger for Power," *Business Standard*, December 29, 1991; Kunal Chattopadhyay, "Run-Up to a Russian Roulette," *Business Standard*, March 23, 1993; Kunal Chattopadhyay, "Fuzzy Power Structure lands Russia in a constitutional crisis," *Business Standard*, September 26, 1993; and Kunal Chattopadhyay, "Yeltsin and the Weimar Syndrome," *Business Standard*, December 16, 1993.

48. On this issue of creating so-called anti-Naxalite groups, see the Press Release by Independent Citizens' Initiative, New Delhi, May 29th, 2006, "Citizens' Panel Warns of Civil War in Chhattisgarh, Calls for End to 'Salwa Judum' Campaign and Judicial Inquiry," and Praful Bidwai, "Waging War Against the People: Dangerous Anti-Naxal Strategy," June 5, 2006, South Asian Citizen Wire, a regular email sent out to subscribers on South Asian affairs by aiindex@mnet.fr, accessible at http://www.sacw.net/article1.html.

49. Antonio Gramsci, *Selections from the Prison Notebooks*, edited and translated by Quintin Hoare and Geoffrey Nowell Smith, New York, 1971, pp. 53–55.

2

FROM RADICAL DEMOCRACY
TO PROLETARIAN DEMOCRACY

I
MARX'S TRANSITION FROM DEMOCRACY TO COMMUNISM

The central political concept of classical Marxism is proletarian self-emancipation. From this flows the idea of workers' democracy, which plays a key role in explaining what Marx and Engels thought about the function of democracy in the liberation of the working class. The discovery of the writings of young Marx and Engels has enabled scholars to make comprehensive studies on the evolution of their ideas. In the present work, the relationship between the positions of young Marx and Engels and their mature selves are neither sharply counterpoised, nor is it argued that Marx's road to communism lay wholly through Hegel or Spinoza.[1] This study aims to show Marx's view on democracy as a totality emerging out of the critiques of German idealist philosophy, French left-wing politics, and political economy, mainly English. Quite long ago, without even going into all the details of the writings of young Marx, Lenin pointed out that Marxism "emerged as the direct and immediate continuation of the teachings of the greatest representatives of philosophy, political economy and socialism."[2] Marxism did not come into existence as a finished theory or philosophy at a given moment. Marx's idea of democracy evolved from an abstract notion of political democracy to proletarian democracy on the basis of concrete historical experiences, the experience of the working class as the most oppressed and at the same time militant class in both France and England, had a great impact on Marx and Engels. Marxism was born as a theory of revolutionary praxis in the course of, as well as in response to, current political struggles. Marx himself remarked in his "Preface" to *A*

Contribution to the Critique of Political Economy (1859), that his criticism of existing state and society did not come out of his philosophy but out of "material conditions of life."[3] So, what made Marx a communist, and what made his communism so distinctive, were human activity and the clash of material interests, which he ultimately saw as class struggle. This does not mean that Marx abandoned philosophy. On the contrary, Hegel's dialectical method made it possible for him to conceptualize class struggle as a global phenomenon. For Hegel, the dialectic was a development of ideas, where each phase emerged within the previous one, developed through contradictions, and in becoming dominant retained the past in subordinate form. While adopting this dialectical method Marx separated it from idealism and made the struggle of ideas subordinate to real social struggles. Without the critique of Hegel, Marx could not have arrived at the concept of the primacy of class struggle and of communism as the end product of workers' own liberation. István Mészáros has argued that in the process of becoming a communist, Marx made an attempt at "situating his type of philosophy in relation to a concrete socio-historical force, and defining its function as both integral and necessary to a successful struggle for emancipation. . ."[4] Marx's evolution shows him settling accounts with Hegel's theory of state in 1843, re-examining the meaning of alienation in 1844, and rejecting all claims for a privileged status of "philosophy" by 1845.

This process began with Marx's adherence to the Young Hegelians. While the Old Hegelians upheld Hegel's conservative political orientation, the Young Hegelians used the dialectical method to mount a rationalist attack on the absolutist state as well as the church. Politically they were constitutionalists who at the same time had hopes on the liberal inclinations of the Prussian Crown Prince, the future Friedrich Wilhelm IV. But his accession in 1840 inaugurated a reactionary phase in the intellectual world and a tight censorship. Marx's friend, the leading Young Hegelian Bruno Bauer, lost his university position. These were years when Marx's ideas were in flux. A sense of discrepancy between what is and what ought to be impelled him to activism.[5] But still trapped within the confines of an idealist outlook, Marx continued to emphasize the philosophical critique of philosophy. His radicalism did not yet lead him to social activism. But soon he lost faith in the Prussian king and he gave up expecting any hero-savior from above. This transition, from constitutionalist liberalism to radical democracy, was quite explicit in Marx's letter to his friend and a fellow democrat, Arnold Ruge. Here he talked about "transition to the human world of democracy." The initiative to change the society into a democratic order was to be taken by the self-confident people themselves, who could feel the necessity of attaining freedom.[6] In moving beyond his liberal friends into becoming a democrat, Marx rejected the model of constitutional monarchy as a "hybrid" and a contradiction. This abandonment of the then current dream of German liberalism made him call for a struggle against the Prussian State.[7]

This shift called for open political activity, which became possible when Rhineland liberals founded the *Rheinische Zeitung* (*RZ*) and allied with the Young Hegelians to run it as a party newspaper. Initially as a correspondent and subsequently as the editor, Marx plunged into a bitter battle against the autocracy, fighting for civil liberties. But it will not be quite fair to call him a "liberal democrat."[8] At this phase his writings for the *RZ* showed his concern for democracy, going beyond demands for civil liberties corresponding to bourgeois-liberal interests. Eventually his democratic outlook and his stress on social aspects of politics made him come into open conflict with liberalism as well as with Hegel's theory of state.

From January to October 1842, Marx concentrated on the issue of freedom of the press. He attacked censorship laws in the name of unfettered freedom of expression, and rejected any limitation on it on the grounds of "permanent immaturity" of the people.[9] It was his consistent emphasis on human self-activity that led Marx to move towards a defense of democracy and critiques of both autocracy and constitutional monarchy. As early as May 1842, he wrote about the lack of control of the electorate over their representatives.[10]

Marx thus related the freedom of press to representative democracy, arguing that such freedom made possible the necessary control from below without which there could be no true representation.[11] In this sense, Marx's critique of the autocracy rejected the limited stand of the bourgeois liberal members of the Cologne Circle, which included leading Rhineland liberals like the financiers Camphausen and Hansemann, industrialists like Mevissen and Melinckrodt. In a letter written around August 25, 1842, to Dagobert Oppenheim, brother of a leading Rhineland banker and one of the managers of the *RZ*, Marx characterized the liberals as people who wanted to win freedom step by step within the constitutional framework.[12] Marx saw the liberal position regarding freedom and democracy as a self-contradicting stand, and criticized it in the following terms:

> The absence of freedom of the press makes all other freedoms illusory. One form of freedom governs another just as one limb of the body does another . . . thus the Sixth Rhine Province Assembly, condemned itself by passing sentence on freedom of the press.[13]

In assessing the debates in the assembly, Marx ruthlessly condemned the "natural impotence of half-hearted liberalism" and the "negligent superficiality" with which the liberals dealt with the issue of freedom of press reducing it to a mere corollary of freedom of trade of the printers. While the liberals targeted the individual bureaucrats who were appointed censors, Marx's target was the institution of censorship itself.[14] But soon he realized that defense of censorship was related to the feudal elements, that is the princes and the knights who regarded "freedom as merely an individual property of certain persons and social estates."[15]

From October 1842, as editor of *RZ*, Marx started writing articles on issues like the law on theft of wood, and another on the distress of the vine-growing peasants of Moselle. In these articles, he was forced to confront the reality of opposed class interests and the role of the state as an agency of domination. The debate over the wood theft law was a particularly instructive case. The gathering of dead wood had traditionally been unrestricted. Gradually, with the development of capitalism, industrial need for wood had increased, which led to the passing of laws to control theft of timber. Over 80 percent of all prosecutions in Prussia dealt with wood. A new law suggested that the wood keeper should be the sole arbiter of alleged offenses and that he alone should assess the damages.[16] In "Debates on the Law on Theft of Wood," (October-November 1842) Marx criticized the state for curtailing the customary rights of the "politically and socially propertyless" and favoring the monopoly rights of the landlords of Trier and Coblenz.[17] Around November-December 1842, the Moselle correspondent of the *RZ* published several articles describing the chronic depression and misery that the grape-growers of the Moselle valley had experienced for years. In publishing the reports Marx probably gave a twist to the contents by claiming that the Prussian bureaucracy had formerly shown a callous indifference to the suffering vine-growers. And it was only the liberalization of the censorship laws that had spared the vine-growers from bureaucratic high-handedness from 1841.[18] The state authorities accused the paper of distorting facts and slandering the officials. Marx's reply, entitled, "Justification of the correspondent from the Moselle," (January 1843), again emphasized the relationship between the freedom of the press and alleviation of social distress. It also provided evidence that a bureaucratic administration had sought to protect its self-interests by telling the peasantry to adjust to the administrative needs. He further claimed that the state had no interest in a permanent remedy of the distress of the vine growers.[19] Marx was thus coming to question the universality of the state which was taking the side of the propertied against the propertyless. His involvement with these social issues led him to realize that the rights of all social groups were not treated on a par by the state, and his break with the Hegelian idealization of the state was hastened when the Prussian state decided to close down the *RZ* from

March 1843. Marx's standpoint during this period may be best described as radical democratic, as opposed to R. N. Hunt's characterization of him as a Young Hegelian and Liberal Democratic.[20] On every issue, he never failed to relate specific freedom to freedom in general, or political democracy, and also to the solution of the problems of social inequality. For liberalism, political equality was always closely related to the defense of private property. Even in his *RZ* days Marx wrote:

> If every violation of property without distinction, without a more exact definition is termed theft, will not all private property be theft? By my private ownership do I not exclude every other person from this ownership?[21]

Moreover, Marx's articles breathed the spirit of peoples' self-activity in opposition to the ideal of bureaucratic reformism. He upheld freedom of expression not merely as a philosopher but to build a "bridge of struggle" between the sphere of the civil society and the sphere of the state. This idea was to be later elaborated in Marx's critique of Hegel's theory of state. In his letter to Oppenheim there was a criticism of the Berlin group of Young Hegelians as people who indulged in "arm chair abstractions."[22] Writing to Ruge, between March and September, 1843, Marx reiterated the necessity of making the people aware of their democratic rights so that they could engage themselves in real struggles. Though, like the Young Hegelians, Marx still felt that philosophy had the leading role to play in injecting consciousness, he was, by now, emphasizing real struggles for democracy, while the traditional Young Hegelian position was tantamount to freedom for the intellectuals. Marx sharply opposed this elitism, when he told Ruge,

> We do not confront the world in a doctrinaire way with a new principle: Here is the truth, kneel down before it. We develop new principles for the world out of world's own principles.... We merely show the world what it is really fighting for and consciousness is something it has to acquire, even if it does not want to.[23]

By this time, Marx was thoroughly disgusted with the liberalism of the reformers in the Rhenish Diet, the hypocrisy and gross arbitrariness of the state, on the one hand, and dissatisfied with the Young Hegelian search for the abstract and absolute on the other. After a prolonged study in Kreuznach he produced a detailed but unfinished critique of Hegel between June and October 1843. In this period he was not only influenced by Feuerbach's humanism and materialist philosophy but was equally moved by the history of the French revolutionary politics. Taking for granted the atheism of the Young Hegelians and the critique of religious alienation, Marx moved on to a more thoroughgoing critique of Hegelian politics. On the one hand, his journalistic activities delayed this project.

On the other hand, the practical experience certainly deepened his democratic convictions. By humanism or human emancipation he started to mean political and social emancipation and urged the revival of the spirit of freedom as the starting point of establishing a democratic state.

Marx's *Contribution to the Critique of Hegel's Philosophy of Law* (hereafter called the Kreuznach manuscript) must be studied against this background. In this attempt at resolving the political dilemmas of modern society, Marx actually attacked Hegel's theory of separation of civil society and state as "a necessary element of the ideas, as absolute rational truth." He struck straight at the core of Hegel's logic by insisting that "the logic does not serve to prove the state, but the state to prove the logic."[24] Hegel had depicted civil society as the site of conflicting social forces. Their particular interests were transcended by the universality of the state. So, according to Hegel, the bureaucracy was the "general estate," and the state was the abstract embodiment of universals which served general interests through this bureaucracy. A major problem with the Hegelian theory, as Marx saw it, was that it described the modern Prussian state but assumed that it was describing the state in general. The contemporary Prussian state was the one that saw massive bureaucratization, a particular form of estrangement of humanity and subordination of civil society to the state. Marx began to historicize his concept of the state, and to use the materialist doctrine to show the social basis of the state, focusing on the feudal institution of primogeniture. Marx identified this institution as the particular manifestation of power of abstract private property over the state. So according to him,

> in the constitution where primogeniture is a guarantee, private property is the guarantee of the political constitution. . . . The political constitution at its highest point is therefore the constitution of private property. The supreme political conviction is the conviction of private property.[25]

And the bureaucracy had a special role to play—it identified the state interest and particular private aims in such a way that "the state interest becomes a particular private aim over against other private aims."[26] Hegel was ruthlessly accused of being through and through infested with the miserable arrogance of the Prussian bureaucracy and of dwindling the society to the point of servility to this state-bureaucracy. The bureaucracy was charged by Marx with ridiculing the "self-confidence" of the people as "mere opinion." Marx criticized Hegel for wrongly assuming that the civil estates acquired political significance in the estates element of the legislature. He argued that all cannot be self-represented, and the "political being" of the civil society showed that the claim of the Prussian "constitutional monarchy" to universality was a false pretense. The state appeared as a different aspect of the same reality of a differentiated society where power was alienated from the mass of society.[27] The only way to do away with this alienation was to overcome the rupture between the state and the civil society, which was only possible in democracy. The Kreuznach manuscript is not merely a down-right rejection of absolutism or constitutional monarchy. It is a crucial text where Marx generalized his experiences, as editor of *RZ*, into a concrete theory in defense of democracy both as a form of rule and in its social content. His counter-position of the two questions— "Sovereignty of the monarch? or Sovereignty of the people?"—posed the issue of democracy without any ambiguity, abstraction, or mystification. Marx argued that in all constitutions, the ultimate prop of the state is the consent of the people. When he wrote that "democracy is the solved riddle of all constitutions,"[28] he meant that popular consent, which was obscured in other constitutions, was explicit here. The state, the law and the constitution all became human manifestations of the process of self-determination of the people. But Marx conceptualized democracy as a unit of political ("formal") and social ("material") principles. First of all he rejected the "political republic" which was nothing but an abstract institutional form of democracy, where political alienation continued to be the nagging political reality for the civil society. So the mere creation of a republic without any social content could not create democracy. Here he substantiated his view by giving the example of North American republic where the property relations were held in an undemocratic way, where with its limited franchise people were enjoying formal democracy without any direct control in the affairs of the state and the Government. "The content of the state lies outside these constitutions."[29] It was only with the application of the democratic principle of both "the right to vote—and to be elected" Marx was arguing that it was only with the application of the democratic principles of "both of the right to vote and the right to be elected" and a positive answer to the question, "Has the people the right to give itself a new constitution?," because if the constitution ceases to be an "expression of the will of the people," it becomes "a practical illusion."[30] This was the crux of his concept of "true" or pure democracy (as opposed to "formal" democracy), where people were not an "undifferentiated or formless mass" but active subjects of history who would transform the institution of government into an instrument for overcoming alienation at the political level. Universal franchise formed the means by which civil society could be transcended to arrive at the political entity by making the people their own rulers, dissolving both the state and civil society as a socially differentiated entity. Marx called for a real revolution in order to obtain a constitution upholding universal suffrage for establishing popular will over the subjective arbitrariness of the hitherto independent executive authority.[31]

For the same reason, Marx criticized Hegel's idea that civil society acquired political significance by sending its delegates to the Diet. For Marx, it was just a "single and transient political act without continuing cohesion, since both the state and the civil society maintain their opposed identity."[32] Such an expression raises the question whether Marx at all favored any kind of representative democracy. It was not his intention to challenge the principle of representation. In his words:

> The question whether *all* should individually "participate in deliberating and deciding on the general affairs of the state" is a question which arises from the separation of the political state and civil society.[33]

The target of Marx's criticism was the Prussian Diet idealized by Hegel. It was a typical estate-based feudal assembly, elected on the basis of a restricted franchise and without the power to control the absolutist monarchy. In this situation civil society certainly could not be adequately represented. What universal suffrage provided was a means whereby all the individuals [read male individuals] could be represented in the state. The duality was overcome through the dissolution of the unrepresentative political state and the unrepresented civil society into a representative parliament.[34] This did not constitute "a masterly critique of even the most radically conceived representative democracy."[35] So universal suffrage was to be the basis of institutionalized radical democracy. Its form, as Marx saw in the Kreuznach manuscript, was to be the dominance of the legislature. He called this "true democracy," where the parasitic state bureaucracy was to dwindle to its proper sphere, losing the attributes of the universal class, imputed by Hegel. As Marx wrote, "The striving of *civil society* to turn itself into *political society*, or to turn *political* society into *actual* society, appears as the striving for as *general* as possible a participation in the *legislative power*."[36] Thus Marx saw democracy as the outcome of the self-activity of the people which presupposed a community of interests of the society as a whole controlling the state. This makes it quite clear that the social basis of this democracy was reflected in its political aspect, the sovereignty of the people. So when Marx rejected democracy, he meant actually its abstract political form that stood on the fundamental dichotomy between the state and the civil society. While this was a remarkably radical position, it was still possible to put it within a Rousseauan framework. Nor did Marx, throughout this book, make a single reference to abolition of private property in actuality. His target was not capitalism, but Hegel's theory of the state and his positive evaluation of liberal constitutional monarchy in a semi-feudal society with a formula that opposed, in brief, all these conservative-liberal elements appearing in Hegel. It was neither communism,[37] nor did it signify a denial of popular sovereignty.[38]

Despite this relentless criticism of Hegel, Marx could not free himself wholly from the Hegelian ideal of statism. He aimed to overcome political alienation through achieving universal franchise. Marx sought his answer in humanism, whose ethics underwent mutations before he could become a communist.[39]

In 1842-43, Marx was still studying communism. But he did not yet become a communist, what he still sought was a universal class that would achieve true democracy. It was later, his experience of the actual proletariat, that would make him turn to communism. This is borne out by his article entitled, "On the Jewish Question." Written in 1843, it was published in 1844 in the *Deutsch-Französische Jahrbücher* (Franco–German Annals). Here, "the political state in its completely developed form" meant the republic.[40] He further claimed that in a democratic republic, moreover, private property was "abolished in idea."[41] At the same time, private property was kept as the natural basis of the existence of civil society, consequently, Marx argued:

> Political emancipation is, of course a big step forward. True, it is not the final form of human emancipation in general, but it is the final form of human emancipation *within* the hitherto existing world order.[42]

If later "Marxist" language were used, this could be expressed as: the democratic revolution was a big step forward, but it did not constitute the final form of emancipation. It only emancipated people from the existing feudal world order, thereby making possible the struggle for the proletarian revolution. The "political emancipation" or democratic revolution, was to free the society from the bondage of the absolutist state, but the contradiction between the propertied and the propertyless would remain even under political democracy. To stop there, would consequently be to implement a "half-hearted" emancipation, which degraded men into "play things of alien power" or subject to the "alien politics" of the liberal state. This alienation was to be brought about through the reinforcement of capitalist property relations.[43] So democracy remained a riddle, that could be solved only when universal human emancipation would be achieved. This total emancipation was defined as democratization of society where man "no longer separates social power from himself in the shape of political power."[44] In the same work, Marx dealt with alienation at a social level as well:

> But the completion of the idealism of the state was at the same time the completion of the materialism of civil society. Throwing off the political yoke meant at the same throwing off the bonds which restrained the egoistic spirit of civil society, political emancipation was at the same time the emancipation of civil society from politics, from having even the *semblance* of a universal content.[45]

Feudal society was resolved into its basic element—"But man as he really formed its basis—egoistic man." Thus, capitalist society developed the egoistic spirit to the utmost, and with that, it developed social alienation further. However, no specific class or gender analysis was made of this alienation. Man, egoistic man, was held to be alienated. This meant the individual capitalist no less than the individual worker.

It was only with the class analysis of the social problem of alienation that Marx could arrive at the conclusion that universal human emancipation was the task of only one class, the universal class of the proletariat. This formed the core of his argument in the "Contribution to the Critique of Hegel's Philosophy of Law. Introduction" (hereafter cited or mentioned as "Introduction"), written in Paris at the end of 1843. Marx, in the course of his intensive study of literature on communism, American republicanism and the French Revolution, at Kreuznach, had already read about the working class and its movements. His letter to Ruge indicated a fairly early awareness so far as the capitalist system of profit, commerce and property was concerned. He did not fail to analyze as early as May 1843 that this system of human exploitation was bound to create economic clashes.[46] In Paris he came face to face with the revolutionary communist secret societies, and the living traditions of the left wing of the French Revolution. Paris being a citadel of European industrialization, was also one of the chief concentration points of migrant German workers, who formed their own organizations. This new social milieu, which was at the same time the worst victim of capitalist development and the participant of the insurrections that had started to sway France since 1831, revolutionized Marx's vision.

"True democracy" was about to be thoroughly reshaped as proletarian democracy. Marx's brief "Introduction" formed a prolog to this idea. This text marked the beginning of Marx's break with Hegelian idealism and emphasized above everything else, "practice" or concrete activity to achieve "general human emancipation." For the first time, Marx identified himself with communism and referred to the proletariat, though primarily concerned with Germany. However, he soon went beyond the territorial limits of Germany to propound a theory of the proletariat as a universal class because of its "universal suffering" as a result of the "drastic dislocation of society" generated by capitalism. It was only this class, Marx came to conclude, which, because of its unique social position of propertylessness, could bring about general human emancipation by creating the universal condition of private propertylessness. He made his position quite clear; the proletariat being the true "negative representative" of the society could not emancipate itself without emancipating all other spheres of society. For Marx:

> By demanding the negation of private property, the proletariat merely raises to the rank of a principle of society what society has made the principle of the proletariat, what, without its own cooperation, is already incorporated in it as the negative result of the society.[47]

By this Marx tried to show the revolutionary potentials of the proletariat. In calling it "a class with radical chains," he implied that the nature of its oppression was such that mere political reforms could not emancipate it. The creation of the modern proletariat had begun a new stage, in social evolution, because reforms within capitalism could not solve its problems. Only in overcoming bourgeois society and thereby abolishing the very principle of private property could this class emancipate itself. Since such universalization of the absence of private property meant a restructuring of the entire society, this class therefore appeared as the universal class capable of leading the flight for general emancipation. But in the article under discussion, the influence of Feuerbachian humanism prevented Marx from drawing the full conclusion. He still thought that "philosophy" as the "head" of the movement was to lead the revolution by providing ideology; and the proletariat as the "heart" was to fight for the revolutionary overthrow of the status quo.[48] So in this "Introduction," proletarian emancipation still remained subordinate to a philosophical idea of communism. The idea that the proletariat was to fight for itself and to formulate its own theory in course of its struggles, was developed by Marx around the year 1844. From a suffering class the proletariat was to become an active revolutionary class. In this transformation an article "Outlines of a Critique of Political Economy," by Friederich Engels, published in the *Franco-German Annals* in February 1844, played a major role. In fact this was the earliest class analysis of the problem of social alienation, which Engels deduced from his critique of political economy. This impact of Engels on Marx was considerable. Although both in critique of political economy and in philosophy it was Marx, who was the hegemonic partner in their joint works yet without the inputs of Engels, the class analysis would not have emerged with as much clarity.

II

ENGELS AND THE PROLETARIAT

This makes it necessary to review briefly the evolution of the ideas of young Engels on politics, political economy and subsequently on proletarian democracy. Engels' political career started with the republicanism of the Young Germany movement. He was drawn close to the democratic-oppositionist writer and journalist Ludwig Búrne. Though he broke with the liberalism of Young Germany movement, he never gave up the democratic demands for a constitution, free press, abolition of religious coercion, and emancipation of women. But it was as a Young Hegelian that Engels presented a radical defense of Hegel's idealism, reason and truth in his pamphlet, *Schelling and Revelation* (around late 1841 and early 1842), as a direct triumph of the "reign of freedom" or democracy.[49] He waged a two-pronged battle against liberalism and absolutist monarchy in the columns of *Rheinische Zeitung* between April and October 1842 without repudiating his demand for radical social reform, freedom of speech and press, and a democratic state. Engels bitterly criticized censorship, especially the Penal Code's Article 151 (of an 1819 Statute) which made it a criminal offense "to excite displeasure and dissatisfaction" with the law code. He pointed out that this amounted to the denial of the right to criticism. He posed a simple yet crucial question in an article, written in 1842, entitled, "On the Critique of the Prussian Press Laws."

> How can one criticise anything without intending to convince others of the . . . imperfection of that which is being criticised, that is awaken dissatisfaction with it? How can I criticise here and praise there. . . ?[50]

Subsequently, in another article for the *RZ*, written in the same year, Engels provided a radical democratic critique of the idealization of the reactionary July Monarchy in France and the Guizot regime which overtly flouted the principles of popular sovereignty, free press, independent jury, and parliamentary government.[51] From this concept of democracy, as freedom and rights for all, Engels proceeded to the analysis, which criticized the Prussian absolutist state for protecting the vested interest of a particular section of the society, though it was much less abstract than Marx's analysis of the social basis of the state. Engels wrote, exposing the vacillating and inconsistent nature of the state and of the king (Friedrich Wilhelm IV), who:

> wants to allow his Prussians all possible freedoms, but actually only in the form of unfreedom, monopoly and privilege. . . . He does not wish to abolish representation, . . . he is aiming at representation of the social estates as already partially carried on in the Prussian provincial diets.[52]

Engels' openness of mind along with a kind of symbiosis of Young Hegelianism and materialism made him embrace a new philosophy— Communism—under the influence of Moses Hess, a Young Hegelian, who was among the first to adopt communist ideas. This was basically a non-proletarian and a sentimental petty-bourgeois socialism, which Marx and Engels later rejected and ridiculed as "True Socialism."

Engels came to England, the bastion of the capitalist world, in the autumn of 1842, to work in the family cotton mill in Manchester. In the year of widespread famine and trade depression, this city became a center of working-class upheavals, political strikes, like the Plug Plot riots led by the Chartists in the summer. (The name "Chartists" was given because of the six-point Peoples' Charter, which was the basic political programmatic text of the movement.) His radical temperament and an almost intuitive sense of perception and comprehension bore rich fruits in the four articles written in late 1842 for the *RZ*. His social and political analysis of England and the concrete situation of the working class reveals that he was making a serious attempt to emancipate his ideas from the domination of Hegelianism. It was only after analyzing the "material position" of the proletariat and not as a blind follower of Hess's prophecy that Engels spoke of an "inevitable revolution" in England. Here, "it will be interest and not principle that will begin and carry through the revolution. Principles can develop only from interests, that is to say, that the revolution will be social, not political."[53] Criticizing the Chartist strategy of "legal revolution," he concluded that a radical and forcible overthrow of the existing social and political set-up would be the only practical solution. And he made it quite clear at the very beginning that radical democracy, upheld by Chartism, was the principle of the working class for emancipation from their dehumanized condition.[54] So young Engels was not at all ambiguous[55] about the social content and the ultimate aim of the political struggle for democracy. The world of Manchester was quite different from that of Paris. Its strategic location made it easy for Engels to assimilate the connections between the modern industry and the modern labor movement. Several years later Engels wrote that his stay at Manchester taught him the importance of economic factors which were the motive force of history, and "they form the basis of the origination of the present day class antagonisms . . . especially in England." They were in their turn the "basis of the formation of political parties, and of party struggles and thus of all political history."[56]

But it took years to generalize the concept. His early writings, starting from a series of articles published in the form of "Letters from London," in the progressive Swiss journal, *Schweizerischer Republikaner*, (May–June 1843), and ending in his celebrated survey of the English proletariat, entitled *The Condition of the Working Class in England*, (September 1844, hereafter referred to as *The Condition of the Working Class*), showed constant ups and downs in Engels' thought. Despite the identification of the interests of the working class and radical democracy, Engels did not immediately conclude that socialism was the outcome of the democratic struggle of the proletariat. He saw three elements in communism: proletarian class interests, political theory, and philosophy. As a result, he felt himself closer to Owenites than to the Chartists. He commented that the communist party can recruit its ranks from "those classes only which have enjoyed a pretty good education; that is, from the universities and from the commercial class."[57] So he went on maintaining the dichotomy between philosophers and workers—the former to lead, the latter to carry on the main burden of the struggle for socialism and democracy.[58] Though he came into close contact with left Chartist leaders like Harney and socialist preachers[59] like John Watts, Engels tended to argue that ". . . the Social evils cannot be cured by Peoples' Charters, . . . Social evils need to be studied and understood."[60] As late as in his earliest joint work with Marx, *The Holy Family* (September 1844), he dismissed Chartism as "nothing but the political expression of public opinion among the workers."[61] This attachment to non-proletarian socialism also explained the temporary spell cast over Engels by the Proudhonist rejection of democracy. But this was only one component in the evolution of young Engels' thought.

Lancashire, and more specifically, Manchester being the hot-bed of the most powerful trade union movements, the focal point of Chartist politics and the stronghold of the socialist movement as well, made Engels aware of the inhuman exploitation brought about by capitalism; the concrete issues of struggle between the proletariat and their oppressors; and the fact that in England the social questions were expressed in a political way since the whole of English politics was fundamentally social in nature.[62] The subsequent merciless critique of political economy and of liberalism gave a new direction and content to Engels' views on the question of democracy. His criticism in the letters from London started with bitter hostility towards liberalism and its empty talks about democracy. His immediate target here, was a lawyer of the Whig government, O'Connell, who now and again talked about democracy—just as Louis Philippe in his days talked about Republican institutions.[63] But it was not "pure Proudhonism,"[64] when Engels bitterly ridiculed a constricted democracy in a bourgeois set-up. For him, political equality could only become meaningful if it was matched with social equality, otherwise it could boil down to hypocrisy, or "regular slavery." Undoubtedly Engels was profoundly inspired by the French left-wing and radical politics but his consequent study of the social premises of liberalism and his first-hand experience[65] of the day-to-day struggle of the working class against their oppressors took him far beyond the limits of Proudhonist radicalism. In his economic studies from "Outlines of a Critique of Political Economy" (hereafter "Outlines"), to his book on the English working class, Engels made a systematic attempt to expose the contradictions built in the immorality and "hypocrisy" of capitalism and showed how incessant competition reduced human beings into "a horde of ravenous beasts," and how private property split the human activity into two eternally hostile sides, viz. labor and capital.[66] For the first time, Engels formulated in "Outlines," the concept of alienation as a direct outcome of the production process which reduced the producers into "dispersed atoms without consciousness of their species,"[67] or into a mere "slave of his own necessaries of life and of the money with which he has to buy them."[68] This concept, developed in *The Condition of the Working Class*, was further elaborated in the same text. Here the modern working class was shown to be forced by the bourgeoisie to sell themselves and their hands as machines and their products as well.[69] The slavery of the proletariat, as Engels argued, was disguised and deceitfully concealed from themselves as well as everyone else. It recognized the right to freedom, at least in outward form. Engels defined its corresponding political form as a parliament elected by the bribes of the rich. The crux of his critique of political economy is that the state was dominated by the propertied class and property constituted the essence of the middle class.[70] It should be pointed out that eighteenth and nineteenth-century political literature including the writings of Marx and Engels, very often made "middle class" the English equivalent of the French word bourgeoisie. Consequently, despite the continuing role of the aristocracy in the political sphere, Engels was pointing out the dominating role of the bourgeoisie and indicating that the English parliament after the reform of 1832 was a bourgeois democracy.[71]

At the very beginning of the "Outlines," Engels rejected the concept of abstract democracy, by writing that it was not enough to counterpose republic to monarchy; one must examine the premises of the state by questioning the validity of private property.[72] So England, where the poor people did not enjoy all the rights of a citizen, where the process of legislation was a mere farce, where the "whole English constitution and the whole of constitutional public opinion was nothing but a big lie which was constantly suppressed and concealed by a number of small lies," was "admittedly a democracy. . . . In the same way as Russia is a democracy."[73] And he prescribed that nothing short of "social democracy" could cure England of the evils of tyranny of private property. It is quite obvious that he made no bones about the class content of this democracy which would help to overthrow the rule of capital. Engels' idea of social democracy was, therefore, much more developed than Marx's concept of true democracy, although at that stage this idea was restricted to England. By it he indicated his understanding of the social implication of Chartism, which was acting on the belief that democracy meant the rule of the working class and therefore made necessary independent working-class politics.[74] It might not be socialist in its program but without it the working class would not be able to handle the democratic machinery as the first step of controlling the state power. Thus as early as 1843, Engels had begun to feel that the interests of the Chartists and the socialists coincided to some extent.[75] When he came to write his book on the English working class, he gave even greater prominence to Chartism, as an independent class movement demanding "proletarian democracy" which was not simply political in nature. Engels did not find it contradictory to bank on the People's Charter to overthrow the aristocracy of money in order to establish working-class democracy.[76]

In Chartism he found the compact form of proletarian opposition to the political power of the bourgeoisie as a stepping-stone to proletarian socialism.[77] Engels in his article series entitled "The Condition of England," (March 1844) claimed that democracy was merely a transitional stage or a means to socialism.[78] But it did not mean that socialism was undemocratic. In saying that the principle of socialism was transcendental over everything of a political nature, Engels was resorting to a Hegelianism which indicated that the previous or democratic stage would be retained in socialism. Real human freedom and a social revolution subordinating to itself the political and philosophical revolutions, so that alienation, which he called "the riddle of our time," could be solved.[79] Here the concept of alienation has a decisive role to play in transforming the idea of socialism as the product of the struggle of the proletariat, which was bound to deepen following the contradictions of capitalism, or its laws, culminating in a social revolution. Broad hints to these ideas which first appeared in "Outlines"[80] were more elaborated in "The Condition of England. The Eighteenth Century."[81] In *The Condition of the Working Class*, Engels portrayed the proletariat as an active class made conscious by the prolonged oppression and impelled towards the revolution by the inner crisis of capitalism. This position was clarified in the two essays he contributed to the Chartist paper, *The Northern Star*: "Further particulars of the Silesian Riots" (June 1844) and "The Late Butchery at Leipzig—The German Working Men's Movement" (September 1844). In the second article, he contrasted the liberals as an inactive group and claimed that the spread of working-class agitation was the only significant element in the struggle for democracy.[82] At times communism was projected as a superior humanistic ideal standing above class struggle. Sometimes it was identified as the revolutionary struggle of the working class for democracy.[83] But the basic ingredients were already present. They only required the theoretical push of historical materialism. This is why Stedman Jones looks upon Engels' contribution as that of a catalytic agent to Marx's theory of historical materialism.[84] Marx referred to Engel's "Outlines" as a "brilliant sketch" which had a profound impact was on him. This made him shift the focus from philosophic communism to the dynamics of the real movement of the working class.

III
COMMUNISM AND DISALIENATION OF LABOR

The year 1844 was indeed crucial for Marx. In February the *Franco-German Annals*, edited jointly by Ruge and Marx, published Engels' "Outlines" and in June the rural domestic-industry weavers of Silesia rose in revolt against their local employers demanding higher rates of pay. Both his German experiences of the struggle of artisanal workers and his readings of the growing dehumanization of this class in England turned him to the "anatomy of bourgeois society" and economy. He intensified his study of the classics of political economy to be found in the writings of Smith, Sismondi, James, Mill, Chevalier, and several others. And the fruit of this labor was a long but unfinished essay, written in three sections, usually entitled *Economic and Philosophic Manuscripts* (April–August 1844, hereafter mentioned as Manuscripts). Instead of making a general assessment of this text, an attempt will be made to focus on those politico-economic issues, which played a decisive role in transforming the proletariat from a passive force into an active agent struggling for its own emancipation, without which Marx and subsequently Engels would not have arrived at the concept of proletarian democracy. It was Marx's first systematic study of and ruthless attack against capitalism as a world historical power. And there was a clear recognition of the developing trend showing the antagonism of the proletariat and the capitalist.

> All wealth has become industrial wealth, the wealth of labour, and industry is accomplished labour, just as the factory system is the perfected essence of industry, that is of labour, and just as industrial capital is the accomplished objective form of private property.[85]

This helped him to take a great step forward in drawing an inseparable connection between the capitalist system of production and the degradation of the workers not merely to a commodity but to "the most wretched of commodities: the wretchedness of the worker is in inverse proportion to the power and magnitude of his production."[86] After a close examination of the factory system, Marx observed that the workers produced goods not as human beings but as a slave class of workers, who were forced to sell themselves and their humanity. Their labor's product confronted them as something alien, as a power independent of the producer; and then "life itself appears only as a means to life."[87] Marx was forced to reject his previous analysis of alienation. So far he had either discussed the concept in terms of political estrangement, that is the alienation of civil society from the state, or located alienation in labor carried on to maintain human existence, that is, alienation in the sphere of exchange relations based on private property.[88] Wage labor, which was detected as the indispensable element of the capitalist mode of production, was for the first time identified as the most concrete form of alienated labor. Alienation occurred at the point of production itself, where the worker was alienated from himself, from his product, and from his life activity.[89] Capitalist (private) property was thus shown as the product of this inhuman production relation of wage labor. Herein lay the basic contradiction of capitalism—"the antithesis between capital and labor," which produced an in-built dynamic of struggle of labor or in Marx's own words "a dynamic relationship driving towards resolution." Marx started his *Manuscripts* with the basic proposition of class struggle: "Wages are determined through the antagonistic struggle between capitalist and worker."[90] Thus the working class ceased to appear a class that would mutely suffer but one that "has to struggle."[91] But this struggle would not be carried out by an individual worker against an individual employer, since alienation had become an universal phenomenon of capitalist oppression, and since an individual worker was also a social being and "sociality" was the defining characteristic of human nature. As early as 1844, Marx spoke of class solidarity among the workers because dehumanization was their common fate. So they felt the need for some kind of association, articulating their common need for liberation from the bondage of capital. "Brotherhood of man is no more a phrase with them but a fact of life,"[92] where wages and private property were both direct consequence of estranged labor. Marx did not take much time in concluding: "the downfall of the one must therefore involve the downfall of the other."[93] Thus class struggle become the motive force of history, continuously pushing it forward towards genuine resolution of this struggle. So both Marx and Engels

> assigned the proletariat the key role in the coming of socialism not so much because of the misery it suffers as because of the place it occupies in the production process and the capacity it thereby possesses to acquire a talent for organization and a cohesion in action which is incommensurable with that of any oppressed class in the past.[94]

At this point, Marx broke with all earlier liberal and socialist concepts of the working class by formulating the concept of a class which was to be the most dynamic and capable of carrying out its struggle to end this alienated existence. And it could achieve it without the leadership of the philosophers. This very struggle by the class itself to achieve disalienation was conceptualized as the positive transcendence of private property since this class could not emancipate itself without the dissolution of private property which was inextricably tied to wage-labor relations. But it was not merely equating the goal of communism with the abolition of wage-labor. Overcoming of alienation meant restructuring productive activity on such a democratic basis which in later terms may be called establishing self-management or workers' control at the point of production, or even associated production.[95] Otherwise communism or the self-rule of the producers, not as alienated beings but as emancipated humans would become utopian idealism. Democracy at the point of production was the crucial starting point to achieve universal emancipation, because the relation of workers to the production was the basic form of all relations of servitude. Hence, his emphasis on the "positive transcendence of private property, as the appropriation of the human essence."[96] This was a more carefully worked out conception than a fleeting glance might suggest. Regaining the human essence meant the positive transcendence of all estrangement. A long discussion is to be found in the *Manuscripts* on this point. Marx wrote:

> *Communism* as the *positive* transcendence of *private property* as *human self-estrangement*, and therefore as the real *appropriation* of the *human* essence by and for man. . . . This communism . . . is the *genuine* resolution of the conflict between man and nature and between man and man—the true resolution of the strife between existence and essence, between objectification and self-confirmation, between freedom and necessity, between the individual and the species, . . . The *human* aspect of nature exists only for *social* man; for only then does nature exist for him as a *bond* with *man* . . . and as the life-element of human reality. Only then does nature exist as the foundation of his own *human* existence.[97]

So, for Marx (and he expressly contrasted himself, in the passage, with Cabet, Owen, etc.), communism was not just the overthrow or abolition of private property. It was a positive act—the creation of a society where the overcoming of alienation at the level of production would lead to the overcoming of all forms of alienation. This is why it was the "riddle of history solved." The types of alienation that were to be resolved included political alienation. The recovery of the human essence was to do away with the perceived contradiction between humankind and nature in capitalist society. As long as humans existed only as "egotistical man," their relationship with nature could not be harmonious. Only "social man," that is humans in communism, were expected to fully understand the bond between nature and the human existence. In that sense, communism was to be a society where human productive activity did not destroy the ecological balance of nature. It was also to be a society where individual liberty was to be harmoniously associated with collective good—in other words, there was to develop a democracy of a socialist nature. Marx, instead of suggesting like Wilhelm Weitling, his contemporary communist and one of the earliest worker-communists in Germany, that collective good should suppress individual liberty, stressed the issue of equality as the political justification of communism.[98] Just as in politics, democracy was the solved riddle of all constitutions, so was communism the resolution of riddles in human society. In writing this, Marx did not aim to create a communist theory through a combination of humanism and naturalism which could be solved merely on the philosophical plane. The *Manuscripts* are not an abstract ethical discussion of communism as the humanist ideal of society.[99] "Developed" communism was not just a suppression of private property and the creation of universal employer vis-à-vis the universal wage-laborers but the practical resolution of social conflict in all spheres of society.

Humanity could be recovered only after the initial abolition of wage labor by the class which has no stake in the capitalist society and the ultimate overthrow of the rule of capital which was the root cause behind the splitting up of humanity into two classes, viz. labor and capital. So the struggle for disalienation had to be a democratic political struggle which was defined by Marx as the "political form of the emancipation of the workers."[100] I. Mészáros has contributed a significant analysis about the political content of Marx's economic prescription,[101] —in fact the keyword "emancipation" was itself a political term. Though at this stage, Marx had not yet arrived at the concept of capture of state power by the working class, it was his earliest formulation of the concept that democratic political struggle of the working class was the essential precondition for achieving universal human emancipation. That he had no confusion about universal human emancipation as the outcome of the "self mediating movement" of the class might be proved by his emphatic and unequivocal statement: "it takes actual private property" and the revolutionary movement would be a "very rough and protracted process." To him, the resolution was by no means merely a problem of understanding, but a real problem of life, which would only be resolved in a "practical way."[102] Thus the communism of Marx was not "formless,"[103] and neither can it be characterized as just a response to the demand of communist negation of private property by the German philosophy on the one hand, nor the *Manuscripts* as "almost totally non-political"[104] on the other. By middle of 1844, in his critique of political economy, Marx had already come out with his formulation though not in later political statement. But the idea was clear enough—communism, which was analyzed as the outcome of the struggle of classes, was to be democratic both in its means and its end. Therefore, it was considered both democratic and proletarian in its political and economic forms. One could not be separated from the other. These were the very crucial formulations of Marx without which his broader concept of proletarian democracy and its political basis, the theory of self-emancipation, cannot be properly understood.

While the *Manuscripts* are Marx's incomplete private notes which were not published in his lifetime, this distinct shift in Marx's stand towards proletarian democracy was made public in his sharp response to Ruge's article wherein the latter made certain disparaging comments about the "feeble" Silesian weavers and their "social revolution" without a "political soul." Marx's response took the form of "Critical Marginal Notes on the Article," by "A Prussian" that came out in *Vorwärts*, edited by Marx's friend Bernays, in August 1844. Here he presented a brief analysis of the social basis of a state and expanded the argument about the relationship between democracy and social emancipation that he had already put forward more briefly in "On the Jewish Question." He also linked it with the conclusions arrived at in the *Manuscripts*. So, one can find a clear political statement that socialism cannot be achieved without the political act of revolution, that is, overthrowing the old political power and relations of production. What is more striking was Marx's claim that only the proletariat could play a dynamic role in the struggle for social emancipation.[105] This idea of the proletariat as the revolutionary class was further confirmed in Marx's letter to Feuerbach, (August 1844), where he wrote, ". . . it is among those "barbarians" of our civilized society that history is preparing the practical element for the emancipation of mankind."[106]

IV

THE PRINCIPLE OF SELF-EMANCIPATION

From the foregoing concept, the emergence of the principle of the proletarian self-emancipation was not far off. But this was a momentous step. There is a major difference between using a section of the toiling masses to ride to power, and organizing the struggle of the masses themselves. From the Greek tyrants of the 7th and 6th centuries B.C., down to Saint-Simon, or Bakunin, there had been various kinds of people who used the aspirations of the exploited and oppressed, offered them palliatives, and on that basis, attempted to or desired to seize power, or impose their "rational" idea of a good society. Marx had, of course, rejected any "saviour from above" model even in his pre-communist days. Now his idea of radical democracy was integrated into his distinctive class analysis.

The Holy Family was a frontal attack on the philanthropic attitude of the Young Hegelian circle of "Critical Criticism" and their attempt to "redeem" the suffering class by changing their "spirit" or "abstract ego," showing that in practice it boiled down to the absurd level of preaching that the workers would cease "in reality to be wage-labourers if in thinking they abolish the thought of wage-labour." Marx ridiculed the Young Hegelians by saying that in their conception the workers were "ethereal beings (who) will then naturally be able to live on the ether of pure thought."[107] Marx on one hand, rejected outright the dominating role of "idea" since in order to carry out ideas "educated" men were needed to transform the ideas into reality. On the other hand, he put forward his radical stand that the proletariat did not require any emancipation from above as their revolutionary potential would emerge from their alienated condition of life. The inferences that Marx had drawn in the *Manuscripts* were expressed in form of concrete conclusions in *The Holy Family*, where the proletariat

> . . . has not only gained theoretical consciousness of that loss, but through urgent, no longer removable, no longer disguisable, absolutely imperative need—the practical expression of necessity—is driven directly to revolt against this inhumanity . . .[108]

The Holy Family also publicly asserted that the working class was in no need of any "first servant of humanity's state" in connection with a discussion of philanthropic socialism in a novel, *The Mysteries of Paris*, by Eugene Sue, a moderate socialist and popular novelist. This novel was highly praised by the Young Hegelians around Bruno Bauer and that was why Marx devoted considerable space to a criticism of the views expressed in it. On the question of ends and means, Marx criticized Sue's standpoint and thereby implicitly that of the Young Hegelians for attempting to turn the proletarians into a passive mass only capable of receiving boons from Rudolf, the hero of the novel, and for claiming that foul deeds were justified if they were carried out for noble ends. Thus by implication, the self-emancipatory struggle as the means and communism as the end were presented here.[109]

By the time they wrote *The German Ideology* in 1845, much of the basic political and social analysis that underlay mature Marxism had been completed (except for the important terrain of a detailed analysis of the capitalist mode of production). *The German Ideology* expressed a detailed statement of "Scientific Socialism." The following arguments show how self-emancipation and proletarian democracy can be derived from the social analysis of this mature Marxism. The argument of the *Manuscripts* was repeated in the analysis showing private property as the product of division of labor and alienation. Out of this contradiction there arose classes and class struggles.

> It follows from this that all struggles within the state, the struggle between democracy, aristocracy, and monarchy, the struggle for franchise etc. are merely the illusory forms . . . in which the real struggles of the different classes are fought out among one another.[110]

There followed a discussion on the class struggle of the proletariat and on communism. The domination of the proletariat through conquest of political power would lead to the abolition of the old form of society—thus, communism equated with the abolition of private property, also became not just an ideal or the final goal or the "real movement."[111] It was portrayed as the world historical activity of the proletariat which alone could carry out the revolution because it was a class which was in itself an expression of the dissolution of all classes.[112]

In the "Theses on Feuerbach" (1845), there is a number of sharpened formulations. "All social life is essentially *practical*." This led Marx to emphasize that revolutionary theory must exist in close unity with practice and must ultimately be derived from practice. It was in the Third Thesis that this view was most cogently presented. Here he opposed the idea of educators from outside teaching the masses, pointing out that any "educator," that is socialist theorist, must oneself learn the meaning of socialism through revolutionary practice. In other words, socialist theory as the ideological change in human beings could only be continuously developed through revolutionary practice which would also change the material circumstances. In the Tenth and Eleventh theses, as well as in the Third, Marx showed that it was by overcoming old materialism including that of Feuerbach that he had arrived at this concept of revolutionary practice to change the world which he would later call the self-emancipation of the working class.[113]

Looking back to his youthful period at the age of sixty-five, Engels wrote that by 1845, Marx and he had developed the materialist theory of history which they now began to elaborate in varied directions. This theory, he wrote,

> was, however, of immediate importance for the workers' movement of the time . . . these movements now presented themselves as a movement of . . . the proletariat . . . as forms of class struggle, but distinguished from all earlier class struggles, by this one thing: that the present day oppressed class, the proletariat, cannot achieve its emancipation without at the same time emancipating society as a whole form division in classes. . . . Communism now (meant), insight into the nature, the conditions and the consequent general aims of the struggle waged by the proletariat.[114]

In other words, Engels confirmed the foregoing argument that the analysis presented in *The German Ideology* had as its political basis the idea of working-class self-emancipation, whatever the philosophical language used.

As they moved away from debates with philosophers to discussions with workers, the Hegelian jargon was entirely dropped. The principle was repeatedly stated in different political contexts. "The Provisional Rules of the International Workingmen's Association," which Marx drafted in 1864 and which was accepted by the International, began with the assertion of this principle.[115] In his letter of November 4,

1864 to Engels, Marx pointed out that he had framed the document so that their view would be acceptable to the current outlook of the workers' movement.[116] So there is no ground for assuming that the formulation itself was a compromise between the Marxist outlook and other ideologies.

How strongly Marx and Engels felt about this principle and its political implications comes out above all in a Circular Letter of 1879 to a number of German Social Democratic leaders. Three members of the outlawed German Social Democratic Party, Hochberg, Bernstein and Schramm, tried to bring out a party journal from Switzerland. An article in the first issue put forward their outlook, which stated that German socialism was, in a too one-sided manner, a working-class movement. The party needed an influx of educated and propertied supporters who alone were fit to represent the party in the Reichstag.[117] Taking up this claim and their further comment about the need to altogether avoid revolution in favor of reform, Marx and Engels criticized these authors as successors of the petty–bourgeois democrats of the 1848 revolution, who had no place in a workers' party and concluded:

> At the founding of the International we expressedly formulated the battle cry: The emancipation of the working class must be achieved by the working class itself. Hence we cannot cooperate with men who say openly that the workers are too uneducated to emancipate themselves, and must first be emancipated from above by philanthropic members of the upper and lower middle classes.[118]

Thus, Marx and Engels, who at different times were willing to work together with English trade unionists, anti-trade union Proudhonists, conspiratorial Blanquists[119] and others, completely drew a line at any kind of cooperation with those who refused to recognize that workers could liberate themselves by their self-activity. This itself showed the centrality of this principle to Marxian politics. It had two sides: on the one hand, it meant that there could be no other liberation of the workers than that which they themselves secured. And on the other hand, it meant that until the workers matured through their own experience of struggle, there could be no talk of communism.

In 1850, when a sharp debate broke out in the Communist League, Marx rejected the view of his opponents, like Willich and Schapper, who wanted to make their desire for revolution the chief motive force. Against their idea of instant revolution, Marx stressed that proletarian self-emancipation would mean that the workers would have to undergo a long period of social conflicts in order to train themselves to become the rulers.[120] So Marx here stressed the dialectical relationship between self-activity and self-education, which, as Norman Geras has pointed out, liberates the proletariat from the need for liberators and gives it an "autonomous class consciousness."[121] The Third Thesis thus formed the crux of Marx's argument that the theory of self emancipation could only be formulated on the basis of experience which the working class acquired from their struggle. Marx did not stop here and proceeded to argue that the dialectics of the theory of self-emancipation gave the class struggle a revolutionary direction. Therefore, instead of being a "slow-motion strategy,"[122] the principle of self-emancipation formed the core of Marx's democratic strategy of achieving communism. In this way Marx saw in the proletariat not only the material basis but also the theoretician of communism who would obviously insist on a revolutionary theory of socialism sweeping aside all those phrases which tended to narrow down the opposition between the bourgeoisie and the proletariat. The alternative would have been to let bourgeois philanthropy paper over the antagonistic relationship between the classes.[123]

V
WORKERS' DEMOCRACY AND LIBERAL DEMOCRACY

Thus, the principle of self-emancipation was at the same time a democratic as well as a proletarian principle. Repeatedly both in their earlier and later phases, Marx and Engels tried to establish a connection between the working class and democracy. Throughout the first half of the nineteenth century, democracy meant a social movement by the bloc of classes below the bourgeoisie for deeper social changes, beyond constitutional and political changes.[124] Only by keeping this class content of democracy in mind could Engels enthusiastically proclaim: "Democracy now-a-days is communism," and categorically counterpose the democratic ideology and politics of the bourgeois.[125] From the same premise of working-class democracy, Marx and Engels made a parallel criticism of liberalism for its very association with capitalism and bourgeois rule, which, by now, it was clear to them, could never accommodate democracy in the sense of their age. In the period of advancing capitalism combining with the political impact of the French Revolutionary and Napoleonic Wars, the establishment of nation-states, it was easier for Marx and Engels to arrive at the position that all states were class states and analyze the real nature of capitalist system of production and politics. Before long they detected a "correlation" between liberalism and capitalism. In *The German Ideology*, the critique of liberalism had therefore taken the form of a merciless attack on the capitalist system where equality and political freedom was looked upon as a hoax. "Liberal phrases are the idealistic expression of the real interests of the bourgeoisie . . . which express the rule of the proprietors."[126] Max Striner, a Young Hegelian, was criticized by Marx and Engels for not realizing that the final goal of the bourgeoisie was to become a perfect liberal, a citizen of the state, safeguarding the basic interests of capitalism through the liberal ideology, which justified a rupture between people's political being and civil being. The way they linked capitalism and liberalism showed that by this period Marx and Engels had given a class analysis to the opposition between democracy and liberal constitutionalism. In other words, from radical democracy, Marx and Engels had reached a point when they were beginning to emphasize class democracy. A thorough study of the history of the French Revolution brought forth to them the idea that throughout the revolution, while the bourgeoisie had striven to overcome feudal particularism by establishing a strong nation-state, it had also aimed to create and maintain a permanent gap between the economic and the political spheres. They concluded that the political rule of the bourgeois class at that time was based on the kind of liberalism that highlighted the individual as a political being or a citizen, while obscuring the social and collective identity of humans.[127] In this way, *The German Ideology* completed their analysis of the symbiosis of capitalism and liberalism. Neither did they have any faith on the contemporary bourgeois states which they depicted as "a committee for managing the common affairs of the whole bourgeoisie,"[128] nor did they have the slightest illusion about universal suffrage in a bourgeois set-up in times of crisis, as Marx showed in *The Class Struggles in France* (1850). He noted that after the elections of March 10, 1850, the principle of universal suffrage was repudiated, a fact that showed that liberal regimes could not easily tolerate democracy. In the same text, Marx showed how repressive and brutal a bourgeois state could be as soon as its upholders and beneficiaries felt themselves threatened by the proletariat. The bloody suppression of the June insurrection in 1848 was one of the examples.[129] Marx had characterized the constitutional republic as the dictatorship of the united exploiters, in which the liberties enshrined in the constitution could only be enjoyed by the possessing classes.

Thus the Third Thesis itself operated in giving the Marxist concept of proletarian democracy a concrete political form. The critique of Hegelian philosophy, and political economy on the basis of actual class struggle experience contributed to the emergence of this concept. It was only with the class analysis of the social problem of alienation that they arrived at the conclusion that a proletarian democracy would lead to universal human emancipation, but only after the application of the principle of self-emancipation. Without the revolutionary principle of self-emancipation, proletarian democracy would not have gotten its political, social and economic implications. The simultaneously proletarian and democratic theory of socialism meant, for Marx, that socialism was the work of the majority in the interests of the majority.

NOTES

1. Different views are held by a number of scholars. That Marx's communism was essentially a product of his Hegelianism is argued by S. Avineri, *The Social and Political Thought of Karl Marx*, pp. 5–12, R. N. Berki, "Through and Through Hegel," pp. 660, 664, 670–71. The influence of Spinoza is emphasized by M. Rubel, "Notes on Marx's Conception of Democracy," *New Politics*, I, no. 2, 1962, pp. 81–82. The view that the standpoint of the mature Marx substantially incorporates that of the young Marx is questioned from two angles: S. Landshut and J. P. Mayer, eds., *Karl Marx der Historische Materialismus*, have claimed that it was the young Marx who was truly humanist and democratic. L. Althusser, *For Marx*, and L. Althusser & E. Balibar, *Reading Capital*, London, 1970, argue that there is an epistemological break between the writings of the young Marx and those of the mature Marx. Consequently, the writings of the young Marx cannot be considered a part of Marxism.

2. "The Three Sources and Three Component Parts of Marxism" in V. I. Lenin, *Collected Works* (hereafter *LCW*), vol. 19, Moscow, 1980, p. 23.

3. K. Marx, "Preface" to *A Contribution to the Critique of Political Economy*, in K. Marx & F. Engels, *Selected Works*, (hereafter *MESW*), vol. 1, Moscow, 1973, pp. 502–4.

4. I. Mészáros, "Marx 'Philosopher,'" in E. J. Hobsbawm, ed., *The History of Marxism*, vol. 1, New Delhi, 1984, p. 120.

5. K. Marx, "Letter to his Father," in *MECW* 1, Moscow, 1975, p. 12.

6. K. Marx, "Letters from the *Deutsch-Franzosische Jahrbucher*," in ibid.: 3, Moscow, 1975, pp. 137–39.

7. K. Marx, "Letter to Arnold Ruge," in ibid.: 1, pp. 382–83.

8. H. Draper, *The Two Souls of Socialism*, Berkeley, 1966, p. 9; M. Rubel, "Notes on Marx's Conception of Democracy," p. 79; D. McLellan, *The Thought of Karl Marx*, London and Basingstoke, 1980, p. 10.

9. K. Marx, "Comments on the Latest Prussian Censorship Instruction" and "Proceedings of the Sixth Rhine Province Assembly. First Article" in *MECW* 1, pp. 109–31, 132–81; see especially p. 153.

10. Ibid., p. 147.

11. Ibid., p. 148.

12. K. Marx, "Letter to Dagobert Oppenheim," in ibid., p. 392.

13. Ibid., pp. 180–81.

14. Ibid., pp. 130–31.

15. Ibid., pp. 138–39, 151–52.

16. For a general discussion, see D. McLellan, *Karl Marx: His Life and Thought*, London and Basingstoke, 1973; Joe Craig, "Karl Marx: Democrat and Republican," in http:/www.socialistdemocracy.org/History/HistoryKarl MarxDemocratAndRepublican.htm, accessed on November 10, 2006. See

further Andrew Vincent, "Marx and Law," in *Journal of Law and Society*, vol. 20, no. 4 (Winter, 1993), pp. 371–97.

17. K. Marx, "Proceedings of the Sixth Rhine Province Assembly. Third Article: Debates on the Law on Thefts of Wood" in *MECW:* 1, pp. 230–35.

18. This editorial twist has been treated in a well-informed way by O. J. Hammen, *The Red '48ers*, New York, 1969.

19. K. Marx, "Justification of the Correspondent from the Mosel," in *MECW* 1, pp. 332–33, 336–41, 343–49.

20. R. N. Hunt, *The Political Ideas of Marx and Engels*, Vol. 1, London and Basingstoke, 1975, pp. 134–39. Hunt believes that Marx's defense of the freedom of the press simply reflected the Young Hegelian idealism about the power of philosophical praxis. But he says that Marx's journalistic ideals were in conformity with the principles of German and European liberalism.

21. *MECW* 1, p. 228.

22. Ibid., p. 392.

23. K. Marx, "Letter to Arnold Ruge," in ibid. 3, p. 144.

24. K. Marx, "Contribution to the Critique of Hegel's Philosophy of Law" in ibid. 3, p. 18.

25. Ibid., pp. 98–108.

26. Ibid., p. 48.

27. Ibid., pp. 70–71.

28. Ibid., p. 29

29. Ibid., p. 31.

30. Ibid., pp. 31, 57, 120–21

31. Ibid., pp. 56–57.

32. Ibid., pp. 111–12.

33. Ibid., p. 118.

34. Ibid., pp. 120–21.

35. C. Pierson, *Marxist Theory and Democratic Politics*, Delhi, 1989, p. 15; similar views are held by B. Hindess, *Parliamentary Democracy and Socialist Politics*, London, 1983; G. Della Volpe, *Rousseau, Marx and Other Writings*, London, 1978; A. M. Melzer, "Rousseau and the Problem of Bourgeois Society," *American Political Science Review*, 74, 1980, and in particular, S. Avineri, *The Social and Political Thought of Karl Marx*, pp. 37–38, where he sees in universal suffrage the abolition of the state. See also L. Colletti, "Introduction" to K. Marx, *Early Writings*, Harmondsworth, 1975, p. 45. For a detailed refutation of the clam that in this work Marx upheld direct democracy, see P. Springborg, "Karl Marx on Democracy, Participation, Voting and Equality," pp. 537–66.

36. *MECW* 3, p. 118.

37. Many scholars like R. N. Hunt, *The Political Ideas of Marx and Engels* vol. 1, pp 74–75; S. Avineri, *The Social and Political Thought of Karl Marx*, pp. 31–39. And R. N. Berki, "Through and Through Hegel: Marx's road to Communism," p. 662 have equated true democracy with communism, treating the latter on an absolutely philosophical level.

38. D. W. Lovell, in his book *From Marx to Lenin*, Cambridge, 1986, pp. 51–53, takes a complicated position which interprets Marxian communism as

a authoritarian one. This communism, according to Lovell, proposes a universal human community, which, while overcoming the duality of the state and the civil society, vexes the issue of democracy by a denial of popular sovereignty.

39. For a different view, whereby Marx's communism is dated before his materialism and associated with his ethics, see M. Rubel, "Notes on Marx's Conception of Democracy."

40. K. Marx, "On the Jewish Question" in *MECW* 3, p. 150.

41. Ibid., p. 153.

42. Ibid., p. 155.

43. Ibid., pp. 153–60. For a thorough discussion see P. Thomas, *Karl Marx and the Anarchists,* London, 1980, pp. 56–121.

44. *MECW* 3, p. 168.

45. Ibid., p. 166.

46. Ibid., p. 141.

47. K. Marx, "Contribution to the Critique of Hegel's Philosophy of Law: Introduction," in ibid., pp. 185–87.

48. Ibid., pp. 176, 187.

49. F. Engels, *Schelling and Revelation,* in ibid. 2, Moscow, 1975, pp. 239–40.

50. F. Engels, "On the Critique of the Prussian Press Laws" in ibid., p. 310.

51. F. Engels, "Centralisation and Freedom" in ibid., p. 355.

52. F. Engels, "Frederick William IV, King of Prussia" in ibid., p. 365.

53. F. Engels, "The Internal Crises," in ibid., p. 374.

54. Ibid., p. 375, see also F. Engels, "Letters from London," in ibid.: vol. 3, p. 379.

55. Engels' attitude to democracy and communism at this stage was still a little hazy. However, when Richard N. Hunt, *The Political Ideas of Marx and Engels,* vol. 1, pp. 130–31 suggests that he was simply a democrat who turned to the proletariat as an instrument of struggle, and whose politics was based on abstract notions of ethics, he is in error. Even here, the link between Chartism as a democratic movement, and its class content, is clear. Gareth Stedman Jones, "Engels and the History of Marxism," in E. J. Hobsbawm, ed., *The History of Marxism,* pp. 308–9, claims that Engels' ethical communism made him treat democracy as an unimportant stage. Actually, Engels was too optimistic about an early victory of democracy. But what he expected was that it was the victory of their struggle for democracy that would teach the workers the necessity of communism for their social emancipation.

56. F. Engels, "On the History of the Communist League" in *MECW* 26, Moscow, 1990, p. 317.

57. F. Engels, "Progress of Social Reform on the Continent," in ibid. 3, pp. 406–7.

58. F. Engels, "Rapid Progress of Communism in Germany" in ibid. 4, Moscow, 1975, p. 236.

59. For Engels' connections with the Chartists and the Owenites, see W. O. Henderson, *The Life of Frederick Engels,* London, 1976, vol. I, p. 22; and R. N. Hunt, *The Political Ideas of Marx and Engels,* vol. I, pp. 106–12.

60. *MECW* 3, p. 407.
61. K. Marx and F. Engels, *The Holy Family,* in ibid. 4, p. 15. For Engels' authorship of only a small part of *The Holy Family,* see editors' notes in ibid., pp. 683–86.
62. F. Engels, *The Condition of the Working Class in England,* in ibid., p. 474.
63. Ibid., p. 391.
64. Draper, in his article, "The Principle of Self-Emancipation in Marx and Engels," in R. Miliband & J. Saville, eds., *Socialist Register,* London, 1971, p. 86, has attached this label to Engels, whose critique of the Whig democracy came to rejecting it altogether by treating it as an "undisguised despotism."
65. That Engels was more and more attracted to actual issues of struggle as a means of empirical knowledge about the working class rather than abstract philosophical discussions was expressed in a letter—see F. Engels, "Letter to Marx," (*MECW* 38, Moscow, 1982, 13), and in his "Preface" *to The Condition of the Working Class in England* (ibid.: 4, p. 297).
66. F. Engels, "Outlines of A Critique of Political Economy" in ibid.: 3, p. 434.
67. Ibid.
68. Ibid., 4, pp. 472–73.
69. Ibid., p. 473.
70. F. Engels, "The Condition of England: The English Constitution" in ibid.: 3, pp. 497–98.
71. R. N. Hunt, *The Political Ideas of Marx and Engels,* vol. 1, p. 108, is however of the opinion that to call the English political system of that period a bourgeois democracy is to commit a "vulgar Marxist crudity" of which Engels was not guilty. Hunt's problem here is his inability to accept that bourgeois political hegemony could include significant political roles by other classes. For other examples of Engels' use of middle class as the equivalent of bourgeoisie, see his article series, entitled "Letters from France," written in 1850, *MECW*: 10, Moscow, 1978, p. 19. In the same series the petty-bourgeoisie was consistently called the "small trading class," ibid., pp. 30–31.
72. *MECW* 3, p. 419.
73. Ibid., pp. 498–512.
74. Hunt, *The Political Ideas of Marx and Engels,* vol. 1, pp. 117–18 fails to realize this class linkage and hence identifies Engels' idea with Marx's concept of true democracy.
75. *MECW* 3, pp. 379–82.
76. Ibid., 476. Both Hunt, *The Political Ideas of Marx and Engels,* vol. 1, pp. 122, 131, and G. Stedman Jones, "Engels and the History of Marxism," in E. Hobsbawm, ed., *The History of Marxism,* pp. 304–9, find a contradiction in this because of their belief that Engels had not rejected his previous philosophical humanist orientation. This comment of Engels shows that both the above-mentioned scholars are in error.
77. *MECW* 4, p. 526, see also F. Engels, "The Condition of England: the 18th Century" in ibid.: 3, p. 467.
78. Ibid., 4 pp. 466–513.
79. Ibid., pp. 464–66, 469.

80. Ibid., 3, pp. 430–34. The importance of the "Outlines" here is that Engels derived socialist conclusion from a critique of political economy that is by pointing to ideological elements in what was supposed to be a neutral science.
81. Ibid., p. 476.
82. F. Engels, "The Late Butchery at Leipzig—The German Working Men's Movement," in ibid., 4, pp. 645–48.
83. Ibid., pp. 583, 646–47.
84. Stedman Jones, "Engels and the History of Marxism," pp. 312, 317, 319. W.O. Henderson, *The Life of Frederick Engels*. vol. I, p. 69, makes an overstatement in saying that at this stage Engels was using dialectical materialism as an intellectual tool for the analysis of English society.
85. K. Marx, "Economic and Philosophic Manuscripts of 1844" in *MECW* 3, p. 293.
86. Ibid., p. 270.
87. Ibid., p. 276.
88. K. Marx, "Comments on James Mill," in ibid., pp. 219–22, 224–25, 228.
89. Ibid., pp. 273–77.
90. Ibid., p. 235.
91. Ibid., p. 237.
92. Ibid., p. 313.
93. Ibid., p. 280.
94. E. Mandel, *The Formation of the Economic Thought of Karl Marx*, London, 1977, p. 23.
95. *MECW* 3, p. 274.
96. Ibid., p. 296.
97. Ibid., pp. 296–98.
98. Ibid., p. 312.
99. A contrary position is held by R. N. Berki, "Through and Through Hegel: Marx's Road to Communism," pp. 666–71. See also G. Therborn, "The Working Class and the Birth of Marxism," *New Left Review* 79, 1973.
100. *MECW* vol. 3, p. 250.
101. I. Mészáros, *Marx's Theory of Alienation*, London, 1970, pp. 127–30, 157.
102. *MECW:* 3, pp. 302, 313.
103. Berki "Through and Through Hegel: Marx's Road to Communism," pp. 662–64.
104. Hunt, *The Political Ideas of Marx and Engels*, p. 77.
105. K. Marx, "Critical Marginal Notes on the Article "The King of Prussia and Social Reform. By a Prussian," *MECW* 3, pp. 202, 205, 206.
106. K. Marx, "Letter to Ludwig Feuerbach," in ibid., p. 355.
107. Ibid., 4, p.53.
108. Ibid., p. 37.
109. Ibid., pp. 163–65.
110. K. Marx and F. Engels, *The German Ideology*, *MECW* 5, Moscow, 1976, pp. 31–2, 46–7.
111. Ibid., p. 49.
112. Ibid., p. 52.

113. K. Marx, "Theses on Feuerbach," in ibid., pp. 4–5.

114. Ibid., 26, p. 318.

115. K. Marx, "Letter to Abraham Lincoln by the General Council of the International," in ibid., 20 Moscow, 1985, p. 14.

116. K. Marx, "Letter to F. Engels," in ibid. 42, Moscow, 1987, p. 87.

117. Quoted in K. Marx and F. Engels, "Circular Letter to August Bebel, Wilhelm Liebknecht, Wilhelm Bracke and Others" in *MECW* 24, p. 264.

118. Ibid., p. 269.

119. Blanquists were called by this term after Louis Auguste Blanqui, a French revolutionary. An incorruptible figure, Blanqui spent thirty-three years in jail. Blanquism was distinguished by its attempts to build conspiratorial organizations and to substitute its own attempts at coups in place of mass revolutionary struggles.

120. *Minutes of the Meeting of the Central Authority* [of the Communist League] in *MECW* 10, p. 626.

121. N. Geras, "Marxism and Proletarian Self-Emancipation," in *Literature of Revolution*, London, 1986, pp. 136–37.

122. A. Gilbert, *Marx's Politics*, Oxford, 1981, pp. 5, 14–15, criticizes those who emphasize the principle of proletarian self-emancipation for advocating a "slow motion strategy."

123. *MECW* 5, p. 469.

124. The class nature of the democratic movement and its strained relationship with bourgeois liberalism is brought out in A. Landy, *Marxism and the Democratic Tradition*, New York, 1946, pp. 75–134.

125. F. Engels, "The Festival of Nations in London," and "The State of Germany," and K. Marx and F. Engels, "Address of the German Democratic Communists of Brussels to Mr. Feargus O'Connor, in *MECW* 6, Moscow, 1976, pp. 5, 29, 58, 59. For details see S. Marik, "Classical Marxism and Proletarian Democracy: The Emergence of a Concept – 1," *Jadavpur University Journal of History*, Vol. 10, 1989–90, pp. 94–95.

126. *MECW* 5, pp. 196–98.

127. Ibid., pp. 199–200

128. K. Marx and F. Engels, *Manifesto of the Communist Party*, in ibid., 6, p. 486.

129. K. Marx, *The Class Struggles in France: 1848 to 1850* in ibid., 10, pp. 62–70. See also F. Engels, "Details About the 23rd of June," "The 23rd of June," "The 24th of June," "The 25th of June," in ibid.: 7, Moscow, 1977, pp. 124–27, 130–33, 134–38, 139–43, for a series of contemporary reports and analyzes in the *New Rheinishe Zeitung*. See K. Marx, "The June Revolution," in ibid., pp. 144–49 for the full of text of the article cited by Marx in *The Class Struggles in France*.

3

CLASS, PARTY, AND FORMS
OF SELF-ORGANIZATION

I
SELF-EMANCIPATION AND ORGANIZATION

While emphasizing that the liberation of the working class could only be the result of its self-activity, Marx and Engels also insisted that the "ruling ideas of an epoch are the ideas of the ruling class."[1] This poses an apparent contradiction. If the ideas of the ruling class are dominant, how can the exploited and alienated proletariat become conscious of its situation and of the need for a revolutionary struggle? The aim of the present chapter is to investigate how far the idea of a communist party, or even a broad-based proletarian party, is compatible with the ideas of self-emancipation and proletarian democracy. One dimension of this reconceptualization of the concept of self-emancipation will be to look at the gender aspect. In other words, did pre-Bolshevik Marxism develop ideas and practices about how to draw women workers into the revolutionary organization or other forms of organizations, and if so, who were the principal figures in this achievement? The investigation needs to be based on an analysis of the writings of Marx and Engels in a historical context, showing the relationship between class democracy and the building of a revolutionary party as it was worked out by them in theory and in practice. On the issue of gendering the organization, we will also look at least two other figures: August Bebel and Clara Zetkin.

The views of Marx and Engels on the revolutionary party emerged during the period between 1844 and 1847. By 1847 they were associated with various political movements and organizations of the working class and also with some movements of the petty–bourgeois democrats, in Brussels, London, Manchester, and Paris, along with Rhineland cities like

Cologne, Barmen, and so on. Their most important task was to clarify and test their theory on the basis of the actual struggles of the working class that were going on in different corners of the continent. As philosophers of revolutionary praxis, Marx and Engels always remained true to the ideas expressed in the Third and Eleventh Theses on Feuerbach, and spared no time in turning to mobilize socialists and communists of various shades, as well as democrats of different countries,[2] to their own revolutionary position of proletarian communism, which was based on the proper functioning of proletarian democracy. They chose Brussels, the capital of a rapidly industrializing country, and located in the middle of a triangle formed by Paris, London and Cologne as the center of their activities. At that moment, Belgium permitted more freedom of expression than any other continental country. Brussels was thus the ideal meeting point for political activists, including those who were in political exile. Similarly, London and Manchester provided Marx and Engels with the opportunity of coming into contact with English Chartists, and also German communists and workers' organizations.

In their attempt to spread their theory of historical materialism and proletarian communism widely, Marx and Engels began to launch organizations as vehicles of the struggle for communism. These were — the Communist Correspondence Committee (January 1846), the German Workers' Association (late August 1847) and the International Democratic Association (September 1847). These were launched to simultaneously propagate communism, to mobilize larger numbers of workers, and to win over the radical–democratic elements of the petty bourgeoisie, as well.[3]

The memoirs of Friedrich Lessener, a German tailor who had become a communist in his youth and was a leader of the international working-class movement, confirm Marx and Engels' orientation of winning over the politically conscious workers to communism through sustained propaganda. Lessener recollects:

> When, as a young tailor's journeyman, I heard a communist speech for the first time in Hamburg in 1846 and then read Weitling's *Guarantees of Harmony and Freedom*, I thought communism would be a reality in a couple of years. . . . But when I heard Karl Marx in 1847 and read and understood the *Communist Manifesto* it was clear to me that the enthusiasm and good will of individuals are not enough to effect a transformation of human society. . . . The Communists who reflected, who were already under the influence of Marx and Engels, condemned all utopian attempts even at that early period.[4]

Thus, as early as 1847, the communism of Marx and Engels contrasted clearly with those of the utopians and others, like Weitling or Blanqui. For the latter, a determined minority was to make the revolution. Marx and Engels believed that the task of the conscious minority was to propagate the necessity and the road to communism and to organize the broad masses. Unlike people like Moses Hess, they also did not feel that propaganda alone would suffice to make the revolution. They used historical materialism to disclose those characteristics of the working class which singled it out as the one oppressed class capable of self-emancipation. First, the working class, in contradistinction to other classes in contemporary capitalist society, had the potential to unite and bring capitalism to a halt, because this class had its hands on the levers of large-scale production. Second, workers were employed in factories and they had to act collectively to produce due to the division of labor. As a result, the workers were disciplined by the capitalist factory itself, and hence capable of learning more swiftly the need for discipline in the revolutionary struggle. Finally, the wage-labor relationship, in terms of which the worker sold his or her labor power to the owner of the means of production, alienated the workers completely. They felt no involvement in the process of production. This alienation made them potentially hostile to the entire economic system, which they would need to overthrow. But historical materialism only indicated a tendency. It showed that the opposites, spontaneous revolution versus instant coup, were both dead ends. However, Marx's concept of alienation was not unproblematic. As long as he was trying to explain that alienation at the point of production was what gave the impetus for revolutionary action, he had a valid point. However, when Marx *defined* alienation solely in terms of paid work (wage-slavery) and the worker, he was overlooking the situation of many women. This comes out clearly in the following extract:

> What, then, constitutes the alienation of labour? First, the fact that labour is external to the worker, i.e., it does not belong to his intrinsic nature. . . . The worker therefore only feels himself outside his work. . . . He feels at home when he is not working, and when he is working he does not feel at home.[5]

While this certainly does not depict the life of the male worker in anything but gloomy terms, the domestic burdens and the pressure of patriarchy on women of working-class families are ignored. For such a woman there was no way to feel at home, since home too was her permanent place of work.[6] At the same time, it would be wrong to say that Marx was unaware of the problem. While alienation as a concept was not effectively extended to women, he did view them as the most exploited. Thus, he wrote:

> The community is only a community of labour, and equality of wages paid out by communal capital—by the community as the universal capitalist. Both sides of the relationship are raised to an imagined universality—

labour as the category in which every person is placed, and capital as the acknowledged universality and power of the community. In the approach to woman as the spoil and handmaid of communal lust is expressed the infinite degradation in which man exists for himself.[7]

For Marx, the proletarian revolution was a possibility, not a historical inevitability. Its potentiality became an actuality as the working class gained self-consciousness. As Hal Draper has correctly argued, Marx's theory looks on the proletariat as an objective agency of social revolution in the process of becoming.[8] Self-emancipation, as already discussed in the previous chapter, is not an automatic process. It very much presupposes the revolutionary class-consciousness without which the working class would not feel the necessity for a political struggle for disalienation. And the formation of this consciousness is not just a spontaneous process. The transformation of the mass of workers from a "class in itself" to a "class for itself" requires a long and protracted struggle where the experience of revolutionary praxis is an indispensable factor. In *The German Ideology* Marx and Engels further argued that the communist proletarians "are determined to change these circumstances at the first opportunity. . . . In the revolutionary activity the changing of oneself coincides with the changing of circumstances."[9]

Thus, the process of struggle and the process of gaining consciousness are interconnected and not separated. However, the two are not identical either. The attainment of consciousness is possible by the mediation of revolutionary theory. This is formulated by the more advanced sections of the class, who recognize the need for a unity of theory and practice, form a revolutionary nucleus, and try to unite the more conscious elements and fight against bourgeois hegemony. The process of revolutionary consciousness cannot be complete without a political party. The political practice as well as writings of Marx and Engels suggest that for them this is a crucial organization, rising from within the more advanced section of the class, whose function is to bridge the gap between a mass of working people, lacking its own class outlook, and a revolutionary class fighting to overthrow the rule of capital.

Marx offered a systematic analysis of the formation of different kinds of workers' associations at different levels of their struggles. *The Poverty of Philosophy* (1847), written as a sustained polemic against Proudhon's individualistic socialism, forms a very useful summary of Marx's and Engels' ideas on party in the phase before the *Communist Manifesto*. Here the basic idea was that it would take long years of struggle to transform the mass of working people into a conscious working class. Their scattered existence, division of labor and above all competition among themselves would stand in the way of a smooth development of class outlook and solidarity. As a result they are forced to be satisfied with the minimum wages, which are often reduced to the lowest level by this competition.[10] Even if, at this stage the workers fought against capital, they could not pose the question of association in class terms due to the nature of their existence and the continued grip of bourgeois ideology over them. But gradually, a recognition of their dehumanized existence as the common factor of all their lives, and participation in common movements for their common interests like the maintenance of wages would lead them to a common effort to nullify their own disunity, because this disunity was the "sharpest weapon against the proletariat in the hands of the bourgeoisie."[11] This common effort could generate the first ideas of a common organization to resist the exploiters. The earliest organizations, or "combinations" (the name "trade union" was coming into vogue, but it was not yet used everywhere), were, according to Marx, the first active forms of class protest against the class of hostile exploiters. The long history of struggles to form unions, marked by many defeats, punctuated by isolated victories, showed clearly the transition from its initial aim of protecting the single workingman against the tyranny and neglect of the bourgeoisie to the more developed aim of establishing class unity in order to launch an out-and-out struggle against the employing class. So, this was a significant pointer to the transition of the working classes from a mere mass of people to a class. Engels vividly portrayed this phase in his book *The Condition of the Working Class in England*. Here he wrote that apart from "keeping alive the opposition of the workers to the social and political omnipotence of the bourgeoisie," the experience of years of struggle would give the proletariat a new feeling of being a class, a power united, and a realization that "something more is needed" to become human beings who "shall not be made to bow to social circumstances, but social conditions ought to yield to them." So these primary associations of the working class played a significant role in transforming their existence from class in itself to class for itself.[12] As Marx pointed out in *The German Ideology*, even a minority of workers who combined and went on strike very soon found themselves compelled to act in a revolutionary way. The interest they defended became class interest and the struggle, one of class against class. Ultimately, Marx concluded in *The Poverty of Philosophy*, such a struggle of class against class was a political struggle. Once the struggle reached this point, the organization of the workers would begin to take on a political character. Marx further observed that the organization of strikes and trade unions went on simultaneously with the political struggles of the workers, who now constituted a large political party—the Chartists.[13] Engels had already analyzed the preconditions and the outcome of the need for political association in the context of England, and was of the opinion that only when the alienated condition of the proletariat and their struggle convinced them that "the sole bond between employer and employee is the bond of pecuniary profit" (i.e. the wage-labor relationship) would they begin to recognize their own interests and would develop independently and cease to be "the slave of the bourgeoisie in his thoughts, feelings, and the expression of his will."[14] As the workers came to recognize the lasting value of organizations, including the identity it conferred on them, they were expected to look beyond the immediate goal of increasing wages, and to value the organization itself. This was, in the opinion of Marx and Engels, the most important role of the trade unions. By themselves, they or the strike-committees (less permanent bodies, set up only as strikes began) could not alter the laws of capitalism. As long as wage-labor relationships remained, the owners could impose wage-cuts, or throw out workers from factories. But by shaping class identity, trade unions could push the workers towards building lasting political organizations on the road to their emancipatory struggles. Once more, the problem of women did not figure as a central issue. In other words, there was no recognition that male and female proletarians did not have identical life experiences, and organizing female proletarians might require specific strategies.

It is obvious that a class that is fragmented cannot achieve unity or class-consciousness all at once, or at the same tempo.[15] Political action and the building of political parties are initiated by one section of the working class. This section recognizes that struggles cannot be confined to the issue of wages. They also understand that there is a need to go forward to the struggle for emancipation, waged as a struggle of one class against another. Once the class struggle reaches this stage it is those who explain scientifically its nature, and try to organize the struggle for a revolution, who deserve to be called communists. The communist party[16] is therefore the association of the revolutionary section of the proletariat.[17] But what is not clear is, what would happen to the gendered nature of the fragmentation? Women workers, as the most oppressed, might be in a more difficult situation, and would require special attention. Nor was it the case that there were no women workers. Engels, in his work on the English working class, wrote at length about the large number of employed women and the dissolution of the family that he thought was following.[18] Why do the communists need a political association? And what strategy did Marx and Engels have concerning drawing women workers into the communist movement or organization? While it is possible to locate sharp condemnations of women's oppression in their writings, as in the passages of Engels mentioned above, no tactical conclusion seemed to be forthcoming.

The question of the communist party preoccupied Marx long before he presented explanations in his lecture series on "Wage Labour" (1847), or in *The Poverty of Philosophy*. This problem was tackled in writings beginning with The *Economic and Philosophical Manuscripts*, and continuing with *The Holy Family* and *The German Ideology*. What he wanted to argue was that an association of communist workers could not merely be a "means" to fight the bourgeoisie but it was also the one place where they could enjoy real freedom, and could find their own existence, not just as alienated beings or extensions of their machines. In *The Holy Family*, Marx and Engels pointed out that organization looked after both the immediate needs of the workers and their needs as human beings.[19] In bourgeois society there could be no humanity, only class. However, the process of organizing enabled the workers to overcome the narrow, dehumanized class identity, and made them appear as the class that through its own emancipation could achieve universal human emancipation. It was this organization that could give them the self-confidence, essential for becoming a class for itself active in their emancipatory struggles. In the course of this they would become aware of their power of cooperation. The growth of this class solidarity would often enable the communists to realize that they would not be able to change their alienated condition by "pure thinking." The organization had the concrete task of struggling for abolition of wage labor and in this sense class organization would become a goal as well.[20] No wonder the workers spent the maximum possible amount out of their pitiful wages on the association, since "out of their revolutionary activity they even make the maximum of their enjoyment of life."[21] Communist organization was thus considered to be a concrete form through which revolutionary practice could be carried out. It was for this reason, among others, that Marx and Engels rejected outright the current they called "True Socialism," for it lacked a "real, passionate practical party struggle."[22] The Communist Party, as early as Engels' 1844 work on the English working class, stood in their eyes as the product of a successful fusion between Chartism and utopian socialism—i.e., between a class movement with a democratic organization and a socialist ideology. His study of the English working class led Engels to conclude that the working class was coming to exercise a hegemonic role in the nation, and he explained that communist leadership should aim at ensuring effective proletarian hegemony.[23] That is, it would make an attempt to break the grip of bourgeois ideology so as to establish proletarian hegemony. It is the political party that can ensure the transition from a purely *Ouvrieriste* attitude to revolutionary consciousness when the working class will recognize that the goal of their struggle is not just taking blind revenge but the abolition of classes altogether to regain their human essence. This is what Engels meant when he declared: "Communism is a question of humanity and not of the workers' alone. . . . The more the English workers absorb Communistic ideas, . . . the more their action against the bourgeoisie will lose its savage cruelty."[24]

What emerged from Marx's and Engels' thought on the need for a party, even at its formative phase, was a dialectical relationship between class movement, its corresponding class-consciousness and formation of appropriate class organizations. Though not in as clear terms as in *The Communist Manifesto*, or other later political tracts, they, in these early writings, indeed saw the political party as a practical and political response to the need for self-emancipation as expressed by the more conscious elements of the working class. In fact, in his confrontation with Proudhonism, Marx all the more tagged the question of political struggle, through associations, with the economic battles of the class. *The Poverty of Philosophy* ends with the following note: "Do not say that social movement excludes political movement. There is never a political movement which is not at the same time social."[25]

This neither means extreme voluntarism nor economic determinism. To Marx and Engels, the success of self-mediating movement or revolution of the class no doubt would depend on the maturation of the productive forces but it could only set the boundary within which the revolutionary class would have to take the initiative to liberate itself. The following claim made in *The Poverty of Philosophy* becomes very significant in this context:

> for the oppressed class to be able to emancipate itself it is necessary that the productive powers already acquired and the existing social relations should no longer be capable of existing side by side. Of all instruments of production, the greatest productive power is the *revolutionary class itself* [emphasis added].[26]

In the same text, he categorically pointed out that as long as the struggle had not assumed a political character and the productive forces not yet sufficiently developed, the communists were mere utopians, but with the development of the proletariat they had to voice its actual aims.[27]

The French scholar Maximilien Rubel has opined that this reflected Marx's sociological concept of a class-based party as distinct from his utopian ethical concept of a communist party.[28] By contrast, Norman Geras has more reasonably argued that the process of self-education and self-emancipation in no way contradicts the Marxist theory of party, since for Marx the party was the instrument of the working class and its own organization for struggle rather than being another external agency over the working class.[29] The necessity of a party is underscored by the impossibility of the entire working class attaining revolutionary consciousness all at once. The class-conscious workers, having become aware of the need for a political struggle, have to band together both to explain this necessity to other workers, and to actually prepare the class to play a hegemonic role in the future revolution. Since class is the lived experience of people, the process of maturation is therefore the process whereby the workers free themselves from the dominance of the ideology and socio-economic pressure of the bourgeoisie through political association. As Lukács puts it, "Organisation is the form of mediation between theory and practice. And, as in every dialectical relationship, the terms of the relation only acquire concreteness and reality in and by virtue of this mediation."[30]

Interpretations of the principle of self-emancipation that tend to rule out the building of a communist party come up against the concrete role of Marx and Engels in the period after the writing of *The German Ideology*. It is therefore necessary to see the kind of class and party relation that the political practice of Marx and Engels reveals, and to relate their programmatic statements with this practice.

In his "On the History of the Communist League," Engels wrote that having discovered materialist dialectics, they believed their duty consisted of not only a scientific substantiation of their view, but also to win over the European—particularly the German—proletariat, to their conviction.[31] For this purpose they established the Communist Correspondence Committee in Brussels. Its aim was explained in a letter from Marx, Gigot, and Engels to Proudhon, as one of organizing correspondence among communists and socialists of different countries, so that "differences of opinion can be brought to light and an exchange of ideas and impartial criticism can take place. It will be a step made by the social movement in its literary manifestation to rid itself of the barriers of nationality."[32] This shows that as yet, the aim was not to form a party of action, but to win over, through discussions, individual socialists. In another letter to G.A. Köttgen, a communist of Elberfeld, Marx and his associates put forward the rules and the style of functioning that they expected. The letter rejected the idea of a communist congress because it was first necessary to create communist societies which had the capacity to act.[33] Clearly the committees were here considered propaganda circles, not yet capable of revolutionary practice.

Among the various groups and individuals with whom this Committee interacted the most important were the left-wing Chartists and the German artisan communists of the League of the Just. Eventually these three forces were to contribute, though not all equally, to the formation of the Communist League and its political outlook.

II

THE COMMUNIST LEAGUE

The League of the Just was the proletarian offshoot of an earlier republican organization, the Outlaws' League. Both in ideology and in organizational concept, the new league, formed in 1836, could be called Babouvist.[34] Under the influence of Parisian secret societies the League of the Just participated in the insurrection of May 12, 1839. After its defeat, some of the leaders like Karl Schapper, Heinrich Bauer, and Joseph Moll set up a unit in London. But while the London group soon renounced conspiracy and insurrection, Wilhelm Weitling in the continent developed a communist theory which still emphasized putsches and dictatorships. In 1845, this led to a sharp clash between Weitling and his former followers. The London leaders emphasized internationalism, the unity of communists and democrats, and strict non-violence.[35] The first two points brought them and Marx close. The idea of pure non-violence divided them. But through the Communist Correspondence Committee, Marx and Engels had targeted "True Socialism," a non-class sentimental socialism which hoped to overcome class conflict through pacifism and the preaching of love (and whose proponents included the German Karl Grün as well as the future anarchist Proudhon). This current had been an alternative ideological pole attracting League members. The campaigns against True Socialism in the long run overcame the League leadership's stand in favor of revolution by pure propaganda.[36] By the end of 1846 or early 1847, the London-based leaders of the League of the Just had rejected not only Weitling's outlook but also the French utopian communist Étienne Cabet's plan for founding a communist colony.[37] This rejection of Cabet brought the League closer to Marx and Engels. In January 1847, Moll was sent to Brussels to invite Marx, Engels, Wolff, and others to join the League. This group had, throughout 1846, "published a series of pamphlets, partly printed, partly lithographed, in which we mercilessly criticized the hotchpotch of the Franco-English socialism or communism and German philosophy, which formed the secret doctrine of the 'League' at the time."[38] Marx was hesitant about joining the League because of his reservations about its politics, but Moll made him overcome these hesitations, by arguing that Marx could expect to best influence the League members if he was a member himself.[39]

This account was written by Marx in a period when he was away from organized politics, and when he was defending the League from the charge of being just another conspiratorial secret society. So it contains some simplifications. Nonetheless, it corroborates the other evidence, establishing the fact that when Marx and Engels joined the League of the Just, they did not succumb to any Blanquist trend. Rather, they won over both the League of the Just, as well as left-wing chartists like George Julian Harney and Ernest Jones closer to their position.[40] In the summer of 1847, the first League Congress took place in London. Here it changed its name to Communist League. This change symbolized a shift from egalitarianism or crude communism to a recognizably Marxist position. The circular issued by the Congress to the League members repudiated the politics of Weitling, Proudhon, and Grün, and submitted a draft manifesto for discussion, in which the emphasis was on the social relations which gave rise to communism.[41]

The Communist League was a landmark in Marx's own political life. Time and again, Marx and Engels treated that experience as the benchmark against which to treat other lesser experiences. So their relationship with the League must be clarified. What status did they enjoy as the ideologues of the League? To this is added a supplementary question about how far the views expressed in *Communist Manifesto* can be taken to be the personal standpoints of Marx and Engels, as distinct from an organizational document bearing the typical marks of an organizational compromise.[42] Second, did Marx and Engels intend the League to be a revolutionary party, particularly a vanguard party? Finally, what sort of a democracy did the League have, both vis–à–vis the proletarian milieu, and with respect to its internal functioning?

The history of the League of the Just shows that the artisan communists like Schapper and Moll, having abandoned ultraleftism, had adopted a more purely propagandistic approach than Marx ever did.[43] Throughout 1847, there was an intensive discussion on the program and organizational perspectives of the League. Two Congresses were held and at least four draft programs were written, two by Engels, one by Moses Hess, and one possibly by Schapper.[44] The Second Congress of the League, held in late 1847, endorsed the standpoint of Marx and Engels and authorized Marx to write the final text in the name of the League. This indicates, on the one hand, that genuinely democratic consultations went on, and on the other hand, eventually Marx had certainly established his ideological domination, for he would hardly have been given a carte blanche to write what otherwise would have been a compromise requiring scrutiny by a committee. At the same time, a formal organizational control was maintained, as existing documents show.[45] The League itself had a definite organizational structure, and certain norms regarding practice. In August, sometime after joining the League, Marx and his friends launched a Workers' Educational Society in Brussels. This structure was used everywhere by the League to organize the broad masses of non-communist workers. The Rules of the League, the Address of the First Congress and the single issue of the journal, *Kommunistische Zeitschrift* show the general acceptance of proletarian democracy in party-building theory.[46]

It is in this light that the *Communist Manifesto* and its discussions on the nature of the proletarian party have to be understood. The chapter of the *Manifesto* entitled "Proletarians and Communists" begins by saying "The Communists do not form a separate party opposed to other working class parties."[47] In this formulation, the word "party" probably does not mean "organization," for the League was of course a separate organization. Their key word was "opposed." As the next sentences explained, the communists did not have narrow interests and sectarian principles, which they put up as interests and principles external to the movements of the proletariat. The specificity of the communist party, according to the *Manifesto*, lay in its internationalism and in its emphasis on the interests of the movement as a whole as opposed to partial or fragmentary interests.[48] In this sense, it is proper to call the League a vanguard party, or more properly, to say the intention of the creators of the League was to set it up as a vanguard party.[49] But the words "vanguard party" need to be used carefully. It would be anachronistic to impute to Marx the intentions of being "for" or "against" Lenin. But he did write that the communists were, on the one hand, practically, the most advanced and resolute section of the working-class parties and on the other hand, theoretically, the far-sighted section.[50]

In the long run, Marx expected the unity of all workers and the creation of one proletarian tendency.[51] Despite the caveat entered by Marx regarding the tendency of such unity being continually upset, the idea itself was problematic. The process of class formation, as Marx's own theory as well as the history of the century and a half since the *Manifesto* was written suggest, could not ensure that the entire class would adhere to only one political current, even in a revolutionary situation. A vanguard party was necessary because of this fragmented existence of the class. The *Manifesto* itself made a distinction between the immediate aim of the communists which they shared with all proletarian parties, and their theoretical conclusions, which, while being based on the experiences of the proletariat, were not immediately understandable or acceptable to all working-class currents.[52]

That the vanguard conception of the *Manifesto* was specifically Marx's contribution becomes clearer when its absence is noted in the draft program adopted by the First Congress of the League and also in Schapper's article. For Marx the proletarian communist current acted as a vanguard because unlike the utopians they did not oppose the actual struggles of the workers but instead embodied the unity of theory and practice. Marx's conception of the vanguard nature of the party therefore fits in with the concept of proletarian democracy. The tasks of the vanguard appeared at this stage as centralizing the experiences of class struggle, drawing out the long-run implications, imparting these to the class as a whole, and trying to lead the class struggles by combining theoretical clarity and practical militancy.

However, unlike many of his successors, at this stage Marx had little to say about the particular form of the party and he was quite alien to the cult of the party that has developed in the twentieth century in the name of Marxism.[53] In writing the *Manifesto,* Marx made three crucial points. The proletariat needed class independence. For this it had to develop forms of self-organization culminating in the party. The goal of a real working-class party had to be the overthrow of bourgeois supremacy.[54]

Written before the actual experience of revolutions, the *Manifesto* is rather abstract regarding concrete tactics and organizational forms. The experience of the revolution of 1848 was necessary to fill in the blanks. The Communist League took part in this revolution with a limited degree of organizational cohesiveness. After the February Revolution, the Central Authority of the League in London transferred its powers and functions to the Brussels Committee; but Marx was almost immediately expelled from Belgium. The Central Authority was reconstituted in Paris.[55] Marx became chairman. When the March Revolution in Germany broke out, the leaders of the League drafted a brief platform specifically addressed to Germany. In April–May 1848, the chief emphasis of the communists was to build open workers' organizations. Two members of the Central Authority, Wallau and Wolff operating from Mainz tried to establish a countrywide network and other members spread out in different places.[56] But the attempt was premature. The sudden forward march of the revolution breaking over a politically inexperienced working class overwhelmed the league cadres. "The few hundred separate League members vanished in the enormous mass that had been suddenly hurled into the movement. Thus the German proletariat at first appeared on the political stage as the extreme democratic party."[57] Most of the communist workers were not rooted in the contemporary German working-class movement. The movement itself was at a rudimentary stage. In this situation, Marx and Engels felt that operating openly and purely as communists would cut them off from the masses.[58] So they adopted a more tactical approach. In a letter to an American correspondent, Florence Kelley–Wischnewetzky, Engels wrote in 1887, "when we returned to Germany in Spring 1848, we joined the democratic party as the only possible means of gaining the ear of the working class."[59] However, in the newspaper they founded, the *Neue Rheinische Zeitung* [*NRZ* hereafter] and in the Democratic as well as proletarian associations in which they participated, their political approach was "that of democracy which everywhere emphasized in every point the specific proletarian character which it could not yet inscribe once for all on its banner."[60] In other words the immaturity of the proletariat in general meant that in developing the theory of proletarian democracy in opposition to petty bourgeois democracy the communists had gone too far ahead of their class. In the revolution of 1848 the German working class participated in politics in a subordinate capacity within the general democratic movement. In such a situation, retaining the Communist League as a secret Communist organization would not have helped in the process of winning over the mass of workers to a standpoint of proletarian class independence. In order to accomplish this task, the Communists had to enter the open and general democratic organization. This was the first time that a proletarian party was taking part in a major revolution. Only this experience could enable future communists to think in terms of flexible organizations capable of functioning both in underground and open conditions. In 1848, the League lacked this experience. On a pan-German scale the organizational work of the Communists proved to be inadequate. When in March 1850, Marx and Engels wrote a quarterly Address on behalf of the reconstituted Central Authority, they acknowledged this inadequacy.[61] In the Address, the conception of the *Manifesto* and the strategic line of 1847 were said to have been proved correct. This was followed by a self-critical passage where it was argued that the League had failed to retain a disciplined revolutionary organization under the belief that the need for a centralized body was over.[62]

The result, as the Address argued, was the hegemony of the petty bourgeois democrats in the general movement. It was felt necessary to reorganize the League quickly through an emissary because a new revolution was impending and an independent workers' party had to be established in time so that this time the working class could avoid being taken in tow by the bourgeoisie.[63] It could be noted that these proposals regarding the party formed only part of a broader political organizational strategy which counterposed proletarian democracy to petty bourgeois democracy. Sometime later, Marx proposed changes in the rules of the League. By the time the new rules were adopted by the new Central Authority located in Cologne, the League had split. An ultraleft faction, led by August Willich and Karl Schapper, had broken away. The Cologne group was Marxist, and accepted Marx's ideological leadership. They adopted the new rules in November 1850, two months after the split. Thus, in a period when Marx is supposed to have recovered from his alleged Blanquism, the first clause of the rules read, in part:

> The League shall represent at all times the interest of the movement as a whole. . . . As long as the proletarian revolution has not attained its ultimate goal, the League shall remain secret and indissoluble.[64]

This impeccably Marxist document therefore emphasizes that—a communist party had to be built to represent the long-term (or overall) interests of the proletariat, and it not only had to continue functioning until the final victory of the proletarian revolution, but also had to have a secret (and not just a public) structure. This implied a continued self-criticism for the mistakes of 1848-49. From the foregoing it can be concluded that Marx did not seek to counterpose the idea of proletarian democracy to the necessity of party building. If one asks, why a secret organization, the answer would be, because of the hostility of states and their police to open revolutionary parties, not because of any cult of secrecy.

However, in continuing the discussion on Marx's activities and ideas regarding the Communist League, it is possible to ask the question whether, in agreeing to the need for a party with a small membership, with an illegal apparatus, and with a plan to work for the overthrow of the existing regime, Marx was not falling into a Blanquist error, or at least making compromises with such a standpoint. To put it in a slightly different form, did the idea of a vanguard communist party mean Blanquism? Such a view is apparently strengthened by the episode of the *Société Universelle de Communistes Révolutionnaires* (hereafter SUCR).

On the basis of a sheet with six signatures,[65] Nicolaievsky claimed that Marx had formed a super-secret society, and was inclined to Blanquism.[66] What we see, in reality, was an attempt by Marx to win over the Blanquists. But to infer from the SUCR document that he had succumbed to Blanquism raises questions about his entire strategy, while Wolfe, who in fact charged Marx with a longer period of infatuation with Blanquism, argues pertinently that Marx's standpoint throughout 1848–51 was consistent, and that the SUCR episode was not an aberration.[67] The signatories were three members of the Communist League (Marx, Engels, and Willich), two Blanquists (Adam and Vidil) and one Chartist (Harney). The names do not reflect specific organizational affiliation. Why was Schapper, one of the oldest League leaders, not a signatory? And what organizations did Adam, Vidil, and Harney represent? Hal Draper points out that "the Chartists" had no organization, nor did the Left Chartists.[68] As for the Blanquists, the historian Arthur Rosenberg pointed out, "At that time there was indeed, no actually flourishing Blanquist organization either in France or in England, but the great name of Blanqui had its effect and was a symbol for the fighting French proletariat. Consequently the French socialist exiles who wanted to differentiate themselves from the bourgeois democrats usually called themselves Blanquists."[69] Draper quotes the historian Plotkin to show that within the refugee organization SPDS (Société des Proscrits Démocrates-Socialists, set up by the left wing of the French emigration in London, in opposition to another organization set up by moderates like Ledru-Rollin and Louis Blanc), there were three separate trends that called themselves Blanquist.[70] Both Nicolaievsky and the French historian Dommanget refer to some further evidence. Dommanget says that the second circular of the Central Authority to the League member alludes to the SUCR.[71] He also cites letters from the London Blanquists to Blanqui. But these documents actually prove something else. Barthelémy's letter to Blanqui, dated July 4, 1850, simply talks about a revolutionary manual being written jointly with the German communists.[72] This was a far cry from launching a world party of socialist revolution. Probably this manual was what the June 1850 Address of the Central Authority to the Communist League also had in mind, for it wrote inter alia that, "The delegates of the Blanquist secret societies are in regular and official contact with the League delegates whom they have entrusted with important tasks in preparation for the next French revolution."[73] But most significant is the letter of October 9, 1950 from Engels, Marx and Harney to Adam, Vidil, and Barthélemy, stating that "we have the honour of informing you that we have, long since, considered the association you speak of, as dissolved, by fact."[74] If on October 9, Marx thought that the SUCR had been *long* dissolved, it could not have had much of an existence. It cannot be used to prove a Blanquist aberration on the part of Marx.

That Marx had not become a Blanquist is proved conclusively by an article that he wrote around the same time (March–April 1850). Reviewing two books, he showed that secret societies are riddled with police spies. While the professional conspirators who formed the core of these societies could not draw in the broad masses of the proletariat in their organizations, they could not keep out the spies. Criticizing them, Marx wrote,

> These conspirators do not confine themselves to the general organisation of the revolutionary proletariat. It is precisely their business to anticipate the process of revolutionary development, to bring it artificially to crisis-point, to launch a revolution on the spur of the moment . . . they are the alchemists of the revolution . . . and have the profoundest contempt for the more theoretical enlightenment of the proletariat about their class interests.[75]

Thus Marx was explicitly counterposing a communist party, capable of explaining theory and organizing the proletariat for struggles, to the Blanquist concept of a party whose task was to create the revolution through a process of substitutionism. The review also shows the lack of democracy both within this kind of society and in the inter-relationship of such organizations with the working class. Discussing the consequences of adventurism, Marx pointed out that the revolutionaries had no future unless they adopted proletarian communism.[76]

In September 1850, there was a split in the Communist League. To Wolfe, this proves that "Marx found the whole outlook [of the March Address] incongruous . . . [and] *condemned* the same estimate and some of the same deductions in his followers in September."[77] Wolfe further remarked that it was only from the time of the split that Marx abandoned the politics of revolutionary will. Lichtheim claims that Marx recognized that the March Address had been Blanquist and thereupon dissolved the League. He wrote that Marx's "tacit renunciation of Blanquism also entailed the abandonment of the vanguard concept . . . [because] this concept had implied at once the dictatorship of Paris over the rest of France, and the dictatorship of the proletariat over the rest of society."[78]

An examination of the documents relating to the split and its aftermath show that there was no change of front by Marx. During an emergency meeting of the Central Authority of the League, Marx accused the members of the Willich–Schapper faction (the minority) of being opposed to the view of the March Address and even of the *Communist Manifesto*. In a second speech, he also pointed out that the March Address had been adopted unanimously, thereby refuting in advance the Marxological myth that it was a compromise between embattled factions.[79] Marx was effectively accusing his opponents of becoming Blanquists and of repudiating the March Address.

The evidence of Peter Roser throws some light on the pre-split situation. In July 1850, Roser, then the president of the Cologne branch of the League, received a letter from Marx, in which he claimed that the differences between his faction and "Willich and his trash" could lead to a split in the League.[80] It was the Central Authority's minority faction, and the majority of émigré members in London, who moved away from the politics of the *Manifesto* to one of conspiracies, leading to the split. As late as February 1851, letters from Marx to Hermann Becker of Cologne (as well as letters to Engels) show him involved in League affairs.[81] Marx proposed the dissolution of the League only after its underground membership in Germany had been almost wholly arrested and the organization smashed. Up to this point, therefore, Marx was trying to organize a proletarian vanguard party, which he took care to distinguish from utopians, Blanquists, and peaceful reformers alike.

The last question that has to be answered is, what sort of democracy was practiced in the Communist League? Both contemporary opponents and modern critics of Marx have often accused him of being an autocrat within the party. In discussing this issue a few preliminary comments are required. In general, an organization that rejects democracy as its normal form of politics within the milieu where it works cannot allow full internal democracy. On the other hand, an organization that is internally democratic has to have some sort of democratic relationship with the masses it tries to influence. Second, in discussing how democratic an organization was, it is necessary to avoid being ahistoric, and to consider the organizational norms of its contemporary rivals and not merely some modern theory of inner party democracy.

Utopians and Jacobins were self-proclaimed believers in the necessity of a dictatorship of the elite over the masses. But even libertarians like Proudhon, usually contrasted to Marx (the alleged authoritarian socialist), did not have democratic organizational concepts. In his writings Proudhon appears to be anti-strike, autocratic and intolerant of dissenting opinion.[82] Further evidence about Marx's "authoritarianism" is that he is supposed to have purged Weitling and the "True Socialist" Kriege from the Communist Correspondence Committee.[83]

The eye-witness account of the Russian P. V. Annenkov only mentions a public debate in which Marx accused Weitling of seeking to provoke uprisings without prior theoretical clarifications and rejected Weitling's criticism that Marx was only an armchair analyst by saying that ignorance never helped anyone. Since Weitling voted against the "Circular against Kriege" at the meeting of May 11, 1846, he must have subsequently become a member of the committee, despite his dispute with Marx.[84] As for the expulsion of Kriege, who was then in America, from a Brussels-based committee, it must have been difficult. The circular does not mention any expulsion, but seeks to refute his version of socialism from a historical materialist viewpoint. Critics of Marx seem to have decided that when Marx defended his own position, he was being an authoritarian.

Against such claims, Marx's letter to Köttgen emphasized the need for durable mutual contacts among communists. It rejected the idea that contributions from supporters should be used for the personal benefit of the leaders and insisted that political capability, not personal considerations, must guide the election of leaderships.[85]

Democracy within the organization was thus Marx's standpoint even before he joined the Communist League. This was the first party-type organization to which Marx and Engels belonged. Though it emerged out of the world of secret societies it was far from being one of them. Looking back at the far-reaching changes that they had effected, Marx told a Social Democratic correspondent in 1877 that Engels and he had joined the League of the Just on condition that its statutes had to be purged of all "superstitious belief in authority."[86]

The typical structure of secret societies, that included one or a group of leaders, a set of mystic cults, elaborate rituals, the concept and practice of execution for breach of trust, were ruthlessly weeded out.[87] As a proscribed organization, the League had to remain secret, but only for objective reasons. The rules show that members were grouped into communities, circles and leading circles, the lower units being subordinated to higher ones and the leaderships of the higher units being accountable to the Congress, which appointed them. The highest executive organ was the Central Authority while the highest legislative authority was the Congress, which was to meet every year with every circle sending at least one delegate or more. The Congress was to decide the location of the Central Authority for the next year. The five-member Central Authority was to be elected by the circle authority of the place where the Central Authority had its seat. Compared to the earlier rules, the most important changes were the following: the abolition of the death penalty for breaking the oath of secrecy, and the establishment of the annual congress in place of the old system of plebiscite among the members. With this, primitive and unsatisfactory democracy was replaced by representative democracy, and control over the leadership by members.[88]

The developing revolutionary situation soon after those organizational changes put the League in trouble, and its headquarters had to be shifted twice and as an emergency measure Marx had to be given discretionary power.[89] Marx reconstituted the Central Authority in Paris. He was supposed to have subsequently dissolved the League using this discretionary power. But the document in question conferred this discretionary power only until the reconstitution of the League. Hence the story of the dissolution cannot be clearly established. Moreover, this alleged authoritarianism on the part of Marx came along at a time when he was supposed to be at his most democratic. So even if the incident were true, it would stand out as an aberration.[90]

The Communist League was reconstituted after the defeat of the revolution in 1850. There is of course a debate over whether it was formally dissolved during the revolution or not, but since it had ceased to function as a collective entity regardless of the formal situation, we are justified in using the term reconstitution. In the September 1850 dispute Marx charged his opponents with having amended in a harmful direction the 1847 rules. In this meeting the Central Authority declared the existing rules (adopted in 1848 under confused circumstances) null and void, and transferred the Central Authority to Cologne. The new Central Authority drew up new rules in November. The basic pattern followed that of the 1847 rules. But in keeping with the March 1850 Address of the Central Authority, the League was proclaimed indissoluble, and greater disciplinary powers were conferred on the Central Authority so that it could implement decisions taken by the Congress.[91]

The foregoing discussion shows that Marx was opposed to an authoritarian internal regime of the revolutionary party. But his initial reaction to hypercentralization had led to an excessive weakening of the executive, a fault that was rectified in 1850. Since observing democratic norms themselves impose a discipline, and since the tasks of a revolutionary party have to be carried out under various circumstances, a distinction had to be made between the members, who could be compelled to carry out decisions arrived at democratically, and the non-members, who could not be so compelled.[92]

A change came after the smashing of the underground structures of the League in Germany. From then until the formation of the International Workingmen's Association (i.e. between 1851 and 1864, hereafter IWA) Marx and Engels did not belong to any party. Some of their personal letters to each other suggest that they were happy about it. But these letters need to be situated in their proper context which was that of a near-complete isolation, since a majority of the London-based German communists supported the Willich-Schapper League. Thus, on February 11, 1851, Marx wrote to Engels, "I am greatly pleased by the authentic isolation in which we two, you and I, now find ourselves," and called his opponents jackasses.[93] Similar sentiments were expressed by Engels two days later.[94] This was a period of a tremendous Europe-wide defeat of all shades of Leftist, radical, or even liberal aspirations. This defeat was followed by an exile worse than that of the pre-1848 period. Now the émigrés were cut off from the workers of their native lands. In such a situation émigré politics was nothing but squabbling among cliques, perpetual intrigues, splits, and pettiness. The politics of proletarian self-emancipation was meaningless when the émigrés were cut off from the proletariat. There was an occasional recognition of this, as when Engels wrote that émigré politics would turn a man into a fool, and that therefore it was necessary to stay away from the pseudo-revolutionism of this politics.[95] Thus, in these years Marx and Engels showed a lack of inclination about forming a proletarian party, and this was a noticeable retreat from the position they had developed in the earlier years. Yet this must be qualified by the fact that wherever they saw real working-class movements, they advised their friends to form workers' parties. This is clear from Marx's letter of November 24, 1857, urging Ernest Jones to form a party by agitating among the industrial workers. This was when the first economic crisis could be felt in world capitalism since the recovery of 1850. Marx felt that unless the English workers got a move on, world capitalism could not be destroyed. That is why he was desirous that Jones, a former left Chartist, and a one-time member of the Central Authority of the League, should organize industrial workers.[96]

Yet it must be admitted that this phase was one of retreat in terms of Marx's ideas about party building. In a letter of February 29, 1860, to his friend, the poet Ferdinand Freiligrath, Marx called the Communist League a party in the "ephemeral sense," compared it with the Blanquist Société des Saisons and explained that he no longer felt the need to build the party in this sense.[97] This was the same meaning that he had attached to the word when he called his program, not a manifesto of the Communist League, but the *Manifesto of the Communist Party*. In the period of the Communist League, though, awareness of the existence of a broader politico-ideological current had not prevented Marx from building a revolutionary vanguard organization. Now he was denying its specificity and legitimacy by equating it with all other types of revolutionary organizations.[98] But the period of retreat came to an end the moment Marx saw the possibility of a new rise in the working-class movement.

III
THE FIRST INTERNATIONAL

Marx played no role in the prehistory of the International. But soon he became its most influential leader. Critics have accused him of being manipulative, of having smuggled in his personal standpoint in an underhand manner, of attempting to impose monolithism on a broad-based organization and even of deliberately destroying the organization or its dissident sections where he could not impose his personal control.[99]

Marx's role in the foundation and during the early years of the IWA can be understood in a different sense if the actual history of the International is kept in mind. Internationalism and attempts to build international organizations were fairly common practices among the Left. At the same time, for several years many such attempts were dominated by Jacobin politics and secret societies of French origin or French inspiration. There had been other types like the English Fraternal Democrats, with whom Marx and Engels had collaborated. But because of their opposition to the secret societies Marx and Engels stayed away from all attempts at revolutionary unity by the secret societies right up to the 1863 conferences in Belgium and Switzerland, even though their friend Johann Phillipe Becker was involved. But in 1864, the two currents converged. British and French labor leaders, strengthened by the revival of working-class movements in the early 1860s, and motivated by both economic considerations like prevention of strike-breaking through the importation of foreign labor, as well as internationalist and democratic political principles, wanted to form an international association. The Philadelphians, a secret society at that time in alliance with Mazzini, also took an interest. Marx was invited to the public meeting on September 28, 1864, at St. Martin's Hall that was to formally proclaim the International. He saw that the International could provide him with the means of influencing the working-class movements in a number of countries. At the same time he realized that the kind of class political movement, which he advocated, was in danger unless the political outlook of the Philadelphians was overcome. Marx's letter to Engels, on November 4, 1864, provides the major source for his critics as well as his supporters. Having described the background of the meeting he told Engels that people who really counted—that is, the real working-class associations and their leaders—were present, and that was why he had agreed to go to the meeting. Elected to the General Council that was established, Marx found the proposed principles and rules to be unacceptable. The rules, put forward by Major Wolff, a Mazzinist, aimed at "really something quite impossible, a sort of central government of the *European* working classes."[100] A part of Marx's "manipulation" consisted of getting the centralist rules thrown out in favor of democratic rules. The organization that Marx wanted to build was to be a flexible association, enabling different kinds of working-class organizations and different political viewpoints to coexist for a considerable period. He also wanted to sharply limit the powers of the leadership. These are brought out by the rules and regulations proposed by Marx. In the draft rules he wrote:

> This Association is established to afford a central medium of communication and cooperation between Working Men's Societies existing in different countries and aiming at the same end, viz., the protection, the advancement and complete emancipation of the working classes.[101]

Membership of the IWA was open to individuals and also to existing workers' associations. The rules also encouraged the combination of scattered workers' societies into national federations. The highest legislative authority was the annual Congress, comprising delegates from every branch or group at the ratio of one for up to five hundred members and more when the membership was higher. The highest executive authority was the General Council. Each Congress was to decide on the location of the General Council and to elect a number of Council members and to authorize them to co-opt further members. As long as the general rules were accepted the sections were allowed to make by-laws suitable to the specific circumstances.[102] Marx also proposed that societies joining the International should have the power to nominate representatives to the General Council subject to the Council's right of ratification.[103] This alternative to the proposal for an international "workers" government in fact showed that Marx did not view the International as a party, but as a broad workers' platform, or united front. It could become the starting point for party building work only after taking into consideration the diversities in the situation of the working class in different countries. Marx, as the builder of the First International, cannot be viewed as the forerunner of the builders of a tightly centralized world party, which was running under orders from an all-powerful executive.[104]

Marx's own letters and his activities show that he considered the International to be a united front organization. This nature of the organization is clearly brought out by Collins and Abramsky in a chapter where Marx's achievement is acknowledged by stating that Marx's "task was to reconcile the irreconciliables."[105] The federal structure was essential if the united front was to function. Engels wrote later that the aim of the International "was to weld together into *one* huge army the whole militant working class of Europe and America. Therefore, it could not *set out* from the principles laid down in the *Manifesto*. It was bound to have a program which would not shut the door on the English trade unions, the French, the Belgian, the Italian, and the Spanish Proudhonists and the German Lassalleans."[106] Marx had no wish to try to drive away the people from the secret societies. At the same time he wanted to combat their politics. Marx's correspondence shows that while he was contemptuous of republicans like Mazzini, Ledru-Rollin, and Karl Blind, he was not so hostile to Le Lubez and other Philadelphians. Indeed the desire to preserve the collaboration of all those who had helped to found the International led Marx to take a moderate stand when a conflict broke out between the Proudhonists and the Philadelphians in Paris. The Proudhonists were opposed to political action. Marx, like the Philadelphians, believed in the crucial importance of political struggles. Yet Marx ultimately sided with the Proudhonists, partly because they had the majority of activists, and partly because he wanted to avoid bureaucratic control over diverse proletarian movements.[107]

In the aforementioned letter of November 4 to Engels, Marx also wrote that he had been able to replace the declaration of principles of Le Lubez and the draft program of Weston, an Owenite, by an address to the working classes. The address was very specific and emphasized the nature of the working class in terms of facts culled from government statements; the consequent class character of the workers' movements and the necessity of internationalism. The St. Martin's Hall meeting had developed out of earlier contacts not only over immediate industrial issues but also over international issues like Italian unification, support to the liberation of slaves in the USA and support for the Polish insurrection of 1863.[108] At the foundation meeting itself George Odger, International Secretary of the London Trades Council, read out an "Address to Workmen of France," in which he called for foreign affairs to be based on reason and moral rights. Despite the vagueness of the words, his speech had argued the need for class unity to strengthen the bargaining power of labor. At the same time there was an attempt at the General Council's meeting of October 11, to merge the International in the Marquis of Townsend's Universal League, which was also in favor of Polish independence. This was why on the issue of class independence Marx had to fight from the beginning. In the Inaugural Address this was done by showing that every improvement in the condition of the worker, such as the Ten Hour Bill, or the successes of cooperatives, was the result of the class struggle. From this the conclusion that he drew was: "the lords of land and the lords of capital will always use their political privileges for the defense and perpetuation of their economical monopolies. . . . To conquer political power has therefore become the great duty of the working classes." In England, Germany, Italy, and France, there were simultaneous revivals, along with simultaneous efforts towards political reorganization of the workingmen's party.[109] Internally Marx opposed the entry of bourgeois figures in the leadership of the International even if they were "honest and sincere"—since he opposed turning the International, a working-class association, into an appendage of bourgeois or aristocratic politics.[110]

Marx's role in the General Council was that of one member among many, and any leadership that he exerted was through intellectual persuasion and hard work. That his style of functioning was not autocratic is exemplified by one recorded case of a polemic, with the old Owenite, John Weston. Weston sought to prove that a general rise in wages was useless and hence concluded that trade unionism for that purpose would have harmful consequences. Marx presented a paper refuting Weston's anti-strike stance, but appreciated Weston's moral courage to articulate it openly in a situation of the strike waves in the continent. When it was a dispute within the working class and when no provable ulterior motives were present, Marx's attitude to political opponents was democratic. Throughout its history, the IWA never sought to gag any viewpoint within it, as long as those who held minority viewpoints did not try to pass off their views as the views of the International.

Within the General Council, the English trade unionists formed the largest group. Of the thirty-four members originally elected, twenty-seven were Englishmen. Odger was elected president, while Cremer, a building workers' leader, became the General Secretary. Marx's closest ally was the old Communist, Eccarius, who was elected Vice President. By the end of the year the expanded General Council of sixty-six members had only seven Marxists, counting Marx himself and including Eccarius, Pfander, Lessener, and Lochner among the Germans, the Frenchman Dupont and the Swiss Jung. From this point to 1869, Marx never made an attempt at direct control. In 1866 he even refused the nomination for the post of President and proposed Odger instead.[111] A year later, the post of President was abolished at Marx's initiative in favor of a rotating chairmanship.[112] Meanwhile, Eccarius had been elected General Secretary, so that Marx enjoyed a strong intellectual influence, as well as some personal influence, but as corresponding secretary for Germany, he was one of several functionaries and could not exercise any dictatorial authority. It is sufficient to note that he did not even attend any of the Congresses of the International before 1872.

In 1888, looking back to the period of the IWA, Engels wrote approvingly that when Marx had written the Inaugural Address, he "entirely trusted to the intellectual development of the working class which was sure to result from combined action and mutual discussion."[113] As two historians of the First International write:

> When, during the Lifetime of Marx, socialism became a world force, it was expressed in his terms and armed with his ideas, rather than those of Mazzini, Proudhon or Bakunin. This was almost entirely due to the International and the effective leadership which Marx brought to bear on the labour movements of many countries at a formative stage is their development.[114]

Marx's own activities and writings show this dual perspective. We have already seen that he wanted to emphasize proletarian self-emancipation and democracy within the organization. But he also wanted to draw lessons from the workers' struggles in order to influence the working class or at least its militant section in a communist direction. Marx drew up the "Instructions for the Delegates of the Provisional General Council" for the Geneva Congress (1866) of the IWA, a document that was eventually presented as the official Report of the General Council. In it he argued that the cooperative movement could succeed only by cooperative production, and not by organizing cooperative stores. He also urged that the trade unions should not consider themselves simply as associations to raise wages and reduce working hours but also as "organized agencies for superseding every system of wage labour and capital rule."[115] As the International grew in strength and benefited from the strike wave of 1866–67, Marx was gradually able to persuade the successive congresses to adopt progressively more socialist policies. The Lausanne Congress of the International (1867) resolved that "the social emancipation of the workers of cannot be effected without their political emancipation."[116] At the Brussels Congress (1868), the Proudhonists scored a victory by getting a resolution passed which saw mutual credit within capitalist society as a means to workers' salvation.[117] However, in the same Congress the Proudhonists were defeated when a resolution was passed advocating collective ownership of land, railways, mines and forest.[118] This victory was consolidated at the Basel Congress of the International in 1869. The importance that Marx attached to the question of land collectivization as an issue of socialist program is incontestable. In England, the General Council with Marx's active support sponsored the Land and Labour League, and Eccarius was even appointed one of the secretaries of the League. In his letter to Engels, on December 4,

1869, Marx mentioned two letters to Robert Applegarth in which he had presented detailed arguments about landed property and its abolition.[119] The address of the Land and Labour League, drawn up by Eccarius, contained a clear program of class struggle, with a demand for the nationalization of land. The aim was clearly to link this to the struggle for political power.[120] In discussions on this issue in the General Council, Marx emphasized both the importance of collective ownership of land, and also the need for persuasion and moderation as far as the small peasantry was concerned.[121] The General Council minutes reveal that people like Élisée Reclus, later to be an anarchist, proposed ignoring the views of peasants, while Marx responded by pointing out that ideological representatives of small property holders (i.e. the Proudhonists) were present in the International, and further that small peasants should not be coerced. Thus it was Marx who emphasized democratic norms and the need to develop consciousness instead of imposing "socialist" dogmas.

When, after the Second World War, the German Social Democratic Party (hereafter SPD) formally dropped all references to Marxism from its program, it referred instead to Lassalle, as the founder of the democratic socialist politics. Variations on this theme are stated even by serious historians like Rosenberg.[122] In analyzing the criticisms of Marx and Engels about Lassalle, scholars have often believed that these were occasioned less by real differences, and more by the rivalry over the leadership of the German working-class movement, a rivalry in which the theoretician Marx was defeated by the practical politician Lassalle.[123]

Lassalle was a German Socialist, who claimed to be a follower of Marx. But the organization which he had set up was radically opposed to Marx's concept of a working-class party. In the early 1860s, the German workers' movement started stirring after over a decade of silence. Workers' Educational Societies were founded in many places. A fledgling national organization was also built up. At this stage, having been rebuffed by the bourgeois liberals whose alliance they had sought, leaders of these organizations turned to Lassalle, who at that time had been likewise rebuffed by the liberals, whose leadership he had tried to gain. The lack of class-conscious self-confidence on part of the workers prompted them to send a letter to Lassalle requesting him to send his views. His response on March 1, 1863, usually known as the *Open Reply*, spelled out his conception of parties and politics.

The General German Workers' Association (hereafter ADAV) that Lassalle founded, gave him dictatorial authority. Indeed, in a secret letter to Bismarck, within a few months, he wrote about the constitution of his empire, as he called the ADAV. He believed that "the working class feels instinctively inclined to dictatorship if it can first be rightfully convinced that it will be increased in its interest."[124] In its politics, despite the call for universal suffrage, the party was hardly democratic, as its tactical line was to concentrate attacks on the bourgeoisie to the extent of forging an alliance with the monarchy. When Lassalle died in 1864, he even tried to bequeath the leadership of the organization through his will to Berhard Becker, a member of the ADAV and a journalist. Eventually the man who became dominant in the ADAV was J. B. von Schweitzer. Between 1865 and 1868 Marx and Engels repeatedly clashed with Becker and Schweitzer over their organizational practices and their politics of support to Bismarck in the hope of getting universal suffrage. A sharp attack on this came in Engels' major pamphlet, *The Prussian Military Question and the German Workers' Party* (1865). Unlike the IWA, the ADAV was centralized, nationalistic, and pro-government. Such an organization could exist only as long as the working class was backward. We should note that in 1868, seven out every nine ADAV members in Hamburg were tailors, shoe-makers, joiners, or cigar-makers, and that resistance to dictatorship within the party came from the Metal Workers' Union and other relatively modern sections of the working class. The long-term effect of Lassalle was to develop a tendency to bureaucratic and authoritarian party functioning, a leadership cult, and worship of the state.[125]

The attitude of Marx and Engels to Lassalle and Lassalleanism can be easily explained in political terms without recourse to questionable psychological hypotheses. The Marx family had indeed known about this side of Lassalle ever since he had visited them in 1862. At that time Marx had criticized Lassalle for behaving like an enlightened Bonapartist.[126] In April 1863, Marx wrote to Engels, on reading the *Open Reply*, that Lassalle was behaving like a workers' dictator. Marx criticized Lassalle for suggesting that the class struggle could be resolved by the workers' agitation for universal suffrage, after which they were to elect people like Lassalle to parliament.[127] Engels' reply to Marx criticized not only Lassalle but the political backwardness of the workers, and suggested the impossibility of forming a modern workers' party by banking on this backwardness.[128] After the death of Lassalle, the correspondence of Marx and Engels reveals their dualistic appreciation of his politics. On the one hand, they could not simply denounce ADAV, which was a workers' party despite all its weaknesses. On the other hand, they were hostile to his dictatorial organizational outlook. In a letter of November 4, 1864 to Engels, Marx criticized Lassalle for behaving like a ruling prince in installing Becker as the president of ADAV.[129]

With the Lassalleans the conflict of Marx and Engels was more acute and public. Sharply counterposing the ADAV to the International, Marx wrote to a friend that in the long run "the whole organisation of the Association will have to be broken up, as its basis is fundamentally wrong."[130] When in 1868, Schweitzer tried to impose a dictatorship over the trade unions, Marx called it a sectarian policy.[131] The contrast could not be sharper. Marx in the International refused to accept even the largely honorary post of President and drafted a democratic constitution for the organization, while Lassalle in the ADAV went in for a personal dictatorship. As with Proudhon, the contrast serves to show that it was Marx who stood for maximum possible expansion of proletarian democracy.

The history of the IWA provides several instances of Marx's approach to workers' democracy. Many of these were issues that came up in the course of his clash with Bakunin. Bakunin himself insisted that democracy was a major issue in the clash, by calling Marx an authoritarian.[132] In the 1860s and 1870s, Bakunin built an organization, variously named at different times and in different documents, but one which Marx knew as the International Alliance for Socialist Democracy (hereafter referred to as the Alliance). Initially, Bakunin took his organization inside the liberal Peace and Freedom League, and tried to get it and the International to merge, presumably because in such a case, as the broker of the unity, he would be an influential figure. When that failed, and the League itself rejected his radical proposals, he split and formed the Alliance as a public organization while retaining a secret inner core as well. The public Alliance was to be an international organization, with elaborate rules. The program stated in its preamble that:

> The socialist minority of the League of Peace and Freedom, having separated itself from the League . . . as a result of the majority vote at the Berne Congress, the majority being formally opposed to the fundamental principle of all workers' associations—that of *economic and social equalisation of classes and individuals*—has thereby adhered to the principles proclaimed by the *workers' congresses* held in Geneva, Lausanne and Brussels. Several members of this minority . . . have suggested that we should form a new *International Alliance of Socialist Democracy,* merged entirely in the great *International Working Men's Association,* but having a special mission to study political and philosophical questions. . . . Convinced, for our part, of the usefulness of such an enterprise that would provide sincere socialist democrats of Europe and America with the means of being understood. . . . We consider it our duty . . . to take the initiative in forming this new organisation.

The rules stated that the Alliance "Constitutes a branch of the International Workingmen's Association," that the Alliance itself would have a central bureau, that Alliance members grouped under their respective national bureaus would ask the central bureau to admit them into the International, and that the Alliance would hold its meetings at the time of the Congresses of the International, but separately.[133]

Marx and Engels were opposed to the affiliation of the Alliance to the IWA, because its founders, beginning with Bakunin, wanted it to be a parallel international organization, whose central leadership claimed the right to mediate between the ordinary members of the Alliance and the International itself. Moreover, by definition, the Alliance claimed to be the theoreticians of socialism, leaving for the International only "practical" tasks. This went directly against the accepted view of the International to the effect that the workers would liberate themselves, and that theoretical development could only be based on practice. In his marginal comments on the program and rules of the Alliance, Marx noted the negative features clearly.

The General Council agreed, and rejected the Alliance's application for affiliation. Bakunin then pretended to dissolve the International Alliance and sought admission for the Geneva branch of the Alliance as a local organization. The General Council, including Marx, fell into this simple trap, and allowed the Trojan horse in.[134] That Bakunin had never dissolved the secret organization was a major charge against him in 1872 at the Hague Congress of the International. That the charge was true can be proved by acknowledgements from his own partisans, like Charles Perron, or James Guillaume.[135] By infiltrating and by creating a parallel and secret body within an independent and democratic International, he was undermining the organization. By recruiting into the Alliance while using the International as a front, he was violating the democratic rights of the International and its members. What is equally important is that Bakunin's own organization was to be an "invisible dictatorship"—as dictatorial as he wanted organizations that he was infiltrating to be loose and chaotic. Arthur Mendel says, "One could not imagine a more rigidly centralized, authoritarian revolutionary organization than the one Bakunin proposed."[136]

Inside the IWA, when Bakunin came into conflict with the members of the Romance Federation (French-speaking Switzerland), it was he who proposed, at the Basel Congress, that the General Council should have the right to suspend existing sections, and that it should be more authoritative.[137] This shows that it was Bakunin who was clashing with all sorts of members of the International, rather than Marx violating democracy, and further that it was at Bakunin's proposal that the powers of the General Council were extended in a way that the majority would ultimately use against Bakunin.

Another related issue is Marx's opposition to anarchism. A scrutiny of the documents leading up to the split show that anarchism was never the real political issue. When Bakunin did create an "anarchist" program, Marx opposed it politically.[138] But he was not opposed to anarchists remaining inside the IWA. He was opposed to any one political–ideological current being proclaimed as the official ideology of the International. He was equally opposed to the transformation of the International into a specifically "Marxist" organization, as he wrote in his letter to his supporter, Paul Lafargue on April 18, 1870.[139]

The contrasting outlooks of Marx and Bakunin were tested by the French events of 1870–71. When the second Empire fell and a Republic was proclaimed, Bakuninists and Blanquists alike hailed the Republic without any caution about its class character, while Marx and the General Council warned that to establish workers' rights, the workers must be cautious about the role of the bourgeoisie. In that sense, the predominance of the non-Marxists in French working-class politics contributed to the unpreparedness of the Paris Commune. Bakunin, for his part, took part in a "revolution" in Lyons, where he "proclaimed" the abolition of the state, and was subsequently chased away by the police of that state.

Later, of course, every left trend claimed the Commune as its own. Marx argued that the Commune represented an attempt by the proletariat to emancipate itself. Bakunin's claim that the Commune reflected the anarchist principle made no sense, because the Commune tried to reconstitute a centralized public order, though under democratic control. Marx did not claim that the Commune represented specifically "Marxist" principles. He wrote that it was the work of "our heroic party comrades in Paris," and Engels later talked of the Commune being a child of the International "intellectually."[140] But by this, they only meant that the Commune was a proletarian revolution, and as such, justified the principles of the International regarding proletarian democracy and self-emancipation.

The final conflict came in 1871-72. Under the difficult situation prevailing in 1871, only a less authoritative Conference rather than a Congress was possible. This London Conference of the International passed a number of important resolutions. One of the most important was that entitled "Political Action of the Working-Class." The resolution linked political action with the struggle for social emancipation. It then went on to assert that class action by the proletariat necessitated the creation of a working-class party opposed to all parties of the propertied classes, so that the social revolution could triumph.[141]

Bakunin and his supporters opposed this call for political action and the formation of political parties. The General Council and the London Conference, by issuing this call, were showing that in their opinion, to establish workers' democracy, politics was essential. Moreover, the resolution indicates that the International itself was not thought of as a party. Marx himself confirmed such a view of the International as a coordinating agency rather than a party immediately after the Conference in a public speech where he said that the task of International was "to organize the forces of labour and link the various working-men's movements and combine them."[142]

Marx's letter of November 23, 1871, to the American Socialist Bolte, and Engels' later comments including the welcome he gave to the foundation of the Independent Labour Party in Britain, confirm that through this resolution, they were not urging the IWA itself to become a disciplined and centralized Communist Party.[143] For them, the International was a united front of diverse working-class currents. What was "Marxist" was Marx's idea of using the united front approach as a necessary stage in building a proletarian party, without imposing ideas as yet unacceptable to militant workers.

The conflict resulted in a struggle for a majority at the Hague Congress of the International. Marx and Engels fought for a majority by urging their supporters to ensure that rules were followed, by getting mandates for trusted people, and in some cases, by ensuring that those elected as delegates could turn up by paying their fares. Marx was naturally concerned with getting a majority. But the letters of Marx and Engels to Wilhelm Liebknecht, Ludwig Kugelmann, Theodore Cuno, Friedrich Adolphe Sorge, etc., show that they were using all the existing rules, and that they were serious about observing the rules.

Marx was accused by the Bakuninists of deliberately choosing The Hague, so that Bakunin could not attend, since he might be arrested in several countries on the way from Switzerland. As a matter of fact, in 1872, so soon after the Commune, the International was a suspect organization to governments and police everywhere, and it could arrange its Congress, which had to be public sessions according to its rules, only in a few places. Moreover, French Communard refugees in England could not go to Geneva, the place the Bakuninists had wanted.[144]

At the Hague Congress, a number of measures was taken to tighten organizational discipline. To the General Council's right to suspend local organizations were added the right to suspend entire national organizations, so that in emergencies it could act decisively. At the same time, Engels, who drafted the new measure, put in a number of clauses to check abuse of power by the General Council.[145] Initially, this resolution was occasioned not by Bakunin, but by the millionaire sisters Victoria Woodhull and Tennie Claflin, who paid a number of membership dues to create spurious local units and take over the New York Federal Council, displacing genuine working-class activists like Sorge.[146] The Woodhull issue has led to much debate. According to Samuel Bernstein, the first historian to discuss in detail the conflicts in the US Federal Council, Marx's position was basically justified. The opposite position has been taken by a recent book, by Timothy Messer-Kruse,[147] while a critical middle-of-the-road stand has been taken by others, such as Paul Buhle.[148] Two distinct issues seem involved here.

Woodhull and her associates in Section 12 of the International in New York, even by the admission of Messer-Kruse, who challenges the traditional interpretation of Bernstein, were composed substantially of non-proletarians, and what is more, they sought to challenge the very basis of the International. Thus, in notes kept by Marx, emphasis was laid on arguments suggesting that social equality was possible within bourgeois society. While there had been repeated statements by Marx against absolute exclusion of non-proletarians from the International, there had also been an understanding that it was ultimately a working-class organization. Section 12 challenged that, and got into a conflict with the old Federal Council. Both sides appealed to the General Council, which ruled that there was to be no *new* American section having less than two-third worker members.[149] The *Marx-Engels Collected Works* provides a footnote, informing us that the version printed in *Woodhull & Claflin's Weekly*, omitted the word "new" before section. The resolution was very clear in explaining its motivation: it wanted to avoid the "intrusion into the *International* of bogus reformers, middle-class quacks and trading politicians."[150]

There was another dimension to the conflict, however. There were many sectarians and faddists, including spiritualists, evidently flocking to the International in the USA. What was seriously questionable was the fact that Marx lumped Woodhull's feminist politics with all these. She had a questionable role, since she was allying herself with sundry reformers and sects. But Marx and Engels seemed to be using class-based arguments not only to reject her class position, but also her feminist assertions. Thus, Marx commented that Woodhull was "a banker's woman, free-lover, and general humbug,"[151] while Engels seemed to imply that the electoralist and bourgeois democratic slogans of Section 12 somehow invalidated its call for "the Political Equality and Social Freedom of men and women alike."[152] But Section 12 put forward a definition of social equality that incorporated control over women's sexuality, opposition to dress codes, etc.; issues no present-day socialist, especially Marxist, can ignore. In the light of contemporary experience, therefore, it is not possible to accept the rather rigid arguments of Marx and Engels, because women's sexuality, the dress code, etc., are not issues important only for bourgeois or petty bourgeois women. Organizing women workers, or other groups not normally within the focus of Sorge and his comrades, as well as incorporating the divergent experiences within the class into programs, was something that was ignored in the fight against Woodhull.[153] So while agreeing on the bourgeois limitations of Woodhull, her electoralist outlook, and so on, it is impossible to give up the suspicion that the rejection of her feminism was also caused by a male bias within the General Council and the Sorge-led Federal

Council. All the material amassed by Marx and Engels provides us with only one text where the right of women's suffrage is acknowledged by a pro-General Council Section in the USA.[154]

Returning to the Hague Congress, we should note that the General Council was empowered to act as the executor of the Congress resolutions. The Hague Congress also reaffirmed the resolution on political action.[155] At the Congress, the Bakuninists did not debate the specifics of the Council's powers. They did not point out which aspects were undemocratic. They called simply for the abolition of the Council, so that no binding decisions could be taken or implemented, however democratically. By this time, Bakunin had shifted from a strategy of conquest from within to a strategy of split at any cost. Until mid-July 1872, Bakunin was trying for a takeover. The first version of the new plan was to boycott the Hague Congress. This was what his Italian adherents then did. But eventually realizing that more supporters might be picked up by going to The Hague and precipitating a split there, such a line was adopted. On August 14, Bakunin drafted a program for a Slavic section that he founded, which stated that it was anarchist, and implied that the International had to be made an anarchist organization. This was of course contrary to the rules, and it implies that in his mind, if not in actuality, Bakunin had already split. By August 31, Bakunin even wrote a letter where the post-split task was defined — to hold a rival Congress at Saint-Imier.[156]

At the Hague Congress, Bakunin and Guillaume were expelled for belonging to the Alliance in violation of the rules of the International. This expulsion proves, not Marx's authoritarianism, but the necessity of discipline as a component part of democracy in any working-class organization, even at the international level.

At the same time, Marx and Engels recognized that the "bubble was bound to burst."[157] What this meant was that the united front that had come into existence at a time when the workers' movement was on the defensive could not last long once the movement forged ahead and different currents drew apart. The Commune split the unity between moderates and radicals, especially after its defeat, when radicals claimed it as their own while moderates moved away. It was only in the USA that the low level of the movement made it possible for the old unity to be kept alive for some more time. Marx hoped that the transfer of the General Council to New York would enable the Council to play the kind of role that it had played in London earlier. This was why Marx proposed the transfer of the Council to New York. An added consideration was probably the fact that in England itself, the International was making no progress in recent years.

The 1876 dissolution of the General Council and the International in Philadelphia also saw the birth of the Socialist Labor Party of the USA.

Though it later became a sectarian organization, in origin this was one of the limited gains of the transfer. In any case, killing off the International was not what Marx wanted. The death was, as Freymond and Molnár suggest, foretold in the manner of its birth.[158]

This however raises some important questions. If Marx and Engels were democrats and if the International was a democratic organization, why did they not try to preserve it in spite of the Bakuninists? In his letter to Sorge, mentioned earlier, Engels provided an answer, which has been neglected. When he said that the "bubble was bound to burst" he was referring to the unity formed on the basis of tactical considerations. The internationalism of most of the components of the International was generally democratic, rather than specifically socialist. Repression by authoritarian governments and the need for solidarity during strikes had been some of the other important factors that had led to the formation of the International in the first place. Thus the International had been a united front rather than a political party. This had been acknowledged both in Marx's letter of November 4, 1864 to Engels, and in Marx's letter to Lafargue written April 18, 1870. A united front by its nature is temporary as it involves an agreement between different trends for specific aims, their strategic differences notwithstanding. Once the struggle of the united front brings concrete successes, differences again assert themselves. This was what happened to the International. The Paris Commune brought fame for the IWA although the latter had not led the former. But it also sharpened the differences because now questions of class power raised by the Commune and the road to power became more important than solidarity for strikers or victims of repression. When basic differences existed on such issues a united organization was no longer possible. In a way the actions of Marx and Engels in this period testify to their recognition of the fact that the entire working class cannot be united into one party. What they now hoped was that those cadres who had adhered to the program of scientific socialism would be able to diffuse those ideas widely so that in future, a Communist International would be built.[159] But their conception of proletarian democracy made them aware that it was not possible to immediately proclaim a Communist International as long as Communist ideas were marginal among the workers of a number of key countries. This is why, for the next decade and a half they opposed such attempts and suggested two different lines of party building. Wherever socialist ideas had become more or less widespread among vanguard workers they were in favor of programmatic clarity in building a communist party. In those countries where even militant workers very often followed bourgeois politicians, they emphasized the struggle for independent political parties of the working class.

IV
THE PERIOD OF THE MASS SOCIALIST PARTIES

In different ways, both Molyneaux and Alan Hunt tend to assume that Marx and Engels envisaged a linear or organic growth from the Labour Party to a socialist party. A fatalist or determinist view of the growth of class-consciousness is supposed to have pervaded their thought.[160] There is indeed a tension between the concept of a party of the class based on democracy and the hegemony of socialist ideas. The problem lies in the fact that in a non-revolutionary period, building a broadly-based working-class party on the basis of workers' democracy would lead the party to dilute itself programmatically. It is true that the writings of Marx and Engels sometimes paid inadequate attention to the problem of reformism as a lasting phenomenon. However, in the first place, their writings including letters on the English labor movement show their awareness of the problem, and in the second place, their writings in any case, do not show them as defenders of the social democratic model of party building. The inadequacy in their conception lay in an (over) emphasis on the program and comparatively less emphasis on the composition and day to day functioning of the party.

Two factors contributing to this one-sidedness were: first, that as exiles for many years, they were not activists of a national party organization, and second, that in the period after the Commune, Marx's failing health made it impossible for him to take part in the day-to-day political activities. The fact that they were not tied to any particular national organization was recognized by Engels in his letter to Bernstein in 1883, when he wrote: "We belong to the German party scarcely more than to the French, American or Russian party and can consider ourselves as little bound by the German programme as by the minimum programme. We attach importance to this our special status as representatives of international socialism."[161] This peculiar status meant that while they could uphold the past programmatic development, they were often cut off from current practices.

Marx's concept of party building thus envisaged two alternative models. One was the creation of a broad-based labor party where class independence was to be the minimum basis of unity. The other model was that of a communist party to be built up when a significant section of the working class became aware of the necessity of communism and began adopting programmatic goals accordingly. The examples are, the Communist League as the prototype of a communist party, and the London Conference resolution on political action as the road from the International to mass labor parties.

In a letter to Bernstein in 1879, Engels complained that the English trade unions, by barring all political action on principle, "thereby also ban participation in any general activity of the working class as a class."[162] Thus in countries like England and the USA, a broad-based labor party had to be built so that the working class got political independence. In a letter to Sorge, on November 29, 1886, Engels wrote, "The first great step of importance for every country newly entering into the movement, is always the constitution of the workers as an independent political workers' party ... that the first programme of this party is still confused ... (is) merely transitory. ... The movement in America is at the same stage as it was in our country before 1848; the really intelligent people there will first have to play the part played by the Communist League among the workers' societies before 1848."[163] This is also an admission that the League was not the mass communist vanguard which was their ultimate goal. A few months later, he was explaining to another American friend that in the USA where class independence had not yet been won, it was better to get a million or two of workers' votes for a genuine class party than to get a hundred thousand votes for a correct program, and a month later he again advised working with the general movement of the class.[164] As late as 1893, Engels was writing to Lafargue that the English workers had to learn to use their strength to form an independent party. He was critical of H. M. Hyndman, the English "Marxist," as he considered the latter to be a sectarian whose party, the Social Democratic Federation, had the distinction of being, along with the German–American Socialists, "the only parties who have contrived to reduce the Marxist theory of development to a rigid orthodoxy. This theory, is to be forced down the throats of the workers at once and without development as articles of faith, instead of making the workers raise themselves to its level by dint of their own class instinct."[165] What matters is not whether every specific judgement of Engels was correct—for example, E. P. Thompson has made out a strong case for William Morris, who was driven close to the Anarchists because of the wrong tactics of Engels and Eleanor Marx-Aveling.[166] The general argument that Engels was making was that at a time when the working class was so lacking in class consciousness that it could not even form its own political parties, but rather remained as left-wing appendages of liberal bourgeois parties, any construction of a communist party in a full-fledged way would turn into a caricature. Violating all norms of workers' democracy, such a party would become an authoritarian or substitutionist organization.

If Engels had stopped here his views would have been very one sided. But in fact, Marx and Engels did not interpret workers' democracy to mean all-inclusive blocs. In 1882, the reformists and the revolutionaries in the French Parti Ouvrier split. Writing to Bernstein (1882), Engels welcomed the split, agreeing with Lafargue that the reformist majority was not a party because it had no actual program. Generalizing from this split he even wrote that every workers' party of a big country could develop only through internal struggle. He considered the split to be inevitable and good.[167]

The insistence on programmatic clarity, once class independence, and a general spread of socialist ideas had been achieved, was even more pronounced in the German case. In Germany two working-class parties had been formed by the late 1860s. The ADAV had survived the death of Lassalle and the initial crisis after it. Meanwhile, Johann Philipp Becker had organized branches of the International which later joined hands with dissident Lassalleans and the *Arbeiterbildungsvereine* (Workers' Educational Association) led by August Bebel and Wilhelm Liebknecht to establish the Social Democratic Workers' Party (SDAP) in 1869 (often called the Eisenachers). Marx and Engels supported this party despite their frequent criticism of Liebknecht. However, they reacted sharply when a merger of the Social Democratic Labor Party was proposed with the ADAV—they felt that united action could have been achieved without a party unity that made a great many ideological compromises with Lassalleanism. When this unity was accomplished and the SPD formed at the Gotha Unity Congress (1875), Marx wrote, that if it was impossible to advance beyond the Eisenach program they should simply have made an agreement about common action.[168] Though the idea of the dictatorship of an individual within the party was dropped, the domination of the parliamentary representatives was still there partly as a strategy to cope with the anti-socialist law. A historian of this party has shown that this model was chosen consciously in opposition to any attempt to build an underground party structure.[169] If this enabled the party to avoid prosecution and the secret society mentality, it was at the cost of party democracy.

Engels in his letter to Bebel wrote even more sharply that a new program was a public banner by which the world judges a party, and hence the retreat was harmful.[170] During the twelve-year period of the anti-socialist law, they were unable to develop this criticism further until 1890. But in 1891, at the time of program revision, Engels published Marx's *Critique of the Gotha Programme* and got Bernstein to write a sharp critique of Lassalle's politics. Once the socialist outlook had spread within the class vanguard they considered it retrograde to dilute it in the name of proletarian democracy.

This is also brought out by the role of Engels in the Second International, when an international socialist congress was planned for the centenary of the French Revolution, and Engels launched a large-scale campaign to make its program Marxist. When this congress gave rise to the possibility of a new International, he fought for the exclusion of both right-wing and ultra-left opponents, who would not accept the Marxist program. Apart from private letters he also collaborated with Bernstein in producing a pamphlet in response to the criticisms of the Social Democratic Federation and its allies, the French opportunist current known as the Possibilists. Entitled *The International Workers' Congress of 1889: A Reply to "Justice,"* the aim of the pamphlet was to defend the exclusion of nationalist and reformist socialist currents.[171] In 1891, the Second Congress of the Second International resolved to exclude the representatives of the anarchists. Engels expressed satisfaction, saying "with this the old International came to an end, with this the new one begins again."[172] It was only when the class movement had not awakened that they considered split on programmatic grounds to be sectarian.

On the question of inner party democracy, the standpoint of Marx and Engels can be explained in the following terms: they supported the broadest democracy within the party, but also called for discipline. Their attitude to various events in the history of the German Party shows this. In 1879, the Reichstag (Parliamentary) faction of the party permitted one of the deputies, Max Kayser, to vote for a tax proposal of Bismarck. Marx and Engels condemned this as a betrayal of party discipline as well as socialist principle. They considered that the program of the party was binding on parliamentary representatives. In the Circular Letter (written to Bebel, Liebknecht, Bracke, and others), they also supported Hirsch, a party journalist, who had criticized Kayser and opposed the attempt of the Reichstag fraction to control the new party journal, *Der Sozialdemokrat,* through an editorial commission which they called a censorship commission. The letter leaves one in no doubt about their hostility to what they considered an attempt by the leadership to escape rank and file control. Finally in the same letter, having criticized Hochberg, Bernstein, and Schramm, for putting forward a petty bourgeois line reminiscent of "True" Socialism they wrote: "In a country as petty bourgeois as Germany, there is certainly some justification for such ideas. But only outside the Social Democratic Workers' Party."[173]

Finally, in 1890-91, Engels made a number of comments regarding inner party democracy. In an oft-quoted letter to Sorge (August 9, 1890) he said: "the party is so big that absolute freedom of debate inside it is a necessity. . . . The greatest party in the realm cannot exist without all shades of opinion in it making themselves fully felt."[174] A little after this, Engels had Marx's *Critique of the Gotha Programme* published. An irate party leadership wanted to impose a censorship on *Neue Zeit,* their theoretical paper, edited by Kautsky. This shocked Engels who wrote to Kautsky that such a proposal whether in memory of the fraction's dictatorship during the anti-socialist law or in imitation of the kind of organization that Schweitzer had built was unacceptable.[175]

V
TRADE UNIONS AND THE COMMUNISTS

If the communist party is the highest form of working-class organization, insofar as levels of consciousness are concerned, if the vast majority of the class is to be revolutionized by revolution itself, then there must be some base-level organizations, formed spontaneously at the primary level of class consciousness, which would make the first attempt to organize the workers as an active class fighting for itself. It is for this reason that both Marx and Engels gave utmost importance to trade union and workers' associations. This emphasis on class revolution made the organization of the whole class a crucial task for them. Moreover, equal emphasis on class action and democracy kept open the possibility of new strategies of party building that linked the party to broader forms of working-class self-activity.

Regarding support to trade unionism, the lead was taken by Engels. His exposure to the English political scene made him pro-union from an early stage. It was, however, in *The Condition of the Working Class* that Engels put forward his defense of trade unions at a time, when the modern, industrial proletariat was just growing up in West Europe, and when opposition to trade unions was quite widespread, even among the socialists and left-wing Chartists. It is a measure of the brilliance of the book that Engels took a position clearer than Marx was to take as late as 1847. The whole tenor on the trade union, as found in the above-mentioned essay, was novel then — an attempt, not to reject trade unions, nor to assume that they are sufficient for the workers' cause, but to accept them as basic institutions of the class that must be integrated into the socialist revolutionary perspective. His emphasis was on the active protest of the workers as human beings against the employers to end their disunity and to raise their wages.[176] A comment made here by Engels is highly significant for it enables us to understand why Marx and Engels took a line of consistent support for unions. He wrote, "that these unions contribute greatly to nourish the bitter hatred of the workers against the property-holding class need hardly be said."[177] For Marx and Engels, this was vital, because their socialism was proletarian socialism.

Marx made a similar assessment of the trade union movements of the 1840s; in his major writings and speeches of 1847-8, viz. *The Poverty of Philosophy*, "Wages," and *Communist Manifesto*. Trade unionism deserved the support of communists, he argued in the *Manifesto*, because it not only meant a fight for wages, but also because its struggles involved "the organisation of the proletariat into a class, and consequently into a political party." It is the *organization* of the workers that transforms apparently "personal" competitions for wages into a struggle of classes. And it is the role of the unions in the beginning of this process that makes them the class organizations of the proletariat par excellence. Initially their victory may be temporary. But the "real fruit of their battles lies, not in the immediate result, but in the ever-expanding union of the workers."[178]

The *Manifesto* is thus a landmark in socialist program, which for the first time emphasized the class nature of the struggle for socialism in which the role of the trade unions are crucial in so far as they transform the suffering class into a revolutionary class. And this role became all the more evident as Marx and Engels exposed the class nature of the bourgeois opposition to trade unionism. In *Capital*, Marx pointed out that even as early as the late eighteenth century, the Le Chapelier Law of 1791 banned trade unionism in the name of Liberty, Equality and Fraternity.[179]

If the struggles for wage are mostly temporary and if the unions are ultimately unable to alter the wages, then why did workers form unions at all? Engels bowed to the consensus of authorities, acknowledging that unions cannot affect the overall application of the law of supply and demand. But he went on to argue that the unions train workers for the class war. While that explains why socialists should support unions, that fails to explain, in objective material terms, why the mass of non-socialist workers should remain so attached to the unions. Richard Hyman fails to note this point. In his commentary, Marx and Engels are simply supposed to have developed an "optimistic theory," where unionization leads to party building and to revolution. Hyman also concludes that Marx's hopes about the radicalization of workers were based on a theory of continuous and growing misery and pauperization of the working class.[180]

Their participation in the IWA and witnessing of the actual role of the unions, as well as the consequent attachment of the workers to the unions, brought about a change in the subsequent defense of trade unionism by Marx and Engels. In the first place, the trade unions functioned as organs of primary resistance. Second, as Marx had gained greater insights into economic functioning, he rejected entirely the ideas of increasing poverty, and of the uselessness of unions in defending wages. In fact, as has been discussed, this was the topic of a debate with Weston in the International. In defense of his stand, Marx wrote a paper asserting that both wages and working hours were ultimately fixed as a result of continuous struggle of the workers organized by the unions.

In *Capital*, Marx again argued that trade unions could set aside the law of supply and demand by using the force derived from the combination of workers, just as capitalism itself relied on force to set aside the law of supply and demand in the colonies.[181]

In 1881, in a series of articles, Engels returned to this issue, "the great merit of Trades Unions, in their struggle to keep up wages and to reduce the working hours, is that they tend to keep up and to raise the standard of life. . . . Without the means of resistance of the Trade Unions the labourer does no receive even what is his due according to the rules of the wages system."[182] So it is not surprising that despite defeat the workers continue to flock to the unions. Engels repeated the same argument in vehement tones in a letter to Bebel, where his critique of the Gotha Program stated that "there is absolutely no mention of the organisation of the working class as a class through the medium of trade unions"[183]. So if the "slavery" of wage-labor is to be abolished then the class "must accept war." And in this way the trade unions become schools of war, required for "the Guerrilla fights between capital and labour," which ultimately become "organized agencies for superseding the very system of wage labour and capital rule."[184]

For Marx and Engels, these associations are also domains where the workers get training in democratic functioning. So they served as the prototypes of workers' democracy in a state. In a letter to the Lassallean leader, J. B. von Schweitzer, Marx wrote:

> a *centralist* organisation, suitable as it is for secret societies and sect movements, contradicts the nature of the trade unions. . . . (in Germany) where the worker is regulated bureaucratically. . . . The main thing is *to teach him to walk by himself.*[185]

However, all this did not lead Marx into a syndicalist stance of supposing that unions *alone* were real class organizations, and that parties were secondary or even irrelevant. In 1869, he is supposed to have told four dissident Lassalleans that "only they [i.e. unions] are in a position to constitute a real workers' party."[186] Draper has shown that despite the quotation marks, it is Hamman's (one of the dissident Lassalleans) paraphrase in the context of Schweitzer's dictatorial control and the reaction to this. Moreover, just at this time, Marx's friends had formed the SDAP, which Marx supported, and it was not based on the trade unions.[187]

Almost at the same time, Engels sharply reacted to the proposal of their friend, Johann Phillipp Becker, that:

> Trades Union must be the real workers' associations and the basis of all organisation, that the other associations *must* only exist provisionally alongside.

Engels wrote in sheer disgust to Marx that this dictatorial proposal was "nothing but the old German Journeyman's desire to preserve his 'inn' in every town, and takes this to be the unity of the workers' organisation."[188] On the contrary, both Marx's and Engels' documented position in a number of writings highlights the limitations of the unions.

Despite his disagreement with Weston on the trade union issue Marx also conceded, at the same time, that there was "a just idea lying at the bottom of his [Weston's] theses," namely, the fact that trade unions fail generally from limiting themselves to "a guerilla war against the effects of the existing system, instead of simultaneously trying to change it."[189]

Moreover, in his letter to Liebknecht in 1878, Marx did not hesitate to point out the current demoralization of the working-class movement in England, in the absence of independent political actions of the trade unions which had almost turned into a "tail" of the Great Liberal Party.[190] The accuracy of Marx's characterization of the financial links between the reformist trade union leaders and the liberal party has been established by the historian Royden Harrison.[191] In England, after 1871, there were no broad movements led by the trade unions. Besides, years of piecemeal victory and improved condition, often injected an inertia in the trade union movement, a dangerous phenomenon, as pointed out by Engels, in an article of 1885. Commenting on the improved condition of the English trade unions since almost 1848, he had observed that in the 1880s they "form an aristocracy among the working class; they have succeeded in empowering for themselves a relatively comfortable position, and they accept it as final." Engels opined that the loss of militancy on the part of the trade union organizations was also responsible for slowing down the pace of the growth of class consciousness among the broad section of the workers, who in turn became hostile to the unions. He therefore stressed that the new International would have to strive to mobilize them.[192]

The call for mobilization did not mean control by the International over every particular class organization, or specifically over the trade unions, as we have already seen, in the context of Marx and Engels' participation in the International Workingmen's Association. So this brings us to the key issue—the trade union movement and the tasks of the communists. Here the guideline comes straight away from the *Manifesto*, where we get the idea that the communists do not form a separate sect imposing their own sectarian principles over the proletarian movement. The idea, if we look at it positively, is that the communists have to act as loyal left wing of the trade union movement. This explains why in the first place Marx wanted to join the International. The communists had two specific tasks, viz., to promote class line and militancy in the movement, and to ensure trade union democracy.

In the International, Marx and Engels wanted to push the working-class movement in a communist direction, but only to the extent that the workers could relate to communist theory, developed out of the political practice of earlier generations of workers, on the basis of their actual experience of struggle. For this, they considered it necessary to develop a radicalized trade union movement, which should pass from purely bread and butter issues to political action.[193]

However, this did not imply that the task of the communists was to present trade unions with an ultimatum of accepting the communist program or face sectarian denunciations. The IWA showed how Marx was prepared to move step by step to combine trade unions with political organizations. Indeed the Reform League, and the political activism of the English unions in general resulted substantially from Marx's endeavors.[194] In the long run, Marx saw his task as promoting the activist elements in the trade union wing to build a political party. Regarding the relationship between the Communist party and the trade union, their idea was quite consistent with the principle of proletarian democracy. The task was neither just to win votes nor to get some recruits. Marx and Engels emphasized bringing as many unionists as possible close to the general political standpoint of the party. Engels specified the dialectics of the union-party relationship in an article praising the German SPD. "A great advantage to the German movement is that the trades organisation works hand in hand with the political organisation. The immediate advantage offered by the trades organisation draw many an otherwise indifferent man into the political movement, while the community of political action holds together, and assures mutual support to the otherwise isolated Trade Unions."[195] So the leading role of the political wing depended on its ability to provide the guidance to the trade unions. This is a difficult political task, steering between the Scylla of party-controlled unionism (forerunner to the Stalinist Red Unionism), and the Charybdys of "trade union neutrality," by which reformist unionists in the next generation meant the withdrawal of support to socialists.[196]

The exact form of the relationship between party and union could not be fixed for good, as both had to evolve. The class movement, as Engels pointed out in a letter to Kelley-Wischnewetzky, must be given time to consolidate. In the same letter he criticized the sectist policy of the Knights of Labor (a secret society established in Philadelphia in 1869) which wanted to control the working-class movement. A few years later, writing to Sorge, Engels again insisted that it has to be revolutionized from within. "Formally, the movement, is first of all a trade union movement" that had taken to politics. So "like everyone else, they (i.e. the unions) learn by their own experiences from their own mistakes."[197]

In 1891, about 20,000 miners in the Ruhr area came out on strike, against the opinion of the SPD leadership, which felt that the government might use this as a plea to reintroduce some kind of anti-socialist law. The party press criticized the miners publicly, at a time when they were subjected to massive repression including the use of the army. Engels felt that even if the assessment of the party was correct, it had no right to dictate the course of a class movement by "a rigid discipline of a sect." To Kautsky, he wrote that "every new group of workers *will be driven toward* us in the course of unwise, necessarily unsuccessful but, under the circumstance inevitable strikes of angry passion."[198]

VI
REVOLUTION AND WORKING CLASS
SELF-ORGANIZATION

For Marx, the working-class movement was not reducible to only two arms—trade union and party. Instead he took into account cooperatives, educational societies, working-class press, or in short, broad workers' association as other significant forms of self-organization of the class. And the question is how communist hegemony is to be established within the framework of proletarian democracy in such diverse organizations.

Naturally this issue in particular cannot predate practice. The whole problem of broader organizations of this class became clarified in the course of 1848 revolution, when the need for such organization became clear. Both in France, where the allegiance of the bulk of the workers lay with the social democratic party including petty bourgeois socialists like Louis Blanc, and in Germany, independent working-class action was hindered as a result of the lack of independent working-class organizations. But it was in Germany that Marx himself put his ideas in practice. The strategic outlook of Marx and Engels dictated the immediate organizational tactical perspective. This outlook, concerning Germany, involved a specific analysis about a revolution in a backward country which however had conditions of a far greater capitalist development compared to the English or French bourgeois revolutions. Against the autocracy the working class had to support the bourgeoisie insofar as the bourgeoisie would fight, ally with Democrats, (of whom, in a way the working class formed the left wing) and at the same time maintain class independence so that the immediate goals of the working class were secured.[199] In order to ensure the future victory of the proletariat, they had to be organized separately. This imposed two tasks—winning them away from bourgeois liberal and more particularly petty-bourgeois democratic ideology and turning their outlook from pre-industrial guild and craft-based association to class association, in both senses highlighting the wage-laborer identity and the need to struggle for its abolition.

The Communist League formulated a 17-point "Demands of the Communist Party in Germany" and planned to use it as the programmatic basis in organizing workers' associations, locally and nationally.[200] On April 23, 1848, the Mainz association even proclaimed itself the provisional Central Committee of the associations. But this attempt failed. According to a historian, the nature of workers' participation in the revolution showed that in agitating for economic demands they often acted along traditional lines, while in political action they as often tended to line up uncritically with the democrats.[201] This became clear to the League leaders who had selected Cologne as the base of operation. In Cologne, the original effort had come from a League member named Gottschalk. But the result had been a craft-divided association. Schapper and Moll took the lead in developing a grass roots movement and restructuring the association so that on the one hand it became more democratic, and on the other hand it became an organization of all workers regardless of craft. Attempts were also made to reach out to rural workers.[202] When Gottschalk was arrested early in July, Moll was elected president, testifying to the growing influence of the "Marx party."

Marx and Engels had realized the impracticability of immediately setting up a national workers' association. Therefore, in order to get a hearing among politicized workers, who were gravitating to the Democrats, they launched the NRZ and also became active participants in the movement of the Democratic Associations. It is now clear that initially they wanted fully independent Workers' Associations and only an alliance with petty bourgeois Democrats. Forced to join in common organizations their line now became emphasizing a distinctly proletarian democratic strategy. This was also done by securing Workers' Associations' representatives on the District Democratic Committee of the Rhine province.

By 1849, regionally at least, the picture had changed. The increasingly sharp class line of the Cologne Workers Association made its subordination to a general democratic line unwarranted. At the same time, an alternative line gradually emerged. Stephan Born, a typesetter who was a member of the Communist League, had gone to Berlin, where he organized the Arbeiterverbruderung (Workers' Brotherhood). Marx had originally stood aloof from this process because Born had organized it along craft lines. Later on, it held a Workers' Congress to set up a national union of German Workers. This attempt was supported by Marx. The Cologne Workers' Association called on all Workers' Associations in the Rhine province to create a separate organization of their own. On April 16, a general meeting of the Cologne association resolved to send delegates to a fresh Congress called by Born. A Rhineland-Westphalian Provincial Congress was actually convened.[203] This provincial congress met on May 6, with one hundred and twenty delegates present. But the all-German Congress could not be held as civil war broke out. The Communists and Democrats faced a difficulty, as they had to fight a civil war for a united Germany but one where the Frankfurt parliament majority wanted a monarchy. Before 1848, the achievement of national unity, democracy and the proletarian revolution had been assumed to be serial developments. But now it was seen that unity might be achieved without democracy, let alone a workers' revolution, for a combination of three factors involving three classes. German bourgeois liberalism feared the proletariat much more than the autocracy, and hence was willing to compromise on rotten terms. The petty bourgeois democrats had proved to be inadequate to the task of leading a democratic revolution, as the entire history of their role both in the Frankfurt Parliament and the Prussian Assembly showed. Finally, the working class was neither adequately organized nor class conscious enough. For communists, the condition of the working class was of paramount importance. Organization of the proletariat was essential in order to develop proletarian hegemony. This was what Marx and Engels explained when they wrote the "Address of the Central Authority to the Communist League" in March 1850.

The Address recognized, unlike the pre-1848 documents of the League, that the multiple stage of consciousness through which workers passed necessitated both a vanguard party and an organization where workers with varying levels of consciousness could interact. By creating such an organization, the communists would be able to defeat the attempt of the petty bourgeoisie to build a multi-class party. They would use this sort of organization in order to ensure proletarian class independence and hegemony. The task of the League was therefore, categorically defined as the establishment of "an independent secret and public organisation of the workers' party." The secret organization referred to the League. But to expect the entire class to align itself with the League was impractical. Hence the need for a democratically structured broad-based public association of the workers "in which the attitude and the interests of the proletariat will be discussed independently of bourgeois influences." So before the revolution, it was necessary to organize the working-class vanguard. During the revolution, in order to defeat counter-revolution and to oppose the treachery of the petty bourgeois democrats, workers' associations would have to be set up. Finally the workers' associations would have to be centralized to promote the development of a proletarian class struggle and to support proletarian candidates in the elections to a national assembly.[204]

Between 1850 and 1870, Marx never returned to this perspective as the class struggle nowhere had developed so far. It was only when the Paris Commune brought revolution back to the agenda in 1871 that Marx reasserted and further developed these ideas. In the first draft of *The Civil War in France*, the defense and vindication of the Paris Commune that Marx wrote on behalf of the General Council in 1871, he commented:

> the Commune is not the social movement of the working class . . . but the organized means of action. . . . It affords the rational medium in which that class struggle can run through its different phases in the most rational and humane way. [205]

By calling the Commune the "organized means" through which the class struggle was to be conducted, Marx was pointing out that the Commune was not itself a communist society. It offered a form whereby the entire working class could be organized in a democratic, non-bureaucratic way, and which was therefore valuable as such organization could minimize the violence involved in class struggle.

It is of course possible to question the correctness of Marx's assessment of the Commune, to ask whether it did reflect working-class aspirations and whether it was a proletarian organization. Indeed, historians have sometimes accused Marx of substituting a myth of the proletarian Commune in place of the real Commune.[206] But Marx's views on the Commune need to be studied carefully, to check how far his ideas developed under its influence, and also to see how he characterized the Commune. In a period of revolution, schematic divisions between class organization and organs of state power are likely to become inseparable in practice because the aim of the organized working class would be to take over state power in its own hands. It was not Marx alone who characterized the Commune as the proletariat's organization. The experience of the February Revolution and of the Second Empire had increasingly made politically-conscious Parisian workers and their leaders aware of the need for organizations to lead independent working-class action. Even Blanqui, the advocate of secret societies, had said, on the basis of the experiences of 1848–51, "the essential need, at all costs, is to be organized."[207] Eugene Varlin, trade unionist, activist of the International and martyr of the Commune, wrote in 1870 that the alternative to an authoritarian state was "for the workers themselves to have the free disposition and possession of the tools of production . . . through cooperative associations in various forms."[208]

During the rising of the Commune itself, the hegemonic role of the proletariat was admitted both by supporters and by opponents. The *Journal Officiel* of the Commune wrote immediately after the uprising, "The proletarians of the Capital faced with the incompetence of the governing classes have understood that the moment has appeared for them to save the situation by taking into their own hands the administration of public affairs."[209] The actions of the Thiers Government and their army also show the class character involved. In arresting Communards and executing them, often without any trial, the working class was singled out. And among those actually accused and tried as Communards, workers and artisans made up the overwhelming majority.[210] Second, the International Workingmen's Association was banned. Contemporaries saw the Commune basically as a working-class organization.

The Commune initially had a wide base. Over 70 percent of the Parisians, who had voted for the election to the National Assembly also voted in the Commune elections, indicating a very high degree of popular support for an obviously rebel institution. But during the by-elections of April 16, the proportion of non-working class voters declined. Moreover the idea of working-class hegemony presupposes the support of the other classes for proletarian self-organization. Marx recognized this when he wrote, "this was the first revolution in which the working class was openly acknowledged as the only class capable of social initiative even by the great bulk of Paris' middle class."[211] As for proletarian forms of organization, we must note that despite considerable industrialization the Parisian working class was still mainly artisanal and small industry based in character, and therefore organizations at the point of production did not exist. However, the trade unions formed an important support base of the Commune, and the Commune tried to promote them.[212]

Marx has been accused of distorting the history of the Commune to appropriate it for the International. This represents a failure to understand Marx's concept of class and party relationship. Marx personally, as well as International's General Council as a whole, had been opposed to a premature uprising in Paris. The General Council expressed this opposition in its Second Address on the Franco–Prussian War, while Marx wrote to Engels a letter, sharply condemning a group of ultra-lefts for desiring to "establish a commune de Paris."[213] Engels in his letter to Sorge, recalled later that the International had not lifted a finger to initiate the Commune, but at the same time he called the Commune a child of the International intellectually.[214] But once the insurrection developed, Marx, Engels, and the International generally, rallied behind it as an expression of class solidarity. At the same time, Marx and his supporters attempted to push the Commune in a more clearly socialistic direction. In Marx's case, this was done by expressing unconscious tendencies as more or less conscious acts, e.g., *The Civil War in France* lays greater emphasis on worker–peasant alliance and proletarian hegemony than did the Commune itself. In Paris, the International and the Federation of Trade Unions issued a joint election wall-poster that called for participation in the elections to the Commune as a precondition for the emancipation of the working class.[215] Among the leaders of the International who played an important role in the Commune were Leó Frankel, Serraillier, Elisabeth Dmitrieff, Varlin, Longuet, and others. Although the Commune survived for only seventy-two days and had to fight for its existence during that period, the socialists still tried to get the Commune to adopt socialist measures as far as possible. Among other things this is shown by the letter of Leó Frankel, who was the Chairman of the Commune's Commission on Labour and Exchange, to Marx (March 30, 1871). Frankel asked for Marx's advice on social reforms, stressing: "We must before all else lay the foundations of the Social Republic."[216] Similarly, Lissagaray wrote an article calling for a program of the Commune, which would have social and political objectives reflecting the hegemony of the proletariat.[217] Socialists were however in a minority in the leadership of the Commune, and supporters of Marx even more so. The majority of the leadership were Blanquists and sundry Jacobin types. Though proletarians or leaders of this class, their ideas of socialism were hazy and often virtually absent.

Later, both Marx and Engels pointed out the non-socialist leadership of the Commune. Marx did this in his correspondence with the leader of the Dutch Social-Democratic Party in 1881, and Engels in his introduction to the edition of the *Civil War in France* published to commemorate the twentieth anniversary of the Commune.[218] But they hailed it as the great movement, greatest ever in their lifetime, of the Parisian working class. Marx, in his celebrated defense of the Commune in the General Council, and even in his interview with *The World* (July 1871) called the Commune the work of the Parisian proletariat, who formed the "advanced guard of the modern proletariat."[219] The Commune indeed posed a complex problem: the question of class power but under a non-socialist leadership. But Marx and Engels, after all their legitimate defense of the Commune (at the moment of its defeat) including class independence and existence of other class parties opposed to communism, did not even once point out the aforementioned contradiction in terms of the failure of the movement. They did not analyze its failure in terms of an absence of a revolutionary leadership organized in the form of a party. Unlike their firm stand in the March Address, the class power and the role of vanguard was not theorized in clear-cut terms. But one should not forget that the Commune was not allowed to live for more than seventy-two days before it was razed to the ground. So the serious tensions, which would have been produced by a working-class power under a non-socialist leadership, could not take concrete shape. It would only be later, with further experience, that Rosa Luxemburg, Leon Trotsky, and Vladimir Lenin would try and develop the two sides of this relationship—a proletarian socialist party on the one hand, and a democratic structure of workers' power on the other.

From the foregoing discussions, we can conclude that there was no single uniform line of party building in Marx's thought, but at all stages he had the idea that the task of advanced communist workers was to build proletarian parties, impart a socialist thrust to them without being sectarian, and also to promote mass organizations where larger masses of workmen could come together for militant struggles. They felt that proletarian self-emancipation made necessary class independence, which in turn could be achieved in the long run through the political hegemony of the communists.

VII
GENDERING COMMUNISM

The one area where neither Marx nor even Engels paid any sort of detailed practical attention was the question of organizing women workers. Paresh Chattopadhyay has sought to make out a case that "throughout his life Marx spoke out against women's 'domestic slavery' and 'exploitation.'"[220] But most of the evidence he cites refers to programmatic issues, and much of it is from drafts never published in Marx's lifetime. So these do not tell us very much about Marx's views on organizing women workers, with which we are concerned in this section. In the early period, as we have sought to show, there was not any special attention. However, in the period of the IWA, we do see a change. During this period, there were more women involved, and we also find Marx attempting to get more women in activist positions. A Mrs. Law became a member of the General Council in 1868, and Marx was quite upbeat in reporting this to his friend Ludwig Kugelmann.[221] In the same letter, he also revealed his own position and criticized the shortcomings of the English and even more, the French trade unions:

> Joking aside, very great progress was demonstrated at the last congress of the American "Labor Union," inter alia, by the fact that it treated the women workers with full parity; by contrast, the English, and to an even greater extent the gallant French, are displaying a marked narrowness of spirit in this respect. . . . [G]reat social revolutions are impossible without the feminine ferment. Social progress may be measured precisely by the social position of the fair sex (plain ones included).[222]

There was a reason for Marx's caustic comment about the French. In 1864, the General Council had voted to admit women to the International. But the French, by a very large majority, opposed this. Proudhon's influence, very strong on them, led to a glorification of the family and of women's domestic role. Ultimately, it was agreed that on this question, each section would be allowed to have its own rule.[223] Individual women who played important roles in the International included André Leó, and Elisabeth Dmitrieff. Dmitrieff was a friend of the Russian revolutionary Nikolai Utin and an opponent of Bakunin, and it was as a part of this group that she joined the IWA. The Russian anti-Bakunin revolutionaries tended to be close to Marx, and had even asked him to represent them in the General Council. When the Paris Commune uprising began, Dmitrieff went off to Paris. Unlike the Proudhonists, she immediately plunged into the work of organizing women workers, and within two weeks, she had organized the biggest women's group in Paris. She secured regular contracts from the Commune and got work for the women. This also involved the women in work like producing uniforms, that is, being involved in the defense of the Commune.[224] Systematic theoretical reflections on women were initiated by August Bebel, and it was only after this that Engels also took up a discussion. Eleanor Marx-Aveling also wrote a significant essay.[225] But it was the German socialist Clara Zetkin who tried to organize masses of women in trade unions, to incorporate women activists in party work, and to develop leading cadres from women. It is to this that we must now turn, even though this means moving away from the writings of Marx and Engels themselves.

A number of Marxist feminists, often examining the record of Stalinized Marxism and its interpretation of earlier Marxism, have at times come to the conclusion that classical Marxism reduced everything to class in such a manner that it left no space for gender. They tend to agree with Heidi Hartmann that the socialist vision was seen in male terms and women's emancipation was believed to be contingent upon the achievement of this male-centered socialism.[226] Maria Mies even argues that Marxism has accepted the patriarchal values of bourgeois liberalism, and treated the gender construct as a biologistic phenomenon. This fatal flaw, according to her, ruined the attempts to organize women in Germany.[227]

In a recent study, Anne Lopes and Gary Roth have sought to rescue August Bebel from a trapdoor of history into which he seems to have fallen.[228] They contend that historical accounts focus on Marx and Engels as the key theoreticians in considering the relationship between Marxism and women's liberation, and on Zetkin as the key figure for the growth of a Marxist women's movement. Bebel is ignored or marginalized in either case. In a juxtaposition between Bebel's *Women and Socialism* (first published in 1879) and Engels' *The Origins of Family, Private Property and the State* (first published in 1884), Lopes and Roth demonstrate that while the book by Engels had nowhere the same level of distribution or history of translation, and while initially it was Bebel's book that seems to have sparked off the Engels work, in the subsequent historiography

Women and Socialism is accorded a "common, or merely documentary" status, while *The Origins* becomes, following a term coined by Hayden White, the "so-called classical text." [229] At the same time, they dismiss Lise Vogel's assertion that the two books constituted a form of silent polemic, by showing that in the twenty-year-long correspondence between the two, Engels never makes criticisms of the book. Vogel's claim that Bebel had shifted to reformism and hence Engels' opposition to him is utterly unfounded. [230] Bebel belonged, even in the early twentieth century, to what has been called the Kautsky–Bebel Centre, not to reformism, and in 1884, he stood very much on the left wing of the outlawed SPD. Equally, one cannot pit Engels against Bebel by asserting that Bebel relied too much on the utopian socialists, for Engels himself had full respect for the latter's position on women's emancipation. Granting the arguments of Lopes and Roth, it is however necessary to recognize that Engels made a kind of theoretical contribution that would be recognized by feminist activists and scholars over time. Gerda Lerner, after making substantial criticisms of Engels, commented: "Yet, Engels made major contributions to our understanding of women's position in society and history: . . . he defined the major theoretical questions for the next hundred years." [231] In assessing the role of Bebel, this perspective should also be borne in mind.

The major claim made by Lopes and Roth is one of a methodological radicalism. This consists first of all of moving away from historical metanarratives to a Nietzschean–Foucauldian stress on genealogy. Thus, instead of seeking to study a metanarrative of the rise of socialism and women's liberation, they focus on Bebel, on the details of his life history, his concerns, and of course on his book. In a way, the central focus is *Women and Socialism*, since their book begins with a note on translators, and then has an entire chapter on the book and its implications and impact. Bebel showed sensitivity to the linguistic dimensions of gender representation, something ignored by his translators. For example, when Bebel uses the German *Menschen*, which should be rendered people or humankind, his translators routinely use mankind. Lopes and Roth believe that it is more important to study how members of the lower classes came to think and act on their own behalf than in the history of large organizations, mass movements, and well-developed theoretical positions. [232] One effect is their conscious decision not to use language associated with Marxist doctrine, which they affirm has become stereotypical. What therefore emerges, even from this preliminary consideration, is that they want to bring to life a fragmentary Bebel, not the leader of the SPD, but only the earlier Bebel, groping his way forward (to what, one wonders, if it is not Marxism).

But an excessive emphasis on subaltern consciousness can lead to strange conclusions. For the twenty-first century reader, it is useful information to learn that *Women and Socialism* came out in fifty-three prints in the German language in Bebel's lifetime, and was translated into twenty languages, and sold over 1,400,000 copies in all. Far more people came to be attracted to socialism through this book than through most of the writings of Marx or Engels. Richard J. Evans called this book Bebel's "lifework," and indeed, he went on revising and improving and altering it all his life. Yet, in that case, what is needed is the writing of the social history of political theory by giving Bebel's book the proper contextual reading. Lopes and Roth emphasize that men's feminism was not a matter of a few individuals, that in Germany it meant the organized support to women's rights by significant men's collectives (like the SPD). "Beginning in the late 1860s, with the development of Marxism as a social movement in its own right, Bebel's feminism developed alongside Marxism's own feminism. Men's feminism, proletarian feminism, and Marxism's feminism are distinct even if overlapping categories. . . . These decades ushered in a brief phase in which Marxism and feminism were . . . identified with one another. It is impossible to retell this history without also retelling Bebel's role in its development."[233] There is an important kernel of truth here. Bebel's book highlighted female agency and introduced a great many working-class activists to socialist theory.

A self-taught working-class socialist thinker himself, Bebel wrote his book in a conversational style, so that his readers could read the book aloud and feel women's oppression. Because the book has simple language and moves with word pictures, even those who have limited education can respond to the book. The testimonies of many women activists, both from the working class and from beyond the working class, show how women responded in reality.

Bebel was evolving from the 1860s to the 1890s, from relatively non-political self-help groups among the working-class men to reach out to women cutting across classes, to male workers, and to socialist activists in particular. The early career of Bebel shows how, functioning within a number of working-class and women's organizations, Bebel's ideas on women's liberation crystallized, and how, by 1865, he had shed his apolitical ideas and had begun collaborating with Wilhelm Liebknecht. From 1865 onwards he takes a clear class orientation. However, his feminism had a non-Marxist origin. Two specific influences on the pre-1865 Bebel need to be mentioned. One was the role of men like Moritz Müller, whose feminism had limitations, but which stressed equal access to education, work and the right to organize. Marxism's ideas on gender, specifically in the German context, were shaped considerably by Müller. But his ideas involved a combination of equality and domesticity. As he expressed it, family life would be improved through the political education of women and their equal access to the public sphere. The other influence on Bebel was that of the middle-class feminists. Their vision of gender equality would gain wider currency in the 1860s and 1870s. They assumed that women had certain feminine traits like emotional sensitivity, avoidance of conflict, etc., and thought that carrying these over to the public sphere would humanize the society. While this perspective was different from that of men's feminism, the fact that the *Allgemeine Deutsche Frauenverein* (German General Women's Association) was in regular touch with Bebel and organizations in which he worked shows that points of contact also existed. Bebel, however, went beyond both. Unlike Müller, he was in favor of full equality of women in political organizations. And unlike middle-class feminists, he did not highlight feminine traits. Even though women's emancipation became an article of faith in the socialist movement, Marxism's feminism, including that of Bebel, seemingly never shook off its faith in domesticity.

One of the recurrent arguments of Lopes and Roth is the relatively greater radicalism of Bebel and the early Marxist movement compared to later conservatism. In the late 1860s the first attempt was made to found a dual-gender union. It was an attempt to go beyond craft unionism as well as to overcome gender segregation. This reflected the openness of the Marxists. By contrast, anarchists, Lassalleans, and liberals, were all opposed to certain manifestations—liberals to anything except educational associations and cooperatives, anarchists to the political, and the Lassalleans were inconsistent on unions and opposed to women's equality. From the 1890s, they write, Bebel's writing became a prop for conservative ideology and practices predating Bebel. This is surprising in many ways. In 1892-3, Zetkin and others would seek to persuade the trade union movement to return firmly to a dual-gender union strategy. At the 1889 International Socialist Congress, the delegates had, while disagreeing with Zetkin's opposition to special protection, still accepted one of her strong recommendations and adopted the following statement: "The Congress further declares that male workers have a duty to take women into their ranks upon a basis of equal rights, and demand in principle, equal pay for equal work for the workers of both sexes and without discrimination of nationality." It seems a singular flaw that the authors of *Men's Feminism* do not recognize that in certain ways, the radicalism of the earlier period was carried forward and deepened in 1891–1907. It is also significant that it was Zetkin, and not Bebel, who recovered the history of this early dual-gender union. Lopes and Roth seem to miss the implication of what they have brought out.[234] In his three-volume autobiography, Bebel misses this union. The period of the dual-gender union was important. Prior to this, Bebel's activities on behalf of women had been more administrative than substantial: he attended meetings, helped arrange logistics at women's conferences, referred inquiries to women's groups, and otherwise associated politically with advocates of women's equality. He was so far publicly silent on gender equality. It was the dual-gender union that changed this. In 1869 he co-authored, with the dissident Lassallean Wilhelm Bracke, the draft program of the Social Democratic Party (the "Marxist" or Eisenach party, as opposed to the Lassallean *Allgemeine Deutsche Arbeiterverein*) and in 1870 his pamphlet *Our Goals* was serialized. The 1869 program did not mention women at all, provoking critical discussion, for example, on the suffrage question. Bebel's call for votes for men was contested by another member who wanted, unsuccessfully, to use the word citizen (though, as women were not citizens under German law, this offered a compromise to the conservatives). In *Our Goals,* Bebel still suffers from contradictions. This is summarized by Lopes and Roth by saying that while Bebel wanted equal work for all in the present, he was in favor of the restoration of domesticity in the socialist future.[235] Thereafter, his ideas evolved piecemeal until he published *Women and Socialism.* The turning points included the Gotha Congress of 1875. When the two socialist parties united in 1875 and adopted the Gotha Program, this program was silent on the question of women's suffrage. Bebel's amendment proposing "the right to vote for citizens of both sexes" was rejected by sixty-two votes to fifty-five. By this point Bebel had moved to the most progressive wing of the movement.

In their discussion on the relationship between Julie Bebel and August, Lopes, and Roth have a desire to show their hero in the best possible light. Julie was, we are told, completely independent. Bebel's *On the Present and Future Position of Women* had emphasized that marriage was a private contract between two fully equal partners, to be dissolved without external constraints when the relationship between them made it necessary. In real life, say Lopes and Roth themselves, "traditional gender roles prevailed in the early years of their marriage."[236] When Bebel was arrested, Julie used to manage his business and served as his political liaison. Bebel's unstinted support to Julie, including when she had a clash with his business partner, is documented. What is however played down is that this involved a reintroduction of domesticity in practice. Nearly every letter of Julie to August includes references to constraints on her time. And in a letter to Engels, she wrote: "I was often very dissatisfied that I couldn't do anything for my intellectual development; but the thought that I could provide a comfortable home for my husband made me happy since this was so important for his intellectual development and work. Because I had to take care of his Party business insofar as I could when he was so often away from home, I was immersed in the spirit of the movement and today remain entirely within it. And so, I must be satisfied with what I have learned."[237]

Reading this recent biography of Bebel, one gets the feeling that Bebel had expunged the term domesticity from his politics while Zetkin brought it all back. It is therefore necessary to underscore the fact that mass recruitment of women in party and trade union, and the development of a considerable layer of middle-cadre leadership, was spurred on by Zetkin and her women comrades.[238] Since Lopes and Roth wish to present Zetkin as a relatively conservative figure, it is worth looking at another assessment. Karen Honeycutt argued:

> Encouraged by leaders like August Bebel, men of the German working-class movement were quick to recognize the political advantages of active support from their wives, sisters, and daughters in the struggle for Socialism. In recruiting these women to their movement, socialist men sought not only to dampen the conservative influence ascribed to women, but to secure helpmates in the working-class struggle and mothers who would transmit socialist values to their children. From the outset, the wives, sisters, and daughters of socialist men constituted an important element of the socialist women's movement. Evidence suggests that most socialist women were married. Many were married to socialists, and probably a majority were housewives rather than factory employees. These characteristics must be kept in mind when considering the development of the socialist women's movement.[239]

In other words, Honeycutt suggests that Bebel's support to women's liberation, or at least the manner whereby he managed to get many other people in the party to agree to support women's rights issues, was rather instrumental. We therefore need to look a little more into how different segments of the German Social Democracy viewed the issue prior to Zetkin. Pre-1889, German Social Democracy was not a monolithic entity. Ferdinand Lassalle had a reputation for being a "champion of women's emancipation" because of his role in Countess Hatzfeld's divorce case.[240] But in the workers' movement, Lassalle and his followers were openly opposed to the employment of women in factories. Obviously, an organization that did not even want women to be employed as factory workers would hardly be willing to organize them.

Nor were the opponents of the Lassalleans always in favor of women's equality. Some of them, like Wilhelm Liebknecht, made some attempts at organizing the women workers in Saxony. But in 1866, the German Section of the International Workingmen's Association published a discussion document which said, among other things, that "The rightful work of women and mothers is in the home and family. . . . The woman and mother should stand for the coziness and poetry of domestic life."[241]

Werner Thönnessen expresses amazement at the fact that an association led by Marx and Engels could have produced such a text.

This presumes that the International was Marxist in the sense that the Communist International was. It also presumes that Marx had already developed an adequate theory of women's oppression and women's liberation. We have already questioned this assumption in connection with Marx's early writings and his attitude to Victoria Woodhull. And there were contending ideas about socialism, or about the emancipation of workers. Indeed, as Thönnessen himself shows, a reactionary viewpoint had its advocates at the First Congress of the International in 1866 (this will be discussed in Chapter 4).

From the late 1880s, socialist women began to ask why there was no proletarian women's movement.[242] In 1889, one of the eight women who attended the international socialist congress in Paris which was to eventually be considered the First Congress of the Second International, was the German delegate Clara Zetkin. Born Clara Eissner on July 15, 1857, Clara was exposed, through her mother, to the feminist ideas of Louise Otto. Eventually, equality interested her in the socialist movement. This led to a break with family and friends. One of her new mentors was a Russian émigré Marxist, Ossip Zetkin, whom she married. On October 21, 1878, the Reichstag passed the Anti-Socialist Law.[243] Everything except parliamentary activity became illegal for the social democrats. Clara worked as an underground activist until 1880. Then, on the expulsion of Ossip as an alien, she followed him to Austria, subsequently moving on to Zurich. In Zurich she met Julius Motteler, the "Red Postmaster," who was in charge of smuggling the illegal party paper into Germany, as well as other leaders of the party. In the mid-1880s, she was becoming well-known, not only as a party activist, but also as a public speaker and writer. In January 1889, Ossip died of spinal tuberculosis. Shortly thereafter, Clara was elected a delegate to the socialist congress. She represented the working women of Berlin. On the sixth day of the congress, Zetkin spoke on the subject of working women. She took on those elements in the socialist movement who wanted to confine women to the home. The protocol of the Congress records her as saying:

> Above all, the Socialists must know that social slavery or freedom rests upon economic dependence or independence. Those who have proclaimed on their banners the liberation of all those bearing a human countenance, ought not to condemn half of humanity to political and social slavery through economic dependence.[244]

At the same time, it is clear that at this stage, on one point she was in agreement with the liberal feminists. Though she made it clear that she was hostile to "the women's movement of the bourgeoisie which allegedly fights for women's rights,"[245] like that women's movement, the working-class women whom she was representing were fighting against a false protectionist attitude. Consequently, at this stage both were proclaiming the absolute equality of the sexes, treating all talk of special circumstance, etc., as a privilege that was the other side of dependence in general.[246] This led Zetkin to make the following statement:

> From this standpoint of principle, we women protest most emphatically against a limitation of women's work. Because we do not want to separate our cause from that of the working class in general, we will not formulate any special demands. We demand no other type of protection than that which labour demands in general from the capitalists.[247]

Subsequently, her work in the bookbinders', tailors', and seamstresses' unions convinced Zetkin about the need to call for special measures for women, because of the double burdens they faced, along with their lower incomes. In opposition to middle-class feminists who argued that legal protection of working-class women degraded them to the status of children depriving them of their freedom and their right to work, Zetkin now insisted that freedom and right to work oneself to death were no freedom and no right at all.[248]

The initial assumption was that all militant workers, regardless of sex, would come into the party. But as Emma Ihrer, a German woman leader, recognized, there were no mass proletarian women's movements even decades after the formation of the SPD. It soon appeared that not only legal barriers, but also male supremacist assumptions within the party, made real equality difficult. Under different circumstances, in both countries, socialist women found that launching women's papers created a space for women workers. In 1891, Ihrer had launched a paper entitled *Die Arbeiterin*, with the aim of developing women cadres, raising their voices against exploitation and inequality and for socialism. After a year, the paper was about to fold up for lack of funds. But the socialist publishing house of Dietz acquired the paper, and made Clara Zetkin the new editor. Renamed *Die Gleichheit* (Equality), this was to become a major voice of proletarian feminism over the years, though Zetkin always disclaimed the term feminism. By 1900, *Gleichheit* had a circulation of four thousand, rising to around seventy thousand by 1907.[249]

Women cadres shouldered the burden of recruitment, partly due to a deep-rooted proletarian anti-feminism entrenched in the party. At the heart of the battle to win more women into the party and to make of them committed fighters for socialism was the endeavor of *Die Gleichheit*. The first issue of the paper had declared that women's subordination was ultimately based on property relations.[250] Editorials explained that the journal would not deal narrowly with "feminine" issues, but with all general issues affecting working-class women. Another editorial, repeated each year throughout the 1890s, stated:

Gleichheit is directed especially to the most progressive proletarians, whether they are slaves to capital with their hands or with their heads. It strives to school these theoretically, to make possible for them a clear understanding of the historical course of development and to make possible for them not only to work consciously in the battle for the liberation of the proletariat but also to be effective in enlightening and teaching their class comrades and training these as fighters with a clear goal.[251]

The paper regularly published articles of a theoretical nature, and also served as a journal of communication for organized women workers. A lot of space was devoted to describing conditions of industries hiring large numbers of women. On the suffrage question, Zetkin published almost thirty articles in the paper. This was therefore a dual policy—on the one hand the party was being made aware that the women's issues were very much class issues, while on the other hand, women were equipped to understand all manner of issues and to take part in all the struggles, rather than remaining confined to a very narrowly defined women's area.

In 1898, Zetkin's support to the left wing in the Revisionism controversy led the right to bring the charges that *Gleichheit* had failed to launch a large women's movement. Zetkin replied that this was the task of the party as a whole, not that of a paper whose task was to produce an ideological influence within the movement. When, in 1900, the Social Democratic women held their first conference in Mainz, resolutions were moved trying to get *Gleichheit* to deal with "popular" questions, which was firmly resisted by Zetkin, Ottilie Baader, etc.

If the paper was not itself the organizer, Zetkin certainly tried to promote the organization of women—in the trade unions and in the party. The 1892 Halberstadt Congress of the trade unions saw a resolution being adopted for the formation of mixed trade unions. But little practical work was done in the next year. This resulted in a major essay by Zetkin.[252] She began by pointing out the indisputable growth of the female proletariat. She pointed out that in a number of areas, mostly where she was already working, women outnumbered men, or formed a significant minority.[253] Quoting reports of factory inspectors, Chambers of Commerce and similar unimpeachable sources, Zetkin commented that this represented only data about those women who were somewhat protected by law, while there were others, in sweatshops, or working as domestic servants, who had no protection whatsoever.[254] She further pointed out that women workers were systematically ill-paid. Zetkin went on to elaborate an argument which can be interpreted in two ways. She asserted that low pay for women hurt men as well as women, for it brought down men's wages as well. As proof she brought up the example of the textile industry, where large-scale employment of women had considerably brought down men's wages, too. But did she thereby simply try to enlist men's support to women's causes by highlighting how that would help men? An alternative interpretation would be that this was one way in which Zetkin attempted to redefine general class goals, incorporating gender issues, showing that such incorporation of gender issues would necessarily affect men as well as women workers. Her awareness of a class and gender intermeshing comes out in passages like this one:

> The transfer of hundreds of thousands of female labourers to the modernised means of production that increase productivity ten or even a hundredfold should have resulted . . . in a higher standard of living. . . . But . . . capitalism has changed blessing into curse and wealth into bitter poverty. . . . Organized labour demanded for a while the prohibition of female labour. . . . Thanks to Socialist propaganda, the class-conscious proletariat has learned to view this question from the angle of its historical importance for the liberation of women and the liberation of the proletariat. . . . Given the fact that many thousands of female workers are active in industry, it is vital for the trade unions to incorporate them into the movement. . . . Where female labour plays an important roles any movement advocating better wages, shorter working hours, etc., would be doomed from the start because of the attitude of these women workers who are not organized. . . . [Moreover] the improvement of the starvation wages of female workers and the limitation of competition among them requires their organisation.[255]

While Zetkin did not at this stage advocate a separate organization of any kind for women, neither did she make the mistake of believing that the male workers' standpoint constituted the general class standpoint while women-specific demands were only petty add-ons or frills. Disappointment at the slow rallying of women workers to the socialist banner, as well as their generally limited responses to oppression, probably contributed to Zetkin's change in attitude. In September 1893 she was writing: "We must keep our feet firmly on the ground of facts, and deal with the situation as it really is. So we have to come to terms at the moment with the fact that women are socially weaker than men."[256] This was the point where, for the first time, a systematic attempt was made within a socialist party to examine the double duties of working-class women. This analysis clearly differentiated socialist women from the liberal feminists, who focussed on women without any analysis of class. This was also a major refinement to any non-gendered concept of class. Since women workers were not part-time women and part-time workers, it meant that they were simultaneously exploited as workers and oppressed as women. As women workers, they could be paid less. They faced the problem of keeping their jobs during pregnancy, childbirth, and the immediate post-natal period, since not only child-bearing but child-rearing was seen purely as women's work. To treat these as marginal issues was to treat half the working class as marginal to the concerns of the working class. At the same time, the "domestic" set-up also involved a class–gender link. Women faced greater hardships when they and their families were working-class members. Double duties meant women could not organize effectively in industries where only women worked, as they had to rush from industrial work to domestic work. On the other hand, where men and women worked together the same conditions meant that the union was primarily male in orientation.

Thus, organizing women workers was possible only through achieving class unity, which in turn was possible when sexism within the working class is overcome. On this issue, according to Maria Mies, Zetkin was wrong to oppose the attempts (for example by some radical German feminists) to organize purely women's unions. But Mies' own narrative shows that the politics of the Central Association of German Girls and Women was similar to that of the radical wing of the liberal feminists. However radical, liberalism is based on individualism, not on class solidarity. Second, Zetkin was not simply turning her back on attempts to organize women, nor "disorganising them" as Mies says. She was insisting that unions had to include both men and women alike on the basis of equality. In order to achieve this goal, she was trying to get the existing unions to reorient themselves.[257] And these efforts bore fruit. The number of women in the trade unions rose from 4,355 in 1891 to 136,929 in 1907. At the same time, it is necessary to stress that a clear articulation of her opposition to sexist and patriarchal values emerge when we look at the efforts to organize women.

> In order to fulfil this task two things are necessary. The male workers must stop viewing the female worker primarily as a woman to be courted if she is young, beautiful, pleasant and cheerful (or not). They must stop . . . molesting them with crude and fresh sexual advances. The workers must rather get accustomed to treat female labourers primarily as female proletarians, . . . and as equal and indispensable co-fighters in the class struggle.[258]

Zetkin is saying here, that class unity can be achieved in a genuine and lasting manner, provided the gender bias, the sexism within the working class is taken up and excised.

Recruiting women in the party was even more difficult. To circumvent the Law on Association, the major hurdle to women's recruitment, Agitation Commissions were set up in different cities in 1889–1895 to coordinate work by trade unions and the party among women. In the course of this work, Zetkin and Baader had to modify another of their original ideas—namely, the complete identity of the struggle for women's liberation with socialism. After originally opposing the reservation of Party Congress delegate seats for women, they had to recognize that without this women were being eliminated from the delegations.

The 1892 Congress had, however, taken serious steps to get more women in the party. In order to get round the precise letter of the law concerning women joining associations, the SPD decided to create a network of *Vertrauenspersonen*, or spokespersons. Individual women could act in a political capacity, and such individual spokespersons were elected, whose task was described as educating proletarian women in political and trade union matters and awakening and reinforcing their class-consciousness. In 1895 the Agitation Commissions were banned, so these individuals became the sole semi-legal vehicles for organizing women in the party until 1907. Between 1901 and 1907 the number of female *Vertrauenspersonen* rose from twenty-five to four hundred and seven. The effect of their work can be gauged by the fact that once the legal restriction on women joining the party was lifted, in 1908, there were 29,468 women in the party, a figure that rose by 1914 to 174,474.[259]

One reason why the women worked so successfully was the fact that, partly due to the legal situation itself, they had to be given a lot of autonomy in working out their tactics, even though the political line was clearly worked out by the entire party. Immediately after the repeal of the Law on Associations, the opportunist elements in the leadership tried to end the so-called separatist tendencies by launching attempts to bring both the women and the youth under tighter control. In 1912 the SPD closed down the women's bureau. The women, like Zetkin, had not thought of the bureau as merely a technical organization. They had seen the potential it had as a forum for political expression by women workers. But precisely this, as well as the fact that Zetkin stood well to the left of the majority of the leadership, made the bureau a target of attack.[260] A different position is held by Tânia Ünlüdağ, who argues that Zetkin simply used alternative structures because there were legal hurdles, and did not resist the party leadership when they shut down the autonomous spaces.[261] According to her, in Zetkin's perception, proletarian women were automatically backward. This just ignores the entire purpose of *Gleichheit*. She seems to think that there has to be an absolute counterposition between popular consciousness and socialist propaganda. When Zetkin was arguing that unless women were brought out into the political movement and mobilized, their petty, mean values would cripple the proletarian movement, she was actually making the point that when women are forcibly kept home as homemakers, they cannot develop politically.[262] Evidently, for Ünlüdağ, not equality but difference is the important factor, for she is even critical of Zetkin for desiring to draw more women into trade unions and party. She calls this a "process of re-education," overlooking the fact that this was a task assigned to the women themselves.[263]

Over the years Zetkin and her women co-thinkers had come to realize that autonomous space provided better opportunities for women workers. So they tried to push in measures to increase this space. One major innovation was the organization of International Proletarian Women's Day. Though this was meant to highlight the struggle for the vote, for Zetkin that struggle was but a step in the direction of the struggle for socialism, to be waged by women and men workers on the basis of equality between themselves. Circumventing the SPD's bureaucracy, she had first got an International Socialist Women's Conference, and then the International Socialist Congress at Copenhagen (1910) to call for the observation of an international day of action by working-class women.[264] March 8, 1908 was chosen because on that date (1908) hundreds of women workers led by the women workers in the needle trades gathered at Rutgers Square in New York's Lower East Side, demanding both the right to vote and to build a more powerful trade union. The success of the gathering drew the attention of Zetkin and other socialist women.[265] This call was then utilized for militant mobilizations of women in every country where the left-wing women were strong in the social democratic parties. Certainly, in 1911, 1912, and 1913, the three major occasions when the Women's Day was observed, German working-class women found a voice in a manner which neither state nor patriarchy liked.[266] In 1912, attendance was a little thinner, and the SPD Party Council promptly used this as a reason to cancel the Women's Day celebration in 1913. Zietz and Zetkin buried the hatchet and fought back. Eventually, a day of demonstrations was sanctioned for March 2–3. Despite the fact that thousands of women participated all over Germany, by pointing to the decline since 1911, the party leadership again tried to call a halt. Once again the women prevailed. It has been suggested that opposition on the part of men may have been a cause for declining attendance. Spontaneous street demonstrations sometimes took place. There was a march in Dresden in 1911 and a very impressive one in Berlin in 1912. There were arrests in Dusseldorf in 1912.[267] All these showed that the women were able to hold on to positions that they had conquered. To assess the Women's Day question just in terms of its impact on decision making is to ignore its impact for the thousands of working-class women who participated in it and sympathized with it. In the face of this strong urge of self-expression sexism in the SPD was in the last resort powerless. Also, it was the one concrete symbol of internationalism for working-class women deprived everywhere of the vote.

The socialists under discussion never thought of themselves as feminists, so they did not set out from the beginning with the aim of redefining class, etc. But they were concerned about bringing more women into the party. Out of this attempt, however, there developed concepts of class struggle, which wanted to avoid turning socialism into a purely male discourse. In the case of Clara Zetkin, this led her, in 1889, into the original position that socialists should fight for the abolition of exploitation over all, but not for special protectionist measures for women. By 1896, however—the year when she gave a major speech on the subject of women workers and the struggle of the socialists, and when the SPD adopted a program for women—she had changed her position. She was arguing that capital's right to exploit all, and the workers' freedom to starve, were the only rights upheld if "protectionism" was rejected. The implications her ideas had for the strategy and tactics of a proletarian revolutionary party will be discussed in Chapter 4.

NOTES

1. *MECW* 5, p. 59.
2. The socialists/communists included the German tailor and well-known communist Weitling, the typesetters Stephan Born and Karl Wallau, the revolutionary agitator and journalist Wilhelm Wolff, a Belgian librarian named Philippe Gigot, the German revolutionary poet Freiligrath, and Joseph Weydemeyer, a socialist journalist. The democrats included people from Germany, France, Italy, and Belgium. Notable among them was Bornstedt, the editor of *Vorwärts*, whose new paper, the *Deutsch – Brüsseler–Zeitung* provided Marx and Engels with a forum to present their views.
3. The Communist League was not just a propaganda organization, so it is not being considered here. It will be taken up in the appropriate context. For a more detailed history of the events of 1844–47, see F. Engels, "On the History of the Communist League," *MECW* 26, pp. 312–21, O. J. Hammen, *The Red '48ers*, pp. 118–51, D. McLellan, *Karl Marx, His Life and Thought*, pp. 128–79; W. O. Henderson, *The Life of Frederick Engels*, vol. 1, pp. 43–101, and B. Nicolaievsky and O. Maenchen–Helfen, *Karl Marx: Man and Fighter*, Harmondsworth, 1976, pp. 100–140.
4. F. Lessener, "Before 1848 and After," in P. Annenkov, *Reminiscences of Marx and Engels*, Moscow, 1956, pp. 149–52.
5. *MECW* 3, p. 274.
6. For an attempt to extend the concept of alienation to women, see Ann Foreman, *Femininity as Alienation*, London, 1977.
7. *MECW* 3, p. 295.
8. H. Draper, *KMTR* 2, New York and London, 1978, p. 51. This comment comes as part of a long and valuable analysis of Marx's concept of the

revolutionary potential of the working class (pp. 33–80). Despite this elaborate analysis, with which it is possible to agree substantially, Draper ignores almost totally the role of the political party of the proletariat in the process of maturation of the working class from its fragmented origins into a united revolutionary class.

9. *MECW* 5, p. 214.
10. Ibid. 4, pp. 376–77; ibid. 6, pp. 210–11. Marx and Engels were concerned with the problem of fragmentation from 1844, when they began writing their critiques of political economy (Engels, *Outlines*, ibid., 3, p. 432; Marx, *The Manuscripts* ibid., p. 238). Engels in his detailed survey of the conditions of the English proletariat showed that this undesirable yet unavoidable phenomenon was not only the outcome of division of labour (skilled vs. unskilled workers) but vast geographical distance between factories, different work, etc., creating different segments of the class.
11. K. Marx, *The Poverty of Philosophy,* in *MECW* 6, p. 210. See also F. Engels, *The Condition of the Working Class in England*, in ibid. 4, p.376.
12. *MECW* 4, pp. 418, 506–7. Marx and Engels attitude to trade unionism as such will be dealt with in a separate section of the present chapter. For the moment the focus is on trade unions as a class organization corresponding to a particular stage of class struggle and consciousness.
13. *MECW* 5, p. 204; ibid. 6, pp. 210–11.
14. Ibid. 4, p. 419.
15. Ibid. 5, pp. 52–53.
16. Here the words organization and association denote what today would usually be called a political party. For most of the 19th century the term party indicated an intellectual current or political trend, rather than a definite organization.
17. *MECW* 5, p. 57; ibid. 6, p. 177.
18. Ibid. 4, pp. 435–39.
19. Ibid. 5, p. 78; ibid. 4, p. 52.
20. Ibid. 3, p. 313.
21. K. Marx, "Wages," in ibid. 6, pp. 435–36.
22. Ibid. 5, p. 457.
23. Ibid. 4, pp. 526–27.
24. Ibid., pp. 581–82.
25. Ibid. 6, pp 209–12.
26. Ibid., p. 211.
27. Ibid., p. 177.
28. In general, Rubel has suggested that there was a tension between the realism of Marx's Sociology and the utopianism of his communism. Instead of Marx's concept of the unity of theory and practice, Rubel's approach continuously sets up two approaches, a voluntarist and a deteterminist one. Rubel's attitude to the Communist Party as an outsider to the working class stems from this analysis. His views are developed in "Remarques sur le concept de parti proletarian chez Marx," in *Revue Francaise de sociologie II*, 3, 1961, pp. 166–76, especially pp. 168–175, in J. O' Malley and K. Algozin, eds., *Rubel on Karl Marx*, Cambridge, 1981, pp. 26–81 and M. Rubel, "De

Marx au Bolchevisme: Partie et conseils," C. Biegalski, ed., *Révolution/Classe/Parti*: Argument IV, Paris, 1978, pp. 12–17.

29. N. Geras, "Marxism and Proletarian Self-Emancipation," p. 138.
30. G. Lukács, *History and Class Consciousness*, London, 1971, p. 299.
31. *MECW* 26, pp. 318–19.
32. K. Marx, "Letter to P. J. Proudhon," in ibid., 38, p. 39.
33. K. Marx and F. Engels, "Letter from the Brussels Communist Correspondence Committee to G. A. Köttgen," in ibid. 6, pp. 54–56.
34. This organizational concept has also been called Jacobin, or Jacobin-Blanquist. In the 1830s it could not be called Blanquist.
35. Minutes of the dispute between Weitling and Kriege on one side, and Schapper and others on the other, have been published in H. Förder, M. Hundt, J. Kandel, and S. Lewiowa, eds., *Der Bunde der Kommunisten: Dokumente und Materialien*, 1836–49, Berlin, 1970. There is no complete English translation but relevant extracts are cited in Nicolaievsky and Maenchen-Helfen, op.cit., pp. 119–21, and A. Gilbert, *Marx's Politics*, pp. 67–73.
36. That it was Marx who stressed armed struggle, while Schapper advocated peaceful transition, is brought out by Schapper's letter to Marx, cited in H. Gemkow, *Karl Marx: A Biography*, New Delhi, 1968, p. 143.
37. *Reminiscences of Marx and Engels*, p. 152.
38. See *MECW* 17, p. 79.
39. Ibid., p. 80.
40. See ibid., 38, p. 158, Marx's letter to Engels. Written in the first half of March 1848 (between March 7 and 12), it shows that up to that period at least, Harney and Jones played quite an active role in the League.
41. "A Circular of the First Congress of the Communist League to the League Members, June 9, 1847" [title given by editors of the *MECW*], and published as an appendix in ibid. 6, pp. 591–92, 598.
42. Boris Nicolaievsky first advanced the hypothesis that there was a sociological dimension to the tussles in the Communist League, between the ultra left-leaning artisans and the intellectuals like Marx whom he wanted to portray as reasonable Social Democrats like he himself. See Nicolaievsky and Maenchen-Helfen, *Karl Marx*, as well as B. Nicolaievsky, "Toward a History of The Communist League": 1847–1852," in *International Review of Social History*, no. 1, 1956, pp. 234–52, and "Who is Distorting History," in *Proceedings of the American Philosophical Society*, vol. 105, no. 2, April, 1961, pp. 209–36. This thesis was taken up by the Social Democratic American scholar, Richard N. Hunt, who argued that the *Manifesto* was a patchwork, with the views of the two groups cobbled together without logic, and hence that this fundamental text cannot be viewed as Marx's text. R. N. Hunt, *The Political Ideas of Marx and Engels*, vol. 1, pp. 147–61, 187–91. For different views see E. P. Kandel, "Iskazhenie istorii bor" by Marksa I Engelsa za proletarskuiu partiiu v rabotakh nekotorikh pravikh sotsialistov," pp. 120–130, and the same author's "Eine schlechte Verteidigung einer schlechten Sache," in *Beiträge zur Geschichte der deutschen Arbeiterbewegung*, Berlin, 1963, vol. II, pp. 290–303. According to D. B.

Ryazanov, the *Manifesto* was purely a creation of Marx, as was the league. See D. B. Ryazanov, ed., *The Communist Manifesto*, Calcutta, 1972, pp. 14, 18–19. Even further to the extreme is the position of R. K. Dasgupta in "Blurred Vision: Gaps in the Communist Manifesto," *The Statesman*, Calcutta, August 19, 1993, where he argues that the relationship between Marx and the League was that between a prophet and his cult, because the *Manifesto* was not democratically adopted. Such fanciful writings are of course hailed as the work of brilliant and sharp minds. See also B. D. Wolfe, *Marxism: One Hundred Years in the Life of a Doctrine*, Madras, 1968, p. 193.

43. At the time of his debate with Weitling, Schapper argued that society was not yet ripe for communism, so a whole period of education was necessary. "Kriege's talk is a mirror for me. That is just how I talked ten or eight years ago, yes, even six years ago [i.e., at the time of the May 1839 uprising]. But now . . . I must entirely agree with what the reactionaries say: 'People are not yet ripe. . . . A truth is never knocked into heads with rifle butts." *Bund der Kommunisten*, Bd. 1, p. 220.

44. F. Engels, "Draft of Communist Confession of Faith," *MECW* 6, pp. 96–103; and "Principles of Communism," ibid., pp. 341–57. For the draft by Hess see Moses Hess, *Philosophische und Sozialistische schriften 1837–1850*, A. Cornu and W. Monke, eds., Berlin, 1961, pp. 336–66. The draft attributed to Schapper was an unsigned leading article in *Kommunistische Zeitschrift*, reproduced in D. B. Ryazanov, ed., *The Communist Manifesto*, pp. 290–96.

45. See the letter from the members of the Central Authority quoted in Ryazanov, p. 21.

46. See *MECW* 6, pp. 589–600 for the Address, especially p. 598 for its repudiation of "barrack-room communism." For the Rules, see ibid., pp. 585–88. The whole issue of the journal is reproduced in D. B. Ryazanov, ed., *The Communist Manifesto*.

47. *MECW* 6, p. 497.

48. Ibid.

49. Given the small size of the League, it is better to call it a nucleus of a vanguard party, as Kandel calls it. R. N. Hunt, *The Political Ideas of Marx and Engels*, vol. 1, p. 163 suggests that since Marx and Engels did not want "the League to remain small by preference, confining its members to revolutionaries by profession, and since they did not assign to the League the task of seizing power through a coup the League could not have been a vanguard organisation." This errs on two counts. First, Hunt assigns to the notion of vanguard party values it does not have. This will be taken up in Chapter 6. Second, Hunt thus sets up a definition of vanguard party from his interpretation of Leninism, and anachronistically attempts to apply those norms to Marx's case.

50. *MECW* 6, p. 497.

51. Ibid., p. 493.

52. Ibid., pp. 497–98.

53. R. Miliband, *Marxism and Politics*, Oxford, 1978, p. 120, has pointed this out correctly. However when he says that for Marx "the party is only the

political expression and the instrument of the class." His formulation is questionable as it seems to suggest that the conscious elements only have the duty of being the instrument of the less conscious.

54. The *Manifesto* has no conception of any working-class party interested in maintaining bourgeois supremacy. So any subsequent socialist party disclaiming the need for a revolution was to that extent a non-Marxist party. See on this point, H. J. Laski, "Introduction" to *Communist Manifesto; Socialist Landmark*, London, 1954, p. 44

55. K. Marx to F. Engels, in *MECW* 38, p. 158.

56. For the events of this period, see O. J. Hammen, *The Red '48ers*, pp. 211–17 and passim and G. Becker, "Karl Marx und Friedrich Engels in Köln 1848–1849," in *Zur Geschichte des Kölner Arbeitervereins*, Berlin, 1963.

57. F. Engels, "Marx and the Neue Rheinische Zeitung (1848–49)," in *MECW* 26, p. 122.

58. Ibid.

59. "F. Engels to Florence Kelley-Wischnewetzky," in K. Marx and F. Engels, *Selected Correspondence* (hereafter *MESC*), Moscow, 1965, p. 400.

60. *MECW* 26, p. 122.

61. J. Molyneux has commented that "in some respect it is in the *March Address* that Marx makes his closest approach to Lenin's concept of a vanguard party." J. Molyneux, *Marxism and the Party*, London, 1978, p. 21. For this very reason scholars who see authoritarianism in Lenin's concept of the party have either accused Marx of succumbing to Blanquism or have suggested that the *Address* did not really reflect Marx's position. See respectively B. D. Wolfe, *Marxism*, pp. 187–88, and R. N. Hunt, *The Political Ideas of Marx and Engels*, p. 236.

62. K. Marx and F. Engels, "Address of the Central Authority to the League (March 1850)," in *MECW* 10, p. 277.

63. Ibid., pp. 277–78.

64. "Rules of the League," printed as an appendix in ibid., p. 634.

65. English translation of the Universal Society of Revolutionary Communists, printed as an appendix in ibid., pp. 614–15. This is an English translation of a French original. The translation is very poor. Compare a part of the original text quoted in Nicolaievsky and Maenchen-Helfen, *Karl Marx*, p. 22. Nicolaievsky's gloss is, however, equally poor.

66. This is the view of Nicolaievsky and Maenchen-Helfen, ibid., pp. 221–23. This view is substantially taken over by B. D. Wolfe, *Marxism*, pp. 191–92, and p. 193, note 6. See also R. N. Hunt, *The Political Ideas of Marx and Engels*, p. 249, note 88.

67. B. D. Wolfe, *Marxism*, pp. 187–88. M. Johnstone, "Marx and Engels and the concept of the Party" in R. Miliband and J. Saville, eds., *Socialist Register*, 1967, cites both Nicolaievsky and Wolfe, but glides over the episode without either accepting or rejecting Nicolaievsky's claim.

68. H. Draper, *KMTR* 3, New York, 1986, p. 201.

69. A. Rosenberg, *Democracy and Socialism*, London, 1939, p. 141.

70. H. Draper, *KMTR* 3, pp. 189–90.

71. M. Dommanget, *Les Idées Sociales et Politiques d'Auguste Blanqui*, Paris,

1957, p. 379.

72. Ibid., p. 383.

73. K. Marx and F. Engels, "Address of the Central Authority to the League (June 1850)," in *MECW* 10, p. 377.

74. Marx, Engels and Harney's letter to Adam, Barthélemy and Vidil, in ibid., p. 484.

75. K. Marx, "Review: *Les Conspirateurs*, par A. Chenu; ex-capitaine des gardes du citoyen Caussidière. Les sociétés secrétes; la préfecture de police sous Caussidière; les corps-francs. *La naissance de la République en février 1848* par Lucien de la Hodde," in ibid., p. 318.

76. Ibid., pp. 319–20.

77. Wolfe, *Marxism*, p. 193.

78. G. Lichtheim, *Marxism, Study*, p. 127. Lichtheim's work is a triumph of the historian's craft. Marx "tacitly" renounces Blanquism—whereas he never adopted it, and, in the last clause, the vanguard party concept is alleged to imply the dictatorship of Paris (with no quotation from Marx).

79. *MECW* 10, pp. 626–29.

80. W. Blumenberg, "Zur Geschichte des Bundes der Kommunisten Aussagen des Peter Gerhardt Roeser," *International Review of Social History* 9, 1964, pp. 81–122. References to the letter appear in p. 99.

81. Marx to Hermann Becker, in *MECW* 38, pp. 273, 282, 308–11; Marx to Engels, in ibid., pp. 273–79, 283–86.

82. For a consideration of a wide range of authoritarian socialisms, see H. Draper, *Two Souls of Socialism*. See also his *KMTR* 3 and *KMTR* 4 (New York, 1990). Authorities who have contrasted Proudhon favorably with Marx include, notably, J. Hampden Jackson, *Marx, Proudhon and European Socialism*, New York, 1962; G. Woodcock, *Anarchism: A History of Libertarian Ideas and Movements*, Cleveland, 1962; and P. Thomas, *Karl Marx and the Anarchists*. By contrast, one should look at Proudhon's own words: in his diaries he gave full rein to his autocratic fantasies. Thus he wrote, "La Revolution, C'est moi"—in conscious imitation of one of history's most autocratic claims. In the associations that he proposed to establish he wanted to "have myself named Director," and "once I have taken my place no one can think of disputing with me." Marx's polemic led an enraged Proudhon to characterise Marx as a Jew and to comment, "The Jew is the enemy of the human race. It is necessary to send this race back to Asia or exterminate it." P. Haubtmann, *Carnets de P.J. Proudhon*, Paris, 1960–74. vol. 3, pp. 39–40, vol. 1, pp. 76, 283, vol. 2, pp. 337, 383.

83. For Marx's "expulsion" of Weitling, et al., see L. Schwarzschild, *Karl Marx: The Red Prussian*, New York, 1947, and R. Payne, *Marx*, New York, 1968, p. 132.

84. P. Annenkov, in *Reminiscences of Marx and Engels*, pp. 270–72.

85. *MECW* 6, pp. 54, 56. Compare Weitling's tendency to personalize issues as mentioned by Annenkov, *Reminiscences of Marx and Engels*, pp. 271–72.

86. Marx to W. Blos, in *MESC*, p. 310.

87. See E. L. Eisenstein, *The First Professional Revolutionist: Filippo Michele Buonarroti (1761–1837)*, Cambridge, 1959. See also A. Lehing, "Buonarroti

and His International Secret Societies." *International Review of Social History*, no. 1, 1956, pp. 122–40. The secret societies began with the Illuminati and the Masonic lodges. Buonarroti, as a survivor of the Société de Egaux of Babeuf, transmitted these to the nineteenth century.

88. *Der Bund der Kommunisten*, vol. 1, pp. 975–85 for the rules of the Outlaws League, and pp. 92–98 and 153–54 for the original and revised rules of the League of the Just.

89. Decision of the Central Authority of the Communist League, March 3, 1848, *MECW* 6, pp. 651–52.

90. See e.g., W. Blumenberg, "Zur Geschichte," p. 89.

91. See *MECW* 10, pp. 626, (Marx's speech), 630 (September 15 resolution) and 634–36 (the new rules).

92. A different view is maintained by R. N. Hunt, *The Political Ideas of Marx and Engels*, pp. 279–83. Hunt sees in Marx's concept of the party, "Athenian democracy in miniature," by which he means the absence of professionals and specialization. He pits against this the Leninist theory of organization, suggesting that such a party can only produce a Red Napoleon. His evidence consists of letters of the period of retreat. Moreover, he adduces no data about Lenin. As for his use of the Athenian democracy as a paradigm, it is questionable, because the instrument of struggle could not be expected to look like a model of the goal of the struggle. I argue in Chapter 5 that the Athenian Democracy influenced his vision of the political arrangements of the future, rather than the structure of the revolutionary party.

93. *MECW* 38, p. 286.

94. Engels to Marx in ibid., p. 290. B. D. Wolfe, *Marxism*, pp. 241–47, has constructed out of these letters a picture of Marx and Engels as intellectual snobs. Though Rubel is more sympathetic to Marx, he also claims that these letters show that the party desired by Marx and Engels was not an organization but an "invisible party founded on real knowledge" (O'Malley and Algozin, p. 72). See also S. Avineri, *The Social and political Thought of Karl Marx*, p. 149 for a counterposing of theoretical research to the practical work of building revolutionary parties.

95. *MECW* 38, p. 287.

96. Marx to Engels in ibid., 40, Moscow, 1983, p. 210. Several letters in this volume show (pp. 113, 133, 209, 219, 223, etc.) how attentive Marx was to economic changes. This certainly shows that only a lack of a proletarian audience held Marx and Engels back, and they were not, despite the attempts to create such pen-pictures of them, any sort of advocate of socialism from above.

97. *MECW* 41, Moscow, 1985, pp. 81–82.

98. See also his book, *Herr Vogt*, where he tried to show that for the Communist League, the main task had been propaganda—*MECW* 17, pp. 78–9. Engels made a better point in an article in the *New York Daily Tribune*, when he wrote that a communist party was an organization of the proletariat, essentially democratic, and compelled to function secretly only because the right of legal organization had been abolished in the continent—F. Engels, "The late trial at Cologne" in *MECW* 11, Moscow, 1979, pp. 388–89.

99. See, e.g. M. M. Drachkovitch, ed., *The Revolutionary Internationals, 1864–1943*, Stanford, 1968, pp. xii–xiii, 25, 29, 30; P. Thomas, *Karl Marx and the Anarchists*, pp. 265–66; B. D. Wolfe, *Marxism*, p. 72 and note 2; S. Rowbotham, "Introduction" to *The Daughters of Karl Marx*, O. Meier, ed., Harmondsworth, 1984, p. xxxvi.

100. *MECW* 42, pp.15–18. See also B. Nicolaievsky's article in M. M. Drachkovitch, ed., *The Revolutionary Internationals*.

101. K. Marx, "Provisional Rules of the International," in *MECW* 20, p. 15.

102. See the "Rules and Administrative Regulations of the International Workingmen's Association," in ibid., pp. 441–46.

103. Ibid., p. 18.

104. G. M. Stekloff, *History of the First International*, New York, n.d., p. 64, believes that the idea of mass affiliation ran contrary to Marx's aim of creating a centralized world party. But he provides no evidence that Marx had such a wish.

105. H. Collins and C. Abramsky, *Karl Marx and the British Labour Movement: Years of the First International*, London, 1965, p. 39.

106. F. Engels, "Preface" to the 1890 German edition of the *Manifesto of the Communist Party*, in K. Marx and F. Engels, *Selected works in 3 volumes*, (hereafter *MESW*), vol. 1, Moscow 1973, p. 102.

107. The foregoing narrative is based on G. M. Stekloff, *History of the First International*, especially part 1, chapters 3, 4 and 5; and B. I. Nicolaievsky, "Secret Societies . . . " in Drachkovitch, ed., *The Revolutionary Internationals, 1864–1943*. Marx's letters of this period are available in *MECW* 42.

108. This internationalist politics is summarised very conveniently by Collins and Abramsky, *Karl Marx and the British Labour Movement*, pp. 17–26.

109. K. Marx, "Inaugural Address of the Workingmen's International Association," in *MECW* 20, p. 12.

110. Marx to Engels, in ibid., 42, pp. 92–93.

111. *The General Council of the First International: Minutes*, (hereafter GCFI) Moscow, 1964, vol. 2, 1966–68, p. 36. This, however, contains an inaccuracy. Marx refused the post of president not because he considered manual workers alone to be suitable, but because he personally was not willing to accept the post. See his letter to Engels, September 26, 1866, *MECW* 42, p. 318.

112. *GCFI*, vol. 2, p. 161; Collins and Abramsky, *Karl Marx and the British Labour Movement*, p. 131.

113. F. Engels, "Preface" to the 1888 English edition of the *Manifesto of the Communist Party*, *MECW* 26, p. 515.

114. Collins and Abramsky, *Karl Marx and the British Labour Movement*, p. vi.

115. *MECW* 20, pp. 190–91.

116. Quoted in Stekloff, *History of the First International*, p. 104.

117. Ibid., pp. 123–24.

118. *GCFI:* vol. 3, 1868–1870, pp. 295–96.

119. *MECW* 43, Moscow, 1988, p. 393.

120. "Address of the Land and Labour League to the Working Men and Women of Great Britain and Ireland" drawn up by G. Eccarius, who was a member

of the Marx circle for many years, in ibid., 21, Moscow, 1985, pp. 401–6.

121. *GCFI*: vol. 3, pp. 120–21, 122–23.

122. A. Rosenberg, *Democracy and Socialism*, pp. 156–61.

123. Among Marx's biographers, even the sympathetic McLellan half accepts this charge. D. McLellan, *Karl Marx*, pp. 315–16. Because of Franz Mehring's role in establishing the Spartacus League, what has been forgotten is that as a socialist, he was originally an admirer of Lassalle. See F. Mehring, *Karl Marx: The Story of His Life*, New York, 1935. Mehring consistently criticizes Marx for his opposition, to Lassalle's authoritarianism.

124. Quoted in H. Draper, *KMTR* 3, p. 99.

125. The foregoing is based on D. Footman, *Ferdinand Lassalle: Romantic Revolutionary*, New York, 1969; R. Morgan, *The German Social Democrats and the First International 1864–1872*, Cambridge, 1965; A. Bebel, *My Life*, Westport, CT, 1983; H. Draper, *KMTR* 4.

126. Marx to Engels, *MECW* 41, pp. 389–90.

127. Ibid., p. 467.

128. Ibid., p. 470. In their letters to each other, Marx and Engels could afford to be cryptic as well as, sometimes, quite abusive. This should be kept in mind when one comes across such terms as "lout" or "rabble."

129. *MECW* 42, p. 15. See also Engels to Marx, in *MECW* 41, p. 558; Engels to J. Weydemeyer, *MECW* 42, p. 38: Marx to Engels, in ibid., pp. 41, 53.

130. Ibid., p. 59.

131. *MECW* 43, pp. 112, 114–18.

132. Bakunin's criticisms of Marx are to be found in a number of works, including his letters. But the summary can be found in *Statism and Anarchy*, parts of which is excerpted in S. Dolgoff, ed., *Bakunin on Anarchy*, London, 1973; and parts in K. Marx, "Notes on Bakunin's Book *Statehood and Anarchy*," in *MECW* 24, pp. 487–526. Scholars who have relied exclusively on Bakunin's version include A. Lehning, "Introduction" to *Archives Bakounine*, vol. I, parts I & II, Leiden, 1961; ibid., "Bakunin's Conception of Revolutionary Organisations and their Role: A Study of his Secret Societies," C. Abramsky, ed., *Essays in Honour of E. H. Carr*, London, 1974; B. D. Wolfe, *Marxism*, p. 72; and H. Gerth, ed., *The First International: Minutes of The Hague Congress of 1872*, Madison, 1958, Introduction.

133. See the "Programme and Rules of the International Alliance of Socialist Democracy," with Marx's marginal comments, in *MECW* 21, Moscow, 1985, pp. 207–11. The preamble is in pp. 207–8, the rules in p. 209.

134. Arthur Lehning presents Bakunin's self-image as absolutely true. Paul Thomas, *Karl Marx and the Anarchists*, p. 318, recognizes that the Bakuninsts were continuing the work of creating a parallel organization inside the International, but claims that this was legitimate because the Alliance itself had always so claimed (pp. 304, 307–314). This is to say that the resolution of the General Council rejecting dual membership, (*GCFI*: 3, p. 54; and K. Marx, "The International Working Men's Association and the International Alliance of Socialist Democracy" in *MECW* 21, pp. 34–36) was invalid, while the claims of an organization that was at that time outside the International, and that got in by a fraud, was democratic and legitimate.

135. For Perron's testimony see E. H. Carr, *Michael Bakunin*, New York, 1975, p. 365. For that of Guillaume, see, H. Draper, *KMTR* 4, pp. 281–82.

136. The quotation is from A. P. Mendel, *Michael Bakunin: Roots of Apocalypse*, New York, 1981, p. 306. For his authoritarian organizations, see also A. Kelly, *Mikhail Bakunin*, Oxford, 1982, pp. 243–45, and passim.

137. Quoted in H. Draper, *KMTR* 4, p. 277 for the proposal. See also pp. 293–94 for a very revealing letter to Herzen.

138. For an instance of his attempt to create an anarchist organization inside the International, see the program of the Slavic section, cited in H. Draper *KMTR* 4, pp. 286–87. For Marx and Engels on the right of ideological anarchists to remain within the International, see *MECW* 44, Moscow, 1989, pp. 309–10, 346.

139. *MECW* 43, p. 485.

140. Ibid. v. 44., p. 131; *Marx-Engels Werke* (hereafter cited as *MEW*) Band 33, Berlin, 1973, p. 642.

141. *GCFI* 3, pp. 231–32; ibid. 4, pp. 444–45.

142. Record of Marx's speech on the Seventh Anniversary of the International, reproduced from *The World*, October 15, 1871, in *MECW* 22, Moscow, 1986, p. 633.

143. Ibid. 44, pp. 251–58; M. Johnstone, "Marx and Engels and the concept of the Party," pp. 132–33; *MECW*: 43, p. 306. However, both Stekloff, *History of the First International*, pp. 219–20, and J. Freymond and M. Molnár, "The Rise and Fall of the First International," in M. M. Dratchkovitch, ed., *The Revolutionary Internationals: 1864–1943*, p. 27, believe that by this, Marx wanted to turn the International itself into a centralized world party.

144. H. Gerth, *The First International: Minutes of The Hague Congress of 1872*, pp. xiv–xvi, claims that Marx "packed" the Congress. For Marx's and Engels' letters to Sorge, Cuno, Liebknecht, Kugelmann, etc., see *MECW* 44, pp. 288–89, 305–12, 373–77, 398, 400–403, 413, 418–420. For discussions in the General Council on the location of the Congress, see *GCFI* 5, pp. 230, 310, 313, 437–38. See also Draper, *KMTR* 4, p. 287

145. K. Marx and F. Engels, "Resolutions of the General Congress held at the Hague," in *MECW* 23, Moscow, 1988, pp. 244–45.

146. *GCFI*, vol. 5, pp. 241–44. For the role of Woodhull, see F. Engels, "The International in America," in *MECW* 23, pp. 177–83, and S. Bernstein, *The First International in America*, New York, 1962, Chapters 7–9.

147. Timothy Messer-Kruse, *The Yankee International: Marxism and the American Reform Tradition, 1848–1876*, Chapel Hill and London, 1998.

148. Paul Buhle, "IWA ('First International')," in Mari Jo Buhle, Paul Buhle and Dan Georgakas, eds., *Encyclopaedia of the American Left*, New York and London, 1990, pp. 380–82.

149. K. Marx, "Resolutions on the Split in the United States' Federation" in *MECW* 23, pp. 124–26.

150. Ibid., p. 126.

151. K. Marx, "American Split," in ibid., p. 636.

152. Ibid., p. 178.

153. H. Draper, *KMTR* 2, pp. 562–63, provides a support for Marx and the

General Council which is very flawed. Draper seems to suggest, by his manner of word-crafting, that since Woodhull's radical feminist phase was a short one, what she said or did even during that phase can be safely ignored or discounted.

154. *MECW* 23, p. 642.
155. *The Hague Congress of the First International: Minutes and Documents*, (hereafter The Hague Congress Documents), Moscow, 1976, pp. 282–91.
156. H. Draper, *KMTR* 4, pp. 286–91.
157. *MEW* Bd. 33, p. 642.
158. Freymond and Molnár, "The Rise and Fall of the First International," pp. 22–23. See also B. Nicolaievsky, "Secret Societies . . . ," p. 233.
159. *MEW* Bd. 33, p. 642.
160. J. Molyneux, *Marxism and the Party*, pp. 30–31. A. Hunt, "Marx, the Missing Dimension: The Rise of Representative Democracy," in B. Mathews, ed., *Marx: A Hundred Years On*, London, 1983, pp. 101–4.
161. *MESC*, p. 358.
162. Ibid., p. 320.
163. Ibid., p. 396.
164. Ibid., pp. 398–99, 400.
165. *F. Engels, P. and L. Lafargue Correspondence* (hereafter Engels–Lafargue Correspondence), 3 volumes, vol. 3, Moscow, n.d.; and *MESC*, p. 474.
166. E. P. Thompson, "English Daughter," *New Society*, March 3, 1977, p. 457. See also, E. P. Thompson *William Morris: Romantic to Revolutionary*, London, 1977.
167. *MESC*, pp. 352–53. See also *Engels–Lafargue Correspondence*, vol. 1, Moscow, 1959, pp. 108–9.
168. K. Marx, "Letter to Wilhelm Bracke," in *MECW* 24, p. 78.
169. For the foregoing see R. Morgan, *The German Social Democrats and the First International*, A. Bebel, *My Life*, V. L. Lidtke, *The Outlawed Party*, Princeton, 1966, especially pp. 97–99, and F. L. Carsten, "The *Arbeiterbildungsvereine* and the foundation of the Social-Democratic Workers' Party in 1869," *English Historical Review*, April 1992, pp. 361–77.
170. *MECW* 24, p. 72.
171. *MEW* 21, Berlin, 1973, pp. 512–22.
172. *Engels–Lafargue Correspondence*, p. 103.
173. *MECW* 24, pp. 259–62, 268.
174. *MEW* Bd., 37, Berlin, 1967, p. 440.
175. Ibid., Bd., 38, Berlin, 1968, p. 41.
176. *MECW* 4, pp. 504, 506–7.
177. Ibid., p. 508.
178. Ibid. 6, p. 493.
179. K. Marx, *Capital*, vol. 1, Moscow, 1986, p. 693. See also *MECW* 4, p. 376; ibid., vol. 6, pp. 209–10, 435–36.
180. R. Hyman, *Marxism and the Sociology of Trade Unionism*, London, 1975, pp. 8, 50.
181. K. Marx, "Value, Price and Profit," in *MECW* 20, pp. 144–49; *Capital*, vol. 1, pp. 599–600.
182. F. Engels, "The Wages System," in *MECW* 24, pp. 380–81.

183. Ibid. 24, p. 70.
184. Ibid. 20, p. 191.
185. Ibid. 43, pp. 134.
186. Cited in H. Draper, *KMTR* 2, p. 586.
187. For a comprehensive discussion, see ibid., pp. 580–90.
188. *MECW* 43, p. 335.
189. Ibid. 20, pp. 103, 149.
190. *MESC*, p. 314.
191. R. Harrison, *Before the Socialists: Studies in Labour and Politics 1861–1881*, London, 1965, Chapter 4.
192. *MECW* 44, p. 172, F. Engels, "England in 1845 and in 1885," in *MECW* 26, p. 299.
193. F. Engels, "Trades Unions," in ibid. 24, pp. 385–86.
194. Collins and Abramsky, *Karl Marx and the British Labour Movement*, Chapter 5. See further V. L. Allen, "The Centenary of the British Trade Union Congress, 1868–1968," in *Socialist Register 1968*, accessed on October 8, 2006, http://socialistregister.com/socialistregister.com/files/SR_1968_Allen.pdf. The National Reform League was set up in 1865 largely at the initiative of the General Council of the International, and there was a considerable overlap in the leadership. The period between the formation of the National Reform League in February 1865 and the passing of the Reform Act in the summer of 1867 was characterized by organized agitations and mass demonstrations with undertones of class disaffection. An address issued by the League in May 1865 stated that "The Working Classes in our Country, the producers of its wealth, are in a degraded and humiliating position. . . . The men who have fought her battles, manned her ships, tilled her soil, built up her manufactures, trade and commerce . . . are denied the most essential privileges of citizens. . . . "At one conference jointly sponsored by the League and trade unions, it was resolved that unless the working class was enfranchised it would be necessary to consider calling a general strike. This was the high point of class radicalization under the inspiration of the International.
195. F. Engels, "The Workingmen of Europe in 1877," in *MECW* 24, pp. 210–11.
196. However, Marx's belief in the need for political action and the politicization of the trade unions did not lead him to propose that "the political party of the proletariat must define the economic tasks and lead the trade union organization itself" (A. Lozovsky, *Marx and the Trade Unions*. Calcutta, 1975, p. 25). Such a definition would concede too much power to the party, power which it need not actually gain through democratic processes, and to retain which it must become authoritarian. Indeed, Lozovsky's definition, originally written in 1933, reads more like a defense of contemporary Stalinist practice. For the attitude of post-Marx social democrats and trade unionists, see C. E. Schorske, *German Social Democracy, 1905–17: The Development of the Great Schism*, Cambridge, MA, 1955, p. 11.
197. *MESC*, pp. 398–99, 407–8.
198. *MEW* Bd. 38. p. 87. See also his letter to Bebel in ibid., p. 95.

199. See K. Marx and F. Engels, Manifesto of the Communist Party, in *MECW* 6, p. 519, K. Marx, "The Communism of the *Rheinische Beobachter,*" in ibid., p. 222, K. Marx, "Moralising Criticism and Critical Morality," in ibid., p. 332, and F. Engels, "The Communists and Karl Heinzen," in ibid., pp. 291–306, esp. 298–99.

200. K. Marx and F. Engels, "Demands of the Communist Party in Germany," in ibid. 7, pp. 3–7.

201. R. Stadelmann, *Soziale and Politische Geschichte der Revolution von 1848*, Munich, 1948, Chapter 12.

202. O. J. Hammen, *The Red '48ers*, p. 221.

203. See "Decisions of the General Meeting of the Cologne Workers' Association Held on April 16, 1849," printed as an appendix in *MECW* 9, Moscow, 1977, p. 494.

204. Ibid. 10, pp. 277–78, 281–84.

205. K. Marx, "First Draft—The Commune," draft, *Civil War in France*, in ibid. 22, pp. 490–91.

206. See e.g., E. S. Mason, *The Paris Commune*, New York, 1967, p. x; and G. Lichtheim, *Marxism*, pp. 118–19.

207. Quoted in E. Schulkind, ed., *The Paris Commune of 1871: The View from the Left*, London, 1972, p. 232.

208. Ibid., p. 64.

209. Ibid., p. 105.

210. The post-Commune terror is summarized by A. Sengupta, *Paris Commune*, Calcutta, 1981, pp. 149–67. He also appends a list of artisans tried as Communards in p. 189.

211. K. Marx, *The Civil War in France*, in *MECW* 22, pp. 336. See further P. Lissagaray, *History of the Commune of 1871*, New York, 1969, F. Jellinek, *The Paris Commune of 1871*, London, 1971, and the books cited in notes 201, 202, and 206.

212. On this see G. P. Morozov, "Professionalnie organizatsii rabochikh parizha i kommuna 1871 goda," in *Voprossi Istorii*, 1961, no. 3, pp. 92–106.

213. K. Marx, "Second Address of the General Council of the International Working Men's Association on the Franco-Prussian War," in *MECW* 22, pp. 268–69; ibid., vol 44, pp. 64–65.

214. *MEW* Bd. 33, p. 642.

215. E. Schulkind, *The Paris Commune*, pp. 111–13.

216. Ibid., pp. 117–18.

217. Ibid., pp. 146–48.

218. *MESC*, p. 338, F. Engels, "Introduction" to *The Civil War in France* (1891 reprint), in *MESW* 2, Moscow, 1977, pp. 185–86.

219. *MECW* 22, pp. 354, 601.

220. Paresh Chattopadhyay, "Women's labour under Capitalism and Marx," *Bulletin of Concerned Asian Scholars*, vol. 31, no. 4 (1999), p. 74.

221. Marx to Kugelmann, December 12, 1868, *MECW* 43, p. 184.

222. Ibid.

223. *GCFI Minutes*, vol. 1, pp. 92–271, cited in T. Cliff, *Class Struggle and Women's Liberation*, London, 1987, p. 37.

224. For the Russian revolutionaries, see F. Venturi, *Roots of Revolution: A History of the Populist and Socialist Movements in Nineteenth-Century Russia*, London, 1960. For Dmitrieff's role in the Commune see "Antje Schrupp: Nicht Marxistin und auch nicht Anarchistin - Frauen in der Ersten Internationale," Ulrike-Helmer-Verlag, Königstein, 1999, http://www.antjeschrupp.de/internationale.htm. Accessed on October 8, 2006.

225. E. Marx-Aveling and E. Aveling, *The Woman Question*, J. Muller and E. Schotte, ed., Leipzig, 1986.

226. H. Hartman, "The Unhappy Marriage of Marxism and Feminism: Towards a More Progressive Union," in *The Unhappy Marriage of Marxism and Feminism: A Debate on Class and Patriarchy*, Lydia Sargent, ed., London, 1986.

227. M. Mies, "Marxist Socialism and Women's Emancipation: The Proletarian Women's Movement in Germany 1860–1919," in *Feminism in Europe: Liberal and Socialist Strategies 1789–1919*, M. Mies, ed., The Hague, 1983, especially 150.

228. Anne Lopes and Gary Roth, *Men's Feminism: August Bebel and the German Socialist Movement*, Amherst, NY, 2000.

229. Ibid., pp. 73–74.

230. Lise Vogel, *Marxism and the Oppression of Women: Toward a Unitary Theory*, New Brunswick, 1983, p. 75.

231. Gerda Lerner, *The Creation of Patriarchy*, Oxford and New York, 1986, p. 23.

232. Anne Lopes and Gary Roth, *Men's Feminism*, p. 23. Given that the book was translated into so many languages, though, a return to the "authentic" Bebel would hardly be useful in understanding how and why the book was so popular.

233. Ibid., p. 32.

234. Ibid., p. 118.

235. Ibid., p. 122. For a discussion of the Eisenach Congress, see Raymond H. Dominick III, *Wilhelm Liebknecht and the Founding of the German Social Democratic Party*, Chapel Hill, NC., 1982, Chapter 5.

236. A. Lopes and G. Roth, p. 145.

237. Quoted in ibid., p. 157.

238. What follows is a summary discussion that I have developed at length in Soma Marik, "German Socialism and Women's Liberation," in *Women in History*, Anuradha Chanda, Mahua Sarkar and Kunal Chattopadhyay, eds., Calcutta, 2003, pp. 169–223.

239. Karen Honeycutt, "Socialism and Feminism in Imperial Germany," *Signs: Journal of Women in Culture and Society*, 5, 1979, pp. 30–41. Accessed on May 2, 2006, available at http://www.st-andrews.ac.uk/jfec/cal/suffrage/document/socigera.htm.

240. However, his role was less shining than contemporary public opinion thought. On Lassalle's murky role in the Hatzfeld case, see D. Footman, *Ferdinand Lassalle, Romantic Revolutionary*, New York, 1969, 54ff.

241. Quoted in W. Thönnessen, *The Emancipation of Women: The Rise and Decline of the Women's Movement in German Social Democracy, 1863–1933*, London, 1976, p. 20.

242. See for example, Emma Ihrer's 1898 article "Working Women in the Class

Struggle," in R. Luxemburg, "Women's Suffrage and class Struggle," in *Selected Political Writings of Rosa Luxemburg*, Dick Howard, ed., New York and London, 1971, p. 216.

243. For the background to the Anti-Socialist Law, its enactment and its impact on the SPD, see V. L. Litdke, *The Outlawed Party.*

244. Clara Zetkin, *Selected Writings*, with an introduction by P. S. Foner, New York, 1984, pp. 45–46.

245. Ibid., p. 46.

246. On the debates between those who stood for strict legal equality and those who advocated welfare measures as a step forwards, see N. Cott, *The Grounding of Modern Feminism*, New Haven and London, 1987, and R. J. Evans, *Comrades and Sisters*, Brighton and New York, 1987. Mies' support to the former position is extreme.

247. Zetkin, *Selected Writings*, p. 49.

248. Quoted in P. S. Foner, "Introduction" to Clara Zetkin, *Selected Writings*, p. 28.

249. See T. Cliff, *Class Struggle and Women's Liberation*, p. 79.

250. *Die Gleichheit*, no. 1, December 1891, p. 1.

251. Quoted in P. S. Foner, "Introduction" to Clara Zetkin, *Selected Writings*, p. 25.

252. C. Zetkin, *Selected Writings*, pp. 51–59.

253. Ibid., pp. 51–53.

254. Ibid., p. 52.

255. Ibid., pp. 54–55.

256. Quoted in Evans, *Comrades and Sisters*, p. 24.

257. M. Mies, "Marxist Socialism and Women's Emancipation," pp. 137–38.

258. Zetkin, *Selected Writings*, pp. 58–59.

259. Ibid., p. 79.

260. Cliff had earlier written his book in the form of a series of articles in his political current's theoretical paper, *International Socialism*. His attempt to rewrite history by asserting that there had existed a separate women's organization solely because of legal technicalities was sharply challenged by Juliet Ash, "Clara Zetkin: A Reply to Tony Cliff," *International Socialism*, 14, Autumn 1981, pp. 120–24. Ash also raises another important issue. She argues that the model of work within the women, developed in the SPD, was inappropriate elsewhere because the SPD was a unique kind of Social Democratic party, which had a range of organizations covering all aspects of working-class lives.

261. Tânia Ünlüdağ, "Bourgeois Mentality and Socialist Ideology as Exemplified by Clara Zetkin's Constructs of Femininity," *International Review of Social History*, 47, 2002, pp. 33–58, pp. 39–40 for the organizational critique.

262. I have discussed this at greater length in S. Marik, "German Socialism and Women's Liberation."

263. Tânia Ünlüdağ, "Bourgeois Mentality and Socialist Ideology," pp. 41–42.

264. C. Zetkin, *Selected Writings*, p. 98, and C. Zetkin, "Internationale Frauentag" in C. Zetkin, *Reden und Schriften*, Bd. I, Berlin, 1957, p. 480.

265. P. Foner, *Women and the American Labour Movement from World War I to the*

Present, New York, 1980, pp. 158–59.

266. R. J. Evans, "Feminism and Female Emancipation in Germany, 1871–1945: Sources, Methods and Problems of Research" *Central European History,* December 1976, pp. 323–51; *Vorwärts,* March 15, 1911, March 21, 1911; R. J. Evans, "German Social Democracy and Women's Suffrage 1891–1918," *Journal of Contemporary History,* 15, 1980, pp. 533–57.

267. For a detailed account of all four years, see R. J. Evans, "German Social Democracy and Women's Suffrage 1891–1918," *Journal of Contemporary History,* 15, (1980), 533–57. A slightly revised version will be found as Chapter 3 of *Comrades and Sisters.*

4

REVOLUTIONARY STRATEGY
AND DEMOCRACY

I
WORKERS'DEMOCRACY AND PERMANENT REVOLUTION

In his graveside speech on Marx, Friedrich Engels said that Marx was "before all else a revolutionist."[1] Consequently, in evaluating the democratic credentials of Marx, a major thrust should be on his revolutionary strategy. The right-wing and fictional image of revolution is very often one of secret conspiracies, clubbing opponents to death; Madame Defarge knitting while the guillotine rises and falls; the rejection of democracy, civil liberties and constitutional means in favor of minority domination. Moreover, revolutions are often thought of as going against the grain of orderly historical progression. Broadly speaking, it can be said that not only Marxism, but any theory of revolution that claims at the same time to speak in the name of democracy or the people, has to answer where it stands on the theoretical issues raised by the popular conception as molded by two centuries of right-wing propaganda. Specifically, these issues can be cast in the form of a set of supposed binaries: a revolution is necessarily a voluntarist action, while the attainment of democracy is a much more determinist process, based on the fulfilment of certain social, economic, and cultural preconditions; revolutionary activism breeds a revolutionary elitism, while majority will and democracy reject such elitism on the ground that it tends to ignore or even to oppose majority will (often by claiming that the existing majority is unenlightened, subjected to ruling class ideological propaganda, etc.); and finally, a commitment to democracy involves abjuration of violence, while revolution means a justification of violence. Investigating and unpackaging these claims with reference to the history of classical Marxism will be the subject of this chapter. While investigating these, we will be also looking at programmatic declarations and mobilization strategies, which will show whether Marx's discourse of socialism was majoritarian or not.

In Marxist political theory, the first and the second of the binaries mentioned above have repeatedly generated divergent, even conflicting answers. It is possible to look at the writings of Marx and Engels themselves and to find the origins of these contradictions. In the "Preface" to *A Contribution to the Critique of Political Economy*, Marx wrote:

> No social order ever perishes before all the productive forces for which there is room in it have developed, and new, higher relations of production never appear before the material conditions of their existence have matured in the womb of the old society itself.[2]

Taken in isolation, this is a statement in favor of absolute economic determinism, and the revolution acts, to carry Marx's metaphor further forward, like a midwife delivering the child at the proper moment. Yet, Marx also proclaimed the impossibility of a bourgeois revolution and the necessity of a proletarian revolution in backward Germany from a very early stage. In the "Contribution to the Critique of Hegel's Philosophy of Law. Introduction," he had written:

> It is not the *radical* revolution, not the *general human* emancipation which is a utopian dream for Germany, but rather, the partial, the merely political revolution. . . . In Germany universal emancipation is the *conditio sine qua non* of any partial emancipation. . . . This dissolution of society as a particular estate is the *proletariat*.[3]

This call for a communist revolution was made, as noted in Chapter 1, by linking communism to a particular class, the proletariat. Any call for a proletarian revolution in Germany automatically raised the question of the level of development of the productive forces and the production relations. The problem of majority will versus elitism also came up when there was a discussion on the prospects of a socialist revolution in Germany, or even in France, in the mid-nineteenth century. The working class was a minority in Germany and France. Consequently, it was not clear how a workers' revolution could be majoritarian, nor how, even if victorious, it could set up durable democratic institutions through which the victorious proletariat could exercise its power. Yet the *Communist Manifesto* asserted: "The first step in the revolution by the working class is to raise the proletariat to the position of ruling class, to win the battle of democracy."[4]

How could a class that was a minority hope to become the ruling class by winning the battle of democracy? Is it the case that despite a formal avowal of democracy, in practice the authors of the *Manifesto* were pushing forward a strategy of minority revolution, especially when the *Manifesto* stated that the communists' ends could be attained only by the forcible overthrow of all the existing social conditions?[5] The conclusion of the *Manifesto* was that Germany was on the eve of a bourgeois revolution that would be followed *at once* by a workers' revolution. So all the way to the *za*, the polarities, determinism vs. voluntarism, and majority will vs. the action of a conscious minority, continue to appear time and again in the writings of Marx and Engels. A survey of their writings from 1844 to 1850 shows several variants being posed. Out of these emerged the theory, or strategy of permanent revolution. But this was not a linear process. The complex path traversed is traced below. And certainly we have to move beyond the texts to the real sites of power, conflicts, and movements of the working class, which had a profound impact on their strategic content of workers' democracy.

To begin with, Marx was primarily interested in the proletarian revolution, that is, conquest of power by the proletariat. There is a crucial difference between the advocacy of a revolutionary seizure of power where the communist party subsumed the working class and an advocacy of a revolution by the proletariat, where a communist party as an instrument of the revolutionary struggle is created by a substantial section of the class itself. The latter necessitated the unity of the working class against the ruling class and its state. Such a political orientation required the break-up of the bourgeois hegemony and creation of the process of counter hegemonization by the proletariat. This could never concretize without the leadership of working-class parties advocating class independence, class struggle and self-emancipation as their basic agendas. Until the development of the revolutionary class, there could be no talk of a revolutionary communist party and its strategy of revolution. However, the objective situation itself did not create the revolution. The necessity of a revolutionary strategy came from the fact that the proletariat comes into the world in an already bourgeoisiefied milieu and is surrounded by pre-bourgeois conditions and ideas. The proletariat can politicise itself, not primarily through preaching, but by engaging in struggles in its own interests, though initially the "interests" might be conceived at a lower plane. Neither democracy nor communism could come automatically as the result of some particular level of economic development. In this way, for Marx and Engels the objective process of history and the subjective role of the revolutionary class were held in a dialectical balance. The function of revolutionary strategy had to be one of showing how democratic struggles of the proletariat could ensure its emancipation once the objective situation made the achieving of that goal possible. But within this framework, Marx and Engels could lean sometimes towards determinism and sometimes towards voluntarism.

In part, this could be a polemical tilt. In part, individual essays could show a genuine slide in one or another side, away from the tension in which the two terms were held together.

The relationship between violence and democracy did not pose so much of a problem to Marx and Engels. However, their justification of violence was couched in distinctive terms. As noted above, the *Manifesto* had called for the forcible overthrow of existing social relations. But a distinction was made and maintained between the violence that might become necessary to establish, defend or extend democracy, and the glorification of violence for its own sake (a position never found in Marx or Engels).[6]

The first Marxist strategy worked out in some detail was unproblematic, for it was a strategy of proletarian majority revolution, chalked out on the basis of the English experience. In an article written in 1845, Engels equated "the masses" with the proletariat, and claimed that democracy had become a proletarian principle. The article reported the formation of the international society of Fraternal Democrats at a meeting held on September 22, 1845, and mentioned the presence of German, French, as well as English speakers. But the real focus of the article was on the English Chartists. The revolution that Engels supported was the revolution that would transfer state power to the working class, and the use of this state power to build communism in the English context.[7] In England, where the industrial revolution had created an increasing proletarian majority, the identification of the masses with the proletariat was quite natural. It was also natural for Engels to assume that a Chartist victory would not only establish democracy but would enable the proletariat to use democracy to achieve its class version of social justice. Right-wing politicians feared the same thing that Engels rejoiced in. In 1842, when the Chartists presented their petition to the parliament, T. B. Macaulay rejected the demand by saying that this would mean "placing capital absolutely at the foot of labour."[8]

The same idea about the democratic and majority nature of the proletarian movement found its way into the *Communist Manifesto*. In what was possibly the first draft of the *Manifesto*, Engels wrote, "The first, fundamental condition for the introduction of the community of property is the political liberation of the proletariat through a democratic constitution."[9]

However, this option was not present in case of chalking out a revolutionary strategy for Germany. Here, the industrial revolution and capitalist transformation were yet to gather full momentum. So the proletariat was numerically small, and possessed, in most areas, a craft consciousness, regional identities, etc. One might say that even the application of a singular, *the* proletariat, was in many ways inappropriate, for such an application presumes a kind of overarching unity, transcending craft, region, gender, to mention three key elements (for the present one would have to add race, color, nationality, etc. in a global context). The German bourgeois revolution had not yet been accomplished and the bourgeoisie could at times (as in the early 1840s) play a considerable oppositional role. So what was immediately on the agenda could only be a bourgeois revolution. Even after the victory of that revolution, the proletariat could not become a majority class overnight. On the other hand, the economic and political evolution of German capitalism was not a mechanical copy of the English or the French cases. The German proletariat seemed able to forge ahead of the bourgeoisie. A complex chain of argumentation, presented in a condensed form in the *Communist Manifesto*, led to an early version of permanent revolution. But that can be understood only by a careful study of the often contradictory development of revolutionary strategy up to 1847.

In Marx's theory, the proletariat was not merely the instrument of communist revolution. It was the vanguard class capable of achieving the emancipation of the entire oppressed humanity. A minority class could thereby become the cutting edge of a majority bloc. In terms of political groups, Marx and Engels directed their criticisms to those whom they tried to win over, and these included people of two sorts: democrats who were not communists, and different communist and socialist ideologues. Through polemics with them, Marx and Engels sought also to peacefully win over the social forces behind them.

In an article, "The Constitutional Question in Germany" (March-April 1847), Engels pointed out that there existed a real contradiction. On the one hand, the workers, the petty bourgeoisie, the peasantry, all were being heavily exploited. A parasitical bureaucracy, a monarchy, and an aristocracy formed the trinity of archaic exploiters. The class on whose shoulders the onus of the struggle should logically fall was the bourgeoisie. At the same time, he pointed out that "no single class has hitherto been strong enough to . . . set itself up as the representative of the interests of the whole nation." This was an incomplete article. The thread of reasoning was picked up and fleshed out in a subsequent article, a polemic against the non-communist democrat, Karl Heinzen. Replying in this article, "The Communists and Karl Heinzen" (October 1847), to Heinzen's criticisms, Engels argued that he and Marx had two legitimate identities—they were communists, and they were also democrats, because the Democracy was a bloc of exploited classes who desired democracy, and whose interests were tied together, against their united oppressors. In a further follow-up of this polemic, "Moralizing Criticism and Critical Morality," Marx argued that the bourgeoisie was not and could not be a part of this bloc, because it found itself in conflict with the proletariat even before the bourgeoisie was fully constituted into a class. Moreover, in backward Germany, land relations had changed gradually, and led to an intertwining of the interests of capitalists and landowners. Land relationships were therefore characterized by Marx as "semi-feudal." And the absolute monarchy, while keeping the bourgeoisie away from power, served it, if necessary with guns in hand, against labor unrest.[10]

This is evidence enough that by this time, Marx and Engels had come to believe that the bourgeoisie could not take up the leadership of the growing struggle against the crown, the nobility and the bureaucracy. The reason was that economically the bourgeoisie had joined with the elements of feudalism instead of pursuing all-out struggle against them. The bureaucratic state, with its estate-based Diet, was the political prop of this combined bloc of exploiters. The political principle that united the bloc of exploited was democracy.

The first criterion of democracy was universal suffrage, which in those days usually meant adult male suffrage. This democracy could be achieved, and social oppression could be ended, by "the conquest of political power by the proletarians, small peasants and urban petty bourgeoisie."[11] The polemics had a dual purpose. In the first place Engels wanted to delineate the revolutionary forces in order to ensure that the democratic revolution was made by the majority. One should add that the subsumption of women under men in this concept of majority through manhood suffrage, though by no means peculiar to Engels or Marx, would subsequently require sustained struggles in the Marxist parties before even the most debilitating aspects were overcome. The second aim was to establish the ideological domination of the proletariat within this bloc by putting forward demands that on the one hand articulated real needs of the peasantry and the urban petty bourgeoisie, and on the other hand had the capacity to relate the struggles of these classes to the proletariat's struggle for emancipation.

Criticizing Heinzen, Engels pointed out that the mass of people would have no interest in fighting for democratic political reforms until they became convinced that the struggle for democracy also involved fighting for their own social gains. Engels also argued that Heinzen had begun by calling for struggles without putting forward any social program. When he was forced to put in social demands those were "such as *Communists* themselves suggest in preparation for the abolition of private property."[12] The problem, as Engels saw it, was that those demands which were for the communists a series of transitional measures, intended to raise the consciousness of the proletariat and the other democratic classes through participation in the implementation of the demands, become in the hands of Democrats like Heinzen, a self-sufficient program. As self-sufficient demands, like, restricting accumulation of capital, the law of inheritance or even competition did not make sense because in a peaceful, bourgeois social order, petty commodity production would always lead to generalized commodity production and the accumulation of capital. They made sense only as transitional measures in a revolutionary situation as steps towards the abolition of private property. In this way, through his criticism of Heinzen, Engels was actually trying to establish the hegemony of the communist line within the Democracy. It was on the assumption of proletarian hegemony within the Democratic bloc that comprised the majority of the nation that Engels could assert:

> In all civilized countries, democracy has as its necessary consequence the political rule of the proletariat and the political rule of the proletariat is the first condition for all Communist measures. As long as democracy has not been achieved, thus long do Communists and democrats fight side by side. . . . Until that time the differences between the two parties are of a purely theoretical nature.[13]

Against the above perspective some articles of both Marx and Engels tend to elaborate a much more stageist outlook. In Marx's article, "The Communism of *Rheinischer Beobachter*" a refutation of feudal socialism (i.e., feudal anti-capitalism with a left rhetoric) was combined with a stageist view. Similarly, when Heinzen replied to Engels, Marx responded in an article, where he stated among other things that the German workers:

> . . . can and must accept the *bourgeois revolution* as a precondition for the *workers' revolution*. However, they cannot for a moment regard it as their *ultimate goal*.[14]

What can create confusion is Marx's insistence in the same article that there was no difference between him and Engels. In fact Marx was practically silent on the issue of the Democratic bloc. Unlike the extreme economic determinism of the "Preface" to *A Contribution to the Critique of Political Economy,* the focus here was not on a fixed succession of long duration economic stages to a linked sequence of political phases. As Michael Löwy has observed, "the stageist dimension remains, but it has been reduced to the somewhat abstract categorical assertion that bourgeois revolution remains the *sine qua non* of revolutionary proletarian politics."[15]

The *Manifesto* was heavily influenced by Engels, but ultimately written by Marx. It contained formulations that could be utilized by both permanentists as well as stageists. On the question of working-class hegemony it adopted the perspective of Engels. The distinguishing feature of communism, it said, was not the abolition of property generally, but the abolition of bourgeois property. It went on to explain that the property of the petty bourgeoisie and the peasants was being destroyed by the capitalist class. This had a peculiar consequence. If those classes were left to themselves, their socio-economic demands would be retrograde. This made them reactionary. However, an alternative revolutionary development was possible.

> If by chance they are revolutionary, they are so only in view of their impending transfer into the proletariat, they thus defend not their present but their future interest, they desert their own standpoint to place themselves at that of the proletariat.[16]

A recurrent theme is the unity of all democrats on the one hand and the distinctiveness of the proletariat on the other hand. Proletarian hegemony could be best established by the resolute struggle of the proletariat, not only for itself but for a majority of the nation. Thus when the *Manifesto* called the proletarian movement the self-conscious, independent movement of the immense majority,[17] it had in mind not the growth of a proletarian majority through decades of industrialization, but the establishment of proletarian hegemony.

Elsewhere in the document, it was explained that within the old society, elements of a new one had been created. Notwithstanding the state forms and the semi-feudal remnants, globally, it was capitalism that was dominant. The only force capable of mounting a global response to capitalism was the proletariat. At the same time, due to the effects of downward leveling of capitalism, the proletariat had the potentiality of leading all the oppressed. This was even presented as an essential task for the proletariat: "the proletariat must first of all acquire political supremacy, must rise to be the leading class of the nation."[18] In other words, the proletariat must acquire state power and it can do so only by placing itself at the head of an anti-feudal and anti-capitalist alliance. The peculiarity of the German situation was emphasized in the following way:

> The Communists turn their attention chiefly to Germany, because that country is on the eve of a bourgeois revolution that is bound to be carried out under most advanced conditions of European civilization, and with a much more developed proletariat than that of England was in the seventeenth, and of France in the eighteenth century, and because the bourgeois revolution in Germany will be but the prelude to an immediately following proletarian revolution.[19]

In the light of the foregoing analysis of the development of a revolutionary strategy, it is possible to view the two passages, not as contradictory, but as complementary elements.[20] Indeed Marx and Engels always owned responsibility for the authorship of the *Manifesto*, and went on reprinting it and recommending it to generations of communists. Hence, it is more useful to consider how the passages may be read as complementary ones.

The immediate tasks of the revolution were anti-feudal ones, by posing anti-feudal, generally democratic and even simply constitutional demands and therefore even the bourgeoisie could theoretically join in the movement. But, "even if Marx and Engels envisioned circumstances in which *tactical* alliance with the bourgeoisie might be necessary, the *strategic* conceptions remained on a clearly permanentist terrain."[21] The question of supporting the bourgeoisie arose if and when they fought in a revolutionary way, while the class independence of the proletariat to the bourgeoisie was to be retained under all circumstances. This antagonism of the proletariat was to be developed politically, so that immediately after the fall of the absolute monarchy the anti-capitalist struggle could begin. Because of the shared hostility of small peasants and urban petty bourgeoisie along with the proletariat to exploitation by the big bourgeoisie, it was expected that the proletariat could maintain the democratic bloc, under its hegemony during the phase of anti-capitalist struggles as well. It should now be evident that Marx and Engels saw no contradiction in calling simultaneously for a majority revolution, a democratic revolution, and a proletarian revolution. These three terms only expressed the numerical, political–institutional and social-hegemonic contents of the same revolutionary process.

If the revolution was to be majoritarian and democratic in character, then why did Marx and Engels assert that a forcible overthrow of all the existing social conditions was necessary for the attainment of communism? In 1846, while arguing with a group of True Socialist artisans, Engels in his letter to the Correspondence Committee defined the aims of communists in the following way:

1. To ensure that the interests of the proletariat prevail, as opposed to those of the bourgeoisie; 2. To do so by abolishing private property and replacing same with community of goods; 3. To recognize no means of attaining these aims other than democratic revolution by force.[22]

This definition was certainly not a comprehensive one. But it served to clarify the relationship between ends and means. This did not take up the political structures of post-revolutionary societies, including the rights of the people there. Giving the central focus to class struggle, Marxist doctrine of proletarian democracy did reject the two other roads to communism, viz., force without democracy or conspiratorial way; and attempts to change society ignoring class struggle, emphasizing the winning over of the hearts of people. In the League of the Just the other two lines coexisted. Its early leader Weitling believed that democracy was the form of government least suitable for bringing about communism. In a debate with his opponents in the League, he saw reactionary policies not as class policies but as the pressure of bad individuals. And in one of his works of this period he wrote, "if we call for communism through revolutionary means, then we must have a dictator."[23] In response to Weitling, Karl Schapper asserted in 1845: "a communist revolution is nonsense — it totally contradicts the principle of communism. Truth needs no physical force."[24]

This debate was a microcosm of the general division within the European left. In France, the line advocated by Blanqui, Barbes, and others was similar to Weitling's outlook. Pacifism was likewise expressed in various ways by Cabet, Proudhon, and others. Consequently, the struggle waged by Marx and Engels against these two lines was an attempt at creating a visible political space for a particular strategic line in the workers' movement. Their criticisms of Blanquism were publicly expressed later because at this stage the workers they were trying to win over had swung away from Blanquist type politics to True Socialism. That was why in 1846-47, they wrote and spoke repeatedly against the latter current. In a letter to the Communist Correspondence Committee in Brussels, Engels described the situation in Paris among the workers: "They have nothing to set against the tailors' communism but popularization a la Grün and green-tinted Proudhon."[25]

The most influential figure of True Socialism was Moses Hess. But Marx and Engels were more concerned with the impact of Grün, who had been able to recruit many communist workers to the True Socialist position. This was the context in which Engels emphasized that the only means of attaining communism was the democratic revolution by force. The only alternative to using force in order to achieve democracy was to hope for a miracle. Thus all the declamations of love covered an opposition to the struggle for democracy. It was not a question of valorizing violence per se. At a more complex level, to emphasize a democratic revolution by force meant emphasizing the centrality of the historic task of the working class of forging an alliance with other democratic classes, in order to achieve democracy. This could be done only through a revolution, i.e., a forcible overthrow of the old order. And the hegemony of the proletariat was a precondition for the growth of the revolution in the proletarian democratic direction.

Available documents show that it was the standpoint of Marx and Engels that prevailed among the German artisan communists of the League of the Just. The clearest indication comes from the only issue of the Communist League's paper, the *Kommunistiche Zeitschrift*, issued in September 1847. The lead article, ascribed to the artisan leader

Karl Schapper, substantially reiterated concepts developed by Marx and Engels over the past two years. The professed task of the journal was to assist the proletariat's struggle for self-emancipation. Utopian communism, abstention from political struggles, and putschism were rejected as false routes. In contrast to Schapper's 1845 position, Engels' formulation about a democratic revolution by force was closely echoed. The period of transition and the future communist order were categorically declared to be democratic orders where individual liberties were to be protected.[26]

This article also discussed the question of an alliance of the oppressed classes, echoing Engels in its criticism of Heinzen. It asserted that the communists stood in the forefront of the battle for democracy. Cabet's scheme for founding a communist Utopia was criticized in a separate article in the same paper, brought out by the League. That this was a direct result of Marx's influence can be easily understood when it is remembered that in 1845, Schapper and his comrades had adopted Cabet's standpoint in order to criticize Weitling's call for a revolution.

A proletarian revolution, as opposed to a peaceful transition to Utopia, was brought back into the agenda, not by the artisans, but by Engels when he wrote (before June 1847) the first draft, of the communist program, the "Communist Confession of Faith." He wrote:

> We are convinced not only of the uselessness but even of the harmfulness of all conspiracies. We are also aware that revolutions are not made deliberately and arbitrarily, but that everywhere and at all times they are the necessary consequence of circumstances/not dependent on individuals or parties/ . . . the development of the proletariat in almost all the countries of the world is forcibly repressed by the possessing classes. . . . If, in the end, the oppressed proletariat is thus driven into a revolution, then we will defend the cause of the proletariat just as well by our deeds as now by our words.[27]

This shows how the London-based leadership was won over. Violence was no longer counterposed to democracy. Rather, it was asserted that the resistance of the oppressors to the course of historical development called for revolutionary action. Far from Marx and Engels being "determinists" and Schapper "voluntarist," it was Schapper who tended, even in 1847, to be a shade too determinist.[28]

In 1884, Engels wrote to Eduard Bernstein, who was then the editor of the *Sozialdemokrat*, the illegal paper of the outlawed German SPD. Commenting on two articles by Bernstein, he wrote:

> The proletariat too needs democratic *forms for the seizure* of power but to it they are, like all political forms, mere means. But if today democracy is wanted as an *end*, one must seek support in the peasantry and petty–bourgeoisie.[29]

Engels did not mean that democracy was unimportant. From the assertions of the *Manifesto* to the stand taken by Engels during the rise of General Boulanger in the late 1880s, they insisted that the workers had to use democracy to push ahead to their social emancipation. Engels' point was that a democratic political system without a social revolution meant a redistribution of power within capitalism, in favor of lesser bourgeois classes. Only if the class struggle was pushed to its culmination by the proletariat could there develop proletarian democracy. So between bourgeois democracy and workers' democracy, despite possible continuity of forms, there would exist a clear social break, complemented by a revolutionary period. This break would be due to the fact that when fundamental social restructuring was on the agenda, i.e., the class struggle had sharpened acutely, formal rules of democracy could not contain social conflicts.

In the *Manifesto,* this strategic task was explained by presenting a critique of two kinds of alleged socialisms, viz., feudal socialism and petty bourgeois socialism. Feudal socialism was a term used to denote reactionary politics which tried to mobilize popular hatred of capitalist exploitation by using anti-capitalist rhetoric. Though Marx and Engels never used this concept later it underlay Engels' explanation of Boulangism in the late nineteenth century. The *Manifesto* explained that in order to get support of the common people the aristocratic opposition to the bourgeoisie had to talk of working-class interests, but in practice such people joined in all coercive measures against the working class.[30]

The *Manifesto* described the anti-capitalism of the peasants and the petty bourgeoisie as petty-bourgeois socialism. This anti-capitalism was capable of showing correctly the economic results of capitalist development—the ruin of the petty bourgeoisie and the misery of the proletariat. But it was incapable of any forward-looking concrete proposal.[31] This chapter of the *Manifesto* has been generally deemed outmoded and consequently ignored. In fact, despite major changes, the historic currents criticized in it remained in existence even at the end of Engels' life. In the 1880s Engels had to involve himself in a long dispute with the "Marxist" Parti Ouvrier in France. This was when an ambitious general named Boulanger was trying to cash in on the increasing corruption in the Third Republic, using an anti-capitalist rhetoric which masked an intention to destroy democracy by using popular discontent with the flaws of the bourgeois democratic system. In this Boulanger was backed by Bonapartists and monarchists. Within the left there were two major responses. Those who wanted to defend democracy failed to take a class line and formed a bloc with anti-Boulanger bourgeois parties. Those like Paul Lafargue, Engels' main correspondent, who were hostile to the bourgeois parliamentary parties, wanted to side with the Boulangist movement hoping to get a part of the power. Responding to this, Engels wrote that while the popular discontent underlying Boulangism was justified, the fact that the workers were willing to throw away their democratic rights in their hatred of the bourgeois leaders showed their immaturity.[32] For Engels the task was never the defense of the bourgeoisie—the task was to wage an independent proletarian struggle in order to defend democracy, defeat the Boulangist war-mongering, and go forward to socialism. He emphasized that there was a third way opposed to both "personal government" and the parliamentary bourgeois regime.[33] He also wrote that if Boulanger became the dictator of France, he would destroy all the democratic institutions and the main victim would be the entire socialist/workers movement. He added (presumably in a fit of irritability) that it would serve them right for ignoring the centrality of the struggle for democracy.[34]

Both the dominant strategy of proletarian independence and hegemony, and the subordinate tactics involving occasional collaboration with the bourgeoisie were tried out in the revolution of 1848 and both were modified in the light of experience. What emerged was the final version of the strategy of permanent revolution explained most elaborately in the "Address of the Central Authority to the Communist League" of March 1850. Two passages from the Address are often juxtaposed to claim a basic contradiction. On the one hand Marx wrote:

> While the democratic petty bourgeois wish to bring the revolution to a conclusion as quickly as possible . . . It is our interest and our task to make the revolution permanent, until all more or less possessing classes have been forced out of their position of dominance, the proletariat has conquered state power . . . and that at least the decisive productive forces are concentrated in the hands of the proletarians. For us the issue cannot be the alteration of private property but only its annihilation, not the smoothing over of class antagonism but the abolition of class.[35]

On the other hand in the same Address, the German workers were said to be unable to attain power and achieve their own class interests without completely going through a lengthy revolutionary development.[36]

As in the case of the *Manifesto*, the problem involved here can be resolved by looking at the writings and activities of Marx and Engels, prior to and during the writing of the Address.[37]

The March Address presented Marx's view of permanent revolution, which was a programmatic slogan that counterposed itself to the revolution that was satisfied with the mere form of the republic. Thus, indicating the difference between Ledru-Rollin and Raspail, respectively the petty bourgeois and proletarian Presidential candidates in France, Engels wrote that the supporters of Ledru-Rollin claimed to be putting forward the same program of permanent revolution as the socialist workers. He was however, skeptical and wrote that once they got political power, they would forget the proletariat unless the armed workers prodded them forward.[38] On the radical side of the spectrum, if permanent revolution was rejected, two other options remained open. One was to agree that socialism was the goal of the future, but see in the immediate future only the possibility of bourgeois rule. The classic case was that of the democrat Ledru-Rollin and the socialist Louis Blanc who did get power briefly in 1848 and whose policies aided not the workers but the bourgeoisie. The other way was Blanqui's way. As Alan Spitzer explains:

> . . . While Marx and his successors were concerned with transforming a middle class (i.e., bourgeois) revolution, Blanqui was attempting to anticipate it. [In Blanqui's view,] for a revolution to end in socialism it had to be begun by socialists.[39]

As the March Revolution broke out, Marx and his comrades opposed the line of the petty bourgeoisie. On the one hand they rejected calls for an all-embracing unity and organized workers' societies. On the other hand they opposed the adventurist scheme of the German Democratic Association for an invasion of Germany. Jenny Marx wrote to Joseph Weydemeyer asking him to publicize the formation of the Workers' Society [40] and to circulate the fact that its leaders "have nothing in common with the German Democratic Society . . . since it will bring the Germans into disrepute."[41] Gilbert is wrong in thinking that the difference between Marx's strategy and that of the Democrats was not just that Marx wanted an armed struggle while the Democrats opposed it. Marx condemned this particular strategy "because he thought that revolutionary violence must flow from a mass German revolution and not from an isolated, returning army of exiles seeking artificially to inspire such a movement."[42] If Marx's own strategy is seen it would become clear that for him insurrections were ruled out until the proletariat had gained its political ascendancy within the Democratic bloc, and this bloc itself was firm enough and numerous enough to expect at least the acquiescence of the majority behind the insurrection once it was launched. That was why Marx's immediate response to the outbreak of the revolution was to elaborate the "Demands of the Communist Party in Germany." This was a seventeen-point transitional program oriented specifically to the German condition. As such its anti-capitalist thrust was less central than in the *Manifesto*, while anti-feudal measures were more prominent. The first demand was for a single and indivisible republic in Germany, that is, for the abolition of feudal particularism. Demands six to nine were anti-feudal demands aimed at reducing the burdens imposed on peasants and small tenants. At the same time inroads were suggested into capitalist property, sometimes linked up with attacks on feudal property. Thus the seventh demand called for the nationalization of feudal estates along with mines. Transport and communication systems were also to be nationalized and the poor allowed free access. There were also to be state guarantee of the livelihood of all workers, a steeply graded income tax and the abolition of taxes on consumption goods.[43] Obviously such a strategy of establishing working-class hegemony meant a much more protracted work of organization and propaganda compared to calls for instant insurrection. Consequently, members of the Communist League saw as their immediate task the setting up of workers' societies and the propagation of the Seventeen Demands.[44] However the low level of political maturity of the majority of the workers forced them to turn to the Democratic Societies at the cost of somewhat downgrading independent working-class action. Their aim was to work within the Democratic Associations in order to win over that large part of the working class which was under the hegemony of the petty bourgeois Democrats.[45] Whenever the relation of force was clearly against the revolutionary people Marx was opposed to insurrection. For instance on September 25, 1848, when the authorities tried to provoke an insurrection, Marx prevailed on the Committee of Public Safety that they had helped to found, to retreat in good order. This may be contrasted with the event of September 11 to 13, when, taking advantage of the popular discontent against the army Marx and other communists, acting through the Democratic Association and the Workers' Society, demanded the mobilization of the civic guard and the direct election based on the universal suffrage of a Committee of Public Safety in order to fight counter revolution. Gerhard Becker points out that this was the only revolutionary governmental organization in 1848 composed of the people themselves. As the name indicates, Marx's aim was to create a revolutionary democratic agency to carry out a thoroughgoing revolution. But the existing popular consciousness at the national level meant that in Cologne, an advanced outpost, he had to proceed slowly[46] In Cologne they followed a policy of building a Workers' Society with its own paper, *Freiheit und Arbeit,* a Democratic Association, and the NRZ. From the beginning the latter functioned as a proletarian mouthpiece of the Democratic bloc in attacking feudal monarchist counter-revolution, but from the very first issue it also criticized the bourgeoisie for not being revolutionary. Even the illusions of the petty bourgeois Democrats were criticized.[47] Alone among the German Democratic press, the NRZ supported the June insurrections in Paris in an impressive show of proletarian internationalism. Engels' first article on it, began by saying, "The insurrection is purely a workers' uprising." Subsequent articles as well as plain reportage took it up as a proletarian issue.[48] Marx's article "The June Revolution," heaped stinging criticism on the official Democrats as cowardly minds, and clearly stated that the democratic republic would not bring the millennium but only create the conditions where open struggle could be waged to resolve the class antagonism. [49]

Within a few months it was clear that the German bourgeoisie was not going to show even the tiniest bit of Jacobin virtue. During the French Revolution the consistent bourgeois revolutionaries (the Jacobins/Montagnards) had shown the willingness to mobilize the common people, thoroughly abolish feudalism and take the sternest of measures against the monarchy and its supporters in order to combat counter-revolution and foreign invasion. The German bourgeoisie preferred to compromise with semi-feudal rulers instead of making concessions favorable to workers, peasants, and petty bourgeoisie. The conclusion both Marx and Engels drew particularly in their subsequent analysis of Bonapartism was that unlike the proletariat, for the bourgeoisie, self-emancipation was not necessary.[50] By late September 1848, Engels was writing, "in Vienna and Paris, in Berlin and Frankfurt, in London and Milan, the point at issue is *the overthrow of the political rule of the bourgeoisie.*" He further explained that the struggle against the Frankfurt Parliament by the German people was a fight against the "Combined landowners and bourgeoisie . . . waged under the red flag."[51] The actual role of the proletariat in fighting for democracy itself made the bourgeoisie more hostile and drove it into the arms of counter-revolution. These conclusions were summarized and explained in details in the important article series. "The Bourgeoisie and the Counter-Revolution," (December 1848). Here Marx argued that with capitalist development, there emerged a trend towards coalescence between aristocracy and bourgeoisie. So, now the latter could hope to gain their ends without a revolution. Above all, fear of the proletariat, whose very growth reflected uneven and combined development in relatively backward mid-nineteenth century Germany, led the bourgeoisie to become "monarchical" and play a counter-revolutionary role in the great movement launched in Germany in 1848 to achieve victory of democracy. Marx further wrote that this revealed a crucial fact of history: ". . . a purely *bourgeois revolution* and the establishment of a bourgeois rule in the form of a *constitutional monarchy* is impossible in Germany, and that only a feudal absolutist counter-revolution or a social republican revolution is possible."[52]

After the failure of the revolution, when the Communist League regrouped in London, the balance sheet was drawn in the March Address. It pointed out that in general in the past revolution the petty-bourgeois democrats had hegemonized the working class. After insisting on the need for a proletarian party, it went on to explain that the workers' party should march together with the petty-bourgeois democrats as long as the existing regime was not overthrown, but should organize separately the working class so that the petty bourgeois leaders could not consolidate the state with a few paltry reform measures.[53] This process of unity and struggle with the petty bourgeois leaders had the aim of consolidating the proletariat and even winning over sections of petty bourgeois masses who at the beginning of the process followed the Democratic Party. The revolution was not to end with the conquest of state power by the proletariat. The immediate aftermath of the conquest of state power was seen as the concentration of the "decisive" productive forces in the hands of the working class. This presupposes that a sector of capitalist or small propertied production was to remain for a time. Moreover, the proletarian revolution would have a worldwide unity. So conquest of power in one country could not bring it to an end. There would begin a period of transition. Throughout this period of permanent revolution the task of the communists was to fight for the establishment and broadening of workers' democracy backed by the proletariat in arms.[54]

Writings of Marx and Engels belonging to the same period show that the perspective of the March Address was their own perspective. In *The Class Struggles in France* (1850), a famous passage explained that the experience of revolution led the proletariat to abandon both the Utopian socialists and the petty-bourgeois socialists, and to organize itself around revolutionary socialism or communism:

> for which the bourgeoisie itself has invented the name of *Blanqui*. This socialism is the *declaration of the permanence of the revolution*, the *class dictatorship* of the proletariat as the necessary transit point to the *abolition of class distinctions generally*, to the abolition of all the relations of production on which they rest . . . [55]

Marx redefined the agenda as well as the strategy of the revolution in the light of the experience of class struggle in France and Germany. The bourgeoisie was using Blanqui as a bogeyman. A supposed Blanquist plot in 1848 became the occasion of recalling the army to Paris.[56] The passage under discussion is important as it reveals that experiential realities pushed Marx to the realization that at the level of parties a merging of flags was hence forth impossible. To win over the petty bourgeois masses and the peasants, the workers' party had to break with the party of petty-bourgeois social democrats. In the same work the idea of hegemony and democratic majority was expressed even more plainly when Marx wrote that the French workers could not overthrow the bourgeois order until the course of the revolution had "aroused the peasants and petty bourgeoisie and moved them behind the proletariat."[57]

Thus, on this point the signed articles of Marx and Engels did not differ from the March Address. While accepting collaboration with the democrats in the struggle to secure democratic rights and to overthrow the common enemy, they tried to emphasize the independent and leading role of the proletariat in a way that the pre-1848 writings had not clearly done. For them, the progressivism of the bourgeoisie and any proletarian collaboration with them remained a tactical and subordinate task.[58]

This overall perspective of permanent revolution was reiterated by Engels again in 1894, when he wrote to Turati, the Italian socialist, that in Italy,

> The *bourgeoisie*, which came to power during and after the national independence movement, would not and could not complete its victory. It neither destroyed the remains of feudalism nor transformed national production according to the modern capitalist pattern . . . they forfeited the last remnant of respect and confidence by involving themselves in the dirtiest bank scandals. The labouring population—peasants, handicraft workers, agricultural and industrial workers—finds itself in consequence in an oppressive position, on the one hand owing to old abuses inherited not only from feudal times but from an even earlier period (take, for instance, the *mezzadria* [share farming], or the *latifundia* of the south, where cattle are supplanting men); on the other hand owing to the most rapacious fiscal system ever invented by bourgeois policy.[59]

Quoting from the *Communist Manifesto* and the *Capital*, he went on to explain that even if the petty bourgeoisie won a victory, the task of the workers' party would not be to become minority representatives in a new government. Instead they would have to fight to a finish the class struggle while impelling the other revolutionary parties to defend the interests of the proletariat by constant pressure.[60] Following Löwy it can be said that the writings of Marx and Engels on the question of revolution in backward countries reveal a double contradiction:

> a contradiction between stagism and permanentism and a contradiction between short term empirical error and historical intuition in the permanentist texts themselves. The reason was that economic development having created a considerable proletariat the bourgeoisie had lost its capacity to play a revolutionary role while the proletariat had not yet matured sufficiently.[61]

II
BLANQUISM, PEACEFUL REVOLUTION VERSUS REVOLUTIONARY STRATEGY

How backward can a country be and still fit into the framework of demands for parliaments elected by universal suffrage, and for the continuation of class struggle within that framework? And did Marx fall into Blanquist strategy by advocating proletarian revolution in backward countries? The first issue came up in Marx's own lifetime, in connection with Russia. Marx's initial interest in Russia was because he saw in the country the bulwark of European counter-revolution. Even when subsequently he came in contact with Russian revolutionaries he did not envisage the same path for Russia and Germany.[62] This was connected to the necessity of two related developments. A proletarian revolution could occur only when industrial capitalism and a large class of proletarians had also developed. Industrialization in Russia came only in the aftermath of the emancipation of the serfs, particularly during the stewardship of Witte. That was why in Marx's lifetime the question of proletarian revolution in Russia was irrelevant while even Engels saw only the beginning of a process.

Turning to the second problem, did Marx ever gravitate to Blanquism? Did he ever abandon the goal of a democratic revolution by a majority under proletarian hegemony? The two experiences of Marx's alliance with the Blanquists suggest that he did not. The differences between Marx and the Blanquists in 1850 have been dealt with in connection with the theory of party.[63] The second period of alliance was after the Paris Commune. In the Commune itself, there was a sharp difference between Marxists and Blanquists and assorted followers of the Jacobin leftist tradition. As G. D. H. Cole puts it: "The Blanquists saw the Paris Commune as the working model of the revolutionary elite in action."[64] In *The Civil War in France*, Marx referred back to his own earlier slogan of "social republicanism" by saying that "the commune was the positive form of that Republic."[65] Blanqui on the other hand, highlighting the hero-liberators (1843, revised 1850), wrote that humanity went forth wearing a blindfold and that progress was always at the cost of the guide.[66] And even after the Commune when groups of Blanquists were being won over by the Marxists, Blanqui himself remained silent when Paul Lafargue invited him to become the standard bearer of a united working-class party.[67] So the gap between Marx and Blanqui remained consistent with Marx only attempting united front tactics to win over the Blanquists.

The course of the entire foregoing discussion raises a question about the further development of the proletarian revolution once universal franchise was achieved. This point was raised very clearly and for the first time by Eduard Bernstein. To him, a violent revolution was proof that the preconditions for socialism were lacking. Such a revolution would result in

> reckless devastation of productive forces, insane experimentalising and aimless violence, and the political sovereignty of the working class would, in fact only be carried out in the form of a dictatorial, revolutionary central power, supported by the terrorist dictatorship of revolutionary clubs. As

such it hovered before the Blanquists and as such it is still represented in the *Communist Manifesto* and in the publications for which its authors were responsible at that time.[68]

Bernstein argued that in principle democracy was the suppression of class government and that constitutional legislation in a democratic atmosphere was the true road to socialism.[69] In the "Preface" to his book, *Evolutionary Socialism* he cited Engels' "Introduction" (1895) to *The Class Struggles in France*.[70]

A close scrutiny of the writings of Marx and Engels, however, reveals a different picture. In one of the drafts of the *Manifesto*, Engels questioned the very counter-position of peaceful revolution to any kind of violence since he was convinced that force would be necessary when the rulers forcibly suppressed the proletariat though as such, the communists would not resist the peaceful revolution. What Engels was bitterly opposed to was substitutionist violence[71] as contradictory to the democratic strategy of proletarian revolution. On law and legal revolution, the *Manifesto* made a sharp and clear-cut statement:

> Your (i.e., the bourgeoisie's) jurisprudence is but the will of your class made into a law of all, a will, whose essential character and direction are determined by the economical conditions of the existence of your class.[72]

In fact, they stated categorically that the aim of the revolution would "be attained only by the forcible overthrow of all existing social conditions."[73]

From the beginning Marx and Engels were aware of the contradictions posed by universal suffrage. They rejected it as the sole means to achieve socialism, nor did they think that proletariat would not have to take the trouble of violent revolution if they could walk along the path of suffrage. This was a false counterposition unless one assumes that universal franchise per se could reform the capitalist system.[74] In *The Class Struggles in France*, Marx pointed out that the bourgeois republic, despite universal suffrage was "bound to turn immediately into bourgeois terrorism." Looking at the French experience of the revolution of 1848-50, he further analyzed the fundamental contradiction of the constitution of 1848—the exploited classes were given political power through universal suffrage, but were expected not to use it for their social emancipation.[75]

In a non-revolutionary period, such a policy could work. Workers accepting capitalism as natural could possibly enjoy the semblance of power, though only political. This was shown by the realignments after June defeat, with workers retreating from real proletarian revolutionaries to doctrinaire socialists and petty-bourgeois democrats.[76]

In a period of steady upswing of the revolution however, elections would take on a different connotation. The proletariat certainly would have to use elections in order to strengthen its party and to secure hegemony in the revolutionary camp. But when in consequence it began to win in the elections, the government, finding an increasing proletarian power in a revolutionary situation, put forward an electoral law which abolished universal suffrage. These bitter experiences in 1850–51, made Marx reject any possibility of smooth gliding over from bourgeois democracy to workers' democracy through the path of suffrage. This transition would require a revolution, which would not be the mere winning of a parliamentary majority, but which would have to set aside universal suffrage and the parliament with its representatives of all classes for a decisive victory of the proletariat-led bloc of the exploited. And this would result in both internal civil war and also an international counter-revolution.[77] In his speech in the September 1850 meeting of the Central Authority of the Communist League, Marx asserted, "you [the workers] have 15, 20, 50 years of civil war to go through."[78] Here obviously the whole period of transition or its earlier part was meant so that until the total defeat of the bourgeoisie the ongoing struggles would have a civil war character.

Nevertheless, the struggle for universal suffrage was not for a moment discarded, nor the need to use it which meant the trappings of political power. But Marx was equally interested in ensuring the suitable conditions without which universal suffrage would be "illusory" to the working class. Both Marx and Engels were aware of a host of such conditions ranging from the need to pay elected representatives so that workers could sit in parliament, to the need to ensure that such things as electoral rolls, etc. were easily available. Without the political preconditions like growing class-consciousness through struggle, simply the "right" to vote would solve no problems.[79] It may be noted that this was said in a period of political defeat of the proletariat. Thus, it was not some particular gain, but a general strategic consideration and commitment to proletarian democracy that motivated Marx to accept universal suffrage as one of the vital means for the proletariat in their road to power.

This also raises the question—how was the universal suffrage won? If the rulers, due to political tactics, made a gift of universal suffrage, and if the workers accepted such a gift with humility, they showed their immaturity and laid the basis for such universal suffrage being revoked later. Thus, behind universal suffrage stood the question, even if not posed explicitly: whose guns defended the constitution? Similar arguments are found in Engels' *The Prussian Military Question and the German Workers' Party*, a programmatic pamphlet, which he wrote in close consultation with Marx around 1864–65. Here he cautioned the Prussian workers not to be swayed by the "Bonapartist trick" of granting universal direct suffrage.[80] Taking into account the need for a guarded tone in a legal pamphlet meant for circulation in Prussia, this was as good as saying that such concessions should be accepted only as elements in a strategic perspective including armed revolutionary struggle.

As strategists of proletarian self-emancipation and class revolution, Marx and Engels never counterposed peaceful political struggles to insurrection. Until the maturation of the proletariat and the development of proper conditions of insurrection, peaceful political struggles were vital but were inadequate. The history of the First International showed that Marx supported the General Council's decision to found the Reform League in 1865 in London to take up the agitation for universal suffrage,[81] while advocating the independent position of the British working class. But the Reform League's agitation was not of the supreme strategic concern for Marx. He saw it as a halfway house where bourgeois reformers also got in.[82]

For Marx, the strategic task was to use legal means to mobilize workers. But the struggle to establish workers' rule would require some amount of force instead of a purely parliamentary road. In his letter to Kugelmann, in 1865, Marx remarked that the issue of "general suffrage" had a "quite different significance" in England than in Prussia.[83] This comment followed a long critique of Lassalleanism which considered the universal franchise as an adequate weapon in a country having a state with a bloated bureaucratic hierarchy. Complete democracy was, according to Marx, "incompatible with the Prussian *bureaucratic* State."[84] This same idea came out even more strongly in a public speech, made by Marx on the seventh anniversary of the International, where he was counterposing the English situation to that of Germany: "England was the only country where the working class was sufficiently developed and organized to turn universal suffrage to its own proper account."[85] This speech came soon after the Paris Commune. In such a time, to say that England alone had a working class capable of utilizing manhood suffrage was apparently strange. Obviously, Marx had in mind some qualification other than the revolutionary inclinations of the workers. It can be suggested that he was hinting at the fact that England at that time had very little in the way of a bureaucratic set up. Nevertheless, immediately after that he went on stressing the question of arms and violence. This reveals that he had very limited faith in the efficacy of universal suffrage as a step to power.

But that did not lead Marx to reject all kinds of political struggle. On the contrary, his proletarian democratic stand came out in his polemics with Bakunin. Here at every stage he supported democratic political institutions and procedures but only after emphasizing their social content. Rejecting Bakunin's attack on the representative system, Marx wrote, "The character of an election does not depend on this name but on the economic foundations, the economic interrelations of the voters."[86] Quoting next a part sentence by Bakunin, "the universal suffrage of the whole people," Marx spontaneously reacted by saying that as long as classes and class struggles would exist, as long as the capitalist order would exist, *the whole people* was a meaningless term, an illusion which hid the reality of class struggle.[87]

In the 1870s, Marx was supposed to have finally given up his Jacobinism and to have been converted to the strategy of "legal revolution." There are two major pieces of alleged evidence. One is the 1872 "preface" to the *Communist Manifesto*. Here they stated that "the working class cannot simply lay hold of the ready made state machinery, and wield it for its own purposes."[88] This has been interpreted to mean that Marx was opposing revolutions. In fact the preface referred to the Paris Commune as the first instance of proletarian state power. The statement quoted indicated that the necessity of smashing the state apparatus was felt because of the experience of the Commune.

The other evidence is documented in Marx's public speech at Amsterdam in 1872, which is frequently cited.[89] Marx was reporting on the just finished *The Hague Congress of the International* and had begun to explain the achievements of the Congress. In this context, he mentioned that the Congress had proclaimed the need for political action, and said, "A group has been formed in our midst which advocates that the workers should abstain from political activity. We regard it as our duty to stress how dangerous and fatal we considered those principles to be."[90] Explaining the reason for this, he said, the workers would have to seize political power, and overthrow the old policy and old institution. But then he added:

> We know that the institutions, customs and traditions in the different countries must be taken into account . . . and we do not deny the existence of countries like America, England, and if I knew your institutions better I might add Holland, where the workers may achieve their aims by peaceful means.[91]

So was he here calling for an end to the revolutionary road? Lenin suggested that by institution, customs and traditions, Marx meant that the extent of bureaucratization and the lack of a standing army in the exceptional cases.[92] Ellen Meiksins Wood suggests that he could also have had in mind English common law.[93] At most, the speech referred to a possibility, and Lenin's argument seems to be quite strong if Marx's speech on the Seventh Anniversary of the International were taken into account. Here he linked workers' power to a workers' army, therefore the absence of a standing army in England could have been a strong consideration for him. So peaceful revolution was not equated with the parliamentary road otherwise it would have been logical to expect him to explain the

Commune as an aberration and to highlight the need to struggle within the parliamentary arena in France. More generally he could have been expected to specifically mention universal suffrage and suggest that after the conquest of universal suffrage workers should proceed peacefully, which he did not. The Act of 1867 in England, rounded off by the Ballot Act of 1872, only enfranchised the lower middle classes and the better-off section of the workers. As late as 1911, out of a population of 40 million in the same territory only 7.2 million had the vote. Moreover, it was only the Parliament Act of 1911 that freed finance bills and other bills relating to expenditures from votes by the House of Lords.[94] Simply this factual side of the matter should be enough to establish that in 1872, Marx could not have had universal suffrage in mind. Marx's speech may therefore be more correctly viewed as a refutation of the anarchist politics of abstentionism (calling for election boycotts and the boycott of all other forms of political struggles in favor of a hoped for insurrection as a matter of "principle"). Engels' speech in the London Conference of the International should be compared at this point as he argued that political freedom was necessary for the workers and that therefore they should fight for it.[95] In the same conference, Marx's comments about the armed forces of reaction opposing the working class and the need to take up arms rebut the claim of the legalistic "mature" Marx.[96]

So Marx was always against unnecessary violence but he always recognized that at some point parliament would become inadequate. In an interview to a newspaper, in the same year, he made the same counterposition stating on the one hand that where peaceful agitation worked faster "insurrection was madness," and on the other hand that as soon as the English bourgeoisie "finds itself outvoted on what it considers vital questions we shall see here a new slave-owner war."[97] Finally in an interview given to the *Chicago Tribune* in 1879, he commented that "no great movement has ever been inaugurated without bloodshed."[98]

More than Marx, it is Engels, who is held up as the father of the peaceful road, above all on the strength of his "Introduction" to *The Class Struggles in France*, as noted above. So his writings of 1883-95 need to be carefully examined. In 1884, he wrote in *The Origin of the Family, Private Property and the State*, that universal suffrage enabled the class struggle to be fought out in a decisive way but that the institution itself could only measure the maturity of the proletariat, and when this maturity reached the boiling point both sides would "know where they stand."[99] In a letter to Bebel, written in the same period, he claimed that in case of a future German revolution the whole of bourgeois and semi-feudal reaction would group around pure democracy, i.e., petty-bourgeois democratic political currents.[100] This implies that at such a moment a purely democratic struggle would become inadequate. In 1889, Engels wrote to the Danish socialist, Gerson Trier, "The proletariat cannot conquer its political domination without violent revolution."[101]

Three or four of Engels' writings of the 1890s are repeatedly cited to show that he suffered a slideback. The real problem lies elsewhere. For Engels, the experience of the revolutions of 1848, supplemented by that of the Commune, remained the touchstone. The impact of the subsequent global changes could not be mastered alone by the aging exile on whose shoulders socialists from all over Europe laid the burden of developing strategy. In an interview with the newspaper, Le Figaro in 1893, he predicted that since Prussia was recruiting its army through conscription, when the socialists became a majority they would inevitably have a majority of the army behind them as well.[102] Here a simple factual error led to theoretical ambiguity. The German army was consciously recruited from non-proletarian strata. On the eve of 1914, only 6.14 percent of the soldiers came from large towns.[103] Without denying the need for violent revolution Engels "visualized the future course of revolutionary development too much along the straight line."[104] Impressed by the growth of working-class power he did not take into adequate account the development of opportunistic tendencies as the result of electoral successes.

Another interview by Engels that is sometimes mentioned, was the one given to The Daily Chronicle (1893), where he predicted the possibility of a speedy parliamentary majority between 1900 and 1910.[105] But this did not mean that he was advocating a parliamentary road to socialism. In his 1891 Critique of the Erfurt program of the SPD, Engels objected to any idea of peaceful revolution in Germany, attacked the growing opportunism in the party and insisted that the working class could only come to power in a democratic republic.[106] In his "Introduction" to The Civil War in France (1891), he clarified that the republic he had in mind would be like the Commune.[107] That even at this juncture Engels had in mind the abolition of the military bureaucratic hierarchy is borne out by his comment:

> How self-government is to be organized and how we can manage without a bureaucracy has been shown to us by America and the first French Republic, and is being shown even today by Australia, Canada and the other English Colonies.[108]

It is however the aforementioned "Introduction" to The Class Struggles in France, that requires a careful scrutiny. To start with, Engels had to agree to tone down what he wanted to write under pressure from the SPD leadership.[109] Even after that chunks were cut out so that in his own words he was made to appear as "a peaceful worshipper of legality at any price."[110] In a letter to Lafargue he explained that the tactics he had proposed were restricted to the present situation in Germany and even then with many reservations, being inapplicable to other countries and perhaps even to Germany in the future.[111] Consequently all interpretations that claim to find in it an awareness of the value of liberal democratic forms[112] are not factually correct, since Germany was neither liberal nor democratic. What needs to be studied here are, did Engels consider the right to vote such a weapon that could in a short time carry the proletariat to power? Did he abandon armed revolution? A detailed study produces a different answer to these questions, than to one assumed by those who have been influenced chiefly by the right-left debate in the SPD after the death of Engels.[113]

The first section was devoted to an explanation of historical materialism. Following came the comment that the February revolution of 1848 had come at a time when conceptions of revolution were still predominantly based on the model of the great French Revolution. Engels wrote self-critically that they had erred, because the historical conditions of proletarian struggles had changed.[114] Unlike revolutions led by new exploiters, the proletarian hegemony could not be based on passive acquiescence by the majority. In addition, Engels observed that the vast potentiality for further capitalist development after 1848-50 showed on one hand why peasants and the petty bourgeoisie had not gone over *en masse* to the proletariat in 1848, and on the other hand the correctness of Marx's opposition to the sects and his hope in the birth of a mass proletarian movement not dependent on a sudden attack.[115] This is a blend of acute historical analysis with a misinterpretation of the past. In 1848-50, the communists had not planned a simple surprise attack, as the discussion on their strategy has sought to disclose. They had hoped to capture power only through protracted struggle. But historical development had indeed created a new situation. The rise of mass parties enabled the open unity of a large section of the proletariat, and the potential to create a majority around the party, in ways unthinkable in 1848. To this perspective of a revolution of the majority "achievable through mass socialist parties, Engels devoted his last writings."[116] After a defeat, in hindsight, analyzing the causes of defeat may not be very difficult. But to claim that therefore the struggle should not have been waged on that ground, is logically untenable. However Engels' attempts to come to terms with the changing situation is more sensible. Since at the moment, the change was occurring in Germany, his insistence on German-specific tactics also becomes understandable. What was wrong was not the attempted proletarian revolution of 1848, but the idea that strategy and tactics derived from 1848 could pass on unchanged into the twentieth century. Perhaps Engels also recognized the danger of codifying Marxism into a dogma with canonical texts and therefore warned against idealizing the old strategy and tactics explained by Marx in his book in

1850. This led him to examine the major new elements. In Prussia, and then in Germany universal male suffrage had existed since 1866, though under an autocratic regime where all real power was concentrated in the hands of the executive of the German Empire. Nevertheless, the German working class had transformed universal suffrage "from a means of deception, which it was before, into an instrument of emancipation."[117]

This really highlights Engels' continuing adherence to the idea of universal suffrage as an instrument of emancipation, not emancipation itself. He then went on to emphasize the gains brought about by the universal suffrage. It enabled the conscious proletariat to measure its strength regularly—the "thermometer" he had mentioned in *The Origin of Family*. Continuing electoral successes demoralized their opponents and acted as a powerful means of propaganda. Third, election campaigns and the Reichstag platform gave a great opportunity to reach out to the people in a big way.[118] Finally Engels said that the scale of the workers' electoral victories wrung out concessions from the bourgeoisie without any concession in return.[119]

It has been observed that there is a tendency to make old Engels into "a whipping boy, and to impugn him any sign that one chooses to impugn to subsequent Marxisms,"[120] or to see in his thoughts an "unconscious preamble and preparation to revisionism."[121] A careful reading of the disputed text shows that nowhere did Engels argue that the right to vote by itself would carry the proletariat to power. His stress on "inevitability" was not meant as an inevitable workers' victory through parliament, but an inevitable growth of the SPD under the then-prevailing conditions. Moreover, Engels wrote very explicitly that "of course, our foreign comrades do not renounce their right to revolution," and when discussing the revolutions of 1848, said that the period of revolutions was concluded "*for the time being*," and that new conditions were being created "under which they were bound to ripen."[122] Even in Germany, where the existing situation enabled the SPD to grow massively, Engels only said that it had "at least in the immediate future," a special task. That task was to organize more and more support for the proletarian revolution. A passage chopped out by Liebknecht reads that the aim was "not to fritter away this daily increasing shock force in vanguard skirmishes, but to keep it intact until the decisive day."[123] What Engels was arguing for was to use legality and the suffrage to win majority as a prelude to a revolutionary struggle for power. The lessons of 1848 and 1871 were that in proletarian revolutions, a semi-conscious mass could not prop up a conscious minority, rather the majority had to be conscious. For this, sustained preparations were necessary.

None the less, Engels has been accused of at least ambiguity in his arguments in the "Introduction" to *The Class Struggles in France* even by some scholars or activists sympathetic to him.[124] But the ambiguity stemmed from the fact that leaders of the German party first requested him to be cautious for fear of a repetition of the Anti-Socialist Law, and even after he had written a carefully worded essay, Wilhelm Liebknecht inflicted substantial cuts without informing him. Since the recovery of the full text in 1930, there is no scope for ambiguity. The recovered passages related to street fighting reveal that Engels, instead of rejecting it altogether, was more concerned with how to make street fighting tactics more effective in the proletarian revolution. He explained that under changed situations, which had become far more favorable for military than for civilian fighters, "open attack" would be preferable to "passive barricade tactics" as the form of insurrection.[125] Politically, this essay anticipates Gramscian strategy related to the contrasting perspective, of "war of position" and "war of manoeuvre."[126] Engels was opposed to any launching of premature insurrection before the revolutionary forces had won a majority in the working class and split the military forces of the state. Universal suffrage and other legal avenues enabled the working class to wage a long war of position, to use democracy to consolidate proletarian power. If the working class went on, as Engels pointed out, increasing its strength, in this way, the bourgeoisie would themselves break through this "fatal legality." They would rather provoke a premature uprising which would be easier to crush than a revolution of the bloc of the exploited. And this reactionary attack would give the proletariat a moral-political advantage of gaining support of the petty bourgeois and the peasantry around proletarian hegemony. For tactical reasons of gaining majority support, offensive attack was changed into a defensive attack.[127] And it was out of a positive evaluation of this new strategy of proletarian struggle and not due to any obsession with legal reforms that Engels remarked in this "Introduction": " . . . the bourgeoisie and the government came to be much more afraid of the legal than of the illegal action of the workers' party. . . "[128] Had Engels been so committed to legality then he would not have reacted so sharply to the comments of Richard Fischer, a leader of the SPD who said that Engels had written a provocative "preface."[129] Engels wrote back on March 8, 1895:

> I simply cannot believe that you intend to sell yourselves body and soul to absolute legality, legality under all circumstances . . . you will gain nothing if you preach the absolute renunciation of revolt.[130]

Still, Engels' writings of the last decade also disclosed limitations. He thought that the majority of the working class had to become conscious before a proletarian revolution was possible. The natural question was, whether electoral battles could adequately educate and give the working class revolutionary consciousness.[131] If the ruling idea of an epoch was the idea of the ruling class, then it was unrealistic to expect that periodic elections would adequately serve to revolutionize the proletariat. Even though the workers might elect or vote for only the candidates of a workers' party, there was no guarantee that its members of parliament would not become wedded to parliamentarism. History has shown that this happens often. Engels at times showed sufficient awareness of this, as when he warned, repeatedly, that democracy would become the catchword of all reactionaries in times of revolution, i.e., they would use the democratic rhetoric to keep in rein the working class, and especially its reformist or opportunist leaders. But he could not see that the revolutionary theory and the day-to-day practice of the German Social Democracy stood increasingly opposed to each other. On this issue, a particularly important point was his attitude to strikes. For Marx and Engels, strikes remained essentially economic weapons. They had ridiculed the anarchist proposal for a general strike for good reason. This was because the anarchists thought of a general strike as a fully organized strike, called by the leadership. Such a strike was either impossible or unnecessary as Engels wrote to Laura Lafargue (1890):

> whenever we are in a position to try the universal strike, we shall be able to get what we want for the mere asking for it, without the round about way of the universal strike.[132]

But to stop here with just criticizing the non-political stance of the anarchists was to fail to indicate how there would be a transition from the level of consciousness that enabled workers to vote for socialist candidates to the level of consciousness that led them to fight for the revolution actively. If the workers were to break out of their alienated existence, struggles, including strikes at the point of production, were also important in generating revolutionary consciousness. The major problem was that, in the absence of big experiences of political strikes, it was not possible for Engels to generalize the theory of political strike in terms of revolutionary democratic strategy of the working class.

III
A STRUGGLE FOR DEMOCRATIZATION

In the "Principles of Communism," Engels made a categorical statement:

> Democracy would be quite useless to the proletariat if it were not immediately used as a means of carrying through further measures directly attacking private ownership and securing the means of subsistence of the proletariat.[133]

Therefore, to say that Marx's and Engels' strategy of revolution was democratic, it is not enough to point to the plans to mobilize a majority, nor to the tactical utilization of democratic forms and legal avenues. It is also necessary to show how far they were consistent in integrating the struggle for democratic rights and civil liberties into the struggle for revolution, that is, to show that they wanted the democratization of the very power structures.

Marx and Engels' own writings and actions showed that they never repudiated the democratic content of their pre-communist activities. In 1843, Engels exposed the hypocrisy of the English constitution which, despite calling itself a constitutional monarchy was "a parody of reality,"[134] where the big leaders devoted their time to discussing democracy and peoples' welfare in order to postpone their actual implementation.[135] The first volume of Marx's projected works,[136] *Gesammelte Aufsätze von Karl Marx*, (published in Cologne in April 1851), contained his attacks on censorship. His criticized the democratic reforms by liberals and petty-bourgeois democrats as hollow and half-measures, devoid of social content of democracy. This criticism was also extended to those radicals like Max Stirner, an anarchist, who regarded democracy as a sham or a meaningless exercise of sovereignty by the people.[137] Marx and Engels responded by fighting for the effective establishment of full popular control over government. It is clear that not only Marx, Engels, or other radicals, but equally, conservative opponents understood that democracy would mean not just universal suffrage, but the establishment of such popular control.[138]

In the revolution of 1848, the line put forward by Marx and Engels was for a thorough-going democracy. But in a country like Germany, the bourgeoisie, though already part and parcel of the surplus extracting mechanism, could still claim to be technically a part of the "people." The urban petty bourgeoisie and the peasantry very much belonged to the stratum of the exploited. The strategy of permanent revolution led Marx and Engels to fight for forms of popular power that would ensure the independence of the proletariat within the general struggle for democracy, so that forces in favor of democracy could be drawn away from the hold of the bourgeois and petty bourgeois hypocrites. In the very first issue of the *NRZ*, Engels wrote that the first task of the National Assembly should have been the proclamation of the sovereignty of the Germans, and the next one the creation of a constitution on the basis of popular sovereignty.[139]

The "Demands of the Communist Party in Germany," were used systematically by the activists of the Communist League in Cologne and elsewhere. As noted earlier, these demands were drawn up in order to simultaneously emphasize the democratic struggle and the proletarian line within it. This resulted in a clash between Marx's faction and Gottschalk's faction. Gottschalk's strategy was one of creating democratic socialist clubs, where effectively petty-bourgeois pink socialists and workers would come together, while Marx emphasized the need for class-based workers' associations, where the socialist ideology would be developed out of class struggle issues. But in the case of elections (because the system was indirect), Gottschalk was in favor of a boycott, while Marx and Engels vigorously campaigned in favor of electoral alliance with the Democrats.[140]

In sustained polemics against the Prussian constituent assembly, the *NRZ* showed the nature of democracy it envisaged. Being supporters of a unitary Germany, Marx and Engels opposed separate constitutions. But their idea of a united Germany was to be based on a democratic constitution dissolving the monarchies.[141] The liberals in the Prussian Assembly were subsequently criticized as they preferred to act in "agreement" with the king rather than in accordance with the will of the people.[142]

The difference between the kind of democracy that Marx advocated and the kind of democracy the "Pale" democrats of 1848 were willing to countenance came up repeatedly. The extreme case was the June days of barricade fighting in Paris, 1848. The German liberals welcomed the crushing of the French working class. As the *Bonner Zeitung*, a left bourgeois paper wrote, criticizing the *NRZ*:

> We want freedom, but we also want order, without which no freedom can exist. Was the *Neue Rheinische* truly defending democracy when it praised a wild insurrection which endangered the republic . . . ?[143]

It was the bourgeois liberal balancing act between democracy and "order" that Marx had challenged in his articles against the Prussian state and its bureaucratic structure many years' back. During the revolution of 1848, his position was a foregone conclusion. The establishment of democracy was only possible through the overthrow of the old "order."

One of the crucial components of a new, democratic order was the unfettered freedom of press. The ex-editor of the *RZ* once more campaigned for freedom of expression in general, of which freedom of the press was a part. This was in response to the attempt of the government to gag the press by using slander provisions in the Penal Code. Taking it as a mortal blow to the revolution, the *NRZ* instantly reacted when the Hansemann ministry submitted an "interim law" to regulate the press. Marx wrote a fiery article, "The Prussian Press Bill," (July 1848) for the *NRZ*, where he commented: "From the day when this Bill becomes law, officials may with impunity carry out any arbitrary act" and contrasted to the Bill the draft German constitution, which stated: "The Censorship can never again be restored."[144] Similarly, Marx violently attacked the Bonapartist regime, which had stated: "The duty of the press is to enlighten the public and not deceive it."[145] To him it was a bid to force the media to support government-sponsored swindles or face the penalty of transportation.[146]

Returning to the German Revolution, it is possible to see how the government tried consistently to defeat the revolution. After the June days in France, an emboldened reaction in Germany increasingly attacked associations. On 28th July, the *NRZ* published an article written by Engels condemning "the reactionary police measures against the right of association." The main aim of the essay was to highlight freedom of associations and the consequent demand that the prohibition of associations should be subject to a court of law initially sentencing such associations. When Mathy, a right-wing deputy to the Frankfurt Parliament, demanded the abolition of these associations because they undermined the basis of a constitution and the entire state edifice, Engels replied:

> The right of association, Herr Mathy, exists just so that one may "undermine" the constitution with impunity, provided, of course one does it legally.[147]

This was a very important statement of principle. Engels was making a distinction between (usually armed) open violation of the constitution on the one hand, and the constitutional right to form associations, which could democratically campaign for the transformation of the constitution. To Marx and Engels, no freedom could be genuine if the opponents of the Government were banned.

For the same reason, Marx in the article, "The Civic Militia Bill" for *NRZ* (July 21–24, 1848), opposed the kind of militia being set up as it deprived its members of political rights through the insistence that they had to obey unquestioningly the orders of the authorities and not enter into any arguments. In other words, asserted Marx, the militia members were being asked to surrender all civic rights. He also pointed out the class bias of the militia for while, "the entire working class and a large part of the middle class are all legally *disarmed*" except during the period of service, "whereas the *bourgeois* section of the civic militia remains at all times in possession of its weapons and uniforms."[148] The militia had always been a slogan of radical bourgeois revolutions, from the struggle of the Italian city republics during the Renaissance to Cromwell's New Model Army and the *levee en masse*. It had been closely related to the central concept of citizenship. What Marx was proposing here, as in the case of the franchise, was to fully extend those rights and duties to the proletariat as well.

Popular control would necessitate forms of organizations capable of exerting pressure or controlling the elected representatives as well as the bureaucracy. This was the basic idea behind all constitutional proposals, put forward by Marx and Engels. When Johann Jacoby, the leader of the left wing in the National Assembly proposed a motion asserting the Assembly's right to pass legally binding decisions without having to await any one's consent, Engels vigorously supported him in an article series, "The Debate on Jacoby's Motion" (*NRZ*, July 18, 19, 23, and 25, 1848).[149] Even earlier, in one of the first articles for *NRZ* (June 1848) it had been stated: "A Constituent National Assembly must above all be an active, revolutionary assembly."[150] He made it quite clear that behind this demand for an active assembly was the implied further assertion of the right of the people to control the assembly.[151] This same concept was reflected in the March Address, where the local workers' societies were asked to set up revolutionary workers' governments which would take over executive functions.[152] Finally, it was this very concept to which Marx returned in describing the Paris Commune to be "a working, not a parliamentary body, executive and legislative at the same time."[153]

In a number of later articles, Marx analyzed the constitutions of certain countries. In a less known analysis of the constitution of the French republic of 1848, which was extensively reproduced in *The Eighteenth Brumaire*, (1852), he exposed the fraudulent character of this apparently democratic constitution. This constitution, after declaring direct and universal franchise, the electoral laws of 1849 and 1850 made provisions for massive disenfranchisement.[154] Specifically, he pointed out that the electoral laws had excluded two-thirds of the French people.[155] Marx denounced another law creating internal passports or labor books in order to exercise de facto control over the workers regardless of their constitutional right.[156] Once more, taking up the liberty of the press, Marx condemned the imposition of security deposits, stamp duties, fines, and the demands that all articles had to be signed by the author. The result, Marx said, was that: "The middle class sat in the jury box and they crushed the working man's press."[157]

Other constitutions were not so elaborately analyzed. But even the briefer analyses brought out significant aspects of the nature of democracy he fought for. Far from considering judicial autonomy to be a bourgeois hoax, he believed it to be a major check on bureaucratic arbitrariness. Commenting on draft constitutions of Schleswig and Holstein and their prototype, the Prussian constitution, Marx wrote:

> The most remarkable paragraphs in these constitutions are two, one of which deprives the courts of law of their ancient right of cancelling administrative decrees.[158]

Analyzing the Prussian constitution further, in later articles, Marx declared that bureaucratization hampered even simple mobility. Through his condemnation of the constitution, it becomes clear that he supported academic freedom, freedom of conscience, social equality, irrespective of feudal caste considerations, etc.[159] Marx was comparatively effusive over the Hessian Constitution of 1831. Apart from the standard defect of having an estate-based election system, the constitution was positive because, "There is no other constitution which restrains the powers of the executive within limits so narrow, makes the Administration, more dependent on the Legislative and confides such a supreme control to the judicial benches."[160] Marx also commented in the same place on the fact that elected councillors supervised the police in Hess in order to highlight popular control over the executive.

The foregoing demands and proposals for reforms put forward by Marx and Engels show that they advocated nothing short of subordination of the executive officials to elected representatives, and the maximization of control from below. They pointed out that the system of representation should ensure that popular will was implemented, and that freedom of the people was not cut short in the name of "national Interest," etc. That is why that Draper is justified in saying that Marx's goal was the "complete democratisation of society."[161]

The question that arises is how far this democratization was to survive the proposed seizure of power by the working class. Though a full answer must await the next chapter, an important programmatic continuity can be indicated. In Engels' letter to Bebel, (March 1875) criticizing the Gotha Programme it was explained that "the first pre-requisite of all liberty" was that "all officials be responsible for all their official actions to every citizen before the ordinary courts and in accordance with common law."[162] Both Engels in this letter and Marx in his Critique criticized the democratic demands of the Gotha Program on the ground that they were so mild that liberals could accept them. They were arguing in favor of extending the democratic demands to the level of proletarian democracy.[163] Similarly, in demanding that the program should insist on the exclusion of government and church from any influence on the school,[164] Marx was emphasizing community control and the increasing freedom of the individual from the coercive agencies of the state.

Marx's committment to the freedom of the individual can be further seen from his attitude to the question of religious beliefs. Despite their own atheism, Marx and Engels, in the "Demands of Communist Party in Germany," insisted only on the separation of the church from the state. In the International they resisted Bakunin's attempts to impose atheism as the central plank of the revolutionary program. Finally, in the critique of the Erfurt program, Engels remarked that the religious communities, "cannot be prohibited from forming their own schools out of their *own* funds and from teaching their own nonsense in them."[165]

So even in Marx's sharpest criticism, there were no suggestions that democracy was to be mocked just because the bourgeoisie made a mockery of democracy, or as Marx once put it, in the case of the United

States, applied "democratic humbug."[166] Similar was the argument put forward by Engels in the 1864 pamphlet, *The Prussian Military Question and the German Workers' Party*.[167] Apparently contradicting this stand in favor of freedom, Marx in "On the Jewish Question," made a distinction between political freedom and rights associated with the "egoistic man."[168] This could be understood as though the sphere of politics would overshadow all other areas in the name of curbing individualism. However, the same idea as explained in the *Manifesto*, is much clearer. Here Marx wrote: "The abolition of bourgeois individuality, bourgeois independence and bourgeois freedom is undoubtedly aimed at."[169] The subsequent explanation shows that he was not talking about the abolition of individual civil liberties under bourgeois rule, but the specifically bourgeois economic rights associated with capitalist private property.

In concluding our discussion on Marx and Engels in this chapter, like in the previous one, we only have to emphasize a greatly neglected issue. Marx and Engels were not merely theorists who accepted the values of democracy. From the very beginning of their political journey, as Young Hegelians campaigning for freedom of the press, to the death of Engels in 1895, they were consistent revolutionary democratic activists. They challenged various models of non-democratic and authoritarian communism/socialism in the 1840s. During the era of the International Workingmen's Association and still later, during the period of growth of mass socialist parties, their influence was crucial in the drive to democratic politics. Insofar as the working class struggles were very important in ultimately ushering in democracy, Marx and Engels were key figures in the organization of this struggle.[170] Failure to recognize this practical side of their life-long commitment leads to serious errors in socialist politics.[171] However, though this is being said in one sentence, one flaw requiring a substantial separate treatment is the considerable lacunae in their programmatic gendering, *The Origin* notwithstanding.[172] It would only be Bebel, Zetkin, and their comrades who would recognize and gradually develop an understanding of the implications of the fact that the working class comes in two basic shapes—male and female— and that achieving class unity necessitates paying special attention to women workers.

IV

EXTENDING DEMOCRACY TO WOMEN

We have noted, in the previous chapter, that Marx and Engels both expressed sympathy for exploited women. But we also saw that their ideas about organizing women came late. The same thing can be said about their programmatic writings on women. Neither the discussions leading up to the *Manifesto*, nor the *Manifesto* itself, had things to say directly about women workers and their double burden, and so on. However, the *Manifesto* did take up another issue very clearly. It argued that the bourgeoisie wanted to impose controls on women's sexuality —for women of all classes. In addition, it argued against idealization of any pre-bourgeois family either: "The bourgeoisie has torn away from the family its sentimental veil, and has reduced the family relation to a mere money relation."[173] Capitalism, they averred, had revealed the pure cash nexus. And this was underscored by the passage, which stated:

> The selfish misconception that induces you to transform into eternal laws of nature and of reason, the social forms springing from your present mode of production and form of property—historical relations that rise and disappear in the progress of production—this misconception you share with every ruling class that has preceded you. What you see clearly in the case of ancient property, what you admit in the case of feudal property, you are of course forbidden to admit in the case of your own bourgeois form of property.
>
> "Abolition of the family! Even the most radical flare up at this infamous proposal of the Communists.
>
> "On what foundation is the present family, the bourgeois family, based? On capital, on private gain. In its completely developed form this family exists only among the bourgeoisie. But this state of things finds its complement in the practical absence of the family among the proletarians, and in public prostitution."[174]

Several points should be noted here. In the first place, here, if nowhere else, Marx no less than Engels (it was, as we saw earlier, Marx who wrote the entire text of the final draft, even though Engels' name is associated for very valid reasons) fully solidarized with the views of the utopians concerning the family. Second, they resolutely oppose attempts to turn the family into a natural or eternal category and assert that it was historically specific, relating it to forms of property. The absolute type of bourgeois family can exist, they assert, only alongside prostitution. Female chastity, marital fidelity of the female, and the nuclear family are preserved by having a differently ordered world by its side. Finally, in this passage, I want to emphasize the word "practical" when they talk about the proletarian family. This suggests that they did not, contrary to a widely accepted reading, suggest that there was no family in the proletariat, only that for all practical purposes, the bourgeois norms were not present in it. However, there is an assumption that the abolition of the bourgeois family will *automatically* lead to the abolition of prostitution. In addition, the sustained survival of patriarchal family forms within the working class as we know today, nearly 160 years after the *Manifesto*, put into question its assumption about the practical disappearance of the working class family, or the view that the abolition of private property will necessarily do away with the non-economic structures of oppression, as in the family. Notwithstanding this problem, the *Manifesto* stood out as a bold programmatic statement on communist aims concerning women.

The words of the *Manifesto* argue that the bourgeois family is oppressive towards children, as parents control and exploit them. It charges the bourgeoisie with controlling female sexuality in all forms—the wife of the bourgeois as "mere instruments of production," and all who are not one's *owned* woman as objects of sexual gratification.[175]

During 1848, there were significant numbers of women active in the revolution.[176] Some of them were socialistically inclined. Many were deeply involved in political agitation in various ways. What we do not find is any significant comment in the writing of Marx and Engels, even though when, in March 1849, the Cologne Democratic Association and the Workers' Society organized a banquet, half the participants were women.[177] It would only be during the period of the First International that Marx would start discussing programmatic issues concerning women. By this time, the question of women's suffrage was very much a subject of discussion, both among bourgeois feminists, and among various working-class organizations, and was even being raised by leading philosophers like John Stuart Mill. But many were opposed to this demand. This included the Lassallean ADAV, whose program demanded, quite consciously, adult male suffrage. Equally motivated partly by straightforward patriarchal values and partly by Lassalle's so-called theory of the iron law of wages, according to which the total wage fund was constant, so that the induction of greater number of workers would lead to the lowering of per capita wages, the ADAV opposed jobs for women. As late as 1867, quite a few years after Lassalle's death, the ADAV adopted a resolution that gives us the full flavor of its ideology:

> The employment of women in the workshops of modern industry is one of the most scandalous abuses of our times . . . because it does not improve the material situation of the working class . . . , and because the destruction of the family in particular reduces the working class population to a wretched state in which even the last remnants of its ideal possessions are taken from it. This gives us all the more reason to reject the current efforts to increase even further the market for female labour. Only the abolition of the rule of capital can ensure the remedy, through which positive organic institutions will abolish the wage-relationship and give every worker the full proceeds of his labour.[178]

This reveals quite a few things about Lassallean ideology. This statement compares unfavorably with the Marxist position against the bourgeois family in the *Communist Manifesto*. Also, it assumes that even under socialism men alone would do factory labor. In the third place the Lassallean position assumed that the class struggle was men's business, and that even under socialism, gender relations would continue as before, or at best become the idyllic bourgeois-patriarchal type without its "distortions."

But anti-Lassalleans were not always exemplary feminists either. The General Council of the International, of which Marx was a member, presented a draft statement on "female and child labour." This draft made a distinction between the exploitative nature of productive work under capitalism, which it denounced, and the fact that women and youth were brought into productive labor, which it considered progressive.[179] This position is itself inadequate, since it has nothing to say about women's domestic labor, but it was based on the position that in socialism, women and men would both be involved in productive labor. But the majority did not support the General Council. It was argued, says Thönnessen, that if male workers received higher wages, all of them could marry, and then all women would have "honourable" positions and would not be driven to prostitution! The fact that the central concern of women's liberation was not to accord women an "honourable status," which is a promise held out by most patriarchal orders with their rhetoric of motherhood, etc., but to struggle for the emancipation of women from legal and social bondage, was missed. Thönnessen even argues that the tenor of arguments against prostitution, then and in later years, indicates that the bourgeoisie were reproached for enjoying liberties forbidden to male workers. In any case, regardless of this particular argument, it should be noted that the International adopted a resolution, which spoke of women's "naturally determined role."[180]

But Marx's collaborative effort in drafting the program of the French Parti Ouvrier, in 1880 was an attempt at ending gender discrimination both at public and private spheres as some of the extracts show:

> In *the Preamble*: "Considering, that the emancipation of the productive class is that of all human beings without distinction of sex or race";
>
> In *the political section*: "Abolition of all laws over the press, meetings and associations and above all the law against the International Working Men's Association. Removal of the livret, that administrative control over the working class, and of all the articles of the Code establishing the inferiority of the worker in relation to the boss, and of woman in relation to man";
>
> In *the economic section*: "Equal pay for equal work, for workers of both sexes."[181]

Written in 1884, Engels' *The Origins* represented a great theoretical stride forward in the late nineteenth century. Its correctness and its legacy are even now highly contested. It is not my intention to enter into that debate here. But Engels did make a major contribution to the understanding of the question of women's oppression from a materialist conception of history. He located the subordination of women in history, rather than in human nature. Thereby, he suggested that in a different social order women might achieve equality. Engels also showed a connection between the monogamous family and private property, as well as between the economic and political dominance by men and their control over female sexuality. By relating prostitution and monogamy as two sides of a compulsion on women, while men enjoyed the benefits of both institutions, his analysis opened up the possibility of a Marxist–feminist analysis. Of course, it is now admitted that he did not carry out the analysis as far as he could have, even with the data at his hand. However, he insisted that in a capitalist society the liberation of women from the status of housewife had to begin with their gainful employment outside their domestic work.[182] But unless women's domestic work was recognized and a programmatic solution found, gainful employment could become a burden rather than the foundation of freedom.

It was indeed August Bebel who, several years before Engels, had laid out in simple terms the dual burden on women for a mass proletarian audience (audience, because the book was meant often to be read out and discussed). We can look at the following passage:

> Husband and wife go to work. The children are left alone or in the care of older siblings who urgently need looking after and educating themselves. . . . Evenings both return tired and exhausted. Instead of an inviting and pleasant domesticity, they find a small, unhealthy dwelling, often without the necessary fresh air, light, or comforts. The woman has her hands full; she must work head over heels in order to put the basics in order. The crying, noisy children are put to bed as soon as possible. . . . The man goes to a bar and seeks there the entertainment which is missing at home; he drinks, and however little he may spend, it is too much for his means. . . . Meanwhile the wife remains at home and fumes; she must work like a beast of burden, there is no break or rest for her; the man uses the freedom which chance has given him—to be born as a man.[183]

This portrayal is convincing because it is drawn from innumerable specific cases, as a synthesis of them all. Of course, this also exaggerates certain trends—a large number of married women, wives of industrial workers, were themselves non-workers. But this mundane narrative is used to focus on gender roles in the family, including the working class family. His depiction is not intended to apportion blame to the individuals, but to suggest that the social system allows little scope for escape by the individual. The emancipation of women is made possible through a struggle to change society.

But once again, concretization of demands and struggles would have to wait until women activists entered the scene. Eleanor Marx was one of them. Eleanor had been viewed too often as the daughter of a great man, hence protected by a second great man, and unfortunately partnered with a third man who was deemed a notorious scoundrel. As a result, her own contributions were often inadequately examined in her own age and in the period immediately after her death.[184] Eleanor was seriously involved in English labor and socialist politics, and helped in organizing workingmen and workingwomen, including in the Gasworkers and General Labourers Union, and among dockworkers. In 1889 she helped set up an association of young working women of the cable factory and rubber plants of Silvertown during their strike. She also helped found an association of working women within the Gasworkers and General Labourers Union. In 1886, Eleanor and her companion Edward Aveling wrote an article, "The Woman Question," in the form of a review of Bebel's book, though in fact the essay went beyond a review. The entire content of the present-day idea, that sexuality is a social construct, was clearly present in the article:

> Society provides, recognizes, legalises for the latter [the men] the means of gratifying the sex instinct. In the eyes of that same society an unmarried woman who acts after the fashion habitual to her unmarried brothers and the men that dance with her at balls, or work with her in the shop, is a pariah. And even with the working classes who marry at the normal time, the life of the woman under the present system is the more arduous and irksome of the two.[185]

She discussed double standards in dealing with adultery and divorce. Discussing socialist policy and prescriptions for the future, Marx and Aveling contended that sex education was essential in order to bring up children properly. "To us, it seems that the reproductive organs ought to be discussed as frankly, as freely, between parents and children as the digestive"[186] since they contended that it was the unwarranted secrecy that resulted in creating morbid or unhealthy ideas and conditions.

Discussing how society imposes norms on women, Eleanor still could not escape the dominant ideas and acknowledged that transgendered identities were unnatural. But she was to say very strongly: "chastity is unhealthy and unholy. . . . The criminal is not the individual sufferer, but the society that forces her to sin and to suffer."[187]

The most important woman activist however, was Clara Zetkin. Maria Mies claims that in the case of Zetkin, "The content of her agitation, apart from the rhetoric of class struggle, was not much different from the content of the bourgeois women's movement."[188] Turning to the suffrage question, such an assessment has to be challenged. From 1891, the SPD, to which Zetkin belonged, called for universal, direct and equal suffrage without discrimination by sex. In 1903, at the Dresden Congress, the Party resolved to campaign for women's suffrage whenever any demand for reform of the suffrage came up.

The Social Democratic women supported votes for women from the very beginning in contrast to the bourgeois feminists who formally committed themselves to female suffrage only in 1902. Of course, in the 1880s and 1890s, the thrust of their campaigns was for better pay, and improvement in the conditions of female factory and domestic laborers. But an 1896 speech of Zetkin, delivered at the Party Congress that year, which, due to the backing given by the party congress, had an almost programmatic stature, stressed that the struggle for equality in the bourgeois sense was also accepted by them, as a means to enable the working-class women to wage class war on the same terms as the men.[189] Two different factors combined to produce a stronger suffrage movement in the twentieth century. The increasing preoccupation of the SPD with the vote as a major means of attaining its goals meant an increased attention paid to the question of votes for women. But women workers, especially the socialists, were also becoming convinced that without the votes, women were in a situation of relative powerlessness.

In 1907, at the International Socialist Women's Conference at Stuttgart, the German delegation led the fight for women's suffrage and opposed both those who treated the suffrage question as one divorced from the class struggles and those who, in the name of realism, opted to support a limited extension of the franchise. Alexandra Kollontai, the Russian Marxist feminist, later wrote a fairly detailed account. She commented:

> One after the other women from Belgium, Austria, Sweden accepted the removal from the agenda of the demand for political rights for women workers and gave their support to an emasculated abbreviated compromise formula for electoral reform. However most characteristic of all was the fact that this opportunist policy was not condemned by consistent and steadfast supporters of socialism but on the contrary, won their sympathy and approval and was even presented to proletarian women in other countries as a model. . . . There are democratic principles which, for the sake of its own interests, the working clans must not sacrifice: there are slogans which the proletariat cannot change without damaging itself even though the change is made in order to achieve the maximum results at any given moment.[190]

The English delegates, or part of them, had expressed the opinion that it was permissible to support limited and qualified voting rights for women. This was supposed to be a stepping-stone to achieving votes for all women. Zetkin was skeptical about such claims. At the International Socialist Congress in Stuttgart, immediately after the Socialist Women's Congress, Zetkin introduced a resolution on women's right to vote and spoke at length on the issue. She said in course of her speech:

> The bourgeois women do not even stand united and determined behind the principle of the full political equality of the female sex. They are even

more reluctant to fight energetically, as one united force, for universal women's suffrage.[191]

Having then gone on to explain the relationship between the struggle for the suffrage and class struggle, she returned to the proposal for limited votes. She explained it in two related ways, not just as a conspiracy. On one hand, she argued, it meant final achievement of bourgeois equality regardless of sex. On the other hand, she said that granting votes to bourgeois women was seen by bourgeois men as counterbalancing votes to proletarian men.

> This was first demonstrated by the events in Norway. When universal suffrage in respect to local elections could no longer be denied to the attacking proletariat which was fighting under the leadership of Social Democracy this reform was vitiated by the introduction of limited women's suffrage. Bourgeois politicians declared candidly that the limited suffrage for women is designed as a counterweight to the universal suffrage for men. . . .
>
> We regard the limited women's suffrage not so much as the first step towards the emancipation of the female sex, [but] as the final step towards the political emancipation of property. . . . There is not one country in which the administrative and legislative bodies have been elected by limited women's suffrage where the politically emancipated women have fought with all of their strength for the civil rights of their poor sisters and for universal women's suffrage.[192]

But if the proposal for a limited suffrage for women was a bourgeois strategy, which the social democracy had to avoid, no less vehement was the reaction of the German left wing to the demand that tactical reasons should compel women at times from raising their demands. This was the issue in both Austria and Belgium. The Austrian Social Democrats had raised the demand for suffrage without distinction of sex as far back as their Hainfeld Programme of 1888-89. In the wake of the Russian revolution of 1905 the Habsburg regime seemed willing to grant concessions. The socialists decided to launch a major struggle for the suffrage, but in order to make it more palatable to the rulers they decided to drop the demand for votes for women, and persuaded the Austrian Socialist women's movement to do the same. Zetkin moved the following resolution at the International Socialist Congress, in the teeth of opposition by the Austrians:

> The International Congress . . . declares that wherever a struggle is to be waged for the right to vote, it must be conducted only according to Socialist principles, i.e., with the demand for universal suffrage for both women and men.[193]

Richard Evans' comments about the way in which the Germans tended to impose rigid policies on the International, which neither they nor the others were ultimately prepared to observe, is not quite a fair statement. The left wing, whether in Germany or elsewhere, had greater commitment to active internationalism. Moreover, opportunism existed within the SPD too. Thus, in Hamburg, a struggle had developed over a rightwing counter-offensive. The Hamburg Senate had introduced a bill to restrict the local franchise into the Citizen's Assembly in order to forestall any SPD victory. The SPD spokesmen, in opposing the bill, did not raise their demand for women's suffrage. The SPD deputy Emil Fischer clearly stated his willingness to compromise on this point if votes for the men were retained. Experience showed this to be a useless attempt. The bill was passed. Fischer in his speech had referred to SPD modesty in not demanding votes for women. Mocking him without naming, Zetkin at the 1907 Congress made the point that:

> It is not the character and extent of the Socialist suffrage demands which will decide the outcome of the battle, but the power relationship between the exploiting and the exploited classes. It is not our clever modesty and restraint which will assure us victory but the power of the proletariat which stands behind our demands.[194]

So the resolutions were the results of hard-fought battles. Of course, they remained of limited value as long as the left was weak. But the battles were not totally fruitless, nor was the stress on class struggle mere rhetoric. Zetkin did not think of the suffrage as a natural right, but stressed its importance as a means of political education.[195] A socialist program, of course neither began nor ended with the suffrage, even though its importance, in contrast to the timidity of bourgeois feminism on the same question, has been highlighted above. But we need to look at the entire re-conceptualization of the woman worker and her double burden.

In 1891 came the Erfurt Congress, which adopted a more Marxist program, drafted by Kautsky and Bernstein. It demanded unequivocally the "universal, equal and direct suffrage with secret ballot, for all citizens of the Reich over twenty years of age without distinction as to sex."[196] The Erfurt program also demanded the abolition of all laws that discriminated against women in the public and the private spheres, along with free education and materials for the same.[197]

At the 1893 International Workers' Congress the attitude of social democrats towards the protection of women came up. Their debates with liberal bourgeois feminism will be taken up later, but it is worth noting here the view of the reporter, Luise Kautsky, that female labor was the "battering ram for the protection of men," since protection of women restricted the degree of their exploitation and therefore indirectly brought about an improvement for all workers. As Thönnessen points out, this meant that "obeisance had still to be made to the men," but it also marks a clear shift from demands for the restriction or abolition of female labor.[198]

In 1894, the social democrats introduced a bill for women's suffrage in the Reichstag, but it was rejected by the Reichstag majority. This was followed by the Breslau Congress of 1895, where the women proposed a further resolution which was passed on to the Reichstag fraction. It demanded that all clauses discriminating against women should be removed from the draft code of civil laws and that unmarried women and their children should be given equal rights. The party further decided to fight for the extension of protection to workers in domestic industry.[199]

At the Gotha Congress of 1896, an eight-point program was adopted to improve the situation of women. It consisted of the following:

> Extension of protection (crèches, paid maternity leave, reduction of working hours); active and passive voting rights for industrial courts; equal political rights; equal education for both the sexes; equal pay for equal work; abolition of the system of servants; equal status in private law; and freedom of occupation.[200]

It is noteworthy that the demands were so formulated that several of them would have covered the interests of women of other classes as well. This flowed from the position developed by Zetkin and others. As she wrote in 1895:

> In Germany the cause of the bourgeois woman has also become the cause of Social Democracy. The German bourgeoisie enjoys the undisputed honour of being among the most backward and narrow-minded of all bourgeoisie. . . . In Germany, therefore, among other things that do not immediately lie in the class interest of the proletariat, the task of solving the question of female emancipation in the bourgeois sense has also fallen to the working class.[201]

In important respects, the SPD and the proletarian women's movement made gains on the basis of this program. In 1890 the working day for women had been reduced to eleven hours and in 1908 it was further reduced to ten hours. From the 1880s the Sickness Insurance Act had been extended to cover a three-week paid maternity leave—later extended to eight weeks.[202] Moreover, demanding a reduction in the working hours of women was often a tactical move to prise open the door to a general reduction in working hours. In part this reflected an acceptance of the idea of female inferiority, e.g. in formulating the demand in the interests of the "weaker sex." In part it no doubt also reflected the hope of male workers that their wives would thereby get more time to keep the household in better order. But it is also clear from the circumstances that Zetkin hoped that a reduction in working hours would enable proletarian women to take a more active part in socialist party building work. Some of the SPD demands went beyond the limitations indicated above. Thus, the demand for equal rights of unmarried mothers and their children or the demands that hinted at a socialization of housework were potential challenges to the flaws in Marx's argument regarding the notion of a male head of household as a typical worker, and the conceptualization of alienation only at the point of waged work. Two views of this movement should be considered here. Tony Cliff attempts to foist an extremely workerist interpretation on the SPD women's movement. We have already seen that in fact the demands of the SPD included some clearly related to specifically women's issues. On the other side there is the trenchant criticism of Maria Mies, who avers that the protectionist demands of the SPD were conservative, and who therefore supports those feminists who opposed protective legislation and insisted that real women's liberation meant no "special privileges."[203] This debate must be put in its historical and theoretical context. In every country where liberal feminism developed a sizeable part of the feminists held that formal equality was to be the sole aim. Given equal legal and political rights they would then work out their futures as individuals. To them it appeared as though protective legislation was an admission of the inferior status of women.

The Marxists responded to this using two arguments. Writing in *Neue Zeit*, Eduard Bernstein wrote (at a time considerably before his revisionist turn):

> It is wrong to cry "No workers' protection for women, which is not also given to men." That is taken from the bourgeois twaddle about women's rights. It contradicts what we, as socialists know. The woman worker, who is socially in a weaker position has need of more energetic social protection than the man. She especially needs it in cases, such as domestic industry, where her particular social status is the cause of special abuses, of greater suppression. She further needs it in her role as the agent of the coming generation, the one who gives birth. . . . If the prohibition of work for women who have just given birth discriminate against them economically, then there is a simple remedy: society should pay compensation. . . . All these things do not constitute exceptional laws against women; they are merely an acknowledgement of actual differences. . . . To deduce legal distinctions from such differences is bourgeois ideology, and this may explain the confusion of bourgeois notions of women's rights.[204]

Calling this ideology bourgeois was not just a way of heaping abuse on it. For bourgeois women, trying to break out of notions of the gentlewoman protected by convention but therewith forbidden from working publicly, plain legal equality was desirable. The gentlewoman was claiming equality with men of her class. For her, that meant a lot. For the woman worker that meant no more than being equally exploited.

In addition, the equal right of the gentlewoman to go out and work could well come about through an intensification of the exploitation of the domestic servant. The rhetoric of gender equality here masked acute class inequality and exploitation, which often came out openly in some feminist writings. Luise Kautsky brilliantly demonstrated the class angle in an article. She cited an American feminist journal, which was opposing special laws for the protection of women workers. There was a proposal to reduce women's workday. The paper opposed this, saying that this would in fact victimize women by putting them in an uncompetitive position. Replying to this she said:

> I am quite sure that the women workers acclaimed the reduction of the work-day. . . . The pained cries of the propertied women in America that their working sisters might not be ruthlessly exploited comes as a worthy close to the debate in the English lower house.[205]

Thus the SPD demands for protective legislation did not mean the SPD was abandoning demands for political and economic equality for women. Further, we have already noted the specific protective laws. These cannot be simply viewed as the product of an acceptance of patriarchy. Mies asks why they did not demand a change in social and sexual division of labor. But from whom ought they have demanded this—the state? Or the individual male? Demands like setting up childcare centers did imply a change from the concept that it was the individual woman's duty to look after the children. The proletarian women's movement was quite conscious that it wanted a different society, free not only of capitalist exploitation but also of women's inequality. But it argued consistently that this fundamental change could only be achieved as a result of the working class taking power in its hands. In the meanwhile, from the existing state of the ruling classes it was demanding not an intervention within the class, but rights against capital. To reject this demand is to imply that demands should not be made to the state. Nor is it meaningful to say that the demand for maternity leave reinforced bourgeois notions of motherhood. The very idea of a paid leave, rather than leaving the job once one became a mother, was radical, as it pushed forward every women worker's right to work.

However, it should not be thought that the Socialist Women's movement was to achieve sustained progress in a linear way. There were also problems. In 1889 Zetkin believed that economic change was swiftly undermining the institution of the family and she saw this breakdown as a positive development. But by 1896 her position had changed drastically. At the 1896 Party Congress, Zetkin was saying:

> Indeed, it must certainly not be the task of Socialist propaganda among Socialist women to alienate the proletarian women from her duties as

mother and wife. On the contrary, she must be encouraged to carry out these tacks better than ever in the interests of the liberation of the proletariat. . . . Many a mother and many a wife who fills her husband and children with class-consciousness accomplishes just as much as the female comrades that we see at our meetings. (Vivid agreement).[206]

The vivid agreement recorded at this point in the minutes (this was, we should remember again, a speech delivered at the party congress) gives the game away. Deeply influenced by bourgeois-patriarchal society, the socialist men were expecting the prime function of women to be family functions, where they would transmit socialist values to their offspring. Women who actually succeeded in overcoming their double burden and attended socialist programs were put in their place by being told that they were no different from, and did not contribute more than, mothers and wives. Zetkin was to admit in 1896 that her previous views on the family had been one-sidedly negative, and that she had since become more positive in her assessment of the family as an institution.[207]

Programmatic issues included the question of relationship with bourgeois feminists. While it was easier to reject such alliances as long as liberal feminism was timid, the situation changed when more radical currents rose among them. It was not possible to say that feminists avoided democratic demands. Instead, Zetkin now emphasized that revolutionary goals of the working-class women necessitated separation from bourgeois feminism.[208]

But *Gleichheit* regularly reported on liberal feminist activities. When the Berlin radical feminists wanted to set up a commission to examine the conditions of women factory workers, Zetkin refused to serve on the commission, with the argument that connection with the SPD would lessen the efficacy of the commission as an instrument for the influencing of government policy.[209]

On one occasion, Zetkin entered into a direct polemic with Wilhelm Liebknecht and the leading party daily *Vorwärts*. In 1895, Adele Gerhard of the SPD, Minna Cauer, and Lily von Gizycki, all three liberal feminists, drafted a petition for mass signature and eventual submission to the Reichstag asking it to request the Kaiser to lift the Law on Associations. *Vorwärts* called for signing the petition. Zetkin opposed this, pointing out that the SPD had submitted a bill on the subject to the Reichstag, which was more democratic than petitioning the Kaiser. She also emphasized that the content of the petition was so clearly tilted in favor of the bourgeoisie, that no collaboration was possible.[210]

If we look at the role of the liberal feminists, our surprise at Zetkin's intransigence might disappear. Even radical feminists like Regina Ruben, or more famously, Lily Braun, were to hesitate for years before ultimately joining the Social Democrats. But they were atypical, and even in their cases theoretical and practical problems remained. Braun was on the verge of joining the SPD by 1895, but was pulled back by social considerations. Joining the SPD would mean, she told Kautsky, "My social equals will all turn their backs on me and I shall lose my income."[211] Other radicals, like Anita Augspurg, wrote bluntly that the trust placed by SPD women in solidarity with the men of their own class rather than with women of all classes, was misplaced.[212] The SPD of the early twentieth century, despite its annual party congresses, its lively press, was characterized by Augspurg as an absolutist organization. This reflected an extreme individualism and opposition to any disciplined and collective work. Quite obviously, this left not only the average woman worker, but also left-wing militants like Zetkin cold.

So what Zetkin was doing can be visualized as an extension of Marx's approach. Marx in the First International was very wary of the League of Peace and Freedom, in which John Stuart Mill played a prominent role. Marx was willing to cooperate with such a group, but only when the organizational and political independence of the proletariat was maintained. Zetkin was doing the same, but with women workers.

NOTES

1. F. Engels, "Karl Marx's Funeral," in *MECW* 24, p. 468.
2. *MESW* 1, p. 504.
3. *MECW* 3, pp. 184–86.
4. Ibid., 6, p. 504.
5. Ibid., p. 509.
6. The most systematic criticism of the Marxian revolutionary project in the name of a linking of socialism with democracy and ethics has come from Eduard Bernstein. In his opinion, social development made possible the democratization of politics and consequently the socialist transformation by peaceful parliamentary and legal action. In this situation, the idea of revolution was nothing but a relapse into Blanquism, subjective politics, or politics of will. For him, revolutionary violence raised the ethical question of whether in modern, civilized times, violence could be at all legitimized. E. Bernstein, *Evolutionary Socialism;* S. Moore, *Three Tactics: The Background in Marx,* accepts a similar argument, but tries to legitimize minority revolutionism by associating Marx with it.
7. *MECW* 6, p. 5–7, 14.
8. Quoted in M. Beer, *A History of British Socialism,* vol. 2, London, 1920, p. 135.
9. *MECW* 6, p. 102.
10. F. Engels, "The Constitutional Question in Germany," in ibid., pp. 75–91, "The Communists and Karl Heinzen," pp. 290–306; K. Marx, "Moralising Criticism and Critical Morality," in ibid., pp. 312–40.
11. Ibid., p. 294.
12. Ibid., p. 295.

13. Ibid., p. 299. This indicates that contrary to the claim of Hunt, Engels did not envisage a period of bourgeois oligarchy. In fact, in order to defend his position, Hunt is compelled to gloss over the quite evident difference between Marx and Engels in the autumn of 1847 over the assessment of the bourgeoisie, the petty bourgeoisie and the peasantry. Hunt combines a small fragment from the article by Engels, discussed above, with two articles of Marx that had a much more stageist perspective, in order to produce a three-stage sequence which cannot be found in any programmatic article by Marx or Engels. See Hunt, *The Political Ideas of Marx and Engels*, vol. I, pp. 181–82.

14. *MECW 6*, pp. 323–33, see also 222.

15. M. Löwy, *The Politics of Combined and Uneven Development*, p. 7.

16. *MECW 6*, p. 494, see also p. 498.

17. Ibid., p. 495.

18. Ibid., pp. 502–3.

19. Ibid., p. 519.

20. Another alternative quite difficult to accept is to conclude that Marx and Engels did not mean what they said in those world-famous lines. Such is the position taken by Richard N. Hunt, *The Political Ideas of Marx and Engels*, vol. I, pp. 176–91. According to Hunt, Marx's strategy aimed at the accomplishment of a democratic bourgeois revolution, while the artisans in the Communist League, seeing the collapse of their class, wanted an immediate communist revolution. The passage quoted above reconciled the two positions formally, but at the cost of analytical consistency. Hunt accordingly suggests that the real position of Marx and Engels is best understood by discarding the *Manifesto* and looking at their signed articles and letters written up to the time Marx actually wrote the *Manifesto*. The same writings, analyzed in the preceding pages, however, do not bear out the position adopted by Hunt.

21. M. Löwy, *The Politics of Combined and Uneven Development*, p. 11.

22. *MECW 38*, p. 82.

23. *Bund Dokumente*, pp. 230–31 and W. Weitling, *The Poor Sinners' Gospel*, London, n. d. p. 186.

24. *Bund Dokumente*, pp. 220–21.

25. *MECW 38*, p. 61. The reference to "tailors' communism" was a double pun, as Weitling and a number of other artisans were tailors. Moreover the prehistory of communism includes Jean of Leyden, a tailor who became the dictator of the Munster uprising in the 16th century. The phrase "tailors' communism, makes it clear that Engels was opposed to it because of its authoritarian nature, see also C. Wittke, *The Utopian Communist: A Biography Of Wilhelm Weitling*, Baton Rouge, 1950, pp. 120, 250, 259–74. The green-tinted Proudhon means the Grün-inspired Proudhon, showing that Engels was linking Proudhon with the True Socialists.

26. D. Ryazanov, ed., *The Communist Manifesto*, pp. 291–94.

27. *MECW 6*, pp. 101–2.

28. Despite being aware of Schapper's article, R. N. Hunt, *The Political Ideas of Karl Marx*, vol. 1, pp. 185–86, peculiarly insists that Schapper was "more insistent"

for communism while Marx wanted a protracted period of maturation. Hunt relates this to his general theory of a basic split in the League between impatient artisans and deterministic intellectuals. The latter supposedly wanted only a bourgeois revolution in Germany. In fact, the stress on the need for a proletarian revolution in Germany came entirely from Marx and Engels. Before them, German communism had had only two options: a communist revolution by a putsch involving whoever was willing to go along, or a protracted period of organization and educational propaganda.

29. *MESC*, p. 371.
30. *MECW* 6, pp. 507–8.
31. Ibid., pp. 509–10.
32. *Engels–Lafargue Correspondence,* vol. 2, p. 340.
33. Ibid., pp. 131, 165.
34. *Engels–Lafargue Correspondence,* vol. 2, p. 238.
35. *MECW* 10, p. 281.
36. Ibid., p. 286.
37. Since this was a party document, Hunt believes that it should not be taken as representing the personal view of Marx and Engels. Hunt, *The Political Ideas of Karl Marx*, vol. I, pp. 235–48. Nicolaievsky also suggests that it was a compromise document only "drafted" by Marx and Engels. This is an untenable theory as it was Engels who republished the document in 1885, acknowledging authorship and saying that the line was still applicable. *MECW* 26, pp. 326–27, Nicolaievsky; "Who is distorting History?" p. 220; F. N. Nicolaievsky's argument is based on one word, "redigier." Since its primary meaning is edited he claims that the document was a compromise, edited by Marx and Engels. Draper's long refutation traces the etymology of "redigieren" and shows that in nineteenth century usage it could also mean "to write." Draper, *KMTR* 2, pp. 611–12. Equally important is the fact that all their lives Marx and Engels emphasized that the line of the document was their line. The most significant case was the split of the Communist League when Marx accused the Willich–Schapper minority of having abandoned the terrain of the March Address and of the *Manifesto. MECW* 10, p. 626. In the same meeting he said that the Address was approved unanimously. See also *MEW*, Band 7, p. 563, *MECW* 38, pp. 384, 389–90, 392–93: and K. Marx, *The Knight of the Noble Consciousness,* in *MECW,* 12, Moscow, 1979, pp. 497–98.
38. F. Engels, "The French Working Class and the Presidential elections," in *MECW* 8, Moscow, 1977, pp. 123–27.
39. A. B. Spitzer, *The Revolutionary Theories of Louis Auguste Blanqui,* New York, 1957, p. 174.
40. See Chapter 2 for the formation and the activities of Workers' Society.
41. *MECW* 38, pp. 539–40.
42. A. Gilbert, *Marx's Politics,* p. 192.
43. *MECW* 7, pp. 3–4.
44. On this see, O. J. Hammen, *The Red '48ers,* pp. 216–17, and E. P. Kandel, "Iskazhenie istorii bor by Marksa i Engelsa" pp. 124–25.
45. Following an economic determinist interpretation of Marx, S. Avineri equates all insurrections consciously prepared with putschism. According

to him the revolution will take care of itself when conditions ripen. S. Avineri, *The Social and Political Thought of Karl Marx*, p. 194. This is a failure to understand the distinction that Marx was making between a putsch organized by a minority and a people's insurrection under proletarian hegemony which would required both the political leadership of communists and democratic forms of organization, embracing the majority.

46. G. Becker, *"Karl Marx und Friedrich Engels in Koln, 1848–1849,"* pp. 122–25, contrary to Lichtheim, who sees Marx as a Jacobin in 1848. It should be noted that Marx's reference to the French Revolution was due to its hold on the popular mind. When he felt that the committee could not function as a revolutionary agency, he got it dissolved. G. Lichtheim, *Marxism: An Historical and Critical Study*, pp. 126–27, 129.

47. F. Engels, "The Assembly at Frankfurt," and K. Marx, "The Democratic Party," in *MECW* 7, pp. 16, 27–29. For a contrary view, see Nicolaievsky and Maenchen-Helfen, *Karl Marx*, pp. 175–78, 193, and Hunt, *The Political Ideas of Marx and Engels*, vol. I, pp. 173–96. The historian Hammen has shown the constant stream of criticism that Marx and Engels directed against the Democrats, O. J. Hammen, *The Red 48ers*, pp. 240–43.

48. *MECW* 7, pp. 124, 128, 130, 133, 138–40, 142–43.

49. K. Marx, "The June Revolution," in ibid., p. 149.

50. For Bonapartism, see H. Draper, *KMTR* 1, for a historical survey of the roads of bourgeois power, see A. Callinicos, "Bourgeois Revolutions and Historical Materialism," *International Socialism*, 43, London, June, 1989, pp. 113–71.

51. F. Engels, "The Uprising in Frankfurt," in *MECW* 7, p. 444.

52. K. Marx, "The Bourgeoisie and Counter-Revolution," in *MECW* 8, Moscow, 1977, pp. 158, 161, 163, 165–167, 178. Nicolaievsky and Maenchen-Helfen, *Karl Marx*, p. 193, claim, "social republicanism . . . meant capitalism still but capitalism in a state in which workers, petty-bourgeoisie and peasants had maximum concessions." A Gilbert, *Marx's Politics*, p. 184 disagrees with Nicolaievsky but claims that such a revolution could only give rise to a very unstable regime and moreover that it could not immediately break the social power of the bourgeoisie. Nicolaievsky's position is obviously wrong because a *social republican* revolution meant a revolution highlighting the social demands of the bloc of Democratic classes, including the proletariat. As for Gilbert's objection it is based on mistaken identification between the establishment of the rule of the working class and the building of socialist society. The *Manifesto* had already mentioned that the proletariat would use its political supremacy to wrest by degrees all capital from the bourgeoisie. *MECW* 6, p. 504. This idea of using political power to expropriate the bourgeoisie step by step thus became a part of permanent revolution.

53. *MECW* 10, pp. 277–80.

54. Ibid., pp. 282–86. Avineri completely misunderstands this strategy and claims that because Marx "offers no directives for an emeute, a putsch, or a coup," therefore the Address "is in no way a blue print for a proletarian revolution." Avineri, *The Social and Political Thought of Karl Marx*, pp. 196–97.

This is to equate proletarian revolution with Blanquism or putschism.

55. *MECW* 10, pp. 127.

56. S. Bernstein, *Auguste Blanqui, and the Art of Insurrection,* London 1971, pp. 167–71 shows that what was planned was a simple demonstration. Draper, *KMTR* 3, pp. 181–83, quotes Louis Blanc to show how this pseudo conspiracy was used to recall the army. This quotation from Marx has been subject to gross misintepretations. S. Moore, *Three Tactics,* p. 29, offers a standard example in this direction. He writes that Marx called the communism of Blanqui the declaration of the permanence of the revolution. As noted above, Marx wrote that the bourgeoisie had "invented" the name of Blanqui. Those who wish to associate Marx with Blanqui like Moore tend to omit these words. See also D. W. Lovell, *From Marx to Lenin,* pp. 39–42. He finds it curious that Marx placed the class dictatorship of the proletariat close to the name of Blanqui. Lovell believes it a mystery, but puts forward conjectures nonetheless suggesting that some sort of elitism was intended. Thus a passage which clearly expressed that the proletariat was moving away from doctrinaires and elitists to an independent class struggle is turned into its opposite.

57. *MECW* 10, p. 57, See also *MESW* 1, pp. 189–91 for F. Engels, "Introduction," to *The Class Struggles in France,* where he talked about the need for a long struggle.

58. See F. Engels, "Revolution and Counter-Revolution in Germany" in *MECW* 11, pp. 7–21, and *MECW* 20, pp. 67–79. H. J. Laski, "Introduction" to *Communist Manifesto,* pp. 58–60, quotes two fragments from the first of the two works mentioned there in order to suggest that the nostalgia of the exiled blurred their realism when they turned to Germany. A careful reading however suggests that, on the one hand, they recognized the existence of real contradictions between the semi-feudal monarchy and the bourgeoisie, and admitted that whenever any section of the bourgeoisie or petty bourgeoisie really fought against the monarchy, the working class should neither remain neutral nor give tacit support to the monarchy, but fight along with the bourgeoisie. On the other hand, they also recognized that because of the conflict between the bourgeoisie and the proletariat, the former would always draw back, and that therefore the strategic line would remain class independence, proletarian hegemony, and the transformation of the democratic revolution into a clearly proletarian revolution.

59. Engels to Filippo Turati, Marxist Internet Archive, accessed on October 8, 2006, http://www.marxists.org/archive/marx/works/1894/letters/94_01_26 .htm.

60. Ibid.

61. M. Löwy, *The Politics of Combined and Uneven Development,* pp. 27–28. That is possibly why Blackburn on the one hand characterizes the scenario depicted in the March Address as unrealistic, and yet says that it provided a remarkable anticipation of certain elements.

62. Both in his polemic with the populist Mikhailovsky, and in the draft of his letter to Vera Zasulich, Marx refused to make Western Europe a necessary model for Russia. He felt that Russian society was not so much a pre-

capitalist society as it was a non-capitalist one enmeshed in ties with the capitalist West. He therefore felt that by appropriating the positive results of capitalism and basing herself on the rural communes, Russia could avoid passing through capitalism. He also tied this to the extension of the revolution in Europe. K. Marx, "Letter to *Otechastvennye Zapiski*," and "Letter to Vera Zasulich in *MECW* 24, pp. 200–201, 346–50, 362, 370–71, 426. After Marx's death Engels gradually become skeptical about the potentials of the *obshchina* and stressed that capitalist development had already begun. *MESC*, pp. 462–65. In this view this made the old perspective outmoded.

63. See the discussion in the third chapter of the present book.
64. G. D. H. Cole, *A History of Socialist Thought*, vol. 2, London, 1955, p. 166. See also H. Draper, *KMTR* 3, p. 275.
65. *MECW* 22, p 331.
66. A. Fried, and R. Sanders, ed., *Socialist Thought, A Documentary History*, New York, 1964, p. 196.
67. S. Bernstein, *Auguste Blanqui*, pp. 347–49.
68. E. Bernstein, *Evolutionary Socialism*, p. 155.
69. Ibid., pp. 143–44, 216–19.
70. Ibid., pp. xii–xiii. Bernstein's argument was two-fold. He believed that force was justified in a bourgeois revolution but not in a proletarian revolution. He also believed that Marx and Engels were Jacobin Blanquist politicians at least until the Paris commune. Similar arguments have been advanced by G. Lichtheim, *Marxism: An Historical and Critical Study*, pp. 151–54 and passim. N. Levine, *The Tragic Deception: Marx Contra Engels*, Oxford, 1975, pp. v and 228 claims that Engels was the first revisionist, while L. Colletti's article "Bernstein and the Marxism of the Second International," in *From Rousseau to Lenin*, London, 1972, pp. 45–48, 105, makes a similar suggestion that the Introduction set the foundation of Bernsteinian revisionism. R. N. Hunt, on the other hand, claims that Marx and Engels throughout most of their lives advocated violent but swift and democratic revolutions against an authoritarian government. But once democracy was established, they stood for peaceful, legal and parliamentary struggles. See in particular R. N. Hunt, *The Political Ideas of Karl Marx*, vol. II, London and Basingstoke, 1981, pp. 325–62. This chapter is clearly designed to rule out general strikes, guerilla warfare or protracted civil or international wars from a Marxist strategy of revolution. According to him, like the reformists, Marx and Engels also desired a legal and peaceful changeover, but differed in assuming conservative resistance to be more likely. Moreover, he equates winning a parliamentary majority with the legal revolution and suggests that until that time Marx and Engels wanted to remain in pure opposition. Finally, in his view, they were actually liberal democrats. And it was a kind of "moral constipation" that prevented them from declaring their basically moral stand, pp. 356–70. See also, S. Hook, "Myth and Fact in the Marxist theory of Revolution and Violence," *Journal of the History of Ideas*, vol. 34, no. 2, pp. 271–80.
71. *MECW* 6, pp. 349–50.
72. Ibid., p. 501.
73. Ibid., p. 519.

74. As had been done by E. Bernstein who highlighted universal franchise as "the alternative to a violent revolution," *Evolutionary Socialism*, p. 145.
75. *MECW* 10, pp. 69, 79.
76. Ibid., pp. 97, 98.
77. Ibid., p. 70.
78. Ibid., p. 626.
79. K. Marx, *The Chartists*, in ibid., 11, p. 335.
80. Ibid., 20, p. 76.
81. *MECW* 42, p. 150.
82. Ibid., pp. 215, 253, 314.
83. Ibid., p. 105.
84. Ibid., p. 104.
85. *MECW* 22, p. 634. Although the term "universal suffrage" was used, until 1891 the socialist movement usually meant by this "adult male suffrage."
86. *MECW* 24, p. 519.
87. Ibid., pp. 519–20.
88. K. Marx and F. Engels, "Preface to the 1872 German edition of the Manifesto of the Communist Party," *MECW*, 23, p. 175, Bernstein *Evolutionary Socialism*, xii, quoted this to assert that this was Marx's approval for moving away from the strategy of one class capturing state power and depriving others of it.
89. Thus E. J. Hobsbawm, "Marx, Engels and Politics," in E. Hobsbawm, ed., *The History of Marxism*, p. 243, refers to it as a contrast to hopes for violent and armed confrontations. D. W. Lovell, *From Marx to Lenin*, p. 55, insists that Marx was emphasizing the possibility of using suffrage to win power and ensure a peaceful transition to socialism. G. Litchtheim, *Marxism: An Historical and Critical Study*, p. 122, interprets the speech in the same way. Finally R. N. Hunt, *The Political Ideas of Karl Marx*, vol. 2, has a long discussion on this speech. Hunt states correctly that Marx mentioned the USA, Britain and possibly Holland as the cases where peaceful revolution was possible. According to him, France, despite having universal suffrage after the Paris commune and the ongoing repression, was not suitable for a peaceful transition, p. 331. In England, he claims, the Reform Act of 1867 made the parliamentary path possible, pp. 325–29. He contends that Marx never advocated or supported violence in democratic countries, p. 334, lumping together class violence with individual terrorism.
90. K. Marx, "On the Hague Congress," *MECW* 23, p. 254.
91. Ibid., p. 255.
92. "The Proletarian Revolution and the Renegade Kautsky," an article summarizing his arguments in the book of the same title, in *LCW* 28, Moscow, 1981, p. 108.
93. E. M. Wood, *The Retreat From Class*, p. 163.
94. A. L. Morton and G. Tate, The *British Labour Movement*, London, 1979, pp. 121–57; K. R. Mackenzie, *The English Parliament*, Harmondsworth, 1950, pp. 185–87; A. Hunt, "Marx—The Missing Dimension: The Rise of Representative Democracy," pp. 101–8, puts forward the claim that Marx and Engels failed to pay adequate attention to the rise of representative

democracy, and that consequently there is no Marxist theory of political democracy. Hunt therefore simply equates the creation of an electorate amounting to less than a fifth of the population with representative democracy. As mentioned above, for Marx, universal suffrage was the crucial starting point for democracy.

95. F. Engels, "On the Political Action of the Working Class," in *MECW* 22, pp. 415–16.

96. "Record of Marx's speech on the Political Action of the Working Class," in ibid., p. 618.

97. K. Marx, Interview with *The World* correspondent, ibid., pp. 602, 606.

98. K. Marx, interview with *The Chicago Tribune* correspondent, in ibid., 24, p. 577.

99. F. Engels, *The Origin of the Family, Private Property and the State*, in ibid., 26, pp. 271–72.

100. *MESC*, pp. 381–82.

101. Ibid., p. 409.

102. *Engels–Lafargue Correspondence*, vol. 3, p. 393.

103. R. Black, *Fascism in Germany*, vol. I, London, 1975, p. 151.

104. L. Trotsky, *Portraits: Personal and Political*, New York, 1977, p. 132.

105. *Engels–Lafargue Correspondence*, vol. 3, p. 400.

106. F. Engels, "A Critique of the Draft Social-Democratic programme of 1891," in *MESW*: 3, Moscow, 1983, pp. 434–35.

107. Ibid., 2, pp. 187–88.

108. Ibid., 3, p. 436.

109. Bebel to Engels, 11, March 1895, In W. Blumenberg, ed., *August Bebels Briefwechsel mit, Friedrich Engels*, Berlin, 1965, p. 795, see also, R. Luxemburg, *Selected Political Writings*, D. Howard, ed., New York, and London, 1971, pp. 120, 383–84, and W. O. Henderson *The life of Friedrich Engels*, vol. 2, p. 667.

110. F. Engels, "Letter to Kautsky," *MESC*, p. 486.

111. *Engels–Lafargue Correspondence*, vol., 3, p. 373.

112. As does D. W. Lovell, *From Marx to Lenin*, p. 88.

113. See H. J. Laski, "Introduction" to *Communist Manifesto*, p. 79.

114. *MESW* 1, pp. 189–90.

115. Ibid., pp. 190–92.

116. E. J. Hobsbawm, "Marx, Engels, and Politics," p. 242.

117. *MESW* 1, p. 195.

118. Ibid., pp. 195–96.

119. Ibid., p. 196.

120. E. P. Thompson, *The Poverty of Theory and Other Essays*, London, 1979, p. 261.

121. L. Colletti, *From Rousseau to Lenin*, London, 1972, pp. 45–51, 105, where he even went to the extent of showing Engels contrasting evolution to revolution, or gradualism to Blanquism. For a contrary view, see P. Kellog, "Engels and the Roots of 'Revisionism'. A Re-evaluation," *Science and Society*, vol. 55, no. 2, Summer 1991, pp. 161–65.

122. *MESW* 1, pp. 201, 192–93.

123. Ibid., p. 201, D. W. Lovell, *From Marx to Lenin*, p. 84, claims that Engels implies that "there is no legal obstacle to the proletariat's assumption of

power through universal suffrage"—the word "implies" shows that Lovell cannot find textual support for his claim. Moreover, Lovell asserts that Engels had turned to liberal democracy, without establishing what this liberal democracy amounted to given liberalism's persistent hostility to democracy, pp. 84–85. For a detailed discussion on the relations between democracy and liberalism, see J. Dunn, *Western Political Theory in the Face of the Future*, Cambridge, 1979, passim.

124. D. Mclellan, *Marxism after Marx*, New York, 1979, p. 17; Hobsbawm, *The History of Marxism*, p. 243.
125. *MESW* 1, p. 199.
126. For A. Gramsci's military strategy see, P. Anderson, "The Antinomies of Antonio Gramsci," *New Left Review*, 100, 1976–77, pp. 5–78.
127. *MESW* 1, pp. 199, 202–3.
128. Ibid., p. 196.
129. Cited in R. N. Hunt, *The Political Ideas of Marx and Engels*, vol. II, p. 350.
130. *MEW* Band 39, Berlin, 1973, pp. 424–26.
131. A. Hunt, "Marx—the Missing Dimension: The Rise of Representative Democracy," pp. 96–101, argues that though Engels thought that in raising the question of elections he was only proposing a change of tactics, he was actually proposing a change of strategy. Participation in electoral struggles, Hunt argues, creates a completely different strategy. However, his argument here, is entirely based on Colletti, *From Rousseau to Lenin*, p. 49. Engels' writings clearly demonstrate that he wanted to use the franchise as an instrument to mobilize the workers, but that he never suffered from the illusion that state power could be transferred from the bourgeoisie to the proletariat through parliamentary decrees. In "Socialism in Germany" an article, written in 1892, Engels expressed the hope that the SPD would get a majority which would enable the SPD to change society peacefully. He wrote: "Time and time again the middle classes have urged us to confine ourselves to propaganda to keep within the law, and to abstain under any circumstances from employing revolutionary means further our cause. . . . But we cannot accept such advice from the middle class." This article is appended to W. O. Henderson, *The Life of Frederick Engels*, vol. II. The quoted passage appears in p. 800.
132. *Engels–Lafargue Correspondence*, vol. II, p. 376. However, on one occasion at least, Engels did envisage that the general strike could also lead to an insurrection. See his letter to Karl Kautsky, November 3, 1893, *MEW* Band 39, p. 16.
133. *MECW* 6, p. 350.
134. Ibid., 3, p. 512.
135. Ibid., p. 39.
136. This collection is referred by R. N. Hunt, *The Political Ideas of Marx and Engels*, vol. I, p. 34.
137. *MECW* 5, p. 333.
138. Lorenz von Stein, author of an influential work on socialism, was confident that democracy, as demanded by the workers of France in 1848, meant a "social dictatorship," in which the workers "had to make the attempt to

usurp the power of the state as a social class in order to attain its social goals," L. Von Stein, *The History of the Social Movement in France, 1789–1850*, Totowa, NJ, 1964, pp. 400, 398, Similarly, E. M. Wood, *Peasant-Citizen and Slave: The Foundations of Athenian Democracy*, London, 1989, p. 27, has shown how the intellectuals of 19th century viewed democracy. She cites the example of Jacob Burckhardt, who claimed that "the fatal flaw" in Athenian democracy was that working people were citizens.

139. *MECW* 7, p. 16.
140. O. J. Hammen, *The Red 48ers*, pp. 218–19.
141. *MECW* 7, p. 116.
142. F. Engels, "The Berlin Debate on the Revolution" in ibid., pp. 73–74.
143. Quoted in Hammen, p. 250.
144. *MECW* 7, pp. 77, K. Marx, "Legal Proceedings against the *Neue Rheinische Zeitung*," and "The Prussian Press Bill," 209–10; 251, 252.
145. K. Marx, "The Financial State of France," in ibid., 15, Moscow, 1986, p. 499.
146. Ibid.
147. Ibid., 7, pp. 288, 289.
148. Ibid., pp. 260, 256–57.
149. Ibid., p. 232.
150. Ibid., p. 49.
151. Ibid., pp. 238–39, 437.
152. Ibid., 10, pp. 283–84.
153. Ibid., 22, p. 331.
154. K. Marx, "The Constitution of the French Republic Adopted November 4, 1848," in ibid. 10, p. 568.
155. Ibid., p. 570–71.
156. Ibid., p. 578–79.
157. Ibid., p. 569.
158. K. Marx, "Arrest of Delescluze," in ibid. 12, p. 421.
159. K. Marx, "Affairs in Prussia," in ibid. 16, Moscow, 1980, p. 77.
160. K. Marx, "Trouble in Germany," in ibid., p. 541.
161. H. Draper, *KMTR* 1, p. 282, see for a contrary view, A. Hunt, "Marx — the Missing Dimension: The Rise of Representative Democracy," pp. 106–7, surprisingly Hunt ascribes all the theoretical and political problems of the various communist parties of the 20th century to deficiencies in the writings of Marx and Engels instead of looking at the concrete historical situation in which each position is developed.
162. *MECW* 24, p. 70.
163. Ibid., pp. 70–71, 95–96.
164. Ibid., p. 97.
165. Ibid., 7, p. 4; vol. 44, p. 16; *MESW* 3, p. 437.
166. Ibid., 41, pp. 561–62.
167. Ibid., 20, p. 77.
168. Ibid., 3, pp. 161–64.
169. Ibid., 6, p. 499.
170. D. Rueschmeyer, E. H. Stephens and J. D. Stephens, *Capitalist Development*

and Democracy, Chicago, 1992, argue this case of working class centrality for the growth of democracy convincingly. My arguments in this chapter parallel, to some extent, August Nimtz, "Marx and Engels–The Unsung Heroes of the Democratic Breakthrough," *Science and Society*, Summer 1999, vol. 63, no. 2, pp. 203–31.

171. See, for example, E. Laclau and C. Mouffe, *Hegemony and Social Strategy*, London, 1995.

172. On this, see the present author's "German Social Democracy and Women's Liberation," in A. Chanda, M. Sarkar and K. Chattopadhyay, eds., *Women in History*.

173. *MECW* 6, p. 487.

174. Ibid., p. 501.

175. Ibid., pp. 501–2.

176. On this, see Whitney Walton, "Writing the 1848 Revolution: Politics, Gender, and Feminism in the Works of French Women of Letters," *French Historical Studies* 18, Fall 1994, pp. 1001–24. See also Jonathan Sperber, *The European Revolutions, 1848–1851*, Cambridge, revised ed., 2005, especially p. 185f.

177. See J. Sperber, *The European Revolutions, 1848–1851*, pp. 186–87. O. J. Hammen, *The Red '48ers*, simply says there were two to three thousand people present, without specifying women.

178. Quoted in W. Thönnessen, *The Emancipation of Women: The Rise and Decline of the Women's Movement in German Social Democracy, 1863–1933*, London, 1976, p. 15.

179. *Der Verbote*, Geneva, 1866, quoted in Thönnessen, *The Emancipation of Women*, pp. 22–23.

180. Thönnessen, *The Emancipation of Women*, pp. 22–23.

181. Karl Marx and Jules Guesde 1880, *The Programme of the Parti Ouvrier*, Marxist Internet Archive, accessed on May 8, 2006, http://www.marxists .org/archive/marx/works/1880/05/parti-ouvrier.htm.

182. I am aware that many of the arguments of Engels are subject to debate. But in making this point, Engels went beyond Marx, for example, in recognizing that not only were women becoming proletarians, but that female-headed proletarian households existed in sufficient numbers to knock out all the claims made to bolster patriarchy. See F. Engels, *The Origin of Family, Private Property and the State*, in *MESW* 3, p. 245.

183. A. Bebel, *Woman in the Past, Present and Future*, trans. H. B. Adam Walters, London, 1988, pp. 58–59.

184. For Eleanor's life, see Yvonne Kapp, *Eleanor Marx*, 2 vols, New York, 1972, 1976; and Chushichi Tsuzuki, *The Life of Eleanor Marx (1855–1898): A Socialist Tragedy*, Oxford, 1967.

185. Eleanor Marx-Aveling and Edward Aveling, *The Woman Question*, p. 19.

186. Ibid., p. 21.

187. Ibid., p. 24

188. Mies, *Feminism*, 151. Mies actually says the same thing in 150, but without naming Zetkin. A page later, she is evidently further emboldened, and can directly take on Zetkin.

189. Zetkin, *Selected Writings*, pp. 77–78.
190. A. Kollontai, *Selected Articles and Speeches*, Moscow, 1984, p. 39.
191. Zetkin, *Selected Writings*, pp. 100–101.
192. Ibid., pp. 104–5.
193. Ibid., p. 98.
194. For Fischer see Evans, *Comrades and Sisters*, 85. For Zetkin see Zetkin, *Selected Writings*, pp. 105–6.
195. This set Zetkin off from Bebel. This is what she said at Stuttgart: "We Socialists do not demand women's suffrage as a natural right with which women are born. We demand it as a social right which is anchored in the revolutionized economic activity and in the revolutionized social state and personal consciousness of women." Zetkin, *Selected Writings*, pp. 99–100. See further the discussion below on the relationship between the socialist proletarian women's movement and the bourgeois liberal or radical feminists.
196. *Protokoll des Parteitages der Sozialdemokratischen Partei Deutschlands*, Erfurt, 1891, p. 5.
197. Ibid.
198. Thönnessen, *The Emancipation of Women*, p. 51.
199. Ibid., pp. 52–53.
200. Ibid., p. 54.
201. R. J. Evans, *Comrades and Sisters*, p. 28.
202. Mies, *Feminism*, p. 148.
203. Ibid., pp. 134–35.
204. Thönnessen, *The Emancipation of Women*, pp. 47–48.
205. Luise Kautsky, "The Women's rightsers and Reduction of the Working-Day for Women" in H. Draper and A. G. Lipow, "Marxist women versus Bourgeois Feminism," R. Miliband & J. Saville, eds., *Socialist Register* (1976), p. 218.
206. Zetkin, *Selected Writings*, pp. 81–82.
207. *Die Gleichheit*, vol. VI, no. 25 (December 9, 1896) and no. 26 (December 29, 1896), pp. 197–200, 203–7.
208. *Die Gleichheit*, vol. 14, no. 13, June 15, 1904, p. 102.
209. Evans, *Comrades and Sisters*, p. 52.
210. Zetkin, *Selected Writings*, 68. For Zetkin's article with the footnotes by (presumably) Wilhelm Liebknecht, and her reply, once again footnote laden, see ibid., pp. 60–71.
211. Lily Braun to Karl Kautsky, May 16, 1895, I. I. S. H., Amsterdam, Nachlass Kautsky, D VI 584. Braun was by marriage Lily von Gizycki, married to Georg von Gizycki, a reformist aristocrat. But by 1896 this marriage had broken up, and she was married to the Social Democrat Heinrich Braun.
212. Cf. Evans, *Comrades and Sisters*, p. 48.

5

DEMOCRACY IN THE PROLETARIAN DICTATURE

I
THE THEORY OF THE DICTATORSHIP OF THE PROLETARIAT

The strategy of revolution calling for a revolutionary and almost certainly violent seizure of power involved a further consideration of the reorganization of the state. The concept of the dictatorship of the proletariat has occupied for a century a central position in discussions of Marx's theory of politics. Scholars do not agree on the implications of this concept.[1] The basic questions are: what did Marx and Engels, as distinct from the varied Marxists of the later generations, mean by the term? What is the relationship between the dictatorship of the proletariat and the transition to communism? How does this idea harmonize with the idea of proletarian democracy? If the dictatorship of the proletariat was a totalitarian state form, then Marxism would have been a typical communist Utopia, which begins by calling for a greater equality and ends with a system imposed from above by the enlightened few. So a thorough examination of the concept of the dictatorship of the proletariat is vital for a comprehensive assessment of the function of democracy in Marx's long-term political goal.

The first concept of revolutionary dictatorship that appeared in the writings of Marx and Engels was that of a "Dictatorship of the Democracy." The writings of Marx and Engels during the revolution of 1848 show that they considered that the workers, the petty bourgeoisie and the peasants as the three classes that needed democracy. The democratic movement was formed by these three classes, and in contemporary parlance they were often called the democratic classes and the movement designated

"The Democracy." Throughout 1848–49, Marx and Engels put forward a concept best classified by the term "Dictatorship of the Democracy." They proposed in 1848 that the democratic classes and their parties should take power, thereby ending the dual power situation prevailing since the March Revolution in Germany. In order to decisively crush the old order and to establish democracy, an energetic use of force would be necessary. Since the rule of the popular masses was continuously attacked by both the monarchists and the liberals, force was an indispensable element of the rule. At the same time, since this was a bloc of three classes, the attainment of proletarian hegemony within it could only be the result of a long-term process whereby the workers democratically won the support of the non-proletarian toiling masses within the bloc. Consequently, workers' rule in the aftermath of the democratic revolution would have to be democratic. Dictatorship in this context did not refer to a form of government, but to the use of force to dictate terms to the vanquished exploiters in an era of the rule of the exploited.

In the first issue of the *NRZ*, Engels prescribed two basic tasks for the National Assembly, viz., immediate and public proclamation of the sovereignty of the German people and the basing of the new German Constitution on this popular sovereignty. For this:

> During its whole session, it should take the necessary measures to thwart all the attempts of the reaction, to maintain the revolutionary ground on which it stands, to safeguard the achievement of the revolution, popular sovereignty, from all attacks.[2]

Ludolf von Camphausen, the liberal Prime Minister of Prussia, responded to such criticisms, emanating from sections of the left, by saying that "The Government did not act in a dictatorial way; it could not and *would not* act in such a way."[3] When Camphausen said that he refused to exercise a dictatorship, what he, no less than Engels (in the *NRZ* article cited above) had in mind was to push through, ignoring the views of the monarchy, the change from an indirect system of voting then in existence to a direct voting system, overriding the semi-feudal electoral law. In other words, Camphausen meant by dictatorship the adoption of energetic measures to establish democracy. Moreover, Camphausen committed the government to an agreement with the Crown over a constitution. So "dictatorship" meant not the arbitrary rule of the monarchy, but the forcible destruction of autocratic laws and the establishment of a democratic constitution. Thus, for conservative liberals, the rule of the people itself (i.e., democracy) signified dictatorship. In an article in the *NRZ*, Marx, while criticizing Camphausen, pointed out that in terms of the old (feudal) law, even the latter's position as a responsible Prime Minister was illegal.[4] What Marx was arguing was that even the establishment of a Liberal cabinet had not come about because of constitutional agitations but because of the March Revolution, which breached feudal legality. The real reason for Liberal objection to the establishment of democracy was not that it was to come through dictatorship, but rather, that this dictatorship would give power to the exploited people. In a subsequent article Marx wrote that the National Assembly:

> only needed everywhere to counter dictatorially the reactionary encroachments by obsolete Government in order to win over public opinion, a power against which all bayonets and rifle butts would be ineffective.[5]

The passage quoted shows Marx desiring that the National Assembly should take up in an authoritative way the opposition to the reactionaries. Significantly, the aim of the dictatorship was to win over public opinion, not just the "bayonets" and "rifle butts" which were set in opposition to it.

Engels, too, in an article explained that what existed in Germany was not a constituted authority but a provisional revolutionary state of affairs in the aftermath of a revolution. This was just another way of describing the dual power. The universal acceptance of the authority of the absolutist state had broken down, but absolutism in alliance with the liberals still retained considerable power. On the other hand, the people had made a revolution and were demanding a new constitution and measures of public welfare. The situation could be stabilized, said Engels, only by a dictatorship,[6] as after the revolution the old legality and its norms were no more. Some power had to take over. Such an emergency assumption of power was a dictatorship. Here, evidently, Engels had in mind the classical Roman idea of a temporary dictatorship in times of crisis. Obviously, if this dictatorship was exercised by the people, through their representative and their institutions, it would be the dictatorship of the Democracy. The words "no matter how feebly it is enforced" indicated that this dictatorship did not have to be very authoritarian. This was further elaborated in an article by Marx in the series "The Crisis and the Counter-Revolution," contributed to the *NRZ* in September 1848:

> Every provisional political set up following a revolution requires a dictatorship, and an energetic dictatorship at that. From the very beginning we blamed Camphausen for not having acted in a dictatorial manner, for not having immediately smashed up and removed the remains of the old institutions.[7]

Marx also considered it impossible for such a dual power to last long. The task of the democrats had to be the installation of a democratic constitution and political order as a precondition for the kind of social welfare that they wanted. This article gave rise to attacks on Marx by contemporary bourgeois critics. According to Franz Mehring, these critics accused the *NRZ* of demanding the installation of a dictatorship. Mehring, however, claimed that the term dictatorship was used by the leftists in 1848 to emphasize the energetic use of force to demolish the remains of the feudal state, and not to indicate a modern "dictatorship."[8]

The concept of the Dictatorship of the Democracy flowed from the strategic aim of building a majority bloc and ensuring its rule. Summarizing his experiences, Engels wrote in his account of the German revolution that if the Frankfurt Parliament had been energetic, it would have immediately dissolved the Diet, elected a Federal Government, declared itself the only legal expression of the sovereign will of the German people, and created its own army in order to suppress the old governments.[9] Of course, the Frankfurt Parliament had not been energetic and it did not take any of those measures. Not only the bourgeois liberals but even the petty bourgeois democrats proved to be hesitant elements. It was clear that without the hegemony of the proletariat and an independent and leading role of the proletarian party, the working class could not expect its emancipation. Just as this realization led to the final formulation of the strategy of permanent revolution, so also did it mean the transformation of the call for a Dictatorship of the Democracy into a call for the dictatorship of the proletariat. If the proletariat was to be the leading class in winning the battle of Democracy, as the *Communist Manifesto* put it,[10] then in essence the rule established would be the rule of the proletariat. To combat reaction, and to establish a new proletarian democracy, such rule would have to be dictatorial in the sense outlined above. This is what links the concept of the "Dictatorship of the Democracy" with the more famous concept of the dictatorship of the proletariat.

The term, the "revolutionary dictatorship of the proletariat," first appeared in Marx's *The Class Struggles in France*, originally published as a series of articles in the *Neue Rheinische Zeitung-Politisch Ökonomische Revue* in 1850-51. In this work, there are references to several kinds of dictatorships. Referring to General Cavaignac's martial law regime, Marx wrote:

> But Cavaignac was not the dictatorship of the sabre over bourgeois society, he was the dictatorship of the bourgeoisie by the sabre[11].

This involved two claims. First, the martial law regime was only the specific form assumed by the bourgeois dictatorship at a moment, only a particular way in which the bourgeoisie exercised coercive powers. Thus class dictatorship was equated with class rule. Second, a dictatorial government, or the government by an individual, was to be distinguished from class dictatorship. Such individual dictatorships were relatively rare occurrences. As Engels explained later, it was in such exceptional cases of individual or bureaucratic dictatorships that state institutions and the personnel in charge of them could exercise greater autonomy.[12] For Marx, the parliamentary democratic regime, dominated by the bourgeois republicans, was the bourgeois dictatorship par excellence. He wrote:

> By repudiating universal suffrage, with which it hitherto draped itself and from which it sucked its omnipotence, the bourgeoisie openly confesses, *"Our dictatorship has hitherto existed by the will of the people; it must now be consolidated against the will of the people."*[13]

Marx's argument here is very precise. A class dictatorship could be based on universal suffrage reflecting the will of the people. This shows that for him, dictatorship was coterminous with rule.[14] In the same text, Marx also referred to the French counterpart of the Dictatorship of Democracy. He referred to the attempt by the petty bourgeois left to unite the workers and petty bourgeoisie. In case of victory it could be transformed into the rule of the proletariat. In February 1849, the democrats, also called the Mountain, that is Alexandre Ledru-Rollin and his supporters, along with different shades of socialists and communists following Louis Blanc, Cabet, and others, attempted to unite into the social-democratic or the "red" party. As in the case of Germany, if the petty bourgeoisie hegemonized this movement, it would not have gone beyond capitalism. But, as Marx described in a passage discussing the condition of the peasantry, it had a different sort of potential:

> Only the fall of Capital can raise the peasant; only an anti-capitalist, a proletarian government can break his economic misery, his social degradation. The *constitutional republic* is the dictatorship of his united exploiters; the *social democratic republic*, the *Red* republic is the dictatorship of his allies.[15]

Though the exact phrase, the dictatorship of the proletariat, is not used, this was the clearest expression of the class nature of the dictatorship. The constitutional republic has been portrayed as a dictatorship because it was a republic committed to the preservation of the rule of the existing dominant social classes, by force if necessary. Clearly what Marx indicated was not an authoritarian form, much less totalitarianism, but a class rule. That democratic republic which adopted a definite social reform program for the exploited was the dictatorship of the allies of the peasants. While the word "allies" could have included the petty bourgeoisie, the first sentence of the previous quotation firmly indicated that the particular "dictatorship of his allies" that Marx would have liked was a "proletarian government," anti-capitalist in character. So the passage as a whole pointed to a dictatorship of the proletariat, in a usage so mild, and so clearly contrasted with bourgeois constitutionalist class rule, that it becomes apparent that the dictatorship of the proletariat meant a class rule as well—the rule of the workers. But it also included the coercive power that such class rule might imply.[16] If this usage is included in a count, Marx used the concept of dictatorship of the proletariat four times in the book. If we exclude this, and stick to the exact phrase, that appears thrice in *The Class Struggles in France*.

The first time the exact term was used was when Marx wrote about the June 1848 uprising. He wrote that only the failure of the uprising convinced the proletariat that social reforms within a bourgeois state was a utopia. As a result, "there appeared the bold slogan of revolutionary struggle: Overthrow of the bourgeoisie—Dictatorship of the working class."[17] It should be noted that Marx talked about a bold slogan in the singular. It is therefore likely that the dictatorship of the working class was his explanatory comment on the slogan, "overthrow of the bourgeoisie."

The second reference to the term came when Marx was describing the politics of the red party. He wrote:

> . . . the proletariat, forced by the terrible material defeat of June to raise itself up again through intellectual victories and not yet enabled through the development of the remaining classes to seize the revolutionary dictatorship, had to throw itself into the arms of the doctrinaires of its emancipation . . . [18]

In this passage the seizure of revolutionary dictatorship by the proletariat was made contingent on its ability to exercise hegemony over all the exploited classes. So the class dictatorship of the proletariat was excluded until it obtained majority support.

The third use of the term, the dictatorship of the proletariat, occurred in the celebrated passage, already quoted more fully in Chapter 4, where Marx commented that the meaning of communism was:

> *the declaration of the permanence of the revolution, the class dictatorship* of the proletariat as the necessary transit point to the *abolition of class distinctions* generally.[19]

This passage is very important because it makes the necessary link between the permanent revolution, the dictatorship of the proletariat, and communism. For the revolution to go beyond mere anti-feudalism to the abolition of capitalist production relations there had to be an intervening period when the proletariat took state power in its hands in order to introduce necessary economic changes and to resist counter-revolution.

It is Hal Draper who best explained why Marx chose to use the metaphor of class dictatorship of the proletariat when he meant class rule. He pointed out that on the revolutionary side, the most common strategic goal was the establishment of an educational dictatorship of the revolutionary elite. Blanqui, with whose followers Marx was trying to forge an alliance, believed both then and later that the immediate goal of the revolution should be the establishment of an educational dictatorship, preferably that of a revolutionary capital (Paris).[20] Marx was attempting to win over the proletarian and semi-proletarian radicals in the Blanquist current and also the Blanquist-type elements in the Communist League itself when he was writing *The Class Struggles in France*. This explains at least in part Marx's choice of the dictatorship metaphor. He was using a tough rhetoric that would appeal to his audience, while ensuring that the content remained his own.[21]

The same reason can explain the next appearance of the term in the preliminary articles setting up the *SUCR*. That Marx, rather than the Willich–Schapper faction or the Blanquists, had been responsible for the term is proved by, among other things, the fact that after the split in the Communist League, the Willich–Schapper group and the Adam–Barthélemy–Vidil current among the Blanquists issued a public statement with quite a different outlook. Here, the words dictatorship of the proletariat did not appear.[22]

The third text in which the term cropped up was in Marx's letter to the "true" Socialist, Otto Lüning. While reviewing *The Class Struggles in France* in his journal, *Neue Deutsch Zeitung*, he criticized Marx for advocating "revolutionary rule, the dictatorship of the working class." He visibly equated the rule of the proletariat with its dictatorship. It is also clear that his objection was to the idea of a "rule of the proletariat"—for he was quite willing to embrace the dictatorship of the revolutionary party "predominantly through the weight of the working class."[23] Marx's letter to Lüning stated:

> In your newspaper's article of June 22, this year, you reproached me for advocating the *rule and dictatorship of the working class*, while you propose, in opposition to myself, the *abolition of class distinctions in* general. I do not understand this correction.[24]

Here Marx made no distinction between rule and dictatorship and claimed to see no contradiction between a proletarian dictatorship, and the abolition of class distinctions. He then cited three of his own works, viz., *The Communist Manifesto*, the article series on France, and *The Poverty of Philosophy*, in order to prove that he saw no difference between working class rule, the dictatorship of the proletariat, and the abolition of class distinctions, since this last could occur only after the establishment of workers' power. The passage from the *Manifesto* stated that if the proletariat became the ruling class it would change the condition of production and thereby overcome the condition of class antagonism and its own supremacy as a class.[25] It is suggestive that Marx referred to the *Manifesto* in a dispute over the dictatorship of the proletariat, though the *Manifesto* did not use the term. It shows that in his own mind, Marx equated the dictatorship of the proletariat with working class rule and saw nothing new in the term. It also reveals that such rule or dictatorship involved the use of force on a transitional basis, so that class society could give way to classless society. The reference to *The Poverty of Philosophy* was even more suggestive. Marx seemed to have in mind its conclusion where he wrote that after the fall of the old society there would not be a new class-domination resulting in a new political power, because the working class could be emancipated only by abolishing all classes. In the new society there would be neither classes nor class struggle. Consequently: "there will be no more political power properly so called, since political power is precisely the official expression of antagonism in civil society."[26]

How Marx claimed that this statement explained the meaning of the dictatorship of the proletariat requires a brief exposition of a few points about his theory of state. Marx and Engels held that the state had originated out of the non-state institutions of the tribal council. At that stage there was no class antagonism. One particular feature of that order was its lack of any specialized coercive apparatus. Such societies were subsequently transformed by the development of private property and the property-based class antagonisms. Society split into irreconcilable opposites and henceforth the unity of society could be maintained only by an agency standing seemingly above the social conflict. Though it arose out of social institutions, its growth was the result of society alienating its powers and handing them over to this agency. In the *Anti-Dühring*, Engels emphasized that the state arose through an organic social process, and was not a "conspiracy" of the rich.[27] So in the Marxist conception all states are class states whose function is to keep class struggle within the bounds of the order of the dominant class. This called for a public authority, no longer identical to the people in arms. The more the class struggle intensified, the more this public power grew.[28] But in the overwhelming majority of cases, the ruling class was a minority class whose form of property included the exploitation of other classes. Such states of minority ruling classes require a specialized public authority with a series of institutions. These include the army, the judiciary, and so on. As Marx wrote in *The Poverty of Philosophy*, politics was the framework within which the conflicts and the relationships between the different classes were regulated. It was always hierarchical in character, and pushed the majority at the receiving end of the alienation. In exceptional cases, equilibrium of class forces might allow real bureaucratic autonomy. In most cases, however, the bureaucratic autonomy was actually subordinated to the general interest of the ruling class. The summary definition of the *Manifesto* was:

"the executive of the modern state is but a committee for managing the common affairs of the whole bourgeoisie."[29] This presupposed that apart from the common affairs there were numerous factional and personal affairs. Unless the managing committee was free from the pressures of those immediate goals, it could not protect overall capitalist domination. Bureaucratization, therefore, appeared as a necessary part of the growth of the capitalist state.[30]

Marx's reply to Lüning indicated, very briefly, the lines along which he was thinking regarding the role of the state after the proletarian revolution. He expected the rule of the proletariat to be more democratic than the rule of the bourgeoisie, because in the absence of exploitative social relations, bureaucratic functions would progressively become less necessary. The aim of the proletarian revolution was to begin a new period, which would culminate, not in a new class society with the proletariat as ruler, but in a classless society. So the workers' state, i.e., the state created by the proletarian revolution, would not be a bureaucratic state where the mass of citizens would continue to be politically alienated. The democracy established under proletarian rule would involve the abolition of hierarchical power relations, because the hierarchy in social relations would disappear as capitalist production relations were transformed by the revolution into associated production relations, and democracy would be extended from the separated domain of politics to society as a whole. In the words of the *Manifesto*, "the free development of each is the condition for the free development of all."[31] So, the whole period of transition to communism was to bring about an increasing democracy, not a totalitarian straitjacket.

Marx again used the term in his letter to his friend, Joseph Weydemeyer, who wrote an article entitled "Die Diktatur des Proletariats" in the New York *Turn Zeitung* (1852). Apart from basically a restatement of the *Communist Manifesto*, Weydemeyer had written towards the end that the proletarian revolution needed a dictatorship similar to that of Cromwell or that of the Committee of Public Safety.[32] In an attempt to straighten him up on the idea of the dictatorship of the proletariat Marx wrote:

> . . . the class struggle necessarily leads to the *dictatorship of the proletariat;* . . .
> That this dictatorship itself constitutes no more than a transition to the
> *abolition of all classes* and to a *classless society.*[33]

Once again, Marx set himself apart from the reigning left orthodoxy, which was to hope for a socialist edition of the Committee of Public Safety, that is, rule by a small band of enlightened leaders. Once again, he linked the dictatorship of the proletariat to the permanent revolution culminating in a classless society. Finally, by saying that the class struggle necessarily led to the dictatorship of the proletariat, he again affirmed that by the term, he primarily indicated a social content, not a particular form.

Marx's theory of state, as discussed so far, however, raises some questions. If politics is always class politics, would not there be constant repression, or what has been called totalitarianism, in the workers' state and in the communist society? Would not all differences be considered manifestations of hostile class viewpoints? Moreover, if administrative systems are to be attacked in the name of bureaucracy, how can a complex society be run? Unlike Rousseau, Marx was committed to industrialization, which he hailed as a great progressive work of the bourgeoisie. So he was also committed to a complex society. So was the workers' state to have only a set of coercive mechanisms? And if not, if it was to display workers' democracy, then how was that theoretically admissible?

II
THE PARIS COMMUNE: THE FIRST WORKERS' DICTATORSHIP

For about twenty years after this, the term dictatorship of the proletariat did not figure in Marx's explanation of the consequences of a proletarian revolution. In his book *Herr Vogt*, devoted to an exposé of a former German liberal as a Bonapartist agent, the term appeared as a quotation from something written by Vogt about Marx. Nor was this surprising, if Draper's thesis about Marx's reason for using the term is accepted. Throughout the period after the ebbing of the revolutionary wave and up to Paris Commune, Marx had no links with the Blanquist movement. His customary term for the rule of the working class was *Herrschaft* (rule). As early as *The German Ideology*, Marx and Engels had written:

> Every class which is aiming at rule, even when its rule, as is the case with the proletariat, leads to the abolition of the old form of society in its entirety and of rule in general, must first conquer political power in order to represent its interest in turn as the general interest.[34]

So, the rule of the proletariat was to lead to the abolition of political power. But the starting point for that was to be the conquest of power by the proletariat, which, as the text makes explicit, had to be based on the consent of the majority as well, since the proletariat was to represent its interest as the general interest, i.e., establish its hegemony in society. The function of violence was not to suppress legitimate oppositions, but to thwart the counter-revolutionary minority and protect the workers' democracy.

In Marx's lifetime, the working class came closest to the conquest of power during the Paris Commune. Indeed, for Marx and Engels, it was the first workers' state, the first living example of the dictatorship of the proletariat. The experience of the Commune showed the validity of having the dictatorship of the proletariat as a programmatic formulation. It also provided lessons about what to expect from the workers' state, what sort of democracy it could develop, and so on.

On this issue, Draper, despite the pioneering work that he has done, seems to be wrong.[35] The dictatorship of the proletariat was not just rhetoric to attract militant activists. It also had a definite programmatic content. Otherwise, it cannot be explained why Marx would go out of his way in a letter to assert that this concept was his own contribution to revolutionary theory. After the Commune, and following the terror against the Communards, Marx was even more decided on this point. In 1871 itself, after the fall of the Commune, Marx asserted in a speech that before any abolition of classes and class rule there would be a need for a workers' army.[36] In 1875, when the German Social Democratic Workers' Party was formed by the fusion of the Marxists and the Lassalleans on the basis of the Gotha Programme, one of Marx's criticisms of that program was that the political transition period corresponding to the revolutionary transformation of capitalist society into communist society "can be nothing but the *revolutionary dictatorship of the proletariat.*"[37] It was Marx who emphasized the above-mentioned passage. The words "can be nothing but" shows that he felt it to be of fundamental programmatic value. Again, when the SPD adopted a new program at Erfurt in 1891, Friedrich Engels hunted up Marx's 1875 critique, which had at that time been suppressed by Wilhelm Liebknecht, and had it published. Moreover, in his own critique of the draft Erfurt Programme, Engels commented that the democratic republic was the specific form of the dictatorship of the proletariat, and immediately went on to argue that a communist society could not be established peacefully.[38]

For Marx, the Commune was the model of the future, the first working experience of working-class power.[39] It showed how a state of the working class could be set up while avoiding the hypertrophy of bureaucracy that accompanied the bourgeois state.[40] What is amazing is the swiftness with which Marx reached his conclusions. His basic analysis of the nature of the Commune appeared in *The Civil War in France* (hereafter *CWF*), which he wrote on behalf of the General Council of the First International, as a defense of the Commune before the English working class. In it, therefore, the term dictatorship of the proletariat did not appear. The Blanquists had so far avoided the International, considering it not revolutionary enough.[41] It was the defense of the Commune by the International that attracted them to it.

Marx's attitude to the Commune is significant for the light it throws on his conception of workers' power. He had believed, not unreasonably, that an untimely insurrection would lead to a massive defeat, while an astute policy could result in major gains for the French workers. He had warned them against an uprising, both publicly, through the "Second Address of the General Council of the International Workingmen's Association on the Franko-Prussian War," and privately through emissaries.[42] But this opposition to an uprising notwithstanding, once it became a fact, Marx took the stand that as an internationalist his task was to express solidarity with the emancipatory movement of the French workers. On March 21, within a few days of the uprising, Engels gave a long speech on the Commune in the General Council. [43] On May 23, Marx told the General Council: "The principles of the Commune would assert themselves again and again until the working classes were emancipated."[44]

In the *CWF*, his magnificent obituary of the Commune, Marx called it "essentially a working class government . . . the political form at last discovered under which to work out the economical emancipation of labour."[45] And, as it has been argued thus far, the "dictatorship of the proletariat" essentially meant working-class rule. Thus, for Marx the Commune was the first historic experience of the dictatorship of the proletariat.

Immediately after the London Conference of the International, a banquet was held in late September 1871 to celebrate the seventh anniversary of the International. Marx presided over the meeting and gave one of his rare public speeches. A summary was reported as part of a news entitled "The Reds in Session" by the *New York World*. According to the report, Marx highlighted the character of the International, then surveyed the worldwide working class movement, in the course of which he said:

> . . . the Commune was the conquest of the political power of the working classes. . . . The Commune could not find a new form of class government. In destroying the existing condition of oppression by transferring all the means of labour to the productive labour and thereby compelling every able bodied individual to work for a living, the only base for class rule and oppression would be removed. But before such a change could be effected a proletarian dictature would become necessary and the first condition of that was proletarian army.[46]

As a newspaper report, the speech contains, in all likelihood, a mixture of quotations, summaries, and paraphrases. Thus, Marx is reported both as saying that the Commune could not find (establish) a new form of class government, and that, before the establishment of a classless society, a proletarian dictature would become necessary. It is likely that he was making his usual point, that the working class would not set up a new exploitative society so that their rule would be the prolog to the abolition of states and class dominations. Draper has correctly drawn attention to the presence of a large number of Blanquists at the banquet.[47] But that is not an adequate explanation for the speech. There can be no doubt that Marx was applying the term proletarian dictature to the Commune.

It was the conquest of political power by the working class, and that to proceed from class society to a classless society it was necessary to have a proletarian dictature. The scale of the White Terror unleashed by the Versailles government made it clear to Marx that the very first condition of the rule of the proletariat had to be the creation of a proletarian army. It may be argued that such an idea was always implicit. But by stating it expressly, Marx made it clear that unless the working class provided the core of the personnel for the coercive apparatus, simply having a workers' government would not mean having the rule of the proletariat. Thus in his letter of April 17, 1871 to Kugelmann, he wrote that given the provocation by Thiers, the alternative to the uprising would have been surrendering without a fight. "In the latter case the demoralization of the working class would have been a far greater misfortune than the fall of any number of 'leaders.'"[48] Thus, the dictatorship of the proletariat became, in the wake of the Commune, even more strongly a programmatic aspect of the Marxist theory of revolution. So important did Marx and Engels consider this, that in the 1872 edition of the *Communist Manifesto*, they wrote that the *Manifesto* had in parts become out of date.[49] Engels explained later in his letter to Bernstein in 1884, that what they had in mind was the experience of the Commune, and approved the Russian edition of the *Manifesto* which also printed parts of the *CWF*.[50]

Quite a few later references to the Commune also made it evident that Marx and Engels went on considering it as a dictatorship of the proletariat, at least in its historic tendency. In his "Introduction" to the 1891 edition of the *CWF* Engels wrote:

Of late, the Social–Democratic philistine has once more been filled with wholesome terror at the words: Dictatorship of the Proletariat. Well and good, gentlemen, do you want to know what this dictatorship looks like? Look at the Paris Commune. That was, the Dictatorship of the Proletariat.[51]

Again, in his critique of the draft Erfurt Programme, Engels wrote:

If one thing is certain, it is that our party and the working class can only come to power under the form of a democratic republic. This is even the specific form for the dictatorship of the proletariat as the Great French Revolution has already shown.[52]

In case of the latter reference, the "Great French Revolution" could mean the revolution of 1789–94. The implication of such a usage will be discussed at the appropriate place. But Draper's alternative suggestion is that Engels meant by this term the Commune of 1871, which was after all the one definite regime that he had previously called the dictatorship of the proletariat, and that also only a few months previously.[53]

To conclude the discussion on this point, Marx and Engels considered the Commune to be the first living instance of the dictatorship of the proletariat. Hence, in any analysis of what they meant by working class rule, the hegemony of the proletariat, the question of ensuring a socialist tendency within the proletarian power, the establishment of institutions of proletarian democracy in the dictatorship of the proletariat, the role of coercion, authority, and terror, must all be heavily dependent on what lessons they drew from the Commune.

It is an important task to find out how Marx thought that an entire class could rule, and how he thought that had happened in the Paris Commune. There have been a number of historians who have challenged Marx's interpretation of the Commune.[54] Unless the value of calling the Commune a workers' state is judged independently of Marx's assumption, the historic worth of the deductions he made on the basis of the Commune cannot be gauged.

The Bonapartist regime in France was overthrown by the revolution of September 4, 1870, in Paris. The newly created provisional government had a monarchist composition. But the pressure of the masses, including the National Guard (which was close to being a popular militia) forced Gambetta, the republican opponent of Napoleon III, to announce the abolition of the Empire.[55] The organizations and institutions that fought most resolutely for the republic were often proletarian and socialist. The Parisian section of the International along with other radical groups formed a Republican Socialist Committee. This Committee demanded, by a manifesto, the municipal elections, the control of the police by the municipalities, the elections and control of all the magistrates, absolute freedom of the press, public meeting and association, and so on.[56] The class conflict was also sharp in the reconstitution of the armed forces. The class interests of the bourgeois leaders of Republican France made them fear the popular patriotism of the National Guard. As a result, there were repeated conflicts and the influence of radicals grew on the Guard. The commanding generals deliberately allowed the National Guard to be killed en masse by the Germans by following poor battle tactics.[57] It was in this situation that national elections were held. The elections were intended to create only a temporary assembly, entrusted with the single task of settling the peace terms with the Prussians. However, as in 1848-1850, so in the elections of 1871, the rural population tended to distrust the left wing republicans, and had consequently voted into the Assembly a huge monarchist contingent. With republicans still viewed with suspicion, as they had been in 1848–50 in rural France, the initial elections resulted in the return of around four hundred monarchists, divided between the two wings, the Legitimists and the Orleanists, and this majority promptly tried to use the Assembly to draw up a new constitution as well. There were a hundred and fifty republicans and a few Bonapartists. Paris stood a long way to the left, and in the elections, Parisian deputies included Victor Hugo, Louis Blanc, Gambetta, Garibaldi, (who had come with volunteers to help the republicans), Delescluze, Rochefort, Félix Pyat, Jules Favre, Henri Tolain, Malon, and the radical journalist Milliere, though the most thoroughgoing left-wing did not gain majority support at the early stages. Thus, Blanqui, Tridon and Eudes, the three leading Blanquists, as well as the leading members of the International, were defeated. But the election of even a relatively inactive person like Louis Blanc reflected popular support for his socialist past, while the conservatives were most offended by the election of Garibaldi. In late February a meeting of some 2000 delegates of the different battalions of the National Guard elected a General Committee, and thereby challenged the sole power of the bourgeoisie and the National Assembly. As Henri Lefebvre has pointed out, a dual power regime was growing.[58] On the early morning of March 18, 1871, the Thiers government made an attempt to seize the cannons of the National Guard. This led to an immediate reaction and a seizure of power in Paris by the National Guard. All the leaders and officials of the Thiers government fled from Paris. The Central Committee did not even attempt to arrest them, or halt the exodus of the regular army. Instead, the Committee kept itself busy in chalking out plans for an election.[59]

The election to the Commune, held on March 26, 1871, was on the basis of equal constituencies and ninety councillors were elected. Over sixty of those elected were revolutionaries of different currents. There were sixteen liberals, i.e., opponents of the revolution. Resignation of the pro-Versailles councillors made necessary supplementary elections in April. Against the assertions that workers did not form a majority, it should be pointed out that no parliament before the Commune and few after it could claim to have more than a quarter working-class members as the Commune did. Contemporary documents also showed the hegemony of the workers. On March 25, 1871, the Central Committee issued a wall poster suggesting that only the election of working people would serve the working people.[60] The *Journal Officiel* of the Commune published a statement by the leaders of the Fifth Arrondissement, which stated in part:

> By leading the Nation to the brink of collapse the other classes have finally exposed the extent of their impotence and decay. . . . Open the door to the enlightened proletariat, the true people, the only class . . . that is capable of saving the country.[61]

The major base of the revolutionaries and socialists was among the workers. The shift was displayed by the mass of petty bourgeoisie, who for the moment had deserted their traditional leaders and followed the lead of the National Guard and the revolutionaries. Out of the forty-three candidates put up by the combined efforts of the International, the Federation of the Trade Unions, and the delegation of the Twenty Arrondissements for the National Assembly elections in February, only three had been elected (Malon, Pyat and Tolain). Twenty-seven of these candidates including Arnaud, Blanqui, Eudes, Frankel, Varlin and others were elected to the Commune in late March. This rise in the socialist vote was due to the acceptance of working class hegemony by the middle class.

The past few months had shown that the French bourgeoisie, in pursuing a narrow class goal, was going against the national interest. In the first place, they refused to put up a resolute defense against the Prussians for fear of a radical revolution. Moreover, in accepting the German terms, including the payment of a massive indemnity, the Thiers government decided to float an internal loan. Newspaper reports claimed that the bankers who were prepared to back the loan also agreed to give Thiers and others 300 million francs as commission. Again, on March 10, 1871, the National Assembly adopted a law on overdue bills which set a seven-month moratorium for payments on security made from August 13 to November 12, 1870. No moratorium was allowed for payment on securities contracted after November 12. This meant that workers, the petty bourgeoisie, small traders and small industrialists were hard hit, while big capital was not. Finally, the National Assembly also refused to defer the payment of house rents any further. Such were the concrete events which pushed the lower middle classes towards the proletariat. But this proletarian hegemony was established partly by default of the upper classes, without adequate preparation on the part of the proletariat itself.

Monty Johnstone has argued that theoreticians of the German Social Democracy wrongly identified the dictatorship of the proletariat with a condition where the proletariat was numerically in an absolute majority.[62] Marx at least did not do so. If the proletariat, in order to rule, had to represent its interests as the general interests of society, then its interests had to be sufficiently broadly defined to incorporate the essential interests of the other major oppressed classes and social groups. "This," Marx averred, "was the first revolution in which the working class was openly acknowledged as the only class capable of social initiative."[63] Both Marx and Lissagaray, the Communard who wrote an authoritative account, stressed that workers' hegemony did not mean the establishment of a regime that looked narrowly after the interests of workers as a corporate group.[64] Turning to the masses outside Paris, the Commune issued a circular, addressed "To the Workers on Farms." Its central slogan was "the land to the farmer, the tools of production to the worker, work for all," and it attempted to explain to the peasants that "the liberation that we demand is your own as well."[65] Johnstone points out, with some truth, that the Commune's actual performance in trying to consciously establish the hegemony of the working class was less impressive than Marx's interpretation.[66] Marx was pointing to the inner tendency, not merely the actual work done. At the same time, by highlighting those particular tendencies, he was also setting forth a program, and explaining that to be victorious, a workers' revolution had to look after the interests of potential allies of the working class as well. In the first draft of the *CWF*, he wrote: "the 'rurals' know that three months rule of the Republican Commune in France would be the signal of the rising in peasantry and the agricultural Proletariat against them."[67]

In the final version, by omitting a theoretical passage on the eventual transformation of the peasants into the rural proletariat, Marx managed to highlight even more strongly the immediate appeals that the Commune had for the peasantry.[68]

To call the Commune a workers' state, however, raises a question about Marx's later judgment. In a letter written to the Dutch socialist, F. Domela Nieuwenhuis, in 1881, Marx wrote:

> the Paris Commune . . . apart from the fact that this was merely the rising of a city under exceptional conditions, the majority of the Commune was in no wise socialist, nor could it be.[69]

This fragment is often quoted as proof of the thesis that for Marx, or at least in Marx's mature judgement, once the euphoria over the Commune was gone, the Commune could not be a dictatorship of the proletariat.[70] But the context of this letter is rarely noted, nor its full text studied. Nieuwenhuis had written to Marx that in its forthcoming Congress, the Dutch Socialist Party intended to raise the question of what legislative measures should be introduced by socialists to safeguard the victory of socialism immediately after they gained power. Marx replied that a socialist government, that is, a government with a definite political program of socialism, could not come to power unless conditions were sufficiently developed. So the discussion here was over the program of a committed and conscious leadership, neither over the social content nor the state form. Marx was suggesting to his correspondent that the Commune's experience did not provide ready-made answers to socialists aspiring to power on a nationwide scale, because in the first place it was an insurrection limited to one city, which had spread only briefly to a few other cities and which had failed to win over the peasantry. Moreover, Marx commented that the leadership of the Commune had not been socialist. This letter was written at a time when most socialists had begun to accept significant elements of Marx's analysis and program. In the Commune, the majority of the leadership was Blanquist, diverse Jacobin types, etc.

For Marx, this was tantamount to the leadership being non-socialist. It is possible to consider on this point the comment of Engels, made in 1874:

> Since Blanqui regards every revolution as a coup de main by a small revolutionary minority, it automatically follows that its victory must inevitably be succeeded by the establishment of a dictatorship—not, it should be well noted, of the entire revolutionary class, the proletariat, but of the small number of those who accomplished the coup and who themselves are, at first, organized under the dictatorship of one or several individuals. Obviously, Blanqui is a revolutionary of the old generation. These views on the course of revolutionary events have long since become obsolete.[71]

In the course of the essay, Engels had also pointed out that by 1874, some Blanquists had arrived at communism by accepting parts of the *Communist Manifesto*.[72] Thus, in the Commune, the existence of a Jacobin–Blanquist majority within the leadership meant the lack of clear socialist ideas among the leaders. At the same time, this did not mean that at a different level, that of the basic class direction, there were no socialist aspirations in the Commune. Marx had written, in the *CWF* itself:

> Yes, gentlemen, the Commune intended to abolish that class—property which makes the labour of the many the wealth of the few. It aimed at the expropriation of the expropriators.[73]

Marx and Engels believed that among their forerunners, the Blanquists did not believe in a class dictatorship and hence had no conception of proletarian socialism, and the utopians had a vision of communism, but no conception of feasible means. They contrasted both groups, not merely to their own ideas, but to the actual experience of the Commune. It had a socialist content, not because of doctrinaires at its helm, but because the struggle was led by the working class, and their instinctive tendency was for socialism. The contrast that Marx made was between the historic tendency embodied by the Commune and the immediate deeds of its leaders.[74]

In the published text of the *CWF*, Marx commented regarding the class measures of the Commune, "Its special measures could but betoken the tendency of a government of the people by the people."[75] The socialist character of the Commune was most clearly proclaimed, not by its specific measures, but by its reiteration of the historic goals of communism, first enunciated by the utopians.

In fact, socialist sentiments were quite openly expressed in the Commune. A letter from a rank and file supporter to Jules Audoyaud, a member of the Central Committee of the National Guard, showed that the masses sometimes pressed for more determined socialistic measures than did the leaders.[76] Even traditional Jacobin republicans were often led through the course of events to express socialist ideas. For example, Paschal Grousset, editor of the paper *l'Affranchi*, wrote that the working class should keep political power in its hands until it completely emancipated itself and created a single class of fraternal producers.[77] Similarly, another Jacobin writer, Albert Grandier, wrote: "This victory [of the Commune] represents the movement for new rights, rising to confront the old divisive political forms and the exploitation of Labour by Capital."[78]

Even in its seventy-two days of existence, the Commune proved that the working class did not lack maturity and that the rule of the proletariat, and the widest application of democracy, did not mean either chaos, anarchy and the end of civilization, or totalitarianism, mob violence, etc. This working class regime had to be crushed by its opponents. That was why, Marx concluded, "the great social measure of the Commune was its own working existence."[79]

III
THE ABOLITION OF THE BUREAUCRATIC STATE

The Commune showed what sort of democracy there could exist in the dictatorship of the proletariat. Indeed, it was a living answer to the often asked question, as to what rule by an entire class, especially the proletariat, would look like in effect.

To start with, Marx and Engels took it to be axiomatic that the dictatorship of the proletariat would be a democratic republic. *The Communist Manifesto* had already talked about the winning of democracy as the first, necessary stage in the struggle for proletarian emancipation. In *The Class Struggles in France*, Marx had written that in a revolutionary period, universal suffrage could only serve as a school of political training.[80] However, this did not mean that as a whole, universal suffrage had no other function. In *The Civil War in France*, Marx wrote:

> [The Empire was] the ultimate form of the state power . . . which full-grown bourgeois society had finally transformed into a means for the enslavement of labour by capital . . . The direct antithesis to the Empire was the Commune. The cry of "Social Republic," with which the revolution of February was ushered in by the Paris proletariat, did but express a vague aspiration after a republic that was not only to supersede the monarchical form of class rule but class rule itself. The Commune was the positive form of that republic.[81]

Since the Empire was bourgeois and authoritarian, its direct antithesis must have been proletarian, democratic, and based on a society where labor was not subordinated to Capital.[82] Marx's exposition of Commune democracy made the following points: that there was universal suffrage; the elected councillors were accountable, and subject to recall; that the principle of election was extended to all spheres, including the election of magistrates, judges and all categories of public servants.[83] So Marx welcomed universal suffrage but did not stop there. As he put it:

> Instead of deciding once in three or six years which member of the ruling class was to misrepresent the people in Parliament, universal suffrage was to serve the people, constituted in Communes, as individual suffrage serves every other employer in the search for the workmen and managers in his business. . . . On the other hand, nothing could be more foreign to the spirit of the Commune than to supersede universal suffrage by hierarchic investiture.[84]

This passage is definite evidence that Marx made a sharp distinction between bourgeois democracy and workers' democracy. In the former, he said, universal suffrage was balanced by a bureaucratic hierarchy. Moreover, the elected members of Parliament were not continuously accountable to the electors. As a result, universal suffrage could not truly serve the people. This was not a campaign for direct democracy nor a Rousseauan critique of representation.[85] That Marx did not have any idea of an impossible direct democracy is further brought out by his description of the Commune's plan for national political organization and his support for it. The Commune had adopted quite belatedly an official program. Its political aspects included the following: consolidation of the republic, autonomy of the Commune, and its extension to every town in France, a national unity based on popular will in place of despotism.[86] Marx adopted this program for his own and expanded on it. He wrote:

> the rural communes of every district were to administer their common affairs by an assembly of delegates in the central town and these district assemblies were again to send deputies to the National Delegation in Paris . . . revocable and bound by the *mandat impératif* (formal instructions) of his constituents. The few but important functions which still would remain for a central government were not to be suppressed, as has been intentionally misstated, but were to be discharged by Communal, and therefore strictly responsible agents.[87]

This passage is significant for many reasons. The election of delegates at each stage, from the smallest village to the nation, ruled out any "direct democracy." At the same time this structure did not suggest localism. As Marx commented, the unity of the nation was not to be broken. Both those who accuse the Commune of trying to break this unity and those who suppose that Marx was advocating federalism, work on a common assumption that centralism necessarily means bureaucratization and the withdrawal of all power from the local communities. What is certainly true is that the Commune modified Marx's idea of centralism in the revolutionary state. During and after the revolutions of 1848, when the task in Germany had been the abolition of feudal particularism, disguised as local autonomy, Marx and Engels had advocated the strictest centralization, as in the Address of the Central Authority to the Communist League (March 1850).[88] In an explanatory note to the 1885 reprint of the Address, Engels felt it necessary to distinguish between the centralization carried out by a Bonapartist regime, and the revolutionary democratic centralization that he hoped for. While advocating the widest extension of local self-government, he asserted that such self-government was not in contradiction to political centralization of the nation. So the function of local self-government was to unite the whole nation democratically from below. Engels admitted that this was a programmatic change brought about as a result of the experience of the bureaucratic centralization of France under Bonapartist rule.[89] It can be taken as a reiteration of Marx's own comments. Shortly after the coup that established the Bonapartist regime in France, Marx wrote his famous work, *The Eighteenth Brumaire of Louis Bonaparte*. In it, he stated,

> But the parody of the empire was necessary to free the mass of the French nation from the weight of tradition and to work out in pure form the opposition between the state power and society. The demolition of the state machine will not endanger centralization. Bureaucracy is only the low and brutal form of a centralization that is still afflicted with its opposite, with feudalism.[90]

In the *CWF*, Marx had again, and much more graphically, contrasted the two kinds of centralization. He characterized the centralized state power as being, on one hand, a weapon in the hands of the nascent bourgeoisie against feudalism, and on the other, as a gigantic bureaucratic and repressive machinery in the hands of the present capitalist class.[91] The Commune was "the reabsorption of the State power by society, as its own living forces instead of as forces controlling and subduing it"[92]. So centralization, as carried out by the Commune, was to be under social control. He believed that capitalist development itself made centralization and national unity inevitable.'[93]

In the first draft he wrote:

> ... Parliamentarism then was dead in France and the workmen's Revolution certainly was not to awaken it from the death. But this one form of class rule had only broken down to make the Executive, the governmental State machinery the great and single object of attack to the Revolution.[94]

The task of the workers' revolution was not to pass from bourgeois authoritarianism to bourgeois democracy, but to fight for the establishment of proletarian democracy, since the Commune was, according to Marx, "the form under which the working class assumes the political power," or "the political form of the social emancipation."[95] The political form is not the life of a class itself, but the way in which a class exercises its domination. This idea of politics is found frequently in Marx's writings. So each class rule must have forms that more or less correspond to its needs. The bourgeois parliament existed together with an executive wing which wielded the real material forces. Since the task of the state was the protection of the general interest of the dominant class and of the mode of production, it was unthinkable that the working class could simply take over the bourgeois legislature and have the executive obeying it meekly. The task of the dictatorship of the proletariat was to overcome the separation of the "economic" and the "political" in capitalism.[96] In the first draft, Marx expressed this idea by saying that the Commune:

> begins the emancipation of labour—its great goal—by doing away with the unproductive and mischievous work of the state parasites . . . on the one side, by doing, on the other, the real work of administration, local and national, for working men's wages. It begins therefore with an immense saving, with economical reform as well as political transformation.[97]

In the final version, Marx asserted that the "Commune was to be a working, not a parliamentary body, executive and legislative at the same time."[98] This was an outright rejection of liberal democracy. The political theory of liberalism, from John Locke to J. S. Mill, has begun with the individual. If they are completely free, clashes of interests between individuals are liable to lead to open warfare. To avoid such a situation, all individuals are supposed to surrender a part of their natural freedom and thereby create the state. So that it does not become too powerful, so that as much of the freedom of the individual as possible is retained, the power of the state is restricted to the purely political realm, and even there, a separation of powers is carried out.[99] The executive in liberal theory, including its liberal democratic extension, is largely a bureaucratic apparatus. Marx, by contrast, called for an expansion of the principle of representation. At the same time, he rejected the separation of legislative and executive powers. This did not make him a theorist of totalitarianism. If the legislature was elected by universal suffrage, then an executive independent of it could not be democratic, but at best plebiscitary. Moreover, Marx and Engels were hostile to checks and balances where they sought to curb mass participation in politics.

In the *Critique of the Gotha Programme*, Marx criticized the draft program for not going beyond what he called the old democratic (petty-bourgeois) littany of "universal suffrage, direct legislation, popular rights, a peoples' militia, etc."[100] Marx's emphasis is clear. The dictatorship of the proletariat had to go beyond the foregoing. So, here, too, a negative definition is presented, namely, that the parliamentary republic was not the form of the dictatorship of the proletariat. The fact that Marx was contrasting bourgeois democracy and proletarian democracy in the critique is evident because he wrote that these demands were a mere echo of certain bourgeois parties, and commented a little later that the democratic republic was the "last form of state of bourgeois society" in which "the class struggle has to be fought out to a conclusion."[101]

Before the Commune, only such negative presentations of their views had existed. By 1875, when the *Critique of the Gotha Programme* was written, this had changed. Engels' letter to Bebel on the Gotha Programme (March 18–28, 1875) had the following to say: "All the palaver about the state ought to be dropped, especially after the Commune, which had ceased to be a state in the true sense of the term."[102]

So the Commune-state was so different in form that Engels even felt it wrong to call it a state. Hence, there can be no doubt that for them the form and content of workers' democracy were quite distinct from those of bourgeois democracy. [103]

However, both Marx and Engels used the term democratic republic to cover bourgeois as well as proletarian republics. Engels' letter to Bernstein (March 24, 1884) argued that democracy was not an abstract concept, for it "changes every time the Demos changes." Engels argued that in the context when workers' rule had not been established, the proletariat needed democratic forms for the seizure of political power, and that "the democratic republic is the *logical* form of bourgeois rule." He also wrote that "the democratic republic always remains the *last* form of bourgeois rule, that in which it goes to pieces."[104] Here he was arguing that the working class can best organize itself, and fight to capture state power, in a democratic state form. But Engels did not believe that capitalist rule would remain democratic to the last, and pass over into workers' democracy, for as he pointed out, when in danger, any capitalist ruling class, including the English, were likely to turn to undemocratic means and forms.[105] It was in this sense that he wrote, in his "Introduction" to the *CWF*, that "the state is nothing but a machine for the oppression of one class by another, and indeed in the democratic republic no less than in the monarchy. . . "[106]

But the democratic republic could have a different content, and a different form, when it was a workers' democracy. In the "Critique of the Erfurt Programme," Engels commented:

> If one thing is certain, it is that our party and the working class can only come to power under the form of democratic republic. This is even the

specific form for the dictatorship of the proletariat, as the Great French Revolution has already shown.[107]

It has been remarked earlier that this can be explained in either of two ways. If Engels was indeed referring to the revolution of 1789–94, the reference to a "dictatorship of the proletariat" cannot mean a reference to the so-called "Reign of Terror." Marx and Engels never glorified the Robespierrist dictatorship. But Daniel Guérin has suggested that Engels was talking about the popular movement, organized in a number of clubs, self-organization of the class, and in the sections of the Commune of Paris of 1792. Later historians have also shown the autonomy of the sans culottes.[108] In other words, Engels was suggesting that from the time of the French Revolution, the working classes (in broader sense than the proletariat, defined in strict Marxist terms) were exerting pressure, even if temporarily, and that the exercise of power by the working classes was possible only when a network of popular democratic institutions was built up. The democratic republic suitable for proletarian rule could be built up by looking at the concrete instances of popular power, from the revolutionary experience of the sans culottes, through the workers' societies of 1848-49, to the Commune of 1871. The crucial difference between the earlier cases and the Commune of 1871 was that in the last case, the working class exercised hegemony so that it did not merely show the possible form for the dictatorship of the proletariat, but was itself an instance of that dictatorship.[109]

All the preceding discussions lead to the ineluctable conclusion that the question of form was not a dispute over democracy versus dictatorship. Rather, this was over parliamentary institutions with democracy restricted by hierarchic and non-answerable bodies versus a pyramid of democratic institutions that not only made law, but implemented it as well, something both possible and necessary in a workers' state.

Marx and Engels never criticized the idea of having representative assemblies. On the contrary, they are on record as having criticized the lack of real power in hands of such assemblies. In his discussion of the Hessian constitution of 1831, Marx wrote approvingly that no other constitution:

> makes the Administration more dependent on the legislature . . . the Representative Chamber selects out of its members a permanent committee, forming a sort of Areopagus, watching and controlling the Government, and impeaching the officials for the violation of the Constitution.[110]

At this level the executive still existed as a separate body, though subject to legislative control. The commune went further. It formed 10 commissions having definite executive functions, and sixty-one of the members of the commune were given some administrative task or other.[111] The committees implemented the decisions arrived at in full council meetings. Even more radical was the call to make all administrative offices elective.

At the national level, a multi-tiered representative system was to be set up. This began with base-level communal assemblies, and went up through regions to the national body.[112] The assemblies at each level were to be modelled on the Paris Commune. They were to be elected by universal suffrage on the basis of equal constituencies, and to perform both deliberative and executive functions. Since the lower levels who were to send deputies to the next level could recall them at will, there was complete popular control.[113]

Though Marx spoke out against the separation of powers, he was in favor of judicial autonomy. Among the opponents of Prussian absolutism in the 1840s, there were three main lines of judicial reform possible. Marx and Engels took up all three. These being, the demand for greater independence for judges; the extension of the jury system and the election of all judges; and finally the expansion of judicial competence in order to exercise some control over executive excesses. In his earliest writings, Marx had objected to the fact that in Prussian criminal proceedings, the judge was not independent, but a government agent.[114] Engels, likewise, stressed the separation of judicial and executive powers in France, England and America, and talked of "the advantages and guarantees offered by the jury system," saying, "that judicial power is the direct property of the nation, which exercises its jurors."[115] Of course, when they became communists, they introduced the caveat that in a class society, no system, including the jury, could produce impartial judgements.[116]

During the revolution of 1848, Marx was vehement in his denunciation of those pseudo-independent Prussian judges who offered no resistance to illegal and authoritarian acts of the crown.[117] In this case, they called for the temporary suspension of the principle of irremovability of the judges like the French revolutions of 1792 and 1848 in order to remove the most servile judges. In his article on the Hessian constitution, Marx praised the fact that the courts of law were "empowered to decide definitively upon all the acts of the Executive."[118]

In the CWF, Marx's position was a continuation of this line of argumentation. Marx was happy that the judges were "divested of that sham independence" which had marked their subservience to executive authority, and he welcomed the fact that judges were henceforth to be "elective, responsible and revocable."[119] But he did not call for merging the judiciary with either the legislative or the executive power.

Subsequently, in their comments on several socialist programs, it is significant that they never objected to the demand for "administration of justice by the people," or "popularly elected judges."[120] While Engels waved away Jules Guesde's objection to the election of judges with the comment that universal suffrage could be abused in other respects as well, and that this did not legitimise any call for abrogating universal suffrage.[121] What emerges from this is that between 1842 and 1891, over a period of half a century, Marx and Engels always, without exception, supported a popular, but autonomous judiciary.

It is possible to sum up the discussion by putting forward a few brief propositions. First and foremost Marx and Engels did not contrast democracy to dictatorship. Rather, they envisaged the dictatorship of the proletariat as incorporating a tremendous expansion of democracy. They also believed that workers' democracy should involve a number of guarantees against excessive hierarchy, or excessive professionalization. These included the elective character of a maximum of official posts, and a ceiling on wages. Moreover, they affirmed that an independent judiciary was a very important check on executive arbitrariness. It was when these conditions had been fulfilled, that universal suffrage could play its desired role in promoting proletarian democracy. In this, Marx and Engels stood in opposition to liberals and libertarians alike. A brief comparison of the positions of John Stuart Mill and the anarchist Mikhail Bakunin would be worthwhile.[122]

Bakunin did write repeatedly about a popular revolution. But he cannot be considered a democratic theorist of any kind, because of his opposition to universal suffrage.[123] He counterposed, to democratically elected national representative bodies a "collective dictatorship of all our allies [i.e. the members of the Alliance for Socialist Democracy] a dictatorship without official rights, and therefore all the more powerful . . . "[124]

Bakunin basically objected to the class rule of the proletariat, on the ground that class rule inevitably meant an exploiting class. In a comment on this passage, Marx wrote that elections as a political form were subject to considerable variations depending on the economic foundations.[125] Marx was thereby pointing out that the social foundations of workers' democracy were different from those of bourgeois democracy. Moreover, Marx asserted that in a Commune-state, with maximization of popular control and democratic institutions, the entire people did rule.[126]

For a liberal like John Stuart Mill, the class struggle, a positive thing before the Reform Bill agitation (1830–32), became a "sinister force" afterwards. Mill was, in the name of liberty of the individual, opposed to democracy as tyranny of the majority. He opposed the rule of the proletarian majority because it did not mean equality. Rather, "one part of the people rules over the rest." Moreover, he asserted that administration should be left to a permanent civil service.[127]

Thus, proletarian democracy differed from both liberalism and anarchism in its emphasis on a thorough-going democratic rule, and the abolition of bureaucracy. The Commune form showed how the working people could directly govern themselves while in the parliamentary form even at its freest Marx and Engels saw the place hunting of professional politicians who were tied in a thousand ways with the capitalist class.

IV
WORKERS' STATE AND COERCION

All the emphasis on expansion of democracy notwithstanding, Marx and Engels also felt the need for coercion and the establishment of proletarian authority by force. Time and again, they emphasized the necessity of class terror. In the *NRZ*, referring to the terrible June days fighting (1848) in Paris, Engels wrote: "after a battle like that of the three June days, only *terrorism* is still possible whether it be carried out by one side or the other"[128].

On the revolutionary developments in Hungary, Engels was happy to note that:

> For the first time in the revolutionary movement of 1848, for the first time since 1793, a nation surrounded by superior counter-revolutionary forces dares to counter the cowardly counter-revolutionary fury by revolutionary passion, the *terreur blanche* by the *terreur rouge*.[129]

Engels was putting forward here the basic condition for the development of any revolution. In effect, he was asking whose force was to prevail — that of the Austrians or that of the revolutionary Hungarians, a question that could be extended to a conflict of capital and labor, as well. Even a movement of the majority in the interest of the majority, as the *Manifesto* considered communism to be, could not achieve power by pure moral persuasion as long as the exploiting classes still manned the guns. But this did not mean that morally the two terrorisms were equivalent. The last issue of the *NRZ* had a defiant editorial, which stated:

> We are merciless; we ask no mercy from you. When our turn comes, we will make no excuses for terrorism. But the *royal terrorists*, the terrorists by the grace of God and Right, in practice are brutal, contemptible and vile, in theory cowardly, underhanded and deceitful, in both respects dishonourable.[130]

In the March 1850 Address of the Central Authority, they argued that class terror was necessary to beat down the resistance of the class enemy. The task of the League was, among other things, the following:

> Far from opposing so-called excesses, instances of popular revenge against

hated individuals or public buildings that are associated only with hateful recollections, such instances must not only be tolerated but the lead in them must be taken.[131]

In all these cases, what is being advocated is the energetic use of force in order to stamp out resistance by the other side, because without that, the class struggle could not be resolved. This has to be distinguished from Marx's opposition to the Jacobin tradition and the distortions grafted by Robespierrism on the legitimate use of force to defend the revolution.[132] In the *CWF*, Marx made a categorical distinction between the politics of revolution by terror, and the necessity of red terror to counter white terror. During the uprising itself, he wrote to Liebknecht and to Kugelmann that the Parisians had shown too great a decency. According to him the military task of crushing the Versailles government when it was weak should have taken precedence over the election of the commune and its peaceful tasks.[133] Even more significantly, Marx's letter to Leó Frankel and Louis Varlin dealt almost exclusively with the problem of defense, although this was in reply to a letter from Frankel where he had asked for Marx's advice on the kinds of social measures the Commune should adopt.[134]

The second chapter of the *CWF* began, "Armed Paris was the only serious obstacle in the way of the counter-revolutionary conspiracy."[135] Page after page of the work described the brutal nature of the growing white terror. In fact, by choosing the title *The Civil War in France*, Marx was highlighting the clash of forces. And one of his intentions was to show that while the proletariat, from a too strong feeling of scruples, hesitated to apply terror, the bourgeois state constantly violated its own laws to crush the working class.[136]

The really massive butchery came after the defeat of the Commune. Marx's burning anger comes through in his description of this phase of the white terror:

> The civilisation and justice of bourgeois order comes out in its lurid light whenever the slaves and drudges of the order rise against their masters. Then this civilisation and justice stand forth as undisguised savagery and lawless revenge.... A glorious civilization, indeed a great problem of which is how to get rid of the heaps of corpses it made after the battle was over.
>
> To find a parallel for the conduct of Thiers and his blood hounds we must go back to the times of Sulla and the two Triumvirates of Rome. The same wholesale slaughter in cold blood, disregard, in the massacre of age and sex; the same system of torturing prisoners, the same proscriptions, but this time of a whole class.[137]

By the time Marx was reading out his essay to the General Council for its approval, the bloodiest phase of white terror had begun. Public criticism of the Commune had to be kept a minimum. So, while in the second draft, Marx had accused the Central Committee of "an excess of moderation bordering upon weakness," in the final version, this moderation was counterposed to the white terror.[138]

Marx defended without any hesitation the armed struggle of the Commune including the shooting of hostages in response to counter-revolutionary violence. And all this could be done, "Paris could resist only because . . . (it had) a National Guard, the bulk of which consisted of working men."[139]

Marx's defense of terror, coercion, etc. was not just an angry reaction to white terror. The logic he put forward was that the exploiting classes would not submit unprotestingly to their expropriation. Workers' democracy could be enforced only if the proletariat showed its ability and willingness to defend that democracy. In late 1872, Marx wrote an article for an Italian journal, edited by Enrico Bignami, who gave it the title "Political Indifferentism." Marx parodied and ridiculed the anarchist stand on political inaction:

> If the political struggle of the working class assumes violent forms and if the workers replace the dictatorship of the bourgeois class with their own revolutionary dictatorship then they are guilty of the terrible crime of *lèse-principe*; for, in order to satisfy their miserable profane daily needs and to crush the resistance of the bourgeois class, they, instead of laying down their arms and abolishing the state, give to the state a revolutionary and a transitory form.[140]

So, the political struggle, leading to the dictatorship of the proletariat, would assume violent forms, and the revolutionary state must be armed to satisfy the needs of the workers and crush bourgeois resistance.[141]

Marx and Engels also rejected the Bakuninist argument that authority equaled authoritarianism and hence the state had to be abolished immediately after the revolution. This was of course a meaningless exercise because some agency would have to be set up to carry out the tasks of the revolution. The Bakuninist opposition to public authority went along with his hankering for a secret dictatorship. As a pamphlet by Marx, Engels and Paul Lafargue pointed out, the secret Bakuninist documents rejected any public organization of the proletariat in favor of a secret coterie, appointed and commanded by Bakunin, who even demanded a "unity of idea." [142]

In a letter to Paul Lafargue, Engels explained the difference more clearly. He wrote that the Bakuninists used the word authoritarian to denounce anything they disliked. By identifying "authority" and "authoritarianism" or anti-democratic functioning, they were, according to Engels, undermining political work, for: "no communal action is possible without submission on the part of some to an external will, that is to say an authority."[143]

This idea was further developed by Engels in the article "On Authority," where he claimed that social and economic complexities ensured that the expropriation of the capitalists would not lead to the disappearance of authority. Because of the division of labor in the factory system of production, workers would have to agree on working hours and various aspects of production. Whether decisions were taken by elected delegates or by votes on different issues, "the will of the single individual will always have to subordinate itself." So Engels took care to distinguish between democratic and publicly recognized authority, and undemocratic authority. That is why, he wrote:

> it is absurd to speak of the principle of authority as being absolutely evil . . .
> the social organisation of the future would restrict authority solely to the
> limits within which the conditions of production render it inevitable.[144]

As against the impractical idea of abolishing authority it suggested controlling authority through elections and through narrowing the limits of authority, as socialism developed.[145] Having emphasized the need for democratizing authority, Engels turned to rebut the anarchist demand for abolition of authority with the following words:

> they demand that the first act of the social revolution shall be the abolition
> of authority. Have these gentlemen ever seen a revolution? A revolution is
> certainly the most authoritarian thing there is; it is the act whereby one part
> of the population imposes its will upon the other part by means of rifles,
> bayonets and cannon—authoritarian means, if such there be as all, and if
> the victorious party does not want to have fought in vain, it must maintain
> this rule by means of the terror which its arms inspire in the reactionaries.
> Would the Paris Commune have lasted a single day if it had not made use
> of this authority of the armed people against the bourgeoisie? Should we
> not, on the contrary, reproach it for not having used it freely enough?[146]

It can therefore be seen that even when arguing in defense of the most democratically constituted authority, Engels was at pains to stress that in defending basic class interests, like the shift of power from one class to another, a period comes when the democratic majority has to use guns and terror to impose its will. In 1883, in a letter to an American working class correspondent, P. Van Patten, Engels again asserted that the task of the working class was to conquer political power, keep down its capitalist enemies, and carry out the transition to socialism "without which the whole victory must end in a defeat and in a massacre of the working class, like that of a Paris Commune."[147] No social order can be held together unless the individuals agree to submit to collective decision. A democratic political system means, simultaneously, a democratic authority. Rejection of such authority outright in the name of individual liberty is actually a rejection of democracy.[148]

V
THE TRANSITION AND THE FUTURE OF THE STATE

This issue of authority is related to Marx's approach to workplace democracy and popular control over the economy during the period of transition. The transitional economy in itself is not the subject of the present study. But there is a persistent claim that Marxism as an ideology "is of such a nature as to require that every branch of economy and form of social expression be subjected to centralized direction and control."[149]

So, Marx's and Engels' views of statization have to be touched upon. In "On Authority," Engels proposed a democratization of work place authority, not the imposition of a bureaucratic state authority. In the most detailed presentation of their view of the future, Engels wrote:

> In making itself the master of all the means of production to use them in accordance with a social plan, society puts an end to the former subjection of men to their own means of production. It goes without saying that society cannot free itself unless every individual is freed.[150]

So it is the society and not the state that would assume mastery over the means of production where a social plan that would guide production, and disalienation in the transitional society would be achieved through workers' management of production. In the same work, Engels emphasized the necessity of the technical conditions that make nationwide coordination and planning of the economy possible.[151] But two political conditions are considered to form essential preconditions. First, the state must become a workers' state. Second, the capitalist relations have to be overcome. The nature of this capitalist relation cannot be separated from alienation. As Marx wrote:

> No special intelligence is needed to understand that, given the free labour that had emerged from serfdom, or wage labour, machines could not effectively *be created*, otherwise than as property confront which was alienated . . . and which . . . was bound to them as capital machines will not cease to be agencies of social production when they become for e.g., the property of the associated workers.[152]

Obviously, intensification of the power of the state could only harm this process. Nicola Badaloni has pointed out that as early as *The German Ideology*, Marx had blamed the division of labor for the fact that production and consumption, labor and enjoyment fell to different persons. It was therefore necessary to overcome division of labor.[153] But that could not be done by retrogression to pre-capitalist economics. What Marx had in mind was overcoming the distinction between worker and manager by democratic control. In his critical notes Marx refuted Bakunin's comment that as soon as some workers became representatives in any capacity in the workers' state: "they will no longer represent the people, but only themselves and their "claims" to govern the people."[154] Marx's position was that any worker elected for a term would still be paid a workers' wage.[155] In a cooperative factory, the manager would be vested with power to run the day to day administration, but would be ultimately controlled by the workers who had the authority to appoint the manager. Marx's juxtaposition of the worker's state means that he called for the universalization of this case to the running of this relationship under the dictatorship of the proletariat. Marx did not deny the need for specialized skills. What he denied was the idea that such skills were possible only at the cost of destroying democratic arrangements.[156] Overcoming the effects of division of labor meant, for Marx, the extension of free time, the possibility of one person learning more than one skill, and above all the systematic extension of workers' management.

The discussion on the political system of the transition period raises the next question. On the one hand, the dictatorship of the proletariat meant some sort of a state. On the other hand, there are well known comments regarding the "smashing" of the state, as well as its "withering away." What is the relationship between the revolutionary state, the smashing of the state, and the withering away?

In class terms, it was the bourgeois state that had to be immediately smashed. In institutional terms, that meant the abolition of bureaucratic autonomy, as stressed by Marx in *The Eighteenth Brumaire*,[157] as well as in his letter to Kugelmann.[158] And in the *CWF*, he commented: "The first decree of the Commune, therefore, was the suppression of the standing army and the substitution for it of the armed people."[159] Likewise, the police "was at once stripped of its political attributes, and turned into the responsible and at all times revocable agent of the commune."[160] To Marx the organized church was another instrument through which the rulers controlled the mass of workers and peasants. He therefore welcomed the disestablishment of the church and the freeing of education from both state and church control.[161] Thus education could become accessible to all and scientific outlook freed of the bond of class and bureaucratic dictates. This was a point to which Marx was long committed, and to which he returned in the course of the *Critique of the Gotha Programme*.[162]

In the "Preface" to the 1872 edition of the *Communist Manifesto*, Marx and Engels wrote that the experience of the Paris Commune showed that the old program had become somewhat antiquated, and quoted the *CWF*, "the working class cannot simply lay hold of the ready-made state machinery and wield it for its own purposes."[163] In other words, the old machinery could not serve a new class. Instead, the working class would have to make a violent revolution and get rid of the hierarchic, parasitic state apparatus before democratization was possible. Engels concurred with this need to smash the state in his "Introduction" to the *CWF*.[164]

But is not the idea of "smashing" the state in contradiction to the idea of a gradual withering away?[165] What had to be smashed was the autonomous military-bureaucratic apparatus of the exploiters' state. But this did not make Marx an anarchist at heart.[166] In *The Housing Question*, written in 1872-73, Engels wrote about "the views of German scientific socialism on the necessity of political action by the proletariat and of its dictatorship as the transition to the abolition of classes and, with them of the state."[167] Just two pages later, he wrote that *every* real proletarian party from the Chartists onward had put forward a policy of organizing the workers in order to establish the dictatorship of the proletariat as their immediate aim.[168]

But since a proletarian revolution was to involve the majority and set up a democracy, the use of force would be against that minority which refused to give up its status as exploiters. To repress them, a full-fledged military bureaucratic apparatus would not be necessary. That was why they reacted sharply to the demand for a "free state" in the Gotha Programme. Engels told Bebel, "a free state is one in which the state is free vis-à-vis its citizens, a state, that is, with a despotic government."[169] Marx commented on the same issue:

> Freedom consists in converting the state from an organ superimposed upon society into one completely subordinated to it, and even today forms of state are more free or less free to the extent that they restrict the "freedom of the state."[170]

This was not a matter of playing with words. For Marx and Engels, the state as a separate entity meant the snatching away of power from society. Though the working class needed a state, that state had to be Janus-faced. It had to repress the former ruling class. As Engels' letter to Bebel explained, during workers rule, the state in the traditional sense remained only in so far as the old exploiters had to be beaten back. But the other face of the workers' state was the massive extension of democracy, and the steady deprofessionalization of the public order. In that sense, the state would wither away.

But this brings the discussion back to the problem of politics under the dictatorship of the proletariat. Miliband has argued that the defense of the revolution would necessitate a strong state. So it is not enough to say that the dictatorship of the proletariat would be more democratic. Institutions would have to be indicated which would strengthen democracy and ensure the subsequent attenuation of the state.[171]

E. Meiksins Wood raises an even more important point. Since according to Marx a crucial task of every society would be to decide how social labor was to be allocated, a kind of public order would remain not only in the transitional society, but also in communist society, and would even grow stronger.[172] In capitalism, this allocation is regulated by the market. If communism meant a planned allocation of social labor, the planning agency would be a powerful public institution. Marx indicated as much, when, in the *Critique of the Gotha Programme*, he referred to "the future state of communist society."[173] Because of its differences with the old state, Engels suggested the replacement of "state" by "commune."[174] But whatever the name, what would be certain is that the very existence of authority would make its misappropriation a possibility. In his letter to Bebel, Engels did consider this problem briefly when he wrote:

> Similarly omitted [from the Gotha Programme] is the first pre-requisite of all liberty—that all officials be responsible for all their official actions to every citizen before the ordinary courts and in accordance with common law.[175]

By adding to this Marx's repeated emphasis on political democratization and popular control over the administration, it is possible to sketch the outline of a Marxist concept of the public order of the future, but it remains hazy due to Marx's well-known reluctance to speculate. However, it is at least certain that Marx's concept of communist freedom did not imply an absence of public order, but the subordination of the autonomous public order to social control. The experience of the Commune had suggested the first important institutions and mechanisms of control—replacement of the standing army by the armed proletariat (and its allies), accountability of all elected officials, minimization of non-elected officials, merger of executive with legislature, payment of officials at worker's wage rates, and so on. That was why Marx said of the Commune "that it was a thoroughly expansive political form while all previous forms of government had been emphatically repressive."[176] The state-like order of future communist society would have to build on such institutions, while shrugging off the last vestiges of the repressive mechanism as class struggle ended.

There remains only one brief criticism. Since Marx and Engels accepted representative democracy and approved the holding of elections in the Commune (their criticism was only over the timing) it may be assumed that they accepted a multi-party system. But their writings provide little clue to an understanding of the role of workers' parties in the period after the seizure of power by the working class, and in relation to the Communes. Moreover, since the transition was to transform the wage-laborers into associated producers, there could remain no place at the end of the process for class parties. At the same time, in any complex society different views, structured around a number of key issues, constitute programs and parties. Since Marx had little to say directly about all this, there remained a gap in his theory of democracy. In itself, this did not create either Stalinism or Social Democratic reformism. These were created by the interplay of social forces. But it would be legitimate to say that many brands of "socialism from above" have tried to subvert the democratic revolutionary ideas of Marx by exploiting such gaps.

NOTES

1. The most famous case is the international debate after the Russian revolution. This had begun with Lenin in *The State and Revolution LCW* 25, Moscow, 1980, 385–497. Karl Kautsky replied with *The Dictatorship of the Proletariat*, Ann Arbor, 1964. Other related writings included L. Trotsky, *Terrorism and Communism*, London, 1975, and K. Kautsky, *The Labour Revolution*, London, 1925. Other contributions included the writings of prominent Bolsheviks like Lev Kamenev and Nikolai Bukharian; Mensheviks like T. Dan and L. Martov; and German and American Social Democrats. Two main issues were involved in the debate: whether the concept of a dictatorship of the proletariat was only a passing phrase of Marx, or a central feature of his theory of the conquest of power by the working and its transition to a classless society; and whether or not the class concept implied the use of coercion against the class enemy. The fact that those claiming political continuity with Marx's ideas differed so radically on this point, and that this difference became associated with their rival assessments of Soviet Russia, shows the necessity of a fresh and clear examination of Marx's own views on the subject.
2. *MECW 7*, p. 16.
3. Quoted in ibid., p. 32.
4. Ibid., p. 32–33.
5. Ibid., p. 50.
6. Ibid., p. 205.
7. Ibid., p. 431.
8. Cited in H. Draper, *KMTR* 3, p. 65.
9. F. Engels, *Revolution and Counter-Revolution in Germany*, in *MESW* 1, p. 334–35.
10. *MECW* 6, p. 504. The *MECW* drops the capitalization.
11. Ibid., 10, p. 76.
12. Ibid., 26, p. 271.
13. Ibid., 10, p. 131
14. D. W. Lovell, *From Marx to Lenin*, pp. 60–61, however, claims that identification of dictatorship with rule creates problems. In p. 69, he writes, "I agree with those who argue that Marx's dictatorship is what it says it is: a dictatorship in the conventional sense. . . . If all class rule is dictatorship . . . then the political forms of class rule are unimportant." He later suggests that this constitutes a sin of omission which Lenin later exploited for his authoritarian purposes (p. 197) Lovell assumes

that words always mean the same thing, and that Marx was aware of the "conventional" meaning of "dictatorship" based on the experiences of the rule of Hilter, Stalin or Pinochet. This anachronism is even more surprising because Lovell cites Draper's "Marx and the Dictatorship of the Proletariat," *New Politics*, vol. 1, no. 4, 1962, pp. 91–104, as well as the unabridged version in *Études de Marxologie*, vol. 6, September, 1962, pp. 5–73. Lovell also cites R. N. Hunt, *The Political Ideas of Marx and Engels*, vol. 1. Both Draper and Hunt have insisted on the need to situate Marx's use of the term in the discourses of his own age. In *KMTR* 3, Draper shows that in the 19th century, "dictatorship" was used to signify the use of coercion. This was rooted in the Roman original. Even in *The Class Struggles in France*, Marx shows an awareness of different forms of government and does not indicate disinterest in that.

15. *MECW* 10, p. 122.

16. Compare, however, R. N. Carew Hunt, *The Theory and Practice of Communism*. According to him "the essence of the dictatorship of the proletariat is . . . the rule of a single section . . . whose mission is to eliminate all other section . . . " (p. 107). He does not provide any reference to Marx.

17. *MECW* 10, p. 69.

18. Ibid., p. 98.

19. Ibid., p. 127.

20. For his idea of educational dictatorship, see A. Blanqui, *Textes Choisis*, Paris, 1971, p. 151. For the dictatorship of Paris see S. Bernstein, *Auguste Blanqui and the Art of Insurrection*, pp. 310–11.

21. In this, Marx was following what were for him standard tactics. When writing for the Chartist press, Marx used the term "working class ascendancy," favored by Chartists. Thus Engels' article "The Ten Hours' Question," published in Harney's paper *The Democratic Review*, repeatedly stated that social gains of the working class depended on the proletarian ascendancy (*MECW* 10, pp. 275–76). The German version of the same article, intended for German communists, used the term proletarian revolution, and explained its consequence to be the rule of the proletariat (ibid., pp. 299-300). The other case, that of Marx adapting his language when drawing up the rules and the Inaugural Address of the International, has already been noted in Chapter 2. This was simply good political tactics, not a change in politics. Yet, just as Marx has been accused of falling a victim to the Blanquist disease, so he has been accused of giving up his revolutionary politics by working with trade unionists in the International. This is to confuse between revolutionary politics and a sectarianism that knows neither compromise nor flexibility, but insists on imposing its points-d'honneur upon the working class.

22. For the SUCR Articles, see *MECW*: 10, pp. 614–15. This is a poor translation although the point about the dictatorship of proletarians (the formulation in this document) is kept intact. See further, *KMTR* 3, pp. 184–87, and p. 404, note 2 for further details. The public statement of the Willich–Schapper League and the Blanquists, "Aux democrates de toutes des nations," is quoted in full in Marx's letter to Engels, December 1, 1850,

MECW 38, pp. 246–47 English translation pp. 247–49.

23. Lüning quoted in *KMTR* 3, pp. 221–22.

24. *MECW* 10, p. 387.

25. Ibid. 6, p. 506

26. Ibid. p. 212.

27. Ibid. 25, pp. 166–67. Omitted here is the role of private property and the formation of classes. This was due to the nature of the polemic with Dühring, who had put forward the theory that the state had been created by force. That Marx and Engels both tied the origin of the state to private property and class formation can be seen by comparing *The Origin of Family*, with L. Krader, ed., *The Ethnological Notebooks of Karl Marx*, Assen, 1974. On the basis of this argument in the *Anti-Dühring*, Draper makes the claim that all states are not class states according to Marx, and that the growing independence of the state could lead to the rise of a ruling class. He, therefore, believes that Marx's pre-communist period characterization of the Prussian bureaucracy as a class could also be admitted in a Marxist framework (*KMTR* 1, pp. 246–48, 488). See however, Engels' characterization of the Prussian bureaucracy as agents of the nobility in *MESW* 1, p. 302.

28. This is taken mainly from F. Engels, *The Origin of Family*, *MECW* 26, pp. 268–70.

29. *MECW* 6, p. 486.

30. Ibid. 26, pp. 270–71.

31. Ibid. 6, p. 506.

32. Cited in *KMTR* 3, pp. 244–45.

33. Ibid., pp. 62–65.

34. *MECW* 5, p. 47, has this translation except for its use of domination to translate *herrschaft*. For the German see *MEW*, Bd. 3, Berlin, 1956, p. 34. Domination is a problematic translation, because it can give the impression of something weaker than rule. The US domination of the world economy in the post-war period would never be translated by using *herrschaft*.

35. "Whatever Marx believed would be, or might be, characteristic of the post-revolutionary period, it was not *this* term that dealt with such problems of a workers' state," *KMTR* 3, p. 213.

36. *MECW* 22, p. 634.

37. Ibid. 24, p. 95.

38. *MESW* 3, p. 435.

39. The majority of scholars who have written on this point dispute the view that Marx considered the Commune to be a dictatorship of the proletariat. The exceptions are: S. H. M. Chang, *The Marxian Theory of the State*, pp. 98–102; H. Draper, *KMTR* 3, pp. 269–74; R. Milliband, *Marxism and Politics*, p. 138; R. Blackburn, "Marxism: Theory of Proletarian Revolution"; M. Johnstone, "The Paris Commune and Marx's Conception of the Dictatorship of the Proletariat," in J. Hicks and R. Tucker, eds., *Revolution and Reaction: The Paris Commune*, Boston, 1973, pp. 82–83; and A. Landy, *Marxism and the Democratic Tradition*, p. 182. For G. Lichtheim, *Marxism: An Historical and Critical Study*, pp. 118–9, the Commune could not be a dictatorship of

the proletariat because (i) it had been elected; (ii) it had mixed political composition including middle-class republicans, as well as socialists of various kind; and (iii) the National Guard also included republicans. He provides no quotation to show that Marx believed a dictatorship of the proletariat had to be unelected, monolithic, and with an armed force in which every member had to be communist. B. D. Wolfe, *Marxism*, relies extensively on Draper's 1962 article, (pp. 206–217), but then asks how and entire class could dictate, rule, or exercise its *herrschaft* (p. 256). Wolfe's implication is that class dictatorship is impossible, and throughout his Chapter 12, he suggests that after the Commune Marx talked of violence only when democratic institutions were absent. Thus he returns to the position that dictatorship refers only to force. See also S. Avineri, *The Social and Political Thought of Karl Marx*, p. 240; D. W. Lovell, *From Marx to Lenin*, p. 81. Lovell even claims that Engels' remarks on the proletarian dictatorship "confused" the issue. This is put even more strongly by N. Harding, *Lenin's Political Thought*, vol 2. London and Basingstoke, 1983, pp. 84–92. According to Harding, Marx had two distinct theories of the future state: the dictatorship of the proletariat as a transitional coercive instrument which to be centralized and the Commune, which was not a state but anarchy, and which was to be quite decentralized. Harding argues that Marx "never identified the Commune as the dictatorship of the proletariat." (p. 91) He holds that Engels made the identification only rhetorically and thereby created a permanent duality in the Marxian theory of state. See futher, D. McLellan, The *Thought of Karl Marx*, pp. 212, 242, and R. N. Carew Hunt, *The Theory and Practice of Communism*, p. 104. J. O'Malley and K. Algozin, ed., *Rubel on Karl Marx*, shows that according to Rubel, Engels distorted Marx's idea in equating the Commune with the dictatorship of the proletariat. Even E. Schulkind, who has edited a volume on the Paris Commune, expressed uncertainty over whether Marx characterized the Commune as a proletarian dictatorship, thought of it in that way, or even whether he was wholly serious in calling it a political form, etc. E. Schulkind, *The Paris Commune of 1871*, pp. 53–54, and E. Schulkind, "Paris Commune," in T. Bottomore, ed., *A Dictionary of Marxist Thought*, Oxford, 1983, pp. 359–60.

40.   A number of commentators have claimed to find a contradiction in the Marxian theory of the state and its future because of the two facets of the state—the state as class power and the state as a bureaucratic apparatus. R. N. Hunt, *The Political Ideas of Marx and Engels*, vol. II, claims that Marx and Engels actually worked with two different theories of state, applying whichever was suitable at a particular moment. R. C. Tucker, *The Marxian Revolutionary Idea*, London, 1970, p. 59, sees a tension between the conception of the state as alienated power, and its functional definition as an organ of class rule. D. W. Lovell, *From Marx to Lenin*, pp. 46–54, mentions a similar contradiction. He however claims that Marx's political project was that of emancipating politics from the state and returning it to "man" [sic] thereby showing that bureaucratic autonomy is central to his understanding of Marx's theory of state. S. Avineri, *The Social and*

Political Thought of Karl Marx, claims to see a basic difference between Marx and Engels. Avineri thinks that for Engels the state is nothing but an external organization for coercion, while for Marx, the existence of the state remained a contradiction between particularity and universality (p. 203). In other words, for him, Marx's theory of state did not change after 1843. All these interpretations and the conclusion, with respect to the dictatorship of the proletariat, are flawed by the inability to see that in their overall theory of the state there could be no contradiction between the concept of the state as the voice of a class and the state as alienated power. See also on this N. Poulantzas, *Political Power and Social Classes*, London, 1973.

41. S. Bernstein, *Auguste Blanqui*, pp. 303–8.
42. *MECW* 22, p. 269, ibid. 44, pp. 73–74. See also a series of refutations of false accusations about Marx or the International as the instigator of the Commune in, K. Marx and F. Engels, "Statement by the General council on Jules Favre's Circular," and F. Engels, "The Address *The Civil War in France* and the English Press," in ibid. 22, pp. 361–66, 375–77.
43. Ibid., pp. 585–86.
44. Ibid., p. 595.
45. Ibid., p. 334.
46. Ibid., p. 634.
47. H. Draper , *KMTR* 3, p. 293.
48. *MECW* 44, p. 137.
49. Ibid. 23, p. 175.
50. *MESC*, p. 366.
51. *MESW* 2, p. 189, Engels' particular target was a rightwing Social Democratic deputy to the Reichstag, Karl Grillenberger, who had repudiated the charge that the Social Democrats wanted to establish the dictatorship of the proletariat. For the whole incident, see Draper, *KMTR* 3, pp. 312–15.
52. *MESW* 3, p. 435.
53. Draper, *KMTR* 3, p. 319.
54. See F. Busi, "The Failure of the Revolution," in *Revolution and Reaction*, J. Hicks and R. Tucker, eds., pp. 19–20. See also D. Thomson, *Europe Since Napoleon*, Harmondsworth, 1982, pp. 395–96, for a popular textbook version.
55. P. Lissagaray, *History of the Commune of 1871*, p. 12.
56. Ibid., p. 15.
57. Ibid., pp. 33–36.
58. H. Lefebvre, *The Explosion: Marxism and the French Revolution*, New York, 1968. See also F. Jellinek, *The Paris Commune of 1871*.
59. Lissagaray, *History of the Commune of 1871*, p. 87.
60. E. Schulkind, *The Paris Commune of 1871*, pp. 107–8.
61. Ibid., p.109.
62. M. Johnstone, "The Paris Commune," p. 81. For an example of such a Social Democratic analysis, see K. Kautsky, *The Dictatorship of the Proletariat*, p. 45.
63. *MECW* 22, p. 336.

64. Lissagaray, *History of the Commune of 1871*, p. 159.
65. Full text in E. Schulkind, *The Paris Commune of 1871*, pp. 152–54.
66. M. Johnstone, "The Paris Commune," p. 81.
67. *MECW* 22, p. 494. See pp. 492–93 for the list of benefits that Marx said the Commune would confer on the peasants.
68. Ibid., p. 337. Compare pp. 494–95.
69. *MESC*, p. 338.
70. Thus Avineri writes: "Marx considered the Commune not a working class affair but a petty bourgeois, democratic radical emeute. He never explicitly states this in the final, published version of the essay, though he hints in this direction." S. Avineri *The Social and Political Thought of Karl Marx*, p. 247. See also ibid., p. 200, and Lovell, *From Marx to Lenin*, p. 59. Avineri thus sets aside Marx's *explicit* utterance, that the Commune was "essentially a working class government" (*MECW* 22, p. 234) and finds "hints" about the petty–bourgeois character of the Commune, though he does not quote and explain those hints.
71. F. Engels, "Programme of the Blanquist Commune Refugees," in MECW, 24, p. 13.
72. Ibid., pp. 16–17.
73. Ibid. 22, p. 335.
74. Ibid. 44, pp. 36–37
75. Ibid. 22, p. 339.
76. E. Schulkind, *The Paris Commune of 1871*, pp. 135–36, See also pp. 128–29, 137–38 for other examples.
77. Ibid., p. 139.
78. Ibid., p. 141.
79. *MECW* 22, p. 339.
80. Ibid. 10, p. 137.
81. Ibid. 22, pp. 330–31.
82. R. N. Hunt, *The Political Ideas of Marx and Engels*, vol II, pp. 132–33, claims at this point that Marx was not differentiating workers' democracy from bourgeois democracy. Hunt treats this difference as a simple expansion of democracy, apart from the issue of violence, noted earlier. He also does not see any counterposition between the parliamentary and the Commune forms (p. 161).
83. *MECW* 22, pp. 331–32.
84. Ibid., p. 333.
85. See C. Pierson, *Marxist Theory and Democratic Politics*, p. 23; E. J. Hobsbawm, *The History of Marxism*, p. 230.
86. E. Schulkind, *The Paris Commune of 1871*, pp. 150–51. With ample class sense, the document attacked the Versailles Assembly, calling it the focus of "the old governmental and clerical world; of militarism, bureaucracy, exploitation, speculation, monopolies and privilege that have kept the proletariat in servitude and led the nation to disaster."
87. *MECW* 22, p. 332.
88. Ibid. 10, p. 285.
89. Ibid., pp. 285–86.

90. K. Marx, *The Eighteenth Brumaire of Louis Bonaparte,* in ibid. 11, p. 193. The last two sentences, and two further sentences, were deleted by Marx in the Second edition of 1869. But the ground that he gave for the deletions was that he had struck out "allusions now no longer intelligible," i.e., he did not repudiate anything.

91. Ibid. 22, pp. 328–30.

92. Ibid. p. 487.

93. Ibid. p. 333.

94. Ibid. p. 487.

95. Ibid. pp. 533, 490.

96. For a systematic treatment of this separation in capitalism, see E. M. Wood, "The Separation of the 'Economic' and the 'Political' in Capitalism," *New Left Review,* no. 127, May–June, 1981.

97. *MECW* 22, p. 491.

98. Ibid., pp. 329–31.

99. For liberal political theory, see the summary in J. Dunn, *Western Political Theory in the Face of the Future,* for a sympathetic account. The classic critical account is C. B. MacPherson, *The Political Theory of Possessive Individualism.* See also N. Wood, *Locke and Agrarian Capitalism;* C. B. MacPherson, *The Life and Times of Liberal Democracy;* G. Duncan, *Marx and Mill,* Cambridge, 1973; A. K. Mukhopadhyay, *The Ethics of Obedience,* Calcutta, 1967. The above is not an exhaustive list, but the main works consulted in putting forward the summary view of liberalism above. Admittedly, liberalism as a whole is more complex, and a case can even be made, as Richard Ashcraft has done, that Locke, one of the founding fathers of liberalism, was more radical than the Marxist tradition, including the MacPherson version, allows. For the present purpose, however, it is enough to note that individual, not class, forms the starting point of liberal theory, and that its main aim remains the protection of the rational individual, such a logic leads to the defense of capitalist property relations. Since the state is by definition not allowed to tamper economic relations. This is the rationale behind Smith's laissez faire. More recently, this is the fundamental principle of liberal theorists like R. Nozick, *Anarchy, State and Utopia,* New York, 1974.

100. *MECW,* 24, p. 95.

101. Ibid., p. 96.

102. Ibid., p. 71.

103. This should be contrasted to Draper's assertion: "Was the council system . . . as a *form of government,* a necessary and inevitable and "permanent" feature of the dictatorship of the proletariat? . . . My sole reason for raising it is—to set it aside. *For this question was not covered by Marx's view of the "dictatorship of the proletariat* which embraced *no idea* about specific governmental form as a necessary part of the concept." H. Draper, *DPML,* pp. 130–31. Draper is obviously confused by the different ways in which Marx and Engels used the term "democratic republic." See also, E. Hobsbawm, "Marx, Engels and Politics," in E. Hobsbawm, ed., *The History of Marxism* p. 234. For a detailed refutation of Draper from a point of view that admits the possibility of state

capitalism" see S. Wright, "Hal Draper's Marxism," *International Socialism,* Sr. II, no. 47, Summer 1990, pp.171–77. Wright however underestimates the extent to which Marx and Engels counterposed bourgeois democracy and proletarian democracy, because he tries to see the counter-position with the "democratic republic," but of a different kind.

104. *MESC,* p. 371.

105. *MESW* 1, pp. 202–3. And "Introduction" to English edition of *Capital:* 1, p. 17.

106. Ibid. 2, p. 189.

107. Ibid. 3, p. 435.

108. For the earlier discussion of this quotation, see text to footnote 57, above. For Guérin's thesis, see D. Guérin, *La Lutte de classes sous la Premiere Republique: Bourgeois et "Bras Nus" (1793–1797),* vol. I, Paris, 1946, pp. 38–41.

109. Marxist historians have strongly emphasized the fact that bourgeois revolutions are the work of a number of classes and strata including the nascent working class. While the upper bourgeoisie tended to agree to a compromise after the initial victories, it was the plebeian and proto-proletarian masses who fought or more radical reforms. This is true of the English Revolution, where democracy was the demand of the Levellers and social justice and equality that of the Diggers. In the French revolution, likewise, lower class pressure led to social and political radicalism. For radicalism in civil war England, see C. Hill, *The World Turned Upside Down,* Harmondsworth, 1975, and B. Manning, *The English People and the English Revolution,* London, 1992. See also, H. N. Brailsford, *The Levellers and the English Revolution,* London, 1961.

110. K. Marx "Trouble in Germany" in *MECW* 16, p. 541.

111. F. Jellinek, pp. 179–80.

112. M. Johnstone, "The Paris Commune," pp. 89–90; and R. N. Hunt, *The Political Ideas of Marx and Engels,* vol. II, pp. 146–47, have argued that elsewhere Marx did not endorse the indirect system of election. This confirms that on this point the experience of the Commune was decisive.

113. At the time of the Paris Commune, large factories were still limited. That is why factory-level committees did not spring up, nor were advocated by Marx, as they have sprung up in a whole series of twentieth century revolutions and major class struggles and were advocated by Marxists. For such cases, see O. Anweiler, *The Soviets,* New York, 1974; D. Gluckstein, *The Western Soviets,* London, 1985. The matter is discussed further in Chapters 5 and 6 below, Alan Hunt, "Marx—the Missing Dimension," pp. 105–107, equates parliamentary democracy with representative democracy, and ignoring the *structure* of the commune, identifies it as an "insurrectionary model." As a result, he misses the significance of Marx's critique of parliamentarism. Compare C. Sparks, "Democracy and the State," C. Harman, ed., *Marxists and the State,* London, 1987, pp. 10–11, where contemporary examples are used to show the necessarily bourgeois character of existing parliamentarism.

114. *MECW* 1, pp. 130 see also pp. 166, 237–38. 384, *MECW* 3, p. 41.

115. Ibid. 2, p. 302 also pp. 136, 141, 307, 359.

116. Ibid. 3, pp. 506–12.

117. Ibid. 7, pp. 201–02, 437; Ibid., 8, pp. 75–80, 197–203, 316–17.
118. K. Marx, "A Prussian view of the War," in ibid. 16, pp. 341–42.
119. Ibid. 22, p. 332.
120. The first is from the Gotha program, the second from the Erfurt program.
121. Engels to Laura Lafargue, February 16–17, 1883; *MEW* bd-35, Berlin, 1968, p. 436.
122. The case of Bakunin is particularly instructive, because he has been hailed as the libertarian alternative to authoritarian Marxism. Thus, Avrich claims that Lenin's espousal of the Commune State was Bakuninism. P. Avrich, "Preface" to *Bakunin on Anarchy*, ed. S. Dolgoff, p. xxi. See also Lovell, *From Marx to Lenin*, pp. 62–64. Non-anarchist writers have also sometimes accepted this division.
123. In his *Statehood and Anarchy*, Bakunin wrote: "the universal suffrage of the whole people to elect its representatives and "rulers of state" — that is the last word of the Marxists and also of the democratic school — is a lie which conceals the despotism of the ruling minority." Quoted in *MECW* 24, pp. 519–20.
124. S. Dolgoff, ed., *Bakunin on Anarchy*, pp. 180–81.
125. *MECW* 24, p. 519.
126. "What does it mean to talk of the proletariat 'raised to the level of the ruling estate?' Will perhaps the entire proletariat stand at the head of the government? There are about 40 million Germans. Does this mean that all 40 million will be members of the government?"
127. J. S. Mill, *Considerations on Representative Government*, London, 1918, Chapter X, p. iv.
128. *MECW* 7, p. 138.
129. Ibid. 8, p. 227.
130. Ibid. 9, p. 453.
131. Ibid. 10, p. 282.
132. For a documentation of this, see H. Draper, *KMTR* 3, pp. 361–67. Marx's and Engels' anti-Robespierrist view point is seldom recognized. See B. D. Wolfe, *Marxism*, p. 20.
133. *MECW* 44, pp. 128, 132.
134. Ibid., pp. 148–49. For Frankel's letter, see E. Schulkind. *The Paris Commune*, pp. 117–18.
135. *MECW* 22, p. 320.
136. Ibid., pp. 323–24, 326–27.
137. Ibid., pp. 348–49.
138. Ibid., pp. 530, 326.
139. Ibid., p. 331. For the shooting of hostages, see pp. 350–52. Likewise, he quoted without disapproval the decree of the Commune which stated that its duty was: "to protect Paris against the cannibal exploits of the Versailles banditti and to demand an eye for an eye, a tooth for a tooth." Ibid., p. 327.
140. K. Marx, "Political Indifferentism," in ibid. 23, p. 393.
141. Draper, by contrast, claims that neither Marx nor Engels *ever* linked the necessity of suppressing the bourgeois resistance to the dictatorship of

the proletariat. *DPML*, p. 134.

142. *MECW* 24, pp. 469–70.

143. Ibid. 44, p. 286.

144. F. Engels, "On Authority," in ibid. 23, pp. 423, 424.

145. D. W. Lovell, *From Marx to Lenin*, p. 74, quotes a turn of phrase ("no matter how delegated") to accuse Engels of relegating the chief area of concern to obscurity. In fact, the turn of phrase came after Engels had discussed *different types of democratic arrangements*. This is one more unfortunate instance of how casually too many scholars pick sentences, and even fragments of sentences, out of the voluminous writings of Marx and Engels to build up cases that would be completely untenable if the texts are studied if full, and in context.

146. *MECW* 23, p. 425.

147. *MESC*, p. 362

148. Consequently neither Marx nor Engels bear any responsibility for those "Marxists" who have used arguments like those presented in "On Authority" to justify the most anti-democratic regimes, or for those "Marxists" who, like the anarchists, oppose democracy for supposedly throttling liberty.

149. R. N. Carew Hunt, *The Theory and Practice of Communism*, pp. 290–91.

150. *MECW* 25, p. 279.

151. Ibid., p. 266.

152. K. Marx, *Grudrisse der Kritik der Politischen Ökonomie*, Berlin, 1953, p. 717.

153. N. Badaloni, "Marx and the Quest for Communist Liberty," in E. J. Hobsbawm, ed., *The History of Marxism*, p. 178.

154. This is from Marx's translation cum paraphrase, in *MECW* 24, p. 520.

155. Ibid.

156. E. Mandel, *The Formation of the Economic Thought of Karl Marx*, pp. 195–97 notes that even the most sophisticated Stalinist theorists differ from Marx on exactly this point. He quotes the East German author, Wolfgang Heise, as saying that the high development of the productive forces requires a high level of "Organization and differentiation of social functions," and therefore it would be "senseless to demand direct democracy in production [i.e. shop floor or factory level assemblies] or the abandonment of authoritarian central planning."

157. *MESW* 1, p. 476–77.

158. *MECW* 44, p. 131.

159. Ibid. 23, p. 331.

160. Ibid.

161. Ibid., pp. 331–32.

162. "*Education of the people by the state'* is altogether objectionable. Defining by a general law the expenditures on the elementary schools, the qualifications of the teaching staff, the subjects of instruction, etc., and as is done in the United States, supervising the fulfilment of these legal specifications by state inspections, is a very different thing from appointing the state as the educator of the people: Government and church should rather be excluded from any influence on the school." *MECW* 24, p. 97. See also ibid.: 22, p. 496,

where Marx wrote that only the working class could convert science from an instrument of class rule (using science in the sense of knowledge) into a popular force, and allow real freedom of thought to scientists. Thus, he was totally opposed to any idea of a "proletarian science" where a "revolutionary" despotism would order scientific research in its narrow interests.

163. *MECW* 23, p. 175. Eduard Bernstein was to quote these lines in order to suggest that thereby Marx and Engels gave up the idea of class power. He even defined democracy as "an absence of class government." E. Bernstein, *Evolutionary Socialism*, pp. 155–56, 142. For a detailed discussion of the revisionist interpretation of this statement, see S. H. M. Chang, *The Marxian Theory of the State*, pp. 14–19, 72–73, 92–93.

164. *MESW* 2, pp. 188–89. H. Draper, *KMTR* 1, pp. 282–83, 334, 463, and *DPML*, passim, makes bourgeois rule almost coterminous with authoritarianism so that democratization itself becomes a leading element in his account of the working-class struggle, without emphasizing different class contexts of democratic political forms.

165. This is how N. Harding, *Lenin's Political Thought*, vol. 2, pp. 89–91, views it.

166. For such claims, see R. C. Tucker, *The Marxian Revolutionary Idea*, p. 85, and S. F. Bloom, The "Withering Away" of the state," *Journal of the History of Ideas*, vol. 7, 1946, p. 121.

167. F. Engels, "The Housing Question" in *MECW* 23, p. 370.

168. Ibid., p. 372.

169. Ibid., 24, p. 71.

170. Ibid., p. 94.

171. R. Miliband, *Marxism and Politics*, pp. 180–90.

172. E. Meiksins Wood, *The Retreat From Class*, pp. 155–56.

173. *MECW* 24, p. 95.

174. Ibid., p. 71.

175. Ibid., p. 70.

176. Ibid., 22, pp. 333–34.

6

VANGUARD PARTY AND REVOLUTIONARY STRATEGY: BOLSHEVISM BEFORE THE FEBRUARY REVOLUTION

Our survey has concentrated so far on Marx, Engels, and the German Social Democracy, because historically, that is how classical Marxism seemed to develop. Marx and Engels of course reflected on revolutionary struggles in different countries, and their theoretical generalizations were based on diverse sources. But the Marxism that was transmitted to hundreds of thousands of European workers in the late nineteenth and early twentieth centuries was the Marxism of the Second International, with the SPD as its biggest, most influential section. Moreover, unlike the French Section of the International (the SFIO) or others, the SPD seemed a model of revolutionary virtues, having repeatedly voted against Bernsteinian revisionism in party congresses. Yet when World War I came, the bulk of the SPD capitulated to imperialism. The heritage of revolutionary Marxism was claimed by different shades of the left wing. The triumph of the October Revolution seemed to prove conclusively that the mantle had fallen properly on the Bolsheviks. Leninism, it seemed, was the Marxism of the twentieth century.

This claim has to be critically re-examined in the context of the relationship between Marxism and workers' democracy sketched out in the foregoing chapters. Ninety years after the Russian Revolution, we are aware of the process of bureaucratization, of the imposition of a dictatorship of a very different sort in the USSR, and we are also aware of the criticisms which argue that Stalinism was not as departure from Bolshevism but its logical culmination. It is therefore necessary to study closely the theory and practice of Bolshevism from 1903 to 1921.

The history of Bolshevism, up to the period when a one-party system of rule was established, can be divided into three stages. These are: the period from its origins to the eve of the revolution of 1917; the revolutionary year (1917); and the early years of Bolshevik power (October/November 1917–early 1921). In the present chapter, the spotlight will be mainly on the first of these periods. The aim will be to study how a theory and strategy of workers' revolution was worked out in backward Russia, and what sort of a political instrument was developed to carry out these strategic tasks.

Russian Marxism began by opposing the Narodnik ideology. The Narodnik ideology had a number of roots. It was an ideology of socialism, but stressing the unique nature of Russia. It based itself on Haxthausen's and Herzen's studies on the Russian peasant communities to argue that it could be possible in the Russian case to bypass capitalism and move to collective production by basing oneself on the traditions of peasant collectivism. One current hoped to achieve this end by propaganda among the peasants, while another hoped for results through direct action including terrorism. At the same time, it was a response to Marx, especially to Marx's *Capital*, which many of the Narodniks saw as a foretelling of what would happen to Russia if capitalism entered that country. At the same time, the Narodniks saw Marx as one of their teachers.[1] So the foundation of an alternative Russian Marxist (Social Democratic) tradition called for protracted ideological struggles against them. It was committed to an elaboration of a Marxist strategy of proletarian revolutionary struggles in a country where the proletariat was not the majority class, and where, moreover, the autocratic regime made legal socialist activities, even at the level possible in Germany during the period of the Anti-Socialist Law, quite impossible. Opposition to Narodnism called for an alternative praxis.[2] This meant the summation of the experiences of proletarian struggle. How this could be done in Russia was a matter of sharp debate, leading to a split among the Russian Marxists. Between 1903, the year of the original split, and 1912, when the Bolsheviks proclaimed themselves to be the real Russian Social Democratic Labour Party (hereafter RSDLP/RSDRP) in opposition to the Mensheviks, a distinctive Bolshevik strategy and organizational politics was developed. It is by examining the nature of this strategy, and this concept of party, that the nature of Bolshevik participation in the revolution of 1917 can best be understood.

At the same time, it is my aim to examine the Russian social democratic (mainly Bolshevik) approach to women workers and their integration in the revolutionary process. For this it will be necessary to look at women workers, the concept of a vanguard party and how far it was gendered, and the question of programmatic issues relating to women.

I

BUILDING A VANGUARD PARTY

In studying Bolshevism, what always comes up first, whether in praise or in criticism, is the Bolshevik party itself. In order to assess the Bolshevik theory of party building, it must be situated in its historical context. It is on the basis of that, rather than a simple comparison of texts, that it must be investigated how far the concept of a vanguard party was in accordance with the principles of proletarian self-emancipation and workers' democracy.[3]

V. I. Lenin is the outstanding architect of the theory of the vanguard party. But the history of Bolshevism cannot be reduced to Lenin's ideas. Nor is it proper to assume that the idea of the party was a tactical one, unconnected to basic Marxist political principles. While there was no direct transmission from Marx to Lenin, the early writings of Lenin reveal, if anything, an excessive veneration for the Marxist orthodoxy. The nature of the Marxist influences on Lenin must, therefore, be understood. His understanding of Marxism was deeply influenced by Plekhanov as well as by the political practice of the German Social Democratic Party especially up to 1914.

In his biography of Lenin, Leon Trotsky wrote correctly that without knowing the works of Plekhanov, Lenin could not have become a Social Democrat.[4] In Russia, most populists considered Marx to be one of their teachers. So a specifically Social Democratic politics involved more than an acceptance of Marx. It meant the acceptance of a proletarian revolution. This called for accepting the certainty of capitalist development, the growth of the proletariat, and its eventual hegemony. Although Plekhanov had a somewhat dogmatic position, he was to pioneer these ideas in Russia. In early polemics against the populists, he asserted that a people are prepared for democracy to the extent of their economic development.[5] At a Congress of the Second International he stated that the Russian revolution would either triumph only as a workers' revolution or it would never triumph.[6] However, in his view, "the hegemonic role of the proletariat stopped short of the seizure of power after the overthrow of Tsarism."[7] In a polemic with Lev Tikhomirov, *Narodnaya Volya* theorist, Plekhanov commented that unlike the Narodniks, the Marxists saw in the proletariat the basic force of the revolution.[8] In other words, there developed a conception of the proletariat as the most powerful agency in the revolution, but the revolution itself was viewed as purely a bourgeois–democratic revolution.

Another influence on Lenin was that of West European Marxist orthodoxy. Lenin's first public writings were preceded by serious studies in Marxism, including *Capital* (he had read vol. II by 1893 and vol. III by 1895 at the latest).[9] He had read major German Social Democratic newspapers and journals like *Neue Zeit* and *Vorwärts*, and other writings of German Social Democrats.[10] Lenin's intellectual roots are in fact, international and Marxist, rather than national and Narodnik.[11] Party building in Russia passed through many stages. In many of these, Lenin was only one of many participants. Long before the emergence of Bolshevism, he showed a clear tendency to base his organizational projects on his overriding political concerns.[12] The need for a political party was by this time a cardinal tenet of European Socialism. In 1895-6, while in prison Lenin wrote in the "Draft and Explanation of a Programme for the Social-Democratic Party":

> The Russian Social-Democratic Party declares that its aim is to assist this struggle of the Russian working class by developing the class-consciousness of the workers, by promoting their organization, and by indicating the aims and objects of the struggle.[13]

He explicitly affirmed that "The emancipation of the workers must be the act of the working class itself."[14] The Social Democratic movement, once it broke out of the circles of radicalized intelligentsia, turned to recruiting workers. But the initial practice of recruitment through study circles limited the Social Democratic work to the narrow upper stratum of skilled workers, who often stood apart from the mass of workers, and who emphasized self-development.[15] The first attempt to overcome this by arousing mass discontent was made by the Vilno activist, Arkady Kremer, who led a strike. In his pamphlet, *Ob Agitatsii* (on agitation) in 1895, he argued that out of the struggles in the factories, a class sense would develop, enabling the workers to attain socialist consciousness.[16] Lenin also took part in such agitational activities.[17] He felt that a declared body of Marxist theory already existed in Russia, with which the revolutionaries could operate. In 1897 he wrote in exile "The Tasks of the Russian Social-Democrats," where he urged that the immediate task was to organize practical work on the basis of existing revolutionary projections.[18]

However, success in factory agitations led to a one-sided development of the economic struggles, which were thought to be self-sufficient and which would lead to a revolutionary consciousness arising within the workers.[19] Those who advocated this one-sided economic struggle to the exclusion of direct political struggles, were called "Economists," and their "deviation" was termed "Economism," by the orthodox Marxists, like Plekhanov, Axelrod, and their followers. Lenin, as one of the leading younger orthodox Marxists, rejected this "Economism" and emphasized that theoretical, ideological and organizational independence of the working class from the bourgeoisie was a burning task, and this could be done only by placing the economic struggles in the historic context of the fight for socialism. He expected the proletariat to become the vanguard fighter for political liberty and, therefore, considered the organizational merging of proletarian and non-proletarian forces as a form of weakening of the political struggle.[20] Thus the vanguard party was to be a proletarian party par excellence. The political independence of the proletariat depended on the existence of a workers' party with a revolutionary program, which "Economist" tactics could not ensure.[21] A party organization, Lenin argued, could not "make" a revolution. But success in a revolution depended on the independent and organized activity of the leaders of the revolutionary class. The localized and "primitive" character of Social-Democratic practical work, which was paralyzing the party's ability to produce the necessary leadership, had to be overcome,[22] so that the mass movement could go on to become a revolution.

Lenin differed from Marx in his analysis of the fragmented character of the working class. Marx had not analyzed in full details the implication of this fragmentation. Lenin argued that the proletariat had several distinguishable strata: the advanced workers, who were the "natural leaders" of the proletariat, and were most receptive to socialist ideas; the "average workers," who, despite the term, were politicized people, who "strive ardently for socialism . . . (but) cannot become fully independent leaders"; and the mass of workers.[23] Ernest Mandel points out that for Lenin, building a proletarian revolutionary party meant fusing the socialist intelligentsia with the advanced workers in one organization.[24] As Lenin said, in the "The Urgent Tasks of our Movement" unless the workers' vanguard was separated, instead of establishing proletarian hegemony the workers would become "the tail of other parties" and betray the principle of self-emancipation.[25]

The actual historical content of Lenin's party-building project needs to be kept in mind at each stage. In the period under discussion, Tsarist Russia lacked utterly all democratic rights. Lenin's article "Where to Begin," which came out in the paper of the orthodox trend in RSDLP *Iskra*, (1901), pointed out that at that time the mass of workers were pressing forward, while the revolutionaries lacked a proper organization. He attacked the "Economists" as impressionists who, as a result of this mass upsurge, were suddenly calling for terror and open assaults on Tsarism.[26] By contrast, he urged the necessity of patient work. Lenin insisted, here too, that the communists were not Blanquists. Lenin did not conceive the task of the vanguard as one of artificially provoking an insurrection or preparing a coup. The question was one of preparing a country-wide revolutionary workers' party and organizational unity through *Iskra* organization and an all-Russian newspaper[27] so that spontaneous upsurges could be given a proletarian direction. In an attempt in 1899 to revive the official party organ *Rabochaya Gazeta,* set up by the First Congress of the RSDLP, Lenin had pointed out that in other countries, the workers had numerous means for public manifestation of their activity. Until the Russian people won political liberty, a broad organization of the movement had to be structured around a revolutionary newspaper.[28] This idea already emerged in "Our Immediate Task," was repeated in 1901, when he wrote:

> A newspaper is not only a collective propagandist and a collective agitator, it is also a collective organizer . . . , which marks the contours of the structure . . . with the aid of the newspaper . . . a permanent organization will naturally take shape.[29]

Contrary to the belief that Lenin only talked of putting theory into workers' heads from outside, he himself did not see the readers of the party press as ignorant. The function of the writer was not to hand out pre-digested and oversimplified generalities to the worker, but to help the reader move to independent ideological–political development.[30] Party literature had to express all shades of opinion and views prevailing among the Social Democrats.[31] Thus the Lenin who emerges shortly before *What is to be Done?* was written, was a revolutionary who wanted to build a workers' party, with the only form of internal democracy feasible in Russian underground conditions, and who believed that class independence was necessary and could be achieved only through a proletarian party.

It is necessary to situate *What is to be Done?* in the course of these arguments, keeping in mind the polemical purpose of the work, which was to defeat "Economism" and to set up a united, orthodox Marxist Party. Where Lenin's polemics were political, the *Iskra*-ists were accused by their opponents of being slanderers, and so on.[32] The central thrust of Lenin's work was neither vilification, nor opposition, but a positive elaboration of the view that the Social Democratic Party had to act as "a political centralizer of fragmentary struggles, sectional experiences and partial perspectives of different layers of the masses."[33] Failing this, the revolutionaries lagged behind this upsurge, both in their "theories" and in their activity.[34] Thus *What is to be Done?*, placed in the context of the ultimate aim of a successful proletarian revolution to be brought about by the organized effort of the class itself, emphasized the shortcomings of the party rather than that of the spontaneous movement of the proletariat.

Opposing "Economism" as one-sided, he argued that consciousness developed only "within" a factory was inadequate. Revolutionary socialist consciousness developed "outside" the factory. A revolutionary was not just a good trade unionist, but a "tribune of the people."[35] All sorts of experiences, the inter-relationship of all classes, and the state, vis-à-vis the proletariat, had to be understood before a socialist consciousness could develop.

The task of *Iskra* was to build the party through a many-sided emphasis on theory, propaganda, agitation, and organization,[36] which would ultimately train a layer of the "professional revolutionary." Lenin explained that the call for professional revolutionaries came from two factors. The conjunctural factor was the total absence of democracy in Russia. In the absence of any elective principle or scope for any open circulation of party decisions, which are essential preconditions for real inner-party democracy, only full-time party activists could ensure stability of the party.[37] The argument about publicity shows that Lenin also desired, in the long run, a transparent class-party relationship. Meanwhile, by releasing militant workers from their jobs, they could be enabled to develop theoretically, as well as to ensure mass participation in the broad movement.[38]

Throughout *What is to be Done?* Lenin repeated that the spontaneous mass movement was forging ahead while the party failed to keep up with its place.[39] The other *Iskra* editors congratulated Lenin for the book.[40] It is necessary to show that his errors at this stage were errors common to orthodox Marxists.

In a celebrated passage of the book, Lenin wrote:

> [W]e have said that there could not have been Social-Democratic consciousness among the workers. It would have to be brought to them from without. The history of all countries shows that the working class, exclusively by its own efforts, is able to develop only trade union consciousness. . . . The theory of socialism, however, grew out of the philosophic, historical and economic theories elaborated by educated representatives of the propertied classes, by intellectuals . . . the theoretical doctrine of Social-Democracy arose altogether independently of the spontaneous growth of the working-class movement.[41]

This elitist notion of the development of revolutionary consciousness was buttressed, a few pages later, with a reference to the authority of Kautsky, who wrote on the draft program of the Austrian Social Democratic party, that:

> Modern Socialist consciousness can arise only on the basis of profound scientific knowledge. . . . The Vehicle of science is not the proletariat, but the bourgeois intelligentsia . . . the task of Social-Democracy is to imbue the proletariat with the consciousness of its position and the consciousness of its tasks. There would be no need for this if consciousness arose of itself from the class struggle.[42]

Later, Lenin was to admit that he had consciously "bent the stick" out of polemical consideration.[43] This and the quotation from Kautsky can be used to "exculpate" him.[44] But that does not solve the problem. The idea that bourgeois science produced socialist theory independent of the struggles of the proletariat was contrary to Marx's view on the revolutionizing character of political practice. Lenin himself would soon become aware of the one-sidedness of his position. In later years he was careful to indicate the historical context of *What is to be Done?* In 1921 he even objected to a non-Russian edition, urging at least good commentaries "in order to avoid false application."[45]

What is to be Done? had little to say about rules of organization. Nor was it perceived as the expression of a special "Leninist" trend in the party.[46] By 1902, work for a second Party Congress had intensified. The First Congress had done little other than proclaiming the RSDRP. The Second Congress was to unite the party, adopt an authoritative program, and lay down basic tactics. Thus, by 1902 Lenin was also paying attention to concrete organizational details and elaborating his ideas.

In his "A Letter to A Comrade on Our Organizational Tasks" (1902), Lenin explained why, at the present stage, he was in favor of having two centers—an émigré ideological leadership and an underground practical leadership. He insisted that as many workers as possible should become "professional revolutionaries."[47] What is important is to note that Lenin here stressed the development of both party and non-party organizations. A secret party was to promote broader organizations. The degree of discipline and secrecy was to depend on the type of work required to be done. Real centralization at the leadership level, he argued, could only be achieved if there was also maximum decentralization of tasks, and direct access of all party units to the central leadership.[48] He also agreed to the suggestion of his correspondent that despite underground conditions, "It should be obligatory to hand over (or forward) to the editors (of the central organ) letters from all who so desire."[49]

II
THE EMERGENCE OF BOLSHEVISM

The split of 1903 was expressly not over *What is to be Done?* Debates in the Congress were on programmatic as well as organizational issues. In the programmatic debates, the entire *Iskra* group was united. Since the *Iskra*-ists were in a big majority, their unity ensured more or less smooth passage of the program. But the organizational clashes were sharp, and led to a split among the *Iskra*-ists. It is therefore necessary to treat them seriously.[50] Lenin had been fighting for a party of dedicated revolutionaries, insisting on the need to push like-minded people into party committees, and achieving considerable success.[51] Nonetheless, at the time of the 1903 Congress the RSDRP was an organization of leaders of workers' struggles, not a militant workers' party.[52] At this stage, Lenin was opposed to an excessive broadening of membership. In the debate over paragraph one of the Party Rules, defining a member, Martov opened the door to sympathizers who need not be integrated into the organizational structure, while Lenin opposed it.[53] This opposition was consistent with his previous standpoint of hegemonic political role of the party along with real inner-party democracy. If a large number of passive members were recruited in an underground party, they would be the people blindly following the leadership, while activists and revolutionaries could be expected to be more independent minded. A spurious "broad party" would dilute the political capacity of the party, while the "broadness" would hamper democratization as passive members would not participate on decision making nor carry out democratically agreed decisions.[54] And in addition, as Martov's supporters explicitly said, it would be in the interests of petty bourgeois intellectuals to keep the rules loose.[55] Plekhanov opposed this saying that this was a concession to the bourgeois individualism of the intellectuals.[56] In addition, we should add, Martov's model would have meant negating the possibility of self-organization and self-activization of the politically conscious workers.

The other category sought to be brought in by Martov were agitating workers. Since both sides believed that the SPD was their ideal, it is worth noting that though the SPD had, by 1905-6, about a million members, about 30,000 functionaries ran the party. The majority of members were active in elections, but not in developing a revolutionary movement.[57] Lenin's call for the formation of a vanguard worker's party was at that time considered by Lenin himself to be a mere adaptation of the "model" German structure to the specific conditions of Russia. In fact, his call had a wider value than he recognized. Unknowingly Lenin and his supporters were laying the groundwork for a revolutionary party, in place of a party of partial struggles, electoralism, etc. Given the greater level of activism of the party ranks, the type of party proposed by Lenin was likely to have more effective internal democracy than a party which had a large inert membership, voting an oligarchic hierarchy, often either petty bourgeois intellectual or paid functionary, repeatedly to power.

The split in the Congress actually took place on the issue of the election of a three member Editorial Board for *Iskra* and a three (or five) member Central Committee (CC). Lenin believed that the existing Editorial Board was inefficient, since Axelrod, Zasulich and Potresov seldom worked seriously as editors.[58] But this proposal was viewed as an insult to these revolutionaries, two of them active since the 1880s. Lenin's opponents, like Tsaryov, delegate of the Don Committee,

Posadovsky, delegate of the Siberian Union, or Trotsky, claimed that the editors who were not elected would feel bad since they would be pronounced superfluous, and that the Congress did not have the moral or political right to do so.[59]

Lenin's reply is significant. He said that election was not a matter of insults. The Congress, as the highest body of the party, had the right to elect, to appoint party functionaries, and to alter the composition of corporate bodies that derived their authority from the Congress.[60] It is even more significant that Lenin, defeated on the question of defining who was to be a party member, submitted to the majority position, while those who were defeated on the issue of re-affirming the old Editorial Board of *Iskra* rejected the decision of the Congress. Thereby they showed that while they were formally proclaiming the Congress as the sovereign institution of the party,[61] they were claiming status as a special category of members who could not be bound by the norms of democracy, or the authority of the Congress.

From the class standpoint, and from inner-party considerations, this dispute is highly revealing. The minority accused Lenin (and Plekhanov) of wanting dictatorship in the party, of desiring domination of the intellectuals. Yet, it was the minority that was most concerned over the fate of professors and students, and that took the tactics of boycotting party institutions, thereby flouting the elementary rule of democracy that majority decisions were binding on members of the association. The tactics of boycott paid dividend, as a worried Plekhanov wanted to invite the Mensheviks back on their terms.[62] Lenin resigned from the Editorial Board in protest.[63] And one of his supporters wrote in disgust:

> What's the use of having congresses if their decisions are ignored and everybody does just what he pleases . . . this is being done by people who . . . want to show, it seems, that discipline is . . . not for them at the top. [64]

Lenin was initially inclined to a compromise.[65] But as the Mensheviks went on attacking him, and called the Congress decision the formation of a "bureaucratic, putschist organisation,"[66] he hardened his stance. However, his activities were within party rules. He first tried to act through the Central Committee, into which he had been co-opted.[67] Subsequently, he won over a number of party committees. The rules adopted at the Second Congress had a provision for an emergency Congress if a certain number of party committees demanded it.[68] Lenin fought for a Third Congress to end the split in the party.[69] Plekhanov, as Chairman of the party Council, and now a supporter of the Mensheviks, did not abide by rules.[70] As a result, in 1905, the Bolsheviks went ahead with a purely Bolshevik Congress.[71] Lenin's campaign for a break with the Mensheviks had been opposed by the Bolshevik dominated Central

Committee. But supported by younger Bolsheviks,[72] the committee men, he fought for the establishment of new party committees, and a new Congress.[73] In insisting on the supremacy of the Congress against both *Iskra* (after it passed to the Mensheviks) and the Central Committee, he had to form a faction that defended the standpoint of the Second Congress. Consequently, his concept of party democracy included both the right to form a faction, and the right to oppose the executive organs of the party if they opposed the standpoint of the Congress.

It was in the middle of this inner-party struggle that he wrote his analysis of the Second Congress proceedings, *One Step Forward, Two Steps Back* (1904). And two powerful criticisms were voiced against some of his ideas that need to be considered in detail. These came from Leon Trotsky and Rosa Luxemburg. In a situation of bitter polemics generally positive arguments too can be enmeshed with not particularly valuable assertions. After the Second Congress, Lenin's opponents had stuck the labels of "Jacobinism" and "Bonapartism" on him. In *One Step Forward, Two Steps Back*, Lenin accepted the "Jacobin" charge, and wrote: "A Jacobin who wholly identifies himself with the organization of the proletariat—a proletariat conscious of its class interest—is a revolutionary Social-Democrat."[74]

Responding to this, Rosa Luxemburg wrote:

> The Social Democratic movement is the first in the history of class societies which reckons, in all its phases and through its entire course, on the organisation and the direct, independent action of the masses.[75]

She stressed that two obstacles dogged the proletarian revolutionary movement: that of degenerating into bourgeois reformism, and that of sectarianism. She criticized Lenin because she felt that his arguments in *One Step* were leading to sectarianism.

There were errors in Luxemburg's views, as Lenin pointed out in a reply to her, sent to *Neue Zeit*, but published only posthumously. The central error of both Luxemburg and Trotsky was concerning whether or not the advanced workers should be organized separately to ensure greater striking power for them.[76]

As long as the rule of a particular class is stable, Marxist theory argues that its ideology will remain hegemonic. In the early stages the mass of workers would not break with bourgeois ideology even when they start fighting the rulers. The process of growing class-consciousness would reach its apogee in a revolution. So, in a pre-revolutionary situation, the vanguard workers had to organize separately in order to create a counter-ideological hegemony vis-à-vis the ruling class. On this point, Luxemburg recognized the validity of Lenin's view later and worked in semi-alliance with the Bolsheviks against the Mensheviks. In her incomplete pamphlet on the Russian Revolution, she wrote, "only a party which knows how to lead, that is, to advance things, wins support in stormy times."[77] Trotsky, likewise, by joining the Bolsheviks in 1917, and by explicit acknowledgement later on, recognized his mistake.[78]

On a number of specific points, Lenin in his reply to Rosa Luxemburg, pointed out that he had not been the initiator of the proposal that gave the Central Committee the right to organize Local Committees, and that he advocated, not a blind subordination of all units to the Centre, but the acceptance of the will of the Congress.[79] Luxemburg and Trotsky, however, had valid criticisms of early Bolshevism. Trotsky argued that the proletarian party had to operate within the gap of the objective factor of class interest and the subjective awareness of that by the workers. This could not be done by substituting party for class.[80] He made a further distinction between the necessity of political centralization and the transformation of that into a permanent organizational technique.[81] Like Luxemburg, he wrote that Social Democracy "consciously wants to be and to remain the class movement of the proletariat."[82]

Lenin had written that workers were disciplined in the factory, and hence opposition to discipline was an intellectual propensity. Luxemburg rejected this, saying that factory discipline imposed from above and conscious self-discipline of the class were antithetical, the one slavish, the other emancipatory.[83]

The opposition of "economic" and "political" struggles, and the idea that Social Democratic consciousness could only come via bourgeois science, were also challenged by Luxemburg and Trotsky. Both of them stressed the potentially conservative role of party organizations in rapidly changing political situations.[84] In his report on the Second Congress written in 1903, Trotsky criticized Lenin's "bureaucratic dream" of achieving a "statutory remedy for opportunism" through Party Rules.[85]

Most important was the view of Luxemburg and Trotsky that reformism and "Economism" were harmful political tendencies, but they emerged from within the movement of the working class. Luxemburg wrote:

> the working class demands the right to make mistakes and learn in the dialectics of history. . . . Historically, the errors committed by a truly revolutionary movement are infinitely more fruitful than the infallibility of the cleverest Central Committee.[86]

The historic experience of the working class would, they expected, lead it to socialist revolutionary politics. Lenin, too, spoke in 1905 of the "spontaneously" social democratic character of the working class.[87]

Before turning to the events of 1905 and Lenin's reassessment, one more aspect of his thoughts on class and party relationship has to be discussed. This is his concept of trade unions. E. Kuskova, an extreme exponent of "Economism," had written an essay or "Credo," to which Lenin responded in 1899. In this article, "A Protest by Russian Social Democrats," he insisted on a continuity with Marx. On one hand, he said that trade unions were essential phenomena under capitalism, an important organization of struggle against capital, and for the abolition of wage-labor. Following the stand taken by the First International, he argued that trade unions must not devote attention exclusively to immediate issues, but should also strive for the general emancipation of the oppressed workers. On the other hand, he insisted that the task of combining the economic and political struggles into one integral whole was a task that fell on the Social Democracy. Without negating the role of trade unions, he rejected the proposal that workers should limit their work to economic struggles, because that would mean the triumph of liberalism and the political suicide of Russian Social-Democracy.[88]

The one-sided emphasis of the "Economists" on spontaneous economic struggle had generated a long period of controversy. In course of this, Lenin coined a term, "trade unionism." By this, he did not mean simply the action of building and working in trade unions, but an ideology within the working-class movement that saw trade union struggles as adequate by themselves.[89] Lenin was bitterly opposed to this. As it often happened in Lenin's polemical writings, the desire to oppose an opponent led him to make deliberately provocative arguments, which he once called "bending the stick." It is possible to see, in his polemics against "trade unionist ideology" in *What is to be Done?* a shift from Marx's position and his own position of 1899, to a "relative devaluation of trade unionism."[90] However, this was more a matter of emphasis, due to a particular historical context, than a substantial shift. He affirmed that the economic struggle could not be waged without trade unions, which were organizations based at the factory and trade levels.[91] He insisted that it was the task of revolutionaries to influence the trade unions.[92] But he did not call for the formal subordination of trade unions to the party, at least at this stage.

III
THE REVOLUTION OF 1905 AND THE RISE OF THE SOVIETS

Before the Third (Bolshevik) RSDRP Congress could meet, a revolution had begun in Russia. The theory and practice of early Bolshevism is best understood when the course of the revolution and role of the proletariat in it is discussed as the background.[93]

Ever since the famine of 1891, there had been a revival of political consciousness. By the beginning of the twentieth century, workers, peasants and students were all in ferment. Between 1894 and 1902 the number of workers in factories with a workforce of 100–150 went up by 52.8 percent. In the big factories employing from 500–1000 workers, the numbers rose by 72 percent. The size of the workforce of the largest factories, which employed over 1000 workers, increased by 141 percent. 458 enterprises employed about 1,155,000 workers. This concentration of workers, and the creation of a skilled labor force, was reflected in the radicalization of the political temper of the mass of workers. In 1884–90, merely 15 percent of those arrested for political offenses were workers. In 1901–1903, the corresponding figure was 46 percent, or almost half. Statistics of the strike movements also show a shift from only or mainly economic strikes to a greater stress on political strikes. In 1901, political strikes accounted for 22.1 percent of all strikes, rising to 53.2 percent in 1903.[94] Rural unrest was also growing steadily in those years, leading to a revival of Narodnik politics and the formation of the Socialist Revolutionary Party [hereafter they will often be mentioned as SRs or SR party].[95] The struggle of workers and radical students had been intensifying and mass strikes developing. Tsarism reacted to this with simultaneous repression and an attempt to form legal workers' societies with police approval. Quickly, however, these legal or Zubatovite unions (so called because of a police official named Zubatov who initiated this policy) became radicalized, and in most cases were disbanded. However, in St. Petersburg, the "Assembly of Russian Factory and Workshop Workers," led by Father Gapon, a prison chaplain, continued. The Gaponist Union opposed class struggle. But in early 1905, a strike began in the giant Putilov works, employing twelve thousand workers. Four workers of Gapon's organization had been sacked. Gapon had to react to stop the erosion of his credibility. As a result, mass meetings were held. A series of general demands were formulated, including an eight-hour day, a general wage rise, etc. The union leaders thought that a petition to the Tsar, and a few benevolent words from the Throne, would be useful to counteract the agitation of radical students. Meanwhile, the Menshevik Petersburg group penetrated the meetings of the Assembly, and succeeded in pushing through several political demands, like freedom of assembly, speech and the press, an end to the Russo-Japanese war, and the convocation of a Constituent Assembly.

By January 7, there was a general strike in St. Petersburg. On Sunday, January 9, 2 million Petersburg workers marched in a peaceful procession to the Winter Palace, and were mown down in a withering fire that killed over a thousand and injured twice as many. An appalled Gapon told the workers, "We no longer have a Tsar."

Within days, a massive protest movement had developed. The patriarchal, loyalist workers had given way to the revolutionary proletariat. The number of workers on strike during January and February 1905 was greater than the total for the ten years preceding.[96] There was a vast growth in working-class assertiveness, and forms of self-organization. An attempt by the government to restore workers' faith in the Tsar led to the setting up of a commission under Senator Shidlovsky. Workers were asked to elect delegates to it. The commission did nothing and was soon dissolved, but the election of delegates (deputies) by the factory taught the workers a valuable lesson in coordinating their own affairs.[97]

Another development was the growth of strike-committees. Differing in name, they were initially set up to bring order into a chaotic movement. In a few cases the strikers won the fight to maintain a permanent representation of deputies.[98] A further step was taken when several factory committees, representing a trade, amalgamated. An example was the Moscow Council of Deputies of the typesetters' incorporating one hundred and ten plants.[99] The final step was the fusion of the economic and political struggles. This resulted in the appearance of general workers' councils (the "Soviets" in the sense usually known). Perhaps the first was the Ivanovo–Voznesensk Soviet. A strike began on May 12. By the 15th, the Soviet (which is simply the Russian equivalent of the word "council") was set up. After the factory owners rejected the worker's demands, the Soviet turned to the Minister of the Interior with a list of requests, going all the way to a parliament based on universal suffrage. By July 18, after repression, the Soviet collapsed.

But it was not the Ivanovo–Voznesensk Soviet that struck popular imagination. That honor fell to the St. Petersburg Soviet. A printer's strike in Moscow was followed on September 27, by a general strike which leaped to St. Petersburg. From September 30, ferment began in the railways. "The strike rushed forward along the rails and stopped all movement in its wake. . . . It used every possible means . . . an entire class obeyed it."[100] From the first day, the October strike had a political character. The Tsar, despite his dislike for Count Witte, sought his help. Under the blows of a strike that had paralyzed the capital, the autocracy was compelled to make concessions. Witte proposed that a document should be issued, but not in the Tsar's own name, since that would have greater legal validity. The Tsar however ignored this technical advice, and issued the Manifesto of October 17, 1905, which guaranteed civil liberties, along with elections to a Duma elected on a fairly wide suffrage, and authorized to enact laws.[101]

The St. Petersburg Soviet sprang up in the course of the strike. It had the precedence of the Shidlovsky Commission, and the Menshevik propaganda of a "revolutionary self-government." On October 10, the Menshevik Committee in St. Petersburg proposed founding a citywide committee to lead the general strike. On October 13, the St. Petersburg Soviet first met at the Technological Institute. On October 15, 226 representatives from ninety-six factories and workshops and five trade unions were present. On October 17, the body named itself the *Soviet Rabochikh Deputatov* (Council of workers' Deputies).[102] It was this example that inspired the setting up of Soviets elsewhere, in Moscow, Odessa, Novorossiisk, Donets, etc. There were also a few instances of Soldiers' Councils and Peasants' Councils.

The Soviet emerged in fulfillment of an objective need for an organization that would represent peoples' authority, an organization that would be flexible enough to encompass hundreds of thousands of workers of various factories, varying age-groups, diverse viewpoints, different level of skills and earnings, without imposing on them so much organizational restraint that this newly won cohesion would break down. While the liberal bourgeoisie had the legal opportunity to work in Zemstvos and municipal dumas, the workers had no existing organization. It was in the factory that they found the natural starting point. Excluded from the least of legal opportunities, they performed an astounding feat of democracy by building the Soviets. The powers of the Soviets lay in the fact that the deputies were elected and that they could function publicly without gaining legal sanction from the State. This set them off from the parties, despite the fact that party activists could be, and usually were, workers or professional revolutionaries dedicated to workers' struggles. As Trotsky, at the age of twenty-six the great mass leader of the 1905 revolution, put it on the basis of his own experience:

> Prior to the Soviet we find among the industrial workers a multitude of organizations. . . . But these were organizations within the proletariat, and their immediate aim was to achieve influence over the masses. The Soviet was, from the start, the organization of the proletariat, and its aim was the struggle for revolutionary power.[103]

Such an organization, in a revolutionary period, was essential if the advanced workers were to influence the masses. But this also required a well thought-out attitude towards the relationship between the party and the Soviets. The Mensheviks, starting with their schematic idea that the current revolution was a bourgeois revolution and hence the working class should not play the leading role in it went on to deny any possibility of the Soviets becoming the basic organs of workers' power, insurrection, and the emerging workers' democracy. They were willing to accord only a modest and temporary role for the Soviets. What they wanted was the creation of organizations that would mobilize the lower classes to put pressure on the government and the liberal opposition. Thus, when the Tsarist government proposed an advisory duma based on a very narrow franchise (the so-called Bulygin Duma) in 1905,

Martov put forward the idea that the workers and all other popular masses excluded from the franchise should elect their "revolutionary deputies" to create an all-Russian forum of self-government organs. When the Soviets appeared, they were hailed as the embodiment of this idea of a "revolutionary self-government." Subsequently, the Mensheviks, notably Larin and Axelrod, proposed a scheme for a workers' congress which was to be structured like a pyramid, with factory committees at the bottom, municipal committees in the middle, and the congress at the top. This congress was to enable the party to get rid of its "sectarianism" and to become a mass party. The Soviets were visualized in this conception as stop-gap organization on the way to mass trade unions and a mass party. Once these organizations were established, the Soviets could no longer have any place.[104] This proposal of setting up "revolutionary self-government" bodies while an autocracy existed was merely playing with the democratic forms without having real democracy. The first pre-condition for democratic (or "revolutionary") self-government was the overthrow of the existing despotic state. Moreover, this slogan tended to dissolve the militant workers in a more inchoate mass of "citizens." The later call for Workers' Congress was equally inappropriate. If the autocracy had not yet been overthrown, then any democratic opening was only temporary. To make it permanent, the struggle to overthrow Tsarism had to be intensified. So the Soviets, as militant organs of workers' united struggle, which had developed as a result of the revolutionary situation itself, could not simply give way to broad, legal parties and unions. Moreover, there could be no prospect of turning a workers' congress into a party without dissolving all existing parties (in 1905 there were already the RSDRP, the SRs, and the Anarchists) and without, consequently, returning to all the problems involved in the idea of a mass party of the entire working class.

The Bolshevik conception too had limitations. P. A. Krassikov, a leading Bolshevik, called the St. Petersburg Soviet a "non-party Zubatovite committee."[105] When the Soviet was formed, a member of the Petersburg Committee, M. M. Essen, exclaimed, "But where do we come in?"[106] At a meeting of the Bolshevik Executive committee of the Neva District of Petersburg said: "On October 29, one of the fifteen members opposed taking part in it at all because the 'elective principle could not guarantee its class consciousness and Social Democratic character.' Four voted against taking part in the Soviet, if it did not accept a Social Democratic programme. Nine were for taking part and two did not vote."[107]

Though the Bolsheviks did not leave the Soviet,[108] it needed Lenin's intervention before the Bolsheviks changed their position. Knuniants-Radin, a party leader, had asked, "Soviet or Party?" Lenin wrote in

"Our Tasks and the Soviet of Workers' Deputies" that this was a wrong question. The real question was how to combine and how to divide the tasks. He also commented: "I think it would be inadvisable for the Soviet to adhere wholly to any one party."[109] Lenin pointed out that the Soviet was carrying on both an economic and a political struggle. He reaffirmed that the economic struggle should not be conducted only by the Social Democrats or only under their banner.[110] On the political struggle, too, he insisted that it was wrong to demand that the Soviet should accept the program of the RSDRP.[111] However, even Lenin at this stage did not see the Soviet as primarily a class organization. He called for co-opting not only soldiers and sailors and peasants, but also the "revolutionary bourgeois intelligentsia."[112]

In late November-early December 1905, Lenin was more cautious, and he wrote in "The Socialist Party and non-Party Revolutionism":

> Is it permissible for socialists to participate in non-party organizations? if so, on what conditions? . . . It would be wrong to say that in no case and under no circumstances should social-democrats participate in non-party (i.e., more or less consciously or unconsciously bourgeois) organizations. . . . Participation can only be temporary . . . permissible . . . if the party as a whole controls and guides its members and groups "delegated" to non-party unions or councils.[113]

The very posing of the question displays a one-sided outlook. If revolutionary socialists refused to participate in non-party organizations, and if the masses created their own organizations, then socialists would end up in a self-imposed ghetto, cut off from many real movements, and restricted in their activities to party propaganda, leaflets, exhortations, etc. But even Lenin's position, calling for some participation in the Soviets, was inadequate. It displays the claim that all non-party working-class organizations were more or less bourgeois organizations. This shows, that in 1905, even Lenin was far from appreciating the Soviets as organs of proletarian democracy.

In 1905, the Social Democrat who had the clearest grasp of the Soviets was Trotsky. He wrote:

> In order to have authority in the eyes of the masses on the very day it came into being, such an organization had to be based on the broadest representation. . . . Since the production process was the sole link between the proletarian masses . . . representation had to be adapted to the factories and plants.[114]

Evidently, Trotsky did not see the non-party character of the Soviets as a weakness. Nor did he conclude that this made them bourgeois institutions. Organizations of the entire class and organizations of the vanguard of the class had to be separate. But they had to work together, and it was in the interests of the vanguard that they did so.

By tracing the actual work of the revolution, Trotsky showed the Soviet functioned as the class organ of the proletariat, and that it could establish proletarian hegemony over the other fighting masses only by that policy. For him, the "Soviet grew as the natural organ of the proletariat in its immediate struggle for power as determined by the actual course of events."[115]

As he explained to the court at the time of his trial, by leading the general strike, disorganizing the Tsarist regime and simultaneously organizing the masses, the Soviet ensured proletarian hegemony.

> We saw how the workers rallied round the Soviet, how the peasants' union, embodying ever-increasing masses of the peasantry, sent its deputies to the Soviet, how the railway and the postal unions united themselves with the Soviet. . . . It was as though the whole nation were making an heroic effort, trying to produce from its deepest core an organ of power that might . . . lay the foundations of a new social system.[116]

In short, he asserted that the "Soviet really was a workers' government in embryo."[117] The principal weapon of the Soviet, the general strike, also showed its class character, and at the same time, it was a weapon in broadening the basis of the proletariat's influence. This also indicated that as against the old power, the Tsarist bureaucracy which was autonomous from civil society, the rising proletarian power would be the centralization of society itself.[118] Finally, Trotsky pointed out that such Soviets could arise only when the existing political order was challenged from below, and itself suffered a crisis at the top.[119] What emerges from Trotsky's analysis of the Tsarist state on one hand, and of the Soviet on the other, is that just as the broad mass of workers could be expected to struggle for socialism only during the revolution itself, so their organization, the Soviet, could rise and become an organ of revolutionary power only during a revolutionary upsurge. The Soviet could not come into existence in a non-revolutionary period, because it was the voice, not of a relatively narrow stratum of vanguard, but of the whole class, or most of it, which remains silent or accepts the rulers in "normal" times. Second, its centralism was not the centralism of a bureaucratic hierarchy, but of society and the creation of a government that would express the constructive will of a nation hegemonized by the proletariat. So said Trotsky in his speech to the court that tried the Soviet. In St. Petersburg, the Soviet's threats forced the regime to negotiate on different occasions. In Moscow, in Novorossiysk, the Soviets coordinated the insurrection. The brief span of the Soviets did not allow a full experience to be gained. Nonetheless, the idea of council power, starting at the factory level and going all they way to the national structure, entered into the consciousness of the workers.

IV
INITIAL BOLSHEVIK RESPONSES TO THE REVOLUTION

This rapidly-changing political scenario put a strain on all existing parties. The Bolsheviks were no exception. The Bolshevik committeemen, trained in underground work, suspicious about Economism, distrusted the Gapon union. S. I. Gusev, a Bolshevik leader, took the line of openly opposing Gapon rather than trying to influence the workers into taking up more radical demands.[120] Even after January 9, the committeemen took a dim view of the spontaneous mass initiative. Joseph Stalin, one of these committeemen, urged the masses to rally round the committees, because "only the party committees can worthily lead us."[121] Lenin's instant reaction was different. At almost the same time, he was writing, "Make way for the anger and hatred that have accumulated in your hearts throughout the centuries of exploitation, suffering and grief."[122] Despite Gapon's Zubatov connections, to Lenin he appeared a real leader of the workers.[123] The St. Petersburg committeemen, by contrast, were totally hostile.

On the rising trade union movement, the Bolsheviks often had a narrow approach. In September 1905, Gusev proposed a resolution at the Bolshevik Odessa Committee's meeting, which counterposed trade unions and the revolution. However, Gusev also proposed trying to gain leadership of trade union. He was opposed by others, one of whom said that the task was to expose and destroy illusion, and there by demolish the unions, not to lead them.[124] Gusev's resolution was passed. But Lenin opposed it. In his letter to S. I. Gusev, (September 30, 1905), he told the Odessa Committee that it was "highly erroneous" and that "we must not stand aloof. . . . Russian Social Democrats should . . . at once create a tradition of Social Democratic participation, of Social Democratic Leadership."[125]

Time and again, the narrow mentality of the committeemen resulted in sectarianism. Thus, Lenin's assertion, made in *What is to be Done?* about the direction of the spontaneous workers' struggles, was now wrenched out of context to claim that "the trade union struggle . . . makes bourgeois notions stick to the proletarians' psychology."[126] Leading Bolsheviks like Bogdanov and Lunacharsky were wary of strikes and counterposed the armed insurrection to the strikes,[127] instead of looking at strikes as movements that united the workers and raised their class-consciousness.

The basic problem was organizational rigidity. The Bolshevik committeemen took one phase of the movement, when there had been only a party of workers' leaders and underground activists, as the permanent character, thereby bearing out the validity of the criticisms of Luxemburg and Trotsky. As Trotsky wrote later,

The negative aspects of Bolshevism's centripetal tendencies first became apparent at the Third Congress of the Russian Social Democracy. The habits peculiar to a political machine were already forming in the underground. The young revolutionary bureaucrat was already emerging as a type.[128]

Even the sympathetic Krupskaya recorded in her memoirs that the committeemen were conservative, opposed to inner party democracy and undesirous of changes.[129] Lenin, from abroad, could see the need to change party tactics,[130] to become more flexible, and get rid of the prerogatives of the committee men and induct more youth, and more workers in the committees.[131] The period when a pre-revolutionary crisis opens up is the period when a revolutionary party has the opportunity to become a mass party. Failure to ensure this transformation is as serious as any attempt to build a mass party when conditions do not permit it. At the Third Congress, Lenin and Bogdanov proposed that workers should be taken into the party at all levels in large numbers.[132] The delegate Gradov (Kamenev) accused Lenin of demagogically raising the question of the relationship between workers and intelligentsia.[133] Reports by Leskov, Filippov and Krassikov made it obvious that workers were not being drawn into the party. One delegate, Mikhailov, even accused in disgust that "the requirements for the intelligentsia are very low, and for the workers they are extremely high."[134]

Lenin had to confront the charge that he was forgetting *What is to be Done?*, and in a subsequent article had to explain that the book was "a controversial correction of 'economist' distortion and it would be wrong be regard the pamphlet in any other light."[135] In attempting to cope with the mechanical vanguardism of his supporters he insisted that hundreds and thousands of workers must be recruited. The party doors should also be open to revolutionary workers who were religious believers.[136]

The dangers of sectarianism and substitutionism, mentioned by Rosa Luxemburg and Trotsky, were evident in the kind of responses to the resolution found among the Bolshevik committeemen. But it was also seen that the revolutionary orientation of the Bolsheviks enabled them to overcome substantially their undemocratic ideas about the role of the party committees and the relationship between the party and the mass organizations, and to reorient the party.

Significantly, Mensheviks, no less than the Bolsheviks, were dependent on the work of the professional revolutionaries. But the Mensheviks saw no special role for them. Lenin, by contrast, viewed the professional revolutionaries and the party machine as a means of increasing the activity of the class vanguard. But their work could succeed only if the gates of the party were opened in revolutionary times. Once a program and basic tactics were worked out, and an organizational structure set up, mass recruitment was deemed necessary, especially during a rising tide of class struggles.[137]

Lenin urged repeatedly in favor of this transition. Events pressed in the same direction. As a result, party cells grew rapidly in factories.[138] Bolshevik recruitment grew at about the same pace as the Menshevik recruitment, and with, on average, a younger and more proletarian composition. Between early 1906 and 1907, both factions had grown massively.[139]

The composition by age showed a younger Bolshevik faction. The Bolsheviks had a good many teenagers, both in the rank and file, and in various "activist" groups. The Mensheviks were on average older. The leadership structure was even more tilted to the Bolsheviks, where Lenin was oldest at thirty-seven, while the average age of the Menshevik leadership was forty-four.[140] As much as 61.9 percent of the 1905 Bolshevik membership was proletarian. In St. Petersburg alone the Bolsheviks had ninety-nine cells among workers (including handicraftsmen). In Moscow in late summer they had forty factory cells.[141] Lenin wrote in January 1907 that only liars "can now doubt the mass proletarian character of the Social Democratic Party in Russia."[142]

At the Fifth Congress of the Party, the last united Congress, the following Social composition of the delegates emerged:[143]

TABLE 6.1

Occupation	Bolshevik		Menshevik	
	Number	%	Number	%
Manual workers	38	36.2	30	31.9
Office and shop-workers	12	11.4	5	5.1
Liberal profession	13	12.4	13	13.4
Professional revolutionaries	18	17.1	22	22.1
Writers	15	14.3	18	18.6
None	4	3.8	3	3.1
Students	5	4.8	5	5.2
Landowners	0	0.0	1	1.0
Total	105	100.0	97	100.4

This shows that the relatively youthful Bolsheviks were able to respond more quickly to the shift in the situation, and draw in a higher proportion of workers into not only the membership, but also the leadership. By contrast, it was the Menshevik faction that retained a higher proportion of full timers and intellectuals, particularly at the upper levels.

V

INNER-PARTY DEMOCRACY IN 1905

In the case of inner-party democracy, Lenin's shift, compared to his centralizing tendency of *One Step Forward*, was more perceptible. The

Third Congress had already adopted the stance that elections, and autonomy of local committees vis-à-vis the Central Committee, should be the norm. The new rules adopted at the Congress gave local organizations autonomy in matters relating to their area of activity (Article 6) and the right to issue party literature in their own names (Article 7).[144]

In St. Petersburg, the new structure was that of an elected conference, due to meet at least twice a month. It was to be elected twice a year, and in turn it was to elect the party committee. Large numbers of members were drawn in the decision-making process. For example, the St. Petersburg party decided to boycott the First Duma by 1168 to 926 votes.[145] Lenin even recommended referenda in case of important political questions.[146] The Bolshevik activist Pyatnitsky recollected a similar widespread application of democracy in Moscow.[147] On the question of the party press, Lenin stressed that here there could be no question of a mechanical "rule of the majority over the minority."[148]

In late 1905, a move for party unity was strengthened. In November 1905, the Mensheviks held a conference. This was followed by a Bolshevik Conference, (December 12–17). The two groups then set up a United Central Committee, with three Bolsheviks and three Mensheviks. Both groups, as well as the new Central Committee, now called for the reorganization of the party on the principle of democratic centralism.[149] At the Fourth (Unity) Congress of the RSDRP, the Menshevik majority brought in a set of resolutions constituting the democratic centralist principles, viewed as a democratic norm of functioning.[150]

Lenin's own understanding of the principle can be seen in the appeal to the party by the Bolsheviks that he drafted. In "An Appeal to the Party by Delegates to the Unity Congress who belonged to the former 'Bolshevik' Group," he asserted that in a revolutionary epoch, experience corrected the line of the party, and this necessitated that members had to fight for open, wide, and free debates on theory and tactics, without disturbing the unity of action.[151] He wrote further that being in a minority would not lead the former Bolshevik faction into boycotting the Central Committee, he upheld party unity, and said that in the united party "there must be wide and free discussion of party questions, free comradely criticism and assessment of events in Party life."[152] He then gave the meaning of democratic centralism as he understood it:

> [G]uarantees for the rights of all minorities and for all loyal opposition . . . all Party functionaries must be elected, accountable . . . and subject to recall . . . a guarantee that the ideological struggle in the party can and must prove fully consistent with strict organizational unity.[153]

The stress is heavily on the rights of minorities, but with an important proviso that the opposition must be a loyal opposition. The concept of a "loyal" opposition was, however, carefully defined to avoid abuse of power. The ideological disputes had to go along with organizational unity, that is, the opposition could not hinder the work of the party. This was further clarified on one occasion, when the Central Committee sent a circular laying down the limits of public criticism. Lenin objected to the circular, saying that it had defined unity of action too broadly, but freedom of criticism too narrowly. He argued that the principles to be adhered were autonomy for local organizations, as well as democratic centralism. This implied "universal and full freedom to criticize, so long as this does not disturb the unity of a definite action."[154] In other words, even after a decision was taken, there could be criticism, but no obstruction to the carrying out of the decision, unless the decision itself was changed. Apart from Lenin's broad definition of the freedom to criticize, the kind of broadening of the rights of members that he was urging could be understood by looking at this act itself. He was publicly challenging the Central Committee. He wrote that the before adopting such a resolution, the C. C. should have discussed the matter in the party.[155] Subsequently, he was to put forward the view that if a real mass party had to be built, rather than a sect, then different lines had to exist, and their open clash had to be viewed as normal.[156] From this conception, he also concluded that like-minded groups had the right to form factions.[157]

An essential component of democratic centralism was the control of the organization by the members, and the existence of local organizations as the basic party units.[158]

Lenin also emphasized that a party wishing to be the class vanguard had to inform the whole class about its activities, about inner party debates. Responding to the charge of factionalism brought by the Socialist Revolutionaries, he said that a mass party had to inform the masses "as to which leaders and which organizations of the party are pursuing this or that line."[159] He also pointed out in an essay of 1907, defending the development of the professional revolutionaries, that due to the development of their network, between 1903 and 1907 the RSDRP had been able to give the public information about the inner party situation, and to build a democratic legal organization with representative Congress when the situation permitted.[160]

VI

PARTY AND UNION: FROM NEUTRALITY TO INFLUENCE

In this period, Lenin's views on party and unions changed gradually. The Third (Bolshevik) Congress called for exploiting legal and semi-legal organizations like trade unions in order to secure in them predominant Social Democratic influence.[161]

The Fourth Congress noted that "The trade union movement is a necessary component of the class struggle and that trade unions are an essential element in the class organization of the proletariat," and that there was a need to combine economic and political struggles. It resolved to assist "the formation of non-party trade unions."[162] Lenin's contribution to the Congress and his subsequent report on the Congress show that on many other issues he was critical of the Mensheviks. That is why, his silence on the trade union question indicates his acceptance of this stand. It was in 1907, in his preface to the collection *Twelve Years*, that Lenin explicitly abandoned his belief in trade union neutrality.[163] This was due to the influence of Bolshevik trade unionists like V. P. Nogin.[164]

Another influence was the developments in Germany. The Free Trade Unions in Germany had been Social Democratic since their inception. However, the long years of peaceful trade unionism, of limited forms of collective bargaining had generated an opportunist form of trade unionism. This was attacked by leftists like Rosa Luxemburg, and also by Kautsky, who in this period was close to the Left. A resolution on the trade unions, moved in 1906 at the Mannheim Congress of the SPD, which sought to be guided by the Social Democratic spirit was actually a retreat. A part of Kautsky's original draft, calling for the accountability of party members in the unions to the party, was dropped, thereby making not only the trade unions "autonomous," but cutting off the route of Social Democratic influence over the Unions as well.[165] Behind this was the reality that at the Cologne Congress of the trade unions, the trade unionists had forced Bebel and other party leaders to make a secret agreement, whereby the party virtually abandoned any attempt to shape trade union policy. Lenin, at that time very much influenced by Kautsky, had in mind the full Mannheim resolution. At the Fifth RSDRP Congress, the Bolsheviks brought a resolution, opposed by Mensheviks and Bundists in the trade union commission.[166] This resolution urged "promoting trade union recognition of the ideological leadership of the Social Democratic party and establishing organizational ties with the party."[167]

While this change was dictated by a legitimate feeling that "trade union independence" was becoming a cloak for reformism and for class collaboration, the call for "establishing organizational ties" was vague. The vagueness could be dangerous, since it was capable of being interpreted in an extremely one-sided way as the organizational subordination of trade unions to party, or the subordination of socialist trade unionists to party committees among whom trade union work was unknown and not seriously understood. The years between 1907 and 1912 saw a struggle on these very issues. Only in the course of struggle could the final picture emerge.

VII
PROBLEMS OF CONSOLIDATION
UNDER REACTIONARY RULE

The period of revolution (1905–1907) was followed by a counter-revolution (1907–1912), in which the first period, 1907–1910, saw the all out offensive of the autocracy and the crumbling of most of the legal institutions. Along with that came an economic depression.[168] This combination led to a dispersal of the proletariat and a severe weakening of the Social Democratic Party.[169] Cut off from the mass of workers, isolated, the leaders forced to return to the hated emigration, the Social Democrats were compelled to reassess their positions from an extremely unfavorable situation. Two vital issues came up again, as the underground structures were being rebuilt. First, what sort of class and party relationship was to prevail, and second, what was to be, the extent, limits, and nature of inner-party democracy. The Bolshevik responses in these cases were clarified in course of their polemics and struggles with two other trends—the Recallists and Ultimatists on one hand, and the Liquidators on the other.

By the second half of 1907, differences had emerged sharply, and to some extent the old Bolshevik–Menshevik line-ups were being reproduced. As the reaction tightened its hold, there emerged an ultra-left trend within the Bolshevik faction itself. One wing of the Bolsheviks led by Alexander Bogdanov, who was supported by Krasin, Lunacharsky, and others, were in favor of boycotting Duma elections, even when there was no prospect of the revolutionary movement posing the question of power, thereby ruling out activity within legal organs as a partial form of struggle. They were also in favor of boycotting trade unions, or forcing unions to toe the line of the underground party committees mechanically, and were further in favor of preaching armed struggle at all times.[170] Opposed to them were Lenin, and a group of younger Bolsheviks, like Gregory Zinoviev, Lev Kamenev, Alexei Rykov, and Mikhail Tomsky. Bogdanov's line was given the title "otzovism" (Recallism) by Lenin. Lenin and his supporters argued that there was no fresh revolutionary upswing, so the task was not to press for sharp class conflicts that could not occur, because the advocacy of armed uprisings would only produce a caricature of Bolshevism.[171] When the masses were not actually entering into revolutionary struggles, legal and semi-legal organizations had to be utilized by the illegal party committee, instead of calling for an open uprising.[172]

The conflict became so sharp, that a meeting of the "Extended Editorial Board of Proletariat" was called in June 1909. The *Proletariat* was the factional paper of the Bolsheviks, and a meeting of the extended editorial board meant in reality a camouflaged meeting of the Bolshevik central leadership. This meeting dissociated Bolshevism from Bogdanov's political line, and expelled Bogdanov from the Bolshevik faction. It is useful to look at Lenin's justification of this action.

> In our Party Bolshevism is represented by Bolshevik section [meaning faction]. But a section is not a party. A party can contain a whole gamut of opinions . . . the extremes of which may be sharply contradictory . . . that is not the case within a section. A section in a party is a group of like-minded persons formed for the purpose primarily of influencing the party acceptance for their principles in the purest possible form. For this, real unanimity of opinion is necessary. The different standards we set for party unity and sectional unity must be grasped by everyone.[173]

Thus, for Lenin, factions were above all political combinations, not groupings created simply to gain majorities and hold power. As ideological currents, even if held together by factional discipline, factions could not hold together by the application of the formal rules of democratic centralism if serious differences arose. The minority in a faction could not be expected to accept factional discipline and keep silent when a major question of party policy came up, as in fact Bogdanov and his supporters showed. At the same time, the faction's majority also had the right to speak in the name of the faction without opposing lines being raised also in the name of the faction. Hence the expulsion of Bogdanov should be viewed as a split in the Bolshevik faction. The Bogdanovists, who organized the paper *Vperyod*, were recognized as a separate faction by the party.[174]

These events should be further juxtaposed to Lenin's view, expressed after the Unity Congress:

> Strictly speaking, these private arrangements at factional meetings are quite natural. . . . Towards the close . . . the composition of the Central Committee was virtually decided . . . not by voting in open Congress, but simply by an "agreement" between the factions.[175]

So he considered these factional arrangements quite legitimate, even though in the case that he was describing it meant that the Bolsheviks got a minority of the seats in the Central Committee.

The other case, the struggle against the Liquidators, showed that there were quite definite limits to democracy, these being set by the party program and basic principles. Following the coup of Stolypin in 1907, there was a massive crackdown on trade union activities as well as on the revolutionary parties. The immediate impact was shattering. In 1907 alone, over one hundred fifty unions were closed down. Some 604 union activists were imprisoned and 357 given terms of administrative exile.[176] The party suffered even more badly. Many party units collapsed.

In this situation, the Mensheviks moved rightwards. By October 1907, the Potresov was writing to Axelrod, "We are undergoing complete disintegration and demoralization."[177]

People like Axelrod and Potresov took the lead in proclaiming the need to liquidate the old underground structure of the party to create an open labor party. Though all Mensheviks did not advocate this, the proposal was based on the fact that Mensheviks collectively tended to see greater prospects for using the remaining legal avenues. The Mensheviks wanted an all-inclusive mobilization to fight the autocracy. Such an inclusive approach had to raise slogans that would be likely to dilute the party program and to propose forms of organization and activity that would go against accepted party principles and policies. The most moderate tendency among the Mensheviks was the proposal and the campaign for a Worker's Congress: "In this ideally favourable case the workers congress will play the role of a proletarian constituent assembly, which will liquidate our old party system and initiate a new party regime."[178]

This was Axelrod in 1907. By 1910, Potresov was proclaiming that the party had ceased to be and hence stood in no need for liquidation.[179] Even Martov, the principal leader of the Mensheviks, while dissociating himself from the extreme pronouncements of the Liquidators, held a picture of the underground as only a skeleton organization, while legal work was to provide the mainstay of party-building work. But the legal opportunities corresponding to such a perspective did not exist. The mass repression meant that a legal worker's congress and a legal new party would not merely be built by jettisoning the underground. It could be built only by abandoning the political principles, like the call for a democratic revolution, a constituent assembly, full democracy based on universal adult suffrage for both the sexes and civil liberties—in short, the core of the party program. This moderation, begun in practice from 1907, was extended to the realm of principles once the final split with the Bolsheviks occurred. The moderation of the Liquidators resulted in their facing much less police attacks. Even a number of Mensheviks were pained at this collapse of party loyalty and program.[180]

Axelrod, Potresov or their cothinkers were rightly accused of "liquidationism." In the name of democratization, they were actually seeking to come into legality only by acknowledging the lawfulness of the Stolypin era. Even as a general proposal, their call was an invalid one. A constituent congress, called without a program, to form a loose workers' congress and an equally loose party, could only be a major step backward after the achievements of the previous years.

However, contrary to a simplification promoted by Lenin, the picture of the party activists and trade unionists inside Russia did not show a simple three-fold division between "Liquidators," Leninists and "Recallists." At the Fifth Conference of the RSDRP, (1908) Lenin moved a resolution on the tasks of the party. It stated that one of the principal tasks was:

> To strengthen the RSDLP in the form it was built up during the revolutionary epoch . . . to struggle against deviations . . . and against attempts . . . to whittle down the slogans of the RSDLP and to liquidate the illegal organization of the RSDLP. At the same time it should be borne in mind that only by promoting the transfer of Party functions to Social Democratic workers themselves . . . and only by setting up and consolidating illegal Party organizations can the Party emerge on the right path of development.[181]

A specific resolution on directives regarding organization repeated that the illegal organization had to have unfaltering influence and arrange all legal and semi-legal work.[182] Lenin's opposition to liquidationism was based on the general consideration that only by strengthening the illegal committees could general political issues, socialist programmatic issues, be systematically related to the specific, limited, and partial issues taken up by the legal organization.[183] Writing extensively against the Liquidators in 1908–1912, Lenin concluded quickly that there had to be a complete split with the Liquidators, since they wanted nothing less than the abolition of the old party and its program, while carrying on their activities in its name with the approval of the autocratic state. Thus in 1911, he called the group round *Nasha Zarya, Dyelo Zhizni,* and *Golos Sotsial-Demokrata* a "serious anti-Party and anti-Social-Democratic force."[184]

In a resolution that he wrote for a Paris meeting of his faction and some supporters, he called his opponents builders of a Stolypin "Labour Party."[185] By this he was attacking their adjustments with the Stolypin regime. Opposing the Liquidator Levitsky, he wrote, "Renunciation of the idea of hegemony, however, is the crudest form of reformism."[186] Lev Kamenev, in a pamphlet entitled *Two Parties,* argued that in fact there were two organizations claiming to be the RSDRP.[187] Lenin's introduction endorsed this stand. This attempt at mobilizing party sentiment for a split with the Liquidators was based on a principled defense of the program.

However, there was another side to the battle. In his customary approach of "stick-bending," Lenin went to put forward a principle of organization that was excessively centralist. Inside Russia, the activists were divided into many trends. While some activists supported the Liquidators, a large group of worker activists, who had been party members in 1905–7, sought to fuse legal work with the underground. Many of the younger Menshevik *praktiki* rejected the Liquidators' proposals. Apart from the Liquidators, there were the "mainline" Mensheviks, supporters of Martov who wanted to retain some underground organization. There were the pro-party Mensheviks, as the group led by Plekhanov were called. There were the Pravdists, supporters of the Vienna-based *Pravda*, brought out by Trotsky, who was also an anti-Liquidator. Even the Bolsheviks were far from being united, since three groups existed. There were *Vperyod*-ists, (Otzovists) the orthodox Leninists, and the Bolshevik "conciliators," i.e., Bolsheviks who wanted to unite all pro-party forces. Many of the practical workers, indeed a majority by most indications, opposed both the Liquidators and the Leninists and Otzovists. By the summer of 1908, for example, in St. Petersburg Otzovists were dominant in the party committee. They tried to exercise veto powers on the work of trade unions.[188] Trade union activists, including Party-minded activists, resented this. Their call was not for liquidationism, but for equal rights in the party, of all those who were really party people. As early as 1908, right-wing Mensheviks were unhappy at the partisan tone of intervention adopted by workers' delegations in legal arenas, like the All-Russian Women's Congress.[189] By 1909 mostly young, single, relatively skilled and committed male workers started joining the RSDLP. Union meetings had high attendances, despite police surveillance. In 1907, one-third of union members considered themselves party members. In the years of reaction, this proportion rose.[190]

There can be little doubt that many of the members shown in the 1907 party congress went on considering themselves as party members, whatever their formal status. In 1909, half the trade union activists (i.e. the organizing core of the unions) considered themselves Social Democrats. In St. Petersburg, in absolute terms, such union-activist-cum Social Democrats therefore numbered around 1500, against 500 organized in underground cells. By 1910, when the Liquidators' outlook was spread out in full, it was seen that "In contrast to Lenin's allegations, however, the proponents of this approach represented a distinct minority within Menshevik ranks."[191] Bonnel, in her well-documented study, emphasizes further that "Most Menshevik Praktiki did not endorse the 'liquidationist' position, calling instead for a combination of legal and illegal methods of struggle."[192]

A majority of Bolshevik praktiki, likewise, seem to have favored this approach. This came out at the extended Editorial Board meeting of *Proletariat*, which expelled Bogdanov. The same meeting heard Rykov, Goldenberg–Meshkovskii and others. These activists demanded the dismantling of the faction and unity based on the principle of combined forms of organizations, legal and underground.

Swain's careful sifting of the evidence indicates that those practical workers who wanted to combine legal and underground work were divided between the Bolsheviks, who were close to Lenin despite differences, and left Mensheviks, closer to Trotsky. Both sides were prepared to work with the underground, and by the end of 1909 and early 1910, such ideas led to the crystallization of a tendency that Lenin called "conciliationism." At the January 1910 plenum of the Central Committee, the conciliators dominated, urging collaboration between the legal activists and the underground.[193]

Lenin and his closest supporters opposed this. In an article, "A conversation between a Legalist and an Opponent of Liquidationism"(1911), Lenin began by equating legal activists with liquidationists.[194] This showed a lack of awareness, or a rejection of the real patterns of struggle. It is necessary to stress, at the same time, the fact that a split was inevitable. From 1907, Axelrod and Martov were in favor of splitting. Dan admitted that he was in favor of unity only because a split at that stage would have been advantageous for Bolshevism.[195] The January 1910 plenum, without endorsing Lenin's position, called for a demarcation of party and Liquidators.[196] But Mensheviks like Martov found it impossible to break with the Liquidators. In refusing to do this, they showed that they were prepared to flout party decisions, democratic norms, and even programmatic guidelines, because without the Liquidators, they would be captives to a strong left wing.

By contrast, Lenin was open in his intentions. When he felt the split necessary, he said so. Having noted this feature, it is also necessary to note Lenin's continued hostility of "Legalism." The plenum, with the collaboration of the Bolshevik conciliators, called for a new party conference, in which participation was to be extended "not only to the raion [a Russian territorial division], factory, and other party cells, but also to those Social Democratic participants in the legal movement . . . who are prepared to resume organizational connection with the party. In organizing the elections, party groups in the legal workers' movement should be included on the same basis as all other party cells."[197] Trotsky, who drafted the resolution, gained the support of a majority of practical workers.[198] Formally, Lenin accepted the resolutions. But his subsequent writings disclosed his continued opposition to much of its content.[199]

On the conciliators' side, the legitimate argument was that legal and underground work had to be united, and for this, the Social Democratic Legal activists had to be drawn into party work. By 1910, the political movement was reviving. Lenin and Zinoviev, the most prominent émigré Bolshevik leaders, had to acknowledge this.[200] But they claimed that conciliationism was merely an émigré circle or an intellectual mood. Hence, when Trotsky took an initiative to organize the conference called by the 1910 plenum, Lenin demanded the annulment of the decisions of that plenum.[201] But Alexei Rykov, sent abroad as a Bolshevik practical worker, opposed Lenin. From this point, Lenin seems to have begun rethinking. He could see how professional union activists like Kanatchikov, Malinovsky, and others were able to do party work in the legal arena.[202]

Consequently, in 1912, when Lenin won over the conciliator Bolsheviks, he held a conference in Prague, which declared itself the party. This was achieved because, on the relationship between the underground committees and the legal activists, the relevant resolution stated:

> Recognizing that the experience of the last three years has definitely confirmed the fundamental provisions of the resolution on the organizational question adopted by the December (1908) conference. . . . The conference finds that: illegal party organizations must participate most actively in guiding the economic struggle (strikes, strike committees, etc.) and in bringing about cooperation between the illegal party cells and the trade unions—especially with the Social Democratic cells in the trade unions and also with various individuals in the trade union movement.[203]

This was a compromise. Recognition of the 1908 decision, bypassing the 1910 resolution, was one way of claiming that the Leninists had been correct. But in the operative part of the resolution, the illegal committees and the "Social Democratic cells" in the trade unions were given equal status.[204] The face of Bolshevism was changed in the aftermath of the Prague Conference. Lenin's struggle against opportunism was now firmly linked with a revolutionary organization built up through the unity of militant activists. A Bolshevik Central Committee resolution of 1913 said:

> Social Democrats must attract into all workers' societies the broadest possible circles of workers without distinction according to party views. But the Social Democrats within these Societies must organize party groups cells and through long, systematic work within all these societies establish the very closest relations between them and the Social Democratic party.[205]

The reasons for the ultimate victory of Leninism may well be located here. Lenin was able to combine his adherence to principle with a willingness to learn from the working class. The conciliators were correct in insisting from an earlier date the need to combine legal and illegal work. But, as Trotsky, the most theoretically articulate conciliator acknowledged later, they had a major weakness. "By striving for unity at all costs, I involuntarily and unavoidably idealized centrist tendencies in Menshevism . . . (this) brought me into still sharper conflict with Bolshevism."[206] Where Lenin had "bent the stick" against even worker conciliators at times, Trotsky, or the Bolshevik conciliators, often failed to recognize the fundamental breach between the Menshevik leaders, who were developing into reformist politicians, and the Bolsheviks, who were adhering to the revolutionary line of the party. In the historic balance, Lenin was certainly right in affirming that the Bolsheviks were the revolutionaries, and the split with the Mensheviks had become a necessity. This was shown in an exemplary way in 1912, when Trotsky organized a counter-conference in Vienna. The Leninist Central Committee boycotted it. As a result, Liquidator and semi-Liquidator ideas became dominant. The *Vperyod*-ists also walked out as a result. Martov and the right wing Menshevik Garvi now began changing the program. The resolution on the coming Duma elections resulted in radical changes. Among the eleven points that the Social Democrats had traditionally included in their election demands, only the call for an eight-hour day remained unamended. The call for a "democratic republic" was replaced by one for "Sovereign popular representation." The demand for land confiscation was toned down to a demand for the revision of the agrarian legislation of the Third Duma. Hopes were expressed that by supporting "left-moving bourgeoisie," the Duma could be turned into a vehicle for political change.[207] Leftists who attended the Vienna Conference were compelled to break with it. Even Trotsky, its initiator, had to do so.

In the wake of the Prague Conference, and owing to a revived workers' movement, the Bolsheviks now forged ahead. In the elections of April 1913 to the executive of the St. Petersburg Metal Workers' Union, ten of the fourteen members elected were Bolshevik supporters. *Luch*, the Menshevik paper, backed Liquidators, and lost heavily.[208] A. Kiselev, the new president, was attacked for his policies by the Liquidators like Abrosimov. A general meeting attended by over two thousand members reelected *Pravda*'s list of candidates by a big margin.[209] During the social insurance campaign, the Liquidators were routed even more.[210] In June 1914, Lenin could report that out of eighteen trade unions in St. Petersburg, the Bolsheviks dominated fourteen, and out of thirteen in Moscow, ten.[211]

The Bolshevik press also got more support. Lenin took over the title *Pravda*, published by Trotsky as an illegal paper, popular in St. Petersburg, and launched a daily of that name from 1912 from St. Petersburg. Its circulation rose to between forty thousand and sixty thousand, much higher than *Luch*, and it got more monetary support from workers' groups.[212] In the area chosen by the Mensheviks, the legal arena, Bolshevism was steadily winning over the majority of vanguard workers. In 1914, when the workers' struggles assumed a near-revolutionary proportion, the Bolsheviks were in the leading position.[213] It was the war that interrupted this process.

It is evident from the foregoing discussion that the Bolsheviks were not monolithic.[214] Moreover, they had become, by 1914, the major working-class party. Finally, they had attained this status by adopting a structure that made possible a democratic relationship between the class and the party. In 1917, the results could be seen.

VIII
INTEGRATING GENDER IN PARTY BUILDING

While my argument so far has been that the Bolshevik-style party was more democratic than other parties, and simultaneously revolutionary, I will now argue that even the Bolsheviks did not go far enough, inasmuch as they did not succeed in examining the hidden gender biases in their concepts of class, class struggle, class demands, and consequently of class vanguard, professional revolutionary, etc., with serious consequences.[215] The women workers' demands and aspirations as members of the mass organizations or even the RSDLP were often treated as backward views. If adopting the viewpoint of the class was the strength of Bolshevism, was this as applicable for women as for male workers?

The first theoretical consideration specifically of women workers came from the pen of Nadezhda Krupskaya, who wrote a pamphlet entitled *Zhenshchina Rabotnitsa* (The Woman Worker) in 1901. This was the first time that the party was urged to turn to women workers as a group and to look at their demands.[216] The pamphlet has a more symbolic value, as the author was subsequently to be a prominent Bolshevik, rather than any intrinsic value comparable to the works of Zetkin. It was Lenin who took a definite step in the programmatic field. Reviewing the first Russian Marxist program (the *Ozvobozhdenii Truda* group's program of 1885) in 1899, Lenin stressed that there was a need to add a demand for complete equal rights for men and women when the program talked about reforms of the laws.[217]

This was however, a limited kind of review, since the law reform under consideration was the change from Tsarist autocracy to bourgeois democracy. Yet Lenin of all persons was certainly aware that the working class had a fragmented character. We have discussed earlier that Lenin's analysis in *What is to be Done?* in favor of centralizing the vanguard workers stemmed from his perception of the fragmented nature of the working class and the tasks of the vanguard. Those militant, class-conscious workers, who were capable of generalizing on the experiences of struggles, and of leading struggles as well as organizing them, were the vanguard workers. Below them came those whom Lenin called the average workers. This was a misnomer, for these too were workers who fought the class enemy, but they did not play such a central role in party building. It was because the working class had a fragmented existence that Lenin emphasized the need to unite and centralize the experience of the vanguard workers.

However, the apparently gender-neutral picture of the working class hid certain unexamined biases. What requires emphasis in the context of my previous discussion is how far this apparent gender-neutrality caused a problem with the Bolshevik strategy of party building.

Since the professional revolutionaries formed the core of the underground party, it is necessary to look at the social composition of the Bolsheviks and examine the women professional revolutionaries. The concept of professional revolutionary itself was one that made possible the development of an active working-class cadre, and was therefore revolutionary and democratic, in contradiction to the "mass parties" where the mass of worker members were actually subordinated to the functionaries, often of petty bourgeois origin. But this very revolutionary democratic dimension of the emergence of professional revolutionaries of working-class origin made the gender imbalance all the more glaring. On the eve of the February Revolution, the Bolshevik Party had twenty-four thousand members. They were subsequently known as the Bolshevik Old Guard, together with approximately four thousand members of two smaller non-Bolshevik groups, a section of the Menshevik Internationalists, and the Inter District Group or *Mezhraiontsii*, who both fused with the party at the time of its Sixth Congress. There were almost two thousand five hundred women members in this list of about twenty-eight thousand Old Bolsheviks. The research by Barbara Evans Clements has brought to light information about the social origins, educational qualifications, professions, etc. of 318 women and 254 men at comparable levels. This constitutes an adequate sample on the basis of which some conclusions can be drawn. At least 62.1 percent of the men had come from worker or peasant families. Among women members, only 36.8 percent had come from these two classes. As many as 37.4 percent of male party members had come from the aristocracy, the intelligentsia, the petty bourgeoisie, and the lower rungs of the bureaucracy, while 37.1 percent of women are recorded as having come from these layers. However, a further 24.5 percent of the women did not give data on social origins, the most likely cause being a desire to erase out an upper- or middle-class background. Among all women members, 8.5 percent were professional revolutionaries, while only 0.8 percent of the men were professional revolutionaries. At first glance it may seem that my previous criticisms were false. But in fact, the 8.5 percent represented a percentage of a much smaller total, since as late as 1917, less than 10 percent of the total membership were women members. There were many worker Bolsheviks, mostly men, who held on to a job and still did regular party work. In addition, it should not be forgotten that most of the women professional revolutionaries were non-proletarian.[218] To become a professional revolutionary always means to take certain difficult decisions. But in the case of women there were dimensions that the men did not face up to. Cecelia Bobrovskaia in her memoirs wrote that she had seen innumerable wives of revolutionaries who had all the qualifications of being a revolutionary, but who were compelled to remain housewives because of the responsibilities about children and the family.[219] The point should be clear. Women had to decide what to do about children when they became professional revolutionaries, a decision male revolutionaries seldom had to take. Some 20 percent chose not to have children. Or, if they had well-to-do families, like those of Inessa Armand and Alexandra Kollontai, they could manage by relying on their families. For women workers, married off by the end of their teens or slightly later at the most, and having children soon after, free choice in these matters seldom occurred. In addition, there exists data that in some cases, party member husbands were opposed to wives becoming party members, possibly because this would involve doubling the contribution to the party funds and having to accept that the wife might get party assignments at times inconvenient for the husband.[220] Such a problem was not unique to the RSDRP, because Clara Zetkin also had to make compromises in these directions. But given the premise of vanguard worker-based party, the matter stands out more sharply in the case of the Bolsheviks. The women who went on to take leading positions in the party, in whichever faction, were seldom workers. This, if anything, tended to reinforce notions concerning backwardness. Women workers were held to be basically backward. And by a tautological statement, it was argued that neither could backward elements be recruited into the vanguard party, nor could the ideas of the backward elements be allowed to dilute "real" class demands. As a result, unlike the considerable number of male worker-Bolshevik leaders, we can think of only two women in comparable positions: Klavdia Nikolaeva, and Alexandra Artiukhina.

But then why did the 2500-odd women join the party? Certainly, like the men, they felt that the Marxist program offered a way out of the exploitative society and the autocratic, despotic Tsarist order. The liberal feminist analysis and the limited reforms proposed only in the field of law and judicial relations seemed poor by the side of the Marxist analysis, which linked the real emancipation of millions of working-class and peasant women with the social revolution. And as women they often brought their own concerns into the party. Consequently, even if the Bolshevik women could not get rid of all the stereotypes at one go, over time their efforts began to undermine previous conceptions. But in the earlier drafts, women often took on the stereotype about rationality, hardness, etc., being typically masculine virtues and tried to cast themselves into such a "masculine" mold. Hardness was a quality chosen as their own symbols by many of the early women recruits. In the Stalin era, there was a great deal of stress on the family, women's natural role in it, etc. This also led to a reassessment, or one could say official portrayal, of the revolutionary women, both worker and non-worker. But after de-Stalinization, Bolshevichki (Old Bolshevik women) who had survived wrote up their memoirs, highlighting their *Tverdost*.[221] To become equals, they had to be more than actual equals, as reports on Stasova, Konkordiya Samoilova, Zemlyachka, Evgenia Bosch, and others show.

Prior to 1905, the party was small and the number of women even smaller. The revolution of 1905 resulted in relatively larger numbers of women coming towards the party. At the same time, with an increase in women's recruitment into industry, the party had to pay more attention to work among women. If we look at the members of the post-1905 period, they fall into three groups: those (a significant part of the ordinary members) who had a paid occupation along with their party work; the underground full-timer activists; and finally the émigrés. Prior to 1917, the City Committee was the most important, after the Central Committee, since provincial committees could not function effectively for long, nor provide sustained leadership. Members and especially Secretaries of the city committees were professional revolutionaries. The usual structure was to have three secretaries—one for the basic political decisions, one for publication of pamphlets and leaflets, and one for the technical work of the committee. From Evans Clements' sample, we find that where women became secretaries, they tended to get the post of the technical secretary. This reflected an internalization within the party structure of a typical gender division of labor. Thus, the most effective technical secretary of the Petersburg Committee was Elena Stasova. Yet, though she filled this post very efficiently for close to four years, the major political decisions were taken by male secretaries, and her correspondence with Lenin dealt with everyday organizational work.[222]

The picture among the émigrés was even clearer. No woman other than Alexandra Kollontai ever got recognition as theoretician. It could be argued that they simply were not theoreticians. This is the sort of argument put forward by Barbara Evans Clements, who argues that women found it more worthwhile to be grassroots activists than to be in the Central Committee.[223] Actually we find the same picture in a number of countries. Rosa Luxemburg had to establish herself as a theoretician by refusing to do women's movement work. No other woman was recognized as a theoretician, primarily because they were usually engaged in other kind of work, e.g., working in the underground, working as couriers, working as assistants, working to earn money so that theoretician husbands need not work, and so on.

And as Elwood's biography of Armand shows, it could be because the party leadership (in this case Lenin) exerted considerable pressure on them, telling them bluntly that as theoreticians they were not serious and that they should do more useful work.[224] From the Second Party Congress of 1903 to February 1917, women theoreticians, Central Committee members, and members of any other émigré committee, whether Bolshevik or Menshevik, all added up to less than a dozen.[225] It was only in the domain of organization that women were found more acceptable. Krupskaya had been the real technical secretary of the *Iskra*, and then of the Bolshevik faction, for many years. Yet people like Bogdanov, Zinoviev or Kamenev, or practicals like Shlyapnikov, or until his exposure as a Tsarist agent, Roman Malinovsky, had become far more famous. Neither in theory development, nor in the making of strategy did many women play a very significant role.

Evans Clements provides a non-explanation by saying that women did not want leadership positions, as they were interested only in sacrifice in the cause of the revolution and wanted to stay away from power struggles.[226] How does one accept this saintly picture of women who projected themselves as hard as rock, and who joined a party that was engaged in one of history's greatest mass struggles for power? Even if true, it would only indicate that the women had internalized a patriarchal assumption about the higher positions in the party automatically falling to the men. And in fact, some women did aspire to other type of work, recognition as theoretically alert people or people capable of making contributions to the development of party strategy. Both Rozalia Zemlyachka and Evgenia Bosch fall in this category. The case of Bosch is perhaps exemplary. During the war, Bosch was in alliance with Pyatakov and Bukharin. The three of them differed on a number of issues with Lenin. Lenin tended to present the differences as at least in part caused by machinations of Bosch.[227] In other words, women who aspire to be independent theoreticians or strategists are of dubious character. It is therefore necessary to make the point that the Bolshevik assumptions about the backwardness of women led them to conclude that not too many women should be in the leading positions. Indeed, unlike Zetkin and her comrades, the Bolsheviks seldom, before the revolution, made conscious attempts to bring more women into the party and into the leading positions of the party. One could mention certain specific experiences. Prior to the revolution of 1905, there had been few workers who were in the leadership of either faction. But during the revolution of 1905, Lenin fought to open the doors of the party, and its leadership, to workers. We have seen that during the liquidationism controversy,

Bolshevik trade unionists resisted Lenin at one point and insisted that underground committees and party workers in trade unions should have the same status. But women workers were ignored. The one group of Bolsheviks who did turn to working-class women, we will see later, were the Bolshevichki themselves. But if we look at the Bolshevik "general line," we would have to conclude that inadequate gendering of the concept of class led them to often underestimate the potentials of women workers, and as a result to take a long time before there would be any systematic effort for the development of women leading cadres. As late as the 6th Party Congress in 1917, out of 171 delegates, only ten were women, even though a large number of well-known women activists had been early supporters of Lenin's line at the time of the April Theses.[228]

IX
THE STRATEGY OF REVOLUTION: THE PROLETARIAT IN THE DEMOCRATIC REVOLUTION

The Marxist opposition to populism began with a rejection of the claim that the Russian Revolution would result in a uniquely Russian path of socialism, bypassing capitalism. The Russian Marxist orthodoxy was formulated by G. V. Plekhanov. According to Plekhanov, the Russian Revolution had to be a workers' revolution. But he did not thereby suggest that he expected the working class to set up its class rule and begin socialist construction. He only expected the leading role of the workers in the struggle against the autocracy.[229] This idea was explained even more clearly by Pavel Axelrod in 1901, when he wrote that "our party will become the liberator par excellence, a center toward which all democratic sympathies will gravitate and where all the greatest revolutionary protests will originate."[230]

This aim was reflected in the programs drawn up for Social Democracy. Social Democracy was viewed as the conscious movement of the working class. At the same time, the goals it set forward were not socialist, but general democratic. These included the purging of the remnants of feudalism in Russia, the introduction of a political order guaranteeing the freedoms of speech and press by a general arming of the people.[231] The working class was to wage this battle because only in conditions of capitalist development under a democratic political system could it fight and win its eventual battles for social emancipation. Only the working class, because of its position in society, could take the lead in this anti-feudal struggle. But the slogans and aims it would put forward would be in the interests of the entire nation. Consequently the working class would be able to establish its hegemony. The Russian bourgeois society would follow it because the overthrow of the autocracy would benefit it. It is, therefore, possible to conclude that the program of the Russian Social Democracy was the following: The bourgeoisie in Russia was incapable of establishing its own hegemony in the anti-autocratic struggle. So the realization of the democratic aspects of the bourgeois revolution was dependent on the establishment of proletarian hegemony. The result of proletarian hegemony, however, was only to clear the path of capitalist development and facilitate capitalist development. Only when capitalist development proceeded considerably further could there be any talk of a proletarian revolution and socialist construction. The term "democratic revolution" reflected this ambiguous situation. It meant a program falling considerably short of the socialist aims, but a bourgeois revolution carried out with the maximum democratic gains that could be achieved without stepping over bourgeois boundaries.

This idea was taken up on the basis of the then prevailing orthodoxy in Marxist political parties generally. It was based on an economic determinist understanding of Marx.[232] Lenin's rise as a leading Marxist theorist in Russia saw him defending these ideas. In this first major polemical work, directed against populism, he wrote:

> in general, the Russian Communists, adherents of Marxism, should more than any others call themselves SOCIAL–DEMOCRATS, and in their activities should never forget the enormous importance of DEMOCRACY.[233]

The draft program written by Lenin in 1895-96 stated that the proletariat's struggle for emancipation was a political struggle, and its first aim was to achieve political liberty.[234] In the detailed series of demands put forward, he explained that the lack of elementary civil rights were the fundamental problems before the workers, because the Tsarist bureaucracy was a "special caste" which was "irresponsible in the full sense of the term."[235]

Both Axelrod, and Lenin, in polemicizing against the "Economists," stressed that if the proletariat waged only economic battles, it would not be able to establish hegemony in the democratic revolution. So the workers' tasks included championing "the interests of every oppressed nationality or race, of every persecuted religion, of the disfranchised sex, etc."[236]

In this and in a number of other articles, Lenin put forward a complex view. On the one hand, he was arguing that the working class had to fight for democracy, and in the course of doing so, to win over a majority. The struggle for democracy was an essential part of the struggle for socialism, because thereby the proletariat could ensure a majority bloc in a country where it was by itself in a minority. This was an argument directed towards the socialist activists and advanced workers. At the same time, he emphasized the democratic content of the immediate program to win over the non-proletarian masses.[237]

In particular, even at this stage, Lenin was turning to the majority of the nation. He wrote that the struggle to achieve political freedom could not be waged in isolation by the working class. The workers' party had to:

> Inscribe in its banner support for the peasantry ... insofar as the peasantry is capable of a revolutionary struggle against the survivals of serfdom in general and against the autocracy in particular.[238]

The orthodox position, in 1898, was stated unambiguously in the manifesto of the First Congress of the RSDRP, held in Minsk. The manifesto stated that the Russian bourgeoisie was weak and cowardly, and the working class had to take up the task of winning political freedom in order to pursue more energetically the struggle against capitalism.[239] Thus the Marxists considered that liberalism was a total failure in Russia. However, this left open the question of what the working class was to do if a liberal movement did develop.

The Second Party Congress in 1903 adopted the draft program put forward by *Iskra*. It reiterated the need for a first stage of the revolution, comprising the overthrow of the Tsarist autocracy and the creation of a democratic republic. One set of demands were addressed specifically to the peasantry, in which feudal rights were sought to be totally abolished.[240]

The program argued that while the Tsarist state was the immediate target, capitalism was already the dominant mode of production. Consequently, the bourgeoisie was not a significant ally, but half an enemy, from whom the rights of the workers had to be snatched away. Two resolutions were moved about the liberals at the Congress. The resolution by A. N. Potresov was initiated by the Mensheviks. The Bolshevik resolution, moved by Plekhanov, expressed the necessity of supporting any oppositional struggle by the bourgeoisie, but stressed the "limited and inadequate" character of the bourgeois liberation movement. It then went on to warn the working class about "the anti-revolutionary and anti-proletarian character of the trend expressed in Mr. P. Struve's organ, *Ozvobozhdenie*." The resolution of Potresov, by contrast, stressed that the party "does not refuse to enter, and, should the need arise, will enter ... into temporary agreements with liberal or liberal democratic trends," provided these latter agreed to stand resolutely alongside the Social Democracy, did not include in their program any anti-working class demands, and took as their battle slogan the call for universal suffrage.[241]

Though at this stage the differences appeared slight, already the Bolsheviks were displaying a greater skepticism about the liberals, and therefore highlighting the anti-working class role of the most prominent liberal political current of the day. By contrast, the Mensheviks were willing to believe in the possibility of the rise of a revolutionary liberalism, one that would side fully with Social Democracy against the autocracy, and even desist from raising any anti-working class demands. Since liberalism was a typical bourgeois ideology, to demand of liberalism that it should not raise anti-working class demands was tantamount to having illusions that the liberals might forego the class interests of the bourgeoisie. This was the starting point of divergence on the question of proletarian hegemony in the democratic revolution. In 1904, war broke out between Russia and Japan. As prominent minister Plehve said, "we need a small victorious war to stem the tide of revolution."[242] The liberals, including *Ozvobozhdenie* edited by the ex-Marxist Struve, initially supported the war. But with the Japanese victories they became defeatist.[243] The *Zemstvo* (rural local self-governmental bodies) Liberals called for a national conference of *Zemstvo* delegates in November 1904. This was followed by constitutional banquets. The Bolsheviks took a sharply negative attitude to these agitations. They saw in these an attempt to strangle the unfolding revolutionary struggles by establishing a moderate, liberal hegemony over the mass radicalization, in order to drive a hard bargain with the autocracy, and to ultimately sell out the lower classes in exchange for the benefits extracted from Tsarism. The Mensheviks took a totally different stand. As the Menshevik controlled *Iskra* wrote:

> as an independent force we do not exist, and thus our task consists in supporting the second force . . . and in no case intimidating it by presenting our independent proletarian demands.[244]

Almost all the leading Mensheviks took this line of abandoning the Menshevik version of "proletarian hegemony." Their previous arguments were, first, that the peasantry as a fighter against the autocracy was extremely unreliable, and second, that liberalism would fight but it would not be able to display an independent, far less a hegemonic role. Thus proletarian hegemony was viewed more as coming by default due to the inability of the bourgeoisie, than because of the conscious struggles of the advanced workers. So once the liberals became politically active, and displayed a clear unwillingness to come under socialist hegemony, the Menshevik theory of proletarian hegemony could not longer be sustained. The only persons close to the Menshevik camp who took a different position were Lev Trotsky, who shared the Bolsheviks' assessment of liberalism, and Alexander Parvus, the Russian-born

Marxist now settled in Germany. In *Iskra*, from which Plekahnov had ensured the ouster of Trotsky, Parvus alone defended the old standpoint that the Russian proletariat would have to play the role of the vanguard in the coming revolution.[245]

The Bolshevik approach was determined by their thorough-going rejection of bourgeois liberalism, along with a recognition that the ideology of liberalism was becoming quite prevalent. The Bolsheviks insisted that if liberalism triumphed, the result would be half-hearted reforms achieved by compromise with the autocracy. Only under proletarian hegemony could the bourgeois revolution triumph as a democratic revolution. Lenin was sharply critical of what he perceived as the duplicity of the liberals, and wanted the party to constantly prod them, and to fight unhesitatingly for the full minimum program of the Social Democracy, so that the liberals were exposed and more and more workers won over from liberal democracy to working-class democracy.[246]

Lenin's economic analysis was still locked within a primarily national framework,[247] according to which there still remained considerable scope for capitalist development in Russia. However, to realize this potential, autocracy and semi-feudalism had to be wiped out. Liberalism with its compromising role was a poor leader for a full-fledged democratic, anti-autocratic revolution. At the same time, the more autocracy and semi-feudalism were wiped out, the greater would be the political scope of the proletariat, and the more its ranks would swell due to rapid development of capitalism.[248] In order to ensure that this happened, the proletariat would have to fight not only Tsarism, but also the vacillating liberals. Thus, not intimidating the liberals meant, in effect, refraining from carrying out Social Democratic political work.[249] By putting forward this anti-liberal line, Lenin did not envisage a minority revolution waged by the proletariat isolated from the rest. Unlike the Mensheviks, he was aware that the pursuit of power was linked to a willingness to overcome the traditional Russian Marxist prejudice about the role of the peasantry. In the early twentieth century, there was a massive escalation of popular protest and government repression in rural Russia. Peasant resistance grew into peasant radicalism. Lenin, who had opposed sending Social Democratic organizers into the countryside in 1901, now urged a turn to the villages. By the end of 1902, he was immersed in studying the peasant question. In 1903, he wrote a pamphlet, *To the Rural Poor*, which was a "real breakthrough in the history of Marxism, especially Russian Marxism."[250]

The central aim of the work was to propagate the Social Democratic program among the peasants and to raise their political consciousness. He began with a description of urban working-class activities, and suggested that peasants should consider the ways in which their lives would change if they could be assured of medical care, education for their children, and decent wages that the factory workers were fighting for. Turning to the specific grievances of the peasantry, he then explained that the eradication of peasant poverty was linked to the struggle to change the political system. Integrating the tradition of belief in the good Tsar being kept ruling justly by evil upper-class advisers, into a Marxian account of class conflict and bureaucracy, Lenin pointed out that the political enslavement of the rural poor was not caused by an individual. With a careful use of statistical evidence and a belief in the potential force of the peasant's hatred of external authority, Lenin attempted to describe the existing situation in vivid terms that peasants would have to link their personal situations with the requirement of the regime.

Thus Lenin, unlike Plekhanov, believed that the common person, whether worker, peasant, or urban non-proletarian poor, could act rationally, and that they could all be mobilized for the revolution. Social Democracy, through its activities as well as the theoretical writings, could raise the peasant from blind anger and frustration. But the pamphlet still reflected the constricting pressures of contemporary Marxist orthodoxy. On one hand, Lenin was willing to form an alliance with peasants. On the other hand, he always insisted that this was a petty bourgeois, or small property owners' struggle. As a result, in his view, the proletarian hegemony over the peasantry could not go further than setting up a democratic republic. But once such a republic is formed, the class struggle in the countryside would develop to its logical conclusion, and a large rural proletariat would emerge under democratic labor laws of the bourgeois state.[251] This explains Lenin's hostility to the politics of the Socialist Revolutionary party, which he attacked for confusing the "primitive peasant idea" of small-scale equality of land tenure with socialist agriculture.[252]

To sum up, by 1905, when the first Russian Revolution began, Bolshevism had a concept of majority revolution that was to be based on a political alliance between workers and peasants. The outer limit of this revolution's progress was set by the petty bourgeois nature of the peasantry. Maximum democratization was to be won within the bourgeois framework, but it was not possible to go beyond that until there was an expansion of the urban proletarian and semi-proletarian population.

In the revolution of 1905, both bourgeois liberalism and peasant radicalism appeared as distinct forces. Left-wing liberals like Struve supported the idea of an All-Russian Peasant Union. The SRs, like Chernov, called for revolutionary expropriation by peasant unions.[253] On the side of the liberals, a number of political associations began to be formed. These crystallized into two political parties—the Union of

October 17, or Octobrists, and the Constitutional Democrats (or Party of Peoples' Freedom), or the Cadets. It was now clear that not only would bourgeois liberalism not accept proletarian hegemony, but also that it was fighting to establish its hegemony over the oppositional movements.

The Mensheviks asserted that the bourgeois nature of the revolution made necessary a bourgeois liberal leadership at the helm of the revolution. The conclusion that Plekhanov drew from the rise of liberalism was that the Social Democrats must not do anything to alienate the liberals, and therefore they must drop their infatuation with insurrections. Schapiro's summary is quite pertinent here: "The Mensheviks, faced with the evident fact that the Cadets were going to think and act for themselves . . . quietly abandoned their once cherished doctrine."[254]

The distinctions between the Menshevik and the Bolshevik concepts of hegemony were twofold. In the first place, as economic determinists, the Mensheviks argued in defense of a theory of the progressive and leading role of the liberal bourgeoisie. Second, the Menshevik theory absolved the party of any particular responsibility in establishing proletarian hegemony. For the Bolsheviks, the liberals were a force of compromise and half-hearted development. A majority revolution thoroughly democratic in character meant a worker-peasant alliance. To achieve this alliance, and to trounce liberalism no less than the autocracy the vanguard workers' party must develop its program and establish its hegemony.

Thus, Lenin wrote that the bourgeoisie as a whole was incapable of waging a determined struggle against the autocracy, because it feared that a complete break with the autocracy would also put its property in danger.[255] The Third Congress of the RSDRP, in 1905, purely Bolshevik in composition, adopted a resolution "On Support of the Peasant Movement." It insisted that Social Democracy had to support every revolutionary struggle against the existing order, and at the same time, it had to work for the independent organization of the rural proletarians.[256] Given this configuration of class forces, Lenin concluded that it was necessary on the part of the proletariat not merely to play an active role, but to fight for the leading role in the bourgeois democratic revolution, and the establishment of a revolutionary provisional government with proletarian participation. Whether or not workers were in the government, the proletariat was to compel it to carry out the minimum program of the workers' party, i.e., achieve a thorough-going democratic revolution with the greatest benefit for the working class and to ensure the best conditions for capitalist development.

This idea of a provisional government carrying out the Marxist minimum program was called by Lenin the "revolutionary democratic dictatorship of the proletariat and the peasantry" in his works of 1905 and later, especially in *Two Tactics of Social Democracy in the Democratic Revolution*. Lenin explained that the provisional government had to be the organ of an insurrection, and coming to power by the overthrow of the autocracy, it would have to carry out a revolutionary democratic program, defend working-class interests, and organize struggles against the counter-revolution. In such a case, entering into a coalition government was not class collaborationism and letting down the interests of the working class.[257] Standing over half a century after the revolutions of 1848, Lenin could show clearly that the capitalist transformation of various countries could be carried out in various ways. What the working class needed was not merely the bourgeois transformation of society, but the democratization of the state.[258]

Throughout 1905, and for years afterwards, Lenin went on reiterating these ideas. He examined the different classes and strata, and insisted that the tactical slogans formulated by the Third Congress could guide not only the proletariat, but also the petty bourgeoisie. He suggested that the bulk of the revolutionary democrats should be sought among the peasantry. Two roads were open before the revolution: a representative assembly called by the Tsar, which would mean a landlord-big bourgeois dominated regime, or a popular insurrection and worker–peasant preponderance.[259] This was because the insurrection was not a path preferred by the bourgeoisie. The proletariat's position in society, on the other hand, compelled it to be consistently democratic.[260] A victory of the revolution meant immediate steps to establish a republic, and get rid of the landlords and the government officials.[261]

Consequently, if the working class acted as the extreme opposition, rather than trying to take power, it would allow the bourgeois–landlord combination to triumph. The fundamental political issue, as Lenin saw it, was who would convoke the Constituent Assembly. If convoked by the Tsar, i.e., without a successful insurrection, it would serve the interests of the upper classes, and the revolution would head for defeat. If convoked by the revolutionary people, arms in hand, after a provisional Revolutionary Government had already begun democratization, the outcome would be a radical republic. Throughout 1905 and afterwards, Lenin returned to the analogy: 1789 or 1848?[262] Both were roads to capitalism, but the road of 1848 would mean the conversion of semi-feudalism into capitalism from above, and the transformation of the muzhiks into landless peasants, and thence into agricultural proletarians.[263]

In supporting the peasant struggles, Lenin attempted to demarcate the Bolshevik program from that of the SRs. The peasants could not be saved from the baneful impact of capitalism. The democratic revolution would not short-circuit capitalist development, but would intensify this development. The SR ideal was to emancipate the peasants through the socialization of land. For Lenin, this was an absurdity. The All-Russian Peasant Union that came up was dominated by middle peasants. At its First Congress, delegates displayed an awareness of the need for a Constituent Assembly along with the need for land. But they also often expressed loyalty to the Tsar.[264] In the summer and autumn of 1905 there was a steady escalation of rural unrest. Its target was the landed gentry.[265] After the publication of the October Manifesto, peasants took it as an open call to seize forest and pasture land.[266]

Lenin enthusiastically supported the growing peasant struggle. Bolsheviks and SRs stood close on tactical matters, just as Mensheviks and Cadets did. Within the SR Party, Victor Chernov at this stage was developing a theory of a two-stage revolution with a long transition period,[267] leading Lenin to say that the only road forward for Chernov was to accept Marxism.[268] Within the revolutionary movement, therefore, Lenin was trying to establish his thesis about a majority bloc comprising worker and peasants by polemicizing against two opponents. Against the populist revolutionaries, he was insisting on the bourgeois limits of the peasantry's goals. Against the Mensheviks, he was defending the need to support the revolutionary thrust of the peasant struggles. At the Fourth (Unity) Congress, Bolshevism was in a minority on this as on other issues. Lenin's position was essentially political. The peasant political actions were threatening the survival of the Tsarist regime and hence should be supported. At the same time, peasants should be told that their claim that everybody should have the right to use the land was achievable only when a democratic republic was established.[269] The Menshevik program, developed by Peter Maslov, planned for the transfer of large landed estates to local democratic organizations, so that, as Dan argued, the land question could only be decided with proletarian participation.[270] Joseph Stalin, present at the Congress as a Georgian Bolshevik, proposed a different program,[271] arguing that it was impossible to ignore the peasantry's desire to divide the land. He asserted that division of the land would neither delay economic development nor check the progress of the revolution. He, therefore, opposed Lenin, because Lenin had put forward a program of land nationalization, arguing that it was not a step towards socialism, but a step to create the most favorable condition for agrarian capitalism. Moreover, nationalization carried out by revolutionary peasant committees would politically educate the peasants.[272]

It is possible to say that by 1906, the Bolshevik strategy of democratic revolution had been adumbrated in full. Having recognized that the peasant majority of the population, rather than the flabby liberals,[273] were the crucial factors in the Russian revolution, the Bolsheviks argued that the experience of opposition to traditional authority might bring the peasants to support a revolutionary democratic movement initiated by the proletariat under the political leadership of the Social Democrats. Unlike the Mensheviks, they welcomed a peasant upsurge. The Bolsheviks viewed the Cadets' role in the State Duma with distrust.[274] The Cadet's agrarian program, though more radical than Stolypin's, yet advocated reforms, i.e., concessions within the existing semi-feudal land relations and State framework, not a peasant revolution.[275] Lenin was much more impressed with the 107 peasant deputies who formed the Trudovik group, and denounced greedy landlords who cheated the poor or used the army to burn down rebellious villages. Trudoviks in the Duma also proved to be more consistent defenders of political liberty. Yet, Lenin and the Bolsheviks went on dismissing the possibility that peasants might fight anti-capitalist struggles. As he put his case repeatedly, the Bolsheviks supported the peasantry to the extent it was revolutionary democratic, and prepared to fight it as it became anti-proletarian.[276]

Several questions were raised by this standpoint. First what kind of mechanisms did Lenin visualize for the worker–peasant revolution? Second, how was the working class expected to limit its hegemonic role through a self-denying program? Third, even accepting the criticism that the SRs suffered from certain simplistic illusions, the very nature of the peasant movement raised the question of whether the peasantry through its allegiance to the community, and its opposition to the growing bloc between bourgeoisie and landlords, could become an ally in the early stages of a workers' revolution to begin socialist construction? While these were important issues, it is incontestable that for all its contradictions, the Bolshevik program by stressing the leading role of the working class and the alliance with the peasantry, returned to Marx's position of 1848-9 and made a revolutionary, yet majority orientation possible. It was in 1917 that the questions posed above began to be answered in concrete terms.

X
ESTABLISHING DEMOCRACY AND DEMOCRATIC RIGHTS IN THE BOURGEOIS DEMOCRATIC REVOLUTION

Though the social composition of the democratic bloc, and hence the social basis of democracy, was of paramount importance for Lenin, it did not mean that Lenin was unconcerned with the institutional mechanisms or the legal codification of political liberty. Every draft program written by Lenin or any other orthodox Marxist in Russia, stressed these elements. The Emancipation of Labour, Russia's first Marxist group, led by G. V. Plekhanov, had formulated a political program, which put

forward a full list of demands including universal franchise, salaries for
elected deputies, inviolability of the person and residence of citizens,
unrestrained freedom of conscience, speech, assembly, etc., freedom of
movement, and full equality of all citizens; the revision of the civil and
criminal legislation involving on one hand the abolition of estate-based
divisions, and on the other hand, the abolition of inhumane laws.[277] At
the end of the century, in 1899, Lenin found it possible to endorse this
section of the program with only a few changes, notably the addition
of the demands for the complete abolition of internal passports, and
"complete equality of rights for men and women."[278]

Lenin always stressed, in his programmatic writings, that institutions
and forms were important. In an 1899 draft, he observed that proletarian
democracy was not identical to direct legislation by the people. He
argued that such direct legislation could degenerate into an imperialist
plebiscite (i.e., a Bonapartist) state.[279]

The program adopted at the Second Congress went into considerable
detail. It expressed the view that the most immediate political task of
the party was the overthrow of the autocracy and its replacement by a
democratic republic. A series of conditions or demands had to be met
to ensure the constitution of this democratic republic.[280] These included
directly political demands as well as social and economic demands
that ensured the personal conditions so that people could in fact use
democracy. It is worth remembering in the light of the discussion on
Liquidationism that this was the democratic program that Lenin was
defending, and the Liquidators were trying to abandon in favor of a
milder one.

Sovereignty of the people was defined as the concentration of
supreme state power wholly in the hands of a unicameral legislative
assembly elected on the basis of universal, equal, and direct suffrage
for all men and women of the age of twenty or above. Parliaments
were to be biennial. Every voter was to have the right to be elected to
any representative body. Representatives were to be paid. From the
days of the People's Charter onwards, these were standard democratic
demands. In accordance with the campaigns of the socialist movement,
the wording was careful so that women's right to the vote was explicitly
recognized. Extensive local self-government was demanded, as well as
regional self-government for national minorities who lived in certain
parts of the empire. The protection of minority rights included the
demand that people must have the right to receive education in their
native language, to express themselves in their language, and to use
these languages on an equal basis with the state languages in all local,
public and state institutions. Finally, since the minorities were nations,
their right of self-determination was acknowledged by placing these

demands under the discussion of the bases of the democratic republic. The program showed that establishment of a real democracy, in its view, was incompatible with the existence of subordinate nations, races, etc.

Other demands called for the establishment of civil liberties and the control of officials by the people. These were inviolability of person and domicile, unrestricted freedom of conscience, speech, publication and assembly, freedom to strike and freedom of association, freedom of travel, abolition of social estates, and equality of rights for all citizens, the right of any person to prosecute any official before a jury, and the creation of elected judges. Apart from those, there were four demands: the replacement of the standing army by universal arming of the people (the most fundamental demand of radical democracy); the separation of church from state (so that religion becomes a private matter) and of the school from the Church (to ensure secular, democratic education); free and compulsory general and vocational education for all up to the age of sixteen with meals, etc., for poor children; and the abolition of indirect taxes and establishment of a progressive income tax. These represented a Marxist program of democracy, with a strong emphasis on liberty.

Bolshevik tactics on various questions of democracy can be judged in terms of this program. The first issue is the demand for an authoritative parliament. As a result of the growing radical struggle in 1905, the Tsarist Government proposed to create a "consultative Duma." Its draft law, prepared by Minister of Interior, Bulygin, gave it the name Bulygin Duma. In an article in the Bolshevik paper *Vperyod* (April 1905), Lenin denounced it for being not a constitutional, but a consultative body. He wrote that since the Tsar's approval of bills could be withheld through vetoes, the Duma did not limit the autocratic regime.[281] Second, the bicameral Duma had an Upper House comprising sixty elected nobles and a number of officials appointed by the Tsar.[282] The Lower House was to have 643 elected members, aged not less than twenty-five years, with the ability to read and write Russian. An elaborate system of indirect election was set up. Lenin pointed out that since representation was estate-based, the working class was completely excluded.[283] Analyzing further the role of various upper class circles, Lenin discerned three trends—the conservatives, the liberals, and the "radicals" who wanted only a "skimpy constitution."[284]

The October Manifesto promised a somewhat broader Duma. But this too was not a proper constitution. Moreover, it came at a time when the organs of popular power were growing in strength. In November 1905, Lenin was therefore arguing that a democratic election could only be conducted by a provisional revolutionary government.[285]

With the arrest of the Soviet of Workers' Deputies in St. Petersburg, and then the defeat of the Moscow uprising, the question of participating in the Duma began to come up in Social Democratic circles. A conference of the social democratic factions and national groups, including Bolsheviks, Mensheviks, Latvians, Poles, the Jewish Bund, and the Revolutionary Ukrainian Party decided, with the Mensheviks dissenting, to call for an active boycott. An active boycott meant taking advantage of the electoral process to propagate the Social Democratic line, participating in election meetings, but to call for boycott of the actual elections. The Mensheviks increasingly called for taking part in the elections at the lower rungs.

On December 11, 1905, a statute containing the new electoral law was published. It increased the number of representatives to be elected by the workers, and even more so by the peasants. The Mensheviks called for participation in the election of electors to form an illegal, alternative assembly. Lenin opposed this on a number of grounds. First, that if free representatives were needed, the freely elected Soviets, rather than a police supervised Duma election, should be chosen. Second, he said, "we too, will take full part in a parliament. But . . . the Duma is not a parliament."[286]

However, Lenin also made it clear that his tactic of active boycott was based on the assumption that the revolution was going to continue to gather momentum. An active boycott meant an immediate slogan of an armed uprising.[287] Eventually, both Bolsheviks and Mensheviks boycotted the elections. But many individual Social Democrats contested and when the Duma met on April 28, 1906, it had fourteen members who united into a Social Democratic group. Later on, Georgian Mensheviks had five more members elected.

At this, Lenin's position was, "our readers know that we were in favour of boycotting the Duma . . . But it goes without saying that, if real party Social-Democrats have now been elected to the Duma on really party lines, all of us . . . will do all we can to help them to fulfil their arduous duties."[288]

At the Stockholm Congress of the RSDRP (April/May, 1906), the Menshevik delegates from Transcaucasia proposed that the party should give up its boycott and nominate candidates to the elections that were still pending. All but one of the Bolsheviks accused the Mensheviks of betrayal. But Lenin voted with the Mensheviks. Subsequently he argued that the boycott tactic was dependent on the specific situation, and should now be lifted.[289] At the subsequent RSDRP conference on July 21–23, 1907, Lenin proposed a resolution against boycott. Bogdanov, speaking for the Bolsheviks, spoke in favor of a boycott. Lenin was opposed by the other Bolsheviks. His draft resolution stated that in the absence of a rapid upswing of the revolution, even the Duma elections could not be abandoned.[290]

The apparent contradiction in Lenin's stand of 1905 and that of 1907, and the conflict between the Bolshevik majority and Lenin can be explained without much difficulty. As long as it seemed that the revolution was on the ascendancy, they concentrated on an armed insurrection, and treated the Duma election as an attempt by the autocracy to divert the revolutionary energy of the workers and peasants. But when full democracy was unattainable, Lenin was willing to take part in relatively undemocratic bodies as revolutionary agitators in the enemy camp. Lenin saw, earlier than his supporters, that the time for an open assault on the autocracy had passed. That was what set him temporarily in contradiction to them.

The rise of liquidationism was not just a matter of changing the party structures. The Liquidators wanted to free the Duma deputies from party control. This came out most clearly after the Vienna conference of 1912, when the Liquidators scored a major victory over the non-Bolshevik leftists. In the elections to the Fourth Duma, the St. Petersburg Social Democrats tried to discuss unity. When *Pravda* first came out it assured its readers that it would be a party paper, not a factional paper (i.e., it would treat the Prague Conference, declaring the Bolsheviks to be the party, as a provisional meeting). As Stalin wrote in *Pravda*'s first editorial, "*Pravda* will call above all else and in the main for unity in the class struggle of the working class."[291] But *Pravda* made it clear that unity would have to be built on the basis of a clear statement of electoral program in line with the traditional Social Democratic stance, and mandatory on all those elected as "electors." At this point, *Luch*, the Liquidators' paper, came out. *Luch* opposed the idea of voting according to a program. Ultimately, the Bolshevik Badaev was elected as the Deputy to the Duma, but only after a split in the workers' electors votes, unlike in the past. The *Pravda* mandate, adopted by the electoral college of St. Petersburg stated in part:

> The demands of the Russian people advanced by the movement of 1905 remain unrealized.... We think, therefore, that Russia is on the eve of mass movements, perhaps more profound than those of 1905.... As was the case in 1905, the Russian proletariat ... will again act as the vanguard.... The only allies it can have are the long suffering peasantry.... The Duma tribune is, under the present conditions, one of the best means of enlightening and organizing the broad masses of the proletariat. It is for this very purpose that we are sending our deputy into the Duma and we charge him and the whole Social Democratic fraction of the Fourth Duma to make widely known our demands from the Duma tribune, and not to play at legislation in the state Duma. We want to hear the voices of the members of the Social Democratic fraction ring out loudly from the Duma tribune proclaiming the final goal of the proletariat, proclaiming the full and uncurtailed demands of 1905.[292]

The uncurtailed demands of 1905 meant the democratic republic, the

confiscation of the landed estates, and the eight-hour day. In course of
these conflicts, emerged the Bolshevik attitude to parliamentarism and
to the parliamentary representatives. From the foregoing, it is possible
to conclude that Lenin did not oppose participation in parliament or
even in the Duma. After the expulsion of Bogdanov the Bolsheviks as
a whole agreed on the need to participate in the Duma. But whether in
the Duma, or in real democratic parliaments, they insisted that Social
Democratic representatives would have to put forward the party line.
They could not claim to be independent of party control.[293]

This survey of the Bolshevik attitude to democratic institutions has
so far revealed that Bolshevik intransigence reflected, not a rejection
of democracy, but a rejection of poor compromises in the name of a
democratic program. Lenin's and Bolshevism's view of democratization
can be further gleaned by looking at a few specific issues. In an
article, written in 1901, Lenin excoriated the government for drafting
183 students into the army for "riotous assembly." The students had
demanded the right to conduct their affairs freely. From this incident, he
moved on to an attack on the authoritarianism of the imperial justice.[294]
Similarly, Lenin took up, in the same issue of *Zarya* which published the
foregoing article, the case of a peasant beaten to death by policemen. The
policemen had been given a short prison term. Lenin exposed the class
nature of the judiciary, but he also emphasized that the judiciary had no
independence, that the case had not been tried before a jury, and then
urged that government officials should be tried by common people.[295]

A fundamental issue in democracy is freedom of the press. In
Bolshevik writings, two sorts of press are mentioned. There was the
party press and party literature, and there was the more general press.
Lenin's approach to the question of freedom of opinion in the party press
was to say that it had to be subordinated to the revolutionary aims of
the party. But in an article of November 1905, he put forward a more
detailed outlook. He wrote that party literature would have to be "part
of the common cause of the proletariat . . . a component of organized,
planned and integrated Social Democratic party work."[296]

This view of all party literature as being a component of *integrated*
party work made Lenin impose stiff conditions. He argued that to
have real freedom of association, those who did not accept the view of
a party could neither stay in it, nor claim the right to write in the party
press.[297] He also wrote that "Newspapers must become the organs of the
various party organizations, and their writers must by all means become
members of those organizations. Publishing and distributive centers,
bookshops and reading rooms, libraries and similar establishments
must all be under party control."[298] This was, in a way, too restrictive,
for it presupposed an extensive party control combined with a party

discipline against what he called "bourgeois anarchist individualism." Lenin also wrote that "there is no question that literature is least of all subject to mechanical adjustment or levelling, to the rule of the majority over the minority."[299]

The article presents a problem. Its core argument, that freedom of press within a party should not mean freedom for anti-party elements, was unexceptionable. However, he did not clearly define "anti-party" views. His definition of the borderline between party and anti-party views included the party program, the party's resolutions on the tactics and its rules and the entire experience of international Social Democracy.[300] But to include tactical differences into definitions of what was "anti-party" meant turning any difference into open enmity, and making inner-party debates very restrictive. Moreover in insisting that workers' democracy wanted (or needed) all literature to be turned into party literature, Lenin was extending (hypothetically) the domain of party and partisan literature too far.

Lenin's own pre-1917 practice shows him to be more flexible than the article suggests. In 1910, when the Central Committee plenum decided to close down the factional papers, it also decided to issue a special discussion bulletin. Lenin took the position that articles defending the party line should be printed in the party press meant as the party's mouth-piece, while articles questioning the party line should be published in the discussion bulletin.[301] During the war years, when censorship tightened everywhere, a suggestion by Lenin showed that he did not actually rule out party activists writing in the non-party press. He only stressed that the official party press must reflect the party line.[302]

In the foregoing pages, it has been demonstrated that the Bolshevik party that emerged by February 1917 was not a personal creation of Lenin. While he was its foremost theoretician, the party was created by protracted interactions between practical workers and theorists, and repeatedly remodeled. The core idea of *What is to be Done?*, which was the idea that since the working class is fragmented and large parts of its subjected to the domination of non-proletarian ideologies, the advanced workers have to be organized separately in order to gain greater striking power, was validated by subsequent experience. At the same time, many ideas and organizational concepts had to be modified and discarded under the pressure of events and under working-class pressure. Moreover, party building meant elaborating a proletarian revolutionary program. Two key elements were well-developed before 1917. One was the necessity of a worker–peasant alliance in order to create a majority for the revolution, and the other was the need to struggle for a consistently democratic polity as the best guarantee for the extirpation of the autocracy and the maximization of the rights of the working class in the new era. A contradiction was, however, set up between the idea of necessarily bourgeois democratic limit on the revolution and a provisional revolutionary government set up as a result of the revolutionary activity of the workers. Only in 1917 was this contradiction solved.

XI
GENDER, PATRIARCHY, PROGRAM AND PRACTICE

When the 2nd RSDRP Congress adopted the program of the party, it displayed a lack of awareness of patriarchy. Even so simple a demand as equal pay for equal work was missing.[303] The demands that were raised concerning women workers included stopping all forms of work harmful to women's health, opening crèches in factories where women worked, paid maternity leave, etc.[304] In fairness to the Russian Marxists, though, it should be said that if their program was more limited, in their case the whole party fought to achieve the demands. During the strike waves of 1905–7, the overwhelming majority of charters of demands showed the recurrence of those demands concerning women workers. So while protecting the weak rather than fighting for equality was the perspective, within that limitation there was no compromise on struggles.[305]

Though Marxists had been aware that there was a "woman question," at least from the time when August Bebel published his celebrated book on the topic, despite Bebel, despite Engels, and despite Zetkin, women continued to be marginalized in the Russian party, as well as most other parties. However, it tended to be assumed in that relatively liberal age that the "backwardness" of women was due to the pressure of bourgeois society and ideology, rather than because of women's innate backwardness. Since Lenin's analysis, too, did not take into account the specific forms of oppression faced by women workers, the general class goals, general class demands, and hence general definition of what constituted the advanced worker, were too easily placed in the mold of the male workers' goals, demands and political consciousness. This is why, even such a fundamental act as drawing up the party program in 1903 saw women's issues remaining marginal. General class demands were supposedly common to all, while the demands of women were specific, and at the margins. With such ideas rooted in the understanding of most party members, there were few attempts to draw women workers into the party prior to the revolution of 1905.[306]

The Bolsheviks, including the Bolshevik women, began as critics of any autonomous women's movement, even an autonomous proletarian women's movement on the German model. During the revolution of 1905, on one hand there was a fair amount of participation by women in strikes, and on the other hand, the Equal Rights Union and other liberal feminist organizations began to make some headway in organizing women. Between 1901 and 1910, the number of women employed in the workforce went up by 18 percent at a time when male employment rose by only 1.3 percent.[307] From 1910, women began to take part in increasingly militant economic struggles in course of the revival of the labor movement. From 1905, women also began participating in a large number of political struggles. Women were elected to the Soviets of Workers Deputies of St. Petersburg and Ivanovo-Voznesensk.[308] As a result of these factors, Social Democrats began to feel a pressure for organizing women workers. At this stage, Alexandra Kollontai was the only member of the party who had proposed separate meetings for women in order to recruit women. But in this work she faced resistance from within the party. Even the most respected woman member of the party, the veteran Vera Zasulich, opposed any attempt to organize women separately. When despite all this Kollontai called an all-women meeting, she found that a notice had been put up cancelling the women's meeting and announcing an all-men meeting instead. How important such all-women meetings were is brought out by Glickman. She shows that the social conditions made women workers diffident, and in mixed meetings, often unwilling even to speak.[309]

In 1908, liberal feminists called the first All-Russia Women's Congress. The feminists who had called the Congress were opposed to the idea of class struggle. But many women workers wanted to take part in the Congress. The official party line, as laid out by the city committee of St. Petersburg, was to boycott the Congress, and when later participation became inevitable, to purely rhetorically "expose" the liberal feminists. Kollontai and a group of women worker-Social Democrats tried to turn the participation of women workers in this Congress into a political education for them. Secret meetings were organized and a forty-five-strong working-class women delegation prepared. Volkova, speaking on behalf of them, told the assembled women that there was a basic difference between the bourgeois and the proletarian approaches to women's liberation, with the proletarian approach stressing fundamental social revolution. She also proposed a very radical set of demands for the immediate future.[310] Apart from mobilizing the women for the purpose of the Congress, Kollontai attempted a theoretical intervention through a book, which however could not come out before the Congress. The book has a curious history. Entitled *The Social Basis of the Woman Question* (in Russian), this book was never reprinted after the Russian revolution, and even in her Russian-language selected works, only the preface is reproduced. A general impression has been created that it was directed only against feminism as such. Kollontai's own assessment was different. Along with liberal feminism she had also criticized the lack of gender consciousness in the Social Democratic party. Rare among Marxist works on women of that period, the book also made questions of sexuality a political issue, to be discussed seriously. By taking up the question of marriage not merely from a legal point, but as a matter of male control over women's sexuality, she placed the discussion on women's liberation in terms where it was not possible to simply repeat a set of demands addressed to government and employer, but to force the class to look inwards. In Russian Marxism, this was the first effort.

This would be followed up by one Bolshevik, Inessa Armand, and her running battle with Lenin over the issue of women's sexuality. Armand's feminism was ignited at least in part by this reality of the life of women workers. Until 1913, her writings do not show any discussion on such issues as prostitution or female sexuality. But by early 1915, we can discern a change. She drafted an outline on the "family question" which she sent to Lenin. Lenin wrote back, saying the draft was unclear, but stressed that "freedom of love" had no place in a Marxist pamphlet. He thereby ignored all the other points in the proposed outline, and focussed on one point with which he declared disagreement. His subsequent controversy with Armand shows Lenin identifying "freedom of love" with freedom of adultery, and Armand arguing that she had not put such a connotation. Lenin's angry response was that bourgeois women meant, by freedom of love, one of the following three things: freedom from seriousness in love, freedom from childbirth, and freedom of adultery.[311] Let us note first of all, that Lenin clubs freedom of adultery with freedom from childbirth. To assume and assert as a "class line" that it is proletarian to desire many childbirths is regressive.

As for the bourgeois women, if by this Lenin was referring to bourgeois feminists, their conception of free love did not mean freedom to commit adultery either. Many of the more conservative currents in bourgeois feminism, in country after country, insisted that the goal must be stricter sexual morality for men, rather than so-called looser morality for women.[312]

To return to the Armand–Lenin debate, for Lenin "free love" meant promiscuity and multiple partners in casual sex (the so-called glass of water theory, which he insisted on foisting on his feminist Bolshevik comrades). But nowhere in Armand's published writings or letters do we get such an interpretation. Rather, she equated freedom of love with a freedom to choose one's marriage partner, with marriage based on personal commitments between two equal people, a relationship free from religious or social hypocrisy. Also, it is evident from Lenin's letters, that she saw these as demands pertaining to all women.[313] Thus, rival strands existed in Bolshevik history. One would find itself elaborated after Lenin's death as *the* Marxist position on women.

The more conservative socialist discourses on sexuality assert that all talk of sexuality is a petty-bourgeois naughtiness, or worse, petty bourgeois individualism seeking to divert and ruin the revolutionary struggle. Against this it is necessary to emphasize a woman's right to control her body. According to the analysis made by Kollontai and Armand, at the same time, the contemporary class-state was the defender of legal marriage and the family. So any talk of women's liberation within the existing state structure would be false. Real women's liberation would be possible in a society where motherhood and the duties of child rearing would fall on society collectively, not on individual women or families. Hence, in Kollontai's eyes, socialism could not be a discourse framed only by male experiences. A sharp ideological struggle must be carried out in order to redefine class struggle and socialism.[314] But even Kollontai could not come out of the ideological pressure of patriarchy fully.[315] In this connection we need to look at how International Working Women's Day came to be observed in Russia. In Russia, apart from the problem of police control, there also existed a deep suspicion in many quarters within the party about such a program. Many members thought it was a kind of separatism aiming to split the class. Kollontai wrote an article, "Zhenskii Dyen," targeting the impact of patriarchy on the working-class movement. She rejected the accusation that observing women's day was a kind of surrender to bourgeois feminism. She highlighted the insensitivity of the male comrades to explain why there was low membership of women in party and mass organizations. She wrote that the prospects of revolution would be more the more conscious fighters grew in numbers. Those women who merely carried out the instructions of their fathers or husbands, or who sat by the chimney the whole day, could not possess consciousness.[316] This was a clear exposition of gender divisions within the class, and an argument that class unity could not be brought about by the dominant gender imposing their will on the dominated.

Kollontai at this stage was a left Menshevik. Women Bolsheviks, like Konkordiya Samoilova, were also pushing the party to organize women. As a result of the initial lack of socialist attention to the struggles by women workers, the strikes and other forms of agitation launched by them often remained unorganized when one looks at the typical models of organization. And yet the women in fact frequently displayed exemplary organization and clarity of purpose. As long as the rational choices in the name of class goals were made exclusively by male workers and from the standpoint of the male workers, the women appeared irrational. In fact, the violence and elemental spontaneity displayed in many women's strikes stemmed from an attempt by the women to put their stamp on the struggles. It also reflected an attempt to break away from the tight constraints of patriarchal control.

A study of strike demands reveal that as the working-class movement became more and more organized, the union and party leaderships tended to impose a uniform demand pattern. There were several reasons for this. On one hand, the growth of local struggles into a more broadly comprehended class struggle meant negotiation and incorporation of the aspirations of different groups. On the other hand, along with the demands forming a discourse shaping the specific nature of the working class, they also constituted a discourse that reasserted male bias. As a result, "general demands" seldom talked about equal wages for men and or women. When the demand for minimum wages was first made in 1905, the demand was for ninety kopecks daily for men and seventy-five for women.[317] When women themselves took a leading role, the demands often changed, as records show. In 1912 alone, in twenty-two strikes in which women were present in a significant or dominant number, an end to sexual harassment in the name of searching workers as they left the factory premises was a major demand. In 1913, this was even the main reason for the strike at the Grisov factory. Centralized charters of demand, though, still did not reflect this. The demands raised by the women workers displayed a growing awareness that standardized "class demands" did not take their specific oppression into account. Sexual harassment by supervisors was one of the prominent demands in a large number of struggles. Equal pay was a very infrequent demand, but it too began to be raised.[318]

The consequence of struggles by women workers was the recognition by a number of Bolshevik women that some kind of special effort should be directed specifically toward the women. The first result was a page in *Pravda*, the legal paper brought out by the Bolsheviks from 1912. Out of this experience there developed the journal *Rabotnitsa*. From emigration Inessa Armand and Nadezhda Krupskaya, and inside Russia Samoilova and Elizarova played a major role. Samoilova had been running *Pravda*'s page on women, and she was the first to take an initiative. At this point Inessa Armand had returned to Russia, and she was also keen to organize work among women workers. The presence of several women close to Lenin has led mythmakers to claim it as chiefly Lenin's initiative, but there is no evidence to that effect. The Central Committee provided no funds. And Krupskaya's memoirs highlight the role of Armand, not that of Lenin. One letter by Krupskaya saying "*we* have" discussed a paper for women is taken to mean Lenin's active interest. In fact, another copy of that letter, kept at the Okhrana archives, is signed by Krupskaya and Armand. In recent years, over-zealous defense of Bolshevism by some Trotskyists like Tony Cliff or Alan Woods have led to a repetition of such Lenin cults. Woods claims: "Lenin constantly emphasized the revolutionary potential of these women proletarians and insisted that the party take special measures to win them to the revolutionary cause."[319] It is a case, here, of ascribing all positive work by Bolsheviks to Lenin. By contrast, while Anne Bobroff also takes the position that the initiative for *Rabotnitsa* belonged to Lenin, unlike Cliff or Woods, she shows that this was the first official commitment of the party to a long-term contact specifically for women.[320] In this context we should also note that apart from *Rabotnitsa*, no other efforts were taken up to organize women workers, certainly not separately, and the demands to this effect were either trivialized or treated in a hostile manner.

The paper saw two lines being pushed. The draft editorial written by Krupskaya for the first issue talked about bringing backward women into the socialist struggle. According to her, "The 'woman' question for working men and working women is a question of how to organize the backward masses of working women," and therefore the sole task of *Rabotnitsa* was to explain to the insufficiently conscious working women what their interests were, indicating the "communality of their interests with the interests of the entire working class."[321] Similar attitudes were expressed by many other Bolsheviks. Thus, during World War I, the Kiev Committee of the party issued a leaflet entitled *To the Working Women of Kiev*. It was a bland call to women workers to join in the struggle already being waged by their male comrades. While acknowledging that women suffered due to family and social oppression, the leaflet had nothing to say about these oppressions, arguing instead that simply joining the struggle, which the men had already discovered, would be enough.[322]

Armand's article, by contrast, stressed that without more encouragement to women's struggles, the struggle for socialism could not go forward. The underground activists were not too keen to write theoretical essays, but in article after article they highlighted the dual oppression faced by women workers.[323] And this experience of bringing out a paper for women also influenced the main party paper, *Pravda*, which began to pay more attention to women workers. There remained however a difference in perception. The *Pravda* reports, often written by male worker-correspondents, contained a patronizing thrust at times missing in *Rabotnitsa*. Thus a 1913 report on the struggle in the James Beck Cotton Mill said: "They all tell tales on one another and try to hurt one another in every way. Gossip and toadying have built a firm nest for themselves."[324] It is important to question this picture of utter disunity and to ask whether it was not substantially serving a negative ideological function— that of obscuring the potential for solidarity and militancy existing among women workers. *Rabotnitsa*, consciously acting as their voice, did highlight precisely those elements. So, this was an arena where Bolshevism moved forward hesitantly. Yet, as we will see in the next chapter, during the year of revolution, some advances were made here, too.

NOTES

1. For Narodnism and its history, there exists a wealth of material. A general survey is available in F. Venturi, *Roots of Revolution: A History of the Populist and Socialist Movements in Nineteenth-Century Russia*. For the relationship between Marx and the Narodniks see T. Shanin, ed., *Late Marx and the Russian Road: Marx and the Peripheries of Capitalism*, London, 1984, and A. Walicki, *The Controversy Over Capitalism*, Oxford, 1969.

2. For early Russian Marxism and its opposition to Narodnism, see the general discussion and further references in Kunal Chattopadhyay, *The Marxism of Leon Trotsky*, Calcutta, 2006, pp. 69–75.

3. In one form or another, a multitude of critics have attempted to highlight Lenin's differences with Marx at this juncture. Richard N. Hunt, *The Political Ideas of Marx and Engels,* vol. 1, pp. 365 and 367 explicitly avows that Marx never advocated a vanguard party (not quite correct, as discussed in Chapter 3) and that a vanguard party would always lead to bureaucratization (a sociological claim requiring careful scrutiny). L. Kołakowski, *Main Currents of Marxism*, vol. 2, Oxford, 1982, p. 390, claims that according to Lenin, the party with its correct theoretical consciousness embodies the proletarian consciousness irrespective of the views of the real proletariat. For D. W. Lovell, *From Marx to Lenin*, pp. 10, 146, 151, 152, Lenin's concept of party was unimportant compared to his theory of state in the rise of Soviet totalitarianism, but never the less , he holds that Lenin used organizational disputes to pin political labels on opponents. S. S. Wolin, *Politics and Vision*, opines that Lenin had a tendency to "sublimate" political thought into organizational theory. His insistence on an organized, vanguard party injects a bureaucratism absent in Marx, (pp. 365, 420–21). A similar view is put forward by A. G. Meyer, *Leninism*, New York, 1962, pp. 23–25; A. Ulam, *The Bolsheviks*, pp. 139–40 and D. Shub, *Lenin*, Baltimore, 1961, p. 72, argued that Lenin's conception of the party led to the stifling of the independent initiative of the masses. Even so sympathetic a writer as Marcel Liebman, *Leninism Under Lenin*, London, 1980, says that the concept of a proletarian vanguard was an "elite concept of the party" (p. 29). The elitist character of Bolshevism has also been stressed in L. Schapiro, *The Communist Party of Soviet Union*; and L. H. Haimson, *The Russian Marxists and the Origins of Bolshevism*, Boston, 1966. R. N. Carew-Hunt, *The Theory and Practice of Communism*, pp. 169, 178, 185–92, says that Lenin was a master tactician who made a revolution through a small, tightly controlled, fanatically loyal party. See further E. H. Carr, *1917: Before and After*, London, Melbourne, and Toronto, 1969, p. 19; and S. Fitzpatrick, *The Russian Revolution*, Oxford, 1984, pp. 25, 81, 98.

4. L. Trotsky, *The Young Lenin,* Harmondsworth, 1974, pp. 151–52.
5. G. V. Plekhanov, *Selected Philosophical Works*, vol. I, Moscow, 1974, pp. 164–65.
6. Ibid., p. 456. See also two versions of the speech in the Plekhanov Archive, Marxists Internet Archive, accessed on October 9, 2006, http://www.marxists.org/archive/plekhanov/1889/07/speech.html.
7. M. Löwy, *The Politics of Combined and Uneven Development,* p. 32.
8. G. V. Plekhanov, *Selected Philosophical Works*, vol. I, pp. 411–50.
9. This is borne out by the references to these volumes in his "On the So-called Market Question" (1893), in *LCW* 1, Moscow, 1977, pp. 80–89 and passim (vol. 2 of *Capital*) and "On the Economic Content of Narodism" (1895) in *LCW* 1, p. 488.
10. For a near-exhaustive study on his West European Social Democratic ideological make-up, see N. Levine, "The Germanization of Lenin," *Studies in Soviet Thought* , vol. 35, no. 1, January 1988, pp. 1–37.
11. For the thesis about Lenin's Narodnik roots, see, for example, R. Pipes, "The Origins of Bolshevism: 'The Intellectual Evolution of Young Lenin,'" in R. Pipes, ed., *Revolutionary Russia*, Cambridge, 1968, pp. 26–52.
12. The view, that for Lenin, organization theory was self-sufficient, comes from simply declaring unimportant his voluminous political writings, and from a very partial (one-sided) reading, *What is to be Done?*, discussed below. See in this context J. Frankel, ed., *Vladimir Akimov on the Dilemmas of Russian Marxism, 1895–1903,* Cambridge, 1969.
13. *LCW* 2, Moscow , 1977, p. 96.
14. Ibid., pp. 112–13, 116–17.
15. See A. K. Wildman, *The Making of a Worker's Revolution*, Chicago, 1967, pp. 31–27.
16. Plekhanov, quoted in T. Cliff , *Lenin*, vol. 1, London, 1975.
17. See V. I. Lenin, "Explanation of the Law on Fines imposed on Factory Workers," "To the Working Men and Women of the Thornton Factory," and "What are our Ministers thinking about?" in *LCW* 2, pp. 33–72, 81–85, 87–92, for examples.
18. Ibid., pp. 323–51.
19. On Economism, see T. Dan, *The Origins of Bolshevism,* New York, 1970, pp. 211–12. See also R. Pipes, *Social Democracy and the St. Petersburg Labour Movement 1885-1897,* Cambridge, 1963, p. 124.
20. *LCW* 2, p. 336.
21. V. I. Lenin, "A Protest by Russian Social-Democrats" and "Apropos of the *Profession De Foi,*" in ibid., 4, Moscow, 1977, p. 181 for class independence, and pp. 171–82, 286–96 for the overall arguments.
22. V. I. Lenin, "A Retrograde Trend in Russian Social-Democracy," ibid., pp. 279–81.
23. Ibid.
24. E. Mandel, *The Leninist Theory of Organisation,* Baroda, 1977, pp. 14–18.
25. *LCW* 4, pp. 367–68, pp. 293–94. Lenin's target was the "Economist" text known as the "Credo." For its text, see in ibid., pp. 172–74. For the links between "Economism" and Revisionism, see T. Cliff, *Lenin*, vol. 1, pp

61–63. For a view that challenges Lenin's analysis of "Economism" see J. L. H. Keep, *The Rise of Social Democracy in Russia*, London, 1963.

26. *LCW* 5, Moscow, 1977, pp. 17–20.

27. Ibid., p. 21.

28. Ibid. 4, pp. 219–20.

29. Ibid. 5, p. 22.

30. Ibid.

31. V. I. Lenin, "Draft of a Declaration of the Editorial Board of *Iskra* and *Zarya*" in ibid. 4, pp. 325–26.

32. Thus M. Liebman, *Leninism under Lenin*, pp. 53–61 argued that the line of intolerance, running from 1902 to 1917, affected events after the revolution. Yet, Lenin's argument of 1902 was only that if some people wished to renounce Marxist orthodoxy and convert the party into a party of bourgeois reforms he wanted, not unity but separation from them. *LCW* 5, pp. 352–55. This hardly differed from Marx's Circular Letter.

33. A. Vanaik, "In Defence of Leninism," *Economic and Political Weekly*, September 13, 1986, p. 1639.

34. *LCW* 5, p. 397.

35. Ibid., pp. 400, 402, 412.

36. Ibid., pp. 423, 420.

37. Ibid., pp. 464–66, 472, 477.

38. Ibid., pp. 464–65.

39. V. I. Lenin, "A Talk with Defenders of Economism" in ibid., pp. 316–18, 373, 396–97, 413–16, 435.

40. See Potresov, cited by T. Dan, *The Origins of Bolshevism*, New York, 1970, pp. 237–38; also A. K. Wildman *The Making of a Worker's Revolution*, p. 234, For Axelrod's acceptance, see A. Ascher, *Pavel Axelrod and the Development of Menshevism* Cambridge, Mass, 1972. pp. 177, 178–79.

41. *LCW* 15, p. 375.

42. Ibid., pp. 383–84.

43. B. Pearce, ed., *1903: Second Congress of the Russian Social Democratic Labour Party (Minutes)*, London, 1978, pp. 158–59.

44. This is done by T. Cliff, Lenin, vol. 1, pp. 80–82 and P. Le Blanc, *Lenin and the Revolutionary Party*, pp. 63, 67–68. Apart from Kautsky, Lenin could also have quoted Plekhanov, *Selected Philosophical Works*, vol. 1, p. 404, or Axelrod, who argued that without Social Democratic interference the proletariat, did not possess a historically elaborated social ideal. On this see N. Harding, *Lenin's Political Thought*, vol. 1, pp. 152–53.

45. V. I. Lenin, "Preface to the Collection *Twelve Years*" in *LCW* 13, Moscow, 1978, pp. 101–8; K. Radek, "On Lenin," *International Socialist Review*, vol. 34, no. 10, November 1973, p. 29.

46. This is in flat contradiction to the claims of L. H. Haimson, *The Russian Marxists*, Chapter 9, that this book, and Lenin's ambitions, caused the split in the party. See also I. Getzler, "The Mensheviks" in *Problems of Communism*, vol. 16, no. 6, November–December, 1967, p. 15.

47. *LCW* 6, Moscow, 1977, pp. 234–35.

48. Ibid., pp. 238–45, 246–47.

49. Ibid., p. 237. In view of the foregoing, it is not possible to accept the view that the aim of this "Letter" was to "transform the Russian committees into obedient instruments . . . of the top leadership of the party," L. H. Haimson, *The Russian Marxists*, p. 168.

50. There is, however, no need to provide a detailed account of the events, which have been often written. For the full proceedings see *Vtoroi S'ezd RSDRP*, Moscow, 1959. The English translation is B. Pearce, ed., 1903; see also L. H. Haimson, *The Russian Marxists*, pp. 171–81.

51. V. I. Lenin, Letters to F. V. Lengnik, and to I. I. Radchenko, in *LCW* 36, Moscow, 1977, pp. 112–13. For the admission of the police general Spiridovich about Lenin's successes, see L. Trotsky, *Stalin*, p. 39.

52. For Martov's admission that this was so, see T. Anderson, ed., *Masters of Russian Marxism*, New York, 1963, p. 101.

53. For Martov's version, see Brian Pearce, ed., *1903*, p. 10. For Lenin's version see p. 311. For Martov's view, that "we should only rejoice if every striker . . . could proclaim himself a party member," see p. 310.

54. Ibid., p. 328.

55. Ibid., pp. 311, 317.

56. Ibid., pp. 321–22.

57. See R. N. Hunt, *German Social Democracy, 1918–1933*, Chicago, 1970, p. 59.

58. V. I. Lenin, "Account of the Second Congress of the R.S.D.L.P" in *LCW* 7, Moscow, 1977, p. 31 for Lenin's justification.

59. B. Pearce, ed., *1903*, pp. 423, 424–25, 426.

60. Ibid., p. 433. See L. H. Haimson, *The Russian Marxists and the Origins of Bolshevism*, p. 179, "To strike the names of Axelrod, Vera Zasulich and Potresov from the roll of Iskra's editors was a deadly insult." Interestingly, Haimson argues in p. 188 that the Menshevik Axelrod was correct in accusing Lenin of creating an elite domination over the proletariat, whereas in fact it was this elite that was rejecting democracy.

61. B. Pearce, ed., *1903*, pp. 10, 334 on the Congress; p. 436 for Martov's refusal to serve on the Editorial Board.

62. L. H. Haimson, *The Russian Marxists*, pp. 182–86.

63. V. I. Lenin, *One Step Forward Two Steps Back*, in *LCW* 7, p. 208.

64. Quoted in ibid., p. 208.

65. See N. K. Krupskaya, *Memories of Lenin*, Moscow, 1959, p. 98.

66. See I. Getzler, *Martov*, Cambridge, 1967, p. 85. See also T. Hammond, "Leninist authoritarianism before the revolution," in E. Z. Simmons, ed., *Continuity and Change in Russian and Soviet Thought*, Cambridge, 1955, p. 147; M. Liebman, *Leninism under Lenin*, p. 40; and J. L. H. Keep, *The Rise of Social Democracy*, p. 151.

67. *LCW* 7, pp. 570–571, for editors' note 146.

68. B. Pearce, ed., *1903*, p. 10.

69. V. I. Lenin, "What we are working for?" and "To the Party" in *LCW* 7, pp. 447–50, 456–57.

70. Thus, when a series of committees called for a Congress, the Party Council refused to convene one. See also V. I. Lenin, "Whom are They trying to Fool?" and "The First Step" in *LCW* 8, Moscow, 1977, pp. 225–27, 239–44.

71. L. H. Haimson, *The Russian Marxists*, does not mention the struggle for the Third Congress, nor the support Lenin got. Instead, he suggests that in 1904–05, Lenin tended to become "the keeper of (a) hopeless and lonely . . . dream" (p. 219). Evidently, the Menshevik émigré leaders alone counted, and not the committees inside Russia, in Haimson's arithmetic.

72. See G. Zinoviev, *History of the Bolshevik Party*, London, 1983, pp. 112–14.

73. See further V. I. Lenin, "To the Central Committee of the R.S.D.L.P" in *LCW* 34, Moscow, 1977, pp. 200–201.

74. *LCW* 7, p. 381.

75. R. Luxemburg, "Organisational Question of Social Democracy," M. A. Waters, ed., *Rosa Luxemburg Speaks*, New York, 1980, p. 117.

76. This does not purport to be a thorough treatment of Luxemburg's ideas. That has been done in S. Marik, "The 'Anti-Leninism' of Rosa Luxemburg: A Reappraisal of her Theory of Party," *Society and Change*, vol. X, no. 1& 2.

77. R. Luxemburg, "The Russian Revolution" in M. A. Waters, ed., *Rosa Luxemburg Speaks*, p. 374. It is worth emphasizing this, since, led by Bertram D. Wolfe, (in his introduction to Rosa Luxemburg. *The Russian Revolution, and Marxism or Leninism*, Ann Arbor, 1961, p. 11), a whole range of scholars portray Luxemburg as anti-Leninist.

78. See L. Trotsky, "Our Differences," in N. Allen, ed., *The Challenge of the Left Opposition (1923–25)*, New York, 1975, p. 263.

79. *LCW* 7, pp. 472–74, See also R. Luxemburg, "Organisational Question," pp. 116–18.

80. L. Trotsky, *Our Political Tasks*, London, 1980, pp. 74–77.

81. Ibid., pp. 8–12, 16, 30–31, 38–94.

82. Ibid., p. 8.

83. R. Luxemburg, "Organisational Question," p. 119. Compare *LCW* 7, p. 474 for a rather weak rejoinder.

84. L. Trotsky, *Our Political Tasks*, pp. 95, 77. R. Luxemburg, "Organisational Question."

85. L. Trotsky, *Report of the Siberian Delegation*, London, 1980, p. 21.

86. R. Luxemburg, "Organisational Question," p. 130. See also L. Trotsky, *Our Political Tasks*, p. 9.

87. V. I. Lenin, "The Reorganisation of the party," in *LCW* 10, Moscow, 1977, p. 32.

88. *LCW* 4, pp. 176–78. See also ibid., p. 180, where he endorses the view that Social Democracy should become class movement of the organized workers.

89. Ibid., 5, pp. 362–65, 397–440.

90. R. Miliband, *Marxism and Politics*, p. 133.

91. V. I. Lenin, "The First Results of Political Alignment," in *LCW* 9, Moscow, 1977, p. 404.

92. V. I. Lenin, "On Axelrod's Pamphlet" and "Denouements at Hand" in ibid., pp. 419, 454.

93. The events narrated are, unless otherwise specified, based on S. Harcave, *First Blood: The Russian Revolution of 1905*, London, 1964; and S. M. Schwarz, *The Russian Revolution of 1905*, Chicago, 1967.

94. A. Woods, *Bolshevism: The Road to Revolution*, London, 1999, pp. 124–25.
95. On rural Russia before and during the revolution of 1905 there is a considerable amount of literature. As it is not central to my aims, I do not discuss it in detail. Interested readers can consult Roberta Thomson Manning, *The Crisis of the Old Order in Russia: Gentry and Government*, New Jersey, 1982, or Maureen Perrie, *The Agrarian Policy of the Russian Socialist-Revolutionary Party from its Origins through the Revolution of 1905–1907*, New York, 1976.
96. O. Anweiler, *The Soviets*, p. 34.
97. L. Trotsky, *1905*, Harmondsworth, 1971, p. 123.
98. O. Anweiler, *The Soviets*, p. 38.
99. G. Kostomarov, *Moskovskii Soviet v 1905 godu*, Moscow, 1955, pp. 65–69.
100. L. Trotsky, *1905*, pp. 106–7.
101. On Witte and the Tsar, see H. D. Mehlinger and J. M. Thomson, *Count Witte and the Tsarist Government in the 1905 Revolution*, Bloomington, Indiana, and London, 1974.
102. O. Anweiler, *The Soviets*, p. 46.
103. L. Trotsky, *1905*, p. 266.
104. See O. Anweiler, *The Soviets*, pp. 65–72; A. Ascher, *Pavel Axelrod*, pp. 232–38.
105. V. S. Voitinskii, *Godu pobedi porazhenii*, Moscow, 1923, quoted in J. L. H. Keep, *The Rise of Social Democracy in Russia*, p. 230.
106. Recollection of B. I. Gorev, a representative of the Bolshevik centre in St. Petersburg, quoted in S. M. Schwartz, *The Russian Revolution of 1905*, Chicago, 1967, p. 180.
107. David Lane, *The Roots of Russian Communism*, Assen, 1969, p. 88.
108. L. Trotsky, quoted in S. M. Schwartz, *The Russian Revolution of 1905*, p. 181.
109. *LCW* 10, p. 19.
110. Ibid., p. 20.
111. Ibid., p. 21.
112. Ibid., p. 23.
113. *LCW* 10, pp. 80–81.
114. L. Trotsky, *1905*, p. 123.
115. Ibid., p. 266.
116. Ibid., p. 407.
117. Ibid., p. 266.
118. Ibid., pp. 270–71, 274.
119. Ibid., p. 414.
120. The Bolshevik activist N. Doroshenko, quoted in S. M. Schwartz, *The Russian Revolution of 1905*, pp. 68–69.
121. J. Stalin, *Works*, vol. 1, Moscow, 1947, p. 80.
122. Quoted in L. Trotsky, *Stalin*, p. 164.
123. N. K. Krupskaya, *Memories of Lenin*, pp. 11–12; V. I. Lenin, "The Beginning of the Revolution in Russia" in *LCW* 8, p. 97.
124. S. M. Schwartz, *The Russian Revolution of 1905*, pp. 157–58.
125. *LCW* 34, p. 359.
126. S. M. Schwartz, *The Russian Revolution of 1905*, p. 153.
127. Ibid., pp. 131–32.

128. L. Trotsky, *Stalin*, p. 62.

129. N. K. Krupskaya, *Memories of Lenin*, pp. 124–26.

130. *LCW* 34, p. 296; V. I. Lenin, "New Tasks and New Forces" in *LCW 8*, pp. 146, 218–19.

131. Ibid. 10, pp. 29, 32, 33; ibid. 8, pp. 145–46; V. I. Lenin, "Eleventh Congress of the R.C.P.(B.)," in ibid. 33, Moscow, 1980, p. 307.

132. V. I. Lenin, "Draft Resolution on the Relations between Workers and the Intellectuals within the Social-Democratic Organisations" in ibid. 8, pp. 409–10.

133. *Tretii s'ezd RSDRP*, Moscow, 1959, p. 255.

134. Ibid., pp. 265, 267, 335, 362.

135. *LCW* 13, p 108.

136. Ibid. 8, pp. 145–46, V. I. Lenin, "Speeches at the Third Congress of the RSDLP," in ibid. 8, pp. 407–15; ibid. 10, pp. 32, 36, p. 23 (for religious workers).

137. Ibid. 10, p. 31.

138. *Tretii s'ezd RSDRP*, pp. 547–53.

139. At the Fourth Party Congress in April 1906 it was Bolsheviks–13,000, Mensheviks–18,000, according to D. Lane, *The Roots of Russian Communism*, pp. 12–13. Another estimate was that for 1907, which gave the Bolsheviks 46,143 and the Mensheviks 38,174 members, according to P. Broué, *Le Parti Bolchevique*, Paris 1963, p. 36. Ernest Mandel questions this set of figures, as well as other similar high figures, suggesting that they included members of party-dominated trade unions, sickness benefit associations, etc. See his letter to P. Le Blanc, in P. Le Blanc, *Lenin and the Revolutionary Party*, p. 126. However, such workers did consider themselves to be Social Democrats, as it was shown by their role in the period of reaction from the Second half of 1907.

140. D. Lane, *The Roots of Russian Communism*, pp. 35–37.

141. Ibid., pp. 25–26 for figure in percentage; p. 116 for the Moscow figures. *Tretii S'ezd RSDRP*, pp. 547–53 for the St. Petersburg figures.

142. Compare J. L. H. Keep, *The Rise of Social Democracy*, p. 287, "The RSDLP, professedly a proletarian party, was in reality an organization of revolutionary intellectuals with only a modicum of popular support."

143. D. Lane, *The Roots of Russian Communism*, p. 40. Evidently, in calculating percentages, there has been some approximation.

144. R. C. Elwood, ed., *The Russian Social Democratic Labour Party 1898–October, 1917*, Toronto, 1974. This is vol. 1 of R. H. McNeal, General Editor, *Resolutions And Decision of the Communist Party of the Soviet Union*, p. 57.

145. V. I. Lenin, "Reorganisation and the End of the Split in St. Petersburg," in *LCW* 12, Moscow, 1977, p. 396; V. I. Lenin, "To All Working Men and Women of the City of St. Petersburg and Vicinity" in ibid. 10, p. 127.

146. V. I. Lenin, "The Social Democrats and the Elections in St. Petersburg," in ibid. 11, Moscow, 1978, p. 434.

147. O. Pyatnitsky, *Memoirs of a Bolshevik*, Allahabad, n.d., pp. 91–92.

148. V. I. Lenin, "Party Organisation and Party Literature," in *LCW* 10, p. 46.

149. R. C. Elwood, ed., *The RSDLP*, pp. 83, 87, 91.

150. See for a Stalinist transformation of this concept into a dictatorial monolithism, J. Peters, *The Communist Party: A Manual on Organisation*, New York, 1935, p. 23. see R. C. Elwood, ed., *The RSDRP*, p. 94 for the unity congress resolution.

151. *LCW* 10, pp. 310–11.

152. Ibid., p. 314.

153. Ibid.

154. V. I. Lenin, "Freedom to Criticise and Unity of Action" in ibid., pp. 442–43.

155. Ibid., p. 443.

156. V. I. Lenin, "But who are the Judges?" in ibid. 13, p. 159.

157. Ibid., p. 323. See also G. Zinoviev, *History of the Bolshevik Party*, pp. 143, 148–51. For an account of the Bolshevik faction after unification.

158. V. I. Lenin, "Social Democrats and the Duma Elections," in *LCW* 11, p. 434, 441, "Report on the Unity Congresses of the R.S.D.L.P." in ibid. 10, p. 376.

159. Ibid. 13, p. 159.

160. Ibid., p. 103.

161. R. C. Elwood, *The RSDLP*, p. 62.

162. Ibid., p. 102.

163. *LCW* 13, p. 108.

164. G. Swain, *Russian Social Democracy and the Legal Labour Movement*, pp. 17–18.

165. For the events, see C. E. Schorske, *German Social Democracy*, Chapter 2. For Luxemburg's position, see her *Massenstreik, Partei aund Gewerkschaften*, in R. Luxemburg, *Gesammelte Werke*, Bd. 2, Berlin, 1990, pp. 154–70. See also J. Nettl, *Rosa Luxemburg*, 2 vols., London, 1966, pp. 248–50.

166. *Pyatyi (Londonskii) S'ezd RSDRP*, Moscow, 1959, p. 639.

167. R. C. Elwood, ed., *The RSDLP*, p. 115.

168. Quite erroneously, Lenin expected the crisis to produce a fresh upsurge, whereas, coming at the tail-end of a revolutionary cycle, it should really have been expected to spread despair, as it did. See V. I. Lenin, "Draft Resolutions for the Fifth Congress of the R.S.D.L.P." in *LCW* 12, p. 142.

169. Thus, the participation of workers in political strikes declined drastically, not only below the 1905–6 level, but in 1908–8, to even below the average for 1895-1904. For this, see V. I. Lenin, "Strike Statistics in Russia" in *LCW* 16, Moscow, 1977, pp. 395–96, 406.

170. See G. Zinoviev, *History of the Bolshevik Party*, p. 153, and A. Bogdanov, *Red Star*, Bloomington, Indiana, 1984, p.131. see also R. Stites, "Fantasy and Revolution: Alexander Bogdanov and the Origins of Bolshevik Science Fiction," in *Red Star*, p. 10.

171. V. I. Lenin, "A Caricature of Bolshevism" in *LCW* 15, Moscow, 1982, pp. 383–84.

172. Ibid., pp. 385–87. The validity of Lenin's assertion can be seen by the fact that the Recallists steadily diminished in influence over the years, failing to build any strong left-Bolshevik alternative.

173. *LCW* 15, p. 430. For a Bogdanovist statement of principle, see R.V. Daniels, *A Documentary History Of Communism* , vol. 1, New York, 1962, pp. 62–63. It should be noted that while for polemical purposes (to discredit the

Marxist credentials of Bogdanov), Lenin went to great lengths to prove that this philosophical "errors" were major issues, he was not expelled from the faction for his philosophy, but for his politics.

174. See the January 1910 CC Plenum resolutions in R. C. Elwood, ed., *The RSDLP*, pp. 138–39.

175. *LCW* 10, p. 323.

176. A. Elnitskii, *Istoriya rabochego dvizheniya v Rossi*, Moscow, 1925, p. 285.

177. Quoted in L. Trotsky, *Stalin*, p. 110.

178. Quoted in A. Ascher, *Axelrod*, p. 237.

179. "Can there exist in sober reality, and not merely as the figment of a diseased imagination, a school of thought that advocates liquidating what has ceased to be an organic whole?" Quoted in A. Ascher, *The Mensheviks in the Russian Revolution*, p. 76.

180. Cf., S. H. Baron, *Plekhanov: Father of Russian Marxism*, London, 1963, pp. 281–86 for Plekhanov's opposition to liquidationism. See also I. Getzler, *Martov*, pp. 125, 126.

181. *LCW* 15, p. 233.

182. *LCW* 15, p. 325.

183. Ibid., p. 354, that this was the crux of the debate is not disputed by defenders of the liquidationists' standpoint. Thus, Israel Getzler, in his article "The Mensheviks," in *Problems of Communism*, writes that "while the Mensheviks strove to educate the primitive Russian working class and to rally it behind limited but achievable objectives, the Bolsheviks laid stress on demagogic appeals to class hatred and millenarian illusions, leading the workers into futile strikes and bloody demonstrations in a reckless attempts to provoke a show down with the regime and create a revolutionary situation." So, if the police set parameters on public activity, violating that is "stressing demagogical appeals to class hatred." Moreover, as Getzler points out in all sympathy with the Liquidators, it was they who were elitists, treating the workers as primitives who had to be educated, while the Bolsheviks strove to induct more workers in their ranks.

184. *LCW* 17, Moscow, 1977, p. 203.

185. V. I. Lenin, "Resolution adopted by the Second Paris Group of the R.S.D.L.P. on the State of Affairs in the Party," in ibid., p. 218.

186. V. I. Lenin, "Reformism in the Russian Social-Democratic Movement" in ibid., p. 233.

187. V. I. Lenin, "Introduction to the Pamphlet *Two Parties*," in ibid., p. 225.

188. See, N. V. Kuznetsov, "Partiya I profsoiyuyz v gody reaktsii," *Voprosy Istorii KPSS*, no. 4, 1958, pp. 92–99.

189. See A. M. Kollontai, *Iz moei zhizni i raboty*, Moscow, 1974, pp. 111–13. See also Swain, *Russian Social Democracy and the Legal Labour Movement*, pp. 47–51.

190. Swain, *Russian Social Democracy and the Legal Labour Movement*, pp. 59–60.

191. V. E. Bonnell, *Roots of Rebellion*, p. 375.

192. Ibid., p. 349, compare Getzler's claim that the practical workers were close to the *Nasha Zaria* group. I. Getzler, "The Mensheviks," p. 21.

193. Swain, *Russian Social Democracy and the Legal Labour Movement*, pp. 93–94.
194. V. I. Lenin, "A Conversation between a Legalist and an Opponent of Liquidationism" *LCW* 17, p. 179. See also pp. 185–87 for parts of the same article where the ideas of combining legal and underground work is turned into a caricature.
195. A. Ascher, *Pavel Axelrod*, pp. 272, 273, 293.
196. Cf., *KPSS v rezolyutsiyakh, resheniiakh s'ezdov, konferentsii i Plenumov Tsk,* Moscow, 1954, vol. 1, p. 291.
197. R. C. Elwood, The *RSDLP*, p. 140. It is noteworthy that neither Tony Cliff, nor Paul Le Blanc, who both defend Lenin at this juncture, discuss in detail either the text of this resolution, or the context. Le Blanc is extremely dismissive of Swain's work, but with no fresh evidence.
198. G. Swain, *Russian Social Democracy and the Legal Labour Movement,* pp. 93–94.
199. Cf, V. I. Lenin, "Towards Unity," "Golos (voice) of the Liquidators against Party," and letter to the Central Committee of the R.S.D.L.P. (May 1910), in *LCW* 16, pp. 147–55, 156–64, 192–93. In pp. 215–16, Lenin expresses his reservations about some parts of the plenum decision.
200. G. Zinoviev, *History of the Bolshevik Party* pp. 165–68.
201. *LCW* 17, p. 106.
202. Malinovsky was to become, from later 1909, a police agent. But his early career was that of a social democratic trade unionist. See R. C. Elwood, *Roman Malinovsky: A Life without a Cause,* Newtonville, 1977. For Kanatchikov, see S. Kanatchikov, *A Radical Worker in Tsarist Russia,* Stanford, 1986.
203. R. C. Elwood, *The RSDLP*, p. 149.
204. Elwood, in ibid., p. 147 saw in the resolution only monolithism and the imposition of Leninist uniformity, completely ignoring the change that Lenin accepted because of working-class pressure.
205. Cited by V. E. Bonnell, *Roots of Rebellion,* p. 391. A different translation of the full text is in R. C. Elwood, *The RSDLP*, pp. 180–81.
206. L. Trotsky, *The Permanent Revolution,* New York, 1976, p. 173.
207. For Trotsky's role in organizing the Vienna conference, see G. R. Swain, *Russian Social Democracy and the Legal Labour Movement,* pp. 144–47. For his rout and the political changes pushed through, see R. C. Elwood, *The RSDLP*, p. 159, and Swain, p. 148. For the hopes on the left bourgeoisie and the Duma, see Swain, *Russian Social Democracy and the Legal Labour Movement,* p. 149.
208. Swain, *Russian Social Democracy and the Legal Labour Movement,* p. 173.
209. Ibid.
210. S. Milligan, "The Petrograd Bolsheviks and Social Insurance, 1914–17," *Soviet Studies,* January 1969.
211. V. I. Lenin, "Objective Data on the strength of the various Trends in the Working-Class Movement," in *LCW* 20, Moscow, 1978, p. 387.
212. On *Pravda,* see W. Bassow, "The pre-Revolutionary *Pradva* and Tsarist Censorship," *The American Slavic and East European Review,* February 1954. See also V. I. Lenin, Letter to G. L. Shklovsky, in *LCW* 36, p. 212; "The

Working Class and its Press" in *LCW* 20, pp. 363, 369.

213. See A. Badaev, *The Bolsheviks in the Tsarist Duma*, London, 1933, pp. 176–77.

214. See the opposite claim of A. G. Meyer, *Leninism*, pp. 92, 93.

215. I am grateful to those who commented on earlier papers dealing with these issues. In particular I would like to thank the American trade unionist and revolutionary activist, Ron Lare, for the detailed comments that he sent.

216. A copy of the pamphlet is kept at the International Institute of Social History, Amsterdam, but without any indication of who the author is. Moira Donald, in her "Bolshevik Activity Amongst the Working Women of Petrograd in 1917," *International Review of Social History*, vol. 27, 1982, pp. 129–60, identifies Krupskaya as the author.

217. "A Draft Programme of Our Party," in *LCW* 4, Moscow, 1977, p. 239.

218. B. Evans Clements, *Bolshevik Women*, pp. 32, 45.

219. C. Bobrovskaia, *Twenty Years in Underground Russia*, New York, 1934.

220. B. Evans Clements, *Bolshevik Women*, p. 135; R. L. Glickman, *Russian Factory Women: Workplace and Society, 1880–1914*, Berkeley, Los Angeles, and London, 1984, p. 209.

221. It is instructive to compare *Zhenshchiny russkoi revoliutsii*, Moscow, 1968, which gives the women's own views, with official histories of even the post-Stalin era, like *Docheri zemli Vladimirskoi*, Iaroslavl, 1982. For a more detailed consideration of these issues see S. Marik, "Gendering the Revolutionary Party," in B. Chatterjee and K. Chattopadhyay, eds., *Perspectives on Socialism*, pp. 13–50.

222. *Perepiska V. I. Lenina i Rukovodimykh im uchrezhdenii RSDRPs partiinymi organizatsiiami 1905-1907 gg*, 3 vols, Moscow, 1982–85, vol. 2, p. 205; *Partiya i Revolyutsii 1905 goda Dokumenty k Istorii I Parti I v 1905 godu*, Moscow, 1934, p. 193. The accounts of how Stasova kept the party tightly run are to be found in Evans Clements.

223. B. Evans Clements, *Bolshevik Women*, p. 138. Even if we accept this rather doubtful assertion, we would be led back to the proposition that patriarchal ideas were absorbed by women themselves.

224. R. C. Elwood, *Inessa Armand: Revolutionary and Feminist*, Cambridge, 1992, pp.101–2; 145–48. B. Farnsworth, *Alexandra Kollontai*, p. 58, makes a similar point when she writes that a pamphlet by Kollontai had to suffer unnecessary editing by Lenin.

225. B. Evans Clements, *Bolshevik Women*, p. 66 and Table 9, p. 67.

226. Ibid., pp. 138–39.

227. See Robert Service, *Lenin: A Political Life*, vol. II, Bloomington, Indiana, 1991. Since many Marxists will question the motivations of Service, we can also refer to Lenin's letters, in, for example, *Polnoe Sobranie Sochinenya*, vol. XLIX, p. 198.

228. T. Cliff, *Lenin*, vol. I, *Building the Party*, p. 90.

229. See G. V. Plekhanov, *Selected Philosophical Works*, vol. 1, p. 456, for the leading role of the proletariat in his conception. See ibid., pp. 266, 267, 308, 309 for his assessment about the future of capitalism in Russia. See also M. Löwy, *The Politics of Combined and Uneven Development*, p. 32.

230. A. Ascher, *Pavel Axelrod*, p. 134.

231. G. V. Plekhanov, *Selected Philosophical Works*, vol. 1, p. 40.
232. For economic determinism in Marx, see Chapter 4, above. See also M. Löwy, *The Politics of Combined and Uneven Development*, Chapter 2, and Kunal Chattopadhyay, *The Marxism of Leon Trotsky*, Chapter 1.
233. V. I. Lenin, *What the "Friends of the People" are and how they Fight the Social-Democrats*, in *LCW* 1, p. 290.
234. Ibid. 2, p. 96.
235. Ibid., pp. 117–18.
236. Ibid. 4, p. 177.
237. See V. I. Lenin, "Our Programme" in ibid., pp. 211, 212, 217, 239.
238. Ibid., p. 242.
239. For the full text, see G. Zinoviev, *History of the Bolshevik Party*, Appendix I, pp. 201–3.
240. B. Pearce, ed., *1903*, pp. 5-6, 8-9.
241. For full texts of both resolutions, see ibid., pp. 465–6. It is a matter of historical record that the delegates, exhausted after the protracted wrangling over the party rules and the elections of the Central Committee and the Editorial Board, considered the political resolutions very briefly and passed both resolutions, so that formally an ambiguity was retained with the official line of the party.
242. Quoted by D. J. Dallin, *The Rise of Russia in Asia*, London, 1950, p. 79.
243. See B. Pares, *A History of Russia*, London, 1937, p. 428.
244. Quoted in G. Zinoviev, *History of the Bolshevik Party*, pp. 107–8.
245. See J. Carmichael, *Trotsky: An Appreciation of his Life*, London, 1975, p. 87, for Parvus's article. See also M. J. Olgin, ed., L. Trotsky, *Our Revolution*, New York, 1918. This contains some of Trotsky's writings of 1905.
246. V. I. Lenin, *The Zemstvo Campaign and Iskra's Plan*, in *LCW* 7, pp. 327–32, 498, 499.
247. By this time, Parvus and Trotsky were beginning to place Russia in an international context, L. Trotsky, *The Permanent Revolution and Results and Prospects*.
248. For an in-depth treatment, see N. Harding, *Lenin's Political Thought*, vol. 1, pp. 213–48, and K. Chattopadhyay, *Leninism and Permanent Revolution*, Baroda, 1987, pp. 27–45.
249. For Lenin's stress on the struggle against the liberals, see *LCW* 7, p. 504. See further ibid., pp. 509, 513–15, for his ideas on the main tasks of the revolution. These included the advocacy of attacks on prisons, police headquarters, etc., not examples intended to soothe the liberal nerve.
250. On Lenin's opposition in 1901, to sending out rural organizers, see V. I. Lenin, "The Workers' Party and the Peasantry," in *LCW* 4, p. 427. For the assessment of *To the Rural Poor* quoted above, see E. Kingston-Mann, *Lenin and the Problem of Marxist Peasant Revolution*, p. 61.
251. Cf., V. I. Lenin, "Revolutionary Adventurism," and *The Agrarian Programme of Russian Social-Democracy* in *LCW* 6, pp. 194–205, 133–4.
252. V. I. Lenin, "Why the Social-Democrats must declare a determined and relentless War on the Socialist-Revolutionaries" and "Vulgar Socialism and Narodism as resurrected by the Socialist-Revolutionaries" in ibid.

pp. 170–73, 261–68.

253. See M. Perrie, "The Russian Peasant Movement of 1905–1907: Its Social Composition and Revolutionary Significance," *Past and Present*, November 1972, p. 15.

254. L. Schapiro, *The Communist Party of the Soviet Union*, p. 82. On the role or the Cadets or Cadets, see C. E. Timberlake, ed., *Essays in Russian Liberalism*, Colombia, Missouri, 1972, especially the articles by J. E. Zimmerman and W. G. Rosenberg.

255. *LCW* 8, pp. 511–12.

256. R. C. Elwood, ed., *The RSDLP*, p. 63, compare the Menshevik conference of 1905, resolution on the peasantry, in ibid., pp. 76–79, which suggested leaving the ultimate solution of the land question of a future Constituent Assembly.

257. V. I. Lenin, *Two Tactics of Social-Democracy in the Democratic Revolution* in *LCW* 9, pp. 28–30.

258. Ibid., pp. 4, 47, 50.

259. Ibid., pp. 47–48.

260. Ibid., p. 51.

261. Ibid., pp. 32, 36, 38.

262. See for example, V. I. Lenin, *Social-Democracy and the Provisional Revolutionary Government* in *LCW* 8, pp. 291–92, 385; V. I. Lenin, "What our Liberal Bourgeoisie want and what they fear," and "Theory of Spontaneous Generation," in ibid. 9, pp. 58–9, 241–252; V. I. Lenin, *The Agrarian Programme of Social-Democracy in the First Russian Revolution 1905–1907*, in ibid. 13, pp. 239, 343, 352. For contrasting statements on the tasks in developed counties and in Russia see V. I. Lenin, "The Revolutionary-Democratic Dictatorship of the Proletariat and the Peasantry," *On the Provisional Revolutionary Government*, in *LCW* 8, pp. 298–99, 471–73, and ibid. 13, p. 242.

263. Ibid. 13, p. 242.

264. Minutes of the first congress of the peasants Union, quoted E. Kingston-Mann, *Lenin and the Problems of a Marxist Peasant Revolution*, p. 86.

265. See discussion in M. Perrie, "The Russian peasant movement of 1905–1907."

266. E. Kingston-Mann, *Lenin and the Problems of a Marxist Peasant Revolution*, p. 87.

267. For Chernov's ideas, see discussion in M. Perrie, *The Agrarian Policy of the Russian Socialist Revolutionary party from its origins through the Revolution of 1905-1907*. See also O. Radkey, "Chernov and Agrarian Socialism before 1918," in E. Simmons, ed. *Continuity and Change in Russian and Soviet thought*, Cambridge, 1955.

268. V. I. Lenin, "Socialist-Revolutionary Mensheviks" in *LCW* 11, pp. 197–206.

269. V. I. Lenin, *The Unity Congress of the R.S.D.L.P.* in *LCW* 10, p. 287; from Lenin's speech on the agrarian program, see also V. I. Lenin, *Revision of the Agrarian Programme of the Workers' Party*, in ibid., pp. 189–94, and 194–95 for the draft agrarian program.

270. *Protokoly: Chetvertyi (ob'edinitel 'nyi) s'ezd RSDRP, aprel'-mai 1906 goda*, Moscow, 1959, pp. 522–23 (Maslow), p. 81 (Dan). See also Plekhanov (pp.

59–61) denouncing Lenin's call for land nationalization on the ground, that if the revolution failed, land nationalization would strengthen the autocracy.

271. Ibid., p. 79.

272. Ibid., pp. 131–33.

273. For further discussion on the role of the Liberals see R. T. Manning, "Zemstvo and Revolution: The onset of the Gentry Reaction 1905–1907." In L. Haimson, ed., The *Politics of Rural Russia in 1905-1914*, Bloomington, 1979, and G. Fischer, *Russian Liberalism from Gentry to Intelligentsia*, Cambridge, 1958.

274. Nearly one-third of the Cadet deputies to the First Duma, when the Cadets were at the peak of their radicalism, were big landlords owning 500 dessyatins or more.

275. Cf., V. I. Lenin, "Cadets and Trudoviks," "The Menshevik Tactical Platform," in *LCW* 12, pp. 191, 257, V. I. Lenin, "On the 'Nature' of the Russian Revolution" in ibid., 15, p. 25.

276. See, e.g., V. I. Lenin, "The Proletariat and Peasantry," in ibid., 10, pp. 42–43.

277. G.V. Plekhanov, *Selected Philosophical Works*, vol. 1, p. 403f.

278. *LCW* 4, pp. 231–32, 239.

279. Ibid., p. 239.

280. B. Pearce, ed. *1903*, pp. 6–7.

281. V. I. Lenin, "The Constitutional Market Place," in *LCW* 8, p. 352.

282. Ibid., p. 353.

283. Ibid.

284. Ibid., pp. 355–56.

285. V. I. Lenin, "The Dying Autocracy and the new organs of Popular Rule, in ibid. 10, pp. 66, 70.

286. V. I. Lenin, "Should we boycott the State Duma?," in ibid., pp. 98–99.

287. V. I. Lenin, "The boycott of the Bulygin Duma and Insurrection" in ibid. 9, pp. 182–83.

288. V. I. Lenin, "The Social-Democratic Election victory in Tiflis," in ibid. 10, pp. 423–24.

289. V. I. Lenin, "The Unsound Arguments of the 'Non-Party' Boycotters," in ibid. 11, pp. 78–81, "The Boycott," in ibid., pp. 141, 145.

290. Ibid. 13, p. 60.

291. J. Stalin , *Works*, vol. 2, Moscow, 1953, p. 255. See also R. G. Suny, "Labour and Liquidators: Revolutionaries and the 'Reaction' in Baku," *Slavic Review*, no. 2, 1975.

292. A. Badaev, *Bolsheviks in the Tsarist Duma*, pp. 21–22.

293. *LCW* 15, pp. 385–93, and V. I. Lenin, "The Faction of supporters of Otzovism and god-building," and "Notes of a Publicists" in ibid., 16, pp. 31–32, 33, 201.

294. V. I. Lenin, "The Drafting of 183 students into the Army" in ibid., 4, pp. 414–19.

295. V. I. Lenin, "Casual Notes" in ibid., pp. 389, 392–93.

296. Ibid. 10, p. 45.

297. Ibid., p. 47.

298. Ibid., p. 46.

299. Ibid.

300. Ibid., p. 67.

301. Ibid. 16, pp. 156–57.

302. V. I. Lenin,"The Collapse of the Second Internationa," in ibid. 21, p. 241.

303. For the Programme, see B. Pearce, *1903*, pp. 3–9.

304. Ibid., p. 7

305. R. Glickman, "The Russian Factory Woman 1890–1914," in D. Atkinson and others, *Women in Russia,* Stanford, 1978, pp. 80–81.

306. Ron Lare, in a personal communication to me, had argued in connection with my paper on German Socialism and Women's Liberation that there is a distinction between the class vanguard and the vanguard party. The argument seems to be that there could well have been many vanguard women workers, who might for some reason be outside the party. I hope I have taken that criticism into account in the foregoing passages. The point is not that the party just happened to have fewer women, but that the party thought that women workers by and large did not cut the mustard, being backward "babas."

307. A. Ryazanova, *Zhenskii Trud*, Moscow 1923, p. 35, citing a factory inspector's report.

308. B. Evans Clements, *Bolshevik Women*, p. 102.

309. T. Cliff, *Class Struggle and Women's Liberation*, pp. 93–4; R. Glickman, "The Russian Factory Woman 1890–1914," p. 81.

310. T. Cliff, *Class Struggle and Women's Liberation*, pp. 95–97 claims that Kollontai's sole reason for participation was to show the working-class women that the liberal feminist approach was wrong. Kollontai's own autobiography says something else. She wanted serious participation in order to politicize women workers. She also had to encounter opposition from both the Bolshevik and the Menshevik factions. See A. Kollontai, *Autobiography of a Sexually Emancipated Communist Woman*, New York, 1971, p. 549. See further B. Farnsworth, *Alexandra Kollontai: Socialism Feminism and the Bolshevik Revolution*, p. 32.

311. V. I. Lenin, *Polnoe Sobranie Sochinenii*, 55 volumes, Moscow, 1958–65, vol. XLIX, pp. 51–52, 54–7. Armand's views have to be reconstructed from what Lenin says, since her letters are not available.

312. The evidence is too vast to present even in summary form here. Readers can profitably consult Richard J. Evans, *The Feminists*, London, 1984 (reprint of revised edition of 1979). One could think of Lucy Stone in the USA, as discussed in Dale Spender, *Women of Ideas*, London, 1988, pp. 355–56; or Charlotte Perkins Gilman, a socialistically inclined feminist, also from USA, for whose views see Josephine Donovan, *Feminist Theory*, New York and London, 2000, p. 67.

313. Armand's history is worth noting for another reason. For several decades, Western historiography, prompted by Bertram D. Wolfe, treated her as Lenin's mistress, and his submissive agent, rather than as a serious Bolshevik activist. It was only when R. C. Elwood worked on the biography of Roman Malinovsky, the agent provocateur who had become

a Bolshevik Central Committee member, that he discovered that at a time when Lenin was supposedly having an affair with Armand in Paris, Malinovsky had in fact been with Lenin. This led to investigations that exploded the entire myth, though few scholars bother to read Elwood, for the Wolfe version reads ever so much more titillating. For Wolfe, see Bertram D. Wolfe, "Lenin and Inessa Armand," *Slavic Review,* vol. XXII, no. 1, March 1963, pp. 96–114. See also Richard Stites, "Kollontai, Inessa and Krupskaia: A Review of Recent Literature," *Canadian-American Slavic Studies,* vol. IX, no. 1, Spring 1975, pp. 84–92.

314. See A. Kollontai, *Izbranii statii i rechii,* Moscow, 1972, pp. 61–79. See also her autobiography. For a discussion, see B. Farnsworth, *Alexandra Kollontai,* pp. 36–37.

315. A. Kollontai, "Zhenskii Dyen," in *Izbranii statii i rechii,* pp. 109–112.

316. Ibid., pp. 109–12.

317. Ibid., p. 159.

318. B. Evans Clements, *Bolshevik Women,* p. 102; S. Smith, "Class and Gender: Women's Strikes in St. Petersburg, 1895–1917 and in Shanghai, 1895–1927," *Social History,* vol. 19, no. 2, May 1994, pp. 145, 159, 160; A. Bobroff, "The Bolsheviks and Working Women 1905–1920," *Soviet Studies,* vol. XXVI, no. 4, October 1974, p. 554.

319. A. Woods, *Bolshevism,* p. 491. I have discussed the origins of *Rabotnitsa* in details elsewhere. See S. Marik, "Biplabi Dal O Linga Samata," in *Loukik Udyan: Manabi Samkhya,* August 1999, pp. 379–406.

320. Anne Bobroff, "The Bolsheviks and Working Women 1905–1920," p. 545.

321. *Women and Revolution,* Fall, 1973, p. 5.

322. J. Riddell, ed., *Lenin's Struggle for a Revolutionary International,* New York, 1984, pp. 267–69.

323. B. Evans Clements, *Bolshevik Women,* pp. 105–6.

324. *Pravda,* February 17, 1913, p. 4.

7

BOLSHEVISM IN 1917

Since Marx, Engels, the Social Democracy, and Bolshevism alike subscribed to the view that the socialist party was an instrument of the proletariat in its struggle for emancipation from the tyranny of capital, it is necessary to study the strategy, as well as the organizational structure and functioning of Bolshevism in 1917—the moment of truth not only for Russian socialists of all hues, but for all who profess socialist creeds of any kind the world over. Yet what is most significant in any study of the events that happened in Russia in that year, is the yawning chasm between most recent specialized academic historiography and the received wisdom of the age—which includes hostile historians who have allowed their outlook to mar their objectivity. Rigorous academic research has substantially vindicated the Bolshevik claims about their adherence to workers' democracy (a statement which should not be confused with the belief that any apologia for Stalinist interpretations will be accepted as a good narrative). But at the same time, even many socialists and communists of earlier years have since 1991 increasingly joined the bandwagon of those who claim that the October Revolution was a coup, and that Bolshevism led ineluctably to Stalinist authoritarianism.

How did Lenin and his supporters, who had rejected all talk of going beyond the bourgeois democratic stage in 1905, shift to a call for socialist revolution while retaining their commitment to a majority revolution? What sort of democratic class and party relations were worked out in course of mass mobilizations in 1917? How were Soviets reconceptualized in Bolshevik theory and in organizational outlook?

Another question, whose answer will be sought in connection with the discussion on class and party relationship, as well as in connection with the October insurrection, is the question of the role of violence. In the discussion on Marx's strategy of revolution, a distinction was made between the possibility of violence to put down the minority who own the means of production and who may refuse to submit to the majority when basic class interests are at stake, and the valorization of violence. It is necessary to examine afresh the widely held "self-evident" view that Bolshevism did not care for democratic norms and was committed to violence as a matter of course.

I

THE PROBLEM OF A MAJORITY SOCIALIST REVOLUTION

In October 1917, the insurrection was carried out in the name of beginning the world socialist revolution, of which the Russian Revolution was to be a part. Yet in 1905, and all the way to 1915-16, Lenin and the Bolsheviks had insisted that the Russian Revolution had to be a bourgeois democratic revolution. Accepting the premise of proletarian hegemony, Trotsky had pointed out in 1905-7 that the liberal bourgeoisie was reactionary and that the proletariat must establish its hegemony and carry the peasant masses behind it in order to achieve its goals. But the scattered nature of the peasantry made it incapable of centralized action at the national level unless the proletariat provided leadership. So the victory must lead to a government under proletarian hegemony. That is, it would be a dictatorship of the proletariat, supported by the peasantry. And even in trying to implement the minimum program, the proletariat would come into conflict with the bourgeoisie, as the experience of 1905 over the struggle for the eight-hour working day had shown. So either the proletarian regime would be forced to go beyond bourgeois democratic measures to lay hands on capitalist property and production relations, or it would have to betray even its minimum program. Finally, he saw from 1905 onwards that the Soviets were organs of workers' democracy, around which the working class could group all its allies.[1]

Lenin had objected to this. As late as 1914, when he wrote *The War and Russian Social Democracy* he was still insisting that the Russian Revolution must limit itself to a democratic republic, confiscation of the landed estates, and an eight-hour working day.[2] Before 1917, he spoke repeatedly in the following vein: "the revolution will strengthen the rule of the bourgeoisie."[3] Lenin had argued that the working class was in a minority, that Russian conditions did not permit the beginning of socialist construction, and that peasant support would not last beyond the bourgeois democratic stage. If that was so, then the same objections held good in 1917, as Lenin's opponents pointed out to him. In addition, Lenin faced the problem of explaining the line of march once the Tsarist state was overthrown.

In the course of his attempts to understand the changed world during World War I, Lenin studied imperialism, and in that context visualized a transition to the proletarian revolution.[4] After the February Revolution, in his "Letters from Afar," he wrote that the fall of Tsarism was only the first stage of the revolution, and that the next stage would be the establishment of working-class rule. In these letters he argued that, far from stabilizing the bourgeois state the proletariat must smash it, and replace it by a different kind of state.[5]

The leading Bolsheviks inside Russia took a different stand. On February 28, 1917 (O.S.), the Russian Bureau of the Central Committee, led by Alexander Shlyapnikov, issued a leaflet, "To All Citizens of Russia." It put forward the traditional Bolshevik program of a provisional government, civil liberties, anti-feudal measures, a Constituent Assembly and universal suffrage.[6] The leaflet did not even mention Soviets.[7] On March 4 the Russian Bureau passed a resolution calling the Provisional Government led by Prince Lvov "in essence counter-revolutionary" and called for a different Provisional Government, "that is democratic in character."[8]

On March 12, following the return from Siberia of Stalin, Kamenev, and Muranov, the political line of the Central Committee became even more moderate. The left Menshevik Sukhanov wrote that *Pravda* "became unrecognisable."[9] On the question of the war, which Lenin had denounced as an imperialist war, Kamenev said that "the war will go on. . . . When an army stands against another army, the most absurd policy would be to propose that one of them lay down its arms. . . . We cannot permit any disorganisation of the military forces."[10] Consequently, the Provisional Government had to be supported with the demand that it should consolidate the achievements of the revolution.[11]

A few days before Lenin's return, the first legal conference of the Bolsheviks began. Joseph Stalin, reporting "On the Attitude to the Provisional Government," explained that power had been divided between two organs, the Soviet, which was the leader of the insurrectionary people, and the government which was fortifier of the conquests by the people.[12] This was an argument for the stabilization of the dual power, instead of calling for the overthrow of the bourgeoisie.

On April 3, Lenin returned to Russia to place his "April Theses" to the party. On the question of majority, and form of democracy, the theses had a clear position—a position that was totally at variance with his earlier position. He averred: "to return to a parliamentary republic from the Soviets of Workers' Deputies would be a retrograde step."[13] He no longer looked upon the Soviets as temporary organs of insurrection, to give way after accomplishing the revolution to bourgeois parliamentary democracy. Now he saw the Soviets as the starting point of a higher form of proletarian democracy.

In 1917, both the Cadets and the SRs had shifted to the right. Even the left-wing Cadet, N. N. Chernenkov, agreed that land reforms should be postponed to the end of the war. Enactment of land reforms involving encroaching on the property of big landowners was described by Cadets as a "political luxury."[14] Likewise at the SR Congress in late May 1917, the party of the peasantry ignored widespread peasant disturbances and defeated the demands of the party's left wing for an immediate peace, end of the alliance with the bourgeoisie, and socialization of land.[15] Even land transactions carried out by landlords so that confiscation of their land could be averted were suspended, as Trotsky wrote, only after the people had taken to the streets.[16] Peasant militancy, and the axis between liberal bourgeoisie and landlords, led to an acute rupture between the peasants and the bourgeoisie. The failure of the parties of moderate socialism to respond to popular aspiration drove workers and peasants alike to militant solutions. The revolutionary process thereby became permanent.

In April, the process was still in early stages, and debates were sharp. Lenin insisted that Tsarism had been overthrown, but its power had not been destroyed. The bourgeois democratic revolution had not been accomplished in the sense he had given to the term so far. Only a bourgeois–landlord bloc had come to power.[17] But it rested on a dual power.[18] From this he concluded that the task was to fight for workers' control over banks and industry,[19] and for creation of a commune-type of state.[20] He insisted that the Provisional Government was an imperialist government, and that a democratic peace, desired by workers, soldiers and peasants, could be brought about only by overthrowing the government.[21] He also emphasized that the peasants' demand for land could be met only by Soviet Government.[22]

Thus, Lenin was now putting forward the idea of a *dictatorship of the proletariat supported by the peasantry*. As to why the peasantry would extend this support, Lenin had two arguments. In the short run, the support given by the proletariat for immediate confiscation of land should secure peasant backing. In the long run, Lenin now expected that peasant communities could become the starting points of socialization of agricultural production. In the amendments that he drafted for the party program, the section on agrarian relations had five new points, which included:

First, the struggle for the immediate complete confiscation of all landed estates in Russia. Second, the transfer of all land to the peasantry, organized in Soviets of Peasants' Deputies or other really democratically elected local self-government bodies. Third, the nationalization of all land, but with the right of disposal vested in local democratic institutions (peasants' committees, etc.). Fourth, the encouragement of the initiative of peasant committees for socially regulated utilization in the cultivation of the land. Finally, he advocated that rural proletarians and semi-proletarians should be urged to turn landed estates into model farms on a communal basis by local Soviets of Agricultural Laborers' Deputies.[23]

Thus Lenin was returning to Marx's insight about the possibility of utilizing the Russian peasant communities in the development of socialism in Russia. He rejected the Mensheviks' claim that Russia's economic backwardness posed an insuperable obstacle to socialist development. In the first place, he held that the Russian Revolution would hasten revolutions in the West, which in turn would help the Russian workers. Second, he said that the concrete problem in 1917 was that Russia's economic difficulties could not be overcome without significant encroachments upon private property.[24] But that meant the first steps towards socialism. Using ideas similar to those of Trotsky that he had previously opposed, he explained that though Russia had not experienced capitalist development to the utmost, the world capitalist development presented prospects of a proletarian revolution backed by the peasantry.

Opponents within the party, like Kamenev, objected to this line on the ground that socialism could not be built in Russia. Lenin responded by arguing that the point was not one of instantly building socialism, but of fighting for proletarian hegemony. Because the bourgeoisie was no longer radical, because only under working-class leadership could democracy be achieved, the revolution would succeed only if the working class succeeded in building institutions of workers' democracy, in hegemonizing the entire plebeian masses of town and country through these institutions, and overthrow bourgeois power. He expected the peasants to support the proletarian revolution out of self-interest, and thereby transform the bourgeois democratic revolution into a proletarian one, with the construction of a classless society as its goal.[25]

While there were marginal differences between how Marx had put the case in 1850, Trotsky in 1905-07, and Lenin in 1917, the essential perspective was the same—a perspective of developing proletarian hegemony and building a community of interests between workers and peasants against the landlords, the capitalists, and the existing state, so that the completion of the bourgeois democratic revolution would become the early stages of the proletarian revolution. Trotsky and Lenin had a greater clarity, because of the experiences of 1905 and 1917, regarding the specific forms of class power and alliances. Both of them saw in the Soviets the organizations that could concentrate the working class and their potential allies, make widely known the central political tasks, bring to bear on the relatively backward elements the influence of the more conscious ones, and thereby ensure a majority for the revolution. Paris in 1871 was still dominated by small workshops, so that the Commune had a purely territorial basis. By contrast, soviets and factory committees in Russia, starting from the factories, grouped together the workers at the points of production and gave hegemony to the workers of large factories. As discussed in the previous chapter, Soviet power would mean the organization of all workers regardless of their party affiliation, and the establishment of class power rather than party power. But such a degree of class militancy does not exist in "normal" times, under bourgeois hegemony. A strategy of building soviets could have serious meaning only if the strategy was one of seizure of power by the soviets.

II
CLASS AND PARTY IN THE FEBRUARY REVOLUTION

The traditional view has been one of counterposing a peaceful, spontaneous February Revolution to a violent, conspiratorial October insurrection. There is only a small element of truth in this. It consists of the fact that none of the parties—whether bourgeois or socialist—who came to leading positions after the fall of the Tsarist autocracy, had expected, desired or prepared for a radical revolution in 1917.

A great number of memoirs, written afterwards, attest to this.[26] But the five-day long agitation, beginning in one area and spreading to the whole of Petrograd, and then beyond it, compelling the Tsar to abdicate, could not be absolutely spontaneous. It had its local leaderships. What it lacked was central leadership. Social historians have increasingly come to argue that while war intensified popular hatred of Tsarism, a revolutionary overturn was becoming a strong possibility even in the immediate pre-war years.[27] This was what Lenin had predicted in "Where to Begin," when he said that a popular upsurge might topple Tsarism, and so the revolutionaries had to be prepared. Being prepared meant being ready for swift changes in the mood of the masses, their rapid radicalization, and a quick reorganization of party strategy to ensure that the revolution received proper leadership. The first step to that, the building of a strong organization of the class-conscious workers, had been accomplished in good measure by 1914. The further task for this vanguard was to participate in larger struggles, win over wider strata of activists, while retaining its organizational independence, so that it could lead without collapsing into momentary illusion. The history of Russia in 1917 was the history of massive and unprecedented mass mobilizations, in Petrograd, and countrywide. Victory of the revolution depended on the direction of these mobilizations. No party which lacked mass support and did not express mass aspirations could win.[28] The February and the October insurrections were two moments of a single revolutionary process, the roots of which lay in the twin processes of intensifying popular radicalization and increasing awareness of the need for a centralized leadership on one hand, and the growing ability of the Bolsheviks in identifying themselves with the aspirations of the masses and thereby providing the leadership, on the other.[29]

The soviets were not created by any party leadership, including the Bolshevik leadership. Nor, however, were they spontaneous. The memory of the 1905 Soviet lived on the minds of the advanced workers. But the rapidity with which the Petrograd Soviet became the most authoritative institution, far more acceptable to the workers and soldiers than the Provisional Government, cannot be explained by the actions of parties or groups. A more social explanation can be suggested on the basis of the changes that had occurred in Petrograd and in urban Russia as a whole.

The autocracy had not been serious in its deal with the upper classes made at the time of the 1905 revolution. The Stolypin era saw it taking power (or the prospects of power) away from the Cadets. Moreover, the further growth of capitalism and the coalescence between landed wealth and capitalism created a situation where the ruling circle was steadily being turned into a narrow clique, and the whole of upper-class "society" was growing hostile to it. During World War I, the isolation of the Tsar and his court clique became near absolute. The Tsar's minister, Protopopov, recorded it on the following words:

> Even the very highest classes become *frondeurs* before the revolution. . . .
> A sense of the danger of this sport did not awaken till the last moment.[30]

The bourgeoisie was becoming the dominant partner in an opposition bloc stretching from the liberal aristocratic opposition at the top, to even many moderate socialist or radical intelligentsia members from below. The semi-constitutional regime, despite all the restrictions, still gave some opportunities to the intelligentsia. They could take part in Duma activities. They could engage in legal journalistic opposition, moderate criticism, could get through the censors, and some public activity was going on. This was a major reason for a turn of the Social Democratic intelligentsia to liquidationism. And they represented only a fragment of the radical intelligentsia. Populists, non-affiliated fellow travellers, likewise found collaboration with the bourgeois opposition desirable. During the war, when the bulk of the radical intelligentsia took a patriotic stand, they co-operated with the "Progressive Bloc," the bourgeois opposition that attempted to run the war in its way, and to organize military supplies, defense production, etc., through the War Industries Committee.

But alongside this, there was the sharpening of the class divide between the workers and the entire bourgeois world. A working-class radicalization had begun slowly from 1910, and had picked up pace in 1912. As many as 550,000 workers participated in political strikes in 1912, the figure rising to 1,059,000 in the first half of 1914. This upset the left intelligentsia. Defeated in trade unions and in insurance board elections, they accused the Bolshevik paper *Pravda* of "strikomania."[31] This radical intelligentsia drew greater comfort from the elections to the Fourth Duma, which had only 185 absolutely pro-government deputies out of a total of 442.[32] Thus, the socialist movement was splitting not only organizationally but also socially, with the majority of worker-activists being anti-liquidators.

The beginning of World War I had a complex result. On one hand, the patriotic fervor gripped even sections of the militant workers. A mass arrest of Bolsheviks in Petrograd, including the Bolshevik Duma members, crippled their top levels. Several thousand militant activist-workers had been drafted into the army as a politically-decided measure to weaken working-class resistance. The first months of the war were marked by political stupor and a renewed ascendancy of the Mensheviks.[33]

But war also meant large-scale expansion of defense related production, and an expansion in those branches of industry. In the capital, industrial output doubled between 1914 and the beginning of 1917. The workforce rose by 135 percent in the metal industry, by 99 percent in the chemical industry, and 44 percent in garment industry. In 1914, the number of factory workers was 242,600. In 1917 it was 392,800 in the city proper, and 417,000 including factories situated on the outskirts of the city. Many of these new workers were not workers from evacuated areas, but peasants (12.3 percent of the metal workers who owned land began working between 1914 and 1917).[34] This initially meant that the more politicized workers were submerged, but taken in conjunction with other factors, this was to result in a renewed outburst.

The other effects included both the factory environment and the surrounding areas. Over 70 percent of the Petrograd proletariat were employed in factories of over one thousand. Just over 6 percent worked in factories employing less then 100 workers. Workers' living conditions were terrible, as were health statistics (nearly 25 percent of all babies born died by the time they were one year old).[35]

The lack of political tradition among the new workers, coupled with the increasing deprivation and hardships as the war went on, resulted in an increasing anger among them. A new strike movement began, but with a less clear political outlook. In 1915 there were 146 political strikes involving 241,373 strikers. In the same year economic strikes in Petrograd numbered 157, with 78,988 strikers. The corresponding Petrograd figures for 1916 were: political strikes–330, strikers–373,969; economic strikes–354, strikers–234,500.[36] In January–February 1917 six times as many workers were involved in political strikes as in economic strikes.[37] In February 1917, therefore, a contradictory situation prevailed. While a central revolutionary leadership was absent, having been beheaded, there was a sharp rise in the class struggle. To the workers, the Tsarist bureaucracy and the court circles, the nobles and the bourgeoisie were one and the same. At the same time, the bulk of them had no clear understanding of the political conflicts between the different socialist parties. The aims of the workers were clear. They demanded a democratic political system along with an equally democratic factory, i.e., one from which the ruthless exploitative laws imposed by Tsarism would go. At this stage, they did not think of taking over all power. Even when the February Revolution was accomplished, they only wanted the socialists to lead them and to bridle the bourgeoisie. Similarly, in the factories they wanted a democratic order, not a complete take-over. Even these demands led to sharp conflicts and the rise of a movement for workers' control. But since, at this stage, the workers did not want the establishment of proletarian rule, nor the take-over of industry, their aims corresponded more to the slogans put forward by the Mensheviks and SRs. Yet this was more an apparent than real unity. The parties of moderate socialism wanted the bourgeois parties to rule. The workers and soldiers wanted that their demands should be met. And they were conscious of this much, at least, that unless they created their own institutions and abolished the worst of the old laws, there would be no real safeguards. As a result, soviets, factory committees and soldiers' committees sprang up. The workers also began to organize their own militia.[38]

It is well known that the Executive Committee of the Petrograd Soviet was set up in an ad hoc manner by moderate socialists, mostly intellectuals. But the question that has come up repeatedly is who started the drive for the Soviets? The official Soviet view, as well as that of many Western scholars who concentrated on Bolshevik documents, emphasizes the key role of the Bolshevik Party. The idea that soviets sprang up all over the country absolutely spontaneously can be discounted. But that does not prove that the Bolsheviks, as a party, created them. This approach to spontaneity vs. organization assumes that workers, as long as they do not follow party leaders, are spontaneous. The Soviets in 1917 were both institutions of working-class power, and terrains within which crucial political struggles were carried out. It is true that the Bolsheviks advocated, after the *April Theses*, the seizure of power by the working class through the Soviets. But this advocacy of April 1917, together with the fact that soviets can become class organizations in a struggle for power does not prove that the Bolsheviks called for them first, nor that they were the key organizers in the early stages. This is to assume what has to be proved, namely, that the Bolshevik tactics of February were anticipating the strategic turn of April. This is to further argue that rank and file workers of many other groups, or even all the other groups, were reformists. The factual side of this problem has been disputed for long. In the Soviet Union, a critical voice was raised by Eduard Burdzhalov, who documented the vacillations and miscalculations of the Bolsheviks, giving rise to a vast debate.[39]

In Petrograd, the agitation began in late January. The Workers' Group of the War Industries Committee, which continued the old liquidator politics, campaigned for "immediate and decisive abolition of the existing regime." This was an expression of the mass hostility to Tsarism. On the occasion of the International Women's Day, February 23) Petrograd women workers of several textile mills struck work, and got the support of metal workers. Once the struggle began, the Bolshevik ranks threw themselves into the fray. On the 24th of February a general strike paralyzed the city. Within two more days, soldiers began to react. By the 27th, most of the garrison regiments joined the revolution.[40] The mood of the masses caught the Bolshevik top leadership unprepared. The Russian Bureau of the Central Committee, headed by Shlyapnikov, Zalutsky and Molotov, thought it to be simply a bread-riot even as late as February 25. A leaflet issued by Shlyapnikov under workers' pressure suggested that the "open struggle" still lay in the future. Moreover, the leaflet ignored the call for a soviet that was already coming up.[41] The Bolshevik Petersburg Committee feared that the increased militancy of the workers might outstrip their organizational abilities. As a result, they suggested that maintaining discipline was more important than making direct call for strikes. The Mezhraionka (a group with links to Trotsky) issued an appeal to the army[42] and distributed a printed leaflet calling on workers to show solidarity with women workers. Their slogan to establish a "provisional revolutionary government" was supported by the Workers' Group.[43] Either the Mezhraiontsi, or the Vyborg District Committee of the Bolsheviks, called for the setting up of a soviet on the same day. But the Russian Bureau's Manifesto of the 27th was still silent on the question of forming a soviet.[44]

Trotsky, in his massive history, emphasized the failure of Shlyapnikov or Vyborg Bolshevik leader Kayurov to look beyond the morrow and to recognize the outbreak of a revolution. But the other issue is not less significant, for it shows the complex interweaving of class and gender. It has been argued previously that the relatively lesser flexibility in the face of women workers was a weakness of Bolshevism. This aspect actually requires a much more elaborate treatment, but some initial attempts will be made below to tackle certain issues.[45] In studying the activities of the different groups and the response of the workers, a number of scholars have suggested that the relationship was manipulative, because the masses were more or less irrational.[46] This fits in with the theory of a Bolshevik coup d'etat in October. But social historians have emphasized long-term trends. The progress from February to October was one of mutual influences between parties and classes. The February events had begun separating the left and the right within the socialist movement. As millions of working people began thinking about their experiences, they engaged in open discussions and debates, and made, what seemed to them, reasonable choices.[47]

It is true that both the Mezhraiontsi and the Vyborg District Committee represented parts of the organized vanguard and both belonged to the revolutionary left. Moreover in the entire process, politicized workers supporting left Menshevik and left-wing SR politics also played a significant role. This is why I have argued that the Soviet was not a created in a purely spontaneous manner. Yet, the swift popular response was also indicative of the natural tendency of the workers to form their own class organizations. But when the Mezhraionka organization issued a leaflet calling for election of delegates to the Provisional Government,[48] they were going ahead of what the masses were willing to do. The mass of workers wanted the socialists to lead them, and were quite willing to see a socialist government. But at this stage they had no conception of establishing their own rule through their elected representatives.

The foregoing discussion shows that at the factory level, or on the streets a united activity of the vanguard workers was developing between late January and the end of the Tsarist autocracy.[49] Within this united battle, the worker-Bolsheviks, or the "Bolshevized" workers, that is, those who had been politically tempered in course of the pre-war struggles, played a very significant role. The fact that in cases when workers wanted arms, or more militant struggles they turned to the Bolsheviks, shows their belief that the latter were more militant. In this sense, it is worth noting Trotsky's conclusion that the February Revolution was led by:

Conscious and tempered workers educated for the most part by the party of Lenin. But we must here immediately add: This leadership proved sufficient to guarantee the victory of the insurrection, but it was not adequate to transfer immediately into the hands of the proletarian vanguard the leadership of the revolution.[50]

The point Trotsky was making can be explained further. The crucial battles were fought by the militant workers, who undertook to ensure grassroots level unity in order to overthrow the Tsarist autocracy. Moreover, the organizations, both the Bolshevik Vyborg District Committee, and the Mezhraionka, were composed of activists who had been close to the Leninist standpoint. But these workers were not in a position to develop a program for the whole country or provide a centralized leadership. As a result, the moderate socialist leaders, who did not wish to push the revolution forward, could thwart the Bolsheviks.[51] They created a Provisional Executive Committee of the Soviet of Workers' Deputies when it was evident that the revolution was going to win, fleshed out this ad hoc executive with some workers, and co-opted large numbers of relatively less politicized soldiers. Fear of getting isolated from soldiers, whose participation had been instrumental in ensuring the success of the uprising, checked even radical workers. The peasant army, in turn initially had great faith in the SR party. Thus developed the Menshevik-SR coalition. It was opposed to any conception of workers' power.

The Bolshevik Party had about 23,600 members at the beginning of 1917. Their social composition was highly proletarian.[52]

TABLE 7.1

	Workers	Peasants	White-collar	Other	Total
Number	14,200	1800	6,100	1,500	23,600
Percentage	60.2	7.6	25.8	6.4	100

In the long run this was the basis of their success. But initially, with hardly any member coming from the intelligentsia, the party felt tremendous lack of journalists, leaflet writers, and other types of intellectuals.[53] The two thousand Bolsheviks of Petrograd could set in motion tens of thousands of Lenin's second category, the "average workers" of *What is to be Done*? But in February, millions had come out. And while their weight was enough to topple the autocracy, two limitations prevented any further development towards the direct seizure of power by the working class. On the one hand, the Bolshevik central leadership was as yet clinging to the view of the nature of the revolution that had been developed during and after 1905. On the other hand, many of the workers who were drawn into agitation for the first time in their lives were politically backward. The party by itself was not in a position to motivate millions of workers across Russia to recognize the need to capture power. It needed a bigger platform, from which it could influence the masses of workers, and in the first place win over the bulk of the advanced workers firmly to its goals. As we will see, this also meant the party would be transformed.

III
CLASS, PARTY, AND SOVIETS

For the situation to change, it was necessary for the working class to develop a concept of class power. It was equally necessary for the development of a political leadership co-ordinating all the struggles of the workers. This was where Bolshevik strategy and theoretical perception revealed a great weakness. All the way to February 28, Bolshevik leaflets had been silent on the soviets. The manifesto "To All Citizens of Russia" had called only for a provisional revolutionary government.

Soviet, or councils, as institutions of workers' democracy, represented the form of possible workers' power in February, because the question of power was posed openly. The Cadets had by then become the principal spokespersons of propertied Russia. For them, the central aim was the protection of bourgeois class interests. Determined opposition to the revolutionary goals of the workers' movement led them to reject even consistent liberal democracy. We have indeed a major paradox. The Provisional Government, seeking to create a stable bourgeois political set up, could not even give it a name. For months, they did not even proclaim Russia a republic. At the same time, there was a peculiarity. The leftward swing in politics marginalized the Nationalist and Octobrist parties. The Cadets found themselves inundated with new members from parties of the extreme right. As a result the left-wing Cadets who wanted to come to terms with the left were defeated in their attempts.[54] The class pressure on the party did not permit such a line.[55] The workers and soldiers detested the Cadets as much as the Cadets detested them. They made no distinction between the bureaucracy, the nobility, and the bourgeoisie. And they showed no inclination to gravitate towards parliamentary structures. There was, in other words, a thoroughly inadequate social base for parliamentary democracy in Russia. As the most eminent historian of the Cadet Party writes, "With their own limited national constituency, the Cadets themselves could never claim to rule on the basis of representative principles."[56]

The soviet experience was new. The Paris Commune had become little more than a ritual to be observed. And in 1905, Trotsky's account of the revolution and Rosa Luxemburg's appreciation of the mass strike were the only serious attempts to analyze the Soviets, or more generally, the institutional bases of working-class power. Socialist theory in general had arrived at a consensus, that the aim was to win a socialist majority in parliament.[57]

Mass participation by workers, peasants and soldiers in the work of government through the soviet would inevitably make the government a less sophisticated affair, and democracy itself would be relatively "primitive." The Mensheviks and the SRs, led by the left intelligentsia, recoiled at the idea of a revolution that would culminate in untrained workers and peasants, unlettered soldiers, collectively taking over the reins of administration. In February, the Executive Committee of the Petrograd Soviet of Workers' and Soldiers' Deputies had a Menshevik-SR majority. The mood of this majority was perfectly expressed by Iraklii Tseretelli, the political exile who became the chief Menshevik ideologue in the Soviet. He said:

> Of course you'll have to talk about the necessity of a compromise with the bourgeoisie. There can be no other road for the revolution. It's true we have all the power, and that the Government would go if we lifted a finger, but that would mean disaster.[58]

Thus, there was created a dual power system. The members of the Fourth Duma, who had attempted to avoid a revolution by securing the abdication of Nicholas in favor of his son or of his brother, had set up a Duma Committee when the revolution was about to sweep away the autocracy. Eventually, this Committee turned itself, with a little alteration, into a Provisional Government, but only after a Petrograd Soviet had been set up.[59] Having proclaimed to the Soviet that this Provisional Government was going to assume power, it was however initially so ambiguous that it did not even publicly assert the fall of the monarchy.[60]

The workers and soldiers in their masses had no faith in the semi-monarchist Committee. They reposed their faith in the Petrograd Soviet of Workers' and Soldiers' Deputies. Sukhanov, the left-wing Menshevik who was influential in the early days of the Soviet, wrote of its first meeting that the chairman:

> had neither a general plan of action nor control of the meeting itself, which proceeded noisily and quite chaotically. But this by no means prevented the Soviet from performing at this very first session its basic task, vital to the revolution—that of concentrating into one centre all the ideological and organisational strength of the Petersburg democracy, with undisputed authority and capacity for rapid and decisive action.[61]

Within hours of its formation, the Soviet had gone beyond the 1905 limits, brought soldiers into its fold, and thereby acquired the power to coerce the class enemy, a basically state-like act. By March 17, nineteen cities had soviets. By June, the number was 519.[62] One of the crucial early tasks of the soldiers supporting the soviets was to push through the General Order Number One. It was practically dictated to Sokolov, a member of the Executive Committee of the Petrograd Soviet, by a group of soldiers. It endowed off-duty soldiers with full civil and political rights, put the units of the capital under the political authority of the Soviet, and stipulated that the decisions of the Provisional Government were to be obeyed only when they did not run contrary to those of the Soviet. Soldiers were to elect their committees. Weapons were not to be turned over to officers.[63] Nothing could show more bluntly the extent to which soldiers hated and mistrusted the old officers' hierarchy. And they, the soldiers as well as the workers, made no difference between that hierarchy, the civilian bureaucracy, and the bourgeois politicians. When the Duma Committee gave way to a formally proclaimed Provisional Government, it dared to take power only after the leaders of the Executive Committee had approached the members of the government and even then, after a formal agreement. Miliukov demanded that the government must be able to proclaim "that it was formed in agreement with the Soviet" and that this text would appear alongside a Soviet Proclamation in *Izvestiya*.[64] So at this stage, workers' power was not established simply because the majority of those leading the workers took a line of compromise with the bourgeoisie.

The dual power system was openly acknowledged. The Order Number One had led to protest by generals that it had legitimized the destruction of the army hierarchy. The War Minister, Guchkov told them sadly:

> The Provisional Government possesses no real power and its orders are executed only in so far as this is permitted by the Soviet of Workers' and Soldiers' Deputies, which holds in its hands the most important elements of actual power, such as troops, railroads, postal and telegraph service. It is possible to say directly that the Provisional Government exists only while this is permitted by the Soviet of Workers' and Soldiers' Deputies.[65]

The refusal of the leadership of the Soviet to take power was a serious problem for the workers. Trotsky explained the nature of the problem in his *History*:

> The political mechanism of revolution consists of the transfer of power from one class to another. The forcible overturn is usually accomplished in a brief time. But no historic class lifts itself from a subject position to a position of rulership suddenly in one night, even though a night of revolution.... The historic preparation of a revolution brings about ... a situation in which the class which is called to realize the new social system, although not yet master of the country, has actually concentrated in its hands a significant share of the state power, while the official apparatus if still in the hands of the old lords. That is the initial dual power in every revolution.[66]

However, the dual power was inherently unstable. And it created the possibility of a further radicalization of the revolution. The masses, not only the workers and the soldiers, but also all kinds of humble people, mechanics, taxi-drivers, janitors, servants, all tended to gravitate to the Soviet.[67] Similar Soviets sprang up in other cities. Everywhere, they became the nodal point of popular power, and challenged, more or less, the official institutions including the city dumas sought to be created by the Provisional Government. This happened in Moscow, Yaroslav, Kazan, Nikolaev, Rostov-on-Don, and other cities.[68] Under the armed protection of the bigger city Soviets, there developed a wide range of popular organs, like district soviets, factory soviets (where the factory was a large one), factory councils, trade unions, various kinds of committees to deal with specific problems, and workers' militias.[69] Perhaps the most important of these were the factory committees, since they begun to restructure production relations from the point of production. Both the soviets and factory councils were elected by mass meetings held at the factories. Thus, within weeks, an outline of a new kind of popular state apparatus was being built up from bottom. The Mensheviks and the Socialist Revolutionaries resisted the growth of council power. The Executive Committee issued an "Instructions to all Soviets," stating:

> The Provisional Government must be regarded as the sole legal government for all Russia. All its decisions, unless protested by the Soviet, must be carried out; all its government organs and commissars must be considered as legal authorities, unless they personally or politically endanger the cause of freedom.[70]

At each step this approach of the Executive clashed with the will of the workers and soldiers, expressed through their representatives at the plenary sessions of the Soviet. Thus, the Executive's response to Order Number One was, according to Hasegawa, the following:

> On one hand, they had tried to avoid exclusive concentration of the insurgents' support for the Soviet, which might inevitably lead to the demand that the Soviet take power. On the other, they found it was necessary to dispel the intense anger and fear felt by the soldiers which might trigger large-scale slaughter of officers.[71]

Again, the workers sought to continue the general strike, which had toppled the monarchy, until an eight-hour day was won. But Chkheidze, the Menshevik Chairman of the Soviet, wanted production to begin at once in the munitions works. Eventually the Soviet leadership was forced by the pressure of the class to negotiate the eight-hour day with the employers.[72]

The Bolshevik Party stood to the left in the debate on the Soviets. But in February-March, the Russian Bureau was unwilling to countenance any strategy that smacked of a call for workers' power. The Petersburg Committee of the Party voted on March 3 "not to oppose the authority of the Provisional Government in so far as its action conform with the interests of the proletariat"—thereby giving the Provisional Government plenty of credit, which at this stage Lenin was totally unwilling to give.[73] The Russian Bureau was enlarged, by adding on to it members of the Petersburg Committee, and as the senior members like Stalin, Kamenev, and M. K. Muranov started returning. They also took over the editorial board of *Pravda* which resulted in further moderation of the line of the party. A comparison of two texts would be instructive. On March 8, the Bureau took a resolution, "on the Attitude toward the Soviets." This said:

> The strength presently represented in the Soviet makes it necessary to support it as the body which can and should create a Provisional Revolutionary Government.[74]

On March 22, the reconstituted Russian Bureau took a resolution, "On the Provisional Government," which while denouncing the government urged that the "Soviets must exercise firmest control over all the actions of the Provisional Government and its agents."[75] Later in March, there began the first of the several All-Russian Conferences of the Bolsheviks, where Stalin called for critical support to the Soviet.[76]

The real turn towards workers' democracy began in the Bolshevik party with the arrival of Lenin. Like his fellow Bolshevik Bukharin, Lenin came to view the bourgeois state as a bureaucratic excrescence.[77] The emancipation of the working class required not only the overthrow of Tsarism, but also the destruction of every element of the emergent bourgeois state, and the establishment of workers' democracy. Emphasizing the strategy of permanent revolution, Lenin now looked on the Paris Commune as the model of workers' democracy, and assimilated it to the Soviets.[78] His *April Theses* asserted that Soviet power was the form of workers' democracy, and that it was more advanced than the most advanced bourgeois democracies.[79] After a sharp conflict within the party, his standpoint was adopted at the April Conference, though in an attenuated form, and with considerable opposition still being expressed. Lenin's view was that the institutional basis of workers' democracy must be quite distinct from that of bourgeois democracy. Workers' democracy should not have an independent coercive apparatus. The latter should be fully subordinated to the representatives. The institutions should be such that the widest expansion of mass participation was made possible. Officials and every kind of representatives had to be elective, displaceable at any moment, and paid at the rate of skilled workers.[80] The April Conference resolution, by contrast, called for the transfer of power: ". . . to the Soviets or to other bodies directly expressing the will of the majority of the people (organs of local self-government, the Constituent Assembly, etc.)."[81]

This obscured the difference between bourgeois democracy

and workers' democracy. This was an apparently purely theoretical problem. Indeed, on March 30, a few days before Lenin returned to Russia, Krassikov, a Bolshevik delegate to the March conference, had been deprived of the floor by the chairperson for raising the question of the dictatorship of the proletariat when practical tasks were under discussion.[82] Lenin clearly considered the clarification of the theoretical position on workers' democracy to be of great strategic significance, not a matter of arcane knowledge. A strategy that aimed at establishing class rule through soviets would be fundamentally different from the one that either confined the revolution to bourgeois democratic stage or retained the bourgeois parliamentary structure of the state.

Anweiler has questioned this, suggesting that Lenin's call for soviets was not due to his commitment to their social and structural characters, but because they could be used for his program of action.[83] This is based on the fact that after July, when there was a refusal of the soviets to take power and when they instigated a witch hunt against the Bolsheviks, Lenin was willing to ignore the soviets because they had become powerless and bureaucratized. Keeping an examination of the July Days in abeyance for now, it is necessary to state, for the moment, that when Lenin initially raised the slogan "All power to the Soviets," he emphasized precisely their social and structural characteristics, above all in the *April Theses* themselves. He raised the demand, at a point of time when its implementation would have brought the Mensheviks and the SRs to power, not his own party. But he raised the call, because it would have legitimized Soviet democracy, and made possible a relatively painless conquest of power under working-class hegemony, but having a new form of class rule. So Lenin's conception of class, party and soviets was the following: the soviets were institutions of workers' democracy, elected from the workplace upwards, and the task of the vanguard party was to win a majority in competition with other parties within the soviet structure by fusing the outlook of the party with that of the majority.

Since the Menshevik–SR bloc did not want to take power, the slogan had mainly educative value. At the same time, the Bolsheviks believed that while the Soviet structure was more democratic than the parliamentary one, what was ultimately vital was the role of the masses. Unless they moved in a voluntary way, even the best of representative forms could develop conservatism and the renewal of the representatives continuously was the only way to cut through this bureaucratization and conservatism.[84]

Organizing the working class and uniting different segments of the class into one coherent whole, ready to fight for class power, came up against various divisions within the class. In recent times, attention has been focused on gender, which posed serious obstacles to the harmonization of unity and equality. Though the war had meant a massive influx of women in industry, women workers' special needs were often ignored. Even in the revolutionary year, this was to come out time and again. Even in that year, when factory committees won a minimum wage clause from the owners in Petrograd, the rates were 5 rubles for men and 4 rubles for women. Likewise, in Moscow, while 220,478 strikers (92.3 percent of all strikers) in 185 strikes (68.8 percent of all strikes) demanded wage rises, only 550 workers participating in two strikes demanded equal pay for equal work, regardless of gender.[85] Women workers were aware of the problems posed by male bias in the unions. At the Petrograd Cartridge Works, after demanding an 8-hour working day, men also demanded overtime payment for work on Saturdays, while women workers resisted this, saying they needed time for domestic work, for standing in queue, or for looking after their children.[86] Since society had not yet been refashioned, and therefore domestic burden remained solely a woman's burden, the overtime would come as a punishment to the women. Tsvetkova, a woman worker in the leather industry, described the situation she faced at her workplace:

> Instead of supporting women workers, organising them, going hand in hand with them, many male comrades regard them not as full and equal members of the workers' family, and sometimes do not even take them into consideration. When the issue of unemployment and lay-offs arises, they try to ensure that they remain in work and that the women are dismissed, relying on the fact that women will not be able to resist because of their weak organisation and helplessness. When we women try to speak and prove to the men that they are not behaving properly, and that we should try to find a way out of the situation together, we are not allowed to speak and the men will not listen.[87]

In Petrograd, the best documented city, Bolshevik women were active in two kinds of work among militant women. One was the formation of the Union of Soldatki (Soldiers' wives). Bolshevik influence over the army was to grow significantly as a result of the Bolshevik women's struggle to organize the Soldatki and to champion their demands. The other work was that of organizing women workers for their demands. The social peace established by the Mensheviks and Socialist Revolutionaries after February was broken for the first time by several thousand women workers in the city laundries. They fought for an eight-hour working day, and for minimum wages. Bolshevik women like Goncharskaya, Novikondratieva, and Sakharova led these struggles. Under the influence of Kollontai, the party press, primarily *Pravda*, regularly reported about the strike. After a month's strike, there was a partial victory of the strike.[88]

But the Bolsheviks were not alone in the field. Pro-war bourgeois feminists were also organizing some working-class women. A meeting of the Executive Committee of the Petersburg Committee of the Bolsheviks gave Slutskaya the task of organizing work among the women.[89] She suggested the necessity of setting up a bureau of working women under the city committee. But at the meeting of the Petrograd Committee itself, despite assurances that this would carry out purely agitational tasks, and that all tasks would be in accordance with the decisions of the Petrograd Committee, there was considerable opposition. The meeting resolved to resume publication of *Rabotnitsa*, but left examination of Slutskaya's proposals for a later date.[90] Eventually very few raion committees set up women's bureaus. The reasons for the non-functioning character of the bureaus can be found in the party's hostility to any kind of feminism.[91] The journal *Rabotnitsa* was revived, and it became the center of agitational and organizational work among women workers. The fact that it was a paper meant it could avoid the charge of "feminist deviation." *Rabotnitsa* enabled two types of women activists— those like Inessa Armand and Alexandra Kollontai on the one hand, and those like Konkordiya Samoilova or others, to coexist. Armand and Kollontai were feminists, even if they did not apply the term to themselves. They were searching for autonomous space for women workers and were keenly aware of how gender intersected class. People like Samoilova were more orthodox, and viewed their work as simply an additive work—bringing more women, therefore more workers, into the party hegemony. As Kollontai wrote later:

> As late as the spring of 1917 Konkordiya Nikolaevna found superfluous the formation of an apparatus in the party for work amongst women. On the other hand she warmly welcomed the rebirth of *Rabotnitsa* as an ideological centre. . . . Comrade Samoilova would not tolerate anything that smacked of feminism and she regarded with great caution any organisational scheme which in her opinion might introduce "division according to sex" into the proletariat.[92]

Kollontai's return to Russia from exile, and the fact that as an enthusiastic supporter of Lenin's *April Theses*, put power behind the work of agitating among women, but she too failed to get the party to agree to the creation of a special apparatus for work among women. When she drafted a proposal modelled on the now defunct German section led by Zetkin, with the help of Klavdia Nikolaeva and Fedorova, this was opposed by Krupskaya, Samoilova, Liudmilla Stal, Zinaida Lilina, and even partially Inessa Armand.[93] After prolonged attempts, Kollontai, Samoilova, and others eventually got the party to agree to a women workers' conference, held on November 12 and 18, in Petrograd and attended by five hundred elected delegates representing over eighty thousand women workers.[94] The aim of this conference was to mobilize the working-class women for the coming elections to the Constituent Assembly, and to prepare the grounds for an all-Russia women's conference. This obviously stemmed from a feeling among some of the women activists that propaganda among women must be organized separately. The paper used bold language, as when an activist, Prokhorova, wrote, "Many women comrades say that everything will be done without us. But comrades, whatever is done without us will be dangerous for us."[95] Many female factory workers sent in short pieces criticizing sexist behavior of male colleagues, not merely overseers. The editors of the paper were no less committed Bolsheviks than their male counterparts. But within their writings and activities it is possible to find the stirrings of a Bolshevik-feminist discourse that went beyond the Bolshevik orthodoxy.

IV
THE BOLSHEVIK PARTY IN REVOLUTION

All through the revolution of 1917, the Bolshevik party was a lively organization, carrying on sharp debates, and having a policy of regular interaction, on the one hand between the top leadership and the cadres, and on the other hand, between the party and the class. The ultimate test of any political party comes when it is in a position of open contest for power. In case of the Bolsheviks, moreover, February 1917 brought the end of a long underground existence, and with it, of all arguments regarding why democracy might have to be limited. So it is necessary to examine what sort of internal party regime existed in 1917, and how that was related to the party's approach to the movements of the working class.

At the time of the March Conference, a three-way struggle ensued. The right wing, led by Voitinsky, wanted unconditional unity with the Mensheviks. The center, led by Stalin, wanted unification based on the political standpoint of Zimmerwald and Kienthal (i.e., a compromise anti-war stand that had temporarily united a revolutionary minority and a Kautskyite majority, but that had been criticized as inadequate by Lenin and the other émigré Bolsheviks, who along with Polish left-wingers like Karl Radek and others had formed a separate Zimmerwald Left). Finally, the left, led by people like Molotov and Zalutsky opposed such attempts at unification.[96]

Lenin had, meanwhile, developed a much more leftist line. Internationally, he was for the foundation of a new International on the basis of a clear-cut communist program, including a split with the centrists, and not merely the open Social Patriots. Within Russia, he was for an absolute rejection of support to the Provisional Government, complete opposition to talks of general unity among socialists, and in favor of a perspective of working-class rule.[97] Lenin's arrival, while the March–April conference was still continuing, had the effect of dropping a bombshell on the party. He even felt that a clean break required breaking with "old Bolshevism," and creating "a proletarian Communist Party" whose "elements have already been created by the best adherents of Bolshevism."[98] At this time, within the leadership (broadly defined) Lenin had only a few supporters. Alexandra Kollontai was his firmest supporter, while Nikolai Bukharin, when he returned to Russia a little later, would also support Lenin.

From this time onward, all the way to the October insurrection, two major lines existed in the party, represented respectively by Lenin and Kamenev. Lenin strove for a party policy winning over the masses for the conquest of power and the establishment of the dictatorship of the proletariat. Kamenev's line was for the development of a militant proletarian opposition to fight for the complete victory of the democratic revolution. Lenin found himself isolated and his *April Theses* were published in *Pravda* as his personal theses.[99] The next day, Kamenev editorially dissociated the party's mouthpiece from Lenin.[100] In the Central Committee, and in the Petersburg Committee, Lenin found few supporters.[101]

Lenin's response was swift. He was aware that a leadership could not be built up overnight. So he had no aim of rejecting the Bolshevik party. But he recognized that a conservative inertia had set in in its upper layers, and decided to overcome that by appealing to the party ranks. Beginning with the publication of the *April Theses*, he launched an open campaign. He could do this with some confidence because while the official program of the party called for a democratic revolution, Bolshevik tactics had highlighted class independence. His action showed that Lenin's conception of democratic centralism did not involve any consideration of subservience to the hierarchy, or any "central committee solidarity," when fundamental issues were involved. It also showed that there existed several trends within Bolshevism. As it has been argued, "Against the old Bolsheviks Lenin found support in . . . the worker-Bolsheviks . . . [who were revolutionary but] lacked the theoretical resources to defend their position."[102]

It was the layer of class-conscious militants, politicized in 1912-14, who overcame the hesitations of the committeemen and the defenders of hierarchy. From this period onward, the party of revolution that Lenin shaped was becoming a much more broad-based workers' party than ever before.

At the Seventh All-Russian conference (April 24–29), while a sizeable block, led by Kamenev and Rykov, fought for old Bolshevism,[103] the crucial resolution "On the Current Moment" won with 71 votes for, 39 against, and 8 abstentions.[104] But on the question of splitting from the Zimmerwald movement, Lenin stood isolated.[105] The critical attitude that he had taken to Old Bolshevism had to be toned down. Finally, in the nine-member Central Committee elected by the Conference, there were three firm Leninists (Lenin, Sverdlov, and Smilga), two supporters of Lenin with qualifications (Stalin and Zinoviev) and four forming the right wing (Kamemev, Nogin, Miliutin, and Fedórov). [106]

The history of this struggle has important lessons. Lenin, the supposed dictator of the Bolshevik Party, found himself isolated at the upper echelons of the party. He could win only after waging a month-long battle, and even then well over a third of the delegates to the Conference were openly opposed to him. At the level of the top leadership the resistance seems to have been greater. The victory of Lenin itself was no foregone conclusion, but it had to be earned through democratic processes in front of the whole party by way of proletarian mobilization against the leading stratum.

Nor did the April Conference bring inner-party discussions to an end. On every occasion important new questions came up. Inner-party discussions were quite wide-ranging, and were interspersed with dialogs with non-party workers and soldiers, the rank and file of the other left parties, etc. In June, when a debate took place over whether to organize a public demonstration calling for an end to the provisional Government, the decision was not taken by the Central Committee alone, which would have been technically legitimate, but by a large gathering which included members of the Central Committee, the Petersburg Committee, the Military Organization, representatives from the trade union- and factory committee-level party cells. It was this meeting that noted the mood of the masses in favor of a demonstration by a vote of 58 for, 37 against, and 52 abstentions, and declared that a demonstration would take place, if necessary defying the Soviet (47 for, 42 against, 80 abstentions).[107] Facing a ban on the demonstration by the All-Russian Congress of Soviets, five members of the Central Committee had to meet on an emergency basis and call off the demonstration with Zinoviev, Kamenev and Nogin voting for calling off and Lenin and Sverdlov abstaining.[108] The party ranks responded by adopting resolutions condemning the Central Committee.[109] Lenin, in a speech before the Petersburg Committee, June 11, 1917, which had become radical due to recomposition in April, said:

> The Central Committee does not want to force your decision. Your right, the right to protest against the actions of the Central Committee, is a legitimate one, and your decision must be a free one.[110]

Similarly, when a pseudo-democratic body, known as the Council of the Republic, was created through assigning blocs of seats to different kinds of organizations, the decision on whether to boycott it or not was not taken by the Central Committee alone. Trotsky, for the boycott, had a majority of one in the Central Committee. But a meeting of the party group at the Democratic Conference, (called to create an institutional basis for the Kerensky regime), decided in favor of entering the Council by seventy-seven votes to fifty. The Central Committee accepted this verdict.[111]

So, right up to the eve of the October uprising, there remained a substantial minority that had a radically different conception of the tasks of the party, and this minority was associated with the highest party bodies. It was never excluded from the executive organs in the name of centralism. At the Sixth Congress of the party, out of twenty-one members elected to the Central Committee, the current associated with Kamenev had several members—Kamenev, Zinoviev, Rykov, Nogin, and Miliutin.[112] Several days before the insurrection, a Political Bureau was elected (for the first time) to carry out day-to-day leadership tasks. It included Lenin, Trotsky, Stalin, Sokolnikov, Bubnov, Kamenev, and Zinoviev.[113] The last two were determined opponents of the insurrection, and even Stalin felt that Lenin's and Kamenev's lines could be reconciled.[114]

The right of the minority was not a mere formal right. A series of events highlight the effective nature of this right. A few cases can be mentioned. At the April Conference, Lenin and Kamenev were co-reporters in the discussion on general policy (reporters get an extended time and the right to speak a second time at the summing up). The personnel composition of party organs included diverse trends. Thus, the new Central Committee, elected by the Sixth Congress, created a new editorial board for *Pravda*, the members being Stalin, Sokolnikov, and Miliutin.[115] And when, at a critical moment, the Central Committee called on party members to stop collaborating with Maxim Gorky's paper, *Novaya Zhizn*, six party members who did collaborate with it wrote to the Central Committee:

> We consider it inappropriate that the CC should take decisions determining the political conduct of this or that group of party members in matters directly concerning them and on which they are better informed without consulting such party members in advance.[116]

This approach can be explained only by a combination of number of factors. In the first place, the general democratic atmosphere in the country made it impossible to install any tight control over the membership, without risking a sharp decline in membership and the transformation of the party into a sect. Second, public agitation by the party, to succeed, had to be a dialog with the masses, not a continuous one-sided propaganda. Thus, the party had to open itself up to mass pressure. Finally, there was the tremendous growth of membership. At the time of the February Revolution, membership was around 23,600. The April Conference represented 80,000 members. The Sixth Congress recorded 240,000 members, that is, a ten-fold growth in six months.[117] This rapid rise in membership meant that what was being built at this stage was not a tightly-knit party of professional revolutionaries, who only formed the core of the party, but a large party of militant workers. Such a massive growth could not be harmonized with absolute discipline, even if the party had attempted to enforce such discipline. In the previous chapter, we had seen how work in the underground, during the years of the Stolypin reaction, had resulted in Lenin insisting on a very tight underground organizational network and its complete control over all open activities. This was only one phase of Leninism, rather than being a timeless essence. From 1912, with the revival of mass movements, it had already been modified. In 1912-14, the activists had already begun to come to the fore. Now, there was a complete triumph of workers' democracy. There can be two ways of looking at this. Trotsky once remarked that this was a "de-Bolshevization" of the party. Or, we can argue that the earlier phase was over. In any case, the party that led the Russian Revolution was not the party as imagined by Lenin in 1910. Table 7.2 shows the kind of growth registered by different committees. In such situations, the old committee hierarchy and its discipline simply could not be maintained.

TABLE 7.2
Growth registered by different committees[118]

Party Committee	Early March	Seventh Conference	Sixth Congress
Petrograd	2000	16,000	26,000
Moscow	600	7,000	15,000
Ivanovo-Voznesensk	10	3,564	5,440
Ekaterinoslav	400	1,500	3,500
Lugan	100	1,500	2,596
Kharkov	105	1,200	—
Saratov	60	1,600	3,000
Kiev	200	1,900	4,000
Ekaterinburg	40	1,700	2,800

One particular issue requiring separate handling here is the matter of women in the party. It has already been noted in the previous chapter that there were far fewer women than men in the party. But these women did work seriously, in a deeply committed way, to compel the party to re-examine whether class unity is automatic, or whether gender fractures class unity, and has to be taken up in each specific case. Formally it was held that since men and women were equal, there was no question of or need for separate organizations for women. But in reality, the women fought throughout the year to carve out such space, from the April Conference to the beginning of November. This struggle was waged, because while they were dedicated revolutionaries, it was as women revolutionaries that they found Bolshevik practice inadequate for their needs, including their need to mobilize greater numbers of women workers for the revolution. Despite all shortcomings, Bolshevism also had many positive things to its credit. If it was a child of its own age, and therefore having some amount of patriarchal values, at the same time, compared to all other proletarian social and political institutions, including soviets and factory councils, women had better representation in the party hierarchy. Of the sample group handled by Evans Clements, data on 159 Bolshevichki show where they were located in the year 1917: 50.9 percent worked directly for the party, 2.5 percent were in the trade unions, and 31.4 percent in the local soviets. Another set of information, covering 182 women, shows that whereas 2.8 percent of them were members of raion or city Duma (municipal organization), and 6.5 percent of raion, city or guberniia Soviet executive committees, 37.3 percent of them were in raion, city or uezd party commitees.[119] And at the highest level, Kollontai was elected to the Central Committee of the party at the Sixth Party Congress, and selected to the program sub-committee, an acknowledgement that women had as much ability as men to reflect on and develop Marxist theory. Though the total presence of women in the Central Committee was limited, this was still higher than other sectors of the working-class movement.[120]

V
"PATIENTLY EXPLAIN": BOLSHEVIK STRATEGY AND THE REVOLUTIONARY CRISES

The concept of Soviet democracy to which Lenin won over his comrades meant that the Bolshevik party would have to fight within the Soviets to win over the majority of the workers and soldiers, in order to carry out their project. At the Petrograd City Conference of the party, held in April, Lenin said:

> We do not have complete political liberty, of course. But nowhere else is there such freedom as exists in Russia today. "Down with war" does not mean flinging the bayonet away. It means the transfer or power to another class. . . . We are still a minority and realize the need for winning a majority. Unlike the anarchists, we need the state for the transition to socialism. . . . The role of the Soviets . . . is that they apply organized force against the

counter-revolution. . . . There can be no dual power in a state. . . . The way out of the war lies through the victory of the Soviet. . . . This is the type of state under which it is possible to advance towards socialism. . . . So long as the Soviets have not seized power, we shall not take it. A living force, however, must impel the Soviets to seize power. . . . So long as the Provisional Government has the backing of the Soviet of Workers' Deputies, you cannot "simply" overthrow it. The only way it can and must be overthrown is by winning over the majority in the Soviets.[121]

This was the essence of the program of action he put forward, and this was what guided the Bolshevik party in the following months. A few incidents show how this line was applied in practice. The first crisis of the revolution came in April. On April 18, Miliukov, the Cadet leader who had become Minister of Foreign Affairs, reaffirmed to the allies Russia's commitment to continuing the war.[122] This resulted in mass demonstration in Petrograd.[123] The leaders of the Soviet attempted compromise. Miliukov's note was offensive to them. But they wanted to avoid any civil war. The Petersburg Committee of the Bolshevik party called for a fresh demonstration with a call, "Down with the Provisional Government." This was not the line of the Central Committee, on whose behalf Kamenev had only proposed that a purely Soviet government should be formed. Lenin was even willing to support the resolution of the Executive Committee calling for an end to demonstrations.

On the evening of April 21st, the Bolshevik Central Committee did its own stock-taking. Their opponents were proclaiming that they were trying to provoke civil war. At that moment, the soldiers and the workers were in fact the most powerful force. The Provisional Government existed because the worker-soldier masses trusted the Menshevik-SR leadership, who counselled faith in the Government. So the power that protected the Provisional Government was that of the popular masses. Any attempt to overthrow the government by force of arms at this stage would have resulted in a minority insurrection and in splitting the masses. That is why, the resolution drafted by Lenin and adopted by the Central Committee insisted that party propagandists must refute the "despicable lie" that "we are holding out the threat of *civil war*," because as long as the government dared not use force against the masses, "*there must be compliance with the will of the majority of the population* and free criticism of this will by the discontented minority." The resolution also called for the use of purely peaceful means of discussions, and called for new elections of delegates to the Soviet.[124] The next morning, another resolution said even more bluntly: "The slogan 'Down with the Provisional Government' is an incorrect one at the present moment because in the absence of a solid . . . majority of the people . . . such a slogan . . . amounts to attempts of an adventurist character."[125]

Again, in the April Conference, in a speech on the current situation, Lenin repeated that the slogan had meant an impermissible use of force.[126] He was insisting, quite correctly, that the capitalists were disarmed. The masses who followed the Menshevik–SR bloc and therefore gave a vote of confidence to the Provisional Government were cheated. For they could not yet see the basic difference in goals between the different socialist parties. But they had to be persuaded. Only when there was a Soviet majority willing to take power could the question of overthrowing the Provisional Government arise.

Related to the April crisis was the crisis in Kronstadt, an island fortress only twenty miles from Petrograd, with a population of eighty-two thousand including twenty thousand soldiers, twelve thousand sailors, and seventeen thousand employees of the war industries. The Baltic sailors, immensely influential, were more proletarianized than the peasant infantry. From the beginning, the Kronstadt Soviet acknowledged only the Soviet Executive Committee, and rejected the authority of the Provisional Government. By late April, the strength of the Bolsheviks had grown massively. Their membership rose to three thousand, and they had over 30 percent of the seats in the Soviet.[127] Miliukov's note to the Allies, affirming Russia's commitment to the war, resulted in an outburst in Kronstadt. The moderate majority in the Soviet had rejected a Bolshevik resolution condemning the government. As a result, large crowds gathered in mass meetings, and passed resolutions calling for the overthrow of the Provisional Government, and the transfer of power to the Soviets.[128]

Re-election to the Soviet resulted in the return of a much more radical executive. The Bolsheviks were dominant, along with left-wing SRs and anarchists. The local Bolsheviks were impatient. On May 13, the new executive committee of the Kronstadt Soviet decided to formally announce Soviet power. On the 14th, Leon Trotsky went to Kronstadt to urge them to put up a militant battle for an all-Russian Soviet power instead of acting locally. Later, when they were being tried, Trotsky spoke for them. The overall Bolshevik line was one of promoting militancy everywhere, while striving to keep the most advanced layers from proclaiming an open rupture with the government (which would have meant some sort of armed action) until the majority was won over. So Kronstadt was not provoked by them. Rather, they sought to rein in the Kronstadt militants. At the same time, their propaganda upheld Kronstadt as a model or symbol of Soviet power. Resolutions were adopted in many places supporting the Kronstadt Soviets.[129]

But this did not mean the Bolsheviks were just like the Mensheviks and SRs, consistently throttling working-class initiative. They were to try and push the mass of workers, so that a collective break would occur between the masses and the moderate leaders. The first clear instance came over the "social peace" and its breakdown. By 1917 women formed 43 percent of the workforce. They had to be organized if the revolutionary movement was to proceed. The first weeks after February saw an unprecedented increase in the number of women organizing themselves to make political and economic demands. The Bolsheviks were active among them. The social peace established by the Mensheviks and Socialist Revolutionaries after February, i.e., their attempt to halt all working-class struggles, was broken for the first time by several thousand women workers in the city laundries. They fought for an eight-hour working day, and for minimum wages. Bolshevik women like Goncharskaya, Novikondratieva, and Sakharova led these struggles. Under the influence of Kollontai, the party press, primarily *Pravda*, regularly reported about the strike. After a month's strike, there was a partial victory of the strike.[130] This incident also shows in an exemplary way the methods whereby the Bolshevik women were mainstreaming gender issues within class politics.

The next such occasion came in June. On the third of that month the first All-Russia Congress of Soviets met. The delegates, voting and non-voting, together represented around 20 million people. The Bolsheviks and their allies formed less than a fifth of the delegates. But in Petrograd their position was growing stronger. In the municipal elections, out of 801 seats, 185 had gone to the Cadets, 299 to the bloc of Mensheviks and SRs, and 156 to the Bolsheviks.[131] This meant that excluding the Cadets, the Bolsheviks got a little over one-third of the votes cast for "the democracy," a term used at that time to designate the parties of the left.

The delegates gave full approval to the policy of the compromising leaders. But the Bolsheviks wanted to show to the provincial delegates the mood of proletarian Petrograd. So, on June 9, there appeared a Bolshevik appeal, which had been preceded by some groundwork. The soldiers of the Petrograd garrison, worried about the threat of a renewal of the offensive, were pushing for a demonstration. Starting with this push, the Bolsheviks decided to add slogans that would draw in workers as well. Since the Congress of Soviets was meeting, they emphasized political slogans like "Down with ten capitalist ministers," "All power to the All Russian Soviet," etc.[132]

The Menshevik leader Chkheidze accused the Bolsheviks of trying to force the hands of the supreme body of the Democracy. The Soviet Bureau issued an appeal, and sent emissaries to the workers' quarters. They reported that the call for Soviet power was being widely made. The reaction of the Congress of Soviets to the call for Soviet power was to ban any public manifestation of the idea. The ban was accepted, but not because of the persuasion by the Congress delegates who went to meet the workers.

> The delegates were met everywhere with extreme unfriendliness and allowed to pass only after lengthy disputes. . . . Neither the Congress nor the Petersburg Soviet had the slightest authority. . . . Only the Bolsheviks were trusted, and whether the demonstration took place or not dependent solely on the Bolshevik Central Committee.[133]

The Bolsheviks were initially not keen to withdraw the demonstration. But the Soviet Congress itself had passed a resolution banning any demonstration for three days. This was motivated by references to a supposed monarchist plot. The party leadership felt it necessary to call off the demonstration. But they had to draft a statement for their followers. The draft prepared by Trotsky, though he was not yet formally a member of the Bolshevik party, was accepted.[134]

The Bolshevik statement explained:

> We hold that the unique institution known as the Soviets of Workers: Soldiers' and Peasants' Deputies is the nearest approach to a popular body expressing the will of the majority of the people, to a revolutionary parliament. On principle we have been, and are, in favour of all power passing into the hands so such a body . . . (but) we cannot recognize the decision of the Soviets as proper decisions taken by a proper government so long as there remain the bourgeoisie.[135]

The statement thus viewed the Soviets as the highest institutions of workers, peasants, and soldiers, objected to the cohabitation of Soviets with the bourgeoisie, and made it clear that the Bolsheviks were submitting to the will of the Soviets, while also asserting that under certain circumstances, the party would have defied the Soviet Congress.[136]

The unexpected sequel to the canceled demonstration of June 10 was a counter-demonstration called for the 18th by the compromisers themselves. They hoped thereby to regain lost ground from the Bolsheviks. But the Bolsheviks successfully utilized this call to propagate among the workers their views once more, and urged them to come out with the slogans originally proposed for the demonstration of 10th June. On the 18th, the vast majority of participants in the demonstration carried Bolshevik or pro-Bolshevik banners, rather than those suggested by the Soviet majority leaders. Despite difficulties, the Bolsheviks had been able to curb the mood for an open blow against the majority leadership, and kept it within bounds as a protest demonstration.

Just over a fortnight later, reining in the mass anger fully was no longer possible. Under pressure of the Entente an offensive had been launched, and its results had been disastrous. When the Provisional Government ordered sections of the Petrograd garrison to the front to shore up the flagging morale, conflict flared up. The First Machine Gun regiment decided it would not go to the front. Leaders of the Bolshevik Military Organization fanned the flames of revolt.[137] Lenin, on the contrary, insisted that it was necessary to be careful, because nationally, the majority still trusted the Mensheviks and the SRs.[138] The Petersburg Committee of the party, and the Military Organization, criticized Lenin for this. Eventually, a situation arose when the First Machine Gun regiment declared that it was coming out in any case. This was on the 3rd of July.[139] The Bolshevik leaders now felt that they had to assume leadership. At the same time, they strove to limit the scope of the movement to that of an armed demonstration, rather than an insurrection. In the Workers' Section of the Petrograd Soviet, Kamenev said:

> We did not summon the manifestation. The popular masses themselves came into the street. . . . But once the masses have come out, our place is among them. . . . Our present task is to give the movement an organized character.[140]

Trotsky later wrote that on the night of July 3, the Bolsheviks and the Mezhraiontsi met debating "not about whether to summon the masses to a seizure of power—as enemies later asserted—but about whether to call off the demonstration the next morning or to stand at the head of it."[141] But as reports came in of workers from Vyborg, and sailors from Kronstadt joining the demonstration, it was decided that calling it off was impossible, and the best thing the party could do was to stand at the head of the movement and give it some order. In the draft resolution on the political situation, Lenin wrote later: "Had our party refused to support the July 3-4 mass movement which burst out spontaneously despite our attempts to prevent it, we should have actually and completely betrayed the proletariat."[142] Lenin drew several conclusions from the July Days. The first was that in Russia as a whole, the Bolsheviks still lacked majority support. Even in Moscow, in the July Days the majority of workers and soldiers did not demonstrate.[143] Second, the slogans were still calling upon the Menshevik–SR leaders to take power, despite the refusal of the Congress of Soviets to do so. This showed a continuing illusion about them even in Petrograd. This illusion had to go before the Bolsheviks could lead a struggle for the conquest of power.[144] Finally, Lenin concluded that a peaceful transfer of power was no longer possible, so preparations had to be made to orient the masses for armed struggle.[145] Trotsky, in his pamphlet, *What Next?* took the same line. He wrote there: ". . . the days of 3–5 day July became a turning point. . . . They exposed the complete inability of the leading parties of the petty-bourgeois democracy to assume power."[146]

In Marx's political lifetime, the Paris proletariat had risen twice. On both occasions, there had been serious weakness. The Provisional Government created by the February revolution of 1848, borne out of an insurrection of workers, had proclaimed the "right to labor." But then, having consolidated its political and military position, it had gone on to give provocations to the workers. The Parisian workers fell into the trap and rose in revolt in June. Without plan, program and leadership, the insurrection was doomed, and it was drowned in a bloodbath. Marx had shown that by helping to crush it, the left democrats and moderate socialists like Ledru-Rollin and Louis Blanc opened the door for Bonapartism. The Paris Commune, for its part, had failed chiefly because of its isolation from rural France. These lessons had been hammered home to countless Marxists by Marx's writings. By placing themselves at the head of the masses during the July Days, the Bolsheviks provided not only slogans, but a program and a leadership. By limiting the movement to a demonstration, they avoided an ill-fated "Petrograd Commune." The value of a centralized vanguard party was fully manifested in this.

VI
FREEDOM OF SPEECH

One issue that requires separate discussion is the question of freedom of the press. As with most other democratic rights, it is a standard bourgeois attack, to the effect that the Bolsheviks were totally opposed to freedom of the press, or at best that they used it cynically when they needed it. As a matter of fact, freedom of the press poses some real problems for a revolutionary socialist party. The Bolshevik predicament can be briefly examined here, for it throws better light than any discussion that focuses on the Civil War. In the free atmosphere of 1917, Lenin's stand about even the party press underwent a change. The existence of several lines within the party made it necessary to have a greater flexibility in the press. Thus, while *Pravda*, in late June–early July was trying to restrain the Petrograd workers, *Soldatskaya Pravda* carried inflammatory articles, e.g., the one by L. Chubunov which practically called for a speedy transition to an insurrection.[147] So in July, while the Central Committee was restraining the masses, other activists and committees were opposing this line. From May to August, the Petrograd Committee fought for its own paper.[148] At the next stage, when the majority began to incline towards insurrection, opponents of the line wrote in *Novaya Zhizn*. In a real atmosphere of democracy, inner party differences had to be allowed much greater scope of expression.

On the broader question of freedom of press for all, it was in 1917 that the question was posed seriously. So far, only the demand had been raised. In 1917, after the July Days, when *Pravda* was banned, Lenin argued that while freedom of press was a democratic slogan, in a near civil-war situation, it could not be applied. He quoted Prince Lvov, the former head of the Provisional Government to show that in

Russia, a civil war was on. He thereupon expressed the view that while the bourgeoisie had unlawfully banned *Pravda*, "The proletariat . . . will close down the bourgeoisie's newspaper after openly declaring by law, by Government decree, that the capitalists and their defenders are enemies of the people."[149] In a subsequent article entitled "Slanderers," he again pointed out the existence of near-civil war conditions, as shown by the fact that "The law on libel in the press has virtually been suspended in Russia."[150] He was making this comment because, at this stage, the Bolsheviks were being accused of being German agents. While it is difficult to construct the outline of a theory on the basis of criticism, at least two points emerge clearly. First, bans on the bourgeois press were envisaged as a part of the intensification of the class struggle during civil wars. Second, in stable situations, laws would regulate the freedom of press.

In an article, "How to guarantee the success of the Constituent Assembly," subtitled "On Freedom of the Press," (September 15, 1917) Lenin wrote that, in capitalist society, capital controlled the press. He showed that while the pro-Kornilov press had a huge circulation, the Bolsheviks, Mensheviks, and SRs, who together commanded 75 percent to 80 percent of the votes in Petrograd and Moscow, had total newspaper circulations less than 25 percent or even 20 percent of the circulation of the bourgeois press. The reason was that the bourgeois press enjoyed plenty of advertisements.[151]

The proposal put forward by Lenin was that private advertisements should give way to a state monopoly on the control of advertisements. This would infringe the right of private property but not the freedom of press. The advertisements could be distributed to all newspapers so any group of citizens showing a minimum number of signatures backing them could have their newspaper, with portion of the state-controlled advertisements ensuring that their paper came out.[152]

This raised the question of newsprint and printing presses. Once again, Lenin argued that control of all presses and all newsprint by the state could benefit freedom of press. These could be distributed by the state, to the big parties, to the smaller parties, and to any group of citizens having a certain number of members, etc. Lenin also suggested that as a step in this direction, before the Constituent Assembly elections, pamphlets reflecting the standpoint of every big party should be printed in millions of copies.[153]

We need to recognize that on the one hand the Marxist critique had a validity, but that on the other hand sometimes the solutions provided were very inadequate. As long as the press was under private ownership, and dependent on private capital for survival, editorial control would be biased in favor of capital. In addition, "freedom of the press" raises the question—freedom for whom? Owners and editors would claim that privilege. Lenin's immediate concern was to secure the right of the socialist parties to put across their views. But the matter goes deeper. Individuals and groups in civil society need space to express themselves no less than political parties. But their wish for self-expression can be thwarted if the owners and editors do not wish to provide them space. So Lenin's call for providing finances to any group of citizen was useful. But too much of the discussion in 1917 was around the immediate perspectives, with an imminent civil war looming large. Even before October, the bourgeoisie wanted to crush the Bolsheviks. So there was little discussion on what would happen in the long run. It could also be said that while Marx was confronted with a relatively powerful liberal tradition, the Bolshevik experience of Russian liberalism did not give them any glimpse of anything positive in liberalism that might be worth supporting. The limitation of Bolshevik thinking on this issue came out after 1917.

VII
THE OCTOBER REVOLUTION AND SOVIET DEMOCRACY

The end game in the class struggles of 1917 was played out in October. The unstable dual power regime was overthrown by an insurrection that handed power to the Soviets. With this there came a permanent split in the world socialist movement. The Bolsheviks claimed that the new regime represented a higher form of democracy. Fedor Dan, the Menshevik, called it a "criminal action" at the time when it had just begun, on October 24.[154] The legitimacy of the October Revolution has ever since been a central issue in the debate over workers' democracy.[155]

Three major possible criticisms have to be considered. First, the Bolsheviks overthrew a democratic regime. Second, they acted through their party, not through the Soviets. Finally, Lenin and Trotsky, particularly Lenin, were said to have been "dictatorial."

The July Days and their aftermath brought about a change in the status of the government. The compromising leaders of the Soviet had refused take power. Moreover, against the pro-revolution soldiers, they had appealed to the officers for "loyal" troops. This discredited them, and enabled the counter-revolution to lift its head.[156] At the same time, in a bid to silence Bolshevism, an attempt was made to ask the government to carry out the program of the Congress of Soviets. The government thereupon resigned, as the bourgeois-landlord elements in it did not want to carry out even a moderate socialist program. Despite this evidence, a fresh coalition was created, but this time with the socialists as the apparently senior partner, and with A. F. Kerensky as the Prime Minister as well as Minister of War.[157]

However, ultimately this did not mean a real swing to the left. On the contrary, by disarming the First Machine Gun regiment, and by endowing the new government with "unlimited powers," the Executive Committee of the All-Russian Soviets (VTsIK) moved to the right. There developed a plan for a Bonapartist coup. It was worked out in two rival headquarters, those of Kerensky, and of the newly appointed Commander-in-Chief, General Kornilov. The Bolsheviks were able to foresee the development of a Bonapartist option, and even the rival ambitions of Kerensky and Kornilov. In his pamphlet of August, mentioned earlier, Trotsky wrote:

> After the collapse of the coalition on the 2nd July the Soviet's refusal to take power excluded the possibility of creating a broad based government. Kerensky's unchecked government is fundamentally a government without a social base. . . . That is the essence of his Bonapartism.[158]

He wrote that the VTsIK had ceased to reflect mass opinion, and the alternatives were "Permanent revolution against permanent slaughter."[159] The strategy of the rightwing was indeed that of slaughter to stop the revolution. Kornilov was their chosen figure and Kerensky had hoped for a coup with Kornilov's support, but it soon became clear to him that Kornilov would not play second fiddle. At the last moment as the coup was about to begin, he broke with Kornilov.[160] This legitimized resistance to Kornilov, though the resistance itself owed nothing to Kerensky. Sukhanov wrote "hundreds of thousands and millions of workers, soldiers and peasants rose up in arms, for defense and for attack, against the class enemy."[161] Trotsky described how while Kerensky was vacillating between negotiations with Kornilov and opposing him in his (Kerensky's) own interests:

> The district Soviets were drawing more closely together and passing resolutions to declare the inter-district conferences continuous: to place their representatives in the staff organized by the Executive Committee, to form a workers' militia. . . . In the total, these resolutions meant an appropriation not only of very considerable governmental functions, but also of the functions of the Petrograd Soviet . . . paralyzed above. . . . The Soviets were reborn again from below at the critical moment under pressure from the masses.[162]

Kornilov's coup was foiled by a tremendous popular upsurge, by the concerted action of Petrograd workers, railway workers and other workers. They combined political agitation with military and technical disorganization of the enemy.

The events connected with the Kornilov coup showed that the government of Kerensky was plotting against the people it supposedly represented. We therefore need to examine it in detail. George Katkov has denounced the idea that a coup was ever intended as a product of Kerensky's imagination.[163] Such a dismissal ignores the tensions that grip left and right alike in a revolutionary period. A right-wing counter-revolutionary coup is a risky venture, just like a left-wing bid for insurrection. Had a coup succeeded, it would have found many friends. Because it failed, as many people as possible rushed to dissociate themselves from it. But the attempt, and the events surrounding it, show that the bourgeois response to the growth of Bolshevism was a plan for shifting the political discourse well to the right, rather than setting up a democratic parliamentary regime. General Kornilov was well-known as an opponent of soldiers committees in the frontline. He had assumed the pose of a "tough" officer, urging the shooting of deserters. So his appointment as Commander-in-Chief was a political signal by Kerensky. He, in turn, demanded and received from the Provisional Government the right to be responsible to his "conscience and the nation" (i.e., he would not be responsible to the government, but only to a vague entity called the nation, rent in two by the impending civil war). At the same time, within the capitalist class as a whole, the July Days brought back a cheer. Lvov, though he had been forced to make way for Kerensky as head of government, now remarked: "It is my firm conviction that our deep breach on the Lenin front has incomparably more importance for Russia than the breach made by the Germans on the South West Front."[164] On July 12, the death penalty was reintroduced. Chernov and Skobelev, the supposedly leftist Ministers of Agriculture and Industry, were trying to reduce the powers of the land committees and the factory committees respectively.

Various capitalist interests were also mobilizing. These include the effort by V. S. Zavoiko, who brought together Petrograd industrialists and bankers, the industrialist A.I. Putilov, who established the Society for the Economic Rehabilitation of Russia, etc. By early August, it was clear that while the Moscow capitalists wanted an economic crisis to force a change in line (this was the content of Ryabushinskii's speech about the "bony hand of hunger"), the Petrograd capitalists wanted a more active role. In brief, there was a fractured capitalist class, but its more determined elements wanted a coup to stamp out the Soviets, including the moderate socialists, not just the Bolsheviks. The lack of any institutional or mass popular base of the government was equally exposed. The first Provisional Government had been a purely bourgeois government, with Kerensky as a decorative "socialist." It had claimed to be an outgrowth of the Fourth Duma. The first coalition had been the institutionalization of the dual power itself. But the new coalition could claim no such legitimacy, however questionable even those institutional bases had been. Nor could it claim popular support. In a bid to create a new base, Kerensky called a State Conference in Moscow. But proletarian Moscow responded with a general strike.[165] The bourgeoisie and the non-Bolshevik socialists were evenly matched, and the Conference served only to expose the lack of a base for the government. The only thing that held back masses was the defeat of the ill-timed July demonstration. After it, the Bolsheviks went into semi-underground. A number of them like Kamenev, Trotsky, and others were arrested, and there was a short period when Bolshevik influence was declining.

Soon, however, popular attitudes began to harden further against the Provisional Government, as well as against the compromisers in the Soviets. There is a wealth of data on this point, and only parts of that data can be reproduced below.

In Petrograd, the Bolshevik slump was very brief. On July 26, six thousand Putilov workers passed a unanimous resolution supporting the Bolsheviks. On August 3 the Bolsheviks replaced the moderates in the sickness fund committees in the Old Lessner and New Lessner factories, having received 80 percent of the votes. Municipal elections everywhere showed them forging ahead of the Mensheviks. In municipal polls in Petrograd on August 20th, they got 184,000 votes against the Mensheviks' 24,000. In Moscow, borough elections in September showed the following: SRs–54,374 votes (14 percent), Mensheviks–15887 (4 percent), Cadets–101,106 (26 percent), and Bolsheviks 198,320 (51 percent, up from 12 percent in June).[166] By August, the battle for the leading stratum of workers was virtually over, with the rout of the Mensheviks. By September, inroads were being made in the SR base of soldiers and less politicized workers.

Following the defeat of Kornilov, there was a brief period when the right wing was completely disarmed. The Bolsheviks again attempted to go over peacefully to Soviet democracy. They recognized that the workers and peasants in their majority wanted a purely socialist government, and proposed that the Menshevik-SR bloc should take power, promising in that case to restrict themselves to peaceful propaganda.[167] Though this perspective had to be abandoned within a few days as the Mensheviks and the SRs began another exercise at building a coalition government, its significance should not be missed. It is obvious that wherever there was a possibility, the Bolsheviks tried to minimize violence and to take power peacefully. It is also clear that this confidence was based on a rising tide in the soviets, factory councils and trade unions, even more than in the municipal bodies. Throughout Russia, from late August, new elections to soviets were being organized. The Bolsheviks made significant gains. Thus, at the Second Congress of the Soviets of Workers' and Soldiers' Deputies of Urals, representing 505,780 workers and soldiers, which met on

August 17–21, the Bolsheviks had 77 deputies against, and 23 for the Mensheviks.[168] On August 31–September 1, the Petrograd Soviet adopted a resolution on power, which led to the resignation of the old executive committee.[169] In Kiev, a Conference of Factory and Shop Committees passed a Bolshevik resolution with 161 votes for, 35 against, and 13 in abstention.[170]

The defeat of the Menshevik–SR bloc in the Petrograd Soviet (279-115 votes) had been questioned by the compromisers. On September 9, the presidium of the Petrograd Soviet insisted that the Soviet must state whether it was changing its line or not, saying it stood for the old line. Both sides had mustered their strength, and the presidium lost by 414 votes to 519, with 67 abstentions.[171]

On September 5, the Moscow Soviet passed a resolution condemning the Provisional Government and the VTsIK by 355 votes to 254.[172] At the Kiev Soviet of Workers' Deputies, the Bolshevik resolution won on September 8th by 130 votes to 66, showing a swing of 35 previously non-Bolshevik delegates to them. On September 10, a regional Congress of Soviets in Finland adopted Bolshevik resolutions by big majorities.[173]

In August, work had barely begun in the rural areas. But by September 21, the Saratov Soviet had 320 Bolsheviks against 103 SRs, 76 Mensheviks, and 34 non-party deputies.[174] In Kronstadt, new elections resulted in a further shift to the left in an already radical Soviet, so that now it had 100 Bolsheviks, 75 Left SRs, 12 Menshevik Internationalists, 7 anarchists, and 90-odd unaffiliated, but mostly left wing, delegates. The right wing of the Soviet spectrum was practically wiped out.[175] Newly elected Soviets in Reval, Dorpat, Wenden, all had a Bolshevik-Left SR majority. In Talinn, the Estonian regional committee elected a little later in October, had 6 Bolsheviks, 4 Left SRs, 1 Menshevik Internationalist, and one rightwing Menshevik.[176]

In Petrograd, Moscow, and the other major centers, the Bolshevik influence grew even more swiftly. From the last week of September, the open struggle between the Bolsheviks and their opponents began for hegemony over the soviets in the final lap of the race for power. The Petrograd Soviet adopted Trotsky's resolution calling for the consolidation and federation of all Soviet organizations and the immediate convocation of the Second All-Russia Congress of Soviets.[177] This unleashed a flood of similar resolutions calling for the assumption of full power by the Congress.[178]

The First Congress of Soviets had stipulated that fresh Congresses were to be called every three months. But the VTsIK now began to hesitate. When, at the urging of the Bolsheviks, it finally decided to call for the Second Congress, scheduling the opening on October 20, 1917, the Executive Committee of the Peasant Soviets, where the Bolsheviks had much less leverage, issued a protest. In the weeks that followed, the supporters of the VTsIK tried to mobilize support for a cancellation of the Congress. At the regional conference of the Donetz Basin and Krivoi Rog area, delegates representing over six hundred thousand workers defeated the Bolsheviks' resolution by 51 votes to 46.[179] But more representative gatherings proclaimed support for the Bolshevik call for a Soviet seizure of power. These included the Moscow regional Congress, the All-Siberian Congress, the regional Congresses at Minsk (Byelo Russia), the Northern Caucasus, provincial Congresses in Vladimir and Tver, etc. But the most important was the Congress of Northern Soviets. Represented in it were Soviets from Petrograd, Moscow, Archangel, Reval, Helsingfors, Kronstadt, Vyborg, Narva, Gatchina, Tsarskoe Selo, the Baltic Fleet, the Petrograd Soviet of Peasant Deputies, the Petrograd District Soviets, and the soldiers' organizations of the Northern, Western, Southwestern, and Rumanian fronts.[180]

The most detailed all-Russia studies, by numerous scholars, disclose that the trend was towards Bolshevism.[181] The Bolsheviks were in the majority in the Workers' Soviets in most industrial cities and in most Soldiers' Soviets in garrison towns, with strongholds in Finland, Estonia, Petrograd, the Northern Front, the Baltic Fleet, the Central Industrial Region (around Moscow), the Urals, Western, and Central Siberia. The Socialist Revolutionaries predominated among the peasants and the frontline committees. Their bases included the black-earth region, the middle Volga, the Western, Southern, and Rumanian fronts. The Mensheviks dominated only in Georgia.

Thus, on the one hand, the Provisional Government continued to lack any democratic base, and on the other, the Soviets became more and more assertive in their bid for power. The last attempt made by the parties of moderate leftism to shore up their position came when they convoked the Democratic Conference on September 14. That Conference, in turn, set up the Council of the Republic, popularly known as the Pre-Parliament. Marc Ferro assesses the significance of the Democratic Conference in the following terms:

> The democratic conference, convoked and organized by the Executive council of the Soviets, reflected in its composition, the great variety of institutions that the Revolution had thrown up rather than their numerical strength or real power. Over thirty types of organization were represented, from the league of clergy and laymen to the Soviets, although the nationalities, for one, had only 43 places out of 1250. . . . [The SR-Menshevik bloc controlling the VTsIK, flouted democracy and] distributed seats as suited them. Workers' and soldiers' Soviets were allotted 230 places, as were the peasant Soviets, whereas the municipal councils took 300, the *zemstva* 200 and the cooperative movement 161.[182]

Notwithstanding all this effort, even this attempt miscarried. The principle of bourgeois participation in government was approved by 766 votes to 688, with 38 abstentions. But then, an amendment excluding the Cadets was also passed with 595 votes against 493 with 72 abstentions.[183] A coalition without the Cadets was a senseless coalition. Kerensky then threatened to resign, refusing to participate in a homogeneous government, and as a result a renewed vote was taken and a Council of Republic created with bourgeois participation. But this was not a genuinely representative body. It was not elected, but nominated by the conference and the government, its composition was the following: 15 percent of all the groups represented in the Democratic Conference, together with one hundred twenty seats for the propertied classes and twenty for the Cossacks.[184] In view of the highly distorted system of representation in the Democratic Conference, it meant that the really representative bodies like the Soviets, peasants' committees, etc., would be underrepresented, while utterly inconsequential bodies would get large representations. As a result, the moderate socialists got far more seats than they could get in Soviets, or in the case of the upper classes, even in municipal dumas (since they were not represented in the Soviets at all). Thus the Council of Republic was not really a representative body. Moreover, the last coalition government which was cobbled together at the same time, was to the right of the previous one. It was more independent of the "democrats." Neither Tseretelli nor the main SR leader Victor Chernov were included in it, unlike in the previous coalition. Instead there were right SRs like Maslov and Avksentiev, and lesser Mensheviks like Skobelev and Prokopovich. With rising Cadet influence, it looked like a potential government of counter-revolution to others besides the Bolsheviks.

This was the context in which Lenin and Trotsky began to work for an insurrection. Lenin's personal role was certainly important, but it was not dictatorial. His central achievement was to make the Bolshevik party and the militant workers understand that however weak the Kerensky government might be, it would not simply give way to a socialist regime. It would have to be forcibly overthrown.

Lenin began calling for insurrection when the Bolsheviks obtained hegemony in the Petrograd and Moscow Soviets by September 1917. This meant, in his view that the active majority of revolutionary elements were with them.[185] As further evidence of the strengthening of the left wing, he cited the growth of internationalist influence among the Mensheviks and SRs. So unlike in April and July when he had attempted to rein in overenthusiastic radicals, he now wanted to spur them forward. As a result, the differences in the Central Committee surfaced anew.[186] Lenin suggested that the large number of party members present as a result of their participation in the Democratic Conference virtually made up a Party Congress, and that they should decide upon the need to steer a course for the revolution.[187]

The struggle in the Central Committee, and throughout the party, was quite serious. A few days' later, Lenin still in hiding, wrote another letter to the Central Committee, entitled "Marxism and Insurrection." He opposed the view that politics of insurrections were always Blanquist. When there was a mass upsurge, when the enemy was in disarray, and when certain other conditions were met, a conspiracy for the technical side of the insurrection was a necessary action, not a Blanquist aberration.[188]

The majority of the Central Committee was hesitant. In its meeting of September 15, the agenda was Lenin's letters. It was decided, with 6 votes to 4 with 6 abstentions, to burn all but one copy of the letter.[189] On September 21, Trotsky's call to boycott the council of the Republic won by single vote, but was overturned by the Bolshevik delegates of the Democratic Conference. Two days' later, the Central Committee, with fifteen members present, voted 8-7 in favor of a proposal to openly confront the moderates' appeal for peace as hypocritical one.[190] But rank and file pressure went to support Lenin and his allies. Bukharin later related that at the Democratic Conference:

> the sailors posted by Kerensky to defend the Democratic conference against us, the Bolsheviks, turned to Trotsky and asked him, shaking their bayonets: "How soon can we get to work with these things?"[191]

Lenin's strategy appreciated this mood and was built upon it. He proposed that the question whether the party was to boycott the Pre-Parliament or not should be made the central plank of a platform for internal elections in the party.[192] Finally, on October 5 the Central Committee decided to withdraw from the Pre-Parliament, with Kamenev expressing his dissent.[193] On October 7, Trotsky, on behalf of the Bolshevik fraction of the Pre-Parliament, read out a statement denouncing the Pre-Parliament as "a new edition of the Bulygin Duma," an unrepresentative and counter-revolutionary body, and said, "we, the Social Democratic Bolshevik group, declare we have nothing in common with this government that betrays the people and with this council which connives at counter-revolution."[194] This was a call for an insurrection.

> The boycott of parliamentary institutions on the part of anarchists and semi-anarchists is dictated by a desire not to submit their weakness to a test. . . . A revolutionary party can turn its back to a parliament only if it has set itself the immediate task of overthrowing the existing regime.[195]

This was the explanation given by Trotsky later. And it corresponded to the view of the boycott taken by observers and opponents. Miliukov wrote that the Bolsheviks spoke and acted like "people feeling a power behind them, knowing that the morrow belonged to them."[196] And Sukhanov wrote that the boycott meant that only one road was left, the road to the barricades. If they cast away the electoral ballot, they must take up the rifle.[197]

The fact that the Central Committee ultimately took its stance unequivocally in favor of an uprising was certainly due to the pressure mounted by Lenin. He was willing to go over its head and appeal to lower bodies. As in April, he used the pressure of those closer to the masses to straighten out the vacillations in the Central Committee. Members of the Vyborg Committee learnt that Lenin had been posing the question of an insurrection. Sveshnikov, a member of that Committee, wrote later in memoirs quoted by Trotsky: "We raised a row. We began to bring pressure on them [i.e., the C.C.]."[198]

However, this was the extent of Lenin's influence. Much is made of certain proposals made by Lenin, so they should be briefly examined. Impatient at what he considered the dilatory tactics of the Central Committee, he put forward a proposal to Smilga, that the latter, as chairman of the Regional Committee of the Army, Navy and Workers of Finland, could call out troops, overthrow Kerensky, and hand over power to the Congress of Soviets.[199] Two days' later, in an article entitled "The Crisis has Matured," he objected to waiting for the Congress of Soviets, on the ground that time would be lost and Cossacks would be mobilized against any seizure of power.[200] He also suggested that the insurrection should be called directly by the party, rather than by the Soviets, and if necessary in Moscow, rather than in Petrograd.[201] He wrote repeatedly that "To 'wait' for the Congress of Soviets is idiocy,"[202] or that "To wait for the congress of Soviets would be a childish game of formalities, a disgraceful game of formalities, and a betrayal of the revolution."[203]

It is not true that with these proposals, he was suggesting that Soviet democracy be rejected in favor of party dictatorship. As the proposal to Smilga showed explicitly, he wanted power to go to the Congress of Soviets. But he was apprehensive that those who were actually opposed to staging the insurrection were taking refuge behind the slogan of waiting for the Soviet Congress. At the same time, his proposals also showed his failure to understand how far the organization of the insurrection could be assisted if it was launched in the name of the Soviets. On this issue his opponent was Trotsky, who devised a different tactical approach to the uprising.

When the old executive committee of the Petrograd Soviet had resigned, Trotsky had been elected the new chairman. From this position, he symbolized Bolshevism to the mass of workers and soldiers. Also, from this position, he was better able to feel the pulse of the workers and soldiers. He was sanguine that for the insurrection to succeed, it had to be made through the Petrograd Soviet. The Central Committee majority, while agreeing on the need for an insurrection, likewise differed with Lenin's tactical proposals. On October 15, there was a meeting of the Central Committee, the Petersburg Committee and other prominent activists. The discussions revealed that many activists, including some who had been to the left of Lenin during the July Days, felt that an uprising in the name of the party would not get adequate popular support.[204] The next day, there was a meeting of the Central Committee which Lenin could at last attend. There too, reports were presented that showed that an uprising organized by the Petrograd Soviet would be more popular than one organized by the party.[205]

This was possible for a number of reasons. As shown earlier, in many Soviets, the majority was left, but not purely Bolshevik. The leftists included Left SRs, anarchists (mainly in factory committees, but also in a few Soviets like Kronstadt), left-wing Mensheviks, etc. The Left SR support was vital above all, for they represented the revolutionary peasantry. Another reason for sticking to the Soviets was that the long established dual power tradition could be used to screen offensive moves. Thus, when a rumor arose concerning a counter-revolutionary plan to abandon the capital, Trotsky formally proposed an all-out opposition to any transfer of seat of the government out of Petrograd. On October 11 he spoke before the Congress of Northern Soviets: "Our government can run away from Petrograd, but the revolutionary people will never leave Petrograd."[206] The Petrograd Soviet became aware that Kerensky was trying to transfer many of the military units out of Petrograd. The Executive Committee of the Soviet decided to respond by creating a Committee of Defence, soon to be renamed Military Revolutionary Committee. This was an executive organ of the Petrograd Soviet, and the tasks given to it included both defensive and offensive ones.[207] Trotsky did not move according to a set plan, but improvised, using events as they came up. A delegation of workers came to him and said that they needed weapons, which an arms factory would supply if the Soviet ordered it. Trotsky gave an initial order for five thousand rifles, which was immediately complied with.[208] In the same way, the Garrison conference of October 18 saw almost the entire garrison declaring their readiness to come out at the call of the Petrograd Soviet.[209] On the same day, Trotsky issued a declaration:

> I declare in the name of the Soviet: we have not been planning any kind of armed initiative. However, if the course of events forced the Soviet to take an initiative, workers and soldiers would respond. . . . At the first attempt . . . to disrupt the Congress of Soviet . . . we shall answer with a counter attack.[210]

This gave the complete definition of the intended insurrection a political offensive under the formula of military defense. The VTsIK postponed the Soviet Congress by six days at the last moment. The Petrograd Soviet put the six days to good use. On the night of October 21, General Polkovnikov, in charge of the Petrograd garrison, refused to allow any access to the Military Revolutionary Committee (MRC). The MRC responded by calling on the soldiers not to accept any directive unless countersigned by the MRC.[211] On October 23, Trotsky won over the garrison at the Peter and Paul Fortress and the Kronverk Arsenal.[212] As yet, every step had been taken by pointing to the quite genuine counter-revolutionary threat and calling for defense. Trotsky's strategy was thus covered by Soviet legality. He was aware that the masses were in favor of action by the Soviets. By the 24th, when the insurrection began, it had been virtually secured. The government's attempt at this stage, to close down the Bolshevik press, provided the perfect scope. The MRC stated, on October 24 that "Two revolutionary papers, *Rabochii put* and *Soldat*, have been closed down by the plotters from the General staff. The Soviet will not tolerate the strangling of free speech."[213] The insurrection had begun. The deceptive ruses were intended for the enemy. For the working masses, at each stage the Bolsheviks proclaimed the goal of Soviet power, and explained that it could be established by overthrowing the Provisional Government.

Later, in his *History*, Trotsky explained the nature of class-party relationship as it had developed on the eve of the revolution:

> The Party set the Soviets in motion, the Soviets set in motion the workers, soldiers and to some extent the peasantry. What was gained in mass was lost in speed. If you represent this conducting apparatus as a system of cog-wheels . . . the impatient attempt to connect the party directly with the gigantic wheel of the masses—omitting the medium sized wheel of the Soviets—would have given rise to the danger of breaking the teeth of the party wheel, and nevertheless not setting sufficiently large masses in motion.[214]

In so far as the October insurrection meant a total rupture with the remnants of the Tsarist state, as well as the emerging bourgeois state, the revolution's victory meant, not a continuity of the old legality, but its destruction, however peaceful the revolution might be. But, the degree of the Bolsheviks' commitment to Soviet democracy and Soviet legality is a different matter. As long as there existed Provisional Government, claiming (though with indifferent success) the allegiance of the troops, it was pointless to imagine that a Congress of Soviets could meet and decide to take over power, without meeting armed resistance from the government. The political decision for the insurrection came from the

Bolshevik party. But the actual work was organized by the Petrograd Soviet. It did so, in full knowledge that what decision the Second Congress of Soviets would adopt depended on who controlled the guns.

At the Second Congress, there were fewer representatives than at the first, for some Menshevik dominated Soviets simply did not participate. But among approximately 650 delegates, the Bolsheviks had 390. All SRs together had about 160 at the beginning. After the walkout of the Right SRs, the Left SRs claimed 179 or 180. Since the Left SRs supported the insurrection, the Congress showed a massive majority for the seizure of power.[215]

By early December, the base of the Soviet regime set up by the Second Congress had expanded further. The old TsIK of the Peasant Soviets had opposed the Soviet seizure of power, but it had to call an emergency Congress on November 23. Out of the 335 voting delegates to the Congress, 195 were Left SRs. Together with 37 Bolsheviks and 22 anarchists, they formed a more than three quarters bloc in favor of he new regime. At the Second All-Russian Peasant Congress which met from December 9 to 25, there were 789 delegates. Among them were 350 Left SRs, 91 Bolsheviks, and 305 Right SRs. The Left SR Maria Spiridonova defeated Victor Chernov to be elected chairperson. On December 17, the right-wing minority split, while the left-wing majority elected an executive committee of 81 Left SRs and 20 Bolsheviks, which merged with the VTsIK elected by the Second Congress of Soviets.[216]

In view of the foregoing, it is possible to accept as genuine the argument put forward by Trotsky, that:

> The relations between the party and the Soviet grew out of the disaccord inevitable in a revolutionary epoch between the colossal political influence of Bolshevism and its narrow organisational grasp. A lever correctly applied makes the human arm capable of lifting a weight many times exceeding its living force, but without the living arm the lever is nothing but a dead stick.[217]

Thus, the Soviet organizational form enabled the politics of Bolshevism to reach out tremendously in the epoch of revolution, but it was Bolshevik politics, as enriched by the influx of continuous fresh blood from the masses, that was responsible for the insurrection. As William G. Rosenberg explains in his contribution to a collection of essays on the revolution:

> Lenin came to power without significant resistance. And here it is . . . the fact that Bolsheviks came to power through and for the notion of Soviet rule—the idea widely believed in October, that Russia's vast network of local and regional councils . . . headed by a national Congress of Soviets was better able to solve the crises of everyday political administration [that is important].[218]

In other words, faith in workers' democracy was not simply limited to the

Bolsheviks. The entire working class, the peasants, and the soldiers had accepted it in preference to parliamentary democracy. The insurrection was only the climactic moment of this attempt to put its principles into practice.

In conclusion, it should be pointed out that the Bolsheviks gave ample evidence of their adherence to workers' democracy. On several issues their program was modified in the light of popular aspirations. For example, the Bolshevik agrarian program did not find much support among the peasants. At the First Congress of Peasant Deputies, the positions taken reflected a pro-SR stance. A model decree was also issued. Since the SRs were unwilling to implement these demands of the peasants, nothing was done until October. Clashes and peasant disturbances increased steadily.[219] It was Lenin who adopted the demands of the peasants and incorporated them in the Decree on Land that he placed before the Second Congress of Soviets. Similarly, the idea of workers' control, through taken up by the Bolsheviks, had originated among the masses, not in the old party program.

The October insurrection was a case of one of history's great mass mobilizations, not a coup. The very success of the mobilization made possible a nearly bloodless conquest of power. All the talk of violence in fact conflates the Civil War with the October Revolution. What came after the revolution showed, not the mindless violence of the Bolsheviks, but the degree to which the former ruling classes were willing to go in order to defend their property and privileges.

NOTES

1. For Trotsky's views see L. Trotsky, *1905*, and L. Trotsky, *The Permanent Revolution*.
2. *LCW* 21, Moscow, 1980, p. 33.
3. Ibid. 9, p. 27.
4. For two studies of the evolution, see N. Harding, *Lenin's Political Thought*, vol. 2, and K. Chattopadhyay, *Leninism and Permanent Revolution*, pp. 46–64.
5. *LCW* 23, Moscow, 1981, pp. 297, 304, 306–7, 323, 325–26, 342.
6. R. C. Elwood, ed., *The RSDLP*, pp. 198–9.
7. This is a fact of some importance, and will be taken up in detail, along with the consideration of this, as well as other leaflets of late February, in section II below.
8. *Pravda*, March 9, 1917.
9. Quoted in T. Cliff, *Lenin*, vol. 2. *All power to the Soviets*, London, 1977, p. 104.
10. *Pravda*, March 15, 1917.
11. See T. Cliff, *Lenin*, vol. 2, pp. 106–7.
12. L. Trotsky, *The Stalin School of Falsification*, New York, 1979, pp. 236–39

13. *LCW* 24, Moscow, 1980, p. 23
14. W. G. Rosenberg, *Liberals in the Russian Revolution*, Princeton, 1974, pp. 128–29.
15. O. Radkey, *Agrarian Foes of Bolshevism*, New York, 1958, p. 194.
16. *Rabochii i Soldat*, July 24, 1917.
17. V. I. Lenin, "The Tasks of the Proletariat in our Revolution," in *LCW* 24, pp. 58.
18. Ibid., pp. 60–62.
19. Ibid., pp. 23–24.
20. Ibid., pp. 68–69.
21. Ibid., pp. 58–59.
22. Ibid., pp. 71–72.
23. For Lenin's defense of collectivist measures, see V. I. Lenin, "The Tasks of the Proletariat in the present Revolution," "Resolution on the Agrarian Question at the 7th (April) All-Russia Conference," and "Draft of the Revised Programme" in *LCW* 24, pp. 23, 168–69, 292–93, 477–78. At the April Conference of the party, he spoke of preaching socialism to the small peasants, while Rykov, one of the "Old Bolsheviks" who opposed him, said that it was impossible to win petty bourgeois peasants to the socialist cause, see *Sedmaia (Aprelskaia) Konferentsiia RSDRP, Petrogradskaia Obshchegorodskaia RSDRP (bol'shevikov,)* Moscow, 1958, pp. 68, 72–73 (Lenin), and 107 (Rykov).
24. *Rabochii Put*, September 16, 1917.
25. V. I. Lenin, "The Dual Power" and "Letters on Tactics" in *LCW* 24, pp. 40, 45, 48–52.
26. See L.Trotsky, *History of the Russian Revolution, 3v*, London, 1967, vol. 1, pp. 145–48.
27. See L. H. Haimson, "The Problem of Social Stability in Urban Russia: 1905–1917," pt 1. *Slavic Review*, vol. 23, December 1964, pp. 619–42; pt. 2, *Slavic Review* vol. 24, no. 1, March 1965, pp. 1–22. See further R. T. Manning, *The Crisis of the Old Order in Russia: Gentry and Government*. For the left and the radicalization, see I. I. Kirianov, "On the Nature of the Russia Working Class," *Soviet Studies in History*, vol. 2, no. 3, Winter 1983/1984: V. E. Bonnell, *Roots of Rebellion*, 393–408, 427–34; R. Zelink, "Russian Workers and the Revolutionary Movement," *Journal of Social History*, vol. 6, no. 2 Winter 1972/73.
28. The view that the February Revolution had no leader is very much a politically motivated picture. It is then counterposed to the picture of a party compelling the working class to move like chess pieces. Both Stalinist and post-Stalinist historiography in the USSR, and right-wing historiography in the west put forward such views. The Soviet version of the "infallible party" of October is sufficiently discredited to require no refutation. But its mirror image is still present, as when Richard Pipes writes: "Lenin, Trotsky, and their associates seized power by forces . . . a violent act carried out by a tiny minority. Furthermore, this power seized was carried out under false pretenses. The coup d'etat of October 1917 was accomplished not on behalf of the Bolshevik party but on behalf of

the Soviets. . . . In reality they used them (i.e., the party used the Soviets) from the beginning as a facade behind which to consolidate their own authority." R. Pipes, "Why the Russians Act Like Russians," *Air Force Magazine,* June 1970, pp. 51–55.

29. See R. G. Suny, "Toward a social history of the October Revolution" *American Historical Review,* no. 88, 1983, pp. 31–52.

30. L. Trotsky, *History of the Russian Revolution,* vol. 1, p. 77.

31. Ibid., p. 49 for the strike figures; G. Swain, *Russian Social Democracy and the Legal Labour Movement,* pp. 70–73 for an account of the anti-strike attitude of the liquidators.

32. G. Swain, p. 168.

33. I. P. Leiberov and O.I. Shkaratan, "K voprosu o sostave petrogradskikh promyshlennykh rabochikh v 97g," *Voprosy isotorii,* no. 1, 1961, pp. 53–54.

34. P. I. Lyashchenko, *History of the National Economy of Russia,* New York, 1949, p. 762. S. A. Smith, *Red Petrograd,* Cambridge, 1983, p. 9–10, 19, Leiberov and Shkaratan, op. cit.

35. Based on S.A. Smith, *Red Petrograd,* Table 2, p.11; J. H. Bater, *St. Petersburg: Industrialisation and Change,* Montreal, 1976; and Smith, p. 13.

36. Based on I. P. Leiberov, "Stachechnaya bor'ba Petrogradskogo proletariata v period pervoi mirovoi voiny (19 iyulya 1914g–16 fevralya 1917g)." *Istoriya rabochego klassa Leningrada,* no. 2., Leningrad, 1963, pp. 166, 177, 183.

37. Ibid., and L. Trotsky, *History of the Russian Revolution,* vol. 1, pp. 55–56. T. Cliff, *Lenin,* vol. 2, provides the data that in 1915, in the country as a whole there were 928 strikes (p. 270).

38. See in this context T. Hasegawa, "The Formation of the Militia in the February Revolution: An Aspect of the Origin of Dual Power," *Slavic Review,* vol. 32, no. 2, pp. 303–22, 1973.

39. His first works were E. N. Burdzhalov, "O taktike Bol'shevikov marte-aprele 1917 goda," *Voprosy Istorii, 1956,* no. 4; and "Eshche O taktike Bol'shevikov v marte-aprele 1917 goda," *Voprosy Isotorii,* 1956, no. 8. "Orthodox" or Stalinist/, neo-stalinist replies, highlighting the "correctness" of the party's role, the speed with which it responded to events, etc. came from I. I. Mints, "Ob osvesheneii nekotorykh Voprosy istroii velikoi Oktyabr'skoi sotsialisticheskoi revolyutsii," *Voprosy istorii KPSS,* 1957, no. 2, February; and E. K. Bartshtein, and L. M. Shalagineva, "Partiya Bol'shevikov vo glave revoliutsionnogo pod'ema mass v period podgotovki i provedeniya fevral'sko burzhuazno-demokraticheskoi revoliutsii,' *Voprosy Istorii KPSS,* 1957. 'Burdzhalov later refined his views and published his *Vtoraya russkaya revolyutsiya,* Moscow, 1967. Mints and a team of his colleagues wrote the official I. I. Mints, *Istoriia Velikogo Oktiabria,* 2 vols., Moscow, 1967. A survey of the Soviet debate of the 1950s and early 1960s is available in L. Schapiro, "Continuity and Change in the New History of the CPSU," in J. L. H. Keep, ed., *Contemporary History in the Soviet Mirror,* New York and London, 1964, pp. 69–82. See also T. Hasegawa, "Bolsheviks and the Formation of the Petrograd Soviet in the February Revolution," *Soviet Studies,* vol. 29, no. 1, January, 1977, pp. 86–107. M. Melancon, "Who wrote what and when?: Proclamations

of the February Revolution in Petrograd,   February 23, March 1917,"
Soviet Studies, vol. 40, no. 3, July 1988, pp. 479–500; D. A. Longley, "The
Mezhraionka, the Bolsheviks and International Women's Day: In response
to Michael Melancon," *Soviet Studies*, vol. 41, no. 4, October, 1989, pp.
625–45; J. D. White, "The February Revolution and the Bolshevik Vyborg
District Committee (in response to Michael Melancon), *Soviet Studies*, vol.
41, no. 4, pp. 602–24. These works carry on a debate over the role of the
Bolsheviks, and in the process show that the revolution of 1917 cannot
be ascribe, to manipulative committeemen.

40. See D. Mandel, *The Petrograd Workers and the Fall of the Old Regime*,
    especially pp. 63–64; L. Trotsky, *History of the Russian Revolution*, vol. 1,
    p. 109 quotes the Vyborg Bolshevik Kayurov as writing that he agreed
    to the strike with reluctance.

41. N. Sveshnikov, "Vyborgskii raionnyi Komitet RSDRP (B)," in *Vogne
    revoliutsionnykh boev: raiony Petrograda dvukh revoliutsiyakh 1917g*, Moscow
    1987, pp. 83–84.

42. L.Trotsky, *History of the Russian Revolution*, vol. 1, p. 125.

43. For the text of the Workers' Group appeal, "Pis'mo rabochei gruppy:
    Tsentralnogo Voino Promyshlennogo Komiteta Abresovannoe brugim
    gruppam Voino-Promyshlennik Komitetov," see D. A. Longley, "The
    Mezhraionka, the Bolsheviks and International Women's Day: In response
    to Michael Melancon," pp. 634–35. For the leaflet of the Inter-Borough
    Organization or Mezhraionka, see ibid., pp. 641–42. Longley believes that
    the call was purely rhetorical. However, it should be kept in mind that the
    Workers' Group was connected to the liberal circles who were speculating,
    before February, about the need to overthrow or remove the autocracy
    from above. The call for a "provisional revolutionary government" did
    not specify the class content of such a government, and it could well have
    been a call to support a liberal government. See further, the Octobrist
    leader Guchkov's letter to General Alexiev in G. Katkov, *Russia 1917, The
    February Revolution*, London, 1967, p. 257. As for the Mezhraiontsi, their
    leader Iurenev later published his memoirs, "Mezhraionka, 1911–1917gg"
    Proletarskaya Revolyutsiya 2, (1924). Longley suggest that in 1924, it was
    the official party line to show that in February, there was no Bolshevik
    leadership, so Iureniev's article depicting his group as standing to the left
    of the official stand of the Bolshevik Russian Bureau only reflected the
    party line. This is a dubious argument. If the authenticity of the leaflets
    in question is not impugned, then their meanings cannot be sought in
    the "line" of 1924, even if it at all existed. The meaning has to be sought
    in the context of the 1917 motivations. The existing evidence shows that
    the Mezhraionka, despite their small size, played a significant role. They
    called for a Soviet quite early. They issued the appeal to the soldiers.
    They had a more flexible approach, because they had no ideological
    commitment to hierarchies in the party. In 1924, moreover, the dictatorial
    clampdown on writing was yet to come, Shylapnikov was able to publish
    his book, which adhered to no "official line," Consequently, the evidence
    must be taken as it stands, namely, the Mezhraiontsi had campaigned

for a provisional government. In their case, this meant something quite different from their the same words meant for the Workers' Group. As allies of the liberals, the latter wanted a liberal government, and the leader of this group, Gvozdev, subsequently became a minister in the Provisional government. The Mezhraionka leaflets show a call to form Soviets. Moreover, they eventually joined the Bolsheviks at the sixth Party Congress.

44. Authorship of these leaflets continues to be disputed. Hasegawa, 'The Bolsheviks,' and I. I. Mints, *Istoriia Velikogo Oktiabria*, pp. 18–19 attribute it to the Bolsheviks. Iurenev's article shows that the Mezharionka had raised the slogan of Soviets. The debate between Melancon and Longley is partly over the relative roles of the Bolsheviks and Mezhraiontsi, while that between Melancon and White is over the leaflet calling for Soviets, with Melancon attributing it the Mezhraiontsi, and White maintaining it was a rank and file Bolshevik leaflet.

45. For a more detailed discussion, the reader is referred to Soma Marik, "Proletarian Socialism and Women's Liberation: The Historical Roots of Socialist-Feminism," in the *Proceedings of the Indian History Congress*, Calcutta Session, Calcutta 2001; and Soma Marik, "Gendering the Revolutionary Party: The Bolshevik Practice and the Challenge before Marxists in the 21st Century," in Biswajit Chatterjee and Kunal Chattopadhyay, eds., *Perspectives on Socialism*.

46. See, e.g., R. Pipes, ed., *Revolutionary Russia*, pp. 119–20, 282; L. Schapiro, *The Communist Party of the Soviet Union*, pp. 175–77; R. V. Daniels, *Red October*, New York, 1967, pp. 19–20, 39–40; S.W. Page, ed., *Lenin; Dedicated Marxist or Revolutionary Pragmatist*, Lexington, 1970, p. 59.

47. There exist several such works, both on the broad canvas, and micro-studies. See, e.g., D. Koenker, Moscow *Workers and the 1917 Revolution*, Princeton, 1981; D. Mandel, The *Petrograd Workers and the Fall of the Old Regime*.

48. Quoted in E. Burdzhalov, *Vtoraya Russkaya Revolyutsiya*, p. 211.

49. M. Ferro, *The Russian Revolution of February 1917*, London, 1972 (hereafter cited as *February Revolution*) despite his intention of writing a social history of the revolution, overlooks the social divide and the aims of the lower ranks, and ends up by contrasting the Bolshevik Russian Bureau, which be calls Leninist (by which he means that it was opposed to Soviets) and the Workers' Group. See pp. 43–48.

50. L. Trotsky, *History of the Russian Revolution*, vol. I, p. 154.

51. See T. Hasegawa, *The February Revolution*, Seattle, 1981, pp. 323, 341

52. T. Cliff, *Lenin*, vol. 2, p. 160; and I. I. Mints, *Isotoriia Velikogo Oktiabria*, vol. 1, p. 319.

53. As late as June, at the Student Congress of Voronezh gubernia, the Bolsheviks had only 16 delegates out of 250.

54. W. G. Rosenberg, *Liberals in the Russian Revolution*, pp. 154–55, 469, Rosenberg believes that this failure of the cadet left-wing alone prevented a successful stabilization of the revolution on a bourgeois democratic basis.

55. For a discussion of the social causes behind the failure of an ultimate

rapprochement between cadets and the moderate left, see R. G. Suny, "Some Thoughts on 1917: In lieu of a Review of William Rosenberg's *Liberals in the Russian Revolution;* in *Sbornik: Papers of the First Conference of the Study Group* on the Russian Revolution," London, 1980, p. 183.

56. W. Rosenberg, *Liberals in the Russian Revolution*, p. 188. For a general discussion on the problems of a parliamentary alternative see Mike Haynes, "Was there a Parliamentary Alternative in Russia in 1917?," *International Socialism*, 76, Autumn, 1997, pp. 3–66.

57. See, for example, K. Kautsky, *The Road to Power*, Chicago, 1909; K. Kautsky, *Selected Political Writings*, London, 1983; M. Salvadori, *Karl Kautsky and the Socialist Revolution: 1880–1938*, London, 1979.

58. Quoted in N. N. Sukhanov, *The Russian Revolution*, London, 1955, p. 258.

59. M. Ferro, *February Revolution*, pp. 50–51.

60. Ibid., p. 53.

61. N. N. Sukhanov, The Russian Revolution, p. 61.

62. M. Ferro, *February Revolution*, p. 79, and M. Ferro, *The Bolshevik Revolution*, London, 1985, p. 183.

63. See G. I. Zlokazov in *Oktyabr' i grazhdanskaya v SSSR*, Moscow, 1966.

64. Quoted in M. Ferro, *February Revolution*, pp. 59–60.

65. Quoted by W. H. Chamberlin, *The Russian Revolution*, vol. 1, New Jersey, 1987, p. 101.

66. L. Trotsky, *History of the Russian Revolution*, vol. 1, pp. 202–3.

67. Ibid., p. 192.

68. M. Ferro, *February Revolution*, pp. 79–80.

69. On the militias see R. A. Wade, "Workers' Militia and the Red Guards," R. C. Elwood, ed., *Reconsiderations on the Russian Revolution*, Columbus, Ohio, 1976.

70. Cited in O. Anweiler, *The Soviets*, p. 130.

71. Cited in T. Hasegawa, *The February Revolution*, p. 402.

72. See D. Mandel, *The Petrograd Workers and the fall of the Old Regime*, p. 87.

73. R. C. Elwood, ed., *the RSDLP*, p. 197.

74. Ibid., p. 200.

75. Ibid., pp. 204–5.

76. Minutes of the Conference, in L. Trotsky, *The Stalin School of Falsification*, pp. 241–42.

77. See Chapter 8 for a discussion.

78. *LCW* 23, pp. 324–25.

79. Ibid., 24, pp. 23, 68.

80. V. I. Lenin, "Political Parties in Russia and the task of the Proletariat," in ibid., p. 100.

81. R. C. Elwood, ed., *The RSDLP*, p. 223. See also *KPSS v rezoliutsiiakh i reshenniakh S'ezdov, konferentsii i plenumov Tsk*, Moscow, 1954, vol. 1, pp. 452–55 for the extent of opposition to Lenin.

82. L. Trotsky, *The Stalin School of Falsification.*, p. 258.

83. O. Anweiler, *The Soviets*, pp. 160–61.

84. L. Trotsky, *History of the Russian Revolution*, vol. 1, p. 329.

85. D. Koenker, *Moscow Workers and the 1917 Revolution*, p. 304.

86. *Rabotnitsa*, no. 3, May 20, 1917.
87. *Golos Kozhevnika*, 4/5, December 1, 1917, 234, cited in S. A. Smith, *Red Petrograd*, p. 155.
88. See M. Donald, "Bolshevik Activity Amongst the Working Women of Petrograd in 1917." See also *Pravda*, May 7, 1917 and May 31, 1917.
89. *Pervyi legalnyi Peterburgskii komitet Bolshevikov v 1917g*, Moscow, 1927, p. 33.
90. Ibid., p. 40
91. Lyudmilla Stal, a prominent Bolshevik woman, made this point later in her memoirs of 1917. See M. Donald, "Bolshevik Activity Amongst the Working Women of Petrograd in 1917," p. 137.
92. Ibid., p. 139.
93. B. Evans Clements, *Bolshevik Feminist: The Life of Alexandra Kollontai*, pp. 111–12.
94. See *Pravda*, November 26, 1917.
95. *Rabotnitsa*, May 30, 1917.
96. L. Trotsky, *The Stalin School of Falsification*, pp. 268 (Voitinsky), 274 (Stalin), 274–75 (Molotov and Zalutsky).
97. V. I. Lenin, "Draft Theses, March 4 (17), 1917," *LCW* 23, pp. 287–88, 292, 303, 334 (opposition to Government); V. I. Lenin, "Letter to Alexandra Kollontai," in ibid. 35, Moscow, 1980, p. 298 (no unity).
98. *LCW* 24, pp. 40, 45, 50.
99. *Pravda*, April 7, 1917.
100. *Pravda*, April 8, 1917.
101. See A. L. Sidorov, et al., eds., *Velikaia Oktiabrskaya Sotsialisticheskaya Revolyutsiia: Dokumenty i materialy*, Moscow, 1957, vol. 2, pp. 15–16
102. L. Trotsky, *History of the Russian Revolution*, vol. 1, p. 306.
103. *Sed'maia (Aprel'skaia) Vserossiskaia Konferentsiia RSDRP (Bolshevikov)* Moscow, 1958, pp. 50, 106.
104. Ibid., p. 373.
105. Ibid., p. 372.
106. Ibid., p. 228
107. P. F. Kudelli, ed., *Pervyi Legalnyi Peterburgskii komitet Bolshevikov v 1917g*, Moscow, 1927, p. 157.
108. Ibid., p. 158, See *Pravda*, June 10, for the Central Committee statement.
109. A. Rabinowitch, *Prelude to Revolution*.
110. *LCW* 25, p. 81.
111. *The Bolsheviks and the October Revolution*, Minutes of the Central Committee of the Russia Social Democratic Labour party (Bolsheviks), August 1917–February 1918, London, 1974, translated by Anne Bone, with additional notes by T. Cliff, p. 67.
112. M. Liebman, *Leninism Under Lenin*, p. 153. Zinoviev had by then clearly come down on Kamenev's side.
113. *The Bolsheviks and the October Revolution*, pp. 88–89, Incidentally, this body, like the Military Centre created on October 16, did not provide any real leadership. That was done by those who led openly, in the Soviet.
114. See ibid., p. 112. See also *Rabochii Put* (the name under which *Pravda* was then being published), October 20, 1917.

115. *The Bolsheviks and the October Revolution*, p. 10.
116. Ibid., p. 41. For the CC's revised decision, see p. 38.
117. The fullest discussion on membership is in T. H. Rigby, *Communist Party Membership in the USSR, 1917–1967*, Princeton, 1968. For the pre-revolution figures, see L. Schapiro, *The Communist Party*, p. 172. The April figures are in *Sedmaia Konferentsiia*. The Sixth Congress figure is in LCW 25, p. 260. Schapiro challenges this, suggesting the lower figure of two hundred thousand, ibid., p. 173.
118. Based on data in *Voprosy Istorii KPSS*, no. 2, 1958.
119. B. Evans Clements, *Bolshevik Women*, p. 126, Table 14 and p. 136, Table 15.
120. For full details see ibid., chapter 3.
121. *LCW* 24, pp. 145–46.
122. R. P. Browder and A. F. Kerensky, *The Russian Provisional Government 1917–Documents*, Stanford, 1961, vol. 2, p. 1098.
123. L. Trotsky, *History of the Russian Revolution*, vol. 1, pp. 318–19.
124. *LCW* 24, pp. 201–3.
125. Ibid., pp. 210–11.
126. Ibid., pp. 244.
127. I. Getzler, *Kronstadt 1917–1921*, Cambridge, 1983, pp. 1, 11, 35; E. Mawdsley, *The Russian Revolution and the Baltic fleet*, London, 1978, pp. 34, 159, 164.
128. *Sedmaia (Aprelskaia) Vserossiskaia Konferentsiia RSDRP*, p. 355.
129. See I. Getzler, *Kronstadt*, p. 73; F. F. Raskolnikov, *Kronstadt and Petrograd* in 1917, London, 1982, pp. 96, 104; L. Trotsky, *History of the Russian Revolution*, vol. 1, pp. 401–2.
130. See M. Donald, "Bolshevik Activity Amongst the Working Women of Petrograd in 1917." See also *Pravda*, May 7, 1917 and May 31, 1917.
131. For the party-wise break up of the Soviet Congress delegates see M. Ferro, *February Revolution*, p. 306. The left vote never rose over 160 out of 1090. For the municipal election, see p. 234.
132. For the full text, see M. Ferro, *February Revolution*, pp. 311–13. *Pravda*, June 10, which was to carry by appeal, came out with a blank space.
133. N. N. Sukhanov, *The Russian Revolution*, p. 395.
134. I. Deutscher, *The Prophet Armed*, London, 1976, p. 268.
135. After the massive rewriting of history in the Stalin era, this was attributed to Lenin. See *LCW* 25, pp. 77–78. See however, Trotsky, *Sochineniia*, vol. 3, Moscow, 1924, Book 1, p. 137 for the text. This is incontrovertible evidence that Trotsky was indeed the author.
136. *LCW* 25, p. 77.
137. See A. Rabinowitch, *Prelude to Revolution*, pp. 131–34, for an inflammatory article in *Soldatskaia Pravda*, the Military Organization's paper, and for a contrast between *Pravda* and this paper.
138. *LCW* 25 pp. 83, 114–15.
139. A. Rabinowitch, *Prelude to Revolution*, pp. 137–38.
140. L. Trotsky, *History of the Russian Revolution*, vol. 2, p. 37
141. Ibid., p. 40.
142. *LCW* 25, p. 316. See also V. I. Lenin, "Constitutional Illusions," in ibid., p.

206: "It was the imperative duty of the proletarian party to remain with the masses and try to lend as peaceable and organized a character as possible to their justified action."

143. D. Koenker, *Moscow Workers*, pp. 122–23.

144. V. I. Lenin, "Lessons of the Revolution" *LCW* 25, pp. 178–80, 196–210, 229–243.

145. V. I. Lenin, "On Slogans," in ibid., pp. 185–92.

146. L. Trotsky, *What Next? And Other Writings from 1917*, London, 1988, p. 3.

147. Cf., A. Rabinowitch, *Prelude to Revolution*.

148. M. Liebman, *Leninism under Lenin*, p. 154.

149. V. I. Lenin, "Our Thanks to Prince G. Y. Lvov," in *LCW* 25, pp 193–95, quotation from p. 195. Moscow, 1980.

150. Ibid., p. 287.

151. Ibid., pp. 379–81.

152. Ibid., p. 382.

153. Ibid; A modern equivalent would be to say that every major party should have equal radio and TV time.

154. See Dan's speech, in M. Jones, *Storming the Heavens: Voices of October*, London, 1987, p. 85

155. L. Schapiro, *The Origins of Communist Autocracy*; R. Pipes, *The Russian Revolution*, p. 491; R. Schlesinger, *History of the Communist Party of the USSR*, Calcutta, 1977, p. 123; E. J. Hobsbawm, "Waking from History's Great Dream," 1990; D. W. Lovell, *From Marx to Lenin* p. 164; M. Ferro, *The Bolshevik Revolution*, pp. 257–58; all hold some sort of view of the October Revolution as a coup. For a critical discussion of the mainstream Western historiography, see S. Cohen, *Rethinking the Soviet Experience.*

156. L. Trotsky, *History of the Russian Revolution*, vol. 2, pp. 118–38.

157. Ibid., pp. 119–21.

158. L. Trotsky, *What Next? And Other Writings from 1917*, London, 1988, p. 12.

159. Ibid., pp. 27–33.

160. The best overall account of the background, the intrigues, and the actual events connected with Kornilov's projected putsch is in L. Trotsky, *History of the Russian Revolution*, vol. 2

161. N. N. Sukhanov, The Russian Revolution, p. 522.

162. L. Trotsky, *History of the Russian Revolution*, vol. 2, p. 223.

163. G. Katkov, *Russia 1917 The Kornilov Affair. Kerensky and the Break Up of the Russian Army*, London, 1980. For a different view see J. D. White, "The Kornilov Affair: A Study in Counter-Revolution," *Soviet Studies*, vol. 20, October 1968, pp. 187–205.

164. Quoted in M. Liebman, *The Russian Revoluion*, London, 1970, p. 189.

165. L. Trotsky, *History of the Russian Revolution*, vol. 2, pp. 149–51.

166. V. V. Kutuzov, ed., *Velikaia Oktiabrskaia Sotsialisticheskaia Revolutsiia—Khronika Sobytii* vol. 3, Moscow, 1957, pp. 29, 79, 248, and O. H. Radkey, *The Election to the Russian Constituent Assembly of 1917*, Cambridge, 1950, p. 53.

167. V. I. Lenin, "On Compromises" in *LCW* 25, pp. 310–14.

168. V. V. Kutuzov, ed., *Velikaia Oktiabrskaia Sotsialisticheskaia Revolutsiia—*

Khronika Sobytii, p. 226. The SRs had forty, giving the Bolsheviks a clear lead over the combined Menshevik–SR bloc.

169. A. Andreyev, *The Soviets of Workers and Soldiers Deputies on the eve of the October Revolution,* Moscow, 1971, p. 260.

170. L. Trotsky, *History of the Russian Revolution,* vol. 2, p. 267.

171. Ibid., pp. 288–90 gives the voting figures.

172. Ibid., pp. 288.

173. Ibid.

174. A. Andreyev, *The Soviets of Workers and Soldiers Deputies on the eve of the October Revolution,* p. 263.

175. L.Trotsky, *History of the Russian Revolution,* vol. 2, p. 286

176. O. Anweiler, *The Soviets,* p. 179.

177. The text of the resolution is in *Vtoroi Vesrossiiskii Sezd Sovetov,* Moscow, 1957, pp. 119–20. It gives September 22, as the date. O. Anweiler, *The Soviets,* p. 181 gives the date as September 21.

178. For a nearly complete checklist, see *Vtoroi Vserossiiskii S'ezd Sovetov,* pp. 121–216.

179. O. Anweiler, *The Soviets,* p. 193.

180. A. Andreyev, *The Soviets of Workers and Soldiers Deputies on the eve of the October Revolution,* p. 304. The Bolsheviks had fifty-one delegates, the Left SRs twenty-four, the Menshevik Internationalists one, and the compromisers fourteen.

181. Apart from Anweiler and Trotsky, see A. Rabinowitch, *The Bolsheviks Come to Power,* New York, 1976; and J. L. H. Keep, *The Russian Revolution: A Study in Mass Mobilisation,* New York, 1976.

182. M. Ferro, *The Bolshevik Revolution,* p. 233.

183. L. Trotsky, *History of the Russian Revolution,* vol. 2, p. 322. M. Ferro, *The Bolshevik Revolution,* p. 233 gives somewhat different figures. The translation is rather poor, and it is not clear on all points.

184. L. Trotsky, *History of the Russian Revolution,* vol. 22, p. 324; M. Ferro, *The Bolshevik Revolution,* p. 233.

185. V. I. Lenin, "The Bolsheviks must assume power" in *LCW* 26, Moscow, 1977, p. 19.

186. R. Schlesinger, *History of the Communist Party of the USSR,* pp. 121–22, rejects the view that Lenin found the Central Committee, or large parts of it, as a hindrance, saying that it is a Trotskyist myth; Trotsky's own detailed account is in L. Trotsky, *History of the Russian Revolution,* vol. 3, pp. 120–58.

187. *LCW* 26, p. 20.

188. Ibid., pp. 22–24.

189. *The Bolsheviks and the October Revolution,* p. 58.

190. Ibid., p. 69

191. Quoted in L. Trotsky, *History of the Russian Revolution,* vol. 2, p. 322.

192. V. I. Lenin, "From a Publicist Diary," in *LCW* 26, pp. 57–58.

193. *The Bolsheviks and the October Revolution,* p. 78.

194. *Rabochii Put,* October 8, 1917, English translation in *The Bolsheviks,* pp. 79–81.

195. L. Trotsky, *History of the Russian Revolution*, vol. 2, p. 324.
196. Quoted in ibid., vol. 3, p. 68.
197. N. N. Sukhanov, *The Russian Revolution*, p. 541.
198. L. Trotsky, *History of the Russian Revolution*, vol. 3, p. 132.
199. *LCW* 26, p. 70.
200. Ibid., p. 83.
201. V. I. Lenin, "Letter to the Central Committee, the Moscow and Petrograd Committees and the Bolshevik Members of the Petrograd and Moscow Soviets," in ibid., pp. 20–21, 58, 80–81, 141.
202. Ibid., p. 141.
203. Ibid., p. 83.
204. See J. Bunyan and H. H. Fisher, *The Bolshevik Revolution, 1917–1918: Documents and Materials*, Stanford, 1934, pp. 69–74.
205. *The Bolsheviks and the October Revolution*, pp. 97–99.
206. *Leon Trotsky Speaks*, p. 59.
207. L. Trotsky, *History of the Russian Revolution*, vol. 3, pp. 99–91.
208. Ibid., pp. 95–96.
209. Ibid., p. 101.
210. M. Macauley, ed., *The Russian Revolution and the Soviet State 1917–1921: Documents*, London, 1988, pp. 119–21.
211. *Leon Trotsky Speaks*, pp. 67–68.
212. N. N. Sukhanov, *The Russian Revolution*, pp. 595–96.
213. Bunyan and Fisher, *The Bolshevik Revolution, 1917–1918: Documents and Materials*, p. 86.
214. L. Trotsky, *History of the Russian Revolution*, vol. 3, p. 264. See as a whole pp. 257–80.
215. O. Anweiler, *The Soviets*, p. 193; and L. Trotsky, *History of the Russian Revolution*, vol. 3, pp. 281, 282, 288.
216. O. Anweiler, *The Soviets*, pp. 204–6.
217. L. Trotsky, *History of the Russian Revolution*, vol. 3, p. 262.
218. W. G. Rosenberg, "Conclusion," in D. H. Kaiser, ed. *The Workers' Revolution in Russia, 1917*, Cambridge, 1987, p. 133.
219. On this, see O. H. Radkey, *Agrarian Foes of Bolshevism*; G. Gill, *Peasants and Government in the Russian Revolution*, New York, 1979; and E. Kingston Mann, *Lenin and the Problems of a Marxist Peasant Revolution*.

8

BOLSHEVISM AND THE EXPERIENCE
OF SOVIET POWER

I
THE BOLSHEVIK THEORY OF PROLETARIAN DICTATORSHIP

The October Revolution was made with the stated goal of the emancipation of the proletariat. But barely two decades later, Leon Trotsky, one of the architects of that revolution, was proclaiming that the state born out of the Russia Revolution had undergone an authoritarian degeneration, and was being juridically liquidated and replaced by a Bonapartist state.[1] Since all Bolsheviks, including Lenin and Trotsky, claimed that the revolution had been consciously made by the revolutionary party, standing at the head of the mass of people, any degeneration has to be examined in relation to the theory developed by the revolutionary party. It is often argued that Lenin's last battle had been against this growing authoritarianism.[2] Despite this, it is necessary to review the nature of the Bolshevik theory of the dictatorship of the proletariat. The need springs from the fact that in 1917, the Bolsheviks declared that a state of a new type had to be set up. A new workers' state was indeed set up after October. But within a very short span of time, the democratic structures of this new state were eroding. In order to grasp the nature of the erosion, it will be necessary to ask whether this erosion was due to inbuilt problems of Bolshevik theory, or whether unexpected, and critical turns in the Russian situation, were more responsible?[3]

Much of the debate on the evolution of Soviet power in the early years of Soviet Russia depends on different answers to the foregoing question. One way of defending the early Bolshevik regime has been the argument that an original democratic impulse was distorted because of the civil war and foreign interventions.[4] Ranged against this is the view that elimination of opposition, and an embryonic authoritarianism, were inherent in the theory of Bolshevism, and that therefore pleas about how the civil war, foreign intervention, and economic crises were responsible for the collapse of democracy, are spurious arguments.[5]

On the question of the kind of working-class political power that would have to be created after the revolution, Bolshevik theory up to 1917 meant essentially the theoretical reflections of Lenin. It will be necessary, however, to look at the RSDRP's tradition as a whole, even if briefly. It will also be necessary to relate briefly the ideas of Trotsky, who joined the Bolsheviks in 1917. And it will have to be done by tracing the degree of continuity or discontinuity with Marx.

Since the publication of Marx's *Critique of the Gotha Programme*, orthodox Marxists regularly used the slogan "dictatorship of the proletariat" to designate working-class rule. But the RSDRP was the first Marxist party to put the phrase in its program. Even the SPD, the leading orthodox Marxist party, had not done so.[6] The reason probably is related to the Revisionist controversy. When Eduard Bernstein launched his attack on Marx's ideas, he called the phrase a "Jacobin" term. Even in a gesture of opposition the SPD leader, Karl Kautsky's authoritative reply to Bernstein evaded the issue by saying that "the decision on the problem of the dictatorship of the proletariat . . . (can be) tranquilly left to the future."[7] Marxists from the Russian Empire, viz., A. I. Parvus (a Russian settled in Germany), or Rosa Luxemburg (a Pole originally from Russian occupied Kingdom of Poland), apart from G. V. Plekhanov, were from the beginning concerned about the issue.[8] So, it is not surprising that when the RSDRP was to adopt a program, the "dictatorship of the proletariat" plank was specifically mentioned. The role of the Revisionist controversy in getting the term incorporated into the program is further confirmed when it is seen that up to 1898, not even Lenin had suggested the term, but when, in 1903, a new program was to be adopted, using the term became a hallmark of Marxist orthodoxy. The program stated that:

> A necessary condition for this social revolution is the dictatorship of the proletariat, that is, conquest by the proletariat of such political power as will enable it to suppress any resistance by the exploiters.[9]

This usage was in line with Marx's view, that corresponding to the economic transformation, there would always be a political transition period, which could be nothing other than the dictatorship of the proletariat. Thus, the RSDRP program, no less than Marx, indicated by the term, primarily the class rule of the proletariat, and second, with that sociological characterization, a need for the proletariat to defend its rule by the force of arms. It is also worth nothing that according to the program, the road to the dictatorship of the proletariat was to pass through a democratic republic. This too was in line with the ideas of Marx and Engels.

On the "dictatorship of the proletariat" plank, there was only a brief debate at the Second Congress, a period when Bolshevism was gradually emerging as a distinct political current. Vladimir Akimov, a right-wing socialist delegate, opposed the program as a whole, and suggested that the program saw the party as active and the proletariat as passive.[10] Rebutting the accusation of Jacobinism, Trotsky said, "it will not be a conspiratorial 'seizure of power,' but the political rule of the organized working class, constituting the majority of the nation."[11] Thus, the supporter of the *Iskra* program clearly equated the dictatorship of the proletariat with class rule.[12]

It should be mentioned that at the Congress, the use of force was clearly advocated in order to establish the full democratic program in critical moments, when class power and forms of rule were to change. The matter came up in connection with the discussions on the prospects of a Constituent Assembly. Plekhanov and another *Iskra*-ist delegate, Posadovsky, argued that the duration of any Constituent Assembly set up on the fall of the autocracy should be subordinated to its potential for fulfilling the democratic program.[13] This, too, was in line with the arguments of Marx and Engels on the need to use force to compel the new post-revolution regime to carry out the democratic tasks promised by the bourgeois democrats before the revolution. But this has nothing to do with the dictatorship of the proletariat, and shows how a democratic republic was to be ensured, even through some critics have used this debate to claim that Russian Marxism was authoritarian from a very early stage.[14]

When in 1905 the tidal waves of revolution turned the attention of the Bolsheviks to the immediate practical tasks of carrying out the democratic revolution under proletarian hegemony, Lenin put forward a concept of the "revolutionary democratic dictatorship of the proletariat and the peasantry." The first occasion when he tried to express these ideas in detail was in *Two Tactics of Social Democracy in the Democratic Revolution*. There, he appended a section entitled "The Vulgar Bourgeois and the Marxist Views on Dictatorship," to argue that the terms dictatorship and democracy are mutually exclusive from the "vulgar bourgeois" standpoint.[15] Thus, his counterposition indicates that he believed in a "dictatorship" which could be democratic in form. However, he confused the issue by the cryptic comment that major questions are settled by force.[16] A limitation that cropped up in his idea was an instrumentalist approach to liberty:

> In general, all political liberty founded on present day, i.e., capitalist relations of production are bourgeois liberty. The demand for liberty

expresses primarily the interests of the bourgeoisie. . . . The proletariat . . . needs political liberty (for it, emancipation).[17]

This left open the question of what the proletariat was to do with liberty after capturing power. This problem was further complicated by a definition of the dictatorship of the proletariat given by Lenin in 1906. In his *The Victory of the Cadets and the Tasks of the Workers' Party* (1906), he wrote: "Authority—unlimited, outside law, and based on force in the most direct sense of the word—is dictatorship."[18] If dictatorship is unlimited, and outside the law, then it can exist only for the interim period between the fall of one regime and the consolidation of the new one. Clearly, Lenin knew fairly little about Marx's use of the term "dictatorship of the proletariat" at this stage, and his own attempt to create a definition was not a happy one.[19] Here he was not even talking of the entire period of transition, since he made it clear that the aim of the democratic dictatorship of the proletariat and the peasantry, the programmatic goal of the Bolsheviks at that period, was to implement the party's minimum program, i.e., achieve a thorough going bourgeois democratic revolution and set up a democratic republic.

Lenin's thought on the question of the stage of the revolution underwent a change during Word War I. Neil Harding has put forward an argument about how Lenin, in his attempt to understand a new the political processes, went back to philosophy and economics. In *Imperialism, the Highest Stage of Capitalism*, Lenin put forward the basic elements of his new socio-economic analysis of capitalism as being essentially a world system, was the theoretical justification for beginning the socialist revolution in a backward country like Russia. He expected the revolution to spread in short order to the more developed countries. The guideline for socialist practice in a workers' state, once it was set up, was provided in *The State and Revolution*.[20]

Though the final version of *The State and Revolution* was written only in the period after the "July Days" in 1917, when Lenin had to go underground, it had a long gestation period. In 1916, Lenin had come into conflict with the left-wing Bolshevik, N. I. Bukharin. The latter had written an article, "Towards a Theory of the Imperialist State." Having discussed the kind of changes effected by imperialism in the capitalist state, he went on to say that humankind was approaching a stage of evolution in the system of production in which the existence of classes would become a fetter on production. He further stressed that the teaching of Marx and Engels on the state had been simplified and distorted by constantly posing as though Marxists were "statists" while anarchists were "antistatists." The Marxists actually wanted economic centralization, but without the state. Marxism, in his opinion, did not stand for the permanence of the state, which would wither away as soon as class differentiation was done away with. The dictatorship of the proletariat was therefore not a state analogous to the bourgeois state, but a transitional moment.[21] After initial objection, his own studies convinced Lenin that leftists, like Bukharin in his party, or the Dutch left socialist Pannekeok, were closer to Marx's spirit than were "orthodox" theorists like Kautsky.[22] The basic ideas of *The State and Revolution*, therefore, were not ad hoc responses to current tactical problems, faced by Lenin in mid-1917. The basic ideas had been worked out prior to Lenin's return to Russia, and they guided his activities. Another major figure who had arrived at these ideas before Lenin was Trotsky. In that sense, these ideas reflected a consensus on the revolutionary wing of Russian, and to a certain extent, international, social democracy.

In his polemic against Lenin in 1904, *Our Political Tasks*, which included a section entitled "Dictatorship Over the Proletariat," Trotsky asserted that "dictatorship over the proletariat" was what Lenin's organizational ideas would lead to, as expounded in *One Step Forward, Two Steps Back*. Regardless of the value of this judgement, his own view is significant:

> The tasks of the new regime will be so complex that they can be solved only through the rivalry of various methods of economic and political reconstruction, . . . by way of a systematic struggle not only between the socialist and capitalist worlds, but also between many trends inside socialism, trends which will inevitably emerge as soon as the proletarian dictatorship poses tens and hundreds of new unsolved problems. No "strong authoritative organisation" . . . will be able to suppress these trends and controversies . . . for it is only too clear that a proletariat capable of exercising its dictatorship over society will not tolerate any dictatorship over itself.[23]

To Tony Cliff this is an idealistic, and presumably worthless argument. By doing so, he ignores the crucial difference between the following: counter-revolution, legal bourgeois opposition, and proletarian and allied opposition to the government. Trotsky was here concerned with setting up a norm. He also wanted to emphasize that substitutionism would weaken the proletariat's struggle for self-emancipation. In this, he stood with the real Marxist tradition, and displayed a more serious concern about the form of the dictatorship of the proletariat, emphasizing the inevitability of a rivalry of various trends, and of debates, in the construction of socialism.

The reason for Trotsky being almost alone in 1905-06 in discussing the concrete problems of the dictatorship of the proletariat is related to his theory of permanent revolution. Because of this theory, he, unlike his contemporaries, was compelled to address the problems of a working-class state. Lenin, Luxemburg and Parvus had all suggested some sort of proletarian domination, but only for the short-term task of destroying the autocracy and setting up a democratic bourgeois republic. Trotsky, by contrast, was arguing that the proletariat, once in power, could not impose some sort of self-limitation. Discussing the likelihood of counter-revolution, he wrote:

> Without the direct state support of the European proletariat the working class of Russia cannot remain in power and convert its temporary domination into a lasting socialist dictatorship.[24]

What is of interest for the present discussion is the final clause. He was urging the conversion of the temporary domination into a lasting dictatorship. By this, he was not advocating a long authoritarian rule. The distinction was one between a brief interregnum when workers would carry out the democratic revolution, and the transition to communism proper. Trotsky spelled out the task of this dictatorship:

> The first measures of the proletariat, cleansing the Augean stables of the old regime . . . supplemented by a democratic reorganization of all social and state relations.[25]

Workers' democracy, introduced quickly, would involve the introduction of a system of elected and responsible officials and a national militia.[26] The struggles of the Russian proletariat had thrown up the form of workers' democracy, the Soviets, which constituted:

> Authentic democracy, without a lower and an upper chamber, without a professional bureaucracy, but with the voters' right to recall their deputies at any moment.[27]

Though Trotsky was not as elaborate as Lenin, nor as careful about checking how far he was adhering to the text of Marx and Engels, in these brief propositions it is not difficult to see agreement with the views expressed in Marx's *The Civil War in France*. Trotsky's concept of the dictatorship of the proletariat was similar to Marx's in claiming that it would establish a new and higher form of democracy, that even at this stage, a working-class armed force would be needed to stop counter-revolution, and that the ultimate goal was not class rule, but the abolition of class rule, and with that, the abolition of the state.

In *The State and Revolution*, and in his public writings and speeches of 1917, Lenin was equally emphatic in developing these ideas. By 1917, he had rejected the idea of a separate bourgeois democratic stage of revolution, and expected that the new organ of power would be the Soviets.[28] Thus, the dictatorship of the proletariat began to be associated, in Lenin's mind, with soviet power.[29] In the third "Letter from Afar," he affirmed:

> We need a state. But *not the kind* of state the bourgeoisie has created everywhere, from constitutional monarchies to the most democratic

republics. . . . The proletariat . . . if it wants to uphold the gains of the present revolution and proceed further, to win peace, bread and freedom, must "*smash*," to use Marx's expression, this "ready-made" state machine and substitute a new one for it by *merging* the police force, the army, and the bureaucracy with the entire armed people.[30]

In these letters, as well as in his writings after returning to Russia, he identified the desired new state with the Paris Commune.[31] In June 1917, he published a pamphlet on the party program. In it, he called for seizure of power by the proletariat, and said that Soviet democracy would be more democratic than bourgeois democracy. Explaining the Soviet model as the broadest possible expansion of class democracy, Lenin pointed out that it would neither require a standing army nor parliament. Workers' power could be exercised by elected officials, paid at the rate of workers' wages, and since the Soviets would combine legislative and executive functions.[32]

In *The State and Revolution*, Lenin made the arguments in a dualistic appreciation of bourgeois democracy. On the one hand, it was the best form of state for the proletariat under capitalism.[33] But it was a democracy that had major limitations. Infrequent parliamentary elections reduce the actual democratic content of representation. Moreover, the parliamentary institutions are not the locus of real power. The role of money power also effects an anti-democratic transformation of parliament, as well as being the class power backing up the state power in the apparatus.[34] This was not a primitive hostility to democracy. This was the basis of his call for the overthrow of the bourgeois state and the establishment of proletarian democracy, which was to be a new and higher form. Lenin insisted that in all this he was only restoring "what Marx really taught on the subject of the state."[35] The first crucial argument that he took over from Marx and repeatedly asserted was that all states are class states. As bourgeois democracy was a democracy primarily for the rich, it could not be replaced through incremental reforms, but the parasite state covered by the democratic trappings had to be smashed.[36] This was the centerpiece of his views:

> We however, shall break with the opportunist; and the entire class conscious proletariat will be with us in the fight—not to "shift the balance of forces," but to *overthrow the bourgeoisie, to destroy* bourgeois parliamentarism, for a democratic republic after the type of the Commune, or a republic of Soviets of Workers' and Soldiers' Deputies, for the revolutionary dictatorship of the proletariat.[37]

It must be realized that Lenin was not counterposing direct democracy to representative democracy. He was arguing that the Soviet form of representation was superior to the parliamentary form. As he wrote:

> Representative institutions remains but there is *no* parliamentarism here
> as a special system, as the division of labour between the legislative and
> the executive, as a privileged position for deputies.[38]

So Lenin was objecting to a system where first, the executive is an
autonomous bureaucracy, and second, the representatives cease to
be under the control of the electorate and become privileged office
holders. These arguments altogether present a defense of expansion
of democracy, not its contraction.[39] Lenin repeatedly emphasized
that all this, i.e., communism, the end of exploitation, the end of the
subordination of groups of people to other groups, could come about
only through a transition period, the starting point of that was working-
class rule.[40] This was to be "democratic *in a new way* (for the proletariat
and the propertyless in general)."[41] It was new and more democratic,
because the Soviet system would allow the electorate to keep a constant
control over the representatives. Moreover the entire proletariat
would be armed,[42] so that there would no longer be a special, minority
apparatus of coercion and consequently the armed forces would lose
their oppressive character.[43] As Lenin wrote:

> [D]emocracy is *not* identical with the subordination of the minority to the
> majority. Democracy is a *state* which recognizes the subordination . . . i.e.,
> an organisation for the systematic use of *force* by one class against another.[44]

The creation of a workers' state would not mean the immediate end of
all bourgeois resistance. That was why even the superior democracy
of the workers' state could not dispense with coercion altogether. The
superiority of workers' democracy over bourgeois democracy lay,
according to him, in the fact that since the working class had nothing
to gain from exploiting any other class, proletarian hegemony would
mean a minimization of the use of force. The destruction of the old
power and the creation of the new power is not simply a question of
the armed force. The armed force is vital, because it guarantees the new
power. But the essence of the proletarian revolution was the end of the
separation and alienation of power from the masses.[45] Lenin admitted
that there could be no question of an instant abolition of the bureaucracy:

> [T]his is *not* a utopia, it is the experience of the Commune, the direct and
> immediate task of the revolutionary proletariat. . . . *We*, the workers, shall
> organize large-scale production on the basic of what capitalism has already
> created. . . . We shall reduce the role of state officials to that of simply
> carrying out our instruction as responsible, revocable, modestly paid
> "foremen and accountants.". . . Such a beginning . . . will of itself lead to
> the gradual "withering away" of all bureaucracy, to the gradual creation of
> another . . . under which the functions of control and accounting, becoming
> more and more simple will be performed by each in turn, will then become

a habit and will finally die out as the *special* functions of a special section of the population.[46]

Working-class power involved certain stages of transition. The first was the transition period, when there would be democracy for the vast majority, along with the suppression of the exploiters. Only following that, when the capitalists as a class were abolished, only when there was no class struggle, could the state cease to exist. However, Lenin insisted that the process of withering away would begin as soon as the new state was set up. As he put it, when the majority suppressed its oppressors, a "special force" for suppression was not necessary. "In this sense, the state *begins to wither* away."[47] Eventually, there would not remain any state, not even a democratic state. This is as argument that bears close scrutiny. At one point he wrote that when there are no classes:

> Only then will a truly complete democracy become possible and be realized, a democracy without any exceptions whatever. And only then will democracy begin to *wither away*, owing to the simple fact that freed from capitalist slavery ... people will gradually *become accustomed* to observing the elementary rules of social intercourse ... without the special apparatus for coercion called the state.[48]

The concept of democracy withering away can be misconstrued. One might think that Lenin was insisting that in the dictatorship of the proletariat, or in communism, there would no longer exist debates, exchange of views, the creation of politics based on the will of the majority expressed in certain formal ways, as well as guarantees regarding rights of minorities. Countless defenders of Stalinism have put forward such a "Leninism."[49] In fact, Lenin was using "democracy" in two ways. At times he meant by it only the adoption of the majority views as the common policy, and related norms. He did not advocate their replacement by a system of enforced unity, on the plea that differences of other way in which he used "democracy" was close to its etymological sense—rules of the proletariat in place of rule of the people (in fact, the lower class people). As a kind of "rule," it encompasses a state, with its coercive apparatus, but one that would be less ferocious than bourgeois states, and would wither away. Thus, polemicizing against Kautsky, he wrote:

> Kautsky has not understood at all the difference between bourgeois parliamentarism, which combines democracy *(not for the people)* with bureaucracy *(against the people)*, and proletarian democracy, which will take immediate steps to cut bureaucracy down to the roots, and which will be able to carry these measure through to the end, to the complete abolition of bureaucracy, to the introduction of complete democracy for the people.[50]

Here, there is no talk of the end of proletarian democracy. Rather, he expected proletarian democracy to lead to complete democracy. So the point was not that the principles of majority decision, protection of the rights of minorities, etc., should be abandoned. The point was that these would, in the communist future, be achieved without an armed force to enforce them, because once basic social (class) interests ceased to divide people, they would follow democratic norms without such implicit threats.

Traditionally, *The State and Revolution*, and the theory of state associated with it, has been considered a much stronger point for Leninism than some of its other aspects.[51] Nonetheless, it is possible to locate a number of theoretical problems in it. The first problem stems from the fact that even in 1917, Lenin did not abandon the previous idea of dictatorship that he had put forward in 1905-6, notwithstanding its evident conflict with his new conceptions. In his *Report of the Current Situation, April 24, 1917*, he wrote that working-class rule would be a dictatorship, because it "rests not on law, not on the formal will of the majority, but on direct, open force. Force is the instrument of power. How, then will the Soviets apply this power?"[52] Taken by itself, such a statement suggests that the workers' state would be run permanently on an ad hoc basis, with decisions not being based on the "formal will of the majority." This kind of a definition could only be applicable in a period when an insurrection overthrew the old state. As there could be no peaceful and completely legal change-over from capitalism and a state protecting capitalist interests to workers' rule the beginning of the transition, a first period when the old law was smashed, and new laws were yet to be put in its place, would intervene. But once the issue of consolidating power came up, the definition of dictatorship of the proletariat as something not resting on the will of the majority contradicted all the talk about how expansive workers' democracy would be. To refer merely to the Soviet form is not enough. Would such a Soviet state have its constitution, written laws, legal mechanisms for balancing between class interests and interests of individuals? Would the act of opposition to the regime be considered automatically to be counter-revolution, and would it be met by force sans laws? To argue that many workers would be drawn into administration is an inadequate response to these queries.

A second problem is terminological. Since Lenin used "democracy" in more than one sense, the idea that democracy would wither away was susceptible to seriously anti-democratic interpretations. A different sort of criticism is one which Lenin anticipated. This is the argument that in the complex world of the modern times, only experts can do some kinds of works, like drawing up proper laws, keeping accounts, running the technical side of most things. Lenin agreed that the coming of the Commune state, or the Soviet state, would lead to a certain loss of sophistication.[53] If in course of ensuring mass participation, in administration, things appeared somewhat rough, unpolished, that would be more than compensated by the social content. Also, technical issues would continue to be tackled by technically trained people, but they would be hired and paid by the workers, so they would remain under proletarian control.[54]

There is, however, another important flaw. This relates to his approaches to "democracy," and to the problems of democratization of the state. Even if the end of classes was to bring about an end of coercive institutions (army, police, most of the penal code, the prisons, and so on), public differences and structures to regulate them would be required. Even if politics, in the classical Marxist sense of class conflict, disappeared, politics, as the articulation of divergent lines of proposed public conduct, would exist. The collapsing of politics into administration is a bad solution, for it leaves no space for critical appraisals of the whole system and policy of administration. Official institutions, which are part of the administration, cannot review its functioning as a whole, from outside its framework, yet within the public domain. This can only be done by non-government, voluntary public organizations, having the right to freely differ from the public authority, to criticize it, to seek to replace those in positions of authority even if they had been elected in a democratic way, and to propose alternative comprehensive policies and seek popular mandate to carry them out. In other words, there would be required parties, trade unions, civil liberties associations, and various associations of groups of citizens.[55] Such a legitimization of opposition, in turn, would illegitimize any notion of the rule of force, unchecked by law. The lack of discussion about the role of political parties in *The State and Revolution* remains a significant flaw. Lenin's account of representative democracy can be criticized for being silent on the question of plurality, rival programs within the workers' state, and on the distinction between counter-revolution and opposition.

Another criticism of Lenin that can be made is that in the article "Can the Bolsheviks Retain State Power" (October 1917), he said that since the revolution of 1905:

> Russia has been governed by 130,000 Landowners [opposing 150,000,000 people] . . . yet we are told that the 240,000 members of the Bolshevik Party will not be able to govern Russia. . . . (though, together with the supporters) we . . . already have a "state apparatus" of *one million* people.[56]

Here, the talk was chiefly of how the Bolsheviks could govern. By taking only of the Bolsheviks and their supporters, the role of the Soviet, and its relationship with parties, was obscured.

Both in *The State and Revolution* and in the article quoted above, Lenin's error was basically one of omission. This can be explained by two factors. On the one hand, Russia had never had a powerful civil society, and Bolshevik practice, as well as Lenin's theoretical reflections, never operated within a functioning civil society. On the other hand, in the absence of the other "classical" model, that of the SPD, (a case of a socialist parliamentary activity in Wilhelmine Germany, which was a semi-autocracy), the role of parties in any representative system was not adequately thought-out by Lenin. Moreover, *The State and Revolution* remained an incomplete work. The experiences of 1905 and 1917 were not summed up. All this was to have some effect later. But it is also worth remembering that other important Bolsheviks in 1917, like Trotsky and Bukharin, had their own views of what constituted the dictatorship of the proletariat. In Trotsky's case in particular, the expectation of pluralism had been clearly spelt out. Even Lenin did assume that other socialist parties, at least, would continue to exist for a whole historical period, something that his concept of a stratified working class indicated. What neither Trotsky, nor Lenin, had expected, was that even the socialist parties would go over to the counter-revolution. This was what happened, however. The collapse of Soviet democracy was related to the fact that most non-Bolshevik parties, who were chosen by the workers, peasants, and soldiers to represent them in the Soviets, decided to turn their backs on the Soviets, and even to join hands with a bourgeois–aristocratic counter-revolution.

II
ECONOMY AND POLITICS: THE OBJECTIVE REALITY OF COUNTER-REVOLUTION

The discussion in the foregoing pages showed that it is not possible to present a model of Soviet history where authoritarianism is derived directly from the theoretical stance taken by the Bolsheviks. Neither the theory of a proletarian vanguard party, nor that of the dictatorship of the proletariat, was necessarily non-democratic. The concept of a vanguard party could lead to elitism only if the party ceased to draw into its ranks the fresh layers of worker militants and if the party began to claim that it would inject the "right" line into the working class. The theory of the dictatorship of the proletariat could lead to authoritarianism, only if one line of argument, normally a subordinate argument, became dominant. This was the argument that unity was essential for a revolution, and that "the" workers' party had to lead the masses. Obviously, if it was assumed that there could be only one workers' party, and if dissent was equated with counter-revolution, then totalitarianism could emerge. But these were hypothetical issues, and they could become real only under specific circumstances.

The defenders of Bolshevism have claimed that those conditions or circumstances are socio-economic as much as political. Basically, they argued that a severe economic dislocation, going back to World War I, together with counter-revolution and imperialist intervention, maimed society, economy, and polity, and thereby contributed to the crisis.

The economic dislocation was quite serious. Tsarist Russia's weak industrial base was hit hard by the war. Russia was ill-prepared to organize either economically or militarily for a long war. Moreover, corruption was rife. So, while the soldiers remained badly equipped and ill-fed, profits were raked in. By the end of 1915, the Germans had captured Courland, Lithuania, Galicia, and Russian Poland. Millions of soldiers died by the end of 1916, and more millions were wounded.

In the interior, the situation was terrible. Prices rose steeply. In 1916, throughout Russia, meatless days were proclaimed regularly to ensure some meat supply everywhere. The long bread queues became a standard scene. By January 1917, forty-year-old men and youth, who should have been called up only in 1919, were being drafted into the army. There was a massive deskilling of sectors of the workforce, as military needs led to recruitment of peasants in large scale into industry. The moral dislocation along with the economic one was equally severe, as enormous fortunes arose out of the bloody foam. There was a lack of bread and fuel, coupled with unparalleled business in luxury goods.

The huge expansion of the Petrograd workforce between 1914 and 1917 took place almost entirely in war related industries like metal, chemical and textiles. [57] But because this was war-related growth, from 1917 the crisis was leading to factory closures and rising unemployment. Between March and July, 568 factories, employing some 104,000 workers, shut down operation. In Petrograd, the number of metal workers who registered with the union as unemployed rose from 37.4 per day in July to 71.3 in October. A shortage of sugar (due to the loss of the beet-producing areas to the Germans) meant an almost total extinction of the confectionary industry.[58]

The transport system, never very good, had declined further. As a result, the supply of coal was poor. Given the paralysis of transport, stocks of fuel and raw materials built up at station platforms. Productivity per worker in the coalmines declined substantially. The causes were technical breakdown, growing lack of skills due to the call up of skilled workers, bad supplies, deterioration of the mines, excessive use of tools, etc.[59] Food supply to the capital was also worsening. In March 1917, bread rationing was begun, with 1½ lb. per day for heavy workers and 1 lb. for others. By the end of April, the ration was reduced to ¼ lb. with no guarantee of supply.[60]

The October Revolution, the Russian cease-fire, demobilization, and subsequently the peace of Brest-Litovsk, intensified the crisis. With war orders gone and their very futures uncertain, factories began to reduce staff, even when workers' control was established. By April 1918, the factory workforce of Petrograd had fallen to about 40 percent of its January 1917 level, and it shrank still further. Thus, in the metal industry, out of 213 factories in Petrograd, 109 had closed by April 1st, 1918, resulting in the decline of workers from 167,192 on January 1, 1917, to 43,129. In the chemicals industry, seventeen out of fifty-five enterprises closed, throwing 16,844 workers (out of 22,535) out of work.[61]

Overall, the Bolsheviks and the Soviet government they headed, had thus inherited a major economic crisis. Moreover, this crisis, accentuating sharply even before October 1917, had so intensified the class struggles that the struggle between revolution and counter-revolution did not have to await October. A bourgeois counter-revolution began from the moment the February Revolution started consolidating gains of soldiers and workers. Bolsheviks, left Mensheviks, other internationalist Social Democrats, left and centrist SRs, etc., were denied passage to Russia. Many, like Lenin, had to return through Germany, taking advantage of Ludendorff's hopes of peace in the East through a left-wing victory in Russia. Others, like Trotsky, were arrested by the "allies" as they tried to make their way back to Russia via allied countries.[62]

From the beginning, this was an international class war. Lenin and Trotsky both made this point. Thus, Trotsky wrote: "The workers' government will from the start be faced with the task of uniting its forces with those of the socialist proletariat."[63] The imperialist powers were not slow in replying to the Bolsheviks. Paleologue and Buchanan, the French and English ambassadors, respectively, made repeated demands to the liberals for the suppression of the Bolsheviks. Buchanan was one of the major props behind Kornilov.[64] The Allied military missions also tried to treat the Russian army separately from the unreliable government.[65] The allies put pressure not only on the right-wing parties, but also on the Mensheviks and SRs, whose rejection of a government of all the socialist parties, based on the Soviets, stemmed in part from this pressure.[66]

Nor did the Russian right wing have to wait for signals from abroad to show their hostility. As class polarities became ever more acute, the working-class struggles came under every kind of bourgeois political offensive. The Bolsheviks were major targets of right-wing anger. Soldiers, who had pushed through the famous Order No. 1, democratizing relationships in the army,[67] were hated by officers trained in a semi-feudal caste hierarchy. Capitalists, uneasy at the revolt of labor, landlords, apprehensive of losing their land — all concentrated fire on the Bolsheviks. Captain Dudarev, assistant Naval Minister, ordered Admiral

Verderevsky to sink pro-Bolshevik ships in the Baltic Fleet if necessary, and to use more disciplined submarines for this purpose.[68] At the time of the semi-insurrection in July (July 3–4), the Ministry of justice announced the discovery of documents supposed to prove that Lenin was a German agent.[69] A spy scare was whipped up. Bolsheviks were persecuted. Lenin and Zinoviev went underground. Trotsky, Raskolnikov and others were arrested. Under pressure from the generals, the death sentence was reintroduced at the front.[70] The official Soviet leaders (Mensheviks and SRs) voted to lift membership rights from anyone indicted by Courts.[71] The offices and presses of several Bolshevik papers were closed down. From July to August, counter-revolution raised its head. Leading financiers and industrialists, officers, the church, all preached the virtues of conservatism. Attempts were made to set up "special action groups." The government was denounced for its supposedly gentle handling of the left. A new type of right wing began to emerge—partly associated with the old Black Hundreds, partly opposing democracy in terms of a modern right-wing (semi-fascist) ideology.

The new government constituted, after the July crisis, was neither rooted in the Duma nor emerged from the Soviets. To legitimize it, Kerensky called a State Conference in Moscow. With far heavier representation from the four Dumas (448) than from the Soviets (229) it was a convention for counter-revolution. General Kornilov, candidate for dictatorship, was hailed as a savior by the right wing. He and his supporters exploited the cult of the glorious dead, exalted ceremonials, called for laws on conscription of labor and the restriction of profits, and continually referred to the supreme interests of the state. Based on an unsteady equilibrium, this was a new right-wing movement, combining elements of military dictatorship, Bonapartism, but also of a fascist type movement, with its anti-Semitic ideology.

The constituent elements of Kornilov's movement can be reviewed briefly. In March, the industrialist A.I. Putilov had set up a secret committee of leading financiers. This group soon became a central anti-Bolshevik headquarters. Among those who joined were N.N. Kutler, a Cadet who was the president of the Urals Mining Company. Kornilov's proposed political adviser for the hoped-for post-coup regime was V.S. Zavoyko, a director of the Russian-Asiatic Bank.[72]

This was the Capitalists' own venture. The officers led by generals like Alexiev, Denikin, and others formed a "Union of Army and Navy officers." These officers were to turn up in 1918 as the leaders of the Whiteguard Volunteer Army. Kornilov came to the fore for two reasons. One was his relatively successful role during the ill-fated July offensive. The other was his public demand for "salvaging" the army by scrapping democracy.[73] As a relatively successful and personally brave general, he was put forward as the opponent of Bolshevik-inspired chaos. Volunteer battalions of picked right-wing officers and specially privileged troops began to be formed. Ostensibly formed for wartime aims, these became, like the *Freikorps* in Germany, the core units of future right-wing militarism. Kornilov wanted to utilize the fall of Riga to bring the Petrograd area into the frontline zones, outlaw and arrest the Bolsheviks, disband the Soviet, and control the government. So he deliberately organized the fall of Riga.[74] For the right wing, national interests were so construed that the class enemy was more important than the foreign enemy.

This same consideration, this same forthright hostility to the Soviets and the Bolsheviks lay behind the activities of right-wing socialists. At the time of the October insurrection, violent measures, based on non-democratic forces at all were proposed by Kerensky. The Menshevik–SR "democrats," on the one hand called for negotiations, and on the other hand, encouraged armed counter-revolution. At the Second Congress of Soviets the Menshevik-Internationalist leader Martov moved a resolution calling for a government which would be recognized by the whole democracy. When the Bolsheviks accepted this, the Mensheviks and SRs rejected it.[75] In response to the will of an overwhelming majority of delegates to the Congress of Soviets, that there should be Soviet power, the Mensheviks and SRs declared the proceedings a coup, and said: "The said conspiracy throws the country into civil war . . . and leads to the triumph of a counter-revolution."[76]

The VTsIK (Central Executive Committee) elected by the First Congress of Soviets, together with the Mensheviks' and SR's Central Committees, rejected the validity of the Second Congress of Soviets. In alliance with the Council of Republic, the City Duma and a few unions, they formed a Committee for the Salvation of the Country and the Revolution. They tried to make it the successor of the Provisional Government.[77]

Kerensky, the head of the Provisional Government left Petrograd, and met a number of generals. General P. N. Krasnov, co-participant in Kornilov's coup, now agreed to help Kerensky. By the morning of October 27, he had occupied Gatchina, thirty miles south of Petrograd. At this stage, arms were being wielded by only small groups. The allegiance of most troops still hung on the balance. As Krasnov's troops advanced on Pertrograd, the Committees for Salvation of the Country and the Revolution appealed to troops not to oppose Krasnov. On October 28, Krasnov took Tsarskoe Selo.[78] To help him, a coup, led by trainee officers of the military schools was planned. Avksentiev and Gotz, respectively President of the Pre-Parliament and President of the Committee for Salvation, signed a joint statement on October 29, calling on all to assist this rising.[79] Thus, their opposition to the workers' revolution drove the generals, the Cadets, and the socialist parties into an alliance, despite all protestations by the Mensheviks and SRs that they were opposed to the right wing.[80]

On the morning of October 29, a coup had begun, led by Colonel Polkovnikov and instigated by the 'Committee for Salvation.' Red Guards and Sailors were thrown against them. About two hundred were killed and wounded on both sides together. Meanwhile at the Soviet Congress, the delegate of the Railway Union (Vikzhel), threatened a railway strike if fighting was not stopped by the night of 29th. Emboldened by this, the Menshevik-SR bloc demanded, on the 29th and 30th, that the VTsIK should be enlarged by the addition of bourgeois representatives (from the city Dumas) and that a government of all the socialist parties should be formed, but not based on the Soviets and from which Lenin and Trotsky would have to be eliminated. On the 30th, Krasnov's Cossacks went into action, but were defeated by the Red forces at the battle of Pulkovo Heights. On November 2, Krasnov was arrested in Gatchina. So mild was Bolshevik rule at this stage that he was released on his word of honor, which he violated immediately, by going to the Don and becoming the leader of a Cossack anti-Bolshevik movement.[81]

The uprising in Moscow saw a more stubborn struggle. In Moscow, a Military Revolutionary Committee (of the Soviet) and a Committee of Public Safety (of the Duma) faced each other. Clashes went on from October 27th to November 2. Victor Serge writes:

> The whites surrendered at 4 p.m. on November 2. "The Committee of Public Safety is dissolved, the White Guard surrenders its arms and is disbanded. The Officers may keep the side arms that distinguish their rank. . . . The MRC guarantee the liberty and inviolability of all." . . . The fighters of the counter-revolution . . . *went free*. Foolish clemency. These very Junkers, these officers, these students, these socialists of counter-revolution, dispersed themselves throughout the length and breadth of Russia, and there organized the civil war.[82]

The process of transfer of power showed that Mensheviks, SRs, and bourgeois oppositions were united in rejecting Soviet power. At Moghilev, the *Stavka*, or army headquarters, attempted to resist the regime. The army chief, General Dukhonin, wanted to move against the Council of People's Commissars (Sovnarkom). But the hesitations of General Cheremissov, the head of the Northern Army, and the resistance of soldiers, prevented this. Dukhonin also kept in touch with Allied Military Missions. Eventually, he was arrested on November 20th. Ensign Krylenko took over in his place.[83]

A more powerful center of resistance was the Cossack region, particular the capitals, Rostov, Ekaterinodar, and Orenburg. General

Kaledin, the Don Cossack Ataman, became the hope of the upper classes, as rightwing politicians and generals made their way to the Don. It was there that the nucleus of the Volunteer Army was formed. In the Ukraine, the Ukrainian Rada, with 213 peasant representatives, 132 army representatives, and one hundred workers, employees, etc., took a formally leftist stand, announcing the confiscation of land, etc. But, having proclaimed an independent Ukraine, it also gave free passage to the troops of the Volunteer Army. Bolsheviks and their allies set up a Soviet power in the Eastern Ukraine, based in Kharkov. The Sovnarkom demanded that the Rada should not disarm Soviet troops while permitting passage to white troops.[84] These events show that in the extremely politically charged atmosphere, neutrality was fast becoming an impossible choice. Those who pretended to be neutral actually helped the extreme rightwing.

It is clearly beyond the scope of the present study to offer a detailed summary of the civil war.[85] But it is important to keep the chronology of the civil war in mind. Within three days of the October insurrection, right-wing forces were being assisted by moderate Socialists in an attempted coup d'etat having far less democratic basis than the Soviet insurrection. Within six weeks, White forces were being organized in Southeastern Russia.[86] Both the Entente and the Germans egged on the Ukraine against the Soviet regime.[87] In Georgia, a Menshevik regime was formed, and it got Entente support.[88] In February 1918, the Volunteer Army left the Don to move on the Kuban. After the Treaty of Brest-Litovsk, the Germans imposed a puppet ruler in the Ukraine, the Hetman Skoropadsky. They also occupied Latvia and Estonia. Finnish independence, confirmed by the Bolsheviks, was followed by a bloody civil war waged by the Whites.

The Finnish Civil War gave a lesson in democracy to the Bolsheviks. When the Finnish socialists won a majority (103 out of 200) seats to the Sejm, Kerensky had it dissolved. Following October, a Council of People's Delegates had been proclaimed in Finland. This revolution was smashed by right-wing armed forces, led by Mannerheim, and militarily under the guidance of Germans led by General Von der Goltz. The defeat of the revolution was followed by mass murder. Some twenty-three thousand Reds were killed.[89] In Helsinki, the Whites made workers' wives and children walk in front of their troops as they recaptured the city street by street. One hundred of them died. In Tavastehus, ten thousand prisoners were interned and many subsequently massacred. In Kummen five hundred were shot after the battle.[90] "In Lahti in one day, some two hundred women were shot with explosive bullets."[91] In Viipuri, six hundred Red Guards were lined up in three rows and machine gunned to death.[92] 8380 captured Reds were killed illegally.[93]

265 "legal executions" were based on "illegal charges."[94] As many as 11,783 prisoners out of the 80,000 or so died due to lack of food, sanitation, living space, etc.[95]

As in Finland, so in Russia too was the counter-revolution actively aided by both imperialist camps. The German ambassador, Count Mirbach, on arriving in Moscow, met a number of members of the Imperial Family.[96] Bruce Lockhart, a British officer, was in contact with Alexiev, Kornilov and Denikin. By April 1918, the Entente had come to the conclusion that they would have to invade Russia and overthrow the Bolsheviks.[97] In April 1918, the British and the Japanese seized Vladivostok. By the end of 1918, there were seventy-three thousand Japanese troops in Siberia.[98] In all, in the course of the civil war the Soviet regime faced the armies of fourteen countries, who at different points supported Kolchak in the East, Yudenich's thrust for Petrograd in the North, and Denikin and the Cossacks' drive to Moscow from the South. By 1919, over two hundred thousand Allied troops were ranged against the Red forces.[99]

White Terror was a brutal anti-poor peasant, anti-worker, and anti-communist policy. The aim of the officers was not to establish parliamentary democracy, but a dictatorship. White-ruled territories were either run as military despotisms, or were given in charge of discredited bureaucrats of the Tsarist era. White Terror was massive; half of an entire captured regiment was shot dead, after being forced to dig their own graves, for being communists.[100] Two orders of Krasnov and Kaledin showed the class nature of White Terror:

> Order No. 2428: It is forbidden to arrest workers. The orders are to hang or shoot them.

> Order No. 2431: The orders are to hang all arrested workers in the street. The bodies are to be exhibited for three days.[101]

In April 1918, General Denikin assumed command of the volunteer army. His advisers, Generals Lukomsky and Dragomirov, openly advocated the restoration of the Romanovs.[102] Denikin himself recognized that this would alienate moderates. But when he abdicated in favor of Baron Wrangel (in 1920) the latter issued a manifesto calling on the Russian people to choose a MASTER (spelt with block capitals to indicate that Wrangel had a Tsar in mind).[103] Their class approach was most clearly expressed in two ways. First, they consistently refused to countenance radical land reforms. Denikin, a relatively politically-alert man, wanted the "creation and strengthening of solid small and middle sized farms."[104] So his was an attempt to continue Stolypin's policy under changes circumstances. But Cossacks, for example, brutally treated the *inogorodni* and even threatened to exterminate them.[105] Second the Whites were committed to anti-democratic politics in White areas. This was seen most clearly in the failure of the SRs to build a democratic regime. On June 8, the Czechoslovak legion, stirred up by the imperialists against the Bolsheviks, rose in revolt. Under their protection, a number of "governments" sprang up. In Samara, the SRs formed a government, the Constituent Assembly Committee. Elsewhere, the right wing formed openly anti-communist and anti-democratic governments. And the Czechoslovaks, who were doing the fighting, insisted that all anti-communists should unite. Under their pressure, a conference of various non-Bolshevik "governments" was held. This conference met in Ufa (September 8–25, 1918). Cadets, SRs, Mensheviks, all united. In place of separate governments, there was created one "directorate" in which SRs collaborated with liberals. Eventually, Admiral Kolchak overthrew this regime and set up his dictatorship.[106]

Another facet of White Terror was its Nazi-style anti-Semitism. According to one estimate, in 1918–21, there were two thousand pogroms, twelve thousand of them in the Ukraine, where one hundred fifty thousand Jews died. Brutal torture, including smashing children against walls, torturing pregnant women, burying people up to their necks and then driving horses over them, was very common.[107] Completely out of sympathy with the common people, the White Generals had a capacity of extreme cruelty and a penchant for orgies.[108] As Leonard Schapiro, an anticommunist historian, summed up the civil war:

> The major factor in Kolchak's defeat . . . was his failure to win over the population, which although far from pro-communist, preferred Soviet rule in the last resort.[109]

The "democratic" parties, i.e., the Mensheviks and the SRs failed to dissociate themselves from the Whites. In October, they were the main forces behind the "Committee for Salvation." Soon after, Mensheviks, SRs, and regional nationalists came together to proclaim a Transcaucasian Republic in February 1918, which shortly after split into three republics—Georgia, Armenia, and Azerbaizan. Baku was then ruled by a Bolshevik-dominated commune. Menshevik-ruled Georgia, in alliance with the British, blockaded Baku and eventually proclaimed a "peoples' dictatorship" there. In August, Stepan Shaumyan and 25 other Bolshevik Commissars of the erstwhile Baku Commune were arrested, and then shot by British soldiers on September 30, 1918.[110]

Inside the Soviet territories, the SRs, Mensheviks, and Cadets set up, in March 1918, the *Soyuz Vozrozhdeniia* (Union of Renewal), which entered into relations with the Allies to cooperate in the overthrow of the Soviet government. Other groups were founded for terrorist action.[111]

In May 1918, the Eighth National Council of the SR Party resolved that in order to get rid of the Bolshevik government, it was permissible to allow the entry of Allied troops in Russia.[112] SRs also assassinated Bolshevik leaders like Volodarsky and Uritsky, while attempts were also made to assassinate Lenin, who survived being shot by Fanny Kaplan, and to blow up Trotsky's train.[113] Sidney Reilly, a notorious British spy, was also involved in Kaplan's attempt to murder Lenin. [114]

It was thus a situation of grim battle unto death. Imperialism, the ultra-right, and even "democrats" were pushing the regime to the wall. In the long run, the regime saw its survival as being dependent on the spread of the world revolution—"Either the Russian Revolution will raise the whirlwind of struggle in the West or the Capitalists of all countries will crush our revolution."[115] But meanwhile, in the months or few years required, as they thought, they had to hold on. The reality that began to unfold was that of a beleaguered fortress awaiting help from outside, but meanwhile imposing a tight discipline and a tight rationing on all inhabitants. Theory and practice had to be matched to that mould. Underestimation of the counter-revolution would lead to a wrong framework for assessing this practice.

III
THE BOLSHEVIKS AND THE CONSTITUENT ASSEMBLY

On the basis of the framework for discussion outlined in the two foregoing sections, it is now necessary to take up specific aspects of the early Soviet regime. The first crucial debate is over the dissolution of the Constituent Assembly.

The RSDRP Programme of 1903 had demanded a Constituent Assembly, elected on the basis of universal suffrage for both men and women. In 1917, the Bolsheviks had called for power to the Soviets. But they had not dropped the call for a Constituent Assembly. In the first place, apart from Trotsky, no one had envisaged the transition from bourgeois democratic to proletarian socialist revolution prior to 1917. As a result, the call for a Constituent Assembly, as the most consistent bourgeois slogan, had been identified with the Bolshevik program. As long as the fate of the revolution was uncertain, as long as workers' power was not actually established, this slogan could not be abandoned as something that had been overtaken by events. Moreover, the Cadets, SRs, and Mensheviks, despite their formal commitment to the Constituent Assembly, were in practice ensuring its postponement. That even the SRs, most closely associated in 1917 with the idea of a Constituent Assembly, were not keen about an early convocation of the Assembly, was later admitted by Boris Sokolov, an SR leader.[116]

As for the Cadets, they did not, in reality, want a Constituent Assembly elected on a universal suffrage. Their support to Kornilov bears this out. In such a situation, the call for election to the Constituent Assembly remained progressive vis-a-vis Kerensky's bonapartism, or Kornilov's attempted coup.

The Constituent Assembly elections were finally held in November 1917, after the October insurrection. Election results were declared by December 30. Out of 707 delegates, 370 were Socialist Revolutionaries, 175 Bolsheviks, 40 Left SRs, 16 Mensheviks, 17 Cadets, 2 Popular Socialists, 86 representatives of National Minorities, including SRs of Minority Nations, and one unknown.[117]

These figures are usually cited as if the SR hegemony is thereby proved. But a thorough scrutiny of the evidence says something else. The SRs who were elected from the non-Russian territories, were considerably to the left of the Russian SRs. So the overall strength of the left wing of the Constituent Assembly would have been much more than the 215 out of 707. Radkey's study suggests that on many issues, these leftists would have acted together, and the right SRs would not have obtained a majority.[118] This shows that the Assembly would have been an unstable body. An analysis of votes polled in 54 constituencies out of a total of 79 showed that taking the country as a whole, the Menshevik–SR block had 62 percent of the popular votes.[119]

However, there were many factors that had to be taken into consideration. First, in the two capitals, Moscow and Petrograd, the Bolsheviks received more votes (837,000) than the combined votes of the SRs and Cadets (733,000).[120] Second, hardly 50 percent of the voters had voted. In some areas, no voting was conducted. In some frontline units, the fall of the Provisional Government was concealed from the soldiers by the officers. In the third place, elections were conducted on the basis of proportional representation for party lists. The high rural votes for the SRs reflected a support for the SR program. But that program was now defended only by leftists in the SR party, who split from the parent party, but only after the electoral lists had been drawn up. As a result, while the much more popular Left SR party collaborated with the Bolsheviks, the Right SRs, due to their control of the party apparatus, dominated the list of SR candidates. The fact that popular support for the SRs reflected chiefly support for the Left SRs was shown by the greater proportion of votes received by the latter wherever they had been able to put up separate lists. Thus, in Petrograd the Left SRs received 16.2 percent of the total votes, the Right SRs, 0.5 percent. In Kazan it was: LSRs., 18.9 percent, SRs., 2.1 percent, and in the Baltic Fleet, Left SRs., 26.9 percent, Right SRs., 11.9 percent.[121] In the fourth place, elections to the Constituent Assembly, with individual citizens being asked to cast their votes, gave results tilted against revolution and self-government, whereas every form of collective agitation, collective meeting, etc., showed a tilt to the Left. Boris Sokolov, the SR leader, recorded that at a Congress of Soldiers, where the SRs had about two-thirds of the delegates, an appeal of the SR leader Avksentiev was turned down by small majority who voted in favor of a resolution calling for power to the Soviets.[122]

Out of these events grew both the practical response of the Bolsheviks, and the theoretical debate that ensued. For Lenin, Trotsky and their co-thinkers, the Constituent Assembly was a bourgeois institution, which no longer corresponded with the current needs of the revolution. This was so, because the Constituent Assembly elections, despite being based on universal suffrage, had many technical deficiencies, like lack of information, etc., and two crucial political shortcomings. One was that due to the late split in the SR party, the SR seats in the Assembly went to rightists who would otherwise have lost to leftist peasant representatives. This was one of the arguments put forward by Lenin in justifying the dissolution of the Constituent Assembly.[123] Radkey, not at all partial to the Bolsheviks, confirms this evaluation of Lenin's.[124] Indeed, Radkey provides data to show that the strength of Bolshevism declined as the distance from the metropolitan centers increased. So, once the activities of the new Soviet Government became more widely known, the popularity of Bolshevism would have grown. "The conclusion is inescapable, that only time was needed to make the more remote fronts resemble the Petersburg garrison."[125]

However, this was not the most important consideration. The major problem lay in the failure to consider the relationship between Soviets and Constituent Assembly. In the speech that Trotsky gave to the Pre-parliament, before walking out, the end was: "all power to the Soviets. All land to the people, . . . On with the Constituent Assembly."[126] This authoritative statement, by the leader most aware of the specific character of Soviets, shows that up to October, the Bolsheviks had not considered sufficiently seriously the question of a conflict between the Constituent Assembly and the Soviets. They viewed the opposition as one between Kerensky's government and both the Soviets and the Constituent Assembly.

Lenin was worried about the practical aspects. After October, Lenin, Trotsky, and Bukharin all raised the question of the relationship between Soviets and the Assembly. However, Bukharin assumed that the problem would go away because of a Bolshevik-Left SR majority.[127] Only Lenin insisted on the need to stop the elections themselves.[128] Amidst this uncertainly among the leaders, the elections were held. But the Constituent Assembly could not be considered in isolation from the class struggle. On December 13(26), *Pravda* published Lenin's "Theses on the Constituent Assembly." In it he argued that the Soviets were institutions of a higher form of democracy. So the bourgeois republic headed by a Constituent Assembly should not be chosen in place of a Soviet state. That would be retrograde.[129] This was the crucial theoretical claim. Lenin poured ridicule on those who argued that there should be first majority vote, and then the beginning of socialism.[130]

The dissolution of the Constituent Assembly gave rise to a major debate. Karl Kautsky condemned the Bolsheviks. He asserted that "Socialism, as such is not our goal, which is the abolition of every kind of exploitation and oppression."[131] His goal was socialist parliamentarism, for, "The control of the Government is the most important duty of parliament."[132] In passing, he even justified the postponement of the elections to the Constituent Assembly, by the Provisional Government.[133] Counterposing Soviets to the Assembly, Kautsky agreed that Soviets played an important role in the development of class struggle, but denied that they were institutions of proletarian democracy.[134] In short, Kautsky rejected the very concepts "bourgeois democracy" and "proletarian democracy." The dissolution, for him, represented a turn to authoritarianism. His definition of democracy is a simple one—universal suffrage and parliament.[135]

Lenin's response, *The Proletarian Revolution and the Renegade Kautsky* (1918), accused Kautsky of obscuring the concept of the dictatorship of the proletariat which Lenin said, required its own special form. In this, Lenin was quite correct. But he then argued that the dictatorship of the proletariat "is rule won and maintained by the use of violence."[136] Thus indiscriminate use of violence shows how a general principle was being transformed into a special idea ("class rule" being substituted by "class violence," and then just "violence"). This was the mentality typical of defenders of a besieged revolution, facing brutal violence from the "civilized" and "democratic" world and its Russian agents. Once this kind of argument was put forward, it became questionable, whether he was in favor of the dissolution of the Constituent Assembly because proletarian (Soviet) democracy was superior, or whether only because the Bolsheviks had failed to get a stable majority, either alone, or in alliance with the Left SRs, in the Assembly.

In 1920, Trotsky replied to Kautsky with the book *Terrorism and Communism*. His arguments were more considered ones, perhaps because he was trying to win over left Social Democrats to communism. He emphasized that democracy should not mean simply counting votes, but taking resolute measures to win the majority. For this, appropriate institutions were needed. This was a principled counterposition. But he also referred to the attitude of the Whites, a contingent issue, to justify dissolution of the Assembly.[137] Finally, in some places, he seemed to be contrasting "dictatorship" to "democracy," as when he wrote that "the dictatorship of the Soviets became possible only by means of the dictatorship of the party."[138]

Rosa Luxemburg participated in this debate. Her critique of the Bolsheviks, made in 1918, is of lasting value. But a distinction has to be made between her positive comments and her own limitations. Luxemburg took issue with a 1918 pamphlet by Trotsky. She hailed the revolution, and acknowledged that democracy could have been saved, not by waiting for formed elections, but by the assumption of power by workers and peasants. But then turning to the Assembly she concentrated on the point made by Trotsky that the Assembly reflected a past stage of consciousness. She asked why in that case fresh elections had not been held. On the question of Soviets versus parliament, her position was at this stage unclear.[139] It was in late 1918-early 1919, when a similar situation arose in Germany, that Kautsky, in the name of socialism and democracy, called for power to the National Assembly in opposition to Workers' and Soldier's Councils. The fundamental point about the dissolution of the Constituent Assembly could then be understood. There was no possibility of combining Constituent Assembly and Soviet, i.e., bourgeois democracy and workers' democracy. One was based on the atomized citizen, the other on the collective producer. Had Soviet power survived, the dissolution would have been only an episode.[140]

IV
THE SOVIET DICTATORSHIP

It has already been discussed, in Chapter 7, that in 1917, the soviets were the real organizations of the people. With the soviets as building blocks, the Bolsheviks hoped to go forward to socialist construction. However, at this stage, they never thought that socialism was an economic system that could be built in one country. Their faith in socialist construction was based on their expectation of a world (primarily European) revolution. In October 1917, when Lenin was trying to convert the Central Committee to the idea of an uprising, he stressed this point repeatedly. On October 1st, he said, "In Germany the beginning of the revolution is obvious."[141] On October 16, at the meeting of the Central Committee, he said, "by acting at that moment the Bolsheviks would have all proletarian Europe on their side."[142]

There was no doubt whatsoever among the Bolsheviks that survival of a workers' government in Russia depended on the spread of the revolution. Even Stalin could summarize the difference between Lenin on one hand and Zinoviev and Kamenev on the other over the October revolution in these words: "There are two lines here: one steers for the victory of the revolution and relies on Europe, the second has no faith in the revolution and reckons on being only an opposition."[143] E. H. Carr concludes that the European revolution's proximity was the factor "on which the confident calculations . . . of every Bolshevik of any account, had been based."[144]

The European revolution was no chimera in this period. It began with the Easter Rising in Ireland in 1916. It continued with the fall of Tsarism. A naval revolt and a general strike in November 1918 overthrew the German Kaiser. Prince Max of Baden tried to assume a regency. But workers and soldiers set up Councils. Revolution had already descended on the streets of Vienna, Budapest and Prague. In Bulgaria, Tsar Ferdinand abdicated, and Stamboulisky, the peasant leader who had just been liberated from jail, got control over the government. Victor Serge writes: "From the Scheldt to the Volga the councils of workers' and soldiers' deputies—the Soviets—are the real masters of the hour."[145] In March 1919, a Soviet government took power in Hungary. In the same year, massive labor unrest shook Britain. For two years massive class struggles convulsed Italy, until a fascist counter-revolution brought Mussolini to power.[146] It was on the basis of these struggles, unprecedented in scope, that the attempts were launched to build a Soviet Europe. By 1920, the Communist International counted in its ranks powerful parties in Italy, Czechoslovakia, France, Bulgaria, Sweden, Germany, Norway, and Yugoslavia.

In January 1919, provocations had resulted in an untimely rising and the beheading of the KPD leadership. But the revolutionary wave was still very strong. "All power to the Councils," and "Dictatorship of the proletariat" became a watch-word of the European working class— for the first and last time in history. As Otto Bauer, an Austrian Social Democratic leader who worked hard to prevent the socialist revolution, explained, the Austrian proletariat (to give one example), "considered the establishment of the dictatorship of the proletariat to be possible."[147] An eyewitness wrote, "An ever widening circle saw in the Workers' and Soldiers' councils, based on the Russian Soviet model, the future structure of representation in Germany."[148]

Eventually, this world revolution was defeated. In 1921, Soviet Russia stood as the isolated, solitary, advanced outpost of a failed revolutionary wave. Counter-revolution was unable to conquer it. But its crisis became acute. The fate of Soviet democracy in Russia was settled as much in Berlin, Vienna, Budapest, or Turin, as in Russia. It is with this in mind that one should turn to the growth and decline of the Soviets. "Given the absence of a freely-elected parliament (in October 1917), the Soviet Congress . . . was certainly the broadest democratic representation in Russia."[149]

This verdict of Anweiler depicts accurately the position in 1917. The struggle for supremacy between the bourgeoisie and working class as reflected in the contest between Soviets and municipal dumas and zemstvos. The Soviet settled twenty-five major and forty minor labor disputed during the early months of the revolution.[150] In Nizhni Novgorod, the Soviet organized local bread supply. In Krasnoyarsk the Soviet introduced ration cards. Bolshevik dominated Soviets in the Urals set up courts, created militias, organized a workers' inspection, established a wage scale, and in some areas even took land from the landlords and put it under social cultivation.[151]

In 1917, the massive economic crisis had led the unions and factory committees to take up demands for democratizing the factories, etc. The borderline between "political and economic" had collapsed. This made the setting up of bourgeois democracy difficult. October legitimized the alternative process of setting up a workers' democracy. The Congress of Soviets had approved in principle of a government of all the socialist parties, but it had also set up its own program in the form of the Decrees on Land and Peace. It had also recognized the Sovnarkom as a government subordinate to the Soviets.

At the Congress, a representative of Vikzhel had threatened to shut out the new government from the railways. A debate ensured, with Kamenev defending the legality of the Second Congress of Soviets and asserting the power of Soviets. Some railway workers also challenged the authority of Vikzhel to speak on behalf of them.[152] The debates appeared confusing, with both sides formally saying that they agreed to a government of the entire "revolutionary democracy," i.e., of all the socialist parties. In fact, there was a clear division, between those who were in favor of subordinating the government to the Soviets and those who opposed such subordination. However, Kamenev, one of the most moderate Bolsheviks, was not firmly in favor of Soviet power on this point. At the second session of the newly created VTsIK (October 29) Kamenev, who was its Chairman, replied to the Vikzhel's ultimatum by saying: "What matters most is not the personal composition of such a government but recognition of the fundamental (decrees) adopted at the (Second) Congress of Soviets."[153]

This showed his willingness to drop Lenin and Trotsky from the government (one of the main demands of the other parties) but it also showed why Kamenev could go along at least partly with the demand to make the government independent of Soviet control. He was willing to concede that the VTsIK should be expanded by including representatives of other institutions. At a meeting of the Central Committee from which Lenin and Trotsky were absent, it was unanimously agreed that the "base of the government has to be widened."[154] The real meaning, it was disclosed three days later, on November 1, when Kamenev made a report on the ongoing negotiations with the other parties, Vikzhel, etc. The "widening" was not envisaged as a process of drawing in other working-class organizations, unrecognized trade unions, and so on. As the Central Committee minutes put it:

> What came out of the proposals was that an organ should be created to which the government would be responsible: consisting of 100 members of the VTsIK, 75 representing the peasants, 80 from the navy, 100 from Peter [i.e., Petrograd] and Moscow (city) Dumas; 15 from Vikzhel, 20 from the All-Russian Trade Union.[155]

This was absurd on both practical and principled grounds. The VTsIK, elected by an All-Russia Congress of Soviets, was to have 100 delegates, while the city dumas of only two cities were to have an equal number of delegates. The All-Russia Trade Union was allotted 20 delegates, while for playing the role of match maker, Vikzhel was granted huge over-representation — 15 delegates. In practical terms such uneven and ill representation meant a negation of democracy. It meant, moreover, a forced combination of working-class organs with bourgeois organs like the city dumas. Kamenev's opponents in the Central Committee pointed this out. Jan Berzin, the Latvian leader, insisted that "we are all agreed that there are points on which we can concede nothing. This applies to the point: all power to the Soviets. This does not exclude the possibility of supplementation but . . . the only enlargement permissible is from Soviets who were not present."[156] Rykov, by contrast, supported Kamenev and said that representation from city Dumas was not unacceptable.[157] So, the debate, both inside and outside the Bolshevik party, was over whether it was to be a Soviet government, or a government of socialist parties. It was the non-Bolshevik socialists who, even when offered posts in the ministry, rejected, as a matter of principle, the authority of the congress of Soviets and the VTsIK.

On the same day (November 1), at the meeting of the VTsIK, Volodarsky spoke on behalf of the Bolsheviks. He asked the VTsIK to consider what the minimum principled basis of agreement should be: agreement on the decrees of peace, land and workers' control adopted by the Soviet Congress, and accountability of the government to the Soviet. Meeting head on the criticism that the Bolsheviks wanted to ignore democratic organs, Volodarsky reminded his audience, that almost half the deputies to the Petrograd municipal duma were Bolsheviks. He therefore affirmed that the defense of Soviet power as a matter of principle was the basic reason for his party's opposition to the creation of a hybrid organ of power.[158] A resolution moved by Volodarsky asked the VTsIK to reaffirm that a coalition among all the socialist parties was possible only on the basis of the acceptance of the program of the Government, recognition of the authority of the Second

Congress of Soviets, accountability to VTsIK, and to expand the VTsIK by including representatives of Soviets, all-Russian trade unions, factory committees, peasant deputies, but not any representative of non-Soviet organizations.[159] Thus, the debate over Soviet power was fought out, and resolved in its favor. In the Central Committee of the Bolshevik Party, Lenin, Trotsky, and Sverdlov initially found themselves in a minority on the question of ending the negotiations.[160]

Eventually, on November 2 after a long battle, Lenin won a majority in the Central Committee. The Central Committee accepted his stand, that if minorities in the Soviets resorted to ultimatums in order to subvert Soviet democracy, acceding to them meant going against proletarian democracy.[161]

The stiff stance taken by Lenin reflected two concerns. On the one hand, the positions that Lenin, Trotsky, Volodarsky, Sverdlov, Avanesov, and others took, whether in the VTsIK or in the Central Committee, showed their commitment to workers' democracy. A second factor was their awareness that the Mensheviks and Right SRs were not serious about any Soviet regime. On November 2, the Central Committee of the Socialist Revolutionary party passed a resolution, in which it said that the basis of agreement had to be, among other things: "The new government shall be made up of the Socialists without Bolshevik representatives."[162]

Serious negotiation with such a party was obviously not on the cards. Lenin's intransigent stand was able to win over the right wing in his own party, and the Left SRs, who ultimately joined a coalition government, because his real opponents were no less intransigent. They had demanded the disarming of the workers, which would have meant depriving the workers' democracy of its armed support. It was not a question of personal intransigence, but of class power.

The establishment of the Soviet government and the dissolution of the Constituent Assembly opened up a fresh period of expansion for the Soviets. A constitution was adopted, and Soviets at the local level grew in power and in numbers.

The Constitution of the Russian Soviet Federated Socialist Republic was created after several drafts. It was adopted in July 1918 by the fifth All-Russian Congress of Soviets. The first four chapters repeated the Declaration of Rights of the Toiling and Exploited People adopted by the Third Soviet Congress. The fifth chapter enunciated a series of general propositions, including the federal character of the republic. The separation of church from state and school from Church, freedom of speech, opinion and assembly for the workers, and series of rights and duties, including the abolition of all discrimination on grounds of race or nationality, and the obligation for all citizens to work.

After this came the practical arrangement of power. The supreme power was invested in the All-Russian Congress of Soviets, comprising representatives of city Soviets on the basis of one deputy to twenty-five thousand voters and of provincial Soviets on the basis of one deputy to every one hundred twenty-five thousand voters. The Congress was to meet every six months.[163] It was to elect the Central Executive Committee (VTsIK) which exercised all power of the Congress when the latter was not in session. VTsIK appointed the Sovnarkom. Subsequent chapters of the constitution dealt with various levels of regional Soviets, Soviet Congress, and their executives.[164]

The Soviet constitution came into existence less through deliberations by constitution makers than through a unity of different practices that were developing. The Marxist theory of the state called for a two-faced working-class state—a state which acted as a ruling class state in opposing bourgeois restorationism, and a state that began to die out. This resulted in a tension between a centralizing and a decentralizing tendency.

Second, the Marxist theory of state claimed that it was necessary to overcome the division between executive and legislative bodies. Thus, neither the Soviet legislative nor the VTsIK were intended to act as parliament. Nor was Sovnarkom a cabinet in that sense. VTsIK could pass laws. But it could also set up its executive organs.[165] In every department or commissariat, the responsible People's Commissar was flanked by members of the VTsIK.[166] Initially the VTsIK had the potential of becoming a powerful body. Its weakening was part of an overall process of growing decay. Up to the Fifth Congress, Soviet Congresses met more or less once in three months, but the constitution provided, instead, for meeting twice in a year. This was due to the difficulty of having the Congress meet regularly in Civil War situations. Likewise, the very nature of the VTsIK as both a legislative and an executive organ meant that many VTsIK members had specific duties, including military work. Finally, the growing polarization and hostility among parties made the VTsIK less effective. The real power devolved upon the VTsIK Presidium, and the Sovnarkom.[167] The growth of the Sovnarkom's power is attested to by the fact that while the VTsIK, between 1917 and 1921, issued 375 decrees, Sovnarkom issued, 1615.[168]

The definition of Soviet power, as conceived in, for example, *The State and Revolution,* called for a voluntary centralization, with an extensive role for local Soviets. These ranged from the volost (district) or city Soviets to uezd congresses and guberniya congress.[169] Robert Abrams' study of the local Soviets shows that in the period 1918–1921, local Soviets were able to displace the old political elite, and create a new political culture with a high degree of input from the lower classes.[170]

In the local Soviets, as late as 1921, the communists were not mostly predominant. In volost executive committees, non-party members predominated. In district city executives, communists were in a slight majority. The advantage of being an organized party was that at the upper level, in the provincial city and congress executive committees, the communists had superiority. However, it has also been noted that the party grew from 24,000 in early 1917 to over ten times by July–August. So even the induction of communists in the Soviets shows the rise of a new layer of administrators. In 1919, the only year for which such statistics are available, only 12.5 percent of the district city executive committees could be considered old Bolsheviks. In the provincial city executive committees in the same years, about 50 percent were old Bolsheviks.[171] The proportion of old Bolsheviks in the uezd congress executive committees, in fact, declined from 12.2 percent in 1919 to 7.6 percent in 1921.[172]

In view of the decline of the other parties in this period, the large-scale entry of non-party activists showed that local Soviets were becoming a base for the creation of a new generation of administrators who came mostly from the workers and the peasants. In the district executive committees in 1919, a sample of 219 gave out that 20.6 percent had no more than a high school education, while only 4.5 percent had university education.[173]

The age composition of local Soviet executive committee members show that in 1919, in a sample of 2662, taken from 30 percent of all local Soviet executive committee members in the district congress and city executive committees, and 40 percent of those in the provincial congress and city executive committees, the age distribution was the following:[174]

Under 25 years	— —	13.7%
25 – 29 years	— —	30.3%
30 – 39 years	— —	44.2%
40 and above	— —	11.8%

These statistics tend to confirm the view that political activity in the early years of RSFSR were not confined either to the old bureaucracy, or to the old parties. The old bureaucracy had been on average better educated. In the new Soviet administration, neither the Tsarist bureaucracy, nor the old "third element" were a major component. The relative youth would indicate that many of these people could not have been eligible for the official posts during the Tsarist era.

Abrams' study further shows that about 50 percent of the district executive committee members held office for all four years (1918–1921). In the provincial executive committees, more than two-thirds maintained their positions throughout the period of War Communism. So these were quite stable institutions. But partly, this was because the Civil War conditions made regular elections difficult. Further, the shortage of able workers made it difficult to organize purges even when necessary.[175]

On the one hand, it is possible to discern in these latter events, a beginning of bureaucratization. On the other hand, the fact that non-party people, young and of ordinary or low educational levels, were coming forward, shows that Soviet democracy did play an important role in the early years.

Studies on the early Soviet period (1917-1918) suggest a turn away from the Bolsheviks in early 1918. Samuel Farber cites a case where the Bolsheviks responded to loss in elections in Vyatka by using force to abrogate the city Soviet election.[176] Certainly, the Soviet system had no chance to grow in a condition of peace. The reverse case, of Baku, saw Bolsheviks handing over power after being defeated, and being murdered soon after. The pressure of civil war made a peaceful democratic contest through the Soviets quite unworkable. But, for a brief period in late 1917, and early 1918, local Soviets did show their potential. Alexander Rabinowitch has written:

> During the first months after the October Revolution, Russia workers, soldiers, and sailors who had supported the overthrow of the Provisional Government in the name of Soviet power—power of ordinary citizens exercised through democratically operated Soviets—participated in revolutionary politics most actively and directly through city and district Soviets.[177]

Rabinowitch's microstudy of one city district Soviet shows how this institution almost entirely displaced the subdistrict dumas and municipal boards. It was not only authoritative, but quite independent of even central Soviet control. A great many function of the soviet included a network of people's courts and an investigating commission. The Soviet had a social welfare section, a legal section, a housing section, a culture and education section, with separate sub-sections for preschool training and children, schools, adult continuing education, and theater and cinema. The First city District Soviet had its own press section, and from April 1918, it put out a substantial district newspaper, the *Vestnik pervogo gorodskogo raiona*. The paper kept residents informed about district Soviet activities and about developments relating to food supply, health and sanitation problems, and various other kinds of detailed information about daily life.[178]

From May 25 to June 5, the District held a workers' conference. Of the 201 voting delegates, 134 were Bolsheviks, 13 Left SRs, 30 Mensheviks and Menshevik Internationalists, and 24 SRs. Among 30 delegates who had voice but no vote, there were six non-Bolsheviks. In the words of Rabinowitch, it was an attempt at "an honest effort to restore meaningful links with the masses despite the stirrings of civil war."[179]

The Bolsheviks still took the Soviets seriously. At the 7th (extraordinary) Congress of the RSDRP(B), held in 1918, (when it renamed itself the Communist party), Lenin said:

> Soviet power is a new type of state without a bureaucracy, without police, without a regular army, a state in which bourgeois democracy has been replaced by a new democracy, a democracy that brings to the force the vanguard of the working people, gives them legislative and executive authority, makes them responsible for military defend and creates state machinery that can re-educate the masses.[180]

As the foregoing discussion on local Soviets shows, this was not mere rhetoric. In this early period, the Soviets did make a beginning in replacing bureaucracy by elected and accountable officials. If, within a year, 25 percent of them at the gubernia level, and 50 percent at the city and volost level were replaced, it shows that despite civil war, this function of training common people remained with the Soviets for quite some time, and was accepted in principle by the Bolsheviks. Thus, when Lenin said that "the socialist character of Soviet, i.e., *proletarian democracy* . . . lies in the fact that . . . for the first time a start is made by the *entire* population in learning the art of administration,"[181] he was not exaggerating greatly. Soviets went on developing everywhere. In the Perm province, about five hundred volost councils were established in the first quarter of 1918. In the Voronezh province, by March, seventy-eight out of eighty-four volosts had Soviets.[182] In the army, the Second, Third, and Tenth armies elected Bolshevik-Left SR majorities in mid-November. The Western Frontline Congress and the regional congress of Western Soviets, held concurrently, gave two-third support to the Bolsheviks. At the Rumanian Front the Executive committee of the army, the Black Sea fleet, and the Odessa oblast (Rumcherod) returned increasingly pro-Bolshevik forces. On December 23, the second Congress of Soviets of the Rumanian front met, with 854 frontline delegates, 106 urban delegates, and 87 peasant delegates. The Bolsheviks had 396 and the Left SRs 220 votes. The Mensheviks and right-wing SRs refused to join the new Rumcherod. On December 25, Soviets took power in Odessa.[183]

However, this growth of Soviet power was soon halted. The most important factor was the isolation of the revolution. No Russian Marxist believed that socialism could be built in one country, least of all in backward, peasant-majority Russia. As early as 1906, Trotsky had predicted that the Russian Revolution would have to seek help from the world revolution, or perish in the face of world counter-revolution. Lenin repeated this view in 1918.[184]

But world revolution could not be hurried along. Meanwhile, from the early months of the revolution, both the domestic right-wing and imperialism had been hostile to the Bolsheviks. The October Revolution was followed by a counter-revolution, which received unstinted support from the imperialists. And almost all opposition parties drew close to the counter-revolution, and failed to demarcate clearly between opposition to the government on the one hand and armed rebellion against Soviet power on the other. Consequently, the democratic forms decayed. In Petrograd the last fully free and democratic elections were held in June 18–24, 1918. The Bolsheviks obtained 48.5 percent of the delegates, the Left SRs 12.2 percent, the Right SRs 17.6 percent, the Mensheviks 11.1 percent and independent 10.7 percent.[185]

TABLE 8.1[186]

Bolsheviks and Soviet Congresses

Party	2nd Congress (Oct. 1917)	4th Congress (March 1918)	5th Congress (July 1918)	7th Congress (Dec. 1919)
Bolsheviks	350	797	868	97%
Left SRs	180	275	470	N.A.
Others	—–	132	87	N.A.
Non-Party	105	22	—–	N.A.

The table above shows how the decline of multi-party Soviet democracy was closely connected to the Civil War, which began in July 1918. The sudden collapse of multiparty democracy[187] turned the Soviets into administrative organs rather than the combination of executive and legislative bodies that Lenin had sought. Working-class participation, however, did rise, not only in the lower levels, but also at the top. In 1918, in twenty of the most important departments of the state economic administration, officials of proletarian origin and delegates from working-class organizations accounted for 43 percent of the total, as against 38 percent with a record in the former Tsarist bureaucracy.[188] But as Soviets collapsed due to Civil War and the dispersal of the proletariat non-elected "revolutionary committees" or expanded party committees, replaced them in many places.[189] Thus, non-elected, unrepresentative bodies began to be set up. With the elected, militant workers being replaced, functionaries now became more important. By the end of 1920, there were 5,880,000 such functionaries, and less than 2 million industrial workers.[190] In Vyatka, Stalin found that out of 4,766 members of the staff of the Soviet authorities, 4,467 were former Tsarist officials.[191]

It was not a Bolshevik drive for complete power that caused this process. On the contrary, the Bolsheviks registered this process with great unease as when Lenin said in 1919, at the Eighth Party Congress:

The Soviets, which by virtue of their programme are organs of government by the working people, are in fact organs of government for the working people by the advanced section of the proletariat.[192]

In a subsequent occasion, he wrote of the "dictatorship of the working class" as being implemented by the Bolshevik party" which had "merged with the entire revolutionary proletariat."[193] Nor was he alone, Zinoviev told the Eighth Congress that fundamental questions "must be decided by the Central Committee of our Party . . . which thus carries these decisions through the Soviet organs . . . of course, cleverly and tactfully."[194] Kamenev told the Ninth Party Congress in 1920 that the Communist Party was the real government, with nobody objecting to this stark description of the reality.[195] Victor Serge spelled out the change with precision and clarity:

> With the disappearance of political debates between parties representing different social interests through the various shades of their opinion, Soviet institutions, beginning with the local Soviets and ending with the Vee-Tsik and the Council of People's Commissars, manned solely by communists, now function in a Vacuum: since all the decisions are taken by the party, all they can do is give them the official rubberstamp.[196]

V
THE RISE AND DECLINE OF WORKERS' CONTROL

The history of the unfolding and eventual crisis of workers' power can be fully comprehended only if several aspects are taken into account. One such is workers' control. Workers' control was a major issue throughout 1917. For Marx, socialism meant disalienation of the working class. Trotsky in 1905-06 had been emphatic in his insistence that in a revolutionary period, there would not be any rigid division between the minimum program and the maximum program, and that the link would be created by workers seeking to enforce the minimum program and coming up against capitalist resistance.

In 1917, that was more or less what had happened. In February, workers did not begin with a specifically socialist program, but they insisted on continuing their struggles until the eight-hour day was won, etc. The desire of the workers for a democratization of relationships in the factory, for less exploitation, and minimum rights, clashed against the capitalist drive for profits, and the government's attitude that the prosecution of the war took precedence over all social demands. Thus, while workers were beginning to embrace the demand for Soviet power, it was for peace and the defense of democratic right, rather than explicitly for socialism. For example, the workers of the Old Baranovskii Machine Construction Factory, quite radical in politics, couched their call to arms against Kornilov in the following terms:

> Believing in our bright future, we raise high the banner of Freedom—long
> live the Great Russian Revolution. To the defense, comrade workers and
> soldiers, of freedom, so dear to us against the executioners, who would
> lead it to slaughter.[197]

Thus, it was not a predetermined socialist goal, but objective
circumstances, that moved the worker. The creation of a "constitutional"
factory, where the foremen were not autocrats, was seen by workers to be
the prerequisite of an enhancement of the status and dignity of workers
within society as a whole. The struggle for the democratization of factory
relations took various forms. First, hated foremen and administrators
fled or were expelled. At the Putilov works, workers thrust Puzanov,
a leader of the factory Black Hundreds (an ultra-right, proto-fascist
Party, protected by Tsarism) into a wheelbarrow, poured red lead over
his head, and threatened to throw him into a nearly canal.[198] Next
came the destruction of factory rulebooks with their punitive fines
and humiliating searches. Then, finally, came the creation of factory
committees, through which workers' control was gradually established.

The movement was created neither by Bolshevik propaganda,
nor by anarchist or chiliastic desires.[199] Up to October, the Bolsheviks
did not put forward the program of full nationalization. For them, the
establishment of the dictatorship of the proletariat was the starting point
of a long road to building socialism. And the process of full-fledged
socialist construction could be actualized in the course of expansion of
the revolution to the West. The radicalization of the workers and the
transformation of the factory committees developed from the struggles.
The first forms of workers control were the ejection of managers. When
factory committees were elected, the right to manage the internal order
of the factory was asserted.[200] In private sector factories, no attempts
were made to immediately set up self-management. There the factory
committees functioned more or less like unions. In state enterprises,
workers often began their own management, but subsequently retreated
to a position of monitoring, or supervising the management.[201]

But lockouts, suspicion of sabotage, and incompetent administration
led to the development to workers control in the private sector.[202] In
April–May 1917, there was an intensification of the conflict between
workers and capitalists. There was a consensus among the upper classes
in favor of a tough labor discipline. The workers also believed, equally
strongly, that capital had to be restrained to avert economic collapse.
Factory committees now demanded supervision over managers at the
plant level, and state regulation at the national level.[203] For workers,
this was even more urgent than peace negotiations.

The Provisional Government sought to tackle the problem by suggesting shifting factories closer to sources of fuel and raw material. This would break the social and political power of Red Petrograd. The workers' section of the Petrograd Soviet rejected this plan on May 31 and suggested that a real economic solution required workers' control from both above and below.[204] On June 1, the First Conference of Factory Committees voted for a Bolshevik resolution (297 votes, or just over two-thirds). The Anarchist proposal got just 45 votes, while the Mensheviks got 85. The Bolshevik resolution spoke of the need to take measures both at the enterprise and national level, and called for transfer of state power to the Soviets.[205] Enterprise level control began to assume actual directing tasks like procurement of raw material, fuel, order, etc.

On the question of workers' control, a relatively broad left-wing bloc had formed, including many left-wing Socialist Revolutionaries and other internationalists, as well as Bolsheviks. This left wing began to put forward an economic program of workers' control, whereby working-class political domination could be exercised over the bourgeoisie. Thus a Left SR called for workers' control to end economic dislocation, and the Vyborg Bolshevik Naumov pointed out that "control is not yet socialism . . . we should direct capitalism along such a path that it will outlive itself. . . . That will lead to socialism."[206] By the end of September, owners had become adamant and unwilling to compromise. The workers responded by calling for stricter economic regulations. At the small Brenner engineering works, the factory committee had to take over the plant. At the V. A. Lebedev airplane factory, the workers forced the removal of the director.[207]

The Bolsheviks, until the seizure of power had no clear-cut economic program. Trade unionist Bolsheviks opposed extension of workers' control. Lenin had an idea of gradual development from workers' control to socialism. Left Bolsheviks urged a swift tempo of workers' management. In any case, no one viewed immediate and full-scale nationalization as the best alternative. Lenin's perspective was extensively argued in "Can the Bolsheviks Retain State Power"? He wrote that by juxtaposing the slogan of workers' control to dictatorship of the proletariat, the slogan was given the meaning of a "countrywide, all-embracing, omnipresent, most precise and most conscientious *accounting* of the production and distribution of goods."[208] The state bank, and similar state organs, were to be nationalized. Industrial capitalism was not to be nationalized. Instead, industrial capital was to be surrounded by members of employees' unions, trade unions, Soviets, consumers' societies, etc.[209] "Confiscation alone leads nowhere, as it does not contain the element of organization. . . . (Instead) we could easily impose a *fair* tax . . . taking care . . . to preclude the possibility of anyone evading assessment, concealing the truth, evading the law, and this possibility can be *eliminated only* by the workers' control of the *workers' state*."[210]

The economic program indicated by the Sixth Party Congress dealt chiefly with immediate tasks. It called for nationalization of banks and a number of syndicated enterprises (where monopolistic blocs had already been formed), the extension of workers' control, the abolition of commercial secrecy, and an eventual introduction of universal labor conscription and planned regulation of productions and distribution.[211] This was not the position of left Bolsheviks, like Skrypnik, Chubar, Antipov, et al. While supporting the idea of control through the workers' state, they placed heavy emphasis on the importance of local initiatives. Moreover, they highlighted the factory committees, rather than the trade unions.[212] Neither Lenin, nor his critics within the party, nor the grass roots activists satisfactorily resolved the problem of the relationship between control through the state and control from below. In fact, the question of the mechanisms of production were not discussed as thoroughly as the question of state power, by any party.

At the factory level, there were two types of organizations. Apart from factory committees, the trade unions came into the open and grew swiftly. Official figures (issued in 1928) claimed that the Metal Workers' Union had 82,000 members in Petrograd on July 1, 1917, and that it rose to 190,000 on October 1. The Textile Workers' Union membership rose almost as swiftly.[213] In Russia as a whole, there were about two million trade union members. Trade unions took a somewhat different attitude to workers' control. The Third Conference of Trade Unions in June 1917 had defined the main function of the union as the conduct of the economic struggle in defense of workers' living standards.[214] Bolshevik trade union leaders like Ryazanov, Lozovskii, Shlyapnikov, and Schmidt put the main emphasis on central planning.[215]

The Soviet seizure of power made it possible to implement the slogan of workers' control. The All-Russian Trade Union Council endorsed a narrow definition of workers' control, emphasizing only the creation of a central apparatus to regulate the economy. The leaders of the factory committee movement, by contrast, used the word "Kontrol," to mean, more or less, management. On November 14th, the VTsIK passed a decree on workers' control, legalizing the defacto system of control. Lenin's draft, which served as the basis, gave considerable prominence to local level power.[216]

The real problem lay in the owners' refusal to come to terms. Rank and file workers felt it necessary to set up a full system of workers' control, from state regulation at the top to local control, without which state regulation was a myth. This was why the narrow definition was inapplicable. If the owner did not respond to suggestions, and either sabotaged production, or refused to increase wages, improve working conditions, and so on, control as "supervision" became meaningless. Even the unions, at the first All-Russian Congress of Trade Unions, in January 1918, called for union involvement in the task of reviving the disrupted productive forces. The resolution also called for the subordination of the factory committees to the unions.[217] Meanwhile, the increasing economic crisis was forcing the workers to take radical measures. Between January 1 and May 1, 1918, the industrial workforce in Petrograd shrunk from 339,641 to 142,915.[218] Workers now began to demand nationalization. Between November 1917 and March 1918, only 5.8 percent of all forms of nationalizations and seizures were by Sovnarkom or the Supreme Economic Council (Vesenkha) set up after the revolution.[219] Pressure for nationalization, in other words, came from below.

Nationalization created fresh problems. Lenin had so far assigned to popular initiative the duty of surrounding the capitalists, supervising their work, and so on. Once the workers' state took over the industries, workers' control was to give way to regulation by trade unions and by state-appointed directors. Since the state was a workers' state, his logic was that managers appointed by it would serve it as they served the bourgeoisie when it hired them. This was to overlook an important aspect of socialist construction. Communism meant the transformation from wage-laborer to "associated producer." Even if this could not be done immediately, the line of march needed to be indicated. Lenin, despite his knowledge of Marx's views, was sometimes to ignore this. While he went on insisting on the need for popular participation, he also advocated, at times, that there was no contradiction between Soviet democracy and the use of dictatorial powers by individuals.[220] The idea of factory assemblies hearing reports, or elected members constituting the majority of the board of directors, did not appeal to him very much.

The Left Communists, a faction that formed in 1918, opposed Lenin on this question. V. V. Osinsky pointed out in April 1918 that nationalization did not equate socialization. To create a socialized economy, the bureaucratic hierarchy of power in the workplace had to give way to local level workers' democracy.[221] In fact, this was felt, if less theoretically, by most workers. That explains why, in 1919, only 10.8 percent of Russian enterprises had come under one-man management. One-man management was justified in the name of efficiency. It is true that nationalizations, without central planning, in a period of economic crisis, caused acute problems. But Trotsky, for example, said:

> The dictatorship of the proletariat is expressed in the abolition of private property in the means of production, in the supremacy over the whole

Soviet mechanism of the collective will of the workers and not at all in the form in which the economic enterprises are administered.[222]

In doing this he was ignoring a major aspect of workers' rule. If workers remained alienated, there could not be socialist construction.[223] Justifying ad hoc responses as real progress to communism showed a dangerous theoretical weakness. The situation was grim enough. Much of industry had collapsed. An equitable town–country exchange system was yet to be set up. The onset of civil war called for an immediate centralization of production for the army. All this led to a pressure for a rapid increase in production. By 1920–21, this led to the terminal crisis of the factory committees. The views of Lenin and Trotsky were secondary, but contributory factors. The balance between bureaucracy and democracy in the labor movement did not depend on "Bolshevization," but on the socio-political conditions as a whole. Marc Ferro has suggested that there was a "bureaucratization" from below, as factory committees refused to submit to re-elections.[224] Smith's study of the sources indicates that Ferro overstated his case. A number of factory committees did submit for re-election, and in most elections a majority of workers took part.[225]

Equally, Smith's own claim about a bureaucratization of the trade unions is questionable. In the summer of 1917, the Petrograd Metalworkers' Union had almost a hundred full timers.[226] This gives a ratio of over 820 workers per full timer–not a very bloated apparatus at all. Moreover, these were mostly trade union full-timers, not party men parachuted into positions of power. In Moscow, trade unions grew equally swiftly (e.g. 111,000 textile workers, 65,000 metal workers, 40,000 municipal employees were unionized).[227] The unions at this stage enjoyed considerable independence from the government. But since both unions and factory committees were trying to regulate production, their mutual relationship had to be clarified. Unionists criticized factory committees of parochialism.[228] In response, the leadership of the factory committee movement called for the boards of the unions to be elected by conferences of factory committees within the branch of industry.[229] Thus, if trade unions were to oversee production, and take part in central policy-making they wanted to make the trade union representatives accountable to the members.

It was the Civil War that, tearing apart the already crisis-ridden economy, destroyed workers' control. The main industrial regions of northern and central Russia remained under Soviet rule throughout the Civil War. But the industries often lacked coal (Donets), oil (Baku), iron (Urals, the Ukraine), cotton (Turkestan), etc. The export–import trade shrank dramatically. Russia's imports fell from 936.6 million poods [1 pood=16.38 kilograms] in 1913 to 178 million in 1917, 11.5 million in 1918, 0.5 million in 1919, and 5.2 million in 1920. Exports fell from 1472.1 million poods (1913) to 59.6 million (1917), 1.8 million (1918), nil in 1919, and 0.7 million poods in 1920. Taking the productivity per worker as 100 in 1913, in 1919, it was 22.[230] Terrible conditions, including lack of food, contributed to absenteeism. Large-scale industry in 1920 provided 18 percent of what it had produced in 1913,[231] and the bulk of this meager production was going to the army. Thus, 40 percent of cotton material, 70–100 percent of their textiles, and 90 percent of footwear produced went to the army in the summer of 1920.[232] With large parts of the peasantry turning hostile due to unequal town-country relations, food suppliers were uncertain. Both the attempt to requisition grain, and the organization of production, made a degree of excessive centralization easy to defend. In fact, this, all the more resulted in economic confusion.[233]

In this situation, centrifugal forces became acute. The journal of the Peoples' Commissariat of Labor described how factory committees fought only to keep their factories supplied with orders and funds, and even tried to use force.[234] They behaved as though they were rival capitalist owners competing against each other.[235] Shlyapnikov, the concerned Commissar, told the VTsIK on March 20, 1918, that there was a total chaos in the railways, and that committees were unable to make the system work.[236]

The curbs on workers' control began with those in the railways (March 20, 1918), followed by industries important for the army, like machine and metalworking plants, leather and shoe factories, etc.[237] The pressure on high productivity led to the introduction of production techniques like Taylorism, i.e., the "scientific management" introduced by F. W. Taylor, which increased workload and speed of work. Thus, "authority," that is, centralization at the cost of the factory committees, developed out of the failure of the committees to protect the industries at a period of acute crisis. With nationalization accomplished, it was no longer possible to view the bourgeoisie as the main enemy. So the content of factory level control came to be questioned. While Mensheviks and SRs gained ground in elections in the spring of 1918, it has been strongly argued that they did not represent a coherent alternative in the eyes of the workers.[238]

As a result of the collapse of opposition parties as well as factory committees, coherent democratic alternatives ceased to be practiced. The demand for one-man management began to be raised on a regular basis rather than as stop-gap arrangements. As late as March 1920, in Petrograd 69 percent of the factories employing over 200 workers were still run by collegial boards.[239] The experience of the democratic factory was not simply given up, whether by the workers as a whole, or by most

Bolsheviks. But as vast numbers of most militant workers, mobilized by the unions, joined the army, the militants of 1917–early 1918 were no longer in a position, by 1919, to assert their standpoint.

As yet, the party did not abandon the goal. The program adopted in 1919 called for an intimate association between the Soviet power and the trade unions.[240] But an unending number of exceptions began to be made: for example, on April 7, 1919, a decree forbade miners from leaving their jobs.

The turning point came in 1920-21. And it came about without any understanding of the gravity of the situation. In February 1920, it became clear to Trotsky that the policy of War Communism had arrived at a blind alley. But when he proposed a shift to a tax in kind, it was ruled out by the central committee.[241] Failing in this, Trotsky, however, did not carry out the struggle. On the contrary, at the Ninth Congress, Trotsky and Lenin developed a policy known in history as the "Militarization of labor." This idea had initially been developed a few months earlier. On January 27, 1920, Lenin urged the creation of a "Labor army" for efficiency.[242] On January 15, the same year, Trotsky issued an "order Memorandum about the Third Red Army—First Revolutionary Labor Army." One aspect of it was laudable—an attempt to turn armies to productive work. But Trotsky also affirmed that "A deserter from work, like a deserter from battle, is contemptible and dishonourable. Both are to be punished severely."[243]

This was the substance of the drafts these spresented by Trotsky on behalf of the Central Committee to the 9th Congress. He called on the trade unions to adopt the "same rights in relation to their members as have been previously exercised only by military organizations."[244] The logic was set forth openly: "our state is a workers' state. . . . Hence the trade unions must teach the workers not to haggle and fight with their own state in difficult times, but by common effort to help it get on the bread path of economic development."[245]

The Ninth Congress fully approved Trotsky's report. A number of important party leaders, including Rykov, Lomov, and Larin, all members of the Supreme council of National Economy, and Tomsky, Nogin and other trade unionists opposed this policy. But it needs to be emphasized that this was a policy of the Central Committee, endorsed by the Party Congress.[246] Trotsky explained to the Party Congress that "The militarization of labour is unthinkable without the militarization of trade unions, without the introduction of a regime under which every worker feels himself a soldier of labour who cannot dispose of himself freely. If an order is given to transfer him, he must carry it out. If he does not carry it out, he will be a deserter who is punished. Who looks after this? The trade union."[247]

Two comments are necessary on this line of approach. Trotsky was putting forward a theory of dictatorship of the proletariat which was at variance, not only with Marx's views but also with those of Lenin and himself expressed in earlier years. Here dictatorship was being opposed to democracy. Nor was Trotsky particularly unique in this. Irrespective of the exact words, Lenin, Zinoviev, Stalin, all the major party leaders in fact, adopted this kind of stand. What made Trotsky's case piquant was the fact that he had warned sixteen years earlier about such substitutionism. Second, Trotsky was seeking to convince the party and the unions of the correctness of his line, by democratic means. In other words, Trotsky was using the institutions of workers' democracy to urge the working class, in the name of saving the workers' state, to give up workers' democracy. The very absurdity of the process enabled a massive opposition to be generated. It was as if workers' democracy, in the last era of its existence, was still compelling the Bolsheviks to acknowledge it.

Thus a large-scale opposition sprang up at all levels.[248] At the Communist fraction of the All-Russian Central Council of Trade Unions, nearly 60–70 members opposed Lenin and Trotsky.[249] At the party Congress, Osinskii said, "what you are doing is implanting bureaucracy under the flag of militarization."[250]

Trotsky was right in saying that all labor is compulsory because people must work in order not to starve. But to equate this general compulsion with militarization of labor, policy making at the top, and compelling workers to give up their interests in the name of the interests of socialism was erroneous. Socialism could not be built by coercing the working class. Perhaps many of the actual measures taken were necessary, one notable case being that of the Central Transport Committees (Tsektran).[251] Between the spring and autumn of 1920, the transport system faced a crisis, and then recovered. Out of seventy thousand versts [old Russian unit of distance, about 1.0668 kilometers] of railroads in European Russia, only fifteen thousand versts were undamaged, and 57 percent of all locomotive were out of order. Engineers even suggested precise dates when the railways would grind to a halt. At the request of the Politbureau Trotsky was appointed by VTsIK as a temporary Peoples' Commissar of Transport Communications. He also became the president of the Transport Commission and the chairman of the Tsektran of railway and water-transport unions. He and his co-workers in Tsektran devised a central plan to revive the railways. It was imposed with considerable coercion. But up to a point, it was successful. By the end of 1920, the railways were put back on their feet. A part of the process, which subsequently earned particular notoriety, was Order No. 1042. It was an order on the repairing of locomotives, through planning and standardization. It and similar orders involved a commandist approach. The railroads' own plants began to over-fulfill the plan from July 1920 until December. But in the long run, production in one sector could not be pushed up even by militarization of labor and by curbing trade union activities. From this, Trotsky was in fact to call for a central plan. But he showed a lack of understanding, that a coordinated central plan or socialist construction needed a willing participation of the working class.[252] Instead, he quite wrongly generalized from his experience in Tsektran to call for a "shake-up" of the trade unions claiming that only union obduracy held up production. Ivan Tomsky, chairman of the All-Russian Central Council of trade Unions, immediately protested. On November 8, 1920, he raised the whole issue in the Central Committee, where Lenin now dissociated himself from Trotsky.

Two drafts on trade union policy were placed by Lenin and Trotsky. However, even at this stage, the differences were limited. Both Lenin and Trotsky stood on the standpoint of the Ninth Congress resolution, which said: "The tasks of the trade unions are principally organizational–economic and educational. The trade unions must carry out these tasks . . . guided by the communist party."[253]

The resolution also said that there should be closer ties between trade unions and Soviets, with unions becoming auxiliary state organs, and that, "the dictatorship of the proletariat and the building of socialism are ensured only to the extent that the trade unions, while formally remaining non-party, become communist in their essence and carry out communist party policy."[254]

Taken in isolation, none of these claims contradicted the principles of workers' democracy. Obviously, once the working class was in power, a purely oppositional role was impossible for trade unions. Equally naturally, a party had the right to try to influence the unions. But the growing monopoly of the Bolshevik party, and the growing bureaucratization of the state, turned these ideas into dangerous ones. Even at the Ninth Congress, Osinskii on behalf of the Democratic Centralist faction and Lutovinov of behalf of those who soon formed the Workers' Opposition, submitted counter-reports.[255] After the split in the central committee over the trade union question in November 1920, these protests became an avalanche. At the same time, as Schapiro has demonstrated, it enabled Zinoviev to pose as though Trotsky alone was a proponent of militarization of labor.[256] In fact, Trotsky had undertaken his authoritarian acts at the request of the Central Committee. As he put it, in defending himself from Zinoviev's demagogic appeals, that it was hypocrisy: "It is not to be tolerated that one man should preach democracy among the workers and when it leads to complications, say to another on the telephone, 'now, the stick if you please, that is your speciality.'"[257] Obviously, he was implying that even after the campaign for trade union rights began, he had been asked by the Central Committee to use force.

However, between December 1920, and March 1921, a bitter debate on the trade union question took place. The Trotsky–Bukharin platform argued that the state control over unions should be pushed to its culmination. The platform of Lenin, Zinoviev, Tomsky and others, while drawing away from this position, said that "rapid" conversion of the trade unions to state institutions would be a major political mistake, but this platform also characterized the unions as a combination of "party as well as non-party" workers. This meant an omission of references to other parties. In a long section on the party and the unions, the platform asserted that "The selection of the executive personnel of the trade union movement should be made, of course, under the directing control of the party."[258]

Thus, with the adoption of this resolution, party control over the trade unions became final. It was in the same period, that is, between 1920 and 1921, that the control of the management by factory committees also disappeared. The new reality was expressed symbolically in 1921, at the Fourth Trade Union Congress.

Shortly before the Congress was to open, the party fraction in the Congress heard Tomsky introducing the draft report. Ryazanov noted that the section on the election of trade union officials did not contain the usual phrase, "normal methods of proletarian democracy." His proposal to put this clause in was accepted by the fraction by one thousand five hundred votes in favor and thirty against. An enraged Party Central Committee (CC) removed Ryazanov permanently from the trade union movement, also removed Tomsky from his position for having failed to carry out the CC's line, and enforced its decisions despite the opposition of a majority of members.[259] In the same month, May 1921, supporters of the faction Workers' Opposition, who had opposed both Lenin and Trotsky over the trade union debate, were removed from the metalworkers' union and loyal people appointed in their place.[260]

In concluding this discussion on the end of workers' control and the destruction of trade union autonomy, a few remarks are necessary. First, this weakness stemmed from an inadequate break with that view of socialism, which put absolute importance on the increase in the total quantum of production.

Apart from the left communist faction of 1918 and the later oppositions no one, neither Lenin, nor Trotsky, saw the proletarian nature of the Russian regime as crucially dependent on working-class self-activity to the point of production (i.e., on workers' self-management of production). They assumed a neutrality of the system of organization, which was "bad" if used by "bad people," and "good" if used for the benefit of many. Of course, scattered in Lenin's and Trotsky's writings there are also other ideas. But it was only after 1923 that Trotsky was to take them up systematically.

Second, the changes of 1920-21 were, once again, conceived as a stop-gap. Trotsky predicted at the Tenth Congress that the new line on trade unions would not last over a year. What they failed to recognize was the fact that after four years of continuous stop-gap arrangements, this action of depriving the trade unions of their autonomy was a blow from which it would be very difficult to recover.

VI
ORGANIZING WOMEN: THE STRUGGLE FOR AUTONOMY

As we noted earlier, Bolshevik women turned enthusiastically to organizing working-class and other toiling women from the early days of 1917. While separate organizations for work among women were not set up despite repeated attempts by some of the women, a staff of leading cadres was assembled. Local level agitation was organized, though organizational terminology remained uncertain. On May 10 *Rabotnitsa* was revived. Kollontai's arrival put extra fire into women's agitational and organizational work.[261]

In the pages of *Rabotnitsa* and *Pravda* the Bolshevik women applied Marxist ideas to specific aspects of the women's question. Their aim was to integrate women with the struggles being planned by the party, and at the same time to integrate women's issues into the general strategy of the party. This also involved organizing women for combat. Richard Stites asserts that there were more armed Bolshevik women involved in the October 25th uprising than there were members of the Women's Battalions organized by the Provisional Government.[262]

Shortly after the October Revolution, there was held the Conference of Working Women of the Petrograd Region. This meeting also heard non-Bolsheviks. Notable among them was a Dr. Doroshevskaya, a spokesperson for the League for Women's Equality. Her separatist feminist position, expressed clearly, found few takers among the assembled working-class and other toiling women.[263] It was Kollontai, Inessa Armand and others, the "Bolshevik feminists," who organized working-class women and strove to incorporate gender equality within class struggle politics in a big way. Richard Stites has a fairly low estimate of what women did. According to him, efforts to include women in political work were often tokenism, and the real pattern was reflected in such situations as in "Trotsky's dictating a sketch of the Russian

Revolution to female stenographers."[264] This is to overlook the serious effort made to create a space for women in party as well as state, and to overlook as well, the changes that came after the end of the civil war. In this section, our aim will be to study the rise and subsequent crisis of the Zenskii otdel (Women's Section). Though the normal chronological structure of the present book should limit discussions to 1921, in this section a few forays will be made to later years.

Yakov Sverdlov, the head of the Party Secretariat immediately after the revolution, as well as the chairperson of the Central Executive Committee of the Soviets, and therefore the head of state, was a communist keenly sensitive to women's subordinate status. He was also the husband of a politically active communist, K.T. Novgorodtseva-Sverdlova.[265] So Sverdlov became a strong ally of Kollontai and the other communist women involved in organizing women. Lenin too felt that the revolution needed women's support in order to succeed. But despite such powerful supporters, the women constantly faced the charge of separatism. Yet the party needed mechanisms to draw in more supporters, and this enabled the Bolshevichki to press forward. In November 1918, Kollontai and other Bolshevik women organized the First All-Russian Congress of Worker and Peasant Women. Some party leaders, like Zinoviev and Rykov, were unwilling to endorse such a non-party women's congress.[266] In order to organize the Congress, the Bolshevik women created a provisional bureau, with Vera Golubeva as the Secretary. Eventually, all the working women who were to be active in the Russian women's movement in the 1920s became part of the bureau. Tireless work by the women resulted in an unexpectedly large turn out of elected delegates–over a thousand of them. One of the key moments came when Kollontai urged the delegates to return home with a new consciousness, so that the word "baba," a derogatory term applied to ordinary adult women, was rooted out.[267] The important programmatic issues raised in the Congress included opposition to domestic slavery, double standards of morality, protection of women's labor and maternity, abolition of prostitution, and drawing women into party and state activities.[268]

Following the Congress, the Women's Bureau was transformed. From a provisional body, it now became an official institution, the Central Commission for Agitation and Propaganda among Working Women. This Commission was attached to the Central Committee of the Bolshevik Party. Later in 1919, the Commission was upgraded by being reorganized into the Zhenskii Otdel (Zhenotdel) or Women's Section (or Department) of the Central Committee. Inessa Armand was made its first director.

It has often been remarked, notably by biographers of Kollontai, that Armand was chosen in preference to Kollontai because she was a safer person. But Armand had been as involved in organizing the 1918 Congress as Kollontai, and had delivered two of the major reports there. Moreover, the organizational technique used with great effect by the Zhenotdel had emanated from Armand at the Women's Congress of 1918. She had proposed that delegates to the Congress should hold meetings of their own on returning home, in order to explain the significance of decisions reached to other women. In the Zhenotdel, Armand and Samoilova took this up and refined it. They suggested that women entering soviet or trade union work should periodically report back to local meetings on their experiences, thereby increasing awareness among women and attracting others to public activity. Armand's biographer, Ralph Carter Elwood, argues that the setting up of the Zhenotdel was not a direct consequence of Kollontai's advocacy of a German style Women's Bureau, *but* the product of an internal restructuring by the Central Committee of the Party, which saw that too many ad hoc bodies had been created to mobilize women, and wanted to replace these by a unified and more authoritative organization. Yet, as Elwood himself recognizes, citing Gail Lapidus, the Zhenotdel, along with the Evsektsiia or Jewish Section, breached the sexual, ethnic, and organizational unity of the party in an effort to reach and mobilize an otherwise inaccessible constituency.[269] So it is surprising that he simply sees this as an attempt to "mobilize" a "constituency." This assumes that it was male government and party figures who worked out the plan for the Zhenotdel in a top down fashion. It is interesting to note that Elwood relies on the testimony of Polina Vinogradskaya, who was aiming to prove that Armand was safe and a non-feminist, after calling Armand "Revolutionary and Feminist" in the title of the biography he has written. It is possible that Kollontai's role in the Left Communist faction may have had something to do with the choice in favor of Armand. But that does not mean that the sustained campaign, not only by Kollontai, but a large number of women, including quite prominently Armand, counted for nothing. This presupposes that Bolsheviks were as authoritarian in 1918 as the CPSU would be in the Stalin era, a supposition that has been consistently challenged in the present study. Moreover, if excluding Kollontai had been a key element of the party's agenda, then there should have been an attempt to push forward someone else when Armand died unexpectedly in 1920. What is much more important is to look at what the Zhenotdel did and how women were politically mobilized and organized.

Zhenotdel worked under difficult circumstances. Anti-women prejudices were not dead in the party, especially after the party had expanded massively in course of 1917. This attitude manifested itself in the term "*Tsentro-Baba*," applied by many to the headquarters of

Zhenotdel. Located in a flat near the Kremlin, the organization initially had a staff of twenty-two paid activists, including the director, a deputy director, and their assistants. The work of the Zhenotdel was extensive. All domains in which women's interests were involved were connected to it, as were women party members who were not active in any specifically women's work.[270] A lot of energy went to mobilizing women for support work in connection with the civil war, the spreading of literacy as a political necessity, etc.[271]

The Zhenotdel work was based on the three levels into which any party work was usually classified: propaganda (propagation of a large number of theoretical ideas to a smaller group), agitation (presenting one idea to a much larger group) and mobilization. *Rabotnitsa* remained the central organ, and *Kommunistika* became the theoretical journal. A number of other journals came into existence at different stages, aimed at different groups of women. Maria Ulyanova, for example, played a considerable role in the development of journalism among women and in encouraging female village and factory correspondents to raise their voices.[272] But printed propaganda was not enough. So agitational techniques included face to face discussions, using "agit-trains" and "agit-boats." But even this could not draw enough women into direct work. So Armand and her colleagues used the delegate meetings. First, women would elect a delegate to the Zhenotdel, with the election itself serving as a political consciousness raising work. The delegate would work in different public bodies. Then at the end of her term she would report back to the women who had elected her. Thus Zhenotdel became a movement of non-party as well as party women. This was a sincere effort to create a state system where "every cook" would become an administrator.[273]

Organizing delegate elections was difficult work, especially in the countryside. And Stites reports that the mostly male administrators were sometimes inclined to shunt off the women to trivial routines. But in general, honest efforts were made to involve the women in public work. At the end of the cycle there were periodic conferences where women of different regions could meet each other and share their experiences.[274]

The death of Inessa Armand in 1920 led to Kollontai's being given charge of Zhenotdel. Extremely important was the work she did in organsing work among the so-called women of the East, that is to say, women of Caucasus, the Volga, and Central Asia. This often involved campaigns against the *Shariat* and the veil. On one occasion, there was the dramatic gesture of Muslim women coming up on a podium and taking off the veil. Quite rightly, the control exercised by religion over women (not just Islam, but equally Christianity) was viewed as a serious obstacle in mobilizing women and fighting for women's equality. This work was difficult, and there would often be ferocious male hostility.

Yet hundreds, and later on thousands of women worked their way into the Zhenotdels in these regions. But Kollontai's role as a leader of the Workers' Opposition resulted in tensions with the party leadership. What must have wounded her was the fact that both Lenin and Bukharin, in attacking her politics, had shifted from political to personal attacks. Bukharin had launched a blistering attack on an article on motherhood that she had written in order to "prove" that her politics were bad.[275] And Lenin had made a snide comment about her past relationship with the Workers' Opposition leader Alexander Shlyapnikov.[276] This was certainly totally unwarranted in a debate over policy in a Party Congress. Soon after, in 1922, she was removed from her position. Angelica Balabanova, Krupskaya, and Stasova all declined this work, as they were not interested in organizing women as such. So Sofia Smidovich followed Kollontai, to be followed by two proletarian women: Klavdia Nikolaeva, who would be a Zinovievist for a brief while in 1925-26, and Alexandra Artiukhina from 1927 to 1930, when Zhenotdel was shut down. As early as 1922, Smidovich was saying that it was better to liquidate Zhenotdel than to give it half a life. Yet, led by Armand, Kollontai, and in some measure even their successors, the Zhenotdel achieved much. It organized masses of women. It raised issues which Kollontai originally said were not feminist issues (and indeed they were not in the contemporary Western sense, since they addressed not the suffrage issue but social and economic rights of women).

The crisis of Zhenotdel cannot be delinked from the crisis of Workers' Democracy in all spheres. But it had a different rhythm. In the first place, the necessity of mobilizing women was acknowledged by the leading sectors of the party, regardless of their attitude to organizing women separately. Zhenotdel played an important role in organizing women for the war effort throughout the Civil War. Its work among non-Russian women was also significant. Stites, by no means an uncritical admirer of Bolshevik work among women, writes that the achievements in the "Eastern" lands alone should earn Zhenotdel a place in social history.[277] But beginning with 1922, Party congress resolutions began combining support for Zhenotdel with criticism of its shortcomings. The Twelfth Congress of 1923 lamented the growth of "feminism." The resolution suggested that the formation of special societies for women could lead to women workers moving away from the common class struggle.[278]

It is significant that the attacks on Zhenotdel intensified with the rise of the Stalinist General Line. We cannot discuss that in detail here. What we need to do, rather, is to look briefly at Soviet policy towards women between 1918 and the 1930s, and relate that to the decline of Zhenotdel. And in doing this, much of the focus will be on the activities and writings of Kollontai.

VII
THE RISE AND DECLINE OF SOCIALIST
STRATEGIES FOR WOMEN'S LIBERATION

At the Second All-Russian Congress of Soviets, Kollontai was elected Commissar of Social Welfare in the new Soviet government. In that capacity she tried to bring about changes, e.g., through the Family Code. Six weeks after the revolution, civil marriage replaced the rule of the Church, and before a year was out the marriage code was produced. This proclaimed full equality of husband and wife, and abolished the concept of illegitimacy by declaring complete equality of illegitimate with legitimate children. Beatrice Farnsworth denies that the code established equality, but the clauses she quotes show that instead of stopping at formal equality, the real inequality was addressed by seeking to bring about substantive equality.[279] The Family Code broke ground in a number of ways. By exclusively recognizing unions recorded in the Civil Registry Office, it broke the historic monopoly powers of the Church to sanctify marriages. By invalidating the old code with its language of domination and submission, by allowing freedom in choosing which surname to use, and by forbidding spousal control in business, friends, correspondence, and residence, in many ways gender equality was greatly advanced.[280] Given the extremely limited forms of contraception available in Russia at that time, a law on abortion was passed in 1920, where abortion was viewed as a major birth control device.[281] This was because the Bolsheviks thought that some limitation on family size was necessary for women's emancipation to be meaningful. However, the abortion law shows different motivations at work. The carefully worded decree stressed that the question of abortion should be decided not from the point of view of the individual but in the interests of the whole collective (i.e., society, race). Legalized abortion would ensure maximum safety for the woman.[282] The economic foundations of the social order that tied women down had to be assailed. This phase however did not last very long. Kollontai's opposition to the treaty of Brest-Litovsk eventually led to her resignation from the Sovnarkom and her ouster from the Central Committee.[283]

By mid-1918, the Civil War had begun. The onset of the Civil War caused worker and peasant women to view the Bolsheviks with some suspicion—after all, their rule had brought more hunger and renewed war. Overcoming this alienation was necessary. Kollontai insisted that if women were to be liberated, their active participation was essential. She felt the war was a catalyst for revolutionary change. In the absence of men, gone off to war, women were taking on new responsibilities. But she also knew that special measures were needed to launch the educational process that would enable women to understand the long-range impact of the revolution. This was one of the motivations behind the First All-Russia Congress of Worker and Peasant Women. Discussions at the Congress, and Kollontai's preoccupations after the Congress, involved questions of family, morality, and economic conditions. Kollontai's speech on the necessary transformation of monogamous family was eventually published as the pamphlet, *The Family and the Communist State*.[284] A resolution at the Congress stressed the need to destroy the old bondage of the family. A specific resolution on the family proclaimed that marriage would become a free comradely union of two equal, self-supporting members of the great working family.[285] Public childcare was demanded to facilitate women's participation in public life. The private burdens were sought to be transformed into public works—through the creation of maternity homes, nurseries, kindergartens, schools, communal dining rooms, communal laundries, mending centers and so on. In 1921, Kollontai gave a speech, where she said:

> The network of social education organizations which relieve mothers of the hard work involved in caring for children includes, apart from the crèches and the children's homes which cater for orphans and foundlings up to the age of three, kindergartens for the three to seven year olds, children's "hearths" for children of school age, children's clubs, and finally children's house communes and children's work colonies. The social educational system also includes free meals for children of pre-school and school age.[286]

In 1923, Kollontai published a book entitled *Women's Labour in the Evolution of the Economy*, in the latter sections of which she discussed gender role transformation in the transition period. There too, she stressed the need for delinking the kitchen from the marriage.[287] At the same time, there were unstated, but powerful prejudices against women, which had to be fought by ideology, not just by law. She was also to stress that a transformation of values was crucial. There was a need to fight the old ideology and culture, and that it was mechanical to expect that the economic transition would automatically bring about a cultural transformation. Women were tied down not merely by economic, but equally by emotional dependence.[288] Her first essays on this theme, after the revolution, had indeed appeared in 1918 under the title *The New Morality and the Working Class*. The Bolsheviks, following Engels and Bebel, argued that when a marriage was freed from economic dependence, it would be based on mutual attachment and be a superior marriage. Kollontai faced frankly the likelihood that, freed from economic concerns and family responsibility, marriages might be less stable. Kollontai was unique in building a theory on this. In the future society, a marriage might be based on emotional affinity, or on transient attraction, without being condemned in either case. She also proclaimed the merit of comradely but short-lived relationships. As for example, she said, it was proper for a bourgeois financier to withdraw money from business during a crisis period in his family's interest, because the bourgeois morality put family first. Compare, she told her readers, the case of the working class. Imagine a strike-breaker wanting to work during a strike for his family's interests. Here the stronger the ties of the family, the poorer would be the outlook for working-class solidarity. Moreover, too strong a family bond would also mean weakness for women's liberation, for women must learn to view love and the emotions within family relationships in the same way as men—that is, as only one part of their total existence, instead of the totality of existence or even as the most important part of the meaning of life.

But this raises an important question. One can understand the argument that the family should cease to be an economic unit, tying women into a subordinate and dependent position, and at the same time weakening class solidarity (though this latter argument itself is questionable, for it seems to suggest that one should fight the family not because it is patriarchal, but because the class identity must be made so uniquely powerful that all other identities must be stamped out). But why should the comradely love be of short duration? Kollontai's answer was not clear. Her vagueness suggested that she had no clear political explanation, but a hunch only that the new women, in the interests of their personal liberation, must not permit themselves to be entangled irrevocably in love for one man. In the commune, there would not exist the heavy weight of spiritual solitude which fostered the bourgeois type of romance, where the chosen man was all. Thus, Kollontai emphasized that the new women, the women of a commune society, must cease to live for the marriage, and must make work the center of their lives, as do men.

When Kollontai joined the Workers' Opposition, she brought to it her distinct gendered outlook. During the first phase of the Workers' Opposition, the focus was on workers' control over production. As noted earlier, while some of the demands were clearly impractical, these demands were based on a realization that the power of the working class had to be based in factory-level organizations. If this did not happen, large sections of less organized workers, including many novice women workers who had learnt to identify with the Party, would be forced off the stage. They would then merely delegate to their Party the immense task of building a new society. Kollontai also felt that there could be no genuinely revolutionary changes in family and sexual relationships until workers' demands were located firmly at the point of production. Nikolai Bukharin, in attacking this faction, sought to link their views on the trade union question and the question of democracy and the road to socialism with Kollontai's views on gender roles, etc.[289]

The second stage of the Workers' Opposition came soon after, when the New Economic Policy (NEP) was introduced. The NEP, Kollontai and Shlyapnikov felt, would mean a new exploitation of the working class. At the end of the Civil War, production had to be restored. This resulted in prioritizing the principle of profitability of firms over the basic rights of class democracy. And the immediate consequence was a growth in unemployment, rising from 175,000 in January 1922, to 625,000 in January 1923, and to 1,240,000 in January 1925. Since unskilled workers were the first to be laid off, and women were for the most part unskilled, they were the worst hit by unemployment. It was found that the principles of equal pay for equal work and the laws protecting female labor were not being observed even in the state enterprises. As subsidies were cut, the communal kitchens and similar services collapsed, and women were being pushed back into domestic slavery. Dislocation, poverty, resulted in a growth of abandoned children. Lack of birth control measures and the renewed economic conditions of individuals tied to families meant that easy divorce laws were turning into burdens for women, as men could walk out easily. A sample of five hundred questionnaires about broken homes discussed at a Vyborg Conference showed that 70 percent of the separations were unilaterally initiated by men, and only 7 percent by mutual agreement.[290] As a result, the Family Code of 1926 was a retreat from the radical position of 1918. Stress was laid on preservation of the family.

At the same time, conservative trends at work, including in the party, saw this as a positive development. Both Trotsky and Kollontai came in for criticism from Polina Vinogradskaia. Kollontai wanted to utilize the changes that had occurred since 1917 to transform the lives of rural women. But for most party members, this seemed one more area where the party regime would come into conflict with the (male) peasantry. Moreover, with NEP, party members who had been fervent revolutionaries were falling victims to bourgeois culture. They were becoming comfort-seeking elements, and people who developed "bourgeois" (we might say strongly patriarchal) notions of family. In order to transform women, it was necessary to build special organizations for women. Here, Kollontai went beyond the Zhenotdel, which was the party's women's bureau. She wrote, in an article in *Pravda* on March 20, 1923, of the need to build feminist organizations involving all kinds of women. She asserted that if feminism sought liberation within a bourgeois framework, it was retrograde, but if it meant the aspirations of women in a workers' state, then male opposition to feminism was incorrect.[291] The setbacks to women's employment under the NEP made reaching out to all women, including housewives, extremely necessary.

Passivity and lack of confidence in their own abilities—these weaknesses of women, had to be overcome through Communist employment of frankly feminist devices (women's clubs and societies, etc).

In a series of articles written in between 1922 and 1923 in the journal *Molodaia Guardiia*, Kollontai expanded on the themes of women's psychological independence, the future of the family, and so on. In one of these, she praised the poet Anna Akhmatova, for her exploration of attitudes towards women. She repeatedly wrote about men's inability to recognize the individuality of the woman he loved, and about the striving of women to combine love with creative work. Men in whom the custom of bourgeois ideology were strong seldom noticed that women, encouraged to live primarily for emotions, were being asked to sacrifice their own worth. In the essay "Make Way for Winged Eros," Kollontai went on to discuss the kind of erotic love that would not entrap and therefore not create the dilemma over a relationship and the need to make one-sided sacrifices for the sake of the relationship. She wrote that during the civil war, the party had been too busy to deal with the question of love, but now a respite had come. In the crisis of war, people notably communists, had time only for "Wingless Eros," hasty physical liaisons that satisfied sexual needs at the biological level. She condemned such relationships as lacking in the spiritual interaction that should characterize love. The "Winged Eros" was eroticism with possessiveness removed. Kollontai saw the development of such love as an integral part of the building of communism. She also wrote a number of stories, the most controversial being the three collected together in *Love of Worker Bees*. The stories dealt with the problem of women's autonomy in the context of the workers' state, including the search for a new sexual morality free from hypocrisy and double standards. The articles and the stories led to a sharp howl being raised. Polina Vinogradskaia was to write a number of critical essays on Kollontai and Trotsky, because both were supposedly wasting time writing about culture and ideology instead of about better communal facilities.[292] In an essay in *Molodaia Guardiia*, Vinogradskaia attacked Kollontai's articles for being non-Marxist and metaphysical. Kollontai was accused of ignoring the practical problems of everyday life, of having a "solid dose of feminist trash," and her stories were said to have reeked of pornography and the gutter. Vinogradskaia took a very mechanical materialist position according to which morality was a simple concomitant of social change. Kollontai, by contrast, consistently believed in the role of morality as a tool in the process of social change.[293] Vinogradskaia asserted that Marxism and sex were mutually incompatible. Sexual love for any reason other than for the birth of children was to be denounced. How humans therefore differed from animals, for which, too, sex is merely a reproductive function was not made clear by Vinogradskaia. Her Marxist love therefore looks very similar to a Christian religious view of love. What Kollontai was emphasizing was that women should create self-definitions that put work at the center, not their male partners. The rejection of this went hand in hand with reinforcing a relatively conservative model of Marxist thought on women, especially women's sexuality. This comes out clearly when we look at the Lenin–Zetkin conversation of 1920, published after Lenin's death by Clara Zetkin. This would be used by even more conservative elements to justify their positions.[294]

Zetkin's essay shows Lenin's very prudish conceptions of sexuality. He objected to the fact that German communists were trying to organize prostitutes, and asked: "Aren't there really any other working women in Germany to organize, for whom a paper can be issued, who must be drawn into your struggles?" He suggested that struggles to rehabilitate prostitutes must wait until after the revolution. The point was of course not that prostitutes were a special militant section of women, but that some woman communist in Hamburg had evidently viewed them as sex workers, and had felt the need to organize them. Given their distinctive position, they could be organized only by work directed specially towards them. For Lenin, in the end, this work becomes mischievous conduct or even degeneration.

Lenin then went on to attack women members of the KPD for discussing issues of sex and marriage. We find Lenin exaggerating (a polemical style quite usual with him, but if we are unaware of it, it can lead to serious misunderstanding) and claiming that while Soviet Russia was surrounded by imperialism, German communist women were doing nothing about such issues, but were simply discussing sexual problems. Moreover, Lenin turns Bebel into an ultimate text. If something is written that is not in Bebel, then it is useless. Without any serious knowledge of modern psychoanalysis, Lenin exclaimed that "Freudian theory is the modern fashion. I mistrust the sexual theories of the articles, dissertations, pamphlets, etc. . . . There is no place for it in the Party, in the class-conscious, fighting proletariat."

And thus we arrive at the most conservative variant of Bolshevism, for which sex issues are best not discussed—if at all, to be finished by reading Bebel, and definitely not by attempts at integrating modern research with working-class life. The real, class conscious working class is so defined that it has no "abnormal sexuality." Zetkin's brief summary of her response and Lenin's reply are interesting. Zetkin argued that the questions of sex and marriage, in an oppressive society, meant problems for all women. War and revolution had intensified the problems. Women were questioning bourgeois hypocrisy. They were also seeking enlightenment by starting from their lived experiences. Confronted by this, Lenin only said that she was behaving like a counsel for her women comrades, and claimed that what had been done in Germany was a mistake. Since there existed no authoritative Marxist text, the serious study she spoke of, was not possible.

But even if we take Kollontai as a radical alternative, at one point, she also displayed a weakness that needs to be considered. She made it clear that the gender division of labor meant a potential, if not actual, discrimination against women. But she did not, from this point, move on to suggesting the need to overcome the gender division of labor from the earliest stage of socialist construction. Possibly this was due to a trace of economic determinism, according to which, socialism would inevitably mean the expansion of production, and the consequent growth in women's employment, and the transformation of the hitherto private domain into a public one, even if women continued to cook, clean, and run crèches in those public spaces.[295] The over-reliance on productive forces to solve all problems allowed Kollontai to suppose that by bringing women into the area of social production to perform the tasks they had hitherto fulfilled privately, their domestic burdens could be relieved. It should however be mentioned that at least on one occasion, during the discussions on the proposed Family Code of 1926, she suggested that "housework also counts for something," and that women's domestic labor should be taken into account and valued.[296]

In the same way, one cannot accept the criticism made by Irina Aristarkhova in "Women and government in Bolshevik Russia." According to her: "After the revolution, the Bolsheviks proclaimed: we promised you the revolution, we gave you the Revolution." In the conclusion, she argues: "Unlike those who argue that there was an emancipation of women in the 1920s that was reversed in the 1930s, I have shown that there was a continuity in Bolshevik policy in relation to women, which at no time sought the emancipation of women . . . [but] the full penetration of the state into the regulation of 'private' life and the subordination of sexuality and gender relations to the purposes of state power."[297]

This is a total misreading, not only of Kollontai, but also of Lenin, Trotsky, and the left-wing Bolsheviks generally. First of all, they did have a genuine commitment to working-class self-emancipation. Aristarkhova makes snide remarks about Trotsky, etc., of having expressed their anger after falling from power. This misses the point that the left wing "fell" from power because they fought for working-class socialism, rather than a bureaucratic "socialism from above," and that Stalinism ultimately ripped through the entire Bolshevik Old Guard. Only then could the bureaucratic state rest content, having atomized the working class and its vanguard. The fact that individuals like Kollontai gave up the battle at a certain stage does not mean that the battle had not been waged by them, nor that they and Stalinism were one and the same.

This leads us to a final point—the effects of the Stalinist counter-revolution. As we have here moved far beyond the general structure of the present chapter and the whole book, I can only provide some basic markers. As early as 1923, when the revolutionary energies had not yet ebbed, we find Stalin highlighting the discourse on motherhood that he would eventually push through. In this, we find him stating: "Finally, working-class and peasant women are mothers who bring up our youth— the future of our country. They can cripple the spirit of a child or give us youth with a healthy spirit. . . . All this depends on whether the woman and mother has sympathy for the Soviet system or whether she trails in the wake of the priest, the kulak, or the bourgeois."[298] So women are necessarily backward, and their importance is that they are mothers, and therefore the task of the party is to take these backward mothers in hand.

VIII
THE RED TERROR AND REVOLUTIONARY LEGALITY

Every emancipatory movement has been forced to confront the problem of coercion. The idea of popular emancipation generates a tendency to liberal, generous attitudes, including to former rulers. But this attitude comes up all too often against the harsh reality of upper-class resistance to social change. In the French Revolution, for instance, the Parisian masses originally displayed a trusting attitude to the moderate leaders, and even to the monarch. But in practically all revolutions, such initial trust had given way to bitterness. There always existed popular anger towards the exploiters. While the revolutions overthrew old elites, there existed the possibility that, contrary to popular democracy aspirations, new elites would control the political system. Once again in the French case, these two trends were displayed by the autonomous movement of the sans culottes on one hand, and the consolidation of a bourgeois elite on the other. While terror was begun by the people to silence feudal counter-revolution and to achieve their major aims, it was subsequently transformed into a bureaucratic terror under the Committee of Public Safety, headed by Robespierre.

Aware of the French precedence, the Russian revolutionaries made conscious efforts to oppose excessive terror. Along with this there was the initial phase of popular generosity, extending even to the leadership. This led even to undue liberalities, as when Krasnov was pardoned after the revolt of early November 1917, or when counter-revolutionaries were freed in Moscow. However, this attitude soon gave way to the Red Terror. Though all acts of coercion in the Red areas are often called Red

Terror, certain distinctions should be made. First of all, the mass terror organized from below was wholly distinct from the formalized terror of the Extraordinary Commission for Combating Counter-Revolution (Cheka). A separation also needs to be made between the Red Terror as a means of class war, the use of terror to hold the army together, and the institutionalization of terror, which aided bureaucratization.

A total rejection to terror, in the broad sense, is a rejection of the right of the Workers' State to terrorize its enemies and thereby keep safe the state. However, even if the right of a revolution to defend itself is admitted, all tactics are not automatically justified. Samuel Farber argues that "The atrocities carried out by the White Terror are assumed to be a given in this context, and are thus of interest only insofar as they may be said, in given instances, to justify or not justify the particular tactics carried out by the Red Terror. From this vantage point, several features of the Red Terror are extremely troublesome and indeed highly distrubing."[299]

The trouble seems to be one of Farber's own creation. By saying that the White Terror is assumed to be "given," in fact he ignores the specific ways in which it provoked Red Terror. The most widespread case of Red Terror occurred after the murders of Volodarsky and Uritsky, and the attempt on the life of Lenin. This was not state terror. This was popular terror, that is, terror organized from below. One of its major constituent elements was the soldiers' and sailors' hatred of the officers. Thus, in Sevastopol, naval officers who had served in 1905-6, (at the time of the ruthless suppression of sailors), were arrested and shot at once. In Crimea, officers, temporarily in control, had shot Bolshevik prisoners. When Red sailors recaptured the peninsula, they took revenge by condemning several dozen officers to death by drowning.[300] Such actions were brutal. But they came as retaliatory brutality.

Point for point, the Red Terror in its popular phase was generous. In the capitals, it was unleashed only on September 2. Carr writes that the terror, "hitherto sporadic and unorganized, became a deliberate instrument of policy."[301] As Lenin told the Seventh Congress of Soviets: "The terror was forced on us by the terror of the Entente."[302]

Farber's explanation for the terror is seriously open to questions. First of all, he makes no distinction between the popular terror and the use of the Cheka. Moreover, he suggests that the Terror was created and perpetrated in order to carry out dogmatically the policies of War Communism. For Lovell, likewise, the White Terror is absent when he points to factors and persons that mediate between Marx and the Soviet state.[303] In Farber's case, there is an explicit statement, that War Communism itself was not a response to a crisis, but a conscious choice.[304]

By contrast, Trotsky offered a cogent explanation of Red Terror. He wrote that "The Red Terror is not distinguishable from the armed insurrection, the direct continuation of which it represents."[305] He pointed out that historically, no new regime, however based on popular support, and however reactionary its enemy, could win by persuasion alone. It needed terror as a supplementary form. The trial and execution of Charles I, and the popular force that destroyed feudal power in England, represented "terror."

The total number of victims of Red Terror were not much more than 10,000. Even adding the executions carried out by the Cheka, they came to around 50,000. "The Red Terror was intended to be and was, in the main, at least in the towns a class terror, directed against the formerly powerful and well to do classes."[306] Chamberlin, the author of these lines, adds that while requisitions and peasant uprisings cost many peasant lives, the picking out of people for execution, that is, a systematic use of political terror to silence the counter-revolution, involved as a rule "people of wealth, education or former social standing: pre-war officers and officials, with members and country squires, priests and merchants."[307]

The intensity of the terror depended on the intensity of counter-revolution. Thus, following the defeat of Kolchak and Denikin, and before the invasion of Russia by Poland, there was a tendency toward mildness.[308] Chamberlain provides the following classification of execution in twenty provinces of Central Russia: participation in uprising–3,082; membership in counter-revolutionary organization–2024; appeals to revolt–455; banditism–643; espionage–102; desertion–102; crimes in office–206; other (including shooting hostages)–1,704.[309]

Quite different in nature was the creation of the Cheka. In the first days of Soviet power, it was the Military Revolutionary Committee of the Petrograd Soviet that looked after security measures. The first formal body for security was the Peoples' Commissariat for Internal Affairs (NKVD). Its first Commissar was Rykov. After his resignation, G. I. Petrovskii became Commissar, with M. K. Muranov as his deputy, and F. E. Dzerzhinsky, M. Y. Latsis, I. S. Unshlicht, M. S. Uritsky, and P. E. Lazimir as Collegium members.[310] By November 25, the Commissariats were sufficiently organized for the MRC to begin winding up. Regarding the struggle against counter-revolution, a Commission had been created as a VTsIK department.[311]

But in the end, on December 7, it was Sovnarkom that created an Extraordinary Commission for Combating Counter-Revolution and Sabotage [usually called Vecheka or Cheka], entrusted with the suppression of all counter-revolutionary acts and attempts, the handing over of saboteurs to revolutionary tribunals, and the carrying out of necessary investigations.[312] A historian of the Cheka points out: "strangely enough, there is no direct evidence that the Bolshevik Party (whose Central Committee minutes for the period are available) played any part in the creation of the Vecheka."[313] He does not provide any "indirect evidence" either.

To start with, the Cheka had a very small staff—120 employees in February 1918. But by the end of 1918 it had a staff of no less than 31,000.[314] By August 1918, the Cheka had formed sub-committees in 38 guberniias and 365 districts, i.e., practically the whole of the territory covered by Soviet rule at that time. The NKVD directed the executive committees of the local Soviets. But on August 29, Dzerzhinsky ordered local Chekas to be completely autonomous.[315]

Soviet institutions contested this. When Peters, a Cheka leader, criticized the suggestion that Chekas should be subordinated to the Soviets, S.I. Dukhovskii, secretary of the NKVD Collegium, asked whether power was to belong to the Chekas or to the Soviets.[316] He wrote that if this went on, the slogan "All Power to the Soviets" should be replaced by "All power to the Cheka." Two days' later, another NKVD official reported that out of 147 local Soviet executives, 118 had favored the subordination of the local Chekas.[317]

One of the infamous cases, often cited, was that of the Nolinsk Cheka, which, on learning that Bruce Lockhart had been arrested and subsequently released, wanted to know why he had not been subjected to the most refined torture.[318] This threat of torture aroused heated controversy. On October 25, 1918, the Central Committee debated the issue, and decided to close down the *Vecheka Weekly Bulletin*, which had published the Nolinsk letter and given it approval, and to censure its editorial board. The VTsIK Presidium for its part made a distinction between terror, which at that stage was held necessary, and torture, which it said was "unworthy, harmful and contrary to the interests of the struggle for communism."[319]

The contrast between the opposed sides could be hardly clearer. Not only individuals like Dukhovskii, but even Lenin had initially attempted to steer clear of terror. On the one hand, as a realist, Lenin had opposed the abolition of the death penalty.[320] But on the other hand, he hoped to avoid using terror. He said in a speech at a joint meeting of the Petrograd Soviet of Workers' and Soldiers' Deputies:

> We are accused of making arrests. Indeed, we have made arrests; today we arrested the director of the State Bank. We are accused of resorting to terrorism, but we have not resorted, and I hope will not resort, to the terrorism of the French revolutionaries who guillotined unarmed men. I hope we shall not resort to it, because we have strength on our side. When we arrested anyone we told him we would let him go if he gave us a written promise not to engage in sabotage. Such written promises have been given.[321]

Antonov-Ovseyenko, who led the Red detachments against the Winter Palace, told the crowd behind him:

> When you kill a White Guard prisoner it is the revolution you kill and not the counter-revolution. I have given twenty years of my life in exile and in prison for this revolution. . . . (It) means something better. . . . In the name of your honours, you should give proof of magnanimity.[322]

In the camp of the Whites, no such tussle existed. The letter of the Nolinsk Cheka raises sharply the question of how excessive power corrupted democratic institutions. No such question can be raised with respect to the Whites. In Kiev, "gigantic five and six storey buildings began to shriek from top to bottom."[323] In Siberia, under Kolchak's jurisdiction there was Ataman Semyonov, whose men "machine-gunned freight cars full of victims at execution fields along the railway."[324] In the Kuban, General Pokrovskii "hanged socialists *en masse* in the courtyard outside his window to improve the appetite."[325]

It was in the Red camp that Cheka's role raised eyebrows. Units of the Cheka did use torture, although examples like scalping of victims, driving rats to gnaw holes into victims' bodies, etc., only came from White propaganda.[326] But the party and the state tried to stamp it out. Time and again Lenin personally intervened to check abuse of power.[327] Apart from the Nolinsk issue, a claim by Latsis in 1918, that whether a suspect was a capitalist or a worker was enough to determine their guilt or innocence is oft quoted.[328] But Lenin's angry rejoinder, "A Little Picture in illustration of big Problems,"[329] is less often considered. Essentially, Leggett notes, whenever the threats to the regime intensified, the Cheka gained the upper hand, while recessions in the crisis led to growth of the powers of the NKIu (Peoples' Commissariat of Justice).[330]

Farber is, however, correct on one point. The Cheka was institutionalized. Once this is done, the point is no longer that of "unavoidable excesses," but of an institution that is basically anti-democratic. But there is little ground for accepting that all, or even most Bolsheviks accepted this for good. Several types of oppositions arose. The NKVD was concerned to control the Cheka. The NKIu, and the Revolutionary Tribunals, wanted to temper justice with mercy. "Most counter-revolutionaries were either sentenced to prison or fined," with only fourteen executions in the early months.[331] Krylenko, in charge of the Tribunals, publicly attacked the Chekas saying that on their reform depend the future development of the revolution.[332] Another criticism came from the Old Bolshevik M. S. Olminsky, who attacked the Cheka for not adhering to legality and for destroying all personal security.[333] For the period of acute civil war, the Cheka could survive all this. But the rot within it was visible. On January 13, 1921, Dzerzhinsky himself wrote, unsolicited, a letter to the Central Committee urging reforms.[334] Victor Serge observed the rapid effects of "professional degeneration" among the Chekists, and Dzerzhinsky himself seems to have suggested shooting some of them.[335]

Lev Kamenev went further than Dzherzhinsky, demanding the transfer of the bulk of the Cheka's process to NKIu. Lenin supported him.[336] Finally, at the ninth Congress of Soviets, Lenin said that it was essential to reform the Cheka, and to emphasize revolutionary legality.[337] At the same Congress the Old Bolshevik V. M. Smirnov moved a resolution, passed by the Congress which stated:

> The Congress considers that the present strengthening of Soviet power within permits the narrowing of the circle of activities of the vecheka and its organs, entrusting to legal organs the struggle against violations of the laws of the Soviet republic.[338]

By 1922, the Cheka was dissolved. Its successor, the GPU, at that stage had limited powers. In line with the idea of establishing a law-based state, the NKVD and NKIu were empowered and GPU made technical, executive organs under them. Nevertheless, the Cheka left behind a dubious legacy. If Farber is wrong in tracing a continuity from 1918 to Stalinist atrocities, John Rees, in his critique of Farber, is too lenient, too prone to overlooking the institutional and not merely personal elements of state terrorism and defiance of democratic norms that the Cheka activities inculcated.[339]

The discussion on the Terror necessitates a consideration of the way civil liberties and democratic rights were handled by the Soviet regime. First of all, there was the issue of freedom of the press. During the insurrection, the MRC attempted to close down a number of papers deemed hostile to Soviet power. Protests were made immediately. On October 27 the Sovnarkom issued a decree stating that only those newspapers would be closed down which called for open insubordination to the government, incited their readers to criminal acts, or "slanderously distorted the facts." Bans were to be authorized solely by Sovnarkom. The decree was to be repealed once normally was restored.[340] This was a temporary measure, and on November 4, the VTsIK met to arrive at a more definitive resolution of the question. Two viewpoints were put forward. Left SRs like Kamkov and Karelin, in alliance with a Bolshevik minority like Larin and Ryazanov, clashed with Lenin and Trotsky. Trotsky argued that the older way of arguing for freedom of press (i.e., simply opposing censorship) was no longer valid because the struggle now was anti-capitalist, and monopoly rights over printing had to be challenged.[341] The crux of Trotsky's argument was that newsprint stocks, and printing presses, should be confiscated and socialized and all groups of workers and peasants should be allowed access to these. Trotsky also pointed out that if a civil war situation raged, they enemy press had to be suppressed.[342]

This was not a repudiation of the freedom of oppositional press. Lenin had, before October, suggested a state monopoly over advertisements, and an equitable distribution. Since the purpose was to provide subsidy and allow people to write without the control imposed by money, the subsidy could be provided more directly by the method proposed by Trotsky. At this stage, neither Lenin nor Trotsky envisaged banning opposition papers. They made a distinction between opposition and enemy. As Trotsky said:

> To demand that all repressive measures should be abandoned during a civil war equivalent to demanding that the war itself should cease . . . when we are finally victorious our attitude toward the press will be analoguous to that on freedom of trade.[343]

The response of Larin, Kamkov, and others centered on the right of minorities.[344] Karelin opposed Trotsky, saying that it would be absurd to distribute publication opportunities in proportion to strength.[345]

The Bolshevik view was approved by the VTsIK. The problem did not lie chiefly in this viewpoint. The problem lay elsewhere. Censorship in 1917–early 1918 was slight. The Cadet paper *Svoboda Rossii* was being published in Moscow until the summer of 1918. Schapiro notes the existence of an extensive Menshevik press until mid-1918.[346] The criticism of Bolshevism was by no means a ground for closing down papers. Two illustrations from leftwing papers will show this. *Novaya Zhizn*, paper of the United Internationalists (e.g., Sukhanov, Bazarov, etc.) edited by Maxim Gorky, wrote the following:

> Lenin, Trotsky, and their companions have already become poisoned with the filthy venoms of power, and this is evidenced by their shameful attitude toward freedom of speech. . . . Blind fanatics and dishonest adventurers . . . consider it possible to commit all kinds of crimes, such as the slaughter outside St. Petersburg, the destruction of Moscow . . . abominations which Plehve and Stolypin once perpetrated . . . the working class . . . will soon (realize) . . . the depth of his (Lenin's) madness . . . his Nechaev and Bakunin brand of anarchism.[347]

The other example comes from *Burevestnik*, an anarchist paper, which in April 1918 attacked the Bolsheviks as "Black Hundreds."[348]

And these were *left* papers. To the right of them stood the majority of Mensheviks and Right Socialist Revolutionaries. Nonetheless, the freedom of press of this period was uneasy. No stabilization of the situation occurred. Instead, with the growing counter-revolution, press freedom was heavily curtailed. But even during the civil war, those who opposed White counter-revolution were permitted to publish.

The Menshevik paper, *Vsegda Vperyed* (Always Forward), came out as a daily for a month in a press run of 100,000 copies. Groups of SRs, Left SRs, and Anarchists continued to publish their papers until 1921. The ban on parties was what finally, and irrevocably shut down the opposition press.[349] The real test came after the Civil War. In 1921, a party member, G. I. Myasnikov, had become a leader of the dissident Workers' Group, a follow-up of the now-banned Workers' Opposition. In a memorandum to the CC in May 1921, he called, among other things, for freedom of press for all "from monarchists to anarchists." He held that freedom of press was the only effective means of checking abuse of power. Undeterred by party threats, he repeated his demands in a pamphlet, and insisted on state subsidy for critical publications.[350] Lenin wrote a long reply to him, which is striking for the shift it shows in Lenin's position. Summing up his arguments, it is possible to discern the following points:[351]

1. There is no pure democracy, hence merely demanding freedom of the press is wrong.
2. Freedom of the press is a basically bourgeois demand, progressive in the era of struggle against feudalism, but not now, when capitalists can buy up papers and create false public opinions.
3. Russia being surrounded by the bourgeois enemies of the whole world, freedom of the press would give them opportunities.

The position was now no longer as it had been, when, during the civil war, Trotsky had replied to Kautsky, that:

> During war all institutions and organs of the state and of public opinion become directly or indirectly, weapons of warfare. This is particularly true of the press. No government carrying on a serious war will allow publications to exist on its territory which, openly or indirectly, support the enemy. . . . This is inhumane, but no one ever considered war a school of humanity.[352]

The distinction is important. At a time of open armed conflict, the enemy cannot be allowed free access in propaganda matters. This has no relationship with one side possessing the whole truth, etc. This is, once again, dictated by the need to survive. But precisely for that reason, once open war ends, this reasoning can no longer be put forward. Imperialist encirclement as a cause for censorship means saying that there would be permanent censorship, until world communism "arrived."

Some of the proposals were "practical" proposals that failed to recognize the central issue. If the party, or one of the state departments, "appointed" non-party people to watch-dog positions, then the party or that department would retain ultimate control.

Freedom of the press, as originally defined by Trotsky, Lenin, and Avanesov in the VTsIK meeting of November 4, 1917, could have been stabilized and developed by creating relevant Soviet organs to oversee the distribution of newsprint, granting access to presses, etc. But this depended also on the acceptance of the legality of the state by the opposition. This is what they did not do. However, even in 1917, the position of Lenin and Trotsky was marked by an inability to specify the boundaries of legality. That is why, despite many utterances about the need to ensure revolutionary legality, it was to remain weak. On the question under scrutiny, the assertion, that the people, not banks, etc., had to be represented by the press, did not settle the question of who the "people" were? Were workers who accepted a bourgeois political line to be granted freedom? Prior to 1921, such issues were theoretical, and in the most critical years, purely speculative. But from 1921, they became vital for the regeneration of workers' democracy. Lenin's reply to Myasnikov shows that he had failed to understand the question itself.

This, of course, raises the problem of socialist legality as a whole. The haziness in Lenin's theoretical framework has been already discussed. In practice, a major effort was undertaken, to simplify the legal system, and to make it an instrument of justice for the people. One action taken was the combination of professional judges and lay judges. The professional judges could be expected to interpret law properly, while lay judges would have served a purpose similar to those of juries, in acting as the voice of the ordinary people. Contemporary accounts of Soviet courts show a strong spirit of compassion and equity. The degree of punishment was generally favorable compared to earlier times (this excludes the Red Terror).[353] The prison system was remarkably improved, including the prisons run by the cheka. One of the pioneering studies of forced labor and prison labor in the USSR recognized that in 1917, "a magnificent experiment" was carried out "to abolish not only prisons but crime itself." And "as long as there were still offenders, they must be cured rather than punished." In the first draft of the new Criminal Code, the maximum penalty was fixed at five years of "deprivation of liberty."[354]

A decree of January 1921 admitted that many prisoners in the Cheka jails were workers, or prisoners arrested for theft and speculation, and urged that only really dangerous people should be kept in jail.[355] Political prisoners had political prisoner status in the jails.[356] At the peak of the Civil War, there were one hundred thousand prisoners, reduced to twenty-five thousand in 1922 and half that in 1923.[357] Some cases of mass executions were recorded, e.g., the case of the Cheka executing prisoners the night before the abolition of the death penalty in 1920.[358] But as a whole, the prison regime was vastly superior to the alternative posed by White Guards, and to the prison regime in many contemporary democracies. The corrective labor code of 1924 said:

> The regimen should be devoid of any trace of cruel or abusive treatment, the following by no means permitted: handcuffs, punishment cells, solitary confinement, denial of food, keeping prisoners behind bars during conversations with visitors.[359]

The problem of legality, however, became acute because of the Bolsheviks' rejection of formality. There was a tendency to suppose that social equality was adequate. Impatience with the principles of the legal process were visible in the early days. During the Civil War, the illusion that War Communism was a real progress toward communism resulted in the closure of bar associations and the banning of private lawyers from courts. In October 1920, the jury system was abolished.[360] Much of this was done by assuming that the things being abolished or modified were liberal principles not required in communism. But the introduction of the NEP necessitated the re-establishment of the bar, of professional legal education, and a degree of stability in the field of civil law.[361] While the Civil War was a major factor in this, theoretical lacunae were also important. Thus, Lenin often defined the dictatorship of the proletariat as "rule that is unrestricted by any laws."[362] This could be stretched to mean that even the laws of the Workers' State could be bypassed in the name of revolutionary expediency.

Another facet in the development of Soviet legality was the relationship between the individual and the state. Evgenii Pashukanis, a prominent Marxist legal theorist, argued that law was based on private property, and the transition to communism meant the dying out of the juridical form.[363] This was at best true of civil law. Even in that case, the dying out of private ownership, and of commodity production, could be a very long, drawn-out process. So legal codes based on the assumption of a rapid abolition of private property would be unsuitable. Moreover, the relationship between the individual and the state covers a lot of terrain. The "withering away of the state" presupposes a growing decline in the powers of the state institutions which interfere in human affairs. For this, there would be the necessity of laws to protect the citizen from the state. A failure to recognize this resulted in the adoption of Guiding Principles on Criminal Law (1919), which suggested that every "dangerous" act directed against the state or its economy and society should be treated as a criminal offense whether or not specifically forbidden by criminal law.[364] In other words, if a person committed an act not forbidden by law, he or she could still be treated as a criminal, if a court decided that his or her act had harmed the state. Instead of protecting the citizen from the state, the state was empowered to protect itself from the citizens. Logically, one could say that even the attempt to ensure that the state withered away could be construed as a "criminal" act. Moreover, the 1922 Criminal Code had no procedure analogous with the writ of habeas corpus. That is, there was no guarantee in Soviet Law that an arrested person would be brought before an ordinary court of law, headed by an independent judge, and that he or she would be duly charged with specific accusations regarding violations of law.[365]

As in everything, however, here also the early years were characterized by a multiplicity of views and practices. One instance is that of the Bolshevik Stuchka, who in Moscow allowed a different line of development, by which lawyers were allowed, but they were not paid by their clients. Clients paid fees according to a fixed rate to a central fund. Lawyers got their money on the basis of numbers and complexities of cases handled. Stuchka, as well as other jurists, insisted on the need for law in the transitional period.[366] It was much later, that a contempt for legality in the name of revolution became a cover for bureaucratic illegality.

IX
THE ELIMINATION OF THE OPPOSITION

Leonard Schapiro in his work on the early Soviet period made the comment that "the attitude of the socialist parties to the Bolsheviks, at any rate after 1918, was not opposition in the ordinary Western political sense of that term at all; it was a struggle for survival."[367] The assumption here is that the socialist parties themselves were not shifting to a counter-revolutionary position, and that destruction of opposition was pre-determined by the Bolshevik program.

Every Bolshevik document prior to October 1917 shows that they did not envisage one-party rule. When, after the July Days, Lenin called for dropping the slogan "All power to the Soviets," he was only referring to the impossibility of any further peaceful development of the revolution. It did not imply a wish to replace Soviet rule by party rule.[368] Here, he was following the idea of Engels, that "The defensive is the death of every armed rising."[369]

Nor did the Bolsheviks envisage partyless Soviets. On being elected president of the Petrograd Soviet, Leon Trotsky said:

> We are all members of parties, and we will be carrying on our work, and more than once we will have to cross swords. But we will conduct the work of the Petrograd Soviet in the spirit of justice and of full freedom for all factions, and the hand of the presidium will never be the hand which suppresses the minority.[370]

The political party against whom the Bolsheviks' hostility was directed from the beginning was the Cadet party. On November 28 (December 11) 1917, Sovnarkom issued a decree banning the Cadets for supporting Kornilov, Kaledin, and Dutov.[371] However, the line between bourgeois parties and others could not be drawn clearly. The right wing of the SRs and the Mensheviks associated with the Cadets, and wanted to topple the Soviet regime in alliance with the Cadets. Radkey even asserts that the Right SR leaders, including many of their delegates elected to the Constituent Assembly were Cadets in all but name, and remained in the SR party because in the Cadet party they would have occupied less important positions.[372] The SR party was also involved very heavily in the Committee for Salvation of the Revolution, as discussed earlier. In connection with the convocation of the Constituent Assembly, the SR attempted to launch an uprising.[373] Despite this, their leadership was not arrested.[374]

Though they lost their strength, there were four SRs in the VTsIK elected at the Fourth Soviet Congress. But they repudiated the authority of the VTsIK and refused to participate in the elections to its presidium.[375] This consistent rejection of Soviet power ultimately culminated in an open bid for alliance with imperialists and rightists. When the Czechoslovak Legion rose in arms against the Bolsheviks, the Right SRs supported it. In Samara, they proclaimed a government under its protection.

It was the SR party that displayed a violent opposition to the Bolsheviks. On October 26 1917, the Central Committee of the SRs resolved, in a secret resolution, to undertake armed action. The carrying out of the plan was entrusted to A. R. Gotz, who, finding that SR activists in Petrograd were unwilling to join an uprising, turned to Cossacks, trainee officers, and finally to Purishkevich, the leader of the Black Hundreds. Defeated, they then joined force with generals. Even Chernov, considered more to be left wing among the SRs, took part in this work.[376]

In November 1917, the SR military commission planned to kidnap Lenin and Trotsky.[377] Individual terrorism, an old SR tactic, was revived. And in May, at the Conference (or Council) of their party, they resolved to "overthrow the Bolshevik dictatorship and to establish a government based on universal suffrage and willing to accept Allied assistance in the war against Germany."[378] Continuing the war against Germany in the face of total opposition from workers and peasants, was thus the plank on which the SRs chose to base their opposition to Bolshevism and their alliance with imperialism. Thus, when on June 14, 1918, the VTsIK excluded the SRs from all Soviets, it was carrying out a necessary act.[379]

It is not necessary to trace in full the subsequent history of the SRs. The SRs were so thoroughly enmeshed with monarchists, Cadets, etc., that Chernov, despite his anti-Bolshevism was "horrified" by the SRs agreement to form a coalition with the antidemocratic forces.[380] This ultra-right turn among the SRs led to splits. Leftist elements continued to break away. In February 1919, some SRs in Moscow and Samara decided to seek a rapprochement with the Soviet regime. But this led to a split, as the Ninth Conference of the party repudiated these "conciliators." The Soviet regime legalized the pro-Soviet wing.[381] The balance-sheet, however, shows that in the conflict between classes both before and after October, the SR party chose, consciously, the camp of counter-revolution.[382]

The Mensheviks had a different, and more complex history. In October 1917, they seemed to be a group of intellectuals without any base. But they staged a comeback in the early months of 1918. Within the party, there was a wide range of views. On October 26 itself, some Mensheviks had been willing to wage an armed struggle against the Bolsheviks. On the other hand, Martov told Axelrod bluntly that what had happened was a proletarian revolution, however much one deplored it.[383] Subsequently, the Mensheviks reappeared in the VTsIK, and their newspapers were often attacked, but these continued to appear. But the Decree of June 14th, 1918 also covered the Mensheviks. This was not wholly justified by the situation. The Mensheviks took part in the VTsIK and in the Soviets. They attacked the Bolsheviks. In May 1918, an openly held Menshevik conference condemned Allied intervention, but also proclaimed their devotion to the Constituent Assembly.[384] They also took a position of "neutrality" at the time of the Czechoslovak rising.[385] While this showed a difference from the SRs, this did not show any attitude of loyalty to Soviet power. However, the Bolsheviks, apparently unwilling to tolerate this vacillation, banned the Mensheviks as well. This was followed by an accentuation of the conflict among the Mensheviks. Not only the Transcaucasian Mansheviks, but also right-wing Mensheviks in Russia, were bitterly anti-communist and called for armed struggle. In some cases, they actually participated in this struggle.[386]

But the majority, led by Martov, recognized the proletarian character of the regime, and called for critical support to it against counter-revolution. They also called for a peaceful agitation for a Constituent Assembly.[387] The VTsIK responded to this spilt by legalizing the Menshevik Central Committee in late 1918.[388] In 1919, the Mensheviks reappeared in the Soviets. They defended the concept of Soviet legality, criticized Red Terror, called for a series of liberalization measures, and above all, defended trade unions and the rights of the workers.[389] As a result, they made important gains in the Soviets. The growing disillusionment with War Communism and hostility to the statization of unions was reflected in Menshevik gains. In 1920, they won 46 seats in the

Moscow Soviet, 205 in Kharkov, 120 in Yekaterinoslav, and 50 in Tula.[390]

In early 1921, there was a growth of mass discontent and a strike wave. The Mensheviks were involved. This was followed by the Kronstadt uprising.[391] An alarmed Bolshevik party, fearful of their isolated situation, resolved to allow no more opposition from outside the party. This was understandable as a panic reaction. But it cannot be justified by referring to crisis. Nor can it be justified by references to *subsequent* actions of the Mensheviks.[392]

There was no formal ban, but rather, a clamp-down on Menshevik activity. However, Lenin's speeches of this period show that the ban was not considered permanent. Though he was quite wrong in calling the Mensheviks a petty-bourgeois party, at the Tenth Party Congress he said, "The choice before us is not whether or not to allow these parties to grow—they are inevitably engendered by petty-bourgeois economic relations. The only choice before us, and a limited one at that, is between the forms of concentration and co-ordination of these parties' activities."[393] Nonetheless, even this imagined restrictive existence was ultimately denied. Though the ban of 1921 was thought to be temporary, it proved to be the final suppression of opposition.

The situation of the anarchists was especially peculiar. On one hand, in 1917, they had collaborated with the Bolsheviks. The anarchist leader Voline, even in his later critical work, noted that in 1917 the Bolsheviks "arrived at an almost libertarian conception of the revolution, with almost Anarchist slogans."[394] Not surprisingly, anarchists supported the dissolution of the Constituent Assembly. The anarchist sailor Zheleznyakov led the detachment that dispersed the Assembly.[395]

This rapprochement was based on Lenin's strong belief in the creative power of the people. Throughout 1917, and early 1918, he was to reiterate that to be successful, insurrection must rely not upon a party, but upon the advanced class, and that after conquest of power a vital task was "to develop (the) independent initiative of the workers, and of all the working and exploited people generally, . . . break the . . . prejudice that only the so-called 'upper classes' . . . are capable of administering the state."[396]

However, many of the anarchists were also sharply critical of the idea of the dictatorship of the proletariat, and the Anarcho-Syndicalists among them were in favor of a fully decentralized workers' control. Within the diffused anarchist arena there were many streams. Some at least had criminal elements in their midst, while others wanted to collaborate with the Soviets. In April 1918, there was a major clash, and several hundred Moscow anarchists were arrested,[397] though there was much hesitation among the Bolsheviks.[398] Some anarchists took part in the Left SR-led July 1918 Moscow rising. In 1919 anarchists and SRs together blew up the Moscow Communist Party headquarters.[399] On the other hand, just a month later, some anarchists fought against the White General Yudenich's offensive against Petrograd.[400]

The most famous case of an anarchist growth was in the Ukraine. Nestor Makhno, an anarchist leader, formed his independent detachment there. Makhno went to the Ukraine in July 1918 with help from Lenin and Sverdlov, when the German puppet Hetman Skoropadsky was still ruling. Makhno organized a partisan Insurgent Army to fight against Skoropadsky and Whites. But in June 1919, it turned against the Red Army, and attacked Bolshevik strongholds, troops, trains and food collectors.[401] It was Denikin's advance against Makhno's territory in autumn 1919 that compelled him to turn to the Bolsheviks once more. But as the White threat was eased, he again turned to hostilities to the Red Army as shown by Chamberlin.[402]

Reports from the Soviet Ukrainian Front gave the same picture of Makhno carrying out raids, shooting Soviet officials, robbing food, and so on.[403] One historian even contends that Wrangel's return in 1920 was possible because of Makhno's activities.[404] It was only when Wrangel advanced on Makhno's base in October 1920 that Makhno concluded an alliance with the Bolsheviks. This time, it was treated as a purely tactical affair by the latter, who turned on Makhno after Wrangel's defeat. Makhno's army was smashed and he fled to Romania in August 1921.

The real social basis of Makhno's movement was not his crude communism.[405] He received peasant support because of his opposition to grain requisitioning by the Soviet state. Politically, his "defense of freedom" involved a form of conscription for his army, to disallow political parties from participating in his "free" elections, and organization of a secret police that was under no law, and that often shot Bolsheviks without giving them any open trial.[406] It is possible to find instances of excessive cruelty during the Bolsheviks' campaign against Makhno but it is difficult to see how they could desist from turning decisively against him.

One final anarchist stronghold was in Kronstadt. Even in 1917, the island-fortress had a political composition that was very leftist. Anarchists and SR Maximalists (a party with a program half-way between traditional narodnism and anarchism) had a strong base. In January 1918, elections to the Kronstadt Soviet gave the Bolsheviks 139 seats with 46 percent votes, the SRs (mostly leftist) 64 seats and 21 percent votes, Maximalists 56 seats and 19 percent votes, Anarchists 15 seats and 5 percent votes.[407] On April 18, 1918, the Kronstadt Soviet denounced the Bolshevik repression of the Moscow Anarchists by 81 votes to 57, with 15 abstentions.[408] Subsequently, the anarchists were suppressed, but continued to function and exercise influence.

Finally, there were the Left Socialist Revolutionaries. They were in alliance with the Bolsheviks. They supported the Second Congress of Soviets but hoped to mediate and create an all-socialist government. Right SR and Menshevik intransigence dashed their hopes, and they joined Sovnarkom. They were opponents of the Treaty of Brest-Litovsk, considering it a surrender to imperialism. They also disagreed with the developing Bolshevik agrarian policy, including the attempt to intensify class struggle in the countryside and requisitioning grain. On July 6, the Left SR Central Committee organized the assassination of Count Mirbach, the German Ambassador, in the hope of relaunching the war against Germany. At the same time they tried to stage an insurrection. They were defeated. But in their case, the party as a whole was not banned. VTsIK passed resolution that permitted as representatives in it those Left SRs who repudiated the action of their Central Committee. As a consequence, there was a break-up in the party and loss on influence, though up to 1920 there were individual Left SRs in the Soviets. Small currents of Left SRs joined the RKP(b).[409]

One major group of Left SRs who joined the Bolsheviks were the Ukrainian Left SRs. They organized themselves as the Communist party of Ukraine (Borot'bists, so called because of their journal, *Borotba*). They were in favor of independence for the Ukraine. They also had deep roots amongst the Ukrainian peasants. The Borot'bists applied for Comintern affiliation in 1919, and again in 1920. A policy of pressure for merger, together with tactful handling, won over the *Borot'bists* to the RCP(b).[410] Christian Rakovsky, the chief Bolshevik leader in the Ukraine, admitted that by this merger, the CP (Bolsheviks) of Ukraine "evolved from the Russian Communist party in the Ukraine into a genuine Communist party of the Ukraine."[411] As Carr notes, this merger gained for the primarily urban, Russian and Jewish CP(b)U several thousand Ukrainian (and often rural) cadres.[412]

The end for all the parties came in 1921. Its background was formed by a growing unrest at all levels. To start with, the economic policies associated with War Communism were turning the peasants hostile. The policy of trying to split poor peasants through separate committees was a failure, because the poor peasant did not form a clearly separated class. Subsequently, the forcible collection of grain though dictated by military necessity, embittered many peasants everywhere. Peasant resistance turned to rebellion. As long as the Whiteguard danger was strong, the peasants put up with the Bolsheviks as the lesser evil. But from 1920, major peasant uprisings swept rural Russia, particularly in Tambov, Saratov, the Ukraine, Northern Caucasus, and Western Siberia. The Tambov rising, in particular, was a massive one, that went on for over a year.[413]

These peasant risings were more popular than Denikin's or Kolchak's rebellion. But the Tambov Uprising's leader, A.S. Antonov, also backed

Wrangel. Both the Green movement, and Red response, were violent and brutal. Bolsheviks were nailed to trees, disembowelled, their eyes gouged out, their sexual organs mutilated, prisoners were buried alive, etc. The Red Army sometimes responded by mass shootings, though they also pardoned many prisoners.[414]

From late 1920, the regime also began to lose parts of its working-class support. The continued economic crisis took its toll. Many workers went to the countryside for good. Others made regular trips to rural areas for food. The impact of the rural disturbances spilled over to them. Moreover, the emphasis on production, and the failure, even if partly due to war necessities, to safeguard workers' conditions made political opposition likely. Eventually, in January 1921, matters came to a head as bread rations, already low, were cut further due to a lack of supplies as food trains from Siberia and Northern Caucasus failed to move due to heavy snow and shortage of fuel.[415] As tension grew, a strike-wave developed. Zinoviev, Chairman of the Petrograd Soviet, proclaimed martial law, and a curfew was imposed. On the 28th of February, the strike-wave reached the Putilov works, which though by now shrunken, was still six thousand-strong. The resolutions passed in factory meetings initially dealt with economic issues. But soon, demands for the restoration of political and civil rights were being put forward forcefully.[416] Menshevik agitators received a sympathetic hearing.[417]

The Kronstadt uprising came as the culmination of this popular opposition to the regime. The Petrograd strikes had shaken the island fortress. Between 1917 and 1920, the composition and political complexion of the Kronstadt garrison had changed. In 1921, it had about fifty thousand people, about half military.[418] In 1917, the garrison had been relatively highly proletarian in composition. By 1920-21, this had changed. A large part of the garrison, including the 16th Rifle Regiment, as well as new recruits to the Baltic Fleet, were peasants.[419]

The impact of peasant disturbances on the sailors is quite evident. Stepan Petrichenko, the leader of the rising, was a peasant who had returned to his native Ukraine between April and the autumn of 1920. He found that "when we returned home our parents asked us why we fought for the oppressors. That set us thinking."[420] A sailor from the *Petropavlovsk*, the battleship that led the rebellion, wrote:

> Ours is an ordinary peasant farm, neither Kulak nor parasitical; yet when I and my brother return from serving the Soviet republic people will sneer at our wrecked farm and say: "What did you serve for? What has the Soviet republic given you?"[421]

Thus, the motivation of the Kronstadt sailors was not too different from that of the peasants everywhere. It showed, as the Tambov rising showed, that the worker–peasant alliance had totally broken down. However, it is also to be noted that political changes had been going on, and that political demands raised had been connected to these changes. In 1919, the Ships' Committees, which had formed the base units of the Centrobalt, had been dissolved.[422] This deprivation of political rights had an impact. Moreover, there were forces in the RCP(b) who were for a long time trying to undermine Trotsky's position. Among them, Zinoviev, Gusev, and others in his faction, as well as a faction round Stalin, campaigned repeatedly about Trotsky's so-called authoritarianism.[423] One effect was to undermine discipline in the Kronstadt garrison.[424]

On February 26, 1921, the crews of the warships *Petropavlovsk* and *Sevastopol* sent delegates to Petrograd. On their return, they reported about the strike wave. At a meeting, a charter of demands was drawn up. It called for a restoration of Soviet democracy, full political freedom for workers and peasants, anarchists and left socialists, and a number of other democratic and economic reforms.[425] However, the logic of confrontation gripped both sides. In Petrograd, Zinoviev's handling had roused anger. Though concessions were offered in Petrograd, the crucial economic concessions that Kronstadt prompted, the tax in kind and the legalization of the grain trade, only came after the suppression of the rebellion. In Kronstadt, too, anger at Zinoviev and Trotsky was channeled into an anti-Semitic direction.[426] While initially the call was for democratic Soviets, there was soon a shift, and the sailors wrote: "There is no middle ground in the struggle against the Communists. . . . One must not be deceived. . . . Victory or death."[427]

The fear of the government was that once the ice melted, Kronstadt would be open to external fleets. An enemy base so close to Petrograd could not be allowed. Moreover, as Avrich has shown, the Whites were preparing to intervene, and anti-communism was pushing Petrichenko towards them. The White National Centre was making plans to use the French navy and Wrangel's seventy thousand soldiers to go to Kronstadt.[428] On March 7, the government forces began to attack. On the 13th, Petrichenko sought Wrangel's help.[429] The revolt was crushed. The historian of the rebellion writes that there is evidence of an agreement with the White after the end of the revolt, and that "one cannot rule out the possibility that this was the continuation of a longstanding relationship."[430]

However, this only serves to show the crisis of the regime. One can well agree with Achin Vanaik that the alternative to Bolshevik rule would have been, not a more democratic socialist rule but White dictatorship.[431] But the events show clearly that in warding off the danger of counter-revolution, the Bolsheviks paid a heavy price. In responding to the

Kronstadt uprising by repressing it, they perhaps had no alternative, since the fortress, so close to Petrograd, had to be recaptured before the ice melted and foreign ships sailed on to Kronstadt and from there posed a threat to Petrograd. But thereafter, in treating the peasant revolts, the workers' unrest, and Kronstadt, as merely conflicts caused by economic distress, they deliberately ignored the political dimension. At the Tenth Party Congress, Lenin's speech contained the following:

> It (Kronstadt) was an attempt to seize political power from the Bolsheviks by a motley crowd or alliance of ill-assorted elements. . . . The movement was reduced to a petty-bourgeois counter-revolution and petty–bourgeois anarchism, . . . invariable hostility to the dictatorship of the proletariat. . . . We must take a hard look at this petty bourgeois counter-revolution with its calls for freedom of trade. . . . In the face of this danger we must understand that we must do more than put an end to party disputes as a matter of form.[432]

In ignoring the specific political demands, Lenin, and the Bolsheviks as a whole, showed how far they had travelled since 1917. Lenin's speech continuously referred to the imperialists, the civil war, and so on. The Civil War had ended only a short while back. The fear of armed attacks was real. Nonetheless, there was no basis for equating all opposition with counter-revolution. In fact this created a political position where an impossible level of unity had to be demanded from the proletariat and where the proletariat, even if it was united to that extent, was to rule over the majority of peasants. In this period, Lenin reverted to the idea that peasants voting and deciding on their own as a majority would mean "nothing more nor less than the restoration of capitalism."[433] He viewed the worker–peasant alliance as a military and economic alliance, but repudiated any idea of reviving workers democracy, by resorting to arguments about "pure democracy."[434] These were not mere statements about the prevailing situation, but a theoretical generalization that could only further damage the prospect of restoring workers' democracy. In fact, the ban on opposition parties and on public dissent led to a stifling of rights within the RCP(b) as well. Notwithstanding their long-term aims, earlier commitments, etc. Lenin, Trotsky and other Bolsheviks in this period (1919–21) contributed to the gagging of opposition parties and thereby to the destruction of workers' democracy. But without workers' democracy, even the vanguard party could not be reinvigorated.

X
THE TRANSFORMATION OF THE BOLSHEVIK PARTY

The last bastion of workers' democracy had been the Bolshevik party itself. In 1917, this party had only a kind of revolutionary discipline

created by adherence to a common revolutionary struggle. Respect
for decisions taken by higher authority was tempered by respect
for the mood of the masses. Lenin himself abandoned the Bolshevik
agrarian program in favor of the actual demands of the peasants, which
corresponded substantially with the SR program.[435] After October, the
pre-October divisions continued to exist, with Zinoviev, Kamenev,
Ryazanov, Lunacharsky, and others opposing Lenin, Trotsky, and
Sverdlov. There was no talk of imposing a unity by fiat. Kamenev's
group insisted on defying the CC resolution and tried to put together
an alliance with the socialist parties. They opposed the hard line
advocated by Lenin, Sverdlov, and Trotsky. At this, ten members of the
CC demanded that the minority must abide by the accepted line and
support a Soviet government. The CC minority thereupon offered to
resign from the CC in order to retain their right to go to the people with
their own views.[436] However, they did not have to resign in the end.
This shows that the CC discipline was not unnecessarily rigid.

Several Peoples' Commissars also resigned, and Commissar for
Labour, A.G. Shlyapnikov, expressed his support for those commissars.[437]
Ryazanov, Kamenev, and Larin, in a letter to the CC, said that "we do
not consider our disagreements with the CC to be a breach of the party
rules . . . we consider that it is totally inadmissible to create a special
regime for particular party members."[438] Another leading activist, S. A.
Lozovsky, objecting strongly to the insistence on retaining Lenin and
Trotsky in the Sovnarkom, wrote:

> I cannot, in the name of the party discipline, submit to the cult of personal
> worship and stake political conciliation with all socialist parties who agree
> to our basic demands, upon the inclusion of this or that individual in the
> ministry.[439]

The conflict that arose over the Brest-Litovsk treaty is another well-
known case.[440] The Soviet government's offer of a general armistice had
been greeted with silence by the Entente powers. The Central Powers
agreed to open armistice negotiations.

The Bolsheviks had originally called for a democratic peace,
with neither annexations nor indemnities. They had also proclaimed
their readiness to fight imperialism to defend a revolutionary Russia.
But when the Central Powers did put forward a set of annexationist
demands, the Bolsheviks faced a crisis. Lenin felt that the commitment
to peace had to be honored, because the soldiers gave no other choice.
If necessary, this would have to involve acceptance of onerous terms.
On this question, the party was split wide open. On January 8th 1918,
at a meeting of the Central Committee members with other leading
activists, three lines were put forward. Lenin urged that peace terms be
accepted. Trotsky called for disbanding the army, proclaiming the end

of the war, but not signing such an insulting peace. Finally, Bukharin called for a revolutionary war. Bukharin's position received 32 votes, Trotsky got 16 votes and Lenin 15 votes.[441]

For six weeks, the party was nearly split. Left Communists even demanded a special Party Conference and threatened to resign from all responsible posts in party and government if a peace treaty was signed prior to such a conference.[442] This Special Conference, which met on January 21, failed to take any clear stand. In the CC, Lenin aligned with Trotsky to block Bukharin. On January 29, Trotsky broke off negotiations, declaring that Russia would not sign the annexationist peace, but was terminating the war.[443]

The Germans responded by ending the armistice and invading Russia.[444] Inside the party, the result was a crisis with the Central Committee first approving the action of the delegation at Brest-Litovsk,[445] and then defeating both a call for revolutionary war[446] and a proposal for signing the peace.[447] Ultimately, on February 18th, Trotsky and his supporters partially sided with Lenin, arguing that if revolutionary war was launched, it would lead to a split in the party, which they could not risk under the circumstances. The proposal for immediate acceptance of German terms were adopted with 7 votes in favor, 4 against, and 4 abstentions.[448]

The CC minutes reveal a tremendous tension. The prospect of split was freely discussed. Yet, it is worth noting how the party acted to heal the wounds. Party unity was indeed considered a vital necessity. But that was not interpreted to mean that disputes should be condemned. Such an issue as war and peace (and the very existence, possibly, of the revolution) was debated with considerable publicity, including a Special Conference. Trotsky, who had some degree of agreement with the war faction, ultimately ensured their defeat, because he knew that if revolutionary war was waged, the party would split immediately, and Lenin's faction might even have to be arrested if they opposed a revolutionary war while war was actually being fought.[449]

Once Lenin's line was assured a victory, his most irreconcilable opponents tendered their resignations from the CC and from Sovnarkom. The response of Lenin and Trotsky was to propose forms of collaboration that allowed maximum flexibility to the minority while retaining them within the party. Lenin called for a guarantee that statements would be published in *Pravda* reflecting the standpoint of the minority. Trotsky's resolution, adopted unanimously, asked the members to "remain members of the leading party body, retaining the right to campaign freely against the decision adopted by the C.C." This meant that the CC members were given the right to publicly differentiate themselves from the official stand of the party on this contentious issue.

Similarly, Krestinsky's resolution on the six Peoples' Commissars who submitted resignations asked them to carry on other work, without feeling bound by cabinet solidarity on the question of the Brest-Litovsk Peace. This was adopted unanimously.[450]

The conclusion is simple, and wholly against the myth of the monolithic Bolshevik party. Even when they were in power, principles and conflicts over principle were seen to be more important for the Bolsheviks than were ambitions or hunger for power. The debates also throw light, in retrospect, on the strength of the Bolsheviks in these early years. Later, as debates were stilled in the name of "unity," it would increasingly become difficult for minorities to become majorities (as Lenin was able to do in 1918) by persuading their comrades.

The Brest-Litovsk treaty was imposed on Russia. Lenin's realism showed him that they had no option but to accept the terms however onerous. It meant not only depriving Russia of most of its coal, iron, and other mining resources, but also withdrawing from the revolutions in Finland or Ukraine. At the same time, it allowed some breathing space to consolidate the revolution. From February to August, there was relative peace until Civil War began.

Within the party, the issue continued to be debated sharply. Bukherin emerged as the Chief spokesperson for the faction of Left Communist at the Seventh Party Congress.[451] He opposed Lenin by claiming that Lenin's policy was betraying world revolution.[452] The significant thing is the widespread discussion, showing how inner-party democracy was considered. Ultimately, Lenin's peace program won by a vote of 30 to 12 with 4 abstentions. But when the Fourth Congress of Soviets ratified the treaty on March 15, 1918, 64 Left Communists abstained. Notwithstanding this, the Seventh Congress re-elected several Left Communists to the CC and Bukharin ranked fifth in the voting, evidence that the party did not treat his difference with Lenin as a cause for "punishment." He and V. M. Smirnov were elected to the program commission as well.[453]

The situation gradually changed with the Civil War and a number of other related factors, including the need to cope with the economic crisis and party expansion. In the first year of the revolutionary power, the party was structurally weak, with the best cadres integrated in the state (Soviet) apparatus.[454] The party organizations had little finance and little apparatus.[455] At the Eighth Party Congress held in March 1919, this situation was deplored. A resolution "On the Organisational Question" criticized the fact that the party's best forces were working wholly as state functionaries. Moreover, they were expected to win influence in the Soviets. Tighter links between local and central party organizations were called for, so that the party could keep itself informed and ensure united work by party members.[456]

The Eighth Party Conference of December 2–4, 1919, held at the height of the Civil War, tightened party discipline. One of the conference resolutions dealt with discipline. Resolutions of party centers were to be "implemented rapidly and accurately," while failure to do so was to be counted as a "party crime."[457] Party fractions in non-party institutions were declared entirely subordinated to the party. Fraction members had to vote unanimously in meetings of the non-party organizations.[458] This meant that whereas in the past, party fractions had debated issues and even changed positions, now only smaller, official bodies, like the CC would direct them. For example, the Bolshevik delegates to the Democratic Conference (in 1917) had voted against the Central Committee majority's call for a boycott, and as a result, there had not been any boycott at that stage. Now such a possibility was being stopped. The centralization process had begun. There were still considerable safeguards. Minorities had the right to challenge majority decisions. But now, the CC decisions had to be carried out. It was no longer possible to reject it in the name of the CC's divergence from the line of the Congress. But this power of the CC was limited by the rule providing for annual congresses, the practice of allowing co-reporters if alternative lines existed, etc.[459]

Until 1923, attempts were made to seriously ensure the authority of the Party Congress. Congresses were held annually from 1917 to 1923. Delegates were more or less freely elected before 1923. There was open discussion and free criticism of the party leadership. Commissions of various kinds were set up, with representation from different trends. In each Congress, standing rules enabled any group of a stipulated minimum (usually forty) number of delegates to present counter reports.[460] Final resolutions showed the result of tough bargaining. In short, the Congress reflected the normal cut and thrust of democratic party functioning.

Democratic Centralism, under the fire of the White Guards' guns, had tilted to centralism. But democracy was not gone. Throughout the period between October 1917 and 1921, the party had different factions. The usual "right" and "left" terms are somewhat inadequate. The factions included those who stressed institutions of popular, participatory democracy (often called the "left"), those who stressed traditional civil liberties and democratic rights (often identified as the "right") and those who turned expediency into theory. The composition of the different trends changed from time to time, though some people, like Kollontai, Osinskii, Preobrazhenskii, etc., remained "left" consistently, while Zinoviev, Stalin, and Molotov remained equally consistently among those who stood for political manipulations (Zinoviev would become left only in 1925-6, partly under pressure of the Leningrad proletariat), and Ryazanov was a more or less consistent "right"-ist, and Lenin and Trotsky, in important respects, had identifications with the "left."[461] But

Lenin was also capable of stiff action against oppositions, especially in 1921-22, while Trotsky in the same period emerged as a major theorist of the domination of the party, and of the CC.[462]

The "left" trends were usually quite vocal. The first of those was the Left Communist faction. They even launched their factional paper, the *Kommunist*. After the final ratification of the Treaty of Brest-Litovsk, their main target was economic policy, where they opposed Lenin's policy of "State Capitalism," one-man management, and the giving of posts of responsibility to bourgeois specialists. Left Communists were also opposed to any shrinkage in workers' democracy, including the abolition of election of officers in the Red Army.[463]

Even civil war did not end the factions. Trotsky's policy of creating a centralized army was opposed from two directions. Localism, by the proponents of partisan warfare (i.e., organization of small guerrilla armies) prompted them to oppose centralization. On the other hand, party members of long standing, moved by a complex set of feelings, partly democratic, partly corporatist, opposed the massive employment of ex-tsarist officers. So strong was this opposition that some of its leaders had to be co-opted in committees to draw up the resolutions, and some of their views had to be conceded.[464]

At the Ninth Congress Lenin was accused of "vertical centralism," and a faction came into existence, calling for Democratic Centralism. Among its chief spokespersons were Osinskii, Bubnov, Sapronov, and V. M. Smirnov. The Workers' Opposition came into existence in 1919. It was formed round an opposition to the party line on the trade union question. At the November 1920 conference of the Moscow Party organization, 124 out of the 278 delegates expressed support for the thesis of the Workers' Opposition.[465] Lenin's prestige and organizational manipulations by Zinoviev and Stalin, were major factors in the ultimate defeat of this opposition. But meanwhile, this opposition was able to publicly air its view in various ways. Alexander Shlyapnikov's "theses" were published in the party's organ.[466] Alexandra Kollontai wrote a more elaborate and extremely powerful pamphlet, *The Workers' Opposition*. It was published in an edition of two hundred fifty thousand copies.[467] This was, however, the last flare-up before extinction. The lid was put on opposition at the tenth Congress, though Lenin suggested that was a temporary affair.

Inner-party democracy up to 1921 was no mere formality. Real inner-party democracy required whole series of conditions: recognition of the real rights of the opposition being the first. The second was the sovereignty of the Party Congress. The CC had to be fully accountable to the Congress. The election of local and regional leaderships had to be freely made. Free confrontation of different opinions, and the circulation of decisions and opinions among the leadership to the rank and file were also necessary. In every issue prior to 1921, serious attempts were made. But Russian reality in 1918–1921 did not create the conditions in which the democratic ideals could be fully applied.

At the Ninth Party Conference, the left wing demanded, and got, more inner-party democratic rights.[468] The party zealously sought to keep intact its rights. This went on until 1920–21. The Ninth Congress had seen Trotsky presenting theses for the militarization of labor. There was a growing challenge to this, resulting, eventually, in several platforms being presented. Apparently, Trotsky persuaded Lenin that an officially sponsored discussion was necessary to establish the democratic credentials of the party.[469]

Already, party democracy was under strain. The Ninth Congress had heard criticism, like how elected local leaderships had been removed. Some cases of assigning dissident party members to distant areas (or diplomatic services) were known.[470]

Alexandra Kollontai drew applause at the Ninth Conference, when she asked Zinoviev what sort of freedom of criticism would be allowed and that party comrades must know whether criticism of party policies would result in their being sent off to a warm climate to eat peaches.[471] The dig was about an attempt by Zinoviev to get rid of Angelica Balabanova from Moscow, to Central Asia for her critical stand.[472] Preparations for the Tenth Congress were democratic. The trade union question was discussed at all levels of the party. But in his opening speech at the Congress, Lenin made it obvious that changes were in the offing:

> We have passed through an exceptional year, we have allowed ourselves the luxury of discussions and disputed within the party. This was an amazing luxury for a party shouldering unprecedented responsibilities.[473]

When the debates began, Lenin's initial move was to treat the Workers Opposition as a group of none-too-serious people. He claimed in his concluding speech on the Report of the Central Committee, that their "arguments about freedom of speech and freedom to criticize . . . have no particular meaning at all."[474] But after Alexandra Kollontai's speech, and after the distribution of her pamphlet, he turned harsh. Kollontai's views, that there was a rapid degeneration of the party, was not novel, as Osinskii and Sapronov had already made that point.[475] But Kollontai expressed the idea in popular terms, and, despite many vital weaknesses, pointed to the danger of monolithism and party dictatorship.[476]

The Workers' Opposition had demanded a Congress of producers. Zinoviev seems to have conceded that 99 percent to such a congress would be non-Bolsheviks, SRs, and Mensheviks.[477] This certainly showed that holding such a congress was dangerous for the ruling party. But it also showed how correct the Workers' Opposition was, in diagnosing the isolation of the party and the growing bureaucratization. Trotsky said that the Workers' Opposition had come forward with dangerous slogans, having put workers' democracy above the historic birthright of the party.[478]

The valid criticism against the Workers' Opposition was that it lacked a clear program. In 1921, with the productive base in disarray, and with the peculiar situation, wherein many long-standing worker militants were in the state apparatus, and many petty-bourgeois elements had entered industry either in the hope of security or to get a "proletarian" identity. As a result, a producers' Congress would not have served the revolutionary purpose that Shlyapnikov or Kollontai hoped for. But their program actually made a valid, though incomplete, analysis of bureaucratization as a negation of self-emancipation. Lenin's action of branding them as an "anarcho-syndicalist deviation" was a seriously damaging act. At the end of the Congress, Lenin moved two resolutions. One was on "the Syndicalist and Anarchist" deviation. Propaganda of this group's idea was declared incompatible with membership of the RCP(b).[479] This concept of a "deviation" had far-reaching implications. It implied that there was a "true" proletarian line, and that all lines that opposed it were not so much opposing lines within the party as oppositions to the party. The party itself, at this stage, was declared to be the repository of the genuine proletarian line in the following terms:

> Marxism teaches . . . the communist party is capable of unifying, teaching and organizing a vanguard of the proletariat and of the entire mass of working people, a vanguard capable of countering the inevitable petty bourgeois waverings of this mass, of countering the traditions of and inevitable backsliding to, a narrow trade unionism or trade union prejudices among the proletariat . . . without this (i.e., hegemony of the party) the dictatorship of the proletariat is unthinkable.[480]

Another resolution adopted was "On Party Unity." It denounced factions and factionalism. It went on to say that "The Congress orders the immediate dissolution . . . of all groups that have been formed on the basis of some platform or other."[481] The final clause of this resolution, kept hidden from the party, empowered the CC to expel even CC members from the party,[482] thereby violating utterly the sovereignty of the Party Congress. The decisions thus taken in haste, and in fear of counter-revolution, were to be of tremendous significance. The conjunctural issues were uppermost in Lenin's mind.[483] But the resultant decisions were not conjunctural. Lenin's definition of "factionalism" as "the formation of group with separate platforms striving to a certain degree to segregate and create their own group discipline"[484] raise an important question. Had he himself not sought to do the same, off and on since 1903? In 1908-9, he had even expelled Bogdanov from the Bolshevik faction, arguing that a party could be a broader organization, but a faction had to be restrictive, because it implied a specific platform. In a mass party, with hundreds of thousands of members, sharp differences could be properly articulated only if factions were permitted. The very premise of banning opposition parties who recognized Soviet power, and of factions in the communist party itself, was substitutionism. The party's line decided by the CC and approved the Congress, was deemed to be the proletarian line. The vast masses outside the party were, by definition, prone to petty-bourgeois wavering. In the name of a hierarchy of knowledge, the self-activity of the working class was reined in. The proletariat itself was viewed as never conscious enough (unless it agreed with the party line) to rule a country or progress to a classless society.

The ban on factions became all the more serious, because of the structural and social changes inside the party. Membership rose from about 23,600 before February 1917 to 240,000 at the time of the Sixth Congress, 390,000 in 1918; 611,978 in 1920 and 732,521 in 1921.[485] Membership break-up by social composition was as follows:[486]

TABLE 8.2

Year	Worker	Peasant	Other
1917	60.2%	7.5%	32.2%
1918	56.9%	14.5%	28.6%
1919	47.8%	21.8%	30.4%
1920	43.8%	25.1%	31.1%
1921	41%	28.2%	30.8%

Up to 1921 party membership was not chiefly a matter of privilege. Members had to be in the forefront of struggles. Thus, in 1920, during the Red Army's march towards Warsaw, the total loss to the army was 33 percent of its forces committed, while the loss of Bolsheviks in the army was 90 percent.[487] At the same time, this vanguard role, played by the worker-Bolsheviks, resulted in a catastrophic decline of party members actually working in the factories. At the Eleventh Congress, it was stated that in big districts, mines, etc., having 10,000–12,000 workers, the party nuclei were often of only six or so members.[488] Naturally, the vanguard nature of the party, dependent on a constant inflow of the grass-roots level militants, began to suffer. In view of its past success in attracting the vanguard to its ranks, the party did not recognize at once that it was being deprived of fresh blood. But steadily, the effect began to be felt. Thus, in rural areas, among the party members formally recorded as "peasants," a high proportion were in fact people who served as officials in local Soviets, party organization or cooperatives and were no longer actually engaged in farming. In Ryazan, in 1922, 78 percent of the party members were such officials.[489] In other words, whether in cities or in the countryside, a large number of members, especially at the leadership levels, were no longer engaged in productive work. Nor were they all party full-timers. Often they were state, trade union, or cooperative functionaries.

During the Civil War, a majority of new entrants were convinced supporters of communism. Even then, Lenin was warning about the dangers of former bureaucrats creeping into the party. To check this, he urged that there should be regular purges and membership renewals. After the Eighth Congress, 10 percent to 15 percent of urban and a greater proportion of rural party members were either expelled or their membership was not renewed.[490] Notwithstanding such attempts, the local and middle level cadres of the party were being more and more enmeshed in administration, and as a result, a gap was growing between them and the ordinary workers. This was the process of bureaucratization at the lower levels. This was also accompanied by the growth of purely commandist style and of smaller institutions at the top.

In the early months of the Soviet power, the CC of the party met very frequently. With the onset of Civil War, this frequency declined steeply. Between April and July 1918, there were only six CC meetings, and none between July and November 1918. To check this tendency, the new rules, adopted by the Eighth Party Conference, insisted that two full meetings of CC had to be held every month.[491] Meanwhile, the Political Bureau, originally set up in late 1917 at a time when the full CC could not meet regularly, and the progress to the insurrection was speeding up, now became a more authoritative body. Another body, the Organizing Bureau, set up to handle organizational tasks of the CC also began to act on behalf of the CC.[492]

In his report to the Ninth Congress, Lenin admitted that "The Political Bureau adopted decisions on all questions of foreign and domestic policy . . . daily work of the Central Committee has been conducted by . . . the Organizing Bureau . . . and the Political Bureau."[493] This trend continued in 1920 and 1921. Thus, between September 1920 and March 1921, the CC met 24 times, the Organizing Bureau 47 times, and the Political Bureau 26 times. Between May and August 1921, there were 9 CC meetings, 39 Political Bureau meetings, and 48 Organizing Bureau meetings. Between September and December 1921, the CC met 5 times, the Organizing Bureau met 63 times and the Political Bureau 44 times.[494] Only when there were acute divisions within the leadership, as during the trade union debate, did the Central Committee meet regularly.

Other party institutions also grew. The secretariat had in the past been a technical apparatus, to carry out Central Committee decisions. But from 15 members in March 1919, its staff strength rose to 602 in

March 1921.[495] One of the most important powers of the Secretariat in conjunction with the section of the party named *Uchraspred* (accounts and distribution section), was the appointment of personnel. In its report to the Tenth Congress, it showed that in a period of just under one year, it had transferred and appointed 42,000 party members.[496] The Secretariat also began to appoint local committees and local party secretaries. This was a clear violation of the norms and to prevent it the Ninth Conference resolved:

> While it is admitted in principle that it is necessary in exceptional cases to appoint people to elective positions, the Central Committee is none the less advised, as a general rule, to use recommendations instead of appointments. . . . Repressions of any sort whatsoever against comrades for the fact that they hold divergent views on certain questions resolved by the party, are impermissible.[497]

Stalin had been a major power in this apparatus even before he became the General Secretary after the Eleventh Congress. With official recognition of his power, as the oppositionist Kossior remarked, the party was reduced to "loading firewood and sweeping streets."[498]

The Central Control Commission was another originally democratic institution that turned into a danger to democracy. The Ninth Conference set up this institution to fight bureaucratic excesses and to receive complaints against party members or organizations, as well as to implement strict party control. Subsequently, control commissions were to hold joint meetings with their counterpart party committees.[499]

In practice however, in 1921, the faction supporting Lenin had its supporters elected almost exclusively to the Central Control Commission. By 1922, this was strengthened. As a result, the Control Commission instead of checking abuses, turned into an abettor of abuses.

Up to 1921, these trends were recognized as undesirable trends, imposed by necessity. Resolutions, like the Eighth Conference change in rules, stressed the need for more democratic decision-making. But in 1921, the ban on factions cut away so important an aspect of the right of party members that it became almost impossible for them to control the leadership. The process of open bureaucratization sprang from this.

NOTES

1. L. Trotsky, *Writings (1935–36)*, New York, 1977, p. 311.
2. See M. Lewin, *Lenin's Last Struggle*, New York, 1968.
3. This line of criticism is less common than criticism of the Leninist theory of organization. There are, however, some critics. D. W. Lovell, for example, says that for Lenin "Political forms are contingent" (p. 169), so that "how the state actually represented the proletariat's interests, and how they

can be determined," is a question that Lenin had avoided (p. 171). He claims that for the Bolsheviks, the Constituent Assembly was a bourgeois institution due to the preponderance of non-Bolshevik socialists, whom they viewed as imperialist agents. (p. 172; see also pp. 173, 175.) The most sharp criticism of Lenin's theory of state comes from A. J. Polan, *Lenin and the end of Politics*. On Lenin's silences, see R. Miliband, "Lenin's *The State and Revolution*," in R. Miliband and J. Seville, eds., *Socialist Register*, 1970. See also A. B. Evans, "Rereading Lenin's *State and Revolution*," *Slavic Review*, vol. 46, no. 1, Spring 1987, pp. 1–19, for an argument that Lenin did not want to abolish the state bureaucracy.

4. See, for example, T. Ali, ed., *The Stalinist Legacy*, Harmondsworth, 1984, pp. 10–11.

5. A major recent work along these lines is S. Farber, *Before Stalinism*, London, 1990.

6. H. Draper, *DPML*, pp. 65–75, makes much of this, and attempts to derive the slogan from Plekhanov's personal "authoritarian" style, which does not explain why the Bolsheviks accepted it .

7. Quoted in M. Salvadori, *Karl Kautsky and the Socialist Revolution*, pp. 65–68.

8. For Bernstein's rejection of the dictatorship of the proletariat, see his *Evolutionary Socialism*, p. 146. For the replies by Parvus see H. Tudor and M. Tudor, eds., *Marxism and Social Democracy*, Cambridge, 1988. For an assessment of his role, see Z. A. B. Zeman and W. B. Scharlu, *The Merchant of Revolution*, London, 1965, pp. 38–42. For Luxemburg's critique of Bernstein, see her *Reform or Revolution ?*, Calcutta, 1993. For Plekhanov's use of the term, see G. V. Plekhanov, *Selected Philosophical Works* (hereafter SPW), vol. 1., pp. 109–10, 302–3. In both cases the stress is on class rule. His response to Bernstein took the form of an introduction to a new edition of the *Communist Manifesto* in 1900, in which he emphasized the necessity of suppressing bourgeois resistance SPW, vol. 2, pp. 472–73. Luxemburg used the term in the following way: "The first act of the socialist transformation must therefore be the conquest of political power *by the working class* and the establishment of the *dictatorship of the proletariat*, which is absolutely necessary for effecting transitional measures." R. Luxemburg, *Gesammelte Werke*, band 1, Zweiter Habband, Berlin 1988, p. 317.

9. B. Pearce, ed., *1903*, p. 5.

10. Ibid., pp. 160–61.

11. Ibid., pp. 170–71.

12. For an opposite view see H. Draper, *DPML*, p. 69.

13. B. Pearce, ed., *1903*, pp. 219–20.

14. See H. Draper, *DPML*, p. 70 for such an allegation.

15. *LCW* 9, p. 130.

16. Ibid., p. 132.

17. Ibid., p. 111.

18. Ibid. 10, p. 244.

19. See H. Draper, *DPML*, pp. 88–93 for a long discussion on Lenin's writings of this period.

20. N. Harding, *Lenin's Political Thought*, vol. 2, p. 84. See further, L. Trotsky, *The Third International after Lenin*, New York, 1980.

21. See, N. I. Bukharin, "K teorii imperialisticheskogo gosudarstva," quoted in N. Harding, *Lenin's Political Thought*, vol. 2, pp. 104–7

22. The shifts in his view can be traced by looking at his letters of late 1916-early 1917, in *LCW* 43, Moscow, 1917, p. 613. See in particular his letter to Inessa Armand: "I have read Pannekoeks discussion with Kautsky in *Neue Zeit* (1912). Kautsky is despicably mean, and Pannekoek, but for some *inacuracies* and slight mistakes, is *almost* right. Kautsky is the acme of opportunism. (p. 613)

23. Quoted in T. Cliff, *Trotsky: Towards October, 1879–1917*, London, Chicago, and Melbourne, 1989, p. 63. The English edition of *Our Political Tasks* omits this section.

24. L. Trotsky, *The Permanent Revolution and Results and Prospects*, p. 105. In M. J. Olgin, ed. , Leon Trotsky, *Our Revolution*, the word "lasting" is translated as permanent. Out of three available translations this was the only unauthorized one. But H. Draper, in *DPLM*, pp. 77–78, launches a sharp attack on Trotsky, based on this word (suggesting that Trotsky revealed thereby an authoritarian tendency). It can be suggested that Draper's special hostility to Trotsky is due to his participation in the 1939–40 split from Trotskyism.

25. L. Trotsky, *The Permanent Revolution*, p. 75.

26. Ibid., pp. 75–76.

27. L. Trotsky, *1905*, p. 268.

28. *LCW* 23. pp. 307–8.

29. It might be argued that in this text Lenin did not use the specific phrase, "dictatorship of the proletariat." But in so far as Lovell, and Draper, both argue that for Lenin "democratic dictatorship" vs. "proletarian dictatorship" referred to the stage of revolution, i.e., bourgeois revolution vs socialist revolution, the reverse must also hold good. That is, if Lenin said that socialism must be built by Soviets, then he must be taken to mean that Soviet democracy is the political form of the dictatorship of the proletariat.

30. *LCW* 23, p. 325.

31. Ibid. 24, p. 68.

32. Ibid., p. 471.

33. Ibid. 25, pp. 398, 403.

34. Ibid., pp. 427–28, 412, 428, 397–98, respectively, for the four points made.

35. Ibid., p. 391.

36. Ibid., p. 414.

37. Ibid., p. 495.

38. Ibid., p. 299.

39. N. Harding, *Lenin's Political Thought*, vol. 2, pp. 134–41 argues that Lenin operated with two separate models, the commune and the "dictatorship"— one democratic, the other authoritarian. This is based on his erroneous claim that Marx did not consider the Commune to be a dictatorship of the proletariat.

40. *LCW* 25, p. 417.
41. Ibid.
42. Ibid., p. 452.
43. Ibid., pp. 466–67.
44. Ibid., p. 461.
45. Ibid., p. 420. Lenin is here quoting a letter of Marx to Kugelmann. This is just one of numerous examples of how closely he followed the idea of Marx and Engels in his writings on the state in 1917.
46. Ibid., pp. 430–31.
47. Ibid., p. 424.
48. Ibid., p. 467.
49. Thus, P. Corrigan, H. Ramsay, and D. Sayer, "Bolshevim and the USSR," *New Left Review*, no. 125, 1981, put forward the view that Stalinism is a phase of Bolshevism, and that there is less scope for a separate polity in socialism (p. 58), leading them to defense of the annihilation of political opposition under Stalinism.
50. *LCW* 25, p. 486.
51. As a result, many critics tend to avoid this work. For Robert Conquest, *Lenin*, London 1972, pp. 86, 87, it is an aberration in being an anarchist-inclined work. R. V. Daniels, *The Conscience of the Revolution*, Cambridge, Mass, 1960, p. 51, treats the work as a treatise in "revolutionary utopianism." H. Draper, *DPML*, in his bid to criticize Lenin for his bad views about the dictatorship, omits this work as not being germane (pp. 96–97).
52. *LCW* 24, p. 239.
53. Ibid. 25, p. 425.
54. Ibid., pp. 431–32.
55. A. J. Polan, *Lenin and the End of Politics*, argues that Lenin claimed that communism would mean unity, so all differences during the dictatorship of the proletariat would reflect class differences. Polan is correct in pointing out the major weakness—non-recognition of public associations existing outside the state structures in *The State Revolution*. But he exaggerates his case in claiming that the work created an ethos of "anti-politics," and the GULAG can be deduced from flaws in this work.
56. *LCW* 26, p. 111.
57. S. A. Smith, *Red Petrograd*, p. 10.
58. Ibid., p. 168.
59. M. Ferro, *The Bolshevik Revolution*, pp. 160–61.
60. Ibid., p. 163.
61. From S. A. Smith, *Red Petrograd*, p. 245, Table 15.
62. For Lenin's return to Russia, see *LCW* 24, pp. 27–29. For Trotsky's internment, see L. Trotsky, *My Life*, Harmondsworth, 1975, pp. 29–94. See A. F. Kerensky, *The Crucifixion of Liberty*, London, 1934, pp. 235–94, for an attempt, as late as 1934, to portray Lenin as a German agent. See further Sir G. Buchanan, *My Mission to Russia*, London, 1923, vol. 2, p. 121 for the complicity of Miliukov and Buchanan himself in Trotsky's internment.
63. L. Trotsky, *1905*, p. 333.

64. Buchanan *My Mission to Russia,* especially vol. 2, pp. 159–63, and pp. 11, 119.
65. Sir Alfred Knox, *With the Russian Army* vol 2, London, 1921, 1914–1917, for his ties with Kornilov.
66. Cf., I. Deutscher, *The Prophet Armed,* pp. 347–48.
67. L. Trotsky, *History of the Russian Revolution,* vol. 1, pp. 263–64.
68. W. H. Chamberlin, *The Russian Revolution: 1917–1921,* vol. 1, p. 179.
69. On this, apart from the texts of Lenin and Kerensky, mentioned in footnote, 63, see L. Trotsky, *History of the Russian Revolution,* vol. 2, and W. H. Chamberlin, *The Russian Revolution: 1917–1921,* vol. 1, p. 179–82. A painstaking attempt to prove the charge is G. Katkov, *Russia 1917.*
70. L. Trotsky, *History of the Russian Revolution,* vol. 2, p. 121.
71. Ibid., p. 122.
72. See e.g., N. Y. Ivanov, *Kornilovshchina i eye razgrom,* Leningrad, 1965.
73. Quoted by M. Ferro, *The Bolshevik Revolution,* p. 41.
74. Ibid., pp. 51–52.
75. L. Trotsky, *History of the Russian Revolution,* vol. 3, pp. 287–88.
76. *Vtoroi Vserossiskii S'ezd Sovetov R.I.S.D.,* Moscow and Leningrad, 1928, pp. 37–40. The 1957 volume, with the same title, that has been cited earlier dose not include these. For a full translation see W. H. Chamberlin *The Russian Revolution: 1917–1921,* vol. 1, pp. 470–71.
77. See J. Bunyan and H. H. Fisher. *The Bolshevik Revolution, 1917–1918: Documents and Materials,* pp. 118–19.
78. Ibid., pp. 149, 150.
79. Ibid., p. 151.
80. See ibid., p. 152.
81. For the clash between Krasnov's forces and the Red forces, see L. Trotsky, *The History of the Russian Revolution to Brest Litovsk,* London, 1919, pp. 100–104. For the uprising in the city, see the eyewitness account in J. Reed, *Ten Days that Shook the World,* New York, 1960. For Vikzhel's role, see Bunyan and Fisher, *The Bolshevik Revolution, 1917–1918: Documents and Materials,* pp. 155–56, 158–59. These negotiations are discussed further below.
82. V. Serge, *Year One of the Russian Revolution,* London, 1992, p. 76.
83. W. H. Chamberlin, *The Russian Revolution: 1917-1921,* vol. 1, pp. 343–47.
84. Ibid., pp. 373–74; V. Serge, *Year One,* p. 116.
85. For summary, see D. Footman, *Civil War in Russia,* London, 1961.
86. On the volunteer Army, see G. A. Brinkley, *The Volunteer Army and Allied Intervention in South Russia, 1917–1921,* South Bend, Indiana, 1966; P. Kenez, *Civil War in South Russia,* 1918, Berkeley, 1971.
87. See T. Hunczak, ed., *The Ukraine, 1917–1921: A study in Revolution,* Cambridge, 1977.
88. See F. Kazemzadeh, *Struggle for the Transcaucasus, 1917–1922,* New York, 1951.
89. A. F. Upton, *The Finnish Revolution: 1917–1918,* Minneapolis, 1980, p. 522.
90. V. Serge, *Year One,* p. 187.
91. Ibid.
92. Ibid.

93. A. F. Upton, *The Finnish Revolution: 1917–1918*, p. 519.

94. Ibid., p. 521.

95. Ibid. In Serge, *Year One*, p. 187, author writes that there were 70,000 soldiers.

96. E. Mandel, *October 1917, Coup d'etat or Social Revolution?* Montreuil, 1992, p. 22.

97. R. H. Bruce Lockhart, *Memoirs of a British Agent*, London, and New York, 1933, pp. 253–54, 265, 273, 283–85.

98. W. Bruce Lincoln, *Red Victory*, New York, 1989, p. 99.

99. Ibid., p. 198.

100. A Whiteguard report, quoted by E. Mandel, *October 1917: Coup d' etat or Social Revolution?*, p. 23.

101. V. Serge, *Year One*, p.331.

102. Cf., P. Kenez, "The Ideology of the white movement," *Soviet Studies*, vol. 32, no. 1. (January, 1980).

103. P. N. Wrangel, *Memoirs*, London, 1930, p. 201.

104. W. H. Chamberlin, *The Russian Revolution: 1917–1921*, vol. 2, pp. 482–83.

105. Ibid., p. 41.

106. V. Serge, *Year One*, pp. 304–7, 336–38.

107. Z. Gitelman, *A Century of Ambivalence — The Jews of Russia and the Soviet Union*, New York, 1988, p. 99–106.

108. See e.g., R. Luckett, *The White Generals*, London, 1971.

109. L. Schapiro, *The Russian Revolution of 1917*, New York, 1986, p. 176.

110. For the Baku Commune, see R. G. Suny. *The Baku Commune 1917–1918*, Princetown, 1972. For the role of the British army, see Major General L. Dunsterville, *The Adventures of Dunsterforce*, London, 1920. See also V. Serge, *Year One*, pp. 401–2.

111. See V. Serge, *Year One*, p. 233, see also, for a general discussion of SR policy, O. H. Radkey, *The Sickle Under the Hammer*, New York, 1963.

112. Ibid., p. 288.

113. Ibid., pp. 289–90, See also, *International Press Correspondence* (Inprecorr), various issues for May–July 1922 which reported on the 1922 trial of the SRs. Their testimony showed the SR party's role and also French complicity.

114. R. H. Bruce-Lockhart, *Memoirs of a British Agent*, pp. 316–23.

115. S. Lovell, ed., *Leon Trotsky Speaks*, New York, 1972, p. 81; see also V. I. Lenin, "Resolution on War and Peace (7th Congress of the R.C.P.(B)," in *LCW* 27, Moscow, 1977, pp. 118–19.

116. Quoted in R. Medvedev, *The October Revolution*, New York, 1979, pp. 03–4.

117. O. H. Radkey, *The Elections to the Russian Constituent Assembly* of 1917, p. 20.

118. O. H. Radkey, *The Sickle under the Hammer*, New York, 1963, pp. 456f.

119. V. I. Lenin, "The Constituent Assembly Elections and The Dictatorship of the Proletariat" in *LCW* 30, accessed on November 26, 2006, http://www .marxists.org/archive/lenin/works/1919/dec/16.htm.

120. Ibid.

121. R. Medvedev, *The October Revolution*, pp. 110 –11.

122. Ibid., p. 108.

123. V. I. Lenin, "Theses on the Constituent Assembly," in *LCW* 26, p. 380.

124. O. H. Radkey, *The Sickle under the Hammer*, p. 301.
125. Ibid., p. 344.
126. *The Bolsheviks and the October Revolution*, p. 81.
127. Ibid., pp. 154–55.
128. L. Trotsky, *On Lenin*, Bombay, 1971, pp. 105–6.
129. *LCW* 26, pp. 379–83.
130. V. I. Lenin, "The Constituent Assembly Elections and The Dictatorship of the Proletariat" in *LCW* 30, accessed on November 26, 2006, http://www.marxists.org/archive/lenin/works/1919/dec/16.htm.
131. K. Kautsky, *The Dictatorship of the Proletariat*, p. 4.
132. Ibid., p. 26.
133. Ibid., p. 61.
134. Ibid., pp. 72–87.
135. It is therefore, one thing to criticize flaws in the Soviet system, quite a different thing to accept Kautsky as a Marxist socialist theorist.
136. *LCW* 28, p. 236.
137. L. Trotsky, *Terrorism and Communism*, London, 1975, p. 66.
138. Ibid., p. 123, also p. 44.
139. R. Luxemburg, *Zur russischen Revolution*, in *Gesammelte Werke*, Bd. 4, Berlin, 1990, pp. 338 (support to Bolshevism), 341 (All Power to workers and peasants), 353–56 (critique of the dissolution).
140. There was little popular outcry at the dissolution, and very little actual support for the Assembly, on this point. See L. Schapiro, *The Origin of Communist Autocracy*, p. 86.
141. *LCW* 26, p. 140.
142. Ibid., p. 192.
143. *The Bolsheviks and the October Revolution*, p. 104.
144. E. H. Carr, *The Bolshevik Revolution*, vol. 3, Harmondsworth, 1966, p. 69. These were not, as Robin Blackburn, "Fin de siecle: socialism after the crash," p. 24, claims, later justifications of the original, Bolshevik seizure of power.
145. V. Serge, *Year One*, p. 319.
146. For Germany, see C. Harman, *Germany: The Lost Revolution*, London, 1982. For the rise of councils in Germany, Italy, and Britain, see D. Gluckstein, *The Western Soviets*. For a general survey, see T. Cliff, *Lenin*, vol. 3, and vol. 4, London, 1978 and 1979 respectively.
147. O. Bauer, *The Austrian Revolution*, London, 1925, p. 9.
148. H. N. Brailsford, *Across the Blockade*, New York, 1991, p. 140.
149. O. Anweiler, *The Soviets*, p. 122.
150. Ibid., p. 136.
151. L. Trotsky, *History of the Russian Revolution*, vol. 2., p. 281.
152. Bunyan and Fisher, *The Bolshevik Revolution, 1917–1918: Documents and Materials*, p. 137; Trotsky, *History of the Russian Revolution*, vol. 3, pp. 316–17.
153. J. L. H. Keep, ed., *The Debate on Soviet Power, Minutes of The All-Russian Central Executive Committee of Soviets*, Oxford, 1979, p. 46.
154. *The Bolsheviks and the October Revolution*, p. 127.

155. Ibid., p. 129.
156. Ibid., p. 131.
157. Ibid., p. 132.
158. J. L. H. Keep, ed., *The Debate on Soviet Power*, pp. 51–52.
159. Ibid., p. 52–53.
160. L. Trotsky, *The Stalin School of Falsification*, pp. 109–22.
161. The *Bolsheviks and October Revolution*, pp. 136–37.
162. Bunyan and Fisher *The Bolshevik Revolution, 1917–1918: Documents and Materials*, pp. 198–99.
163. T. Cliff, *Lenin*, vol. 3, p. 146. This was the reduction from the original plan of quarterly meetings.
164. Based on E. H. Carr. The *Bolshevik Revolution*, vol. 1, Harmondsworth, 1966, pp. 134–59.
165. Bunyan and Fisher, p. 578.
166. E. H. Carr, *The Bolshevik Revolution*, vol. 1, p. 158.
167. For the growing power and stature of the presidium, see C. Duval, "Yakov M. Sverdlov and the All-Russian Central Executive Committee of Soviets (VTsIK)," *Soviet Studies*, vol. 31, no. 1, January 1979.
168. G. Vernadsky, *A History of Russia*, New York, 1944, p. 319.
169. It is a defect of most general works on Soviet history that they ignore this. O. Anweiler, *The Soviets*, and J. Hazard, *The Soviet System of Government*, Chicago, 1964, have good though short discussions on the subject. The works of Koenker, Mandel, Suny, and Raleigh take up particular areas.
170. R. Abrams, "Political Recruitment and Local Government: The Local Soviets of the RSFSR: 1918–21, *Soviets Studies*, vol. 19, no. 4, April, 1968.
171. M. Vladimirsky, *Sovety ispolkomy i s'ezdy Sovetov: Materialy k izucheniiu srtoeniya i devatelrosti organov mestriogo upravleniya*, vol. 1, Moscow, 1920, p. 7.
172. Ibid., and R. Abrams, "Political Recruitment and Local Government," p. 576, citing other surveys.
173. M. Vladimirsky, *Sovety ispolkomy i s'ezdy Sovetov; Materialy k izucheniyu stoeniya i deyatelrosti organov mestviogo upravleniya*, vol. 1, p. 6 Even if the high school figures include some university dropouts, this would not materially alter the picture.
174. Ibid., pp. 4–5; see also R. Abrams, "Political Recruitment and Local Government: The Local Soviets of the RSFSR: 1918-21," p. 577, note 25 for a comparison with 1920–21.
175. R. Abrams, "Political Recruitment and Local Government: The Local Soviets of the RSFSR: 1918–21," pp. 578–79.
176. S. Farber, *Before Stalinism*, p. 24.
177. A. Rabinowitch, "The Evolution of Local Soviets in Petrograd, November 1917–June 1918: The Case of the First City District Soviet," *Slavic Review*, vol. 46, no. 1, Spring 1987, p. 20.
178. Ibid., pp. 22–24.
179. Ibid., pp. 30–32, 37.
180. *LCW* 27, p. 133.
181. V. I. Lenin, *The Immediate Tasks of the Soviet Government*, in ibid., p. 272.

182. O. Anweiler, *The Soviets*, p. 219.
183. Ibid., pp. 202–3.
184. "Regarded from the world-historical point of view, there would doubtless be no hope of the ultimate victory of our revolution if it were to remain alone." *LCW* 27, p. 95
185. D. Mandel, *The Petrograd Workers and the Soviet Seizure of power*, p. 406.
186. T. H. Rigby, *Lenin's Government: Sovnarkom 1917–1922*, Cambridge, 1979, pp. 161–62; O. Anweiler, *The Soviets*, pp. 193, 230; Trotsky, *History*, vol. 3, pp. 281, 282, 288.
187. The fate of the parties is traced below, in a separate section.
188. E. H. Carr, *The Bolshevik Revolution*, vol. 2, Harmondsworth, 1966, p. 187.
189. Out of a total of 6,000,000 workers who joined the Red Army, 180,000 were killed. Three million workers lost their jobs. M. Lewin, *The Making of the Soviet System*, London, 1985, p. 212.
190. T. Cliff, *Lenin*, vol. 3, p. 158.
191. J. Stalin, *Works*, vol. 4, Moscow, 1953, p. 220.
192. *LCW* 29, p. 183.
193. Ibid., p. 559.
194. *Vosmoi S'ezed RKP(b)* Moscow, 1933, p. 230.
195. *Deviatii S'ezed RKP(b)*, Moscow, 1963, p. 307.
196. V. Serge, *Year One*, pp. 265–66.
197. Quoted in D. Mandel, *Factory Committees and Workers' Control in Petrograd in 1917*, Montreuil, France, 1993, p. 5.
198. S. A. Smith,"Petrograd in 1917," p. 63, in D. H. Kaiser, ed., *The Workers' Revolution in Russia 1917*.
199. For such interpretation, see P. Avrich, *The Russian Anarchists*, London, 1973; especially pp. 142–49. J. L. H. Keep, *The Russian Revolution*, p. 64 and S. P. Melgunov, *The Bolshevik Seizure of Power*, Santa Barbara, 1972, pp. 22–23.
200. Cf., *Revoliutsionnoe dvizhenie v Rossii posle sverzheniya samoderzhaviya*, Moscow, 1957, pp. 491–92.
201. Ibid., pp. 575–77.
202. See D. Mandel, *Factory Committees*, pp. 13–14.
203. See *Oktybr'skaya revoliutsiai i Fabzavkomy*, P. N. Amosov, et al., eds., Moscow, 1927, vol. 1, p. 114.
204. *Izvestiya*, June 2, 1917, quoted in D. Mandel, *Factory Committees*, p. 14.
205. *Oktybr'skaya revolyutsia i fabzavkomy*, vol. 1, p. 107. This voting pattern is ignored by those who see in workers' control an anarchist movement.
206. Ibid., vol. 1, pp. 113, 126.
207. S. A. Smith, *Red Petrograd*, pp. 177–79. At this point, it is necessary to argue against the views of F. I. Kaplan, *Bolshevik Ideology and the Ethics of Soviet Labour*, New York, 1968; or J. L. H. Keep, *The Russian Revolution*, who claim that the Bolsheviks were centralizers who only opportunistically used the factory committee movement to seize power, and then destroy the movement.
208. *LCW* 26, p. 105.
209. Ibid., pp. 106–7.

210. Ibid., p. 108.

211. R. C. Elwood, ed., *The RSDLP*, pp. 25–27.

212. Cf., S. A. Smith, *Red Petrograd*, pp. 158–59.

213. Ibid., p. 105, Smith, however, feels that the figures are exaggerated.

214. Ibid., p. 216.

215. Ibid., p. 158.

216. See *Dekrety Sovetskoi Vlasti*, vol. 1, Moscow, 1957, pp. 77–65, and *Obrazovanie v razvitie organov Sotsialisticheskogo Kontrol v SSSR (1917–1975)*, Moscow, 1975, pp. 21–23, see also, I. A. Gladkov, ed., *Natsionalizatsiya promyshlennosti V SSSR 1917–20gg*, Moscow, 1954, pp. 76–84, for a broad definition of workers' control used by factory committees.

217. S. A. Smith, *Red Petrograd*, pp. 217–18.

218. D. Mandel, *Factory Committees*, p. 33.

219. S. A. Smith, *Red Petrograd*, pp. 235–39.

220. V. I. Lenin, "The Achievements and difficulties of the Soviet Government," in *LCW* 29, Moscow, 1980, p. 70, and ibid. 27, p. 268.

221. Ibid., pp. 575–77.

222. L. Trotsky, *Terrorism and Communism*, p. 170

223. However, the centrality of the political process cannot be denied. Both Yugoslav "self-management" and Maoist practice stressed some sort of factory-level workers' participation. In the absence of Soviet democracy, these became mere cosmetic claims.

224. M. Ferro, *The Bolshevik Revolution*, p. 194.

225. See S. A. Smith, Review of M. Ferro's *The Bolshevik Revolution*, in *Soviet Studies*, vol. 30, no. 3; 1981, pp. 454–59, and S. A. Smith, *Red Petrograd*, pp. 205–6.

226. Ibid., p. 202.

227. D. Koenker, *Moscow Workers*, pp. 374–75.

228. S. A. Smith, *Red Petrograd*, pp. 219–20.

229. Ibid., p. 222.

230. L. N. Kritzman, *Die heroische periode der grossen Russischen Revolution*, Frankfurt am Main, 1971, pp. 80, 293.

231. J. Bunyan, *The Origin of Forced Labour in the Soviet State: 1917–1921*, Baltimore, 1967, pp. 173–74.

232. L. N. Kritzman, *Die heroische periode*, p. 265.

233. M. H. Dobb. *Soviet Economic Development since 1917*, London, 1948, p. 114.

234. Quoted in F. I. Kaplan, *Bolshevik Ideology*, pp. 129–30.

235. See the sources cited in ibid., and T. Cliff, *Lenin*, vol. 3, p. 117, notes 19 and 20.

236. Quoted in J. Bunyan, *The Origins of Forced Labour*, pp. 20–21.

237. Ibid., p. 26.

238. See R. Medvedev, *The October Revolution*, Chapter 12, and V. Brovkin, "The Mensheviks' Political Comeback: The Election to the Provincial City Soviets in Spring 1918," *The Russian Review*, vol. 42, no. 1, January 1983, pp. 1–50, esp. pp. 37–38. Some of Brovkin's contentions are challenged by W. G. Rosenberg, "Russian Labour and Bolshevik Power After October," *Slavic Review*, vol. 44, 1983, pp. 213–38. See also S. A. Smith, *Red Petrograd*,

chapters 9 and 10; Rosenberg is correct in pointing out that in voting against the Bolsheviks, the workers were not so much rejecting the program but hoping that Mensheviks and SRs could prove to be "better" Bolsheviks.

239. S. A. Smith, *Red Petrograd*, p. 242.
240. N. Bukharin and E. Preobrazhenskii, *The ABC of Communism*, Harmondsworth, 1989, p. 448
241. *Desiatii S'ezd RKP(b)*, pp. 451–52.
242. V. I. Lenin, Speech delivered at The Third All-Russia Congress of Economic Councils, in *LCW* 30, accessed on November 26, 2006, *http://www.marxists. org/archive/lenin/works/1920/jan/27.htm*.
243. Quoted by T. Cliff, *Trotsky: 1917–1923, The Sword of the Revolution*, London, Chicago, and Melbourne, 1990, p. 163.
244. Ibid., p. 165.
245. Ibid., quoting a speech of February 25, 1920, to the Ekaterinburg membership of the party.
246. The necessity of emphasizing this is Soviet historiography, which always insisted on treating statements by Trotsky as deviations, betrayals, etc. Contemporary Stalinist and Maoist writing tends to do the same.
247. J. Bunyan, *The Origin of Forced Labour*, p. 121.
248. See *Deviatii S'ezd RKP(b)*, Moscow, 1963, for the wide-ranging debate in the party congress.
249. J. Bunyan, *The Origins of Forced Labour*, p. 92.
250. Ibid., p. 123.
251. The following account is based on I. Deutscher, *The Prophet Armed*, pp. 487–88, 501–3; T. Cliff. *Trotsky: 1917–1923*, pp. 169–71; and L. Trotsky, *The New Course*, in N. Allen, ed., *Leon Trotsky; The Challenge of the Left Opposition (1923–25)*, New York, 1975, pp. 109–117.
252. Trotsky changed his position quickly. But this whole episode left a damaging legacy.
253. R. Gregor, *Resolutions and Decisions of the Communist Party of the Soviet Union*, vol. 2, *The Early Soviet Period*, Toronto, 1974, p. 101.
254. Ibid., pp. 101–2.
255. *Deviatii S'ezd RKP(b)*, pp. 115–27, (Osinskii), 239–42 (Lutovinov).
256. For a full documentation of this point, see L. Schapiro, *The Origins of Communist Autocracy*, pp. 253–60, and passim.
257. *Desiatii S'ezd RKP(b)*, p. 453.
258. R. Gregor, *The Early Soviet Period*, pp. 126–28.
259. *Odinnadtsatii S'ezd RKP(b)*, Moscow, 1963, pp. 277–78.
260. J. B. Sørensen, *The Life and Death of Soviet Trade Unionism, 1917–1928*, New York, 1969, pp. 167–69.
261. N. D. Karpetskaia, *Rabotnitsy i Velikii Oktyabr*, Leningrad, 1974, pp. 41–44. For Kollontai apart from sources cited earlier, in chapter 7, see A.M. Itykina, *Revolyutioner, tribun, diplomat: ocherk zhizni Aleksandry Mikhailovny Kollontai*, Moscow, 1964, pp. 81–83.
262. Richard Stites, *The Women's Liberation Movement in Russia: Feminism, Nihilism and Bolshevism 1860-1930*, Princeton, New Jersey, 1978, p. 306.

See further N.D. Karpetskaia, *Rabotnitsy i Velikii Oktyabr*, p. 114.

263. See *Rabotnitsa*, 12 (1917), pp. 10–15 for the conference, and *Rabotnitsa*, 13 (1917), pp. 10–12, especially p. 11 for Doroshevskaya.

264. Richard Stites, *The Women's Liberation Movement in Russia*, p. 327.

265. K. T. Sverdlova, *Iakov Mikhailovich Sverdlov*, Moscow, 1957, is her memoirs of her life with her husband. About Sverdlova herself, see Aleksandra Arenshgein, "Kamnia Tverzhe (K. T. Novgorodtseva-Sverdlova)," in L. P. Zhak and A. Itkina, eds., *Zhenshchiny Russkoi Revoliutsii*, Moscow, 1968, pp. 304–19.

266. See A. M. Kollontai, *Iz moei zhizhni i raboty*, p. 355.

267. In this see B. Farnsworth, *Aleksandra Kollontai*, pp. 149–50. Farnsworth also has a detailed discussion of the First All-Russian Congress of Worker and Peasant Women. More elaborate is the Russian work E. D. Emelyanova, *Revoliutsiya, partiya, zhenshchina: opyt raboty sredi trudyashchikhsya zhenshchin (oktyabr 1917-1925 gg.)*, Smolensk, 1971, pp. 74–87. Tony Cliff, *Class Struggle and Women's Liberation*, p. 142 puts the figure at 1,147.

268. T. Cliff, *Class Struggle and Women's Liberation*, p. 142.

269. R. C. Elwood, *Inessa Armand: Revolutionary and Feminist*, pp. 241–42, and G. W. Lapidus, *Women in Soviet Society: Equality, Development and Social Change*, Berkeley, 1978, p. 72.

270. Richard Stites, *The Women's Liberation Movement in Russia*, pp. 334–35.

271. Tony Cliff, *Class Struggle and Women's Liberation*, pp. 143–44.

272. For Maria Ulyanova, see D. A. Ershov, *Mariya Ilinichna Ulyanova*, Saratov, 1965.

273. For a more detailed discussion of the system and how it brought in women, see V. A. Moirova, "Women's Delegates' Meetings and their Role in the Work of the Party among Working and peasant Women," in S. Smidovich, et al., *Work Among Women*, Communist Party of Great Britain, London, p. 19, 1924.

274. Stites dismisses the conferences as "demonstrations of solidarity and celebrations of communist consciousness" rather than "forums of free debate." Richard Stites, *The Women's Liberation Movement in Russia*, p. 338. It is reasonable to agree that as in other areas, here too the democratic space shrank during the Civil War. But it is not reasonable to write of the voices of women as nothing but a replication of male voices of the same sort. The present writer's research on Indian communist women, including a considerable number of interviews, has shown that women becoming communists, or becoming active in communist-led women's or students' organizations, were not motivated by exactly the same set of ideas as the men, and moreover that a sense of autonomy developed among them, for all their rejection of "feminism." See on this Soma Marik, "Interrogating Official and Mainstream Discourses: Communist Women Remember the Forties," *Jadavpur University Journal of History*, 2003-2004, pp. 77–98.

275. B. Evans Clements, *Bolshevik Feminist*, p. 201.

276. *LCW* 32, Moscow, 1977, pp. 195–96. B. Evans Clements, *Bolshevik Feminist*, p. 200, suggests this contained as reference to the relationship between Kollontai and Shlyapnikov.

277. Richard Stites, *The Women's Liberation Movement in Russia*, pp. 339–40.
278. *KPSS v rezoliutsiiakh i resheniiakh s'ezdov, konferentsii i plenumov Tsk*, vol. 1, Moscow, 1954, pp. 754–55.
279. B. Farnsworth, *Aleksandra Kollontai*, pp. 157–58. For the text of the Family Code of 1918, see *Sobranie Uzakonenii i rasporiazhenii rabochego i krest'ianskogo pravitel'stva. Sbornik dekretov 1917–18 gg*, no. 76–77, art. 818, Moscow, 1920, pp. 953–59.
280. For a more critical view of the code, see R. Stites, *The Women's Liberation Movement in Russia*, pp. 363–66.
281. B. Farnsworth, *Aleksandra Kollontai*, p. 159.
282. B. Evans Clements, *Bolshevik Feminist*, pp. 168–69 has a discussion.
283. *The Autobiography of a Sexually Emancipated Woman*, p. 40. For the Left Communists, see R. V. Daniels, *The Conscience of the Revolution*. For the inner-party debate over the treaty of Brest-Litovsk, and the nature of the German aims, see J. W. Wheeler-Bennett, *Brest-Litovsk: The Forgotten Peace*, London, 1939. A consequence of Kollontai's persistent opposition to Lenin's line, which won in the end, was her being dropped from some of the leading positions.
284. For a translation, see A. Kollontai, *Communism and the Family*, Calcutta, 1992.
285. For reports see *Pravda*, November 17, November 19, November 21, 1918.
286. Alexandra Kollontai, "The Labour of Women in the Evolution of the Economy," accessed on August 20, 2005, http://www.marxists.org/archive/kollonta/works/1921/evolution.html. This is part of the set of her speeches published in 1923 and mentioned in the next footnote.
287. A. M. Kollontai, *Trud Zhenshchiny v Evoliutsii Khoziaistva*, Moscow and Petrograd, 1923.
288. B. Farnsworth, *Aleksandra Kollontai*, p. 169.
289. For Bukharin's attack, see *Desiatyi s'ezd RKP(b): Stenographicheskii otchet*, Moscow, 1963, p. 325.
290. Tony Cliff, *Class Struggle and Women's Liberation*, p. 147.
291. B. Farnsworth, *Aleksandra Kollontai*, pp. 313–14.
292. Polina Vinogradskaia, "Voprosy byta," *Pravda*, July 26, 1923.
293. For Vinogradskaia, see further, B. Evans Clements, *Bolshevik Feminist*, pp. 232–34; A. Holt, *Selected Writings of Alexandra Kollontai*, London, 1977, p. 205.
294. Clara Zetkin, *Lenin on the Women's Question*, accessed on August 20, 2005, from http://www.marxists.org/archive/zetkin/1920/lenin/zetkin1.htm.
295. This proposal, of inserting women into public life yet retaining gender specific duties, had been made many times by her. See for example her speech in the 8th Party Congress, cited in T. Cliff, *Class Struggle and Women's Liberation*, p. 142.
296. Evans Clements, *Bolshevik Feminist*, p. 238.
297. Irina Aristarkhova, *Women and Government in Bolshevik Russia*, WORKING PAPERS, Centre for Comparative Labour Studies, Department of Sociology, University of Warwick, no. 4, August 1995, accessed on July 3, 2003, http://www.csv.warwick.ac.uk/fac/soc/complabstuds/russia/irawp.doc., p. 24.

298. K. Marx, F. Engels, V. I. Lenin, J. Stalin, and Mao Tse-tung, *Women and Communism*, Calcutta, 1978, p. 75.

299. S. Farber, *Before Stalinism*, pp. 117–18.

300. V. Serge, *Year One*, pp. 111–20.

301. E. H. Carr, *The Bolshevik Revolution*, vol. 1, p. 176.

302. V. I. Lenin, "Seventh All-Russia Congress of Soviets," in *LCW* 30, accessed on November 26, 2006, http://www.marxists.org/archive/lenin/works/1919/dec/05.htm. J. L. H. Keep, "Lenin's Letters as Historical source," in B. W. Eissenstat (ed.), *Lenin and Leninism: State, Law and Society*, Lexington, 1971, p. 259, claims that Lenin unleashed the terror on August 9th to suppress peasants. S. Farber, *Before Stalinism*, p. 116, accepts this view.

303. D. W. Lovell, *From Marx to Lenin*, p. 20.

304. S. Farber, *Before Stalinism*, pp. 44, 47.

305. L. Trotsky, *Terrorism and Communism*, p. 78.

306. W. H. Chamberlin, *The Russian Revolution: 1917–1921*, vol. 2, p. 72.

307. Ibid.

308. Ibid., p. 73.

309. Ibid., p. 76, these include shootings by Cheka.

310. *Dekrety Sovetskoi Vlasti*, vol. 1, p. 583, for the decree confirming Petrovsky's appointment.

311. G. Leggett, *The Cheka: Lenin's Political Police*, Oxford, 1981, p. 16, see also J. L. H. Keep, ed., *The Debate on Soviet Power*, p. 66. This shows that on November 2 the VTsTK was contemplating this.

312. See, for a version of the text, *Pravda*, December 18, 1927. For a translation, see G. Leggett, *The Cheka*, p. 17.

313. Ibid., p. 21.

314. T. Cliff, *Lenin*, vol. 3, p. 151, quoting the Cheka leader Latsis.

315. Quoted in G. Leggett, *The Cheka*, p. 124.

316. *Pravda*, October 18, 1918.

317. Quoted in G. Leggett, *The Cheka*, p. 128.

318. Ibid., p. 130; S. Farber, *Before Stalinism*, p. 130. Unlike Leggett, an academic writer, Farber, a former leftist moving right to "democratic socialism," has an axe to grind. So while Leggett gives detailed accounts of oppositions to this sort of thing, Farber mentions them very briefly, highlighting Cheka abuses.

319. For the CC decision see G. Leggett, *The Cheka*, p. 130. For the VTsIK decision see *Dekrety Sovetskoi Vlasti*, vol. 3, p. 451.

320. Quoted in T. Cliff, *Lenin*, vol. 4, London, 1979, p. 18.

321. *LCW* 26, p. 295.

322. Quoted in E. Mandel, *October 1917: Coup d' etat or Social Revolution?*, p. 31.

323. W. Bruce Lincoln, *Red Victory*, p. 323.

324. Ibid., p. 256.

325. Ibid., p. 210.

326. Quoted in G. Leggett, *The Cheka*, p. 197. Leggett admits that neutral sources do not bear out these extreme charges.

327. See Leggett, pp. 168–69.

328. S. Farber, *Before Stalinism*, p. 134 has a single sentence to differentiate Lenin

from Latsis, with a whole section devoted to proving that this difference was negligible.

329. *LCW* 28, p. 389: "One need not go to the same absurd lengths as Comrade Latsis [who said] 'Don't search [!!?] the records for evidence . . .'"
330. G. Leggett, *The Cheka*, p. 171.
331. L. D. Gerson, *The Secret Police in Lenin's Russia*, Philadelphia, 1976, pp. 202–3.
332. Ibid., pp. 214–15.
333. Ibid., pp. 194–95; see also the files of *Pravda* for November 1918–March 1919, where a number of critical articles appear.
334. Quoted in G. Leggett, *The Cheka*, pp. 340–41.
335. V. Serge, *Memoirs of a Revolutionary, 1901–1941,* London, 1963, pp. 80–81.
336. G. Leggett, *The Cheka*, p. 342.
337. Ibid., p. 343.
338. For the text , see *S'ezdy Sovetov V Dokumentakh* Moscow, 1959, p. 184.
339. J. Rees, "In Defence of October," *Society and Change*, pp. 55–57. It is to be noted that Dzerzhinsky was later to advocate during the NEP that strikers should be reported to the GPU, a proposal that brought Trotsky to recognize the gravity of the situation and write his October 8th 1923, letter to the Central Committee that opened the conflict between the left opposition and party apparatus. Dzerzhinsky was also a strong supporter of Stalin until his death. His successor, Menzhinsky, used the GPU apparatus to spy on the United Opposition of 1926–27, and to discredit them. For this, see the documents appended in M. Reiman, *The Birth of Stalinism*, London, 1987.
340. *Dekrety Sovetskoi Vlasti,* vol. 1, pp. 24–25.
341. J. L. H. Keep, ed., *This Debate on Soviet Power*, p. 72. As Keep recognizes in his note, p. 295, the reference to "programme-maximum" meant socialization of production. S. Farber, *Before Stalinism*, p. 94, rejects just this point, for he objects to the suppression of the bourgeois press on the ground that it meant a suppression of the bourgeoisie.
342. J. L. H. Keep, ed., *The Debate on Soviet Power*, p. 71. S. Farber, *Before Stalinism*, p. 94 sees simply cynicism and duplicity in Trotsky's proposal. Farber's own proposal, in p. 110, calling for socialization of the bigger media and placing them at the disposal of the parties, councils, etc., in rough numerical proportion, and allowing private use of smaller media (PCs, duplicating machines, home videos), is little more than a contemporary version of Trotsky's proposal. So the accusation is more a prejudged one than a reasoned rejection of Trotsky's views.
343. J. L. H. Keep, ed., *The Debate on Soviet Power*, p. 71. This was, however, a weak response in one sense. Marx had opposed such a coupling, as we saw in chapter 2.
344. See, e.g., Kamkov, in ibid., p. 69.
345. Ibid., pp. 72–73; S. Farber, *Before Stalinism*, p. 94, surprisingly has no objection to Karelin's criticisms though they are, consequently, equally, criticisms of Farber own views as expressed in pp. 110–11.
346. E. H. Carr, *The Bolshevik Revolution*, p. 77; L. Schapiro, *The Origin of the*

Communist Autocracy, p. 192.

347. M. Gorky, *Untimely thought,* London, 1968, p. 35. The whole article, entitled "To the democracy" was an attack on Sovnarkom for having kept the bourgeois ministers of the Provisional Government under detention. The "Slaughter outside St. Petersburg" was a reference to the battle of Pulkovo Heights. Presumably the Bolsheviks should have surrendered to Krasnov. As for the "destruction of Moscow," this kind of hysterical hyperbole was replied to, by Bukharin, newly arrived from Moscow, in his speech to the VTsIK: "Some Comrades who call themselves radicals, socialists, and even three-quarter Bolsheviks, like *Novaya Zhizn,* have recorded (destructions in Moscow, including) . . . St. Basil's and other cathedrals. . . . The same sort of papers in Moscow reported that in Petrograd the soldiers got *drunk en masse,* that the women's shock battalion had been raped. . . . and so on, The sole purpose of such reports is to sow dissension." J. L. H. Keep, ed., *The Debate on Soviet Power,* p. 95.

348. Cited in M. Liebman, *Leninism Under Lenin,* pp. 238–39.

349. For the opposition press, see V. Broido, *Lenin and the Mensheviks,* Aldershot, England, 1987, pp. 114–15; L. Schaprio, *The Origin of the Communist Autocracy,* pp. 126, 163, 186–87.

350. For Myasnikov's career and views, see P. Avrich, "Bolshevik Opposition to Lenin: G. I. Miasnikov and the Worker's Group" *The Russian Review,* vol. 43, no. 1, January 1984.

351. *LCW 32,* pp. 504–9.

352. L. Trotsky, *Terrorism and Communism,* p. 79. See also p. 80, "we are destroying the press of the counterrevolution, just as we destroyed its fortified positions." S. Farber, *Before Stalinism,* pp. 101–2, objects to this on the ground that "even in a time of civil war, there was still a difference between ideological and forms of struggle," and that Trotsky's view necessarily led to an elite proclaiming itself as a vanguard. It is not understandable how one can proclaim war, and allow freedom of press to the enemy camp.

353. There are a number of studies. See J. N. Hazard, *Settling disputes in Soviet Society,* New York, 1960; P. H. Juviler, *Revolutionary Law and Order,* New York, 1976; P. H. Solomon, Jr., "Soviet Penal Policy, 1917–1934: A Reinterpretation," *Slavic Review,* vol. 39, no. 2, June 1980. See also M. McCauley, ed.., *The Russian Revolution and Soviet State, 1917–1921: Documents,* London, 1975. For a short survey, see E. H. Carr, *Socialism in one Country,* vol. 1, Harmondsworth, 1970, pp. 78–101.

354. D. J. Dallin and B. I. Nicolaievski, *Forced Labour in Soviet Russia,* London, 1948, pp. 149–51.

355. R. Medvedev, *Let History Judge,* Oxford, 1989, p. 650.

356. On this, see B. Kagarlitsky, *The Thinking Reed,* London, 1988, p. 653.

357. G. Leggett, *The Cheka,* pp. 176–82. A. Solzhenitsyn, in *The Gulag Archipelago,* quoted in J. Rees, "In Defence of October," p. 53, suggests that such executions were normal. Dallin and Nicolaievsky, *Forced Labour in Soviet Russia,* Chapter VIII, provide quite a different picture for the first decade of Soviet rule, despite their evident hostility to Lenin and Bolshevism.

358. M. McAuley, *Bread Authority, State and Society in Petrograd, 1917–1922*, Oxford, 1991, p. 391.
359. Quoted in R. Medvedev, *Let History Judge*, p. 502.
360. E. Huskey, *Russian Lawyers and the Soviets State*, Princeton, 1986.
361. See R. Sharlet, "Stalinism and Soviet Legal Culture," in R. C. Tucker, ed., *Stalinism: Essays in Historical Interpretation*, New York, 1977.
362. *LCW* 28, p. 236.
363. P. Beirne and R. Sharlet, eds., *Pashukanis: Selected writings on Marxism and Law*, London, 1980, especially pp. 37–131, containing *The General Theory of Law and Marxism*.
364. I. Lapenna, "Lenin, Law and Legality," in L. Schapiro and P. Reddaway, eds., *Lenin: The Man, the Theorist, the Leader*, New York, 1967, p. 261.
365. J. N. Hazard, *Settling Disputes in Soviet Society*, p. 314.
366. For Stuchka, see P. Berne and R. Sharlet, *Pashukanis*, editors "introduction," p. 20–30, and E. Huskey , *Russian Lawyers and the Soviets State*, pp. 59–61 on the Moscow legal system. For other jurists, like J. Slavin and M. A. Reisner, see S. Farber, *Before Stalinism*, pp. 155–56.
367. L. Schapiro, *The Origin of the Communist Autocracy*, p. 13.
368. "All hopes for a peaceful development of the Russian revolution have vanished for good. This is the objective situation—either complete victory for the military dictatorship or victory for the workers' armed uprising." *LCW* 25, p. 179. It should also be remembered that Lenin's position was not fully endorsed by the party.
369. *MESW* 1, p. 377.
370. S. Lovell, ed., *Leon Trotsky Speaks*, p. 55.
371. *Dekrety sovetskoi Vlasti* vol. 1, pp. 165–66.
372. O. H. Radkey, *The Sickle Under the Hammer*, pp. 291, 491.
373. L. Schapiro, *The Origin of the Communist Autocracy*, p. 150–51, quotes Boris Sokolov to asset that it was a peaceful demonstration. But Schapiro's own facts show a plan for a military coup, which the SR Central Committee called off at the last moment.
374. Ibid., p. 150, n. 4.
375. Ibid., p. 151. Also O. Radkey, *The Sickle and the Hammer*, pp. 373–74.
376. See O. Radkey, *The Sickle and Hammer*, pp. 18–39, 73–74, 88.
377. Ibid., p. 332.
378. J. Bunyan, ed., *Intervention, Civil war and Communism in Russia, April–December, 1918*, Baltimore, 1936, p. 187.
379. *Dekrety Svetskoi Vlasti*, vol. 2, Moscow, 1959, p. 430–31.
380. Quoted in D. Footman, *Civil War in Russia*, p. 117.
381. M. Liebman, *Leninism Under Lenin*, p. 246.
382. Schapiro, *The Origin of the Communist Autocracy*, pp. 152, 169, attempts to show that the SRs were not supporters of the counter-revolution. It is a hair-splitting argument. It is incontestable that SR Council offered support to Western imperialism. It is also incontestable that the Czech rising was not a "democratic" rising but part of an imperialist intervention. They also took part in the All-Russian Directorate. Schapiro presents it as a democratic instrument (p. 159). But as he admits, the white army was

never willing to submit to the SR politicians. Thus, it was the SRs who provided a democratic facade for the counter-revolution.

383. See Bunyan and Fisher, p. 190; O. Anweiler, *The Soviets*, p. 270; V. Serge, *Year One*, p. 89.

384. O. Anweiler, *The Soviets*, p. 294.

385. D. Footman, *Civil War in Russia*, pp. 101–2.

386. Ibid., pp. 103, 113.

387. O. Anweiler, *The Soviets*, p. 294; I. Getzler, *Martov*, pp. 184–89.

388. See *LCW 28*, 190–91.

389. O. Anweiler, *The Soviets*, p. 294; I. Getzler, *Martov*, pp. 185–98.

390. O. Anweiler, *The Soviets*, p. 295.

391. These events are discussed below.

392. In fact, the Mensheviks retained an ambivalence. Axelrod, Abramovich or Nicolaievsky, among others become strongly anti-communist, Dan, on the other hand, took a "left" stand, tending to a rapprochement with the Stalinist regime.

393. *LCW 32*, p. 230.

394. Voline, *Nineteen-Seventeen*, London, 1954, p. 69.

395. M. Liebman, *Leninism Under Lenin*, p. 198.

396. Ibid., p. 409.

397. V. Serge *Year One*, pp. 213–15.

398. P. Avrich, *The Russian Anarchists*, p. 184, 369.

399. Ibid., p. 188.

400. V. Serge, *L'Ani de la revolution*, quoted in M. Liebman, *Leninism Under Lenin*, p. 253.

401. M. Palij, *The Anarchism of Nestor Makhno*, Washington, 1976, p. 177.

402. W. H. Chamberlin, *The Russian Revolution 1917–1921*, vol. 2, p. 237.

403. Ibid., pp. 273–78.

404. W. Bruce Lincoln, *Red Victory*, New York, 1989, p. 327. See also M. Palij, *The Anarchism of Nestor Makhno*, p. 214 for the appraisal of the white colonel Noga of the effect the Makhno Movement.

405. P. Avrich, *Anarchist Portraits*, New Jersey, 1988, p. 120–21, describes him as failing to win over many workers, because he never understood the complexities of industrial economy.

406. J. Rees, "In Defence of October," p. 61, writes that Makhno's peasant communes had only a few hundred peasant families. But the policy of the forced grain collection got him adherents. On this see M. Palij, *The Anarchism of Nestor Makhno*, pp. 213–14. On the politics of Makhno, see P. Avrich, *Anarchist Portraits*, pp. 114, 121; on Makhno's secrets police, see W. H. Chamberlin, *The Russian Revolution: 1917–1921*, vol. II, pp. 232, 234; F. Sysya, "Nestor Makhno and the Ukrainian Revolution" in T. Hunczak, ed., *The Ukraine 1917–1921, A Study in Revolution*, p. 240, and D. Footman, *Civil War in Russia*, pp. 282, 288.

407. I. Getzler, *Kronstadt, 1917*, p. 183.

408. Ibid., p. 186.

409. Apart from O. H. Radkey, *The Sickle Under the Hammer*, see R. V. Daniels, *The Conscience of the Revolution;* V. Serge, *Year One*, pp. 261–66.

410. J. Borys, *The Russian Communist Party and the Sovietization of the Ukraine*, New York, 1960, pp. 259–60.

411. Quoted in ibid., p. 261.

412. E. H. Carr, *The Bolshevik Revolution*, vol. 1, p. 290.

413. For War Communism, see S. Malle, *The Economic Organisation of War Communism, 1918–1921*, Cambridge, 1985; for peasant responses see O. Figes, *Peasant Russia, Civil War*, Oxford, 1989. For the Tambov uprising in particular, see O. H. Radley, *The Unknown Civil War in Soviet Russia: A Study of the Green Movement in the Tambov Region, 1920–21*, Standford, 1976. See also S. Singleton, "The Tambov Revolt, 1920–21," *Slavic Review*, September, 1966.

414. W. Bruce Lincoln, *Red Victory*, pp. 468–71; S. Farber, *Before Stalinism*, pp. 122–23, claims that dogmatically embracing war communism caused the uprising. Moreover, Farber mentions the shootings by the Red Army, but not the pardons, and he omits the Green Terror. This creates a totally unbalanced picture.

415. P. Avrich, *Kronstadt, 1921*, New York, 1974, p. 35.

416. Ibid., pp. 39, 42.

417. Ibid., p. 45

418. Ibid., pp. 51–54.

419. E. Mawdsley, "The Baltic Fleet and the Kronstadt Mutiny" *Soviets Studies*, vol. 24, no. 4, April, 1973, p. 509; J. Rees, "In Defence of October," p. 63. The Kronstadt rebellion has provoked a large-scale controversy between Trotskyists and Anarchists. The Trotskyists, beginning with Trotsky in the 1930s, have asserted that the relative peasantization of Kronstadt led to the uprising. Some of this argument is discussed in the main text. Here it is only necessary to note that S. Farber, *Before Stalinism*, pp. 192–93, writes that this is misleading and that this sociological analysis is "far-fetched."

420. Quoted in W. Bruce Lincoln, *Red Victory*, p. 495.

421. Quoted in I. Getzler, *Kronstadt, 1917–21*, pp. 209–10.

422. Ibid., p. 191.

423. For the military opposition, see *Pravda*, November 29, 1918 (V. Sorin, "Commanders and Commissar in the field Army"); *Pravda*, December 25, 1918 (A. Kamensky, "It is high time"), *Pravda*, January 11, 1919 (Trotsky's letter); *Petrogradskya Pravda* April 3, 11, and 13, 1918 (S. I. Gusev, "How to build the Soviet army). See also A. F. Ilyin–Zhenevsky. *The Bolsheviks in Power*, London, 1984, pp. 63–72; J. Stalin, *Works*, vol. 4, pp. 194, 213–17.

424. For Zinoviev's personal role in 1920–21, see L. Schapiro, *The Origin*, pp. 258–59. This seriously undermined discipline.

425. P. Avrich, *Kronstadt, 1921*, pp. 72–74.

426. Ibid., pp. 179–80.

427. Ibid., pp. 242–43.

428. Ibid., pp. 240.

429. Ibid., pp. 107, 121–22.

430. Ibid., pp. 110–11.

431. A. Vanaik, "Socialist democracy and the Question of Leninism" (paper presented at a seminar on the Russian Revolution at the Indian Institute

of Advanced Studies) Simla, 1993, p. 8.

432. *LCW* 32, pp. 184–85.

433. Ibid., p. 485. This was a speech at the Third Congress of the Communist International.

434. Ibid., pp. 486–96.

435. V. Serge, *Year One*, pp. 81–82. Surprisingly, Marc Ferro, *The Bolshevik Revolution*, pp. 270–71, treats this acceptance of the democratic will of the peasants as a dictatorial step.

436. See *The Bolsheviks and the October Revolution*, pp. 129, 138–40, 140–41.

437. Ibid., pp. 141–42.

438. Ibid., p. 147.

439. Quoted in N. Allen, ed., *Leon Trotsky: The Challenge of the Left Opposition (1923–25)*, p. 236.

440. For a detailed history of the Brest-Litovsk negotiation, see J. W. Wheeler-Bennett, *Brest-Litovsk*.

441. *The Bolsheviks and the October Revolution*, p. 173.

442. Ibid., pp. 188–89.

443. J. W. Wheeler-Bennett *Brest-Litovsk*, pp. 227–78.

444. I. Deutscher, *The Prophet Armed*, pp. 382–83.

445. J.W. Wheeler-Bennett, *Brest-Litovsk*, p. 237.

446. *The Bolsheviks and the October Revolution*, p. 202.

447. Ibid., pp. 204–5.

448. Ibid., pp. 218 –19, 223.

449. See I. Deutscher, *The Prophet Armed*, pp. 389–92. Deutscher suggests that fears of a repetition of the internal blood-letting of the French Revolution that had taken place during the Revolutionary wars guided Trotsky.

450. *The Bolsheviks and the October Revolution*, pp. 236–37, for Lenin's and Trotsky's statements and resolution, p. 232 for Krestinsky's resolution, and p. 236 for the unanimous adoption of the resolution.

451. *Sedmoi ekstrennyi S'ezd RKP(b) Mart 1918 goda: Stenograficheskii otchet*, Moscow, 1962, pp. 24–40.

452. Ibid., pp. 20, 31.

453. L. Schapiro, *The Origin*, pp. 131, 133, S. F. Cohen, *Bukharin and the Bolshevik Revolution*, Oxford, 1980, p. 81.

454. L. Schapiro, *The Communist Party*, p. 246.

455. M. Liebman, *Leninism Under Lenin*, p. 279.

456. R. Gregor, ed., *The Early Soviet Period*, pp. 84–5, 88–89.

457. Ibid., p. 96.

458. Ibid., pp. 47–48.

459. Ibid., pp. 96, 92, 93.

460. Ibid., p. 8. The exceptions were the 7th Congress and the 9th Conference, at which it was decided that any ten delegates could do so. See *Deviataia Konferentsia RKP (b) Sentiabr' 1920 goda, Protokoly*, Moscow, 1972, p. 3.

461. At the 11th Congress, which Lenin was too ill to attend regularly he called for a slogan that was in tune with the concerns of the Workers' Opposition, while Stalin and Zinoviev favored a greater turn to the peasants. See

Odinnadtsatii S'ezd RKP (b), pp. 380–410, for the speech of Zinoviev.

462. See his speech to the 10th Congress, in *Desyatii S'ezd RKP (b) Mart, 1921, goda, Stenograficheskii Otchet*, Moscow, 1963, pp. 350–51, (full text, 349–59).

463. For a detailed account see R.V. Daniels, *The Conscience of the Revolution*, pp. 84–86. For the platform of the Left Communists, see Bunyan and Fisher, op. cit., pp. 560–64. On their attitude regarding the Red Army, see Daniels, p. 104.

464. *KPSS V Rezolutsiiakh*, vol. II, Moscow, 1970, p. 35 gives the figures of 301 delegates with a deciding vote. As many as 174 voted for Trotsky's resolution, 95 for the resolution of V. M. Smirnov, so 32 must have abstained.

465. R. V. Daniels, *The Conscience of the Revolution*, p. 138.

466. *Pravda*, January, 1921.

467. *LCW* 32, p. 256. However, Kollontai, speaking to the Tenth Congress said that in fact only 1,500 copies had been printed, and that with difficulty; *Desyatii S'ezd RKP (b)* p. 103. Anti-communist historians systematically ignore the civil war conditions. Thus, D. W. Lovell, *From Marx to Lenin*, p. 185–86, ridicules "defenders of the Soviet regime" for their defense of communist violence or their attempts to explain that violence. But he has not a sentence on the tremendous level of right-wing violence. He hides these forces under the softer term "opposition." L. Schapiro, *The Origin* is likewise remarkable for the absence of any systematic account of the Civil War.

468. R. V. Daniels, *The Conscience of the Revolution*, p. 117.

469. L. Schapiro, *The Origin of the Communist Autocracy*, p. 238.

470. See A. Rosmer, *Lenin's Moscow*, London, 1971, p. 131.

471. *Deviataia konferentsiia RKP (b)*, p. 188.

472. A. Balabanoff, *My Life as a Rebel*, New York, 1968, p. 238–39. On Kollontai and the Workers' Opposition, see B. Farnsworth, *Alexandra Kollontai: Socialism, Feminism and the Bolshevik Revolution*, Standard, 1980, pp. 12–248.

473. *LCW* 32, pp. 168.

474. Ibid., p. 200.

475. For Sapronov and Osinskii, see *Deviatyi S' ezd RKP (b)*, pp. 50–53, 215–27, 139–42.

476. See A. Kollontai, *The Workers' Opposition*, Calcutta, 1992.

477. *Desyati S'ezd RKP (b)*, pp. 350–51.

478. Ibid., p. 352.

479. R. Gregor, *The Early Soviet Period*, p. 124.

480. Ibid., p. 122 (emphasis added).

481. Ibid., p. 121.

482. Ibid.

483. *LCW* 32, pp. 168–95; see also, ibid., pp. 241, 254.

484. Ibid., pp. 248.

485. T. H. Rigby, *Communist Party Membership in the USSR, 1917–1967*, p. 52.

486. Ibid., pp. 85.

487. W. Bruce Lincoln, *Red Victory*, p. 416.

488. T. Cliff, *Lenin*, vol. 3, p. 180.

489. T. H. Rigby, *Communist Party Membership*, p. 416.

490. Ibid., p. 77.

491. R. Gregor, *The Early Soviet Period*, p. 93.

492. Thus between April and October 1919, the CC met six times, the PB met twenty-nine times, and the OB met 110 times. M. Liebman, *Leninism under Lenin*, p. 283.

493. V. I. Lenin, *Ninth Congress of the R.C.P.(B.)*, in LCW 30, accessed on November 26, 2006, http://www.marxists.org/archive/lenin/works/1920/mar/29.htm#fw2.

494. R. Gregor, The *Early Soviet Period*, p. 13.

495. *Vosmaia Konferentsiia RKP (b)*, Moscow, 1961, p. 221; and T. Cliff, *Lenin*, vol. 3, p. 187.

496. Quoted in ibid.

497. R. Gregor, *The Early Soviet Period*, p. 110.

498. *Odinnadtsatii S'ezd RKP (b)*, p. 143.

499. See R. Gregor, *The Early Soviet Period*, pp. 113–14. 124–26, 185.

9

BUREAUCRATIZATION AND BOLSHEVISM

From the foregoing discussion, it is evident that March 1921 marked the near-total ending of all features of workers' democracy in Russia. Yet, in 1921, it seemed to be only another temporary measure. Lenin pleaded for time, thereby creating the impression that eventually, in one or two years, matters would change. But the effect of the changes of 1921 was devastating. The danger of bureaucratization had been ever present from the early days of the revolution. Once workers' democracy was throttled, this bureaucratization could proceed unhindered. A brief survey of the process is necessary, in order to draw up a balance-sheet about the extent and nature of Bolshevik responsibility for the destruction of democracy and the rise of Stalinism.

The bureaucracy had its roots in the exigencies of the civil war, cultural and technological backwardness of Russia, and the failure of world revolution to develop, thereby condemning Russia to isolation and backwardness. But subjective factors, i.e., institutional errors and wrong decisions, also aided the process. As workers' democracy wilted, undemocratic centralization went on space. It crystallized mainly out of the elements of the old ruling class, but also out of the working class. It arose in state and in party organs. Prior to 1921, however, the situation was far from hopeless. During that period, there developed a functional separation within the working class. This developed later into a full-fledged bureaucracy aided by the weight of the old Tsarist apparatus. This functional separation was therefore dangerous.

In a remarkable analysis, Christian Rakovsky wrote that when a revolutionary class became the ruling class, the entire class was not always absorbed into government and administration. In Russia, he wrote, Soviet democracy went into a decline. As a result, there were particular sections of the proletariat who began to wield the attributes of power, instead of the whole class wielding them.[1] The differentiation in function caused significant modifications in the structure of the working class itself. "Thus, for example, a factory director playing the 'satrap' despite the fact that he is a communist, despite his proletarian origin, despite the fact that he was a factory worker a few years ago, will not epitomize the best qualities of the proletariat in the eyes of the workers. . . . Power is a cause, in the party as much as in the working class, of the same differentiation revealing the seams existing between the different social strata."[2] Thus, in Rakovsky's analysis (later substantially incorporated by Trotsky in *The Revolution Betrayed*) bureaucratization was shown to be a process internal to the working class, a process which unfolded as a result of the decline in democracy. It cannot be seen just as a matter of former Tsarist bureaucrats, extending their hands for more money, power, etc.

The virtual breakdown of the economy, the Tambov and Volga peasant insurgencies, the Petrograd strikes, and the Kronstadt insurrection compelled the Bolsheviks to look for a new road. The illusions of War Communism had to be shed. Money, a substantial free market, and a principle of company profitability had to be brought about. There was a steady growth of a new capitalist class—the private traders, the kulaks, the speculators, all the symbols hated by the Bolshevik left when it talked of NEP Russia. But along with this came fresh thrusts for bureaucratization.

Earlier, there had been three ways in which bureaucracy had grown. First, the collapse of workers' control meant a decision by a majority of the party leaders in favor of one-man management. Prior to 1920, success in this field was limited. But in 1920-21, management had become much stronger. With the coming of NEP and introduction of the principle of *khozraschet* (cost accounting), managers had to be given the power to "rationalize," i.e., to sack workers. Dobb shows that from the summer of 1921 to that of 1922, the number of railway employees declined from 1,240,000 to 720,000 (i.e., 520,000 or a 42 percent reduction in one year).[3]

The number of unemployed workers rose from 175,000 in January 1922 to 1,240,000 in January 1924.[4] It was not so much in the Civil War period, but in the NEP period, that on one hand the powers of the "Red managers" grew in ways intolerable to the workers, and on the other hand, their privileges grew swiftly. In August 1922, the trade union paper *Trud* attacked managers, asking: "Have our managers so far entered into the role of the 'masters' that they prefer unorganized workers to organized and disciplined members of trade unions?"[5]

This was the beginning of the seven-decade-long tussle over the right of the management to control workers, hire and fire at will and so on. The economic bureaucracy, or industrial management, could not go beyond very narrow limits up to 1921, for two reasons. Prior to the introduction of NEP, workers were paid more in kind (like food, etc.) than in wages. Moreover, they could not be dispensed with as long as the Civil War dictated centralized military-oriented production. Second until 1921, there was still a strong degree of trade union independence.

After 1921, the introduction of NEP did necessitate changes. The Eleventh Party Congress adopted a new resolution on the role and tasks of the trade unions under NEP. It admitted the contradictions. It stated that trade unions had to adapt themselves to the masses, while they "must not indulge in the prejudices and backwardness of the masses."[6] Nonetheless, the power of the unions, even vis-à-vis state authorities, were much reduced. In industry, the principle of "economic accountancy" or *khozraschet*, which Lenin described as a transition to commercial principles was the legal basis of the demand of the management for sacking excess workers.

The second sphere was general administration. The civil war years had sapped democracy, and administrators had become more and more accustomed to command and demand unconditional submission to their orders. Over the years, a large number of specialists of bourgeois origin had to be inducted, and for this, they had to be given privileges. By the time the NEP began, officials numbered close to six million.

The attitudes of these officials are of considerable interest. A confidential inquiry of 1922, involving 270 engineers and technicians in responsible positions in Moscow made interesting revelations. Among those surveyed, there were two kinds of people. One group had been in the upper strata of the administration before the revolution, while the other group comprised ordinary engineers, or technically skilled people, who had not enjoyed the benefits obtained by the first group in the Tsarist period. We know that 91 percent of the first group were unsympathetic to the Soviet government, while 87 percent of the second group were unsympathetic to it. While 70 percent of the first group believed that their work had no social value, only 25 percent of the second group had such a belief. Finally, 75 percent of the first group and 70 percent of the second group believed that it was permissible to take bribes.[7]

The technical aspects of the survey are not clear, i.e., whether the sample was representative, whether the group was chosen at random, etc. But some conclusions of exceptional significance may still be drawn. The tremendous hatred of the regime and the rampant corruption are preserved in these dry statistics no less than in the fictional representations. In addition, however, it showed a clear distinction between the attitudes of the two groups. Ordinary educated middle-class elements, shut out from the corridors of power in caste-ridden Tsarist Russia, found their status improving and their work being appreciated in the new era. Having thus secured a niche in the state, they turned increasingly to the party. With party and state distinctions blurred, not only was the party becoming a party-state, but the state apparatus was penetrating the communist party. Bureaucratization of party and state speeded up. These new, confident bureaucrats of petty bourgeois origin wanted to twist the new society to their use.

A third source of bureaucracy was the army. In February 1917, the Tsarist army had nine million soldiers under arms. Mass desertions followed the February Revolution. After October, demobilization was not only part of the Bolshevik program, but an inevitability. An official history of the Civil War estimated that only some thirty thousand to fifty thousand of the soldiers remained under the banner of the revolution.[8] The Red Army had to be built from scratch. This was done step by step. First, a core of committed proletarian soldiers was built up by calling for a voluntary army. At this stage, officers at all levels were elected by soldiers, as a Sovnarkom decree proclaimed.[9] By April 1918, the Red Army numbered nearly two hundred thousand men, drawn almost wholly from the urban proletariat.[10] At the next stage, Trotsky, as the People's Commissar for War, moved a decree in the VTsIK on compulsory military training. By July the Red Army had grown to 725,383.[11] Only when the proletarian base was firmly set up did the soviet power move to recruit poor and middle peasants en masse. Thus by the end of 1919, the Red Army was three million-strong.[12] But with this, an element of instability entered the army. As the famous anecdote goes, the peasants supported the Bolsheviks, who had given them land, but opposed the Communists, who requisitioned grain. Discipline could no longer be voluntary, proletarian discipline. On the one hand, Trotsky tried to use political persuasion against deserters.[13] On the other hand, he also had to use punishments.[14]

The core of the army was communist workers. An order of May 9, 1920 said: "the conduct of communists in the Red Army had decisive significance for the morale and the combat capacity of units."[15] But this only gave special duties, not special privileges, as an order of December 11, 1918 explained.[16] An estimated two hundred thousand communists perished at the front. The Red Army was certainly a different kind of army. Its soldiers had to take an oath to serve the revolution, not the state. Soldiers were taught to read and write. The Soldiers' Handbook taught that the ordinary enemy soldier was a misguided class brother who had to be told the truth and won over.[17] Moreover, it taught:

> Your leaders are brothers who are more experienced than you. In battle, in exercise, in the barracks at once, you must obey them. As soon as you are out of the barracks you are absolutely free.[18]

Thus, a realm of democracy in the army was sought to be clearly set up. Along with that came related items, like, Trotsky's appeal to Red Army men, not to shoot prisoners in vengeance.[19]

But full-fledged workers' democracy could not be extended. Trotsky insisted that like any other sort of specialist, military specialists, that is, Tsarist officers had to be recruited.[20] During the Civil War, 48,409 people were taken into the Red Army, and 10,339 into the military administrative staff. To this was added the medical personnel and ex-Tsarist non-commissioned officers. All together, a total of 314,181 were taken in. Against this, there were 39,914 graduates of command courses, but of them, 26,585 graduated only in 1920.[21] Of the commanders, 95 percent were non-communists.[22]

Thus, at the bottom, there were many peasants in the army, and the nature of War Communism, the conflicts with peasants, etc. precluded full democracy in the army. At the top, bourgeois specialists had to be employed. So election of commanders could not be continued. But to ensure the loyalty of these commanders, their families were treated as hostages, and political commissars were appointed, whose consent was necessary for actions taken by commanders.[23]

Notwithstanding this, Tsarist officers did bring with them the old culture of privilege and hierarchy. Trotsky had to fight a battle on two fronts. He opposed the attitude of those party leaders who feared the experts because of their own lack of expertise and their own love for personal privileges.[24] Such, for example, was the attitude expressed by Lashevich, a CC member who threatened to use and throw away the officers.[25] But Trotsky also opposed all attempts to bring back the old culture, e.g. the use of "ty" and "vy," (the familiar and the honorific forms of "you") in the army.[26] Admitted that inequality could not be immediately abolished he called for abolition of its unjust aspects, useless aspects.[27]

However, Trotsky's aims did not reflect the actual condition in the army. The army that was built had to be centralized. It had to have a supreme command. A mass of ex-Tsarist officers with their ideological baggage came in. Moreover, as a centralized army was needed, some of the democratic institutions got quickly corroded. On October 25, 1918, it was decided that the party structure in the army would no longer be an elective structure above the level of the party cell.[28] This would give the party leaders a flexibility and a swiftness in military affairs. But it also created a basis for bureaucratic control. Trotsky, even in 1923-4, did not use his power in that area for such a rightwing purpose. But the step itself was a negation of the previous attitude to armies and military hierarchies. In retrospect, Trotsky wrote that the demobilization of the Red Army released many officers who assumed leading posts in Soviets, in the economy, in education, and everywhere they thought they could succeed by using the methods learnt in the army.[29]

Even the party leaders were not immune. An entire group was molded by the military experience. At the Tenth Party Congress, among Stalin's associates who had military careers, a large number were elected either as full or as candidate members of the CC. They included Frunze, Voroshilov, Ordzhonikidze, Yaroslavsky, Mikhailov, Komarov, Tuntul, Molotov, Petrovsky, Gusev, Kuibyshev, Kirov, and Chubar.

Yet, until 1921, despite all harassment, opposition parties did exist. Inner-party democracy also survived. Together, these kept a check on the burgeoning bureaucracy. But after 1921, with opposition parties illegalized and inner-party factions banned, the state and party bureaucracy merged swiftly, and the power of the bureaucracy within the party grew at an ever-increasing rate. At the Eleventh Party Congress in 1922, it was recorded that only 22 percent of the Moscow party members came from factory cells.[30]

Membership data from other sources and other regions corroborate this picture. In Ryazan province, over three-quarters of members were officials in local soviets, party or cooperative network.[31] The fact that a high proportion of local soviet officials came up from the ranks has been discussed earlier. But from 1921, they tended to form closed hierarchies. In the Red Army, party cells came to consist overwhelmingly of officers and political staff. At the end of 1921, privates and non-commissioned officers formed half the communists in the army. By 1924, this proportion had fallen to 20 percent.[32]

From the foregoing, it is possible to suggest that the process of bureaucratization had developed as a result of many factors—the dispersal of the proletariat, the decline, albeit temporarily, of the towns and metropolitan cities, the absorption of leading workers into full-time administration, and the rise of bourgeois experts. It would, in fact, be wrong to single out the last as the most important factor. In the spring of 1918, the total population of Petrograd numbered no more the one and a half million, as against two and a half million a year previously. In Moscow, in the same period the population had fallen from two million to one and a half.[33] In Petrograd, in 1921–22, many of the workers were former students, shopkeepers, etc. who joined industry to evade military service.[34] All over Russia, the number of industrial workers had fallen by 58.7 percent between 1917 and 1921–22.[35]

However, the danger of bureaucratization seems to have been perceived very slowly. The Bolsheviks were fearful of counter-revolution and restoration, but they thought in terms of foreign imperialism, or Kulaks, NEP men (traders), etc. Bureaucracy as a specific social force evaded the perception of most leading Bolsheviks. At the Second

All-Russian Congress of Miners in 1921, Lenin himself turned down references to bureaucracy as demagogy.[36]

Thus, in 1921-22, the proletarian revolutionary line of the Bolsheviks depended on the fact that in the past they had built up a proletarian revolutionary party. Marx had explained that there was a difference between a class in itself and a class for itself. A class could be well rooted in the production process and yet be unaware of its strength. Conversely, in Russia in 1921, the class had lost most of its economic power, but it still retained its political dominance because the dominant party was formed of formerly vanguard workers. But this anomalous situation could not last for long. The cohesion of the old Bolsheviks could be an important instrument, if it was used swiftly to rebuild the proletariat and increase its consciousness. But in case of an inordinate delay, the result could be the triumph of the bureaucracy.

It might be said, that the revival of a healthy workers' state depended on two factors. One was rebirth of the proletariat, so terribly reduced and its consciousness shattered as a result of the process traced so far — war, economic crisis, Civil War, closure of industries, absorption in the army, etc. Only gradually, through a patient process of education could it recreate a vanguard layer. The other factor was the need for democratic institutions, both in the party and outside it. As long as the democratic structure remained strong, bureaucratic privilege and power could be contained. In 1921, the Workers' Opposition could secure a fair hearing. Yet in 1923–4, and in 1926–7, a much more powerful Left/United Opposition found itself isolated. Its social base, able to express support only by attending clandestine meetings, could not act effectively. After 1921, in other words, bureaucratic domination changed qualitatively in character. Yet, most Bolsheviks did not realize what they were doing at the Tenth Party Congress.

One reason for this domination of the bureaucracy was advanced by Rakovsky in terms of functional separation. Following him, David Rousset has called this the "organic splitting of the working class" into a work force and a managerial force.[37] By 1922, a profound unease had gripped Lenin, but he had not yet understood that uprooting the vanguard from the production process, and integrating it with the state apparatus, was the basic malaise. In his speech at the Eleventh Party Congress, Lenin commented that the four thousand, seven hundred communists in positions of the responsibility in Moscow were not leading, but were being led.[38] So the functional separation was leading to a social separation. The bureaucracy, not habits, red-tape (i.e., bureaucratism), but a distinct social layer, was trying to maintain its social and political privileges. It had two immediate aims — the conquest of the party leadership, and the transformation of the emergency regulations of the civil war era into a system of normal rule. The Tenth Congress had, along with the ban on factions, passed a resolution on "workers' democracy" so that there should be "a constant control by the public opinion of the party over the work of its leading organs and a constant interaction in practice between the latter and the whole party in its entirety together with the furtherance of strict accountability of the appropriate party committees not only to the higher, but also to the lower organizations."[39] But this attempt to shore up the faltering institutions of party democracy were swept aside. At the Twelfth Party Congress, Stalin bluntly rejected Preobrazhenskii's suggestion that the restrictions should be reconsidered.[40] By 1922 over 97 percent of the party consisted of members who had joined it after the victory of the revolution, and in 1923, the figure was 99 percent.[41]

Meanwhile, a careful selection at the upper levels went on. Leonard Schapiro carefully documents the early bureaucratic attempts by Zinoviev and Stalin. After the Tenth Congress, Krestinsky, Serebryakov, and Preobrazhenskii, who had favored freedom of discussion,[42] were removed from the Secretarial and even the Central Committee.[43] Members of the Workers' Opposition were persecuted. At the Eleventh Party Congress, when Lenin, with his failing health, attended only the opening and closing sessions, Zinoviev and Stalin's persecution of the Workers' Opposition became evident, though at this stage it was still much resisted.[44]

How far did Bolshevik theory contribute to this process? This question can be divided into a number of parts. First, did Bolshevik theory display a reluctance to engage in democratic election process? Second, was there a counterposition of democracy and dictatorship? Third, how did Bolshevik theory contribute to the imposition of monolithism?

It has been shown that prior to the October Revolution, the Bolshevik theory did not contain any explicit hostility to democratic process. On the contrary, the critique of bourgeois democracy proceeded from the belief that greater democracy would be needed, and would be provided by workers' democracy. However, there were also silences, which may be taken as evidences of basic weakness.

In January 1918, S. A. Lozovsky was expelled from the party. Lenin's draft resolution included the following:

> That joint work in the ranks of a single party is impossible with a person who does not understand the necessity for the dictatorship of the proletariat . . . that is, without a systematic, ruthless suppression of the resistance of the exploiters.[45]

Here, the immediate necessity was already becoming theorized. The dictatorship of the proletariat in this passage refers, not to class rule, but to "a systematic ruthless suppression of the resistance." At the Third Soviet Congress, Lenin rejected the Left SR slogan of "dictatorship of democracy" as a phrase as absurd as "iron snow."[46]

In utter disregard for his own views stated earlier Lenin even said that "Democracy is a form of bourgeois state. . . . We were for democracy, but as soon as we saw the first signs of socialism. . . . We took a firm and resolute stand for the dictatorship of the proletariat."[47] There can be no doubt that the grim situation was conditioning the ideas. But nor can there be any doubt that some of these statements were made as theoretical propositions, not just ad hoc responses to the crisis.

On other occasions, the distinctions between the current crisis and general theory were made. For instance, in a polemic with Kautsky over the use of force in Georgia, Trotsky wrote that the Georgian Menshevik regime had its own special security police, no less than the Bolsheviks. The difference lay in the class the two police forces served.[48] So it was not the police force but the class rule behind it that constituted the dictatorship of the proletariat according to Trotsky.

Thus, it is not correct that Bolshevik theory created Red Terror, or the harshness of the Civil War. On the contrary, the program of the RCP(b), adopted in 1919, specifically stated that "deprivation of political rights and any kind of limitation of freedom are necessary as temporary measures. . . . The party will strive to reduce and completely abolish them."[49] But it was in the non-programmatic texts, the polemics, that the strain of civil war was converted into theory.

The Lenin-Kautsky-Trotsky debate has often been viewed as a debate over democracy versus dictatorship. But Kautsky's defense of democracy was a defense of parliamentarism, pure and simple. For him, Soviet meant unorganized and formless masses. Bureaucracy could not be deprived of power; it could only be subjected to the supervision of Parliament.[50] Kautsky in his polemics against the Bolsheviks rejected the very concept of a proletarian democracy. For him, "The dictatorship of the lower classes opens the way for the dictatorship of the sword."[51]

Lenin therefore had a choice of replies. He could concentrate on workers' democracy. But as we saw, in his *The Proletarian Revolution and the Renegade Kautsky* he argued that "The revolutionary dictatorship of the proletariat is rule won and maintained by the use of violence by the proletariat against the bourgeois rule that is unrestricted by any laws."[52]

Now it was no longer the winning of power by violence. The violent conflicts were twisting the theoretical pronouncements. So the very maintenance of workers' rule was to be, by means, unrestricted by any laws. This opened up a prospect of changing laws in the name of revolutionary expediency. While Lenin's justification of specifically undemocratic acts took into account the violence of the counter-revolution, he put forward arguments that bolstered false assumptions. Using his logic, it could be proved that a bureaucratized state, if a majority of its personal were ex-workers, remained a dictatorship of the proletariat that must be unhesitatingly supported by the working class, not just against imperialism, but even against all demands for democratization. While false theory did not create bureaucratization, after 1921 the bureaucracy could use parts of Lenin's argument to put itself forward as the true heir of October.

Lenin and Trotsky (in *Terrorism and Communism*) as well as other Bolshevik leaders, committed a fundamental mistake. At each stage, whenever they were compelled by circumstances to take undesirable and undemocratic steps, they fumbled, and instead of openly admitting that those steps were retrograde steps to be quickly dispensed with, they often put forward false theories justifying those actions in the name of Marxism. Some of the more important cases have been discussed in detail, e.g., the argument that once the state was a workers' state, it did not matter whether in the factories there was collective or one-man managements; the claim that the Mensheviks were a petty-bourgeois party; the claim that dictatorship of the proletariat should not be bound by laws, etc.

It was the great, and unique achievement of Rosa Luxemburg, that on the one hand she identified with the Bolsheviks in their revolutionary struggle, and at the same time, explained that the Bolsheviks' actions should not be regarded as a shining example of socialist policy "toward which only uncritical administration and zealous imitation are in order."[53] For Luxemburg, the dictatorship of the proletariat was identical with socialist democracy, and the dictatorship consisted in energetic attacks on bourgeois rights. It had to be a class dictatorship.[54] She warned that without a full public life, without freedom of press and assembly, elections, and the open clash of ideas, democracy would die out, and a group of energetic leaders would replace revolutionary democracy, leading to a bureaucratization of society and polity.[55] The objective situation certainly forced many of the measures. But

> The danger begins only when they make a virtue out of necessity and want to freeze into the theoretical system the tactics forced on them by these circumstances, and want to recommend them to the international proletariat as a model of socialist tactics.[56]

The responsibility of Lenin, Trotsky, or the Bolshevik party as a whole for the bureaucratization of soviet society is therefore a very complex one. They were not bureaucratic rulers who intended to establish totalitarianism. Nor is it right to say that their theory was the principal cause of bureaucratization. There were errors in Bolshevik practice, often forced by the pressures of the circumstances they faced. But it is possible to say that while there was no prospect of immediate revival of democratic electoral processes in 1919 or 1920, the Bolsheviks did show a tendency to justify that on principled grounds. Moreover, claims for absolute unity of the proletariat or it least its class-conscious vanguard overlooked the difference between uniting for military purposes against imperialism or White Guard counter-revolution, and uniting under one party and its leading stratum for an entire historical epoch.

Bureaucratization meant a deep regression in all spheres. Women's rights were among the spheres where regression was profound. Between 1928 and 1943, all the progressive measures concerning gender and sexuality were to be heavily pushed back. Trotsky put it aptly in 1936 in *The Revolution Betrayed*: "The most compelling motive of the present cult of the family is undoubtedly the need of the bureaucracy for a stable hierarchy of relations."[57]

In 1934 homosexuality was made a crime again, punishable with up to eight years' imprisonment, and an energetic countrywide campaign was launched against sexual promiscuity, quick and easy marriage, and adultery. Motherhood became a central theme of propaganda. Schlesinger quotes several statements of this period, like this: "A woman without children merits our pity, for she does not know the full joy of life. Our Soviet women, full-blooded citizens of the freest country in the world, have been given the bliss of motherhood."[58] Divorce laws were severely tightened up. In 1935-36, fees of 50, 150 and 300 rubles were introduced for the first, second, and subsequent divorces. They also required that the personal documents of the people concerned must record these divorces. This reached its climax in 1944, when a judicial process of divorce was instituted and fees were hiked to between 500 and 2000 rubles. Courts were given the right to reject the divorce suit, bringing back not merely financial but overt state control over sexuality. The same law re-established the distinction between legitimate and illegitimate children. The latter could not claim the support or the inheritance of the father.[59] By 1943, education in schools was gender segregated and different types of courses for boys and girls were being planned and justified in the name of developing the proper masculine and feminine traits.[60] The historic socialist goal of abolition of the family was now denounced as a plot by "The enemies of the people, the vile fascist hirelings—Trotsky, Bukharin, Krylenko and their followers," who had allegedly "covered the family in the USSR with filth," and the theory of the dying out of the family was equated with "disorderly sexual cohabitation."[61]

Like many of the extreme atrocities of the Stalin era, these would be modified later. But two opposed trends came into existence in the name of socialism. One upheld modified patriarchy in the name of class struggle and real, existing socialism, and harnessed the more Victorian comments of Lenin into service while overturning all real achievements of the Lenin era.

To stop here, however, would be inadequate. Any attempt at drawing up a balance sheet must also look at the nature of Bolshevik response to bureaucratization. Even at the Tenth Congress, a resolution was passed on workers' democracy, which called for:

> Constant control by the public opinion of the party over the work of its leading organs and a constant interaction in practice between the latter and the whole party in its entirety, together with the furtherance of strict accountability of the appropriate party committees not only to the higher, but also to the lower organizations.[62]

Lenin from 1921, was to make repeated attacks on bureaucracy, though his analysis was inadequate. At the Tenth Congress, when Shlyapnikov criticized bureaucratic methods, Lenin responded by offering to put Shlyapnikov in place of Tsyurupa, the Peoples' Commissar whom Shlyapnikov had criticized.[63] This was a failure to go as deep Shlyapnikov had done. Where the latter wanted to approach the bureaucracy as a system, created by structures that strengthened non-proletarian forces, Lenin was only concerned with the elimination of red tape or objectionable behavior traits.

Throughout 1921, and part of 1922, he was still looking for means to curb bureaucracy. But that did not involve the restoration of public opposition. Instead, he proposed further induction of workers, the setting up of model departments, the use of the press to curb the bureaucracy, regulations providing for officials to submit themselves to "control" by the public and above all the creation and strengthening of Rabkrin.[64] The Rabkrin, or Commissariat for Workers' and Peasants' Inspectorate, was to have elected members who would work in it for short period, so that everyone was rotationally drawn into this work of checking. While such an approach could stop petty theft, it was hardly the answer to the social malaise. By the end of 1920, it had virtually failed.[65] But Lenin continued to bank on its reorganization, though by 1923, it had over 12,000 employees and had become yet another cog in the bureaucratic wheel.[66]

At this stage, (1921–23), a more serious critique of bureaucratization was begun by Trotsky. He, too, was bound by the legacy of the previous years. So he also did not start by calling for the restoration of democracy. But he could recognize that unless a politically conscious working class was revived, there was a major danger. To overcome this problem quickly, a multifaceted approach was needed. So he rejected Lenin's proposal about Rabkrin, saying its functionaries "are mainly officials who have come to grief in various other fields."[67] He called for a coordinated economic plan for the growth of industry and with it, the proletariat. A planned growth would also reduce bureaucratic confusion.[68] At the same time, he also emphasized the need to extend proletarian hegemony in culture and to create the material and intellectual bases of socialist culture.[69]

In this unsettled situation, Stalin was gradually setting forth as one of the key leaders of the emerging bureaucracy. He could play this role well because of his part as an old Bolshevik. By 1922, Stalin, with Moltov and Kuibyshev as his chief collaborators, had become the master of the secretariat. The Central Control Commission, meant as a check on party bureaucracy, had Soltz, Shkiryatov, Korostelev, and Muranov, four Stalinists out of seven, elected to it. With these institutions under control, Stalin and Zinoviev set out to control the CC. At the Twelfth Congress, Stalin's speech clearly enunciated the attitude and aims of the bureaucracy:

> After a correct political line has been given it is necessary to choose staffs in such a way as to fill the various posts with people who are capable of carrying out the directives, able to understand the directives as their own and capable of putting them into effect.[70]

From Lenin's definition of the party as the class vanguard, and of the communist as a "tribune of the people" the party had indeed come a long way.

The new definition of Bolshevism, put forward by Stalin, was that the essence of Bolshevism was the centralized political machine. In his "Lenin as Organizer and Leader the Russian Communist Party," he acclaimed Lenin primarily as an organizer and only secondarily as a political leader. Among with this went the glorification of the party's (i.e., the apparatus's) "sacred gift of infallibility."[71]

But the rise of Stalin was not as surprising as Trotsky tried to argue later.[72] He approached every step to power carefully. He was one of the top ranking Bolsheviks, an important leader. At the same time, he embodied typical characteristics of the bureaucracy, as Lenin recognized too late—rudeness, intolerance, disloyalty, etc..[73]

The process whereby a bureaucratic commanding staff was created intertwined with, and substantially influenced a second process, namely, the transformation of the "temporary" subversion of workers' democracy into a whole way of bureaucratic centralism. In 1922, 72 percent of all RCP(b) members were Great Russians,[74] a fact that contributed to national chauvinism, conflict with non-Russians, and the clamping down of bureaucratic order on them. The nationality question, defended by Lenin as a democratic task, was become a testing ground for bureaucratic

power. First, there was a forced Sovietization of Georgia, to which Lenin
was also a party. Then, Lenin's cautious approach of trying to form a
coalition with Mensheviks like Jordania[75] was rejected. Between 1921
and 1923, local autonomy of party and state alike in Georgia was put
under extreme attack. In 1923, Stalin called for the incorporation of the
non-Russian Soviet republics (Ukraine, Byelo-Russia, Transcaucasia)
into the R.S.F.S.R.[76] Though this was not absolutely novel for Stalin,
who had, even in 1918 opposed the declaration of an independent
Ukrainian republic,[77] this time the proposal was much more aggressive.
When the Politbureau of the RCP(b) formed a committee to determine
the relationship between various soviet republics, Stalin proposed that
the independent republics should merge in the RSFSR, and once the
decision to this effect was adopted, it should not be publicly stated, but
communicated to the republican party Central Committees, who would
get that very proposal "passed" by the republican Central Executive
Committees or Soviet Congresses, so that the decision could be shown
as the will of the republics.[78] This sheer cynicism was opposed in
committee by leaders of Ukraine[79] (Rakovsky and Petrovsky) and of
Georgia (Mdivani).[80]

Despite resistance, from the Georgians, from Rakovsky, and from
Lenin, Stalin and his ally Ordzhonikidze could deal a severe blow. The
Georgian Central Committee, under provocation, resigned and was
promptly replaced by pliant people. At the Twelfth Congress, Lenin had
planned to attack Stalin on the national question. Though he suffered
another stroke and was completely paralyzed, Stalin made a tactical
retreat. Having put in many of Lenin's criticisms into his own report,
he obtained Trotsky's silence (an event which historians have concurred
in calling a great tactical blunder by Trotsky), and thereafter Stalin
managed to defeat Trotsky's ally Rakovsky. Rakovsky had proposed
that the Chamber of Nationalities, the suggested second chamber in
the new USSR constitution, should be so arranged that no republic (i.e.,
RSFSR) should have more than 40 percent of the seats. That would have
ensured greater national and federal autonomy.[81] This was defeated,
and a thoroughly centralist state was created.

Lenin and Trotsky both mistrusted this process. Trotsky had
criticized the Sovietization of Georgia from above, and Lenin in
1922-early 1923, came to see in Stalin's role a danger. But as noted above,
Lenin was ill, and Trotsky made a poor deal. While mass pressure still
existed, both inside and outside the party, it was no longer organized
through institutions of workers' democracy. The fact that one or two
individuals, like Lenin and Trotsky, had become so important in ensuring
the defense of the rights, is evidence enough that ordinary people no
longer had the power they possessed in 1917. After his return to work

in 1922, Lenin was able to see the dramatic extension of bureaucracy. Virtually a prisoner of the man he wanted to remove, he entered into a secret faction with Trotsky. But his proposals remained ambiguous and often self-defeating.[82]

Basically, Lenin proposed that the size of the Central Control Commission should be increased, with the addition of workers and peasants, that the CC and the expanded Control Commission should assemble as a conference every two months, that a large CC and the Control Commission would be more in touch with the masses. As technical measures they were useful. But, to succeed, they had to be based on the democratization of the Soviets and party and the activity of the workers. That was where Lenin's strength lay in 1917. With the Party Congress becoming a hand-picked body controlled by the Secretary, the cooption of rank and file workers would, in fact, help the General Secretary to overcome the Old Bolsheviks. As a result, all of these proposals were adopted by the 12th Congress, but with Ordzhonikidze as Control Commission Chairman, they became a mockery.

Though Trotsky was slow in taking up the struggle, he took a more long-term view. At the Twelfth Congress, he was silent, partly because he was afraid that in Lenin's absence, his attacks on Stalin could be misconstrued, party because of Stalin's agreement to incorporate many of Lenin's criticisms, and partly because (as many scholars have argued) Trotsky underestimated Stalin. But a fourth factor that restrained him was the silence of the proletariat. Always very sensitive to the danger of substitutionism, Trotsky felt that without the active role of the proletariat, the bureaucracy could not be fought. In part, this seems to have paralyzed him.[83]

Later in 1923, when the working-class agitations increased, the GPU (the reconstituted Cheka) sought to crush them. And at the same time, the unfolding German revolution gave an opportunity for Russian to end its isolation. Trotsky and a number of prominent Bolsheviks formed the Left Opposition. At each stage in the history of the Left Opposition the struggle for proletarian democracy played an important role. In 1923, they demanded the abolition of the ban on factions, and fought for inner-party democracy.[84]

It was by massive rigging of party elections that this opposition could be defeated.[85] In 1924, Trotsky published his *Lessons of October*,[86] in which he pointed out that the revolution had been made in the name of Soviet democracy, not party autocracy. He argued that a party was essential for proletarian revolution,[87] but also that Soviets would be the organs of state power.[88] In 1924, this was so provocative a position that the book came under tremendous attack.[89] In 1926, the United Opposition was formed between the Left, and the Zinovievist Opposition, which with its considerably proletarian base in Leningrad, had fallen out with the bureaucracy. In an article, "Party Bureaucratism and Party Democracy," written in mid-1926, Trotsky wrote that the Stalinist concept of party democracy represented the bureaucracy's attempt to control the party by getting rid of free discussion, control by the party of it leading bodies, and the election of responsible individuals and collective bodies.[90]

The declaration of thirteen members of the CC and the Control Commission to the CC asserted that forms of workers democracy rule out any systematic practices of appointment from above, and called for a democratization of state and party.[91] The program of the United Opposition demanded more explicitly the revival of the soviets through more frequent elections, the accountability of officials to workers and the right to publicly express different views.[92] It was, however, only in the 1930s, that even Trotsky was able to not merely demand a return to workers' democracy, but acknowledge that the 1921 actions of banning opposition parties and inner-party factions had facilitated the rise of the bureaucracy,[93] and that a regeneration of socialism necessitated the legalization of soviet parties chosen by the workers themselves.[94]

However, it is also necessary today to go beyond asking just how the Soviet Revolution failed, and also to ask how workers' democracy is to survive and be transformed into what form, if a classless society is created. The historical experience of the Russian Revolution shows that a party built for the overthrow of the old order has to be militant. But the period of transition had a Janus-like character. One aspect of politics in this period was the continuing class struggle against the exploiters, including the international dimension of that struggle. Another aspect, however, was the struggle for cultural development, for the transformation, in course of the building of a collective economy, of the proletariat and working peasants into associated producers. Marxist theory insists that this process could be finally achieved only through the victory of the world revolution. But it has to begin immediately after the proletariat captures power even in one country in order to launch a slow but steady attack against the last vestiges of bourgeois values and ideology.

This politics has to be politics of a different kind. Here, the "vanguard" qualities required would not be qualities that enable the party to lead a struggle to frontally defeat the class enemy, but qualities that enable a party to better conceptualize the socio-cultural and economic forces and strive to assert its hegemony in building classless society. Even this process would be, in Marxist terms, a class struggle, since the ideology of the previous ruling classes would have to be overcome and assimilated within a new, higher system of classless democracy. But this would be class struggle on an ideology plane, and would abate as classes die down. It is a well-known Maoist claim, that even the complete economic disappearance of classes would not lead to the dying out of class struggle because class ideologies would still remain. This vision of a class ideology hovering like the smile of a Cheshire cat was unknown to Czechoslovak and impermissible by his method. In the classical Marxist concept, the politics of such a classless society would no longer be "alien politics," nor would it be class politics. But it would not entail uniformity. Economic and cultural policy issues would generate differences and give rise to differences in political lines. But as class exploitation would give way to a basic social solidarity such politics would not require huge systems of coercion. This idea was most graphically described by Trotsky in the closing pages of *Literature and Revolution*.[95]

NOTES

1. C. Rakovsky, "The Professional Dangers of Power" in T. Ali, ed., *The Stalinist Legacy*, pp. 47–49.
2. Ibid., p. 53–54.
3. M. H. Dobb, *Soviet Economic Development since 1917*, p. 42.
4. Ibid., p. 46–47.
5. Quoted in T. Cliff, *Lenin*, vol. 4, p. 147.
6. R. M. Gregor, *The Early Soviet Period*, pp. 156–57.
7. L. Kritzman, *Die heroische periode*, p. 233.
8. Quoted in T. Cliff, *Trotsky: The Sword of the Revolution*, p. 64.
9. W. H. Chamberlin, *The Russian Revolution: 1917–1921*, vol. 1, pp. 489–90.
10. T. Cliff, *Trotsky: The Sword of the Revolution*, p. 66.
11. Ibid., p. 67.
12. Ibid., See also on this L. Trotsky, *How the Revolution Armed*, vol. 1, London, 1979, p. 115.
13. L. Trotsky, *My Life*, pp. 428–29.
14. L. Trotsky, *How the Revolution Armed*, vol. 1, p. 486.
15. Ibid., vol. 3, London, 1980, pp. 173–74.
16. Ibid., vol. 1, p. 242.
17. Quoted in E. Mandel, *October 1917*, p. 49.
18. Ibid.
19. *Leon Trotsky Speaks*, p. 113.
20. Ibid., pp. 10, 23, 38.
21. T. Cliff, *Trotsky: The Sword of the Revolution*, p. 74.
22. F. Benvenuti, *The Bolsheviks and the Red Army, 1918–1922*. Cambridge, 1988, p. 209.
23. L. Trotsky, *How the Revolution Armed*, vol. 1, London, 1979, pp. 557–58.
24. Ibid., pp. 223.
25. Quoted in A. F. Ilyin-Zhenevsky, *The Bolshevik in Power*, London, 1984, p. 71. See also J. Stalin, *Works* vol. 4, pp. 194, 213, 216–17.

26. L. Trotsky, *How the Revolution Armed*, vol. 4, London, 1981, pp. 194–95.
27. Ibid., vol. 2, pp. 116–18.
28. Quoted in T. Cliff. *Trotsky: The Sword of the Revolution*, p. 152.
29. L. Trotsky, *The Revolution Betrayed*, New York, 1987, pp. 89–90.
30. *Odinnadtsatii S'ezd RKP (b)*, p. 443.
31. T. H. Rigby, *Communist Party Membership*, p. 109.
32. Ibid., p. 245.
33. M. Liebman, *Leninism under Lenin*, p. 223.
34. This case was argued by Lenin in his letter to Molotov, March 26, 1922, in *LCW* 33, p. 256.
35. T. Cliff, *Trotsky: The Sword of the Revolution*, p. 187.
36. *LCW* 32, pp. 67–68.
37. D. Rousset, *The Legacy of the Bolshevik Revolution*, New York, 1982, pp. 37–50.
38. *LCW* 33, p. 288.
39. *Desyatii S'ezd RKP (b)*, pp. 565–66.
40. J. Stalin, *Works*, vol. 5, Moscow, 1953, pp. 358.
41. See Leon Trotsky, *The Challenge of the Left Opposition* (1923–25), N. Allen, ed., p. 32; and L. Trotsky, *Stalin*, 385.
42. See Preobrazhenskii's article in *Pravda* 22, January 1921. Criticizing the Petrograd Organization (led by Zinoviev) for its hostile tone of debate.
43. L. Schapiro, *The Origin*, p. 322.
44. See *Odinnadtsatyi S'ezd RKP (b)*, pp. 188, 196, 547, 693–700. The Congress refused to expel Shlyapnikov. L. Schapiro, The *Origin*, p. 336, remarks, "police method of search, censorship, and interrogation were . . . being used against the opposition."
45. *LCW* 42, Moscow, 1977, p. 50.
46. Ibid. 26, pp. 473–74. For the Left SR view, see O. H. Radkey, *The Sickle under the Hammer*, pp. 144.
47. *LCW* 26, p. 473.
48. L. Trotsky, *Social Democracy and Wars of Intervention in Russia, 1918–1921*, London, 1975, p. 44.
49. R. Gregor, *The Early Soviet Period*, p. 59.
50. K. Kautsky, *The Dictatorship of the Proletariat*, pp. 4, 19, 26, M. Salvadori, *Karl Kautsky and the Socialist Revolution*, pp. 23–24.
51. K. Kautsky, *The Dictatorship of the Proletariat*, p. 58. See also ibid., pp. 63–65, and 72–87.
52. *LCW* 28, p. 236.
53. R. Luxemberg, *Zur Russischen Revolution*, in *Gesammelte Werke*, Bd. 4, Berlin 1990, pp. 365, 334–35.
54. Ibid., pp. 363–64.
55. Ibid., pp. 360–62.
56. Ibid., pp. 364.
57. L. Trotsky, *The Revolution Betrayed*, New York, 1987, p. 153.
58. R. Schlesinger, *Changing Attitudes in Soviet Russia: The Family in the USSR*, London, 1949, p. 254.
59. Tony Cliff, *Class Struggle and Women's Liberation*, pp. 149–50.

60. R. Schlesinger, *Changing Attitudes in Soviet Russia*, pp. 364, 393–94.
61. K. H. Geiger, *The Family in Soviet Russia*, Cambridge, 1968, p. 104.
62. Cited in E. H. Carr, *The Bolshevik Revolution*, vol. 1, p. 209. For the ban on factions see Chapter 7.
63. *LCW* 32, p. 206–7.
64. See for example, V. I. Lenin, "Rough Draft of Rules for the Administration of Soviet Institutions," in ibid., 28, pp. 349–52.
65. V. I. Lenin. "Our Foreign and Domestic Position and the Tasks of the Party," in ibid. 31, pp. 423.
66. E. H. Carr, *The Bolshevik Revolution*, vol. 1, p. 233.
67. L. Trotsky, "Comments on Lenin's proposal concerning the work of Deputies," in R. Block, ed., V. I. Lenin, and L. Trotsky, *Lenin's Fight Against Stalinism*, New York, 1975, p. 79.
68. J. Meijer, ed., *The Trotsky Papers*, vol. 2, The Hague, 1971, pp. 820–22.
69. See L. Trotsky, *Problems of Everyday Life*, New York, 1973.
70. J. Stalin, *Works*, vol. 5, p. 213.
71. See on this V. Gerratana, "Stalin, Lenin and 'Leninism'" *New Left Review*, no. 103, May–June 1977, p. 67.
72. L. Trotsky, *Stalin*, pp. 334–37.
73. R. Block, ed., *Lenin's Fight Against Stalinism*, p. 65.
74. L. Colletti, "The Question of Stalin," in R. Blackburn, ed., *Revolution and Class Struggle*, p. 70.
75. V.I. Lenin, "Letter to G. K. Orjonikidze," in *LCW* 32, p.160.
76. See M. Lewin, *Lenin's Last Struggle*; *International Marxist Review*, vol. 4, no. 2, Autumn, 1989; and K. Chattopadhyay, "Stalinbad, Soviet Union Gathan, O Jatiyotar Samasya," (Stalinism, the Formation of the Soviet Union, and the Nationality Problem) in A. W. Mahmood, (ed). *Itihas Anusandhan*, 7, Calcutta, 1993.
77. R. Medvedev, *Let History Judge*, p. 16.
78. This document is available as an appendix to V. I. Lenin, *Sochinenya*, vol. XLV, Moscow, 1965, pp. 557–58. The English works of neither Lenin nor Stalin append it.
79. Although Rakovsky was included in the committee as a CC member and it was Petrovsky who came in as the Ukrainian representative, Rakovsky's role at the Twelfth Party Congress shows that he was acting on behalf of the Ukrainians. See on this, K. Chattopadhyay, "Christian Rakovsky and the 1923 Ukrainian Opposition in the RCP(b)," *Proceedings of the Indian History Congress*, 47th Session, New Delhi, 1987.
80. On the Georgians see M. Lewin, *Lenin's Last Struggle*.
81. C. G. Rakovsky, "Speech at the Twelfth Congress," *International Marxist Review*, vol. 4, no. 2, pp. 57–66.
82. See, e. g., *LCW* 33, pp. 482, 484–85.
83. For Trotsky's own account, see *My Life*, pp. 509–14, see in particular the fact that he did not refer at all to the 12th Congress itself. See also I. Deutscher, *The Prophet Unarmed*, p. 93. For Trotsky's underestimation of Stalin, See *Stalin*, p. 387. For his sociological approach, see *Stalin*, pp. 387, 403–4, See also K. Chattopadhyay, *The Marxism of Leon Trotsky*, Calcutta,

2006, Chapter 4.

84. See the documents of the Left, including its Platform or the letter of the 46, in N. Allen, ed., *Leon Trotsky, The Challenge of the Left Opposition (1923–1925)*.

85. *Documents of the Left Opposition*, London, 1980. See *Trinadsatsaia Konferentsiia RKP(b)*, Moscow, 1963, for the extent of the opposition's actual strength. See especially Sapronov's speech in pp. 131–33 for evidence of rigging.

86. See N. Allen, ed., *Leon Trotsky, The Challenge of the Left Opposition (1926–1927)*, pp. 199–268.

87. Ibid., p. 252.

88. Ibid., p. 249.

89. See, especially, the collection *Za Leninism*, Moscow, 1925, with articles by Kamenev, Zinoviev, Krupskaya, Bukharin, and others.

90. N. Allen and G. Saunders, eds., *Leon Trotsky: The Challenge of the Left Opposition (1926–27)*, New York, 1980, pp. 62–72.

91. Ibid., pp. 75, 81–84.

92. Ibid., pp. 340–44, See also pp. 349–61 for a demand for party democracy.

93. L. Trotsky, *The Revolution Betrayed*, pp. 104–5.

94. L. Trotsky, *The Death Agony of Capitalism and the Tasks of the Fourth International*, New York, 1970, pp. 39–40.

95. C. Wright Mills, *The Marxists*, New York, 1963, pp. 285–89.

BIBLIOGRAPHY

PRIMARY SOURCES

A. Writings of Marx, Engels, Lenin and Trotsky:

Blumenberg, W., ed. *August Bebels Briefwechsel mit Friedrich Engels*. Berlin, 1965.

Engels, F., Paul Lafargue, and Laura Lafargue. *Correspondence*. Vols. 1–3. Ed. W. Blumenberg. Trans. Y. Kapp. Moscow, 1959-63.

Krader, L, ed. *The Ethnological Notebooks of Karl Marx*. Assen, 1974.

Landshut, S., and J. P. Mayer, eds. *Karl Marx, der Historische Materialismus*. Berlin, 1932.

Laski, H. J., ed. *Communist Manifesto: Socialist Landmark*. London, 1954.

Lenin, V. I. *Collected Works*. Vols. 1–13, 15–17, 19–21, 23–28, 30, 32–34, 36, 42–43. Moscow, 1977–1988.

— — —. *Sochinenya*. Vol. 45. Moscow, 1965.

Lenin, V. I., and L. Trotsky. *Lenin's Fight Against Stalinism*. Ed. R. Block. New York, 1975.

Lovell, S., ed. *Leon Trotsky Speaks*. New York, 1972.

Marx, K. *Capital*. Vols. 1–3. Moscow, 1986.

— — —. *Early Writings*. Harmondsworth, 1975.

Marx, K., and F. Engels. *Collected Works*. Vol. 1–12, 15–17, 20–26, 38–44. Moscow, 1975–1989.

— — —. *Selected Correspondence*. Moscow, 1965.

— — —. *Selected Works*. Three vols. Moscow, 1973–1983.

— — —. *Werke*. Band 3, 21, 33, 34–35, 37–39. Berlin, 1956–1973.

Marx, K., F. Engels, V. I. Lenin, J. Stalin, and Mao Tse-tung. *Women and Communism*. Calcutta, 1978.

Marx, K., and J. Guesde. The Programme of the Parti Ouvrier, available on the MIA website at www.marxists.org/archive/marx/works/1880/05/parti-ouvrier.htm

Meijer, J., ed. *The Trotsky Papers*. 2 vols. The Hague, 1971.

Ryazanov, D. B., ed. *The Communist Manifesto, by K. Marx and F. Engels*. Calcutta, 1972.

Trotsky, L. *1905*. Harmondsworth, 1971.

— — —. *The Challenge of the Left Opposition: 1923–25*. Ed. N. Allen. New York, 1975.

— — —. *The Challenge of the Left Opposition: 1926–27*. Eds. N. Allen and G. Saunders. New York, 1980.

— — —. *The Death Agony of Capitalism and the Tasks of the Fourth International*. New York, 1970.

— — —. *History of the Russian Revolution*. 3 vols. London, 1967.

— — —. *The History of the Russian Revolution to Brest-Litovsk*. London, 1919.

— — —. *How the Revolution Armed*. 5 vols. London, 1979–1981.

— — —. *My Life*. Harmondsworth, 1975.

— — —. *On Lenin: Notes Towards a Biography*. Bombay, 1971.

— — —. *Our Political Tasks*. London, 1980.

— — —. *Our Revolution*. Ed. M. J. Olgin. New York, 1918.

— — —. *The Permanent Revolution, and Results and Prospects*. New York, 1976.

— — —. *Portraits: Personal and Political*. New York, 1977.

— — —. *Problems of Everyday Life*. New York, 1973.

— — —. *Report of the Siberian Delegation*. London, 1980.

— — —. *The Revolution Betrayed*. New York, 1987.

— — —. *Social Democracy and the Wars of Intervention: 1918–1921*. London, 1975.

— — —. *Stalin*. London, 1946.

— — —. *The Stalin School of Falsification*. New York, 1979.

— — —. *Terrorism and Communism*. London, 1975.

— — —. *The Third International After Lenin*. New York, 1980.

— — —. *What Next? And Other Writings from 1917*. London, 1988.

— — —. *Writings (1935–36)*. New York, 1977.

— — —. *The Young Lenin*. Harmondsworth, 1974.

B. Contemporary Writings:

Anderson, T., ed. *Master of Russian Marxism*. New York, 1963.

Badaev, A. *The Bolsheviks in the Tsarist Duma*. London, 1933.

Balabanoff, A. *My Life as a Rebel*. New York, 1968.

Bauer, O. *The Austrian Revolution*. London, 1925.

Bebel, A. *My Life*. Westport, 1983.

— — —. *Nari: Ateet, Bartaman, Bhabishyat*. Trans. by Kanak Mukhopadhyay. Calcutta, 2003.

— — —. *Woman in the Past, Present and Future*. Trans. H. B. Adam Walters. London, 1988.

Beirne, P., and R. Sharlet, eds. *Pashukanis: Selected Writings on Marxism and Law*. London, 1980.

Bernstein, E. *Evolutionary Socialism*. London, 1909.

Blanqui, A. *Textes Choisis*. Paris, 1971.

Bobrovskaia, C. *Twenty Years in Underground Russia*. New York, 1934.

Bogdanov, A. *Red Star*. Introd. R. Stites. Bloomington, 1984.

Bruce Lockhart, R. H. *Memoirs of a British Agent*. London and New York, 1933.

Buchanan, G. *My Mission to Russia*. London, 1923.

Bukharin, N. I., and E. A. Preobrazhenskii. *The ABC of Communism*. Harmondsworth, 1989.

Cornu, A., and W. Monke, eds. *Moses Hess, Philosophische und Sozialistische Schriften, 1837–1850*. Berlin, 1961.

Dolgoff, S., ed. *Bakunin on Anarchy*. Pref. P. Avrich. London, 1973.

Dunsterville, L. C. *The Adventures of Dunsterforce*. London, 1920.

Fotieva, L. Vospominaniya o V. I. Lenin. Moscow, 1964.

Gorky, M. *Untimely Thoughts*. London, 1968.

Gramsci, A. *Selections from the Prison Notebooks*. Ed. and trans. Q. Hoare and G. N. Smith. New York, 1971.

Haubtmann, P., ed. *Carnets de P. J. Proudhon*. 4 vols. Paris, 1960–74.

Howard, D., ed. *Selected Political Writings*. New York and London, 1971.

Jellinek, F. *The Paris Commune of 1871*. London, 1971.

Kanatchikov, S. *A Radical Worker in Tsarist Russia*. Stanford, 1986.

Kautsky, K. *The Dictatorship of the Proletariat*. Ann Arbor, 1964.

———. *The Labour Revolution*. London, 1925.

———. *The Road to Power*. Chicago, 1909.

———. *Selected Political Writings*. London, 1983.

Kerensky, A. F. *The Crucifixion of Liberty*. London, 1934.

Knox, A. *With the Russian Army, 1914–1917*. London, 1921.

Kollontai, A. M. *Autobiography of a Sexually Emancipated Communist Woman*. New York, 1971.

———. *Communism and the Family*. Calcutta, 1992.

———. *Iz moei zhizni i raboty*. Moscow, 1974.

———. *Izbranii statii i rechii*. Moscow, 1972.

———. "The Labour of Women in the Evolution of the Economy," available on the MIA website at www.marxists.org/archive/kollonta/1921/evolution.htm

———. *Selected Articles and Speeches*. Moscow, 1984.

———. *Selected Writings of Alexandra Kollontai*. Ed. A. Holt. London, 1977.

———. *The Workers' Opposition*. Calcutta, 1992.

Krupskaia, N. K. *Memories of Lenin*. Moscow, 1959.

Lehning, A., ed. *Archives Bakounine*. Vol. 1. Leiden, 1961.

Lessener, F. "Before 1848 and After." In *Reminiscences of Marx and Engels*, ed. P. Annenkov. Moscow, 1956.

Lissagaray, P. O. *History of the Commune of 1871*. New York, 1969.

Luxemburg, R. *Gesammelte Werke*. Band 1–5. Berlin, 1988–90.

———. "Organisational Question of Social Democracy." In *Rosa Luxemburg Speaks*, ed. M. A. Waters. New York, 1980.

———. *Reform or Revolution*. Calcutta, 1993.

———. *Selected Political Writings*. Ed. D. Howard. New York and London, 1971.

Marx-Aveling, E., and E. Aveling. *The Woman Question*. Eds. J. Muller and E. Schotte. Leipzig, 1986.

Meier, O., ed. *The Daughters of Karl Marx. Family Correspondence, 1866–1898*. Introd. S. Rowbotham. Harmondsworth, 1984.

Plekhanov, G. V. *Selected Philosophical Works*. Vol. 1. Moscow, 1974.

Pyatnitsky, O. *Memoirs of a Bolshevik*. Allahabad, n.d.

Radek, K. "On Lenin," *International Socialist Review* 34, no. 10 (November 1973).

Rakovsky, C. "The 'Professional Dangers' of Power." In *The Stalinist Legacy*, ed. T. Ali. Harmondsworth, 1984.

———. "Speech at the Twelfth Congress," *International Marxist Review* 4, no. 2.

Raskolnikov, F. F. *Kronstadt and Petrograd in 1917*. London, 1982.

Reed, J. *Ten Days that Shook the World. New* York, 1960.

Rosmer, A. *Lenin's Moscow*. London, 1971.

Serge, V. *Memoirs of a Revolutionary, 1901–1941*. London, 1963.

———. *Year One of the Russian Revolution*. London, 1992.

Shlyapnikov, A. Semnadtsatyi God. Vol. 2. Moscow, 1925.

Stalin, J. *Works*. 5 vols. Moscow, 1947–1953.

Sukhanov, N. N. *The Russian Revolution 1917. London*, 1955.

Sverdlova, K. T. *Iakov Mikhailovich Sverdlov*. Moscow, 1957.

Tudor, H., and M. Tudor, ed. *Marxism and Social Democracy*. Cambridge, 1988.

Vinogradskaia, P. "Voprosy byta." *Pravda*. (July 26, 1923).

Voitinskii, V. S. *Godu Pobedi Porazhenii*. Moscow, 1923.

Voline. *Nineteen-Seventeen*. London, 1954.

Waters, M. A., ed. *Rosa Luxemburg Speaks*. New York, 1980.

Weitling, W. *The Poor Sinner's Gospel*. London, n.d.

Williams, A. R. *Through the Russia Revolution*. Moscow, 1967.

Wrangel, P. N. *Memoirs*. London, 1930.

Wolfe, B. D., ed. *Rosa Luxemburg: The Russian Revolution and Marxism or Leninism*. Ann Arbor, 1961.

Zetkin, C. *Lenin on the Women's Question*, available on the MIA website from www.marxists.org/archive/zetkin/1920/lenin/zetkin1.htm

———. *Reden und Schriften*. Band I. Berlin, 1957.

———. *Selected Writings*. Introd. P. S. Foner. New York, 1984.

Zinoviev, G. *History of the Bolshevik Party*. London, 1983.

———. *Za Leninism*. Moscow, 1925.

C. Documents:

Amosov, P. N., et al., eds. *Oktyabrskaia Revolutsiya i Fabsavkomy*. 2 vols. Moscow, 1927.

Ascher, A. *The Mensheviks in the Russian Revolution*. London, 1976.

Bernshtam, M. S., ed. *Nezavisimoe rabochii dvizhenie v 1918 godu, Dokumenty i Materialy*. Paris, 1981.

Blumenberg, W. "Zur Geschichte des Bundes der Kommunisten Aussagen des Peter Gerhardt Roser," *International Review of Social History*, no. 9 (1964).

Browder, R. P., and A. F. Kerensky. *The Russian Provisional Government 1917– Documents*. Stanford, 1961.

Bunyan, J., ed. *Intervention, Civil War and Communism in Russia, April–December 1918*. Baltimore, 1936.

———. *The Origin of Forced Labour in the Soviet State: 1917–192.* Baltimore, 1967.

Bunyan, J., and H. H. Fisher. *The Bolshevik Revolution 1917–1918: Documents and Materials.* Stanford, 1934.

Daniels, R. V. *A Documentary History of Communism.* Vol. 1. New York, 1962.

Elwood, R. C., ed. *The Russian Social Democratic Labour Party 1898–October 1917,* Volume 1 of R. H. McNeal, General Editor, *Resolutions and Decisions of the Communist Party of the Soviet Union.* Toronto, 1974.

Förder, H., M. Hundt, J. Kandel, and S. Lewiowa, eds. *Der Bund der Kommunisten: Dokumente und Materialien, 1836–49.* Berlin, 1970.

Frankel, J., ed. *Vladimir Akimov on the Dilemma of Russian Marxism, 1895–1903.* Cambridge, 1969.

Fried, A., and R. Sanders, eds. *Socialist Thought: A Documentary History.* New York, 1964.

Gerth, H., ed. *The First International: Minutes of The Hague Congress of 1872.* Madison, 1958.

Gladkov, I. A., ed. *Nationlizatsiya Promyshlennosti v SSSR, 1917–20 gg.* Moscow, 1954.

Golder, F., ed. *Documents of Russian History.* New York, 1927.

Gregor, R., ed. *"The Early Soviet Period 1917–1929.* Vol. 2 of *Resolutions and Decisions of the Communist Party of the Soviet Union,* ed. R. H. McNeal. Toronto, 1974.

Harding, N., ed. *Marxism in Russia.* Cambridge, 1983.

Jones, M., ed. *Storming the Heavens: Voices of October.* London, 1987.

Keep, J. L. H., ed. *The Debate on Soviet Power: Minutes of the All-Russian Central Executive Committee of the Soviets.* Oxford, 1979.

Kudelli, P. F., ed. *Pervyi legalnyi Peterburgskii Komitet Bolshevikov v 1917g.* Moscow, 1927.

Kutuzov, V. V., and A. L. Sidorov, et al., eds. *Velikaia Oktiabrskaia Sotsialisticheskaia Revoliutsiia—Khronika Sobytii.* Moscow, 1957.

McCauley, M., ed. *The Russian Revolution and the Soviet State, 1917-1921: Documents.* London, 1975.

Pearce, B., ed. *1903: Second Congress of the Russia Social Democratic Labour Party (minutes).* London, 1978.

Pokrovskii, N. N., et. al, eds. *Vtoroi Vserossiskii S'ezd Sovetov R.i.S.D.* Moscow and Leningard, 1928.

Riddell, J., ed. *The German Revolution and the Debate on Soviet Power.* New York, 1986.

Ryazanova, A. *Zhenskii Trud.* Moscow, 1923.

Schulkind, E., ed. *The Paris Commune of 1871: The View from the Left.* London, 1972.

Vladimirsky, M., ed. *The Bolsheviks and the October Revolution. Minutes of the Central Committee of the Russian Democratic Labour Party (Bolsheviks), August 1917–February 1918.* Trans. A. Bone. Notes T. Cliff. London, 1974.

———. *Sovety ispolkomy i s'ezdy Sovetov: Materialy k izucheniiu srtoeniya i devatelrosti organov mestriogo upravleniya,* tom. 1. Moscow, 1920.

———. *Dekrety Sovietskoi Vlasti.* 3 vols. Moscow, 1957–59.

— — —. *Desiatyi S'ezd RKP(b): Mart 1921 goda,* Stenograficheskii Otchet. Moscow, 1963.

— — —. *Deviataia Konferentsiia RKP(b), Sentiabr' 1920 goda,* Protokoly. Moscow, 1972.

— — —. *Deviatii S'ezed RKP(b).* Moscow, 1963.

— — —. *Directivy Komandovaniia frontov Krasnoi Armii (1917–1072).* Moscow, 1978.

— — —. *Documents of the First International: The General Council of the First International, Minutes.* 5 vols. Moscow, 1964.

— — —. *Documents of the Left Opposition.* London, 1980.

— — —. *The Hague Congress of the First International: Minutes and Documents.* Moscow, 1976.

— — —. *KPSS v rezoliutsiiakh i resheniiakh s'ezdov, konferentsii i plenumov Tsk.* 2 vols. Moscow, 1954–1970.

— — —. *Obrazovanie i razvite organov Sotsialisticheskogo Kontrol v SSSR (1917–1975). Moscow,* 1975.

— — —. *Odinnadtsatii S'ezd RKP(b). Moscow,* 1963.

— — —. *Partiya i Revolyutsii 1905 goda Dokumenty'k Istorii i Parti I v 1905 godu. Moscow,* 1934.

— — —. *Perepiska V.I. Lenina i Rukovodimykh im uchrezhdenii RSDRP s partiinymi organizatsiiami 1905–1907 gg.* 3 vols. Moscow, 1982–85.

— — —. "Positive Action and Party Building Among Women," Resolution of the Fourth International. *International Marxist Review,* no. 14 (Winter 1992).

— — —. "Citizens' Panel Warns Of Civil War In Chhattisgarh, Calls For End To 'Salwa Judum' Campaign And Judicial Inquiry," Press Release by Independent Citizens Initiative, received from aiindex@mnet.fr (May 29, 2006).

— — —. *Protokoll des Parteitags der Sozialdemokratischen Partei Deutschlands.* Erfurt, 1891.

— — —. *Protokoly: Chetvertyi (ob'edinitel'nyi) s'ezd RSDRP, aprel-mai 1906 goda.* Moscow, 1959.

— — —. "Protokoly i rezoliutsii Biruro Tsk RSDTP (b) (Mar 1917g)," *Voprosy Istorii KPSS,* no. 3 (1962).

— — —. *Pyatyi (Londonskii) S'ezd RSDRP.* Moscow, 1959.

— — —. *Revoliutsionnoe dvizhenie v Rossii v Aprele 1917g.* Moscow, 1959.

— — —. *Revoliutsionnoe dvizhenie v Rossii posle sverzheniya samoderzhaviya.* Moscow, 1957.

— — —. *Sed'maia (Aprel'skaia) Vserossiskaia Konferentsiia RSDRP(Bolshevikov), Petrogradskaia Obschegorodskaia RSDRP (Bol'shevikov): Petrogradskaia Obschegorodskaian RSDRP (bol'shevikov), protokoly.* Moscow, 1958.

— — —. *Sedmoi ekstrennyi S'ezd RKP(b), Mart 1918 goda,* Stenograficheskii Otchet. Moscow, 1962.

— — —. *S'ezdy Sovetov v Dokumentakh.* Moscow, 1959.

— — —. *Sobranie Uzakonenii i rasporiazhenii rabochego i krest'ianskogo pravitel'stva. Sbornik dekretov 1917-18 gg,* no. 76-77, art. 818. Moscow, 1920.

— — —. *Tretii S'ezd RSDRP.* Moscow, 1959.

———. *Trinadsatsaia Konferentsiia RKP(b)*. Moscow, 1963.
———. *Vosmaia Konferentsiia RKP(b)*. Moscow, 1961.
———. *Vosmoi S'ezd RKP(b)*. Moscow, 1933.
———. *Vtoroi S'ezd RSDRP*. Moscow, 1959.
———. *Vtoroi Vesrossiiskii S'ezd Sovetov*. Moscow, 1957.
———. *Vtoroi Vserossiskii S'ezd Sovetov R.I.S.D.* Moscow, 1928.
———. *Zhenshchiny russkoi revoliutsii*. Moscow, 1968.

II. SECONDARY SOURCES: BOOKS AND ARTICLES

Abrams, R. "Political Recruitment and Local Government: The Local Soviets of the RSFSR, 1918–21," *Soviet Studies* 19, no. 4 (April 1968).
Abramsky, C., ed. *Essays in Honour of E. H. Carr. London*, 1974.
Ali, T., ed. *The Stalinist Legacy*. Harmondsworth 1984.
Althusser, L. *For Marx. London*, 1977.
Althusser, L., and E. Balibar. *Reading Capital. London*, 1970.
Anderson, P. "The Antinomies of Antonio Gramsci," *New Left Review* 100 (November–December 1976 and January–February 1977).
Andreyev, A. *The Soviets of Workers' and Soldiers' Deputies on the Eve of the October Revolution. Moscow*, 1971.
Anweiler, O. *The Soviets. New* York, 1974.
Anweiler, O., and J. Hazard. *The Soviet System of Government. Chicago*, 1964.
Arenshgein, A. "Kamnia Tverzhe (K. T. Novgorodtseva-Sverdlova)." In *Zhenshchiny Russkoi Revoliutsii*, eds. L. P. Zhak and A. Itkina. Moscow, 1968.
Aristarkhova, I. *Women and Government in Bolshevik Russia*, Working Papers, Centre for Comparative Labour Studies, Department of Sociology, University of Warwick, no. 4 (August 1995), available on the University of Warwick website from www.csv.warwick.ac.uk/fac/soc /complabstuds/russia/irawp.doc
Ascher, A. *Pavel Axelrod and the Development of Menshevism*. Cambridge, 1972.
Ash, J. "Clara Zetkin: A Reply to Tony Cliff," *International Socialism, 14,* Autumn 1981.
Avineri, S. *Hegel's theory of the Modern State*. Cambridge, 1972.
———. *The Social and Political Thought of Karl Marx. New* Delhi, 1977.
Avrich, P. "The Bolsheviks and Workers' Control," *Slavic Review* 22, no. 1 (1963).
———. *The Russian Anarchists*. London, 1973.
———. *Kronstadt 1921*. New York, 1974.
———. "Bolshevik Opposition to Lenin: G. I. Miasnikov and the Workers' Group," *The Russian Review* 43, no. 1 (January 1984).
———. *Anarchist Portraits*. New Jersey, 1988.
Badaloni, N. "Marx and the Quest for Communist Liberty." In *The History of Marxism*, ed. E. J. Hobsbawm. Bloomington, 1982.
Baitalsky, M. *Notebooks for the Grandchildren*. New Jersey, 1995.
Balibar, E. *On the Dictatorship of the Proletariat*. London, 1977.
Bandyopadhyay, T. K. *Concept of the Party from Marx to Gramsci*. Calcutta, 1992.
Baron, S. H. *Plekhanov: Father of Russian Marxism*. London, 1963.

Bartshtein, E. K., and L. M. Shalaginova. "Partiya Bol'shevikov vo glave revoliutsionnogo pod'ema mass v period podgotovki i provedeniya fevral'sko burzhuazno-demokraticheskoi revoliutsii," *Voprosy istorii KPSS*, 1957, no. 1 (January).

Bassow, W. "The Pre-revolutionary *Pravda* and Tsarist Censorship," *The American Slavic and East European Review* (February 1954).

Bater, J. H. *St. Petersburg: Industrialisation and Change*. Montreal, 1976.

Becker, G. *"Karl Marx und Friedrich Engels in Koln, 1848–1849."* In *Zur Geschichte des Kölner Arbeitervereins*. Berlin, 1963.

Beer, M. *A History of British Socialism*. 2 vols. London, 1920.

Benvenuti, F. *The Bolsheviks and the Red Army 1918–1922*. Cambridge, 1968.

Berki, R. N. "Through and Through Hegel: Marx's Road to Communism," *Political Studies*, no. 38 (1990).

Bernstein, S. *The First International in America*. New York, 1962.

———. *Auguste Blanqui and the Art of Insurrection*. London, 1971.

Bhattacharyya, B. *Dictatorship of the Proletariat: The Current Debate*. Calcutta, 1985.

Bidwai, P. "Waging War Against The People: Dangerous Anti-Naxal Strategy," South Asian Citizen Wire, received from aiindex@mnet.fr (June 5, 2006).

Biegalski, C., ed. Argument IV: *Révolution/Class/Parti*. Paris, 1978.

Black, R. *Fascism in Germany*. Vol. 1. London, 1975.

Blackburn, R. "Marxism: Theory of Proletarian Revolution." In *Revolution and Reaction: The Paris Commune*, eds. J Hicks and R Tucker. Boston, 1973.

———, ed. *Revolution and Class Struggle*. Glasgow, 1977.

———. "Marxism: Theory of Proletarian Revolution." In *Revolution and Class Struggle*, ed. R. Blackburn.

———. *"Fin de Siecle: Socialism* after the crash," *New Left Review 185* (January–February 1991).

Bloom, S. F. "The 'Withering Away' of the State," *Journal of the History of Ideas* 7 (1946).

Bobroff, A. "The Bolsheviks and Working Women 1905–1920," *Soviet Studies* 26, no. 4 (October 1974).

Bonnell, V. E. *Roots of Rebellion*. Berkeley, 1983.

Borys, J. *The Russian Communist Party and the Sovietization of the Ukraine*. New York, 1960.

Bottomore, T., ed. *A Dictionary of Marxist Thought*. Oxford, 1983.

Bowles, S., and H. Gintis. "The Crisis of Liberal Democratic Capitalism: The Case of the United States" *Politics and Society* 11, no. 1 (1982).

Brailsford, H. N. *The Levellers and the English Revolution*. London, 1961.

———. *Across the Blockade*. New York, 1991.

Brinkley, G. A. *The Volunteer Army and Allied Intervention in South Russia 1917–1921*. South Bend, 1966.

Brinton, M. *The Bolsheviks and Workers' Control: The State and Counter–Revolution*. Montreal, 1975.

Broido, V. *Lenin and the Mensheviks*. Aldershot, 1987.

Broué, P. *Le Parti Bolchévique*. Paris, 1963.

Brovkin, V. "The Mensheviks and NEP Society in Russia," *Russian History / Histoire Russe, no.* 2-3 (1982).

— — —. "The Mensheviks' Political Comeback: The Elections to the Provincial City Soviets in Spring 1918," *The Russian Review* 42, no. 1 (January 1983).

Bruce Lincoln, W. *Red Victory.* New York, 1989.

Buhle, P. "International Workingmen's Association." In *Encyclopaedia of the American Left*, eds. M. J. Buhle, P. Buhle and D. Georgakas. New York and London, 1990.

Burdzhalov, E. N. "O taktike Bol'shevikov v marte-aprele 1917 goda," *Voprosy Istorii, no.* 4 (1956).

— — —."Eshche o taktike Bol'shevikov v marte-aprele 1917 goda," *Voprosy Istorii, no.* 8 (1956).

— — —. *Vtoraya russkaya revoliutsiya.* Moscow, 1967.

Busi, F. "The Failure of the Revolution." In *Revolution and Reaction: The Paris Commune*, eds. J. Hicks and R. Tucker.

Buzgalin, A. "Russia: Signs of Change," *International Viewpoint*, no. 340 (May 2002).

Callinicos, A. "Bourgeois Revolutions and Historical Materialism," *International Socialism, 2nd se*r., no. 43 (June 1989).

Carew Hunt, R. N. *The Theory and Practice of Communism.* Harmondsworth, 1978.

Carr, E. H. *The Bolshevik Revolution. 3* vols. Harmondsworth, 1966.

— — —. *1917: Before and After.* London, Melbourne, and Toronto, 1969.

— — —. *Socialism in One Country. Vol. 1.* Harmondsworth, 1970.

— —. *Michael Bakunin.* New York, 1975.

Carmichael, J. *Trotsky: An Appreciation of his Life.* London, 1975.

Carrillo, S. *"Eurocommunism" and the State.* London, 1979.

Carsten, F. L. "The *Arbeiterbildungsvereine* and the Foundation of the Social Democratic Workers' Party in 1869," *English History Review (*April 1992).

Carver, T. *Marx and Engels: The Intellectual Relationship.* Brighton, 1983.

Chamberlin, W. H. *The Russian Revolution: 1917–1921.* 2 vols. New Jersey, 1987.

Chang, S. H. M. *The Marxian Theory of the State.* Delhi, 1990.

Chattopadhyay, K. "Christian Rakovsky and the 1923 Ukrainian Opposition in the RCP(b)," *Proceedings of the Indian History Congress, 47th Session.* New Delhi, 1987.

— — —. "Fuzzy Power Structure lands Russia in a constitutional crisis," *Business Standard* (September 26, 1993).

— — —. "The German Reunification and the Left." In *Europe in the Second Millennium: A Hegemony Achieved?*, eds. R. Mukherjee and K. Chattopadhyay. *Calcutta*, 2005.

— — —. "Hunger for Power," *Business Standard*. December 29, 1991.

— — —. *Leninism and Permanent Revolution.* Baroda, 1987.

— — —. "Marx, Engels and the Peasant Question," parts I–III, *Jadavpur University Journal of History* 5–7 (1985–1988).

— — —. *The Marxism of Leon Trotsky.* Calcutta, 2006.

— — —. "Run Up to a Russian Roulette," *Business Standard* (March 23, 1993).

— — —. "Stalinbad, Soviet Union Gathan O Jatiyotar Samasya." In *Itihas Anu-sandhan*, vol. 7, ed. A. W. Mahmood. *Calcutta*, 1993.

— — —. "Yeltsin and the Weimar syndrome," *Business Standard* (December 16, 1993).

Chattopadhyay, P. "Women's labour under Capitalism and Marx," *Bulletin of Concerned Asian Scholars* 31, no. 4 (1999).

Chossudovsky, M. *The Globalisation of Poverty*, Mapusa, Goa (Indian Edition), 2001.

Cliff, T. *Lenin.* Vol. 1, *Building the party.* London, 1975.

— — —. *Lenin.* Vol. 2, *All Power to the Soviets. London*, 1977.

— — —. *Lenin.* Vol. 3, *The Revolution Besieged. London*, 1978.

— — —. *Lenin.* Vol. 4. London, 1979.

— — —. *Trotsky: Towards October, 1879–1917.* London, Chicago, and Melbourne, 1989.

— — —. *Trotsky: The Sword of the Revolution 1917–1923.* London, Chicago, and Melbourne, 1990.

— — —. *Class Struggle and Women's Liberation.* London, 1987.

Coggiola, O. *"The Quieter of the Two: Friedrich Engels and Political and Interna-tionalist Marxism."* Unpublished article.

Cohen, S. F. *Bukharin and the Bolshevik Revolution.* Oxford, 1980.

— — —. *Rethinking the Soviet Experience: Politics and History Since 1917.* New York, 1985.

Cole, G. D. H. *A History of Socialist Thought.* Vol. 2. London, 1955.

Colletti, L. *From Rousseau to Lenin.* London, 1972.

— — —. "Introduction" to K. Marx, *Early Writings.* Harmondsworth, 1975.

— — —. "Lenin's *State and Revolution.*" In *Revolution and Class Struggle*, ed. R. Blackburn.

— — —. "The Question of Stalin." In *Revolution and Class Struggle*, ed. R. Blackburn.

Collins, H., and C. Abramsky. *Karl Marx and the British Labour Movement.* London, 1965.

Conquest, R. *Lenin.* London, 1972.

Corrigan, P., H. Ramsay, and D. Sayer. "Bolshevism and the USSR," *New Left Review*, no. 125 (1981).

Cott, N. *The Grounding of Modern Feminism.* New Haven and London, 1987.

Coulter, J. "Marxism and the Engels Paradox." In *Socialist Register*, eds. R. Miliband and J. Seville. (1971).

Craig, J. "Karl Marx: Democrat and Republican" *Socialist Democracy*, available on the SD website at www.socialistdemocracy.org/History /HistoryKarlMarxDemocratAndRepublican.htm

Dallin, D. J. *The Rise of Russia in Asia.* London, 1950.

Dallin, D., and B. Nicolaievski. *Forced Labour in Soviet Russia.* London, 1948.

Dan, T. *The Origins of Bolshevism.* New York, 1970.

Daniels, R. V. *The Conscience of the Revolution: Communist Opposition in Soviet Russia.* Cambridge, 1960.

— — —. *Red October.* New York, 1967.

Dasgupta, R. K. "Blurred Vision: Gaps in the Communist Manifesto," *The*

Statesmen. Calcutta, 1993.

Della Volpe, G. *Rousseau, Marx and other Writings*. London, 1978.

Desai, A. R., ed. *Communism and Democracy*. Bombay, 1990.

Deutscher, I. *The Prophet Armed*. London, 1976.

―――. *The Prophet Unarmed*. New York, 1959.

Dobb, M. H. *Soviet Economic Development Since 1917*. London, 1948.

Dominick III, R. H. Wilhelm Liebknecht and the Founding of the German Social Democratic Party. Chapel Hill, 1982.

Dommanget, M. *Les Idées Sociales et Politiques d'Auguste Blanqui*. Paris, 1957.

Donald, M. "Bolshevik Activity Amongst the Working Women of Petrograd in 1917," *International Review of Social History* 27, 1982.

Donovan, J. *Feminist Theory*. New York and London, 2000.

Drachkovitch, M. M., ed. *The Revolutionary Internationals 1864–1943*. Stanford, 1968.

Draper, H. *The "Dictatorship of the Proletariat" from Marx to Lenin*. New York, 1988.

―――. *Karl Marx's Theory of Revolution. 4 vols*. New York, 1977–1990.

―――."Marx and the Dictatorship of the Proletariat," *New Politics* 1, no. 4 (1962).

―――. "The Principle of the Self-Emancipation in Marx and Engels,." In *Socialist Register*, eds. R. Miliband and J. Seville. 1971.

―――. *The Two Souls of Socialism*. Berkeley, 1966.

Draper, H., and A. G. Lipow. "Marxist Women versus Bourgeois Feminism." In *Socialist Register*, eds. R. Miliband and J. Seville. (1976).

Duncan, G. *Marx and Mill*. Cambridge, 1973.

Dunn J., ed. *Democracy: The Unfinished Journey*. Oxford, 1992.

―――. *Western Political Theory in the Face of the Future*. Cambridge, 1979.

Duval, C. "Yakov M. Sverdlov and the All-Russian Central Executive Committee of Soviets (VTsIK)," *Soviet Studies* 31, no. 1 (January 1979).

Eisenstein, E. L. *The First Professional Revolutionist: Filippo Michele Buonarroti (1761–1837)*. Cambridge, 1959.

Eisenstein, Z., ed. *Capitalist Patriarchy and the Case for Socialist Feminism*. New York and London, 1979.

Eissenstat, B. W., ed. *Lenin and Leninism, State, Law and Society*. Lexington, 1971.

Elnitskii, A. *Istoriya rebochego dvizheniya v Rossi*. Moscow, 1925.

Elwood, R. C., ed. *Reconsiderations on the Russian Revolution*. Columbus, 1976.

―――. *Roman Malinovsky: A Life Without a Cause*. Newtonville, 1977.

―――. *Inessa Armand: Revolutionary and Feminist*. Cambridge, 1992.

Emelyanova, E. D. *Revoliutsiya, partiya, zhenshchina: opyt raboty sredi trudyash-chikhsya zhenshchin (oktyabr 1917-1925gg)*. Smolensk, 1971.

Ershov, D. A. *Mariya Ilinichna Ulyanova*. Saratov, 1965.

Evans, A. B. "Rereading Lenin's *State and Revolution*," *Slavic Review* 46, no. 1 (Spring 1987).

Evans, R. J. "Feminism and Female Emancipation in Germany, 1871–1945: Sources, Methods and Problems of Research," *Central European History* (December 1976).

— — —. "German Social Democracy and Women's Suffrage 1891–1918," *Journal of Contemporary History* 15 (1980).

— — —. *The Feminists.* London, 1984.

— — —. *Comrades and Sisters.* Brighton and New York, 1987.

Evans Clements, B. *Bolshevik Feminist: The Life of Alexandra Kollontai.* Bloomington and London, 1979.

— — —. *Bolshevik Women.* Cambridge, 1997.

Farber, S. *Before Stalinism.* London, 1990.

Farnsworth, B. *Alexandra Kollontai: Socialism Feminism and the Bolshevik Revolution.* Stanford, 1980.

Ferro, M. *The Russian Revolution of February 1917.* London, 1972.

— — —. *The Bolshevik Revolution.* London, 1985.

Figes, O. *Peasant Russia, Civil War.* Oxford, 1989.

— — —. *A People's Tragedy: The Russian Revolution 1891–1924.* London, 1996.

Fischer, G. *Russian Liberalism from Gentry to Intelligentsia.* Cambridge, 1958.

Fitzpatrick, S. *The Russian Revolution.* Oxford, 1984.

Foner, P. *Women and the American Labour Movement From World War I to the Present.* New York, 1980.

Footman, D. *Civil War in Russia.* London, 1961.

— — —. *Ferdinand Lassalle, Romantic Revolutionary.* New York, 1969.

Foreman, A. *Femininity as Alienation.* London, 1977.

Freymond J., and M. Molnár. "The Rise and Fall of the First International." In *The Revolutionary Internationals,* ed. M.M. Drachkovitch. Stanford, 1968.

Fukuyama, F. *The End of History and the Last Man.* New York, 1992.

Gay, P. *The Dilemma of Democratic Socialism.* New York, 1952.

Geiger, K.H. *The Family in Soviet Russia.* Cambridge, 1968.

Gemkow, H. *Karl Marx: A Biography.* New Delhi, 1968.

Geras, N. "Marxism and Proletarian Self–Emancipation." In *Literature of Revolution,* ed. N. Geras. London, 1986.

Gerratana, V. "Stalin, Lenin and 'Leninism,'" *New Left Review,* no. 103 (May–June 1977).

Gerson, L. D. *The Secret Police in Lenin's Russia.* Philadelphia, 1976.

Getzler, I. "The Mensheviks," *Problems of Communism* 16, no. 6 (November–December 1967).

— — —. *Martov.* Cambridge, 1967.

— — —. *Kronstadt 1917–1921.* Cambridge, 1983.

Gilbert, A. *Marx's Politics.* Oxford, 1981.

Gill, G. *Peasants and Government in the Russian Revolution.* New York, 1979.

Gitelman, Z. *A Century of Ambivalence–The Jews of Russia and Soviet Union.* New York, 1988.

Glickman, R. L. "The Russian Factory Woman 1890–1914." In *Women in Russia,* eds. D. Atkinson, et al. Stanford, 1978.

— — —. *Russian Factory Women: Workplace and Society, 1880–1914.* Berkeley, Los Angeles, and London, 1984.

Gluckstein, D. *The Western Soviets.* London, 1985.

Gramsci, A. *Selections from the Prison Notebooks.* New York, 1973.

— — —. *Selections from Political Writings 1910–1920.* London, 1977.

Guérin, D. *La Lutte de Classes sous la Première République: Bourgeois et "Bras Nus" (1793–1797)*. Paris, 1946.

―――. *Class Struggle in the First French Republic: Bourgeois and Bras Nus, 1793-1795*. London, 1977.

Haimson, L. H. "The Problem of Social Stability in Urban Russia: 1905–1917, pt. 1." *Slavic Review* 23, no. 4 (December 1964).

―――. "The Problem of Social Stability in Urban Russia: 1905–1917, pt. 2." *Slavic Review* 24, no. 1 (March 1965).

―――. *The Russian Marxists and the Origins of Bolshevism*. Boston, 1966.

―――, ed. *The Politics of Rural Russia in 1905–1914*. Bloomington, 1979.

Hammen, O. J. *The Red '48ers*. New York, 1969.

Hammond, T. "Leninist authoritarianism before the revolution." In *Continuity and Change in Russian and Soviet Thought, ed*. E. J. Simmons. Cambridge, 1955.

Hampden Jackson, J. *Marx, Proudhon and European Socialism*. New York, 1962.

Harcave, S. *First Blood: The Revolution of 1905*. London, 1964.

Harding, N. *Lenin's Political Thought. 2 vols*. London and Basingstoke, 1983.

Harman, C. *Germany: The Lost Revolution*. London, 1982.

―――, ed. *Marxists and the State*. London, 1987.

Harrison, R. *Before the Socialists, Studies in Labour and Politics, 1861–1881*. London, 1965.

Hartmann, H. "The Unhappy Marriage of Marxism and Feminism: Towards a More Progressive Union." In *The Unhappy Marriage of Marxism and Feminism: A Debate on Class and Patriarchy*, ed. Lydia Sargent. London, 1986.

Hasegawa, T. "The Formation of the Militia in the February Revolution: An Aspect of the Origin of the Dual Power," *Slavic Review* 32, no. 2 (1973).

―――. "The Bolsheviks and the Formation of the Petrograd Soviet in the February Revolution," *Soviet Studies 29*, no. 1 (January 1977).

―――. *The February Revolution: Petrograd 1917*. Seattle, 1981.

Hayek, F. A. *The Road to Serfdom*. Chicago, 1950.

Haynes, M. "Was there a Parliamentary Alternative in Russia in 1917?," *International Socialism* 76 (Autumn 1997).

Hazard, J. N. *Settling Disputes in Soviet Society*. New York, 1960.

Henderson, W. O. *The Life of Frederick Engels. 2 vols*. London, 1976.

Hicks, J., and R. Tucker, eds. *Revolution and Reaction: The Paris Commune*. Boston, 1973.

Hill, C. *The World Turned Upside Down*. Harmondsworth, 1975.

Hindess, B. *Parliamentary Democracy and the Socialist Politics*. London, 1983.

Hobsbawm, E., ed. *The History of Marxism*. Bloomington, 1982.

―――. "Marx, Engels and Politics." In *The History of Marxism*, ed. E. Hobsbawm. Bloomington, 1982.

―――. "Waking from History's Great Dream" *Independent on Sunday* (February 4, 1990).

Honeycutt, K. "Socialism and Feminism in Imperial Germany," *Signs: Journal of Women in Culture and Society*, 5 (1979).

Hook, S. *Towards the Understanding of Karl Marx*. New York, 1933.

―――. Myth and Fact in the Marxist theory of Revolution and Violence,"
    Journal of the History of Ideas 34, no. 2.
Hunczak, T., ed. *The Ukraine, 1917–1921: A Study in Revolution*. Cambridge,
    1977.
Hunt, A. "Marx the Missing Dimension: The Rise of Representative
    Democracy." In *Marx: A Hundred Years On*, ed. B. Mathews. London,
    1983.
Hunt, R. N. *The Political Ideas of Marx Engels*. 2 vols. London and Basingstoke,
    1975, 1981.
―――. *German Social Democracy: 1918–1933*. Chicago, 1970.
Huskey, E. *Russian Lawyers and Soviets State*. Princeton, 1986.
Hyman, R. *Marxism and the Sociology of Trade Unionism*. London, 1975.
Ilyin-Zhenevsky, A. F. *The Bolsheviks in Power*. London, 1984.
Ivanov, N. Y. *Kornilovshchina i eve razgrom*. Leningrad, 1965.
Johnstone, M. "Marx and Engels and the Concept of the Party." In *Socialist
    Register*, eds. R. Miliband and J. Seville. 1967.
―――. "The Paris Commune and Marx's Conception of the Dictatorship of
    the Proletariat." In *Revolution and Reaction: The Paris Commune*, ed. J.
    Hicks and R. Tucker.
Juviler, P. H. *Revolutionary Law and Order*. New York, 1976.
Kaiser, D. H., ed. The Worker's Revolution in Russia, 1917. Cambridge, 1987.
Kagarlitsky, B. The Dialectic of Change. London, 1992.
―――. *The Thinking Reed*. London, 1988.
Kandel, E.P. "Iskazhenie istorii bor'by Marksa i Engelsa za proletarskuiu
    partiiu v rabotakh nekotorikh pravikh sotsialistov," *Voprosi Istorii*, no. 5
    (1958).
―――. "Eine Schlechte verteidigung Einer Schlechten Sache." In *Beitrage zur
    Geschichte der deutschen Abeiterbewegung*, vol. 2. Berlin, 1963.
Kaplan, F. I. *Bolshevik Ideology and the Ethics of Soviet Labour*. New York, 1968.
Kapp, Y. *Eleanor Marx*. 2 vols. New York, 1972–1976.
Karpetskaia, N. D. *Rabotnitsy i Velikii Oktyabr*. Leningrad, 1974.
Katkov, G. "The Kronstadt Rising." In *St. Anthony's Papers*, no. 6, ed. D.
    Footman. London, 1959.
―――. *Russia 1917: The February Revolution*. London, 1967.
―――. *Russia 1917: The Kornilov Affair. Kerensky and the Break Up of the Rus-
    sian Army*. London, 1980.
Kazemzadeh, F. *Struggle for the Trans-Caucasus, 1917-1922*. New York, 1951.
Keep, J.L.H. *The Rise of Social Democracy in Russia*. London, 1963.
―――, ed. *Contemporary History in the Soviet Mirror*. New York and London,
    1964.
―――. "Lenin's Letters as Historical source." In *Lenin and Leninism: State,
    Law and Society*, ed. B.W. Eissenstat. Lexington, 1971.
―――. *The Russian Revolution: A Study in Mass Mobilization*. New York, 1976.
Keig, N., ed.: *Women's Liberation and Socialist Revolution*. New York, 1979.
Kellogg, P. "Engels and the Roots of 'Revisionism': A Re-evaluation" *Science
    and Society* 55, no. 2 (Summer 1991).
Kelly, A. *Mikhail Bakunin*. Oxford, 1982.

Kenez, P. *Civil War in South Russia, 1918.* Berkeley, 1971.

— — —. "The Ideology of the White Movement" *Soviet Studies* 32, no. 1 (January 1980).

Kingston-Mann, E. *Lenin and the Problem of Marxist Peasant Revolution.* Oxford, 1983.

Kirianov, I.I. "On the Nature of the Russian Working Class," *Soviet Studies in History* 2, no. 3 (Winter 1983–1984).

Koenker, D. *Moscow Workers and the 1917 Revolution.* Princeton, 1981.

Kołakowski, L. *Main Current of Marxism.* Vol. 2. Oxford, 1982.

— — —. "Marxist Root of Stalinism." In *Stalinism*, ed. R. C. Tucker. New York, 1977.

Kostomarov, G. *Moskovskii Sovet v 1905 godu.* Moscow, 1955.

Kritzman, L. N. *Die heroische periode der grossen Russischen Revolution.* Frankfurt am Main, 1971.

Kuznetsov, N. V. "Partiya i profsoiuzy v gody reaktsii" *Voprosy Istorii KPSS*, no. 4 (1958).

Laclau, E., and C. Mouffe. *Hegemony and Social Strategy.* London, 1995.

Lane, D. *The Roots of Russian Communism.* Assen, 1969.

Landy, A. *Marxism and the Democratic Tradition.* New York, 1946.

Lapenna, I. "Lenin, Law and Legality." In *Lenin: The Man, the Theorist, the Leader,* eds. L. Schapiro and P. Reddaway. New York, 1967.

Lapidus, G. W. *Women in Soviet Society: Equality, Development and Social Change.* Berkeley, 1978.

Le Blanc, P. *Lenin and the Revolutionary Party.* New Jersey and London, 1990.

Lefebvre, H. *The Explosion: Marxism and the French Revolution.* New York, 1969.

Leff, G. *The Tyranny of Concepts: A Critique of Marxism.* London, 1961.

Leggett, G. *The Cheka: Lenin's Political Police.* Oxford, 1981.

Lehning, A. "Buonarroti and his International Secret Societies," *International Review of Social History,* no. 1 (1957).

— — —. "Introduction" to *Archives Bakounine.* Leiden, 1961.

— — —. "Bakunin's Conceptions of Revolutionary Organisations and their Role: A Study of his Secret Societies." In *Essays in Honour of E. H. Carr,* ed. C. Abramsky. London, 1974.

Leiberov, I. P. "Stachechnaya Bor'ba Petrogradskogo proletariata v period pervoi mirovoi voiny (19 iyulya 1914g–16 fevralya 1917g)" *Istoriya Rabochego Klassa Leningrada,* no. 2. Leningrad, 1963.

Leiberov, I. P., and O. I. Shkaratan. "K voprosu o sostave petrogradskikh promyshlennykh rabochikh v 1917g," *Voprosy Istorii,* no. 1 (1961).

Lerner, G. *The Creation of Patriarchy.* Oxford and New York, 1986.

Levine, N. "The Germanization of Lenin," *Studies in Soviet Thought* 35, no. 1 (January 1988).

— — —. *The Tragic Deception: Marx Contra Engels.* Oxford, 1975.

Lewin, M. *Lenin's Last Struggle.* New York, 1968.

— — —. *The Making of the Soviet System.* London, 1985.

Lichtheim, G. *Marxism: An Historical and Critical Study.* London, 1961.

Lidtke, V. L. *The Outlawed Party.* Princeton, 1966.

Liebman, M. *The Russian Revolution.* London, 1970.

———. *Leninism Under Lenin*. London, 1980.

Locke, J. *Two Treatises on Government*. Ed. P. Laslett. Oxford, 1980.

Longley, D. A. "The Mezhraionka, the Bolsheviks and International Women's Day: In Response to Michael Melancon," *Soviet Studies* 41, no. 4 (October 1989).

Lopes, A., and G. Roth. *Men's Feminism: August Bebel and the German Socialist Movement*, Amherst. New York, 2000.

Lovell, D. W. *From Marx to Lenin*. Cambridge, 1986.

Löwy, M. *The Politics of Combined and Uneven Development*. London, 1981.

Lozovsky, A. *Marx and the Trade Unions*. Calcutta, 1975.

Luckett, R. *The White Generals*. London, 1971.

Lukács, G. *History and Class Consciousness*. London, 1971.

Lyashchenko, P. I. *History of the National Economy of Russia*. New York, 1949.

Macpherson, C. B. *Democratic Theory. Essays in Retrieval*. Oxford, 1973.

———. *The Life and Times of Liberal Democracy*. Oxford, 1977.

———. *The Political Theory of Possessive Individualism*. Oxford, 1962.

Mahmood, A. W., ed. *Itihas Anusandhan. Vol. 7*. Calcutta, 1993.

Malle, S. *The Economic Organisation of War communism 1918–1921*. Cambridge, 1985.

Mandel, D. *Factory Committees and Workers' Control in Petrograd in 1917*. Montreuil, 1993.

———. *The Petrograd Workers and the Fall of the Old Regime*. New York, 1984.

———. *The Petrograd Workers and the Soviet Seizure of Power*. New York, 1984.

———. "Revolution, Counterrevolution and Working Class in Russia: Reflections for the Eightieth Anniversary of the October Revolution." In *Europe in the Second Millennium: A Hegemony Achieved?*, eds. R. Mukherjee and K. Chattopadhyay.

Mandel, E. *Beyond Perestroika*. London, 1990.

———. *The Formation of the Economic Thought of Karl Marx*. London, 1977.

———. *Late Capitalism*. London, 1978.

———. *The Leninist Theory of Organisation*. Baroda, 1977.

———. *October 1917: coup d'etat or Social Revolution?* Montreuil, 1992.

———. *Power and Money*. London, 1992.

Manning, B. *The English People and the English Revolution*. London, 1992.

Manning, R. T. *The Crisis of the Old Order in Russia. Gentry and Government*. Princeton, 1982.

———. "Zemstvo and Revolution: The Onset of the Gentry Reaction 1905-1907." In The *Politics of Rural Russia in 1905-1914*, ed. L. Haimson. Bloomington, 1979.

Marik, S. "Classical Marxism and Proletarian Democracy: The Emergence of Concept - 1," *Jadavpur University Journal of History* 10 (1989–90).

———. "The 'Anti-Leninism' of Rosa Luxemburg. A Reappraisal of her theory of Party," *Society and Change* 10, Nos. 1 and 2 (April–September 1995).

———. "Biplabi Dal O Linga Samata," *Loukik Udyan: Manabi Sankhya* (August 1999).

———. "The Bolshevik and Workers' Democracy: 1917–1927. The Ideological

Crisis of Russian Communism and the Rise of Stalinism" *Proceedings of the Indian History Congress*. 52nd session. Delhi, 1992.

— — —. "Bolshevikbad O Nari Sramik: Prayoger Aloke Tatver Punarvichar." In *Itihas Anusandhan, vol. 13*, ed. G. Chattopadhyay. Calcutta, 1999.

— — —. "Gendering The Revolutionary Party: An Appraisal of Bolshevism." In *Perspectives on Socialism*, eds. B. Chatterjee and K. Chattopadhyay. Calcutta, 2004.

— — —. "German Socialism and Women's Liberation." In *Women in History*, eds. A. Chanda, M. Sarkar, and K. Chattopadhyay. Calcutta, 2003.

— — —. "Interrogating Official and Mainstream Discourses: Communist Women Remember the Forties," *Jadavpur University Journal of History* (2003–2004).

— — —. "A Pioneering Male Socialist Feminist: The Recovery of August Bebel," *Against the Current* (March–April 2004).

— — —. "Proletarian Socialism and Women's Liberation," *Proceedings of the Indian History Congress*, 61st session. Calcutta, 2001.

— — —. "The Withering Away of Stalinism," *Society and Change* VI, nos. 3 and 4 (October 1989–March 1990).

Mason, E. S. *The Paris Commune*. New York, 1967.

Mathews, B., ed. *Marx: A Hundred Years On*. London, 1983.

Mawdsley, E. "The Baltic Fleet and the Kronstadt Mutiny," *Soviet Studies* 24, no. 4 (April 1973).

— — —. *The Russian Revolution and the Baltic fleet*. London, 1978.

McAuley, M. *Bread and Authority, State and Society in Petrograd 1917–1922*. Oxford, 1991.

Mclellan, D. *Marx Before Marxism*. London, 1970.

— — —. *Karl Marx: His Life and Thought*. London and Basingstoke, 1973.

— — —. *Marxism After Marx*. New York, 1979.

— — —. *The Thought of Karl Marx*. London and Basingstoke, 1980.

Medvedev, R. *Let History Judge*. Oxford, 1989.

— — —. *The October Revolution*. New York, 1979.

Mehlinger, H. D., and J. M. Thomson. *Count Witte and the Tsarist Government in the 1905 Revolution*. Bloomington and London, 1974.

Mehring, F. *Karl Marx: The Story of his Life*. New York, 1935.

Melancon, M. "Who Wrote What and When?: Proclamations of the February Revolution in Petrograd, February 23–March 1917," *Soviet Studies* 40, no. 3 (July 1988).

Melgunov, S. P. *Bolshevik Seizure of Power*. Santa Barbara, 1972.

Melzer, A. M. "Rousseau and the Problem of Bourgeois Society," *American Political Science Review*, 74, 1980.

Mendel, A. P. *Michael Bakunin: Roots of Apocalypse*. New York, 1981.

Messer-Kruse, T. *The Yankee International: Marxism and the American Reform Tradition, 1848–1876*. Chapel Hill and London, 1998.

Mészáros, I. *Marx's Theory of Alienation*. London, 1970.

— — —. "Marx 'Philosopher.'" In *The History of Marxism*, ed. E. J. Hobsbawm. Bloomington, 1982.

Mies, M. "Marxist Socialism and Women's Emancipation: The Proletarian

Women's Movement in Germany 1860–1919." In *Feminism in Europe: Liberal and Socialist Strategies 1789-1919*, ed. M. Mies. The Hague, 1983.

Miliband, R. "Lenin's *The State and Revolution."* In *Socialist Register,* eds. R. Miliband and J. Seville. 1970.

———. *Marxism and Politics.* Oxford, 1978.

———. *The State in Capitalist Society.* London, 1973.

Mill, J. S. *Considerations on Representative Government.* London, 1918.

———. *On Liberty.* New York, 1956.

Milligan, S. "The Petrograd Bolsheviks and Social Insurance, 1914–17," *Soviet Studies* (January 1969).

Minz, I. I. *Istoria Velikogo Oktyabria.* 2 vols. Moscow, 1967.

———. "Ob osveschenii nekotorykh voprosov istorii Velikoi Oktyabr'skoi sotsialisticheskoi revolyutsii," *Voprosy Istorii KPSS,* 1957, no. 2 (February).

Moirova, V. A. "Women's Delegates' Meetings and their Role in the Work of the Party among Working and Peasant Women." In *Work Among Women,* eds. S. Smidovich, et al. London, 1924.

Molyneux, J. *Marxism and the Party.* London, 1978.

Moore, S. *Three Tactics: The Background in Marx.* New York, 1963.

Morgan, R. *The German Social Democrats and the First International, 1864–1872.* Cambridge, 1965.

Morozov, G. P. "Professionalnie organizatsii rabochikh Parizha i Kommuna 1871 goda," *Voprosy Istorii,* no. 3 (March 1961).

Morton, A. L., and G. Tate. *The British Labour Movement.* London, 1979.

Mukhopadhyay, A. K. *The Ethics of Obedience.* Calcutta, 1967.

Nettl, J. P. Rosa Luxemburg. 2 vols. London, 1966.

Nicolaievsky, B., and O. Maenchen–Helfen. *Karl Marx: Man and Fighter.* Harmondsworth, 1976.

Nicolaievsky, B. "Toward a History of the Communist League: 1847–1852," *International Review of Social History,* no. 1 (1956).

———. "Who is Distorting History?," *Proceedings of the American Philosophical Society* 105, no. 2 (April 1961).

Nimtz, A. "Marx and Engels–The Unsung Heroes of the Democratic Breakthrough," *Science and Society* 63, no. 2 (Summer 1999).

Nozick, R. *Anarchy, State and Utopia.* New York, 1974.

O'Malley, J., and K. Algozin, eds. *Rubel on Karl Marx.* Cambridge, 1981.

Ostroumov, S. S. *Prestupnost i eye prichiny v dorevolyutsinnoy Rossii.* Moscow, 1960.

Page, S. W., ed. *Lenin: Dedicated Marxist or Revolutionary Pragmatist.* Lexington, 1970.

Palij, M. *The Anarchism of Nestor Makhno.* Washington, 1976.

Pares, B. *A History of Russia.* London, 1937.

Payne, R. *Karl Marx.* New York, 1968.

Pełczyński, Z. A., ed. *Hegel's Political Philosophy.* Cambridge, 1971.

Perrie, M. *The Agrarian Policy of the Russian Socialist Revolutionary Party from its origins through the Revolution of 1905-1907.* Cambridge, 1976.

———. "The Russian Peasant Movement of 1905–1907: Its Social

Composition and Revolutionary Significance," *Past and Present* (November 1972).

Peters, J. *The Communist Party: A Manual on Organisation.* New York, 1935.

Petras, J., and H. Veltmeyer. *Globalisation Unmasked,* Halifax, 2001

Pierson, C. *Marxist Theory and Democratic Politics,* Delhi, 1989.

Pipes, R., ed. *Revolutionary Russia. Cambridge,* 1968.

——— *Social Democracy and the St. Petersburg Labour Movement, 1885–1897.* Cambridge, 1963.

Pipes, R. "The Origins of Bolshevism: The Intellectual Evolution of Young Lenin." In *Revolutionary Russia,* ed. R. Pipes.

———. *The Russian Revolution. London,* 1990.

———. "Why the Russians Act Like Russians," *Air Force Magazine* (June 1970).

Plamenatz, J. *German Marxism and Russian Communism.* London, 1954.

Polan, A. J. *Lenin and the End of Politics.* London, 1984.

Popper, K. R. *The Open Society and its Enemies.* 2 vols. London, 1962.

Rabinowitch, A. *The Bolsheviks Come to Power.* New York, 1976.

———. "The Evolution of Local Soviets in Petrograd, November 1917–June 1918: The Case of the First City District Soviet," *Slavic Review* 46, no. 1 (Spring 1987).

———. *Prelude to Revolution.* Indianapolis, 1968.

Radkey, O. *The Agrarian Foes of Bolshevism.* New York, 1958.

———. "Chernov and Agrarian Socialism before 1918." In *Continuity and Change in Russian and Soviet Thought,* ed. E. Simmons. Cambridge, 1955.

———. *The Election to the Russian Constituent Assembly.* Cambridge, 1950.

———. *The Sickle Under the Hammer.* New York, 1963.

———. *The Unknown Civil War in Soviet Russia: A Study of the Green Movement in the Tambov Region 1920–1921,* Stanford, 1976.

Rees, J. "In Defence of October," *Society and Change* 8, no. 2 (July–September 1991).

Reiman, M. *The Birth of Stalinism.* London, 1987.

Riddell, J., ed. *Lenin's Struggle for a Revolutionary International.* New York, 1984.

Rigby, T. H. *Communist Party Membership in the USSR 1917–1967.* Princeton, 1968.

———. *Lenin's Government: Sovnarkom 1917-22.* Cambridge, 1979.

Rosenberg, A. *Democracy and Socialism.* London, 1939.

Rosenberg, W. G, *Liberals in the Russian Revolution.* Princeton, 1974.

———. "Russian Labour and Bolshevik Power After October," *Slavic Review* 44, 1983.

Rousset, D. *The Legacy of the Bolshevik Revolution.* New York, 1982.

Rowbotham, S., H. Wainwright and L. Segal. *Beyond the Fragments.* London, 1979.

Rubel, M. "De Marx au Bolchevisme: Parties et conseils." In Argument IV: Révolution/Classe/Parti, ed. C. Bielgaski. Paris, 1978.

———. "Notes on Marx's Conception of Democracy," *New Politics* I, no. 2 (1962).

———. "Remarques sur le concept de parti proletarian chez Marx," *Revue*

Francaise de Sociologie II, no. 3 (1961).

Rueschemeyer, D., E. H. Stephens, and J. D. Stephens. *Capitalist Development and Democracy*. Chicago, 1992.

Salvadori, M. *Karl Kautsky and the Socialist Revolution: 1880–1938*. London, 1979.

Sargent, L. ed. *The Unhappy Marriage of Marxism and Feminism: A Debate on Class and Patriarchy*. London, 1986.

Schapiro, L. *1917: The Russian Revolutions and the Origin of Present Day Communism*. London, 1984.

———. *The Communist Party of Soviet Union*. London, 1970.

———. "Continuity and Change in the New History of the CPSU." In *Contemporary History in the Soviet Mirror*, ed. J. L. H. Keep. New York and London, 1964.

———. *The Origin of the Communist Autocracy*. London, 1966.

———. *The Russian Revolution of 1917*. New York, 1986.

Schapiro, L., and P. Reddaway, eds. *Lenin: The Man, the Theorist, the Leader*. New York, 1967.

Schlesinger, R. *Changing Attitudes in Soviet Russia: The Family in the USSR*. London, 1949.

———. *History of the Communist Party of the USSR*. Calcutta, 1977.

Schorske, C. E. *German Social Democracy, 1905-1917: The Development of the Great Schism*. Cambridge, 1955.

Schrupp, A. Nicht Marxistin und auch nicht Anarchistin—Frauen in der Ersten Internationale, Ulrike-Helmer-Verlag, Königstein 1999, available on the Antje Schrupp website at www.antjeschrupp.de

Schwartz, S. M. *The Russian Revolution of 1905*. Chicago, 1967.

Sengupta, A. *Paris Commune*. Calcutta, 1981.

Service, R. *Lenin: A Political Life*. Vol. 2. Bloomington, 1991.

Shanin, T., ed. *Late Marx and the Russian Road: Marx and the Peripheries of Capitalism*. London, 1984.

Sharlet, R. "Stalinism and Soviet Legal Culture." In *Stalinism: Essays in Historical Interpretation*, ed. R. C. Tucker. New York, 1977.

Shub, D. *Lenin*, Baltimore, 1961.

Singleton, S. "The Tambov Revolt, 1920–1920," *Slavic Review* (September 1966).

Sirianni, C. *Workers' Control and Socialist Democracy*. London, 1962.

Slovo, J. *Has Socialism Failed?* London, 1990.

Smith, S. A. "Class and Gender: Women's Strikes in St. Petersburg, 1895–1917 and in Shanghai, 1895–1927," *Social History* 19, no. 2 (May 1994).

———. "Petrograd in 1917." In *The Worker's Revolution in Russia, 1917*, ed. D. H. Kaiser. Cambridge, 1987.

———. *Red Petrograd*. Cambridge, 1983.

———. Review of *The Bolshevik Revolution, by M. Ferro. Soviet Studies* 30, no. 3 (1981).

Solomon, Jr., P. H. "Soviet Penal Policy 1917–1934: A Reinterpretation," *Slavic Review* 39, no. 2 (June 1980).

Sørensen, J. B. *The Life and Death of Soviet Trade Unionism, 1917–1928*. New York, 1969.

Spender, D. *Women of Ideas*. London, 1988.

Sperber, J. *The European Revolutions, 1848–1851*. Revised ed. Cambridge, 2005.

Spitzer, A. B. *The Revolutionary Theories of Louis August Blanqui*. New York, 1957.

Springborg, P. "Karl Marx on Democracy, Participation, Voting and Equality," *Political Theory* 12, no. 4 (November 1984).

Stadelmann, R. *Soziale und Politische Geschichte der Revolution von 1848*. Munich, 1948.

Stedman Jones, G. "Engels and the History of Marxism." In *The History of Marxism*, ed. E. J. Hobsbawm.

von Stein, L. *The History of Social Movement in France, 1789–1850*. Totowa, 1964.

Stekloff, G. M. *History of the First International*. New York, n.d.

Stites, R. "Fantasy and Revolution: Alexander Bogdanov and the Origins of Bolshevik Science Fiction," in *Red Star*, by A. Bogdanov. Bloomington, 1984.

— — —. "Kollontai, Inessa and Krupskaia: A Review of Recent Literature," *Canadian-American Slavic Studies* 9, no. 1 (Spring 1975).

— — —. *The Women's Liberation Movement in Russia: Feminism, Nihilism and Bolshevism 1860-1930*. Princeton, 1978.

Suny, R. G. *The Baku Commune: 1917–1918*. Princeton, 1972.

— — —. "Labour and Liquidators: Revolutionaries and the 'Reaction' in Baku," *Slavic Review*, no. 2 (1975).

— — —. "Some Thoughts on 1917: In Lieu of a Review of William Rosenberg's *Liberals in the Russian Revolution*." In *Sbornik: Paper of the First Conference of the Study Group on the Russian Revolution*. London, 1980.

— — —. "Toward a Social History of the October Revolution," *American Historical Review*, no. 88 (1983).

Sveshnikov, N. "Vyborgskii raionnyi Komitet RSDRP (B)." In *Vogne revoliutsionnykh boev: raiony Petrograda dvukh revoliutsiyakh 1917g*. Moscow, 1987.

Swain, G. *Russian Social Democracy and the Legal Labour Movement 1906–14*. London and Basingstoke, 1983.

Talmon, J. L. *The Origins of Totalitarian Democracy*. New York, 1960.

— — —. *Political Messianism: The Romantic Phase*. New York, 1960.

Therborn, G. "The Working Class and the Birth of Marxism," *New Left Review* 79 (1973).

Thomas, P. *Karl Marx and the Anarchists*. London, 1980.

Thompson, E. P. "English Daughter," *New Society* 3 (March 1977).

— — —. *William Morris, Romantic to Revolutionary*. London, 1977.

— — —. *The Poverty of Theory and Other Essays*. London, 1979.

Thomson, D. *Europe Since Napoleon*. Harmondsworth, 1982.

Thönnessen, W. *The Emancipation of Women: The Rise and Decline of the Women's Movement in German Social Democracy 1863-1933*. London, 1976.

Timberlake, C. E., ed. *Essays in Russian Liberalism*. Columbus, 1972.

Toussaint, E. *Your Money or Your Life: The Tyranny of Global Finance*. Chicago, 2005.

Tsuzuki, C. *The Life of Eleanor Marx (1855–1898): A Socialist Tragedy*. Oxford,

1967.

Tucker, R. C. *The Marxian Revolutionary Idea. London,* 1970.

———, ed. *Stalinism: Essays in Historical Interpretation.* New York, 1977.

Ulam, A. *Lenin and the Bolsheviks.* London, 1969.

Ünlüdağ, T. "Bourgeois Mentality and Socialist Ideology as Exemplified by Clara Zetkin's Constructs of Femininity," *International Review of Social History,* 47 (2002).

Upton, A. F. *The Finnish Revolution, 1917–1918.* Minneapolis, 1980.

Vanaik, A. "In Defence of Leninism," *Economic and Political Weekly* (September 13, 1986).

———. "Socialist Democracy and the Question of Leninism." Unpublished seminar paper, presented in the Indian Institute of Advanced Studies. Shimla, 1993.

Venturi, F. *Roots of Revolution: A History of the Populist and Socialist Movements in Nineteenth-Century Russia.* London, 1960.

Vernadsky, G. *A History of Russia.* New York, 1944.

Vincent, A. "Marx and Law," *Journal of Law and Society* 20, no. 4 (Winter 1993).

Vogel, L. *Marxism and the Oppression of Women: Toward a Unitary Theory.* New Brunswick, 1983.

———. *Woman Questions.* New York and London, 1995.

Vogt-Downey, M., ed. *The USSR 1987–1991: Marxist Perspectives. New* Jersey, 1993,

Volkogonov, D. *Triumph and Tragedy.* Vol. 1. Moscow, 1989.

Wade, R. A. "Workers' Militia and the Red Guard." In *Reconsiderations on the Russian Revolution,* ed. R. C. Elwood.

Walicki, A. The Controversy Over Capitalism. Oxford, 1969.

Walton, W. "Writing the 1848 Revolution: Politics, Gender, and Feminism in the Works of French Women of Letters," *French Historical Studies* 18 (Fall 1994).

Wheeler-Bennett, J. W. *Brest-Litovsk: The Forgotten Peace.* London, 1939.

White, J. D. "The Kornilov Affair: A Study in Counter-Revolution," *Soviet Studies* 20 (October 1968).

———. "The February Revolution and the Bolshevik Vyborg District Committee (In response to Michael Melancon), *Soviet Studies* 41, no. 4 (October 1989).

Wildman, A. K. *The Making of a Workers' Revolution.* Chicago, 1967.

Wilson, E. *To the Finland Station.* London, 1960.

Wittke, C. *The Utopian Communist: A Biography of Wilhelm Weitling.* Baton Rouge, 1950.

Wolfe, B. D. *Three who Made a Revolution.* Boston, 1955.

———. "Lenin and Inessa Armand," *Slavic Review* 22, no. 1 (March 1963).

———. *Marxism: One Hundred Years in the life of a Doctrine.* Madras, 1968.

Wolfenstein, E. V. *The Revolutionary Personality. Lenin, Trotsky, Gandhi.* Princeton, 1967.

Wolin, S. S. *Politics and Vision. Princeton,* 1960.

Wood, E. M. "The Separation of the 'Economic' and 'Political' in Capitalism" *New Left Review,* no. 127 (May–June 1981).

————. *The Retreat from Class*. London, 1988.

————. *Peasant-Citizen and Slave: The Foundations of Athenian Democracy*. London, 1989.

Wood, N. *John Locke and Agrarian Capitalism*. Berkeley, 1984.

Woodcock, G. *Anarchism*. Cleveland, 1962.

Woods, A. *Bolshevism: The Road to Revolution*. London, 1999.

Wright, S. "Hal Draper's Marxism," *International Socialism*, 2nd ser., no. 47 (Summer 1990).

Wright Mills, C. *The Marxists*. New York, 1963.

Zeman, Z. A. B., and W. B. Scharlau. *The Merchant of Revolution*. London, 1965.

Zhak, L. P., and A. Itkina, eds., *Zhenshchiny Russkoi Revoliutsii*. Moscow, 1968.

Zlokazov, G. I. *Oktyabr'i Grazhdanskaya v SSSR*. Moscow, 1966.

NEWSPAPERS, PERIODICALS AND JOURNALS:

Against the Current
Air Force Magazine
American Historical Review
American Political Science Review
Bulletin in Defence of Marxism
Bulletin of Concerned Asian Scholars
Business Standard
Canadian-American Slavic Studies
Central European History
English History Review
Études de Marxologie
French Historical Studies
Independent on Sunday
International Marxist Review
International Press Correspondence
International Review of Social History
International Socialism
International Viewpoint
Istoriya rabochego Klassa Leningrada
Izvestiya
Journal of Contemporary History
Journal of the History of Ideas
Jadavpur University Journal of History
Journal of Women in Culture and Society
Loukik Udyan: Manabi Sankhya
New Left Review
New Politics
New Society
Past and Present
Political Studies
Political Theory
Politics and Society

Pravda
Problems of Communism
Revue Française de Sociologie
Russian History/Histoire Russe
The Russian Review
St. Anthony's Papers
Science and Society
Slavic Review
Social History
Socialist Register
Society and Change
Soviet Studies
Soviet Studies in History
Studies in Soviet Thought
The American Slavic and East European Review
The Statesmen
Voprosy Istorii
Voprosy Istorii KPSS
Women and Revolution
Work Among Women

INDEX